Soldier of the South

SOLDIER OF THE SOUTH

Lieutenant General Richard H. Anderson at War and Peace

Edward J. Hagerty

THE UNIVERSITY OF SOUTH CAROLINA PRESS

Published by the University of South Carolina Press
Columbia, South Carolina 29208

uscpress.com

Printed in the United States of America

Library of Congress Cataloging-in-Publication Data can be found at
http://catalog.loc.gov/.

ISBN: 978-1-64336-622-7 (hardcover)
ISBN: 978-1-64336-645-6 (ebook)

Contents

List of Illustrations

Introduction

On January 13, 1871, the clerk of the United States District Court in the sleepy town of Sumter, South Carolina received a sheaf of legal documents from the law firm of Haynesworth and Fraser. The file bore a name instantly recognizable to any South Carolinian, particularly one from Sumter, as it pertained to their neighbor and local war hero, "Richard H. Anderson, Bankrupt." In the devastated South of that period, tragic financial situations were commonplace and few escaped the consequences of the recent civil war. A "Notice of Sale by Assignee in Bankruptcy" later appeared in *The Sumter Watchman* on November 29, 1871. "Fighting Dick" Anderson, late lieutenant general in the Confederate Army, was about to lose possession of all the lands inherited from his father and brother. Not only was Anderson's family home on the auction block, he also stood poised to lose his father's 2,500-acre plantation known as Riverton, as well as the plantation known as Hiwassee, which had been left to him in his brother's will.[1] Had the nation exacted such a toll as the cost of treason, the loss might have seemed less pitiful. Instead, it simply reflected the sadly turbulent conditions then prevailing in the southern United States.

Richard Heron Anderson was a professional soldier for most of his life. One of South Carolina's most illustrious military figures, he was rivaled in stature only by his nominal junior in rank, Wade Hampton, a state legislator with extensive landholdings whose political career was advanced by his notable service in General Robert E. Lee's Army of Northern Virginia. Southerners considered Anderson and Hampton to be heroes who fought with much distinction, each achieving the rank of lieutenant general. Both were elected officers of the State Survivors' Association upon its formation in Charleston in 1869—Hampton as president and Anderson as vice president—positions they retained for several subsequent years. Over time, however, Hampton's extraordinary wealth and postwar career far eclipsed that of the unassuming Anderson, and Hampton outlived him by nearly twenty-three years. Nonetheless, Anderson played a prominent role in the fortunes of the southern armies from Charleston Harbor to Pensacola Bay and from the Virginia Peninsula to Sailor's Creek.

General Robert E. Lee selected Anderson to lead the Army of Northern Virginia's First Corps after his "Old Warhorse," Lieutenant General James Longstreet, fell wounded at the Battle of the Wilderness in 1864. Anderson was an experienced soldier, having served as a dragoon officer in the old Army since graduating the United States Military Academy at West Point in 1842 with classmates and future Confederate generals like Longstreet, Daniel Harvey Hill, and Lafayette McLaws. Including his time at West Point, Dick Anderson was in uniform continuously from the age of sixteen. He knew little else but a life in the saddle. He fought in Mexico and served dutifully at dreary outposts on the inhospitable western plains with the 1st and 2nd Dragoons. It was a career marked by hardships and long absences from family and loved ones, but it was nothing in comparison to the heartache he suffered and the devastation he witnessed as a Confederate officer. His upbringing, family ties, and his devotion to his native state led him to side with South Carolina in March 1861, being careful to observe what he considered the required honorable proprieties in ensuring acceptance of his resignation from the Army prior to leaving his post.

Despite his privileged cotton plantation upbringing as the son of a noted physician and member of the planter elite, however, there is no evidence that Anderson bore any malice towards northerners even during the tumultuous series of antebellum crises that plagued the nation. Likewise, there is no indication that he was a vociferous or even an avid defender of slavery, though he expressed support for the South's right to secede from the Union. The latter compelled him to offer South Carolina his sword in its time of crisis. His support for secession as a remedy for the internecine disagreements plaguing the nation, however, implicitly embodied support for slavery, the primary reason for secession in the first place. Anderson was acutely aware of the tensions simmering since the unsatisfactory Compromise of 1850, which provoked the ire of South Carolinians even to the eve of secession a decade later. He certainly must have read carefully his state's declared causes for secession, leaving no doubt that—Constitutional issues aside—the issue boiled down to South Carolinians' conclusion that the Republican Party intended to wage a war against slavery "until it shall cease throughout the United States."[2]

Despite his awareness of the causes, there is no evidence that he defined the crisis exclusively in those limited terms. Instead, Anderson set the issue primarily in the context of his duty to his native country, meaning his allegiance to the state of South Carolina rather than to the United States. Such nuanced parsing of one's loyalty is difficult to comprehend today, but it was a critical element of the foundation of Anderson's life, as it was for many other nineteenth century southerners who chose to side with their states when conflict came. While there is no need to rehash the myriad causes for secession here, it suffices to say that southerners tied their perceptions of continual assaults on their rights and their political power within the Union directly to northerners' efforts to undermine slavery as a viable economic institution and labor system, and to define it instead as a moral abomination. Thus, for southerners, supporting secession necessarily meant tacit agreement with the complaints that led to secession. The South's inflexible embrace of slavery and northerners' increasingly aggressive opposition to it lay at the heart of all of those complaints. Men like Anderson undoubtedly viewed South Carolina's right to secede as an inviolable one, and they accepted the seemingly lucid Constitutional arguments for its legality as legitimate. Only the sword would resolve the question of legitimacy, but when Anderson resigned from the US Army in March 1861, no one knew with certainty whether war would ensue or what the outcome might be. What he did know, however, was that he could not support the federal Union in any effort to subjugate South Carolina or to attempt to prevent it from exercising its right to depart that Union. That would have meant a rejection of the way of life that had nurtured him in his youth and established the foundation upon which he based his life, while simultaneously meaning acceptance of the possibility of wholesale destruction of his family's source of wealth and prestige as members of the planter elite class.

By 1860, in addition to his 150-acre home property known variously then as Hillcrest or the Homestead, situated in the village of Stateburg,[3] Anderson's father owned and managed nearly 150 enslaved persons on a 2,500-acre plantation on the Wateree River known as Riverton. Those holdings placed the family in the top eight percent of large planters in South Carolina's Sumter District, whose population was nearly 71 percent black in 1860.[4] Dick Anderson's brother, Mackenzie, owned a 1,900-acre plantation known as Hiwassee located about three miles from the Homestead. Failure to sustain that social and economic status by force of arms meant the family's financial ruin, and ultimately that of Dick Anderson as well. As the eldest son, he stood to inherit the bulk of his father's vast estate, including the significant capital investment in enslaved workers. Despite his lengthy separation from his parents and siblings during his time in the Army, Anderson remained deeply attached to his home and all the trappings of the southern plantation system. Among other considerations, his decisions were thus inextricably bound to the potential impact on his family, yet he did not make those decisions lightly, and, as the evidence indicates, perhaps even with some degree of regret at having to do so.[5]

Other factors assuredly affected Anderson's decision in 1861. The influence of his wife's northern upbringing and the example provided by her prominent Democratic family in Pennsylvania, coupled with his gratifying days at the Carlisle Barracks in the Keystone State shaped his worldview, as did his exposure to people, cultures, and places far beyond just those of the South Carolina planter elite. His time on the western plains, and his interaction with the common soldiers of his regiment, many of whom were immigrants, put Anderson in contact with the same class of poorer whites he would have associated with the "Sandhill tackey" people familiar to him in regions near his family's plantation.[6] One can only speculate as to how he viewed the hardships of daily life for enlisted dragoons on the prairie in comparison to what he observed of the lives of enslaved workers near his family's village house and the larger plantation at Riverton.[7] It seems probable that Anderson saw those enslaved workers engaged in the "task" system of labor organization, which set specific tasks for enslaved laborers to accomplish and, once those tasks were completed, sometimes allowed them time to engage in other activities, such as maintaining gardens to supplement the food allotments given to them by their enslavers or even engaging in small-scale market exchange of goods and services.[8] Tasking was sometimes used on Upcountry cotton plantations and is often set in contrast to the "sun-up to sun-down" labor organization of the gang system. While it is true that the task system did at times allow enslaved people to "re-claim" a portion of their time, both systems were used as a means of organizing, regulating, and disciplining the working time of enslaved people. They were also often used in conjunction with one another as the needs of plantation work, and the ability of enslavers to enforce one or another system of labor discipline, dictated.

Regardless of the precise labor patterns on Dr. Anderson's plantation—which remain elusive based on available evidence—it is apparent that Richard Anderson was accustomed to seeing those serving under him in any capacity hard at work and subservient to his commands, and that mirrored his own values and helped form his expectations as an army officer.

Like many children raised on southern plantations, it would not have been unusual for the Andersons to have had several young members of the plantation's enslaved community as playmates, at least until their differences in status became too awkward to ignore. As with many aspects of slavery, the experience varied and the nature of the Anderson's relations with enslaved children is undocumented. Accounts from other locations in the area describe the plantation's white children tasked with the happy work of handing out the yearly allotment of new shoes and clothing to the enslaved workers gathered around the big house. Perhaps the Anderson children did so as well. Undoubtedly, they had close contact with nursemaids and the family's household staff, though only vague notions of the dynamics and parameters of the family's interactions exist.

Anderson would also have been acquainted with his nearby Stateburg neighbor, William Ellison Jr., a formerly enslaved man who had purchased his freedom decades earlier and started a very successful business building cotton gins that made him one of the wealthiest black men in South

Carolina. Ellison was able to purchase his own wife and children, but, in seemingly incongruous circumstances, he eventually owned nearly seventy additional enslaved persons himself. Ellison was keenly aware that an 1841 state law prohibited the freeing of any enslaved person, and the unfortunate man was thus unable to set even his own wife and children free. Despite his strong advocacy for slavery, the senior Dr. Anderson respected Ellison as an artisan and businessperson, and even sponsored his admission to the local Episcopal Church. Dr. Anderson was open to conducting business with Ellison and had confidence in his financial acumen, even jointly entering into a loan from Francis Sumter for over $1,000 to be repaid in three yearly installments between 1846 and 1848.[9] Those kinds of examples and diverse experiences put Dick Anderson in touch with a wide range of class, race, and wealth categories that broadened his views and rendered easy or simplistic conclusions difficult. Finally, they might have tempered any inclination to express an unequivocal position on slavery.

Anderson's career as a Confederate officer, while distinguished in a strictly military sense includes words and actions indicating that he also came to understand the futility of the cause and questioned whether his state's position on the issues leading to the conflict was correct. A close examination of his wartime comments and actions frequently imparts a sense of despondency and sadness from which one may surmise that he harbored some degree of ambivalence towards his cause and that he was a man of great sensitivity. The losses among his own family—an infant child, a brother, a sister—were sufficient to cast anyone into despair, and the wholesale slaughter around him left him appalled. Though it was a level of human devastation that touched his own family early in the conflict, it was one in which he nonetheless continued to play a prominent role because he saw it as his duty to do so and was cognizant of the potential impact of failure.

Each year of the war brought some devastating personal tragedy. Anderson suffered his most grievous loss on a battlefield when his younger brother fell mortally wounded while serving as a volunteer aid on his staff at Williamsburg. His father's death in 1864 and his temporary estrangement from his wife's family in Pennsylvania were losses that also weighed heavily on him, as did the death of an infant daughter in 1861 and his sister Mary in 1863. Though he was always a church member, there is scant evidence of Anderson being a deeply religious man. Unlike his brother Benjamin, whose diary clearly reflects his deep religious sentiments, there is almost nothing similar in Dick Anderson's surviving writings. Faith sustained many of his contemporaries who accepted divine providence and professed a resignation to God's will, but no evidence supports his wholehearted embrace of that era's widely held sentiment. Baptized in the Episcopal Church, Anderson sought solace in the Bible, as illustrated in a story from his first biographer who describes him reading the book before bedtime.[10] Nevertheless, his pragmatic nature sometimes led him to fret over events that were beyond his control, and to question the rectitude of his own choices and of the South's cause. Such internal conflicts were not conducive to unhindered performance. He was a man prone to occasional stretches of melancholy that sapped his energy and led to inertia. His unquestioned acceptance of the role of divine will in his life is somewhat doubtful as a result.

Anderson always strove to do his duty, whether it was in the United States Army or the Confederate one. At times, he appeared equally dissatisfied with his situation in either position, and he was especially distraught at his disquieting role in quelling violence and disputes between his countrymen amidst the turbulence of "Bleeding Kansas."[11] Such conflict did not comport with his nature, though he was at one point compelled to challenge a fellow officer to a duel after that officer egregiously violated social norms by virulently attacking southerners and slavery while at table in Anderson's quarters. The quarrel likely owed as much or more to the outrageous social insult rendered to Anderson in his own home as to the opinions expressed in the officer's intemperate words. Still, Anderson persisted in the old Army, doing his duty there and later with the Confederacy even though the latter required adherence to the morally repugnant goal of preserving slavery and the related conditions that sustained the lifestyle of elite southern planters, including the Andersons.

Returning to his ancestral home near Stateburg after Lee's surrender, Anderson discarded the only career he had ever known and embarked on the mission of saving his family's plantation. The postwar collapse of the South's economy, social structure, and labor system all combined with the usual vicissitudes of farming to consign the effort to failure. The year 1865 was not a propitious time for a man who had soldiered all his adult life to turn suddenly to cultivating the soil. Dick Anderson, his brother Wallace, and their widower brother-in-law Frederick Childs, had little experience in running a large plantation. Salvaging the plantation in the chaotic labor and economic conditions then prevailing in the South required men with far greater aptitude in the intricate details of business and agriculture. Moreover, it required greater capital, which was not easily available to them. They had neither skills nor money to sustain a property already mired in debt. Much of the inheritance from Dick Anderson's father derived its value from Confederate bonds or currency, enslaved persons, and other investments that were lost to him. Borrowing even more money proved his downfall as he attempted to sustain the plantations. In the immediate aftermath of the war, however, the defeated general bore his losses stoically and asked for nothing. He put the war behind him quickly as he turned his attention to agriculture. Within a few years he held office in the state's veteran association, but he did not dwell on the war or seek recognition for his role in the conflict. He recognized and honored the sacrifices of those with whom he served, but unlike others among the officer corps of the Army of Northern Virginia, including Lee and Jubal Early, he wrote nothing that contributed to the eventual revisionist Lost Cause version of history.

That he could have capitalized more fully on his reputation and stature was undeniable. Many others did so, riding their fame to various political offices and lucrative positions. He eschewed politics, rejecting nomination for mayor of Charleston in the spring of 1871, at the very nadir of his financial collapse when such a position might have rescued him. He avoided appealing to others until driven by desperation, but when he did try to discretely lean on his military reputation the results were not entirely favorable. His invariably dignified bearing and demeanor befitted a former army officer who had served honorably in two causes and performed his duties as best he understood them. Anderson paid a price for his honor and modesty, though, as illustrated by the grievous economic decline of an officer of such stature and fame.

By contrast, Wade Hampton overcame all obstacles and rose to the governorship of South Carolina in 1876. Hampton's son-in-law, John Cheeves Haskell, who, along with his several of his brothers, served on Anderson's staff at various times, became a state legislator in 1877. The absence of any known communication from the Haskells, particularly since they viewed Anderson with some fondness, is noteworthy. In a December 1864 letter to his sister, for example, Joseph Haskell remarked on their brother Langdon "Lally" Haskell's transfer to Anderson's staff. Joseph noted that Lally's new position "ought to be pleasanter, as Genl. Anderson is one of the finest men I know."[12] Either Anderson never made his financial woes known to them, or they were not yet in a position to assist him in the war's immediate aftermath.

By 1871, the reduced circumstances of his native South entwined with Dick Anderson's personal fate. At the risk of engaging in cliché, one may say that his life was an apt metaphor for the history of that section of the country. From a background of prestige and wealth, he soon found that failure, embarrassment, and ruin stared him in the face. Mounting debts reached well into the thousands of dollars.[13] Little remained in the way of valuable personal property save the fine sword that had been presented to him on the eve of civil war by the state of South Carolina "as an expression of its appreciation of his gallant and meritorious service" during the war with Mexico. On the sheath was a golden shield bearing the state's coat of arms; the hilt appropriately bore a figure of John C. Calhoun, the South's foremost architect of ruin and desolation. Though all else was lost to him, Anderson carefully preserved the cherished sword.[14]

Misfortune dogged Anderson after the collapse of the family's fortunes. His poverty and his search for employment took him to Charleston and then to Camden, South Carolina, where he worked for the South Carolina Railroad as a railroad agent, a position very much beneath his capacity and stature. His financial condition frequently kept him separated from his two children, and his beloved first wife died tragically in 1872 after periods of both mental and physical decline. In 1879, fourteen years after the close of the war and two years after the collapse of political Reconstruction, Wade Hampton finally helped to rescue Anderson from joblessness, and he was tendered a newly created position as state phosphate agent. He relocated to Beaufort and lived briefly with his second wife in a local boarding house until his premature death at the age of fifty-seven.[15]

Despite his post-war decline in fortunes, Dick Anderson's story encompasses all the elements of a life marked by adventure, controversy, romance, sadness, and joy. Like any man, Anderson had imperfections, including his decision to rally to his state's cause under the banner of "duty" and throw his support behind secession and the perpetuation of slavery. However, it is not the intention of this biography either to impugn his motives in the absence of a clear understanding of his rationale, or to excuse a flawed personal choice. It is instead preferable to try to understand the context, circumstances, and conditions that led to such choices, which might simultaneously shed more light on his reasoning process.

He was a privileged son of the South whose formal training at the United States Military Academy reinforced the same ideas about manhood, duty, and honor, inculcated from his youth, and which took their place alongside his devotion to his family and his native state. Like other senior leaders who led men on the field of battle, Anderson was part of an elite group drawn from the highest levels of southern society. Those men were educated, often wealthy, frequently politically connected at some level, and "in many cases were descendants of the very men who forged our country." Their devotion to duty, like Anderson's, was unquestionable. The mortality rate for southern general officers was three times higher than that of northern generals. Anderson was fortunate in that regard, suffering two relatively minor physical wounds. The psychological trauma may well have been more severe.[16]

Writing about Dick Anderson has not been an easy task. The colorful anecdotes that dot so many biographies of prominent Civil War characters are largely absent. Even the painstaking research and depth of knowledge of so renowned an historian as Douglas Southall Freeman failed to uncover much, leading Freeman to write in his Foreword to Volume I of *Lee's Lieutenants* with Anderson in mind, that "certain of Lee's Lieutenants were unsensational in behavior or had emotional control so complete that they seemed colorless or even stolid." Freeman lamented the scant information available about some characters, but he shunned the "painful artificiality" of Carlyle's method of painting quick portraits through "catchword descriptions." I have adopted Freeman's views on this point and embraced his advice that "lesser writers" than Carlyle should avoid that method. Still, in nearly the same breath Freeman reduced Anderson to "that modest gentleman, the easy-going, generous 'Dick' Anderson."[17] It requires little effort to follow Freeman in respect to that pithy description of Anderson, as one quickly perceives that he was both modest and a gentleman.

Quiet and self-effacing, rarely sententious, and immune from irascibility, Dick Anderson did not seek the limelight to inflate his reputation—especially at the expense of another officer. Alas, the meek did not inherit the laurels of the Lost Cause, and Anderson faded into relative obscurity for a time. A man as modest as Anderson would also have recognized his own limitations. Historians have justly viewed his overall performance in command of the First Corps as competent, but not spectacular, as was the case later at Sailor's Creek where the failures of his tiny Fourth Corps were associated with the disintegration of substantial elements of Lee's army. Lee's choices for the position of corps commander were few in the spring of 1864, and those he appointed were not yet quite the equals of their predecessors. There was indeed a crisis in command at that time. Still, Anderson was a sound and logical choice given the options Lee had, yet it is also true that Lee would discover that a heightened level of oversight and direction was required to get the best performance from his subordinates at that time. Moreover, circumstances by 1864 had changed dramatically. The war had become one of persistent movement and maneuver in response to Union pressure that saw Lee's vastly outnumbered army constantly skirting the edges of catastrophe. Lee could ill afford to leave much to chance, and his leadership style had to adapt to the abilities of his recently elevated corps commanders and the level of threat the army faced.

Dick Anderson's story is that of a soldier who did his duty and did his best, even though that degree of effort was sometimes insufficient to achieve his goals. In leadership courses, students frequently learn as much from inferior leadership as they do from truly great leaders. From flawed leadership examples, they will learn what *not* to do, they will observe the consequences of weak decisions, and they will be able to brainstorm various options that might have led to a more desirable outcome. In Anderson's case, there is a great deal to learn from his successes, his character, and his sound leadership traits, but we can also learn from examples where his efforts and his decisions did not quite live up to expectations. The modest Dick Anderson would have been pleased to know that he was able to be of some assistance to students of leadership in that respect, and from our modern perspective we are left only to lament that for four years of civil war his courage and skills were worthy of a better cause.

Chapter 1

The High Hills of Santee

Good habits formed at youth make all the difference.

—Aristotle,
Nicomachean Ethics

Land near the village of Stateburg, South Carolina, passed through several hands since King Charles II first granted 450 acres to William Hilton in 1758. The grant encompassed one of the most desirable locations in the area, with a hilltop building site along the King's Highway to Charleston commanding a view of the vicinity known to locals as the High Hills of Santee. Around the foot of that hilltop site a small village named Claremont developed, and was referred to more colloquially as "The Borough." Nearby, the Wateree River provided an important means of transportation for foodstuffs and timber, and later for the cotton crops that eventually covered much of the landscape. On the hilltop overlooking the village, Hilton constructed a two-story dwelling that served as a tavern and way station for travelers along the road to Charleston. Subsequently known as Hillcrest, or as the Homestead among the family members in the nineteenth century, it was later styled The Borough House in the early twentieth century and preserves that name today. In Hilton's day, it was a small, wooden-frame structure measuring about 30 by 48 feet. Little in its original functional design and appearance indicated that it would one day be considered one of the finest plantation homes in the area and noted as the birthplace of Confederate Lieutenant General Richard H. Anderson. In 1792, Thomas Hooper bought the dwelling and seventy-five acres. Hooper had arrived from Charleston around 1789, and he was steadily amassing landholdings in the area. By that time, the vast expanse of American lands had been wrested from British hands after a bitter revolutionary struggle during which the High Hills of Santee saw their share of conflict. Hooper's new home had played a central role.[1]

During the Revolution, the King's Highway saw the passing of General Nathanael Greene's Continental Regulars and colonial militia commanded by local resident, General Thomas Sumter. Dust rose from the footsteps of Lord Cornwallis' British "lobsterbacks" and the thundering hoof beats of Lieutenant Colonel Banastre Tarleton's green-coated cavalry. After Tarleton burned Sumter's plantation, the Patriot general brazenly held forth with his partisans, fighting on his own terms and "adhering casually to the instructions or advice of the Continental generals." Fighting in the Southern colonies had all the trappings of a civil war pitting Loyalist residents against their Patriot neighbors and even setting some families at odds.[2]

General Greene chose the Borough House as his headquarters in the summer of 1781. One of the nearby springs on the property provided fresh water for troops bivouacked near the home. The spring was arched over with rock and has ever since been called "Greene's Spring." A giant white oak tree near the Borough House took on the name "The Spy Oak" after Sumter hanged two Tory spies from its branches. Another reminder of the presence of the Continental Army was left indelibly marked in the rear door of the Borough House, where a soldier reputedly burned the initials "C. A." into the wood with a red-hot poker.[3]

Thomas Hooper, a Harvard lawyer, had been a Loyalist in Charleston but remained neutral during the Revolution. It is testimony to his diplomacy that the former Loyalist procured a judgeship for the county and blended well with his neighbors after moving west in 1789. Thomas married Mary Heron in 1778. Her father had been Captain Benjamin Heron of the Royal Navy.[4] The Hooper family prospered after the war, as did the little town of Claremont and its residents. Bypassed during the search for a state capital, the village then known as Stateburg continued to flourish, surrounded by large plantations marked by stately homes. The area grew increasingly reliant on the cultivation of cotton. Sped by the invention of the cotton gin in 1793, South Carolinians moved steadily toward the coronation of that staple as the southern "King." Enslaved workers supplied the labor force that created a cotton aristocracy in the South, and several of Stateburg's plantations were among South Carolina's largest and wealthiest. The enslaved population grew correspondingly, and many area residents counted themselves among slavery's staunchest defenders.

Stateburg's prosperity naturally attracted new citizens, with much of the Lowcountry aristocracy fleeing temporarily to the region when disease and oppressive summer heat transformed the coastal areas into an inhospitable miasma. The High Hills of Santee provided a more enticing climate than that offered on the coast. Some relocated to the Stateburg area permanently, however. Young Dr. William Wallace Anderson, who would one day sire Richard Heron Anderson, became one of the newest full-time residents when he headed south in 1810 from his family's Maryland home. He probably did so largely at the instigation of his father, Richard, who had passed through the area during the Revolution.

At the start of the Revolution, Richard Anderson, grandfather to the future General Richard H. Anderson, joined the Continental Army as a first lieutenant of the Maryland Line. His heroic action at the Battle of Germantown, near Philadelphia, brought him much acclaim. Wounded and nearly captured at the Battle of Camden after reaching South Carolina in August 1780, he won distinction again by capturing British artillery pieces at the Battle of Cowpens.[5]

Wounded severely in the left elbow during the fighting at Guilford Courthouse in North Carolina a few months later, Anderson soon recovered and in 1787 married Ann Wallace, who claimed descent from a brother of the thirteenth-century Scottish chieftain, William Wallace. If true, the descendants of Ann Wallace and Richard Anderson had the blood of revolutionaries coursing through their veins. The first child to feel the pulse of that rebel blood was a son, William Wallace Anderson, born on April 19, 1789. William was not destined to be a military man, instead graduating the University of Pennsylvania in 1810 with a diploma and certificate "certifying to his attendance for two seasons upon the practice of Physicians of the Pennsylvania Hospital." He soon struck out for South Carolina, and the High Hills of Santee by which his father must have been so impressed during his sojourn years earlier.[6]

For nearly eight years, Dr. Anderson practiced medicine in Stateburg, eventually marrying Mary Jane McKenzie on January 30, 1818. Mary Jane was the daughter of John McKenzie and Elizabeth Heron, sister of Mary Heron Hooper. Mary Heron Hooper and her husband Thomas adopted Mary Jane after Elizabeth died prematurely. Sometime after Mary Jane's marriage to Dr. Anderson, the couple moved into the Hooper home, by then known as Hillcrest. Mary Heron Hooper died in 1820, and her husband Thomas in 1798, so Mary Jane likely inherited the house upon Mary's death. Dr. Anderson's medical practice was a successful one, and soon he was able to begin enlarging and improving the original structure. The growing family needed more space, and already by 1820, there were fourteen enslaved males and fourteen enslaved females on the plantation. Richard Anderson was born on October 7, 1821. A younger sister, Mary Heron Anderson, died in infancy soon after Richard's birth, and Dr. Anderson added the name "Heron" to Richard's name in her memory. Edward McKenzie Anderson was born in 1823, and the following year saw the birth of William Wallace Anderson, Jr. Another daughter, Mary Hooper Anderson, came into the world in 1826, followed by a fourth son, Franklin, in 1828. The couple's last child was John Benjamin, born in 1831. Despite his considerable medical skills, Dr. Anderson's family was plagued by the same fate as that suffered by many in that era. It was common for several members of a family not to survive to adulthood because of injuries for which there was no suitable treatment or illnesses for which there was no known cure. The Anderson's were no exception. Besides

Mary Heron, who died an infant, the family also lost Franklin when he was just over four years old. The year 1832 was one of dual tragedies for the family, for Richard Anderson's mother Mary Jane died as well, but the household was not long without a woman's touch. Dr. Anderson married Elizabeth Waties in October 1833. John Benjamin, the family's youngest son, reached the age of twenty-six before dying of illness in 1857.[7]

In addition to medicine, Dr. Anderson dabbled in the study of botany and architecture with considerable skill. He kept himself well informed through subscriptions to several local and state newspapers and continued throughout his life to acquire books on botany. In the year his son Richard was born, the doctor set about enlarging the original home and constructing a series of outbuildings and dependencies on the property. He made significant changes to the house, adding two substantial single-story wings to the main structure, the beginning of a carefully planned and executed five-part classical Palladian design. The doctor's study of architecture led him to develop a fascination with the construction method known as pisé de terre. He took this opportunity to try the method, which consisted of the construction of wooden forms into which clay soil was hand-packed and rammed to create a wall. The thick finished walls were then covered on the outside with a layer of heavy stucco for protection. Dr. Anderson also added a two-story Greek Revival portico to the front of the home, while from the rear porch the grandeur of the house was complemented by a view down a broad avenue that descended gently through the trees nearly a mile. Dr. Anderson also built a pisé medical office adjacent to the road, while nearer the main house he erected a two-room pisé schoolhouse surrounded by a colonnade with twenty-four Tuscan columns. The construction efforts that began in 1821 vindicated Dr. Anderson's reliance on the pisé method. The buildings remain even today among the oldest pisé structures in the country and the only surviving structures of that type with any classical architectural significance. Undoubtedly, enslaved workers comprised the primary source of labor for all his building projects.[8]

Dr. Anderson's wife likely brought a few enslaved persons to the marriage through her inheritance from the Hoopers, but the first record of Dr. Anderson purchasing an enslaved worker was in 1818, when he paid $150 for a "wench" named Clarky. The plantation records are dotted with receipts thereafter documenting the purchases of black male and female workers. Some were older, such as the $500 purchase in 1824 of a "male slave named Jim about 40 years of age." By 1835, Dr. Anderson began buying several enslaved persons from his sister-in-law Anna Waties. He bought "a certain negro boy named Oscar" from her that year for $500. Young men of prime working age were more valuable, and in 1837, Dr. Anderson paid Anna Waties

$1,500 for "two young negro men slaves named Canada & Sanday." He continued to make capital investments in enslaved persons, paying Waties as much as $1,000 for a single "male slave Monday" in 1839. Two days after that he gave her $900 for "Nanny, an old woman, Frederick her son a boy about eight years old and Rose a girl between four & five years old." Family, friends, and neighbors seemed to comprise the sources of his purchases, rather than random agents specializing in the sale or purchase of enslaved persons. In early 1845, he paid his neighbor Francis Sumter $500 for "one negro man slave named Hampton," and later that summer he made one of his single largest investments in human chattel when he bought twelve enslaved persons from Thomas Bracey in Stateburg. He paid $3,700 for Sampson, Binah, Bob, Silvia, Isaac, Tilda, Dolly, Peggy, Samuel, Linda, Adam, and Jefferson. He continued to increase his roster of enslaved workers into the next decade, paying neighbor Jane Rees $900 in early 1854 for Lucas, "a carpenter by trade, about thirty-two years of age, said to be rheumatic." In early 1856, Henry, another new addition, was worth only $500. Naturally, there would have been some variation in pricing of enslaved persons over the decades between 1818 and Dr. Anderson's death in 1864, but it is clear from the record of his purchases that male field hands in their prime were worth most, with women, children, and the elderly worth less. Next to prime field hands, however, a so-called "breeding wench" would have been of highest value due to the natural increase she would bring to the plantation's enslaved population. Despite her value, that dehumanizing slur would constitute her primary identity and purpose on most plantations.[9]

By the time young Richard, called Dick, was old enough to be aware of his surroundings, the plantation on which he lived looked a great deal different from the one on which he was born. Though little is known of the boyhood activities of Richard and his closest brothers Edward—called McKenzie—and William—called Wallace, one surviving anecdote indicates that hunting occupied an important place in the boys' lives. The story also illustrates that Dick Anderson had already begun to develop the modest and gentlemanly qualities that would mark his adulthood. While hunting with a friend and giving the boy some pointers on the proper handling of a firearm, he soon saw an opportunity for a shot at their prey. Rather than taking the shot himself, however, he graciously handed over the rifle to his companion who fired the first shot of his life with the gun steadied on Anderson's shoulders.[10]

It is likely that the practices documented on many southern plantations applied to the Anderson's as well. If so, the Anderson children would have played and interacted closely with enslaved children around their same ages. By 1830, when young Dick was nine years old, there were fifty-four enslaved persons on the plantations, some of whose parents must certainly have lived in close proximity to the family home where they served their immediate needs as house servants, gardeners, and others whose skills were needed for daily life. Five of the children were boys under the age of ten, while ten girls were also in that age range.[11] Surely, some of those enslaved children must have played with the Anderson children, and since their home was located in the village of Stateburg, other plantation homes were not far away. All their neighbors either had, or—in the case of the Ellison family immediately next door—were enslaved persons.

Though the practice of interracial play was common, the experiences varied, but in all cases, the white children learned their role as "masters" while black children were compelled to accept their subservient status. Thus, many young enslavers learned at an early age the powerful differences in their status, even at times lording their superiority over their playmates or dispensing violent punishments if such was the example they observed from their elders. Existing recollections from other plantations vary widely but nonetheless provide examples of what might have occurred. Elizabeth Keckley, an enslaved woman who published a memoir in 1868, recalled from the age of four already having to take care of her enslaver's infant child, thus becoming both caretaker and playmate. Henry Gladney's owner gave Gladney to his grandson, who sometimes treated him well and abused him at other times. "It 'mused him to pet or kick me, as it pleased him," Gladney recalled. Others had warm memories of idyllic childhood days in the company of both black and white children who spent their time "roaming from plantation to plantation, not knowing or caring what things were going on outside [their] little realm."[12]

Whether Dr. and Mrs. Anderson set a paternalistic example in their interaction with enslaved servants and field laborers is unclear, but there is no evidence to conclude they were physically violent. If the gentlemanly nature Dick Anderson exhibited routinely in all his interpersonal relations later in life is any indication, it seems he absorbed little if any of the rougher lessons of slavery he might have observed on his family's plantation as a youth. In any case, relationships between children changed radically as they grew older and, as the eldest child, Dick Anderson would have been the first to make the transition to a more regulated distinctiveness that separated him fully from his former Black playmates and cemented in his mind the roles of enslaver and enslaved. The effects of that separation were even greater for the enslaved children. Previously on a more "democratic footing," in the words of one white Virginian, those children encountered suddenly "the first bitter consciousness of being a slave: and nothing can be sadder than to see the poor little things wandering about companionless and comfortless."[13]

The concept of paternalism is another facet of plantation life that might have influenced Dick Anderson's views on slavery as an institution, although enslavers and enslaved frequently held conflicting views regarding social conditions wherein self-reported evidence of white paternalism proved contradictory to enslaved persons' memories. Enslaved persons' narratives typically support such conclusions. Nonetheless, the only available evidence based on their known actions seems to support the idea that Dr. Anderson and his family might have embraced the goal of acting as paternalistic owners, though the range of that quality's characteristics can vary widely. Without direct evidence, we cannot know whether Dick Anderson observed the use of harsh punishments or even verbal abuse, or whether he was aware that his father might have sold slaves due to their recalcitrance, on speculation, or because economic circumstances compelled him to do so. If not involved with the sale of his own enslaved workers, it is also possible that Dr. Anderson played at least a supporting role in providing certificates verifying the physical soundness of others.

The letters of slave trader A. J. McElveen from Sumter[14] in the fall of 1856 indicate that the sales and purchases of enslaved persons in that area were brisk, and competition among traders was intense. We do not know whether sales meant the separation of any of the Anderson plantation families, a particularly horrendous and unforgettable event for enslaved spouses, parents, and children whose memories of such tragedies pepper their recollections with disturbing frequency. Any of those incidents, if they occurred, certainly would have contributed to Dick Anderson's conception of slavery as it developed in the cultural and economic milieu of his youth. What we must acknowledge, however, is one element of that milieu that without doubt infused the minds of southerners with the determination to embrace and defend slavery, and that is racism. Indeed, the concept of paternalism is not possible to grasp in the context of slavery without first acknowledging that it existed because of racism. Racist views strengthened enslavers' ability to classify themselves as paternalists and led to diversity in how they understood the meaning of the term. For some, once they convinced themselves that they enhanced the well-being of enslaved blacks simply by supplying the example of civilized benevolence through their presence and influence, paternalism could take many forms. In all, however, it was a white supremacist view governed ultimately by the self-interest of the enslaver and the unequivocal acceptance of the notion that they always knew what was best for their supposed inferior enslaved charges.[15]

In their treatment of the enslaved people on their plantation, the scanty evidence available shows that the Andersons exhibited the qualities sometimes described as paternalistic, despite the doctor's intensely strong sentiments regarding the propriety of the institution. Antislavery agitation led some slaveholders to embrace their peculiar institution with greater fervor and to rationalize their position by taking steps to improve the material treatment of their "people." Dr Anderson's agreement to sell his butler, Dick, to Stephen Decatur Miller, father of Mary Boykin Chesnut may provide one specific example of his paternalistic attitude. Dick had married one of the Millers' slaves by the name of Hetty, although no legal basis for the marriage of slaves then existed under South Carolina law. The two families agreed to sell to the other "whichever consented to be sold." Hetty did not wish to leave the Millers, and the Andersons thus agreed to sell Dick so he could be with his wife. "This was magnanimous on their part, for Hetty was only a lady's maid, while Dick was a trained butler, on whom Mrs. Anderson had spent no end of pains," recalled Mary Chesnut later. "As a butler he is a treasure," she noted, and Dick was clearly proud of his exalted position in the household, where "his duties were managerial rather than physical, involving the assessment of household requirements and the delegation of labor to lower-ranking house slaves." Dick never forgot the kindness shown by the Andersons and always maintained some affection for the Anderson family, particularly for the General. During the war, Dick once inquired about General Anderson, remarking, "He was my young Master once. I always will like him better than anybody else." The incident also illustrates the closer relationship white enslavers typically had with domestic slaves rather than with field hands. Distance from daily family interaction most likely tempered equally paternalistic treatment of those who labored in the fields. Nonetheless, Dr. Anderson's willingness to see an enslaved family united in this specific case speaks well of his treatment of the issue.[16]

Despite their perceptions of paternalism, white plantation owners, vastly outnumbered by the enslaved blacks among whom they lived must have harbored some degree of fear for their safety that also influenced their interaction with their enslaved charges. While the administration of brutal punishment sometimes set an example and deterred transgressions, even the most paternalistic of enslavers stood a chance of encountering violence from discontented blacks. Mary Chesnut, for example, claimed in 1861 that she had never thought of being afraid. "I had never injured any of them," she naively wrote. "Why should they want to hurt me? Two-thirds of my religion consists in trying to be good to negroes because they are so in my power, and it would be so easy to be the other thing." After her Cousin Betsey was "murdered by her own people[,] her negroes," Chesnut felt suddenly "that the ground is cut away from under my feet." "Why should they treat me any better?" she pondered. To that tale, she added reminiscences from the previous year when a brother of one of her acquaintances, "always declaiming about the 'beneficent institution.'" was also "murdered by his negroes." Chesnut described Betsey as "a saint on earth," as she bemoaned her cousin's fate. Alas, however, she was unable to resist casting some blame on Betsey for having so indulged her household staff that they grew insolent, "like spoiled children. Simply intolerable." The criticism calls into question her previous comments about "trying to be good to negroes." While it was "easy to be the other thing" in cases where enslaved workers were recalcitrant, it was clearly much easier to try "to be good to negroes" in cases where they gave no cause for dissatisfaction. Chesnut is among the southern women who emerge from her diary, in the words of historian Elizabeth Fox-Genovese, as one of the "remarkably attractive people who tried to do their best by their slaves," but who nonetheless "accepted and supported the social system that endowed them with power and privilege over black women." The latter universally proclaims the outlook of female southern enslavers, and such views must therefore have permeated the atmosphere of the Anderson home as well.[17]

Dick Anderson's youngest brother John Benjamin, known as Benjamin, took over management of the family's large plantation at Riverton in 1853, after his graduation from South Carolina College. The enslaved man Canada purchased by his father in 1837 became one of his most reliable and capable assistants among the more than one hundred enslaved workers on the property. Canada was a stable family man living with a wife, Lucy, and her four children. Much to the satisfaction of the avidly religious Benjamin, Canada also embraced religion and was baptized at the Episcopal Church of the Holy Cross in 1846. Benjamin's diary entries mention Canada frequently. In late 1856, for example, he noted that he "was impressed tonight with Canada's evening devotions. They did him credit." Despite that, Canada was sometimes troublesome and Benjamin administered various punishments as a result. On one occasion the punishment was not noted except to record that Benjamin found "Canada guilty of stealing & punish[ed] him & Lucy into confession." Once, Canada was frightened when a neighboring plantation owner came to Riverton in search of a stolen hog. Fearing that he would bear the blame, Canada ran off to the Homestead. He returned the next night seeking pardon. The next day was Sunday, and after church services Benjamin administered "a few strokes with the whip for running away." The following spring Mackenzie came to Riverton "to see Canada safely up & plead his cause for him. He told him to stay with Hampton last night [most likely at the Homestead], but it seems he declined going into the house with Hampton." His diary noted no punishment in that case, but later that month Canada apparently ran off briefly once more and returned. "Canada comes back tonight," wrote Benjamin. "I pardon him unconditionally." Benjamin was most likely following the examples he had learned in his youth through his observation of his father's management of the plantation and his instructions to overseers regarding corporal punishment. The administration of such discipline is remarkably scarce in Benjamin's journals, from which one may conclude that the enslaved workers gave little cause for complaint and that Benjamin carried out punishment with some reluctance. His diary entries frequently mention other enslaved persons by name and the work they did. He recorded births and deaths in a manner that indicates that he was anything but detached from the lives of the workers for whom he was responsible. If it is true that Benjamin was acting in a manner that reflected his observation of his father's treatment of their enslaved workers, then it is likely that his brothers, including Dick, had observed the same behaviors.[18]

Other family members frequently inquired after servants in their letters and dealt equally leniently with the enslaved persons with whom they interacted. Nonetheless, it seems that close association with house servants sometimes taxed the patience of even the most genteel family members. Dick's brother Wallace, writing from New Orleans Barracks in May 1855 to his future wife Mary Virginia Childs, whom Wallace called Jennie, tread carefully in probing her willingness to even approach the task of training new servants. "Have you a knack and fondness for the training of servants," he inquired. "If so you can have an opportunity, perhaps before long of trying your skill and patience in that way. Will three of all sizes be too many for your powers of endurance?" Wallace had already written his sister Mary at the Homestead asking her to "bestow some preliminary instructions" on those whom she selected for service with Wallace's fiancée. At least one of those chosen proved highly unsatisfactory. Writing from New Mexico in 1857, Jennie complained to her mother that one of the servants was "the trial of my life," who was "breaking up my supply of china ware as vigorously as usual." In this case, she expressed some hard and vengeful feelings. "I comfort myself by thinking what a breaking in he will get when I have him put on the plantation, as I intend to do when I get home." The threat of such consequences indicates the perceived superiority of being engaged as a house servant in comparison to backbreaking labor in the fields, but it also could have entailed separation from loved ones and all that was familiar, and thereby led to resentment and discontent.

For the Anderson and Childs' staff, moreover, service in the household also meant service in the life of an army officer, often at far-flung outposts. Even the more experienced Mary Anderson encountered difficulties with her house servants. In early 1861, she wrote her mother-in-law, Ann Childs, about her frustration with Allen, whom she had gladly dispatched to her brother Wallace's care. "He said Allen does about as well as any of the boys he had to wait on him which means I suppose he will be glad to be rid of him since both of the other boys he sent back to the plantation." Making the transformation from field hand to house servant or butler might have been a desirable promotion for some, but it was apparently quite a challenging ordeal. "Allen had 3 years faithful drilling and training to make him a house servant but all without avail; he will never get any higher than hoeing corn & taters! Every day and night I am thankful he is not here. I hope I may never meet his like again."[19]

The marriage of Wallace to Mary Virginia Childs, and that of her brother Frederick L. Childs to Mary Heron Anderson, closely bound the two families. Their backgrounds were somewhat different however. Fred and Mary's father, Brigadier General Thomas Wells Childs, a northern-born career army officer, had died in 1853. The Childs family resided at Fort McHenry, Maryland during the 1850 Census, and three servants were listed in the household: a mulatto coachman, a Black waiter, and a Black female with unspecified duties. All three were born in Maryland, and none were enslaved.

A separate slave schedule listed three enslaved workers, two males and one female. Thomas directed that at least two them named in his will were to be freed and given $300 upon his wife's death. The family was accustomed to having servants attend to their needs and apparently acquired other enslaved servants after Thomas' death. Their letters indicate the Childs had little trouble with their own enslaved workers and they seemed satisfied with their efforts. Writing to his mother in the summer of 1858, Fred welcomed the opportunity to see the family's enslaved servants again and observe, "how much Selina is disposed to become the grand young lady Albina is. I am sure if she follows her mistress's command & ties up her head neatly in a handkerchief as becomes a servant, she will appear far more respectable than Albina with wool tortured into love locks."[20] Still, their experience was limited, and neither Fred nor Mary had ever associated with the large numbers of enslaved persons found on the Anderson plantations and households. With both Wallace and Fred serving in the army, the Childs' interaction with enslaved persons remained confined to personal servants. That would only change later when they found themselves faced with the absentee management of the family's plantations upon the senior Dr. Anderson's death, and of course it would change when they found themselves negotiating with formerly enslaved workers after 1865 as they attempted to manage those plantations in person. As for Dick Anderson, from the age of sixteen his army career likewise excluded him from extensive contact with the rigors of running a plantation and the management of an enslaved workforce. Benjamin was the only son with extensive experience, but he died of some unspecified illness in 1857. Mackenzie, trained as a lawyer, also purchased and managed the Hiwassee plantation in 1859, but he was to live only another three years. That lack of family expertise proved telling after emancipation.

The record does not indicate whether the Anderson family ever feared violent retribution from disaffected enslaved workers, but the possibility that such thoughts plagued them is real. Both Mackenzie and Benjamin were members of the local militia company, and Benjamin noted occasionally that he was on patrol on certain dates. Most likely that was a reference to the slave patrols that were common in the Antebellum period and which sought to preserve order and ensure no enslaved persons were off their plantations without proper authorization. Chesnut's 1860–1861 diary entries depicted events that also must have occurred with similar frequency when she and Dick Anderson were young. The Denmark Vessey rebellion in Charleston occurred only a year after Dick's birth and long plagued the collective memory of enslavers. Nat Turner's 1831 rebellion in Virginia led to panic in nearby counties that spread to other states. Southern newspapers covered those events closely, and state legislatures in the South enacted a series of laws further proscribing the activities of free blacks and enslaved persons. Nevertheless, conspiracies regarding slave revolts, real or imaginary, were constantly uncovered throughout Dick Anderson's youthful years, and thus the prospect of internal threats to domestic order—whether organized or individualized—must have occupied at least some space in the thoughts of antebellum southerners.[21]

Finally, the labor system his father employed likely colored Dick Anderson's conception of his family's plantation, although one must also consider that the 150-acre property surrounding the Homestead was situated in the village of Stateburg and was not the primary plantation where the majority of the family's enslaved field hands labored—that was Riverton. Prior to his departure for West Point at the age of sixteen, Dick Anderson would have observed and conducted interactions with the house servants and other enslaved persons working near the family's home. While he must have seen the family's extensive cotton plantation at Riverton, situated about six to eight miles from the Homestead, it could not have been a major component of his daily life given his age and school commitments for most of the year. The facts are incomplete, but there is evidence that the Andersons relied primarily on the "task system" of labor, at least at the Homestead. This system differed considerably from the "gang labor" system where the intensive effort dictated by the demands of the growing season required enslaved workers to labor as a group from sunup to sundown under the supervision of a white overseer and a black foreman, known as a "driver." The "task system" that was widely used for rice and long-staple cotton cultivation in the Lowcountry and on some Upcountry cotton plantations like that of the Andersons required enslaved laborers to complete a specific daily task typically involving the amount of work that could be completed in around eight to nine hours. Upon completion, they were usually free to use their time in whatever way they saw fit. Deemed less harsh than gang labor, the task system reduced the workload and allowed enslaved people to raise gardens, sell or trade produce, and accumulate money or goods. Some plantations, perhaps Anderson's, relied on a combination of both systems, pushing enslaved laborers to work more intensively at planting, hoeing, and harvesting times, while switching to a task system in off seasons when less concentrated effort was required. The Homestead property likely had no use for the gang system because no intensive, large-scale agricultural operations there required it. At Riverton, it is likely that the gang labor system was in use at various times. That system lent itself readily to the cultivation of cotton, whose low growing tendencies made it simple for a mounted overseer or driver to observe large numbers of enslaved workers. In any case, Dick Anderson's experience in his youth might have exposed him to the more brutal reality of gang labor for at least part of the year. If so, he might have viewed the lives of the enslaved simply and naturally as bound in hard work and long hours, with far too little freedom to accomplish much else. Black laborers on his family plantation might have served no purpose other than to exhaust themselves in the service of their enslavers. While such observations would have contributed to the formation of his perceptions of the institution and of blacks in general, if Anderson's experience was mostly of workers laboring under the task system, he may have developed a different view that carried a more benign interpretation of slavery that included memories of a fairly contented enslaved community. It is difficult to determine which system he saw predominantly, but whether blacks labored eight or nine hours a day or from sunup to sundown, they toiled arduously.[22]

In addition to observing his father's treatment of enslaved persons on the plantation, Dick Anderson also saw how his mother and sister engaged them in the home. As noted above, interaction with household staff could sometimes be fraught, though many enslaved women serving as nannies were universally well loved. In many cases they formed bonds of lifelong attachment, as attested to by letters home written by adult children inquiring about the well-being of their former nannies. Still, female enslavers on large plantations faced challenges in the home that rendered their experience with their enslaved household staff very different from that of the relations their husbands and sons had with workers outside the home. Dr. Anderson, for example, though obviously involved in overseeing the efficient performance of his farming operations, could separate himself from the closest daily contact with slavery first through an overseer and driver, then later through his son

Benjamin's management of plantation operations. Though the white male enslaver was the dominant power in the southern family, he was "not the controlling force within the plantation household." The absence of overseers or drivers in the home combined with daily contact at close quarters created more intimate connections between the mistress and her house servants, but also presented more opportunities for conflict in her domain. These circumstances placed white women in a difficult position, unable to resort to the authority of their husbands to settle disputes with servants without simultaneously undermining their own control over the household. Nevertheless, they wielded a great deal of power in the home, but more than that, the presence of the mistress in the home "made it a civilized place." The work of early twentieth century Progressive historian U. B. Phillips has undergone much criticism and seen the alternating discrediting and acceptance of his ideas about slavery over the ensuing century, but he was unquestionably on target when he wrote of the plantation mistress that, "Her presence made the plantation a home; her absence would have made it a factory."[23]

Young Dick Anderson found observations of his mother and sister's interactions with the household staff instructive, but he also learned about the role and position of white women in a patriarchal southern society. Most women were not the delicate creatures often portrayed in depictions of the moonlight and magnolia antebellum South. Most often, they were a hardworking, integral part of the labor system that kept the plantation household running smoothly. As a result, they rose early and began their day supervising in the kitchen and carrying out the constant, demanding task of managing the household staff. In addition to the kinds of problems with servants cited above as expressed by Mary Anderson and Jennie Childs Anderson, female enslavers struggled constantly with household undercurrents that included servants' ongoing struggle to define their own needs and to exert some level of control over their lives within the context of slavery. The record does not reflect what, if any, level of force the female family members exerted to maintain control over the servants in the Anderson household, but all the children would have absorbed whatever lessons were imparted. The presence of complaints about sub-par performance in the surviving letters from female family members and the total absence of any mention of corporal punishment of household staff may indicate that physical violence was not a part of the Anderson household. One wonders how Dick Anderson later handled the subject when first exposing his northern wife to the intricacies of managing an enslaved household staff.[24]

Like most young boys of his class in the antebellum South, Dick Anderson and his brothers learned much about horsemanship, and Dick especially developed a love for the animals as well as substantial expertise in their handling. Conversely, if his academic standing at West Point is any indication, he devoted insufficient energy to mastering other more mundane aspects of his early education, conducted at nearby Edgehill Academy. There, all of the young Anderson boys endured the strict discipline of a dour New England schoolmaster, Willard Richardson, who charged $120 tuition for the three older Anderson boys in 1834. Richardson emphasized to his charges a study of the classics, particularly Virgil's *Aeneid*. The next year Dr. Anderson paid $135 for tuition and books that included Xenophon, Bakewell's Philosophy, Latin readers, Pike's Arithmetic, and others. The philosophy text most likely refers to Frederick C. Bakewell's recently published book entitled *Philosophical Conversations: In Which Are Familiarly Explained the Causes of Many Daily Occurring Natural Phenomena*. If so, Richardson was clearly a devoted teacher who kept pace with current trends in the subjects he taught. Bakewell's was a book designed specifically to "to keep up the attention of young people." Mostly, the author hoped, it would teach them to "think, and . . . acquire the habit of investigating the causes of things." A teacher could ask for little more, but Dick Anderson, aged fourteen in 1835, was probably like most young men in that era, for whom the popular novels of William Gilmore Simms or Sir Walter Scott were of more interest. Simms set his romantic novels in various periods of Southern history with chivalric aristocrats and rugged frontiersmen as their main protagonists. Scott's *Waverly* novels were widely read, and the 1819 publication of *Ivanhoe* especially helped plant notions of chivalry into the imagination of more than one southern boy. The generational impact of such novels is apparent. Jousting tournaments with competitors styled as Knights were highly popular among South Carolinians, and as late as the 1870s Dick Anderson's own son was a participant in such events. Despite his gruffness, "Old Bull," Richardson proved to be both a kind and patient teacher, and young Dick Anderson made some effort to master the required work. Two of his schoolbooks still among those at the Borough House library are Greek and English copies of the aforementioned Xenophon's *Cyropaedia*, or *Education of Cyrus*. One can imagine Richardson slyly trying to capture the boys' attention with such a reading by explaining that it was one of the earliest historical novels, at the same time subtly downplaying the Greek historian's didactic purposes. Whether Dick Anderson absorbed the underlying moral regarding good government, or whether the life of Cyrus the Elder proved as interesting to him as that of Ivanhoe remains a mystery.[25]

One certainty is that Anderson never developed a fondness for poetry, later telling a relative "that nothing was ever said in poetry that could not have been better said in prose." Books and recitations did not entirely occupy school days, however. Richardson once entered the classroom "with a large rattlesnake wrapped around his arm which he had just killed, and after spouting that passage from Virgil which describes Leoquon in the folds of the serpent he said with glee 'Now boys we will eat him!'" Anderson later recalled that the rattler was "as good as a young chicken." It was not the only time in his life he would sample rattlesnake. He later recalled a dinner of rattler and nettles while serving on the Plains during his antebellum Army career, claiming he found the meal "equal to bacon and greens."[26]

The genteel nature of life at the Homestead included the finely cultivated art of entertaining, and the house was a frequent destination for the well-heeled traveler as well as for socially prominent neighbors. As previously noted, the Andersons knew Governor Stephen Miller, for example, whose daughter Mary Boykin Miller would one day wed US Senator James Chesnut. Mary Boykin Chesnut's diary kept during the Civil War years and cited above contains insightful and perceptive observations about prominent figures and events of the era. In a July 1862 entry, Mary referred to the general as "Fighting Dick Anderson, one of the playfellows of my childhood." They remained friends and Dick Anderson's wife became a member of Mary's social circle in Richmond during the war.[27]

Among the most prestigious visitors to the Anderson home was a close family friend, Joel Roberts Poinsett. Poinsett traveled extensively in Europe and South America before returning in 1816 to serve in the South Carolina legislature. He and Dr. Anderson shared an interest in botany, and Poinsett's later tenure as US Minister to Mexico enabled him to bring back several specimens of a subtropical plant of the euphorbia family, christened Poinsettia in his honor. On one visit, Poinsett planted a Camelia Japonica near the rear portico of the Anderson home, which thrives there today. Appointed Secretary of War in 1837, Poinsett held that post until 1841, during which time young Dick Anderson received his appointment to the Military Academy at West Point.

Dick Anderson's grandfather and namesake, Colonel Richard Anderson, lived at the Homestead for several years. The entire Anderson family might have accompanied the old soldier to Camden in 1825, where he and former Revolutionary comrade Marquis de Lafayette were pallbearers when the remains of their fallen comrade Baron Johann de Kalb were reinterred. Also living in nearby Camden was Dick's second cousin, Dr. Edward Anderson, the eldest son of Grandfather Richard Anderson's brother. In 1830, Edward assisted Dick Anderson's father in performing one of the most noted surgical procedures of the time on an enslaved man named Tom who belonged to a neighbor. Tom had received a severe blow to his jaw some years before, after which a small tumor appeared and began to grow steadily. By the time Dr. Anderson examined him the tumor had grown so large that Tom's chin projected ten inches beyond his neck. His distended upper lip made it impossible for him to close his mouth. The deformity displaced and confined his tongue so that he had difficulty making himself understood in speech. "Altogether the disease exhibited a loathsome and frightful appearance, and rendered the life of the poor Negro almost insupportable," Dr. Anderson recalled.[28]

In a difficult operation, Dr. Anderson and his cousin Edward successfully removed the tumor. It weighed nearly three pounds. Tom had recovered so well within a few months that he was able to begin work once more. He was so thankful for the cure that he constantly expressed his desire to live at Dr. Anderson's plantation. Finally, Anderson did purchase Tom, and he lived and worked for many years afterward at the Homestead. The case was widely noted as the first successful removal of a cancerous jawbone. Accounts appeared in *The American Journal of the Medical Sciences* in 1832 and in Gibson's *The Institutes and Practice of Surgery* in 1845.[29]

Wallace eventually took up the study medicine as well, but if their father harbored any hopes of a medical career for his eldest son Dick, they went unrealized. Wallace graduated South Carolina College and attended medical school at the University of Pennsylvania. He passed the exam given by the Army Medical Board in May 1849, and was selected to fill one of three vacancies for surgeons. His service in Texas and New Mexico provided opportunities to pursue his own interests in natural history. Among materials he forwarded to the Smithsonian Institution in Washington, DC was a new species of that bird commonly known as Virginia's Warbler, named in honor of his wife Mary Virginia Childs, whom he married in 1855. With a facile talent for art as well, Wallace's landscape drawing of "The Needles," a distinctive rock formation lying between the Cayetano Mountains and San Juan River, appeared in Captain Randolph B. Marcy's 1859 guidebook for westward-bound pioneers entitled *The Prairie Traveler*. Other drawings that survive today include miniature portraits of his children and a view of New Mexico's Cantonment Burgwyn.[30]

Their brother Mackenzie studied law and practiced in Sumter, dividing his time between a boarding house there and the Homestead until 1859, when he purchased the 1,900-acre Hiwassee plantation. Benjamin, as noted previously, took over responsibility for management of his father's Riverton plantation until his premature death in 1857.

Dick Anderson showed no early evidence of scientific skills or interests, though his service on the western plains later compelled him to take an interest in the natural world. Meantime, when he reached his later teen years convenient circumstances related to Joel R. Poinsett's career influenced Dr. Anderson's calculations regarding his eldest son's future. Poinsett's appointment as Secretary of War presented a unique opportunity for him to do a good turn for his friend Dr. Anderson by appointing his son to the United States Military Academy at West Point, New York. That Poinsett acted on his behalf is very likely, particularly since no formal application from Anderson is located in the records of the military academy. However, Poinsett and other political figures who nominated candidates typically provided only the opportunity for the consideration of nominees. Nominees also had to be physically fit and have some proficiency in reading, writing, and arithmetic, and they had to pass an entrance exam given in June. With free tutoring provided, along with a second chance to pass in August unless a congressional representative nominated a replacement immediately, over 90 percent of the antebellum nominees became cadets. Still, academic deficiencies led to the dismissal of more than 25 percent of those admitted. Young Dick Anderson, aged sixteen years and nine months, entered the class of 1842 on July 1, 1838, thereafter embarking on an association with military life that would span twenty-seven years of service.[31]

Chapter 2

From West Point to Mexico

Reared as we are, in quiet and in peace
Now all at once we're thrown upon the world

—Goethe,
An Lottchen

When Dick Anderson arrived at the United States Military Academy at West Point, New York in the summer of 1838, it was an institution in the midst of turmoil.[1] The lackadaisical leadership of the former commandant of cadets left morale at a low point. Disciplinary problems abounded. Former adjutant First Lieutenant Charles F. Smith now held the post. By September, Major Richard Delafield stepped into the position of Superintendent. Delafield found the institution in frightful condition and its cadets much in need of firmer discipline. Together, Smith and Delafield were just the men needed to restore discipline and morale at the institution.[2]

Delafield had the scholarly look of a New England Transcendentalist, and his parsimonious nature along with his ardor in enforcing regulations soon led many cadets to develop a dislike of the officer. He acquired the nickname "Dicky the Punster" because of the frequent sarcasm he used when addressing cadets. He was indefatigable in his efforts to restore discipline, however, and he acted just as strictly in protecting the government's funds. Cadets sometimes purchased uniform items on credit after trading their issued government clothing to local civilians in exchange for food, tobacco, or alcohol. Delafield prohibited plebes from drawing new garments on credit. Instead, he recommended they learn to mend their worn items. Dick Anderson thus honed the sewing skills that he later practiced "for relaxation" during quiet times in camp, even after he became a general officer in the Confederate Army.[3]

With many issues corrected by the fall term in 1838, small additional steps made a cadet's life more comfortable, though it remained an austere existence. Cadet Anderson would have slept on a pallet spread on the drafty floor of his room until completion of the entrance exams. After that he would have been permitted the use a narrow iron bedstead at the cost of twenty cents a month. Mattresses remained folded and bedding was placed in a bag during the day to deter cadets from sleeping during study hours.

Cadet rooms remained closely monitored, with inspections several times daily. Eating and smoking there were prohibited. Unless excused, cadets were restricted to their rooms when not attending classes, and they were required to be in uniform even when in their quarters. Regimentation governed nearly every aspect of their daily lives. They marched under supervision to classes and meals, and paraded seven days a week in addition to special parades held for distinguished visitors.[4]

Saturday night marked the only time during the week when cadets were free to engage in organized entertainment, but amusement was scarce and makeshift. Cadets uninterested in the exercises of the Dialectic Society, cadet theatrical performances, or the band concerts that constituted the usual Saturday evening fare might even leave the post to indulge in a variety of prohibited activities, but at the risk of dismissal. The infamous nearby tavern owned by Benny Havens was the most notorious of the local drinking establishments, but not the only one. Whether Cadet Anderson ever succumbed to those enticements is not a matter of record. Havens and other local citizens sometimes managed to smuggle liquor onto the post as well, where cadets might be tempted to combine illicit drinking with two other favorite but prohibited activities: smoking and cooking in the barracks rooms. Each of the Spartan chambers in the barracks during Anderson's time at the Point was equipped with a coal-burning fireplace for heating. With food foraged from the mess hall or from the officer's barnyards, cadets sometimes cooked up an improvised feast that, if not tastier than their usual fare, was at least a change from the monotonous diet of bread, beef, and potatoes. Cadets frequently complained of the food during Anderson's time, noting in addition to its generally abysmal taste the presence of various bugs and other foreign matter not suited for ingestion.[5]

Algebra, Geometry, and Trigonometry constituted the primary focus of the cadets' first year, along with study of the French language. One text used was Jean-Jacques Barthélemy's four-volume *Voyage du jeune Anacharsis en Grèce*. Cadets were to cover two volumes of the young Scythian's adventures that year before continuing with the same course in their second year. As was the case with Dick Anderson's earlier classical education, one may ponder whether many heeded the underlying message regarding the quest for knowledge and instruction, but the presence of such works in the secular canon of young American men at that time illustrates the importance given to further shaping their character. Third class cadets—those in their second year—continued with French and moved on to Calculus, Surveying, and more Geometry. Added that year were classes in English Grammar and drawing of the human figure and topography. As second classman, or their third year as cadets, drawing continued with more emphasis on landscape and topography, and the academic focus turned to science. Natural and Experimental Philosophy included such topics as Astronomy, Optics Electricity, and Mechanics. Along with that was a full year of Chemistry. Finally, in their senior, or first-class year, cadets began their study of the military arts. Classes in Mineralogy and Geology were important to the officers in their explorations of the West, while Ethics classes taught Rhetoric, International Law, and Moral Philosophy. For many cadets, interest in those classes paled in comparison to Artillery and Infantry Tactics. They learned the artillery business from the role of individual gun crewmembers through the maneuvering of entire artillery batteries, along with technical details about projectiles and powder. The Infantry course similarly progressed through the school of the soldier from individual manual arms and drill to the maneuvering of units up to brigade size. Finally, in what was probably the most critical component of a young cadet's academic career at the Academy, they began to learn Engineering and the Science of War from Professor Dennis Hart Mahan. The Academy was designed to produce engineers, and the courses taught in 1842 by Mahan and his two assistants included not only the subjects of "Military Engineering" and "Field Fortifications," but also classes on "Civil Engineering," that covered architecture, stone cutting, and machines. Moreover, each year cadets engaged in practical exercises through the Department of Tactics. Those included infantry and artillery drills as well as fencing and equitation on alternate days.[6]

Three distinct branches existed in the regular army structure during this period: the scientific corps, the general staff, and the line. The largest percentage of graduates from the Military Academy found themselves assigned to the scientific corps. War Department policies reserved assignments there for graduates with the highest class standing, and top cadets found themselves in the prestigious ranks of the corps of engineers, the topographical engineers, or the ordnance corps. The next most enviable assignment was to the artillery, which combined elements of science with those of a combat function. Finally, fewest graduates went to the least desirable line positions, among which were postings to infantry or dragoon regiments, the latter considered more elite than the infantry.[7]

When he graduated the Academy on July 1, 1842, Richard H. Anderson stood an undistinguished fortieth in his class of fifty-six. His highest standings on his final exam in 1842 were in the subject of "Ethics" and "Engineering," in which he was ranked thirty-fourth. The lowest standing was in "Mineralogy and Geology," where his order of merit was forty-seventh. Dick also accrued sixty-three demerits in his final year at West Point, placing him 118th on the conduct roll of the entire corps of cadets. He received an appointment as brevet second lieutenant in Company D of Colonel Stephen

Watts Kearny's 1st Dragoons, and he was ordered to report to the Cavalry School for Practice located at Carlisle Barracks, Pennsylvania. The small staff of dragoon riding instructors at West Point undoubtedly had their eyes open for suitable equestrians among their pupils. A handful of cadets who finished higher in the class standings but whose horsemanship might have proved deficient in the eyes of the dragoon instructors were not so lucky, and they found themselves in the infantry.[8]

Just behind Anderson stood George Sykes of Maryland, who received a posting to the 3rd Infantry. Sykes eventually commanded the Union Fifth Corps in 1863. Sykes earned the moniker "Tardy George" in the Old Army for his lack of dash and initiative. Most of those finishing ahead of Anderson carried on the tradition of being posted to more prestigious assignments. Cadets like William S. Rosecrans, Gustavus W. Smith, Mansfield Lovell, John Pope, Seth Williams, Abner Doubleday, and Daniel Harvey Hill took their places with the army's engineers or artillerists. Classmates finishing nearer the bottom included Lafayette McLaws, Earl Van Dorn, and James Longstreet, all of whom received infantry assignments. By 1861, of the thirty-seven surviving members of the Class of 1842, thirteen cast their lot with the Confederacy; twenty-one with the Union.[9]

Like many graduates, Anderson took a leave of absence before embarking on a career that would separate him from family and friends for extended periods. He was authorized leave until the end of September, after which he was to report for duty at Carlisle. As a school for practice, Carlisle Barracks saw most of the Army's new dragoon officers pass through its gates on a "period of probation, or rather preparation, . . . ere they are fitted to encounter the buffetings of a rude and extremely practical world." It was the "trooper's nursery," as one of them fondly recalled, and it taught the new men much.[10]

> The profuse hospitality and proverbial geniality of the good citizens of Carlisle threw much light upon the subject of dining out; the wit and beauty of the belles of Cumberland County rendered the study of human nature and the refinements of society comparatively easy and delightful; while the old-time reputation of Pennsylvania whiskey made experiments with alcohol a pleasing and extremely popular branch of chemistry. But the jolly fellows one by one passed out into the life of adventure, privation, and peril to which Carlisle was but the introduction; a life spent—perchance too quickly—in a dragoon saddle and in "the rough service of the horse."[11]

In addition to learning the rudiments of dragoon service, it is likely that Dick's duties included organizing recently assigned men and their equipage for the westward journey to join their companies, which were frequently scattered among various posts since the regiments were rarely intact. Dick began preparations in November 1842 after receiving orders to join his company at Fort Gibson, Indian Territory. The standard route of that day would have taken him by train to Harrisburg, thence by canal to Pittsburgh, where a steamer took him down the Ohio River to the Mississippi. From there, dragoons going to the headquarters at Fort Leavenworth traveled northward to the Missouri River. Anderson and those going to forts in the Indian Territory headed south on the Mississippi to the Arkansas River, then westward—in Anderson's case to the very gates of Fort Gibson. He arrived at the lonely frontier outpost two days before Christmas to find himself serving as third officer in Company D, commanded by 1st Lieutenant Abraham R. Johnston, an Ohioan who had graduated in the class of 1835. The 2nd lieutenant, John W. T. Gardiner of Maine, had been transferred to the company just a few weeks before and had graduated with the class of 1840. Company D's rolls included two sergeants, four corporals, two buglers, forty-two privates, and a farrier.[12]

Also at Fort Gibson was Company H, commanded by Captain Nathan Boone, son of the famous frontiersman Daniel Boone. Nathan was an elderly scion of the frontier by then, highly respected for his knowledge of the plains and its Native American inhabitants. With Boone was First Lieutenant Robert Hall Chilton of Virginia, who would later serve the Confederacy as General Robert E. Lee's chief of staff. Company H's newly assigned second lieutenant was another Virginian, Anderson's classmate Armistead T. M. Rust who graduated thirty-first in the class.[13]

Built in 1824, Fort Gibson lay on the Grand River, three miles above the Arkansas near present-day Muskogee, Oklahoma. A nearly impenetrable canebrake on three sides, and the river on the fourth, protected the fort. The rock ledge on the riverbank provided a perfect natural landing for the boats bringing soldiers and supplies. Established to protect the Native American tribes that had emigrated from the East, Fort Gibson housed the troops expected to halt feuding between the Osage and the more-recently arrived Cherokee. After Congress authorized the formation of a regiment of mounted troops in March 1833, the fort also became a base for dragoons protecting the Santa Fe Trail.[14]

By the time Dick Anderson arrived there in December 1842, men like Captain Nathan Boone had already spent the better part of their lives learning the ways of the Native Americans and exploring the vast expanses of the American West. Assignment to Boone's company would have been beneficial, and though it was not the case, Dick learned much through his subsequent association with the captain. That connection began in the spring of 1843, when Boone led an expedition in search of the great salt plain. The party included Anderson's company. Born in Kentucky in 1782, Boone grew up on the frontier, acquiring many talents that distinguished him from the average officer. His service as captain in a battalion of volunteer mounted rangers raised in 1832 led to an appointment with the 1st Dragoons. One trooper who joined Boone's company in 1839 had nothing but the greatest admiration for his captain.

> He was then about 60, spending his life in exploring the country, and surveying, in intercourse with the various Indian Tribes, he knew them all, could speak the dialect of each, had passed nearly the whole of his life in the open air, so as to give some plausibility to the opinion so commonly expressed, that he knew every inch of the land from the Mississippi River to the Rocky Mountains. And yet with this experience, he was the most kind, affable, and strictly honest man, simple in his habits and manners, not refined except in that politeness which good nature inspires.[15]

Boone gladly passed along his knowledge to his men. He had their complete confidence, and they trusted that "he could find his way where few others could." He taught them how to guide by the sun or to tell direction from the growth of "superior foliage or mosses on the South side of large trees." It was on the treeless prairie where his talents gave the men a real edge though. He showed them how they could determine directions by observing the Pilot Grass, which grew always with the edges of its leaves faced north and south, and the flat of the leaves to the east and west. Though it was not abundant on the plains, one typically found it several times a day in the course of travel. Boone was proficient in the common sign language of the Native American tribes, and was able to speak several dialects well enough to communicate with almost anyone his troop might encounter. He was the perfect commander for a company of dragoons, not only because of his unparalleled skills and experience, but as one contemporary put it, because of his "unflinching perseverance, combined with personal courage, and an integrity which nothing could shake."[16]

Boone's goal in April 1843 was to observe and map the area of the "great salt plain" and "accurately lay down the exact Latitude and Longitude of a certain Salt Rock which had hitherto only been known to Indians." What Boone was looking for was the area of present-day north-central Oklahoma encompassed by the Great Salt Plain State Park. Modern travelers could cover the distance in a matter of a few hours. On May 14, Boone set out with Company H, while three days later, thirty-one troopers of Company D headed out in a heavy rain to join him. At the head of Company D was Lieutenant Johnston, with Dick Anderson second in command. Lieutenant Gardiner remained at Fort Gibson.[17]

Catching up with Boone on the banks of the Arkansas River, they found him preparing to ford the half-mile-wide river. Boone had the men build a bark canoe to transport the provisions. It took ten trips to transfer the supplies the next morning, with the soldiers wading across the river on foot and pulling the canoe along with them. Teams hauled the three wagons over without incident, and the troopers forded with the water level up to the horses' saddle skirts. Anderson undoubtedly learned a great deal from observing the process.[18]

The men marched early the next morning, following "the great Osage hunting trail." The landscape quickly changed as they traveled westward with the prairie grass disappearing almost entirely, giving way to short buffalo grass. Timber appeared only along the banks of streams. "On leaving one creek it was like putting out to the open sea until we rose the ridge," Boone noted, "when a narrow skirt of trees would point out the position of the next."[19]

By Saturday, May 27, they began to see recent signs of buffalo, particularly in places where salt seemed to effloresce from the prairie floor. Just after sunset, a dark cloud appeared in the northwestern skies and soon brought a fearful thunderstorm with hailstones said to be the size of hen's eggs. The horses stood it until the storm had nearly subsided, when many panicked suddenly and broke for the open. The herd roamed the plains all night, but the frightened beasts returned on the run at daylight. The following day they met a group of about forty friendly Osages, the Wah-sha-she. They led the soldiers to their camp, where more Osages were busily attending to twenty-five buffalo they had recently killed. Boone learned from them that one of the salt plains for which he was searching was within twenty miles, and he decided to camp that night with the Osage and obtain a guide the next day.[20]

Unfortunately, morning revealed several horses and mules missing from the camp, with only their cleanly sliced lariats remaining as a clue to their fate. The Osage reported that Pawnees had come in the darkness and stolen some of their horses as well. After a fruitless chase led by the Osage the trail was lost among the buffalo tracks on the plain. Boone's suspicion, however, was slowly focusing on the Osage themselves. When Boone agreed to another joint search for the mounts, Osages eventually pointed out a trail that only heightened the soldiers' suspicions. It was clear that a group of shod horses made the tracks, but there was not a single unshod hoof print among them. Had Pawnee stolen the horses, they would have been riding their own unshod mounts and leading the army horses behind. Boone then sprang another trap for the Osage. One of the dragoons came forward with a knife found near the missing horses. The soldier handed it to the Osage chief saying that he found it during the pursuit and asking whether it belonged to the Osage. "Oh yes, Wa-sash-ay" replied the grateful chief. When told that the soldier had found the knife near the spot where the missing horses had been tied, the wily chief claimed that their trader also traded with the Pawnee and they had knives just like the Osage. Despite his frustration, Boone wisely elected to drop the matter and return to his mission of exploring the salt plain. Anderson's opportunity to observe interactions with the duplicitous Osage was an experience that added to his comprehension of human nature, and subsequent events soon reinforced his appreciation for the behavior of his fellow man.[21]

A few days later, after finding the salt plain, the soldiers surprised another party of Osages. One of them was riding an Army mule stolen from the dragoon camp. Boone had his men take away the Osages' guns and their bows and arrows. The officers requested permission to take four ponies from the party to replace the four privately owned horses that were among those stolen. Boone promised the Osages that he would return them in exchange for the original animals, but they never saw them again. The incident was thus imperfectly resolved. That night the dragoons camped on the nearly treeless expanse of plain on the north side of the Arkansas and feasted on a freshly killed antelope, which they found "very tender and delicate." Only the presence of a large number of mosquitoes spoiled the otherwise pleasant night around the campfires, during which the mildly satisfying conclusion to the mystery of the stolen animals was undoubtedly a topic of discussion.[22]

By Wednesday, June 7, having been out for twenty-five days, Boone's force reached the Santa Fe Trail. Some were disappointed to find that the celebrated trail was "no made road at all, but an immense mire, in some places more than a mile wide, where the original prairie ground had been so worn by the [wagon] trains passing, that others following were obliged to take a wider range onto new grounds."[23]

With their rations nearly exhausted, Anderson and Boone with a small hunting party spent the following Sunday searching for buffalo. They traveled nearly twenty miles before falling in with a herd of the beasts, quickly killing and dressing a number of the animals before loading the meat onto spare horses and arriving back at camp at 2 AM the next morning. Men and horses rested that day while the buffalo meat cured over smoky fires. The following day's hunt proved more eventful when Lieutenant Johnston rode back into camp after his gun accidentally discharged and sent a ball completely through his foot. The wound was dressed and Johnston placed in a wagon while the men moved nearer the Arkansas River. There they encountered Captain Phillip St. George Cooke with three companies of dragoons from Fort Leavenworth escorting traders on the Santa Fe Trail. That evening, thousands of buffalo surrounded the dragoon's camp and munched complacently on the grass, while soldiers easily killed several more of them.[24]

Over the next few days, storms collapsed tents, stampeded horses, and churned the Arkansas into a raging torrent that prevented a crossing. Boone remained encamped for several days after the storms while the waters receded, and one evening the dragoons "heard a heavy rumbling sound, resembling something like underground thunder." An immense herd of buffalo soon appeared. Soldiers ran for their carbines, anxious for the chance to shoot one. Once again, stampeding beasts crushed tents to the ground and several horses broke their lariats and ran off. The men, however, cared only for the thrill of the hunt and the chance to bag one of the majestic animals. The dragoons were fortunate no one was shot accidentally in the crossfire. When the herd passed, forty dead buffalo lay strewn on the prairie. "But this was wanton destruction," recalled one soldier, "as we did not require or could not use 1/100th part of the meat. The rest was left to the prairie wolves or other wild animals."[25]

Boone's reaction to the slaughter went unrecorded, but a few days later, the grand sight of nearly 10,000 buffalo grazing on the plain below their hilltop vantage provided a memorable vista. The animals stretched as far as the eye could see, and the soldiers stood mesmerized as a dozen wild horses ran playfully through the unfazed herd. The soldiers passed the July 4 holiday roasting buffalo meat and generally enjoying themselves, but two days later they experienced their first loss when a private died in camp. He had been riding in a wagon since they left the banks of the Arkansas, but finally succumbed to what one trooper recalled as "a disease of the brain of old standing." They buried him under a cottonwood tree on the bank of a creek, and one of the men carved his name into the tree.[26]

On July 18, Lieutenants Johnston and Anderson reached the spot where they were to part with Boone and continue on to Fort Washita. With the injured Johnston still riding in the company wagon, Anderson took over command of the troop. Despite having spent over a month at the side of the master and absorbing Boone's extensive knowledge, Anderson promptly got lost and was in danger of running out of provisions altogether. Leaving Johnston with five men, he struck out to find the confluence of the Canadian and Little River. A few miles up the Little River, he knew he would find Edwards Trading Post. After a trek of forty-five miles, Anderson replenished his supplies there, recovered his bearings, and returned to Johnston before continuing on to Ft. Washita without further incident.[27]

As Dick Anderson's first great adventure on the plains came to an end, he could reflect on what he had learned. Crossing swollen streams, surviving on the land, interacting with Native Americans—all of those were experiences he would put to good use throughout his career in the West, and his foray with Boone had laid a solid foundation for a life on the plains. It might even have reinforced what became a longstanding habit with Anderson. Self-sufficiency was essential to survival on the frontier. Dick mastered the ability to maintain his clothing and equipment—a habit begun of necessity at West Point—and he apparently found enjoyment in it. Much later when he was a Confederate general, one member of his staff noted that on first waking, Anderson had the habit of frequently "sitting on his bed and proceeding to mend and patch his belongings out of a well-filled tailor's 'necessaire' he always carried." The officer noted that from mending clothes to repairing tack, "everything came handy to him. He caught me once watching this work," the staff officer later recalled, "and said, smiling good naturedly: 'You are wondering, I see; so did my wife when first married. She thought she should do the mending, but I told her I ought to have a little recreation occasionally.'"[28]

Anderson's company rested at Fort Washita, spending a relatively inactive summer and fall in the Red River country. Meanwhile, Lieutenant Gardiner joined them there in August, no doubt to Dick's welcome relief, as Lieutenant Johnston was in no condition to assist with the day-to-day routine of commanding a dragoon company.[29]

Eventually, Anderson received orders to take thirty men and escort Cherokee Indian Agent Pierce Mason Butler to the Red River. At age sixty-five, the former Army officer and veteran of the Seminole War was an influential and prominent figure in Anderson's home state, having served two years as South Carolina's governor before receiving an appointment as Indian Agent at Fort Gibson. Butler would soon don his uniform once more and fall at the head of the Palmetto Regiment at Churubusco, Mexico in 1847. Anderson—just recently turned twenty-two years of age—Butler, and the dragoons set out from Washita on November 30, 1843. Over the course of the next two weeks, Anderson cultivated Butler's friendship and left a lasting impression on the influential older man. Butler later wrote Dick's father about the "pride & satisfaction I felt with the association & acquaintance with your son Lt. R. H. Anderson of the Army last winter." Butler congratulated Dr. Anderson "upon having such a son," and went on to compliment him on Dick's fine attributes: "He is Sir a young man of high personal qualities. As a Soldier and a Gentleman he has no superior. It was my pride as a Carolinian to hear from every quarter 'Lt Anderson of South Carolina is a Gentleman' of high moral worth & a soldier of high promise. I hope he will continue in the service. I left him in good health & fine spirits."[30]

By the following July Anderson was transferred to the 2nd Dragoons at Fort Jessup, Louisiana, where a year elapsed before the annexation of the Republic of Texas in July 1845 led to increased tensions with Mexico. Fort Jessup's garrison was soon on its way to the border. The dragoons were to make a cross-country march to join the "Army of Observation" assembling near Corpus Christi, Texas. Around 500 men in seven companies, commanded by Colonel David E. Twiggs, set off from Ft Jessup on July 25 with a train of sixty wagons. "Anticipations and predictions of a disastrous march for the dragoons, on account of the drouth [*sic*] and warm season, were rife among certain wiseacres," recalled one participant. Twiggs avoided much of the summer heat by marching the men at about 3 AM, or sometimes midnight, and terminating the day's trek before the daytime temperatures rose. Nonetheless, three men died from heat-related illnesses, and a number of other men deserted. Some placed blame for several of the desertions on the fact that over the first six days of the march many horses could not be ridden because of newly adopted Army saddles causing severe soreness of the horses' backs. A number of troopers were thus trudging along on foot. Moreover, by the time the regiment neared Corpus Christi, there were already fifty men listed as sick. That quickly changed with the prospect of a fight. As the dragoons crossed the Nueces River, they heard what they supposed was a salute being fired at Corpus Christi. When the "distant reports" continued unabated, the men concluded that the town must have come under attack. "'To horse' was immediately sounded, then 'the advance.'" The men who were sick and convalescent were ordered to remain with the wagons, but "when we were fairly under way . . . the officer left in charge reported that there were no sick, *the number having suddenly been reduced from fifty to nothing*!" Dick Anderson and the excited dragoons had gone about three miles before encountering General Taylor on his way to greet them. They "soon discovered that instead of the enemy we were about to meet a violent thunderstorm." They professed to be "not much vexed, as the occurrence displayed to us the alacrity with which our men would prepare to meet the enemy."[31]

Arriving at Corpus Christi on August 27, the dragoons thought the camp idyllic, "probably one of the healthiest and pleasantest spots in the world." Nights were cool while refreshing sea breezes kept daytime heat and mosquitoes at bay. Fish were plentiful in the surrounding waters. The men drilled and enjoyed hunting, racing, and a makeshift theater. Lieutenant Anderson likely accompanied dragoon patrols "into the interior on 'tours of observation.'" The idyllic setting eventually proved anything but that when fall arrived with frequent overnight turns in the weather. The soldiers called them "northers," and the "instantaneous transit from the torrid to the frigid zone" often left water buckets iced over and tent canvas shrouded in sleet. "The beauty of this climate is decidedly in the summer," concluded one of the discomfited dragoons. The effect on Dick Anderson, then commanding Company D in the absence of Captain Lawrence P. Graham, was telling. After falling ill with a debilitating case of typhoid pneumonia, he eagerly grasped an opportunity to return home in early 1846. Anderson was listed among the regiment's sick men throughout February, and on March 6, he procured a sixty-day leave of absence and left immediately for home to recover his health. Two days later his regiment departed Corpus Christi for the Rio Grande near Matamoras. After arriving home, Anderson traveled to Sullivans Island on the South Carolina seacoast, probably at the insistence of his father, who may have advised salt air as part of his treatment. It seems unlikely that the family would have sent their long absent son away on his own, and perhaps his parents and siblings took the opportunity to enjoy the delightful spring weather by the sea as well. Vacationing on Sullivans Island was something they would enjoy over the next several years, most likely renting a house until the spring of 1848, when Dr. Anderson purchased a home known as the Wilkes House for $260.[32]

Chapter 3

The Mexican–American War

Broad is the road that leads to death,
And thousands flock together there.

—Isaac Watts,
hymn "The Almost Christian"

The United States declared war on Mexico on May13, 1846 after Mexican soldiers surrounded and overwhelmed a dragoon squadron led by Captain Seth B. Thornton at La Rosia. Captains Thornton and William J. Hardee were captured, along with a lieutenant and forty-six enlisted men. Eight men died in the lopsided fray, including Anderson's Academy classmate Lieutenant George T. Mason. Anderson by then believed his health was "sufficiently reestablished" and was soon on his way back to his company despite being authorized leave until June 6. He claimed he "traveled night and day" in an effort to reach his command, yet he was only as far as Mobile, Alabama by July 2. There he fired off a required monthly status report before continuing on to New Orleans. When he reached the Crescent City, Anderson encountered Company H of the 2nd Dragoons, its troopers full of exciting tales of events south of the border. He was dismayed to find himself transferred to Company H, with instructions to return east for recruiting duty at the small town of Abingdon, in the mountains of southwestern Virginia. Four other disappointed officers of the Second Dragoons were performing similar duty around the country at that time.[1]

Anderson was soon relieved from recruiting duties and he reached Camargo, Mexico by early October where he found Captain Nathaniel W. Hunter leading Company H. The Second Dragoons continued to operate in much the same manner it had on the Plains. The regiment was seldom together and companies instead frequently deployed to separate locations, while squads were further broken out from the companies to engage in specific missions. While his classmates were gaining laurels leading infantry or artillery units, mounted officers performed vital, yet often less conspicuous duties. Things began to change after Major General Winfield Scott landed his army at Veracruz, Mexico in March 1847, but in the meantime, the dragoons acted as couriers, scouts, and skirmishers.[2]

Camargo had been the assembly point for American forces advancing against Monterey. In the summer of 1846, it became a vast sea of misery,

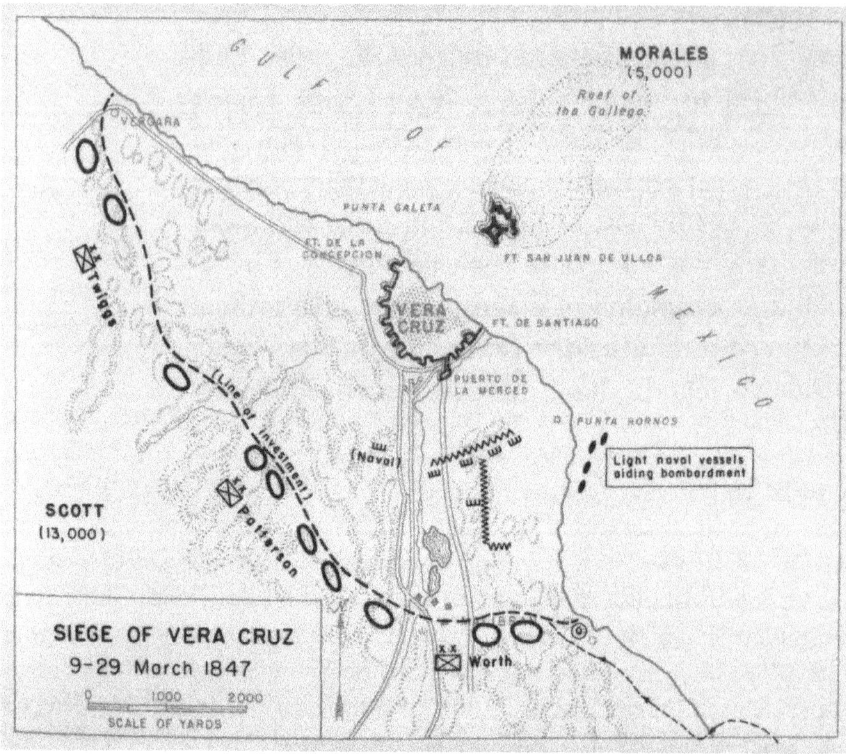

Figure 1. Map of the Siege of Vera Cruz. *The West Point Atlas of American Wars* (1959). Library of Congress Geography and Map Division.

sickness, and death. A plethora of diseases for which young men from rural areas had no previous exposure or immunity decimated volunteer regiments before ever firing a shot. The climate and camp conditions had less effect on the regulars, and Anderson was fortunate to have fallen ill earlier when he could still leave the regiment to recover. When he arrived there in October, it remained a forlorn place. Everywhere one looked the freshly dug graves of once eager volunteers sat baking in the scorching sun. Lieutenant Anderson was undoubtedly glad to leave northern Mexico to accompany Scott's force when he transferred to Captain Hardee's Company C in late January. On February 25, 1847, Anderson finally began to move towards Veracruz.

The dragoons embarked at Brazos Santiago "on small coastal vessels chartered for the occasion." After joining General Scott, they would sail past Veracruz to an anchorage two miles south of the city. Scott put 10,000 men ashore on March 9 with no resistance from the defenders of Veracruz, and over the next few days he began landing supplies and extending his lines. Then the weather threatened what had been an amazingly smooth amphibious operation. "Northers" blew in and halted the operation. The dragoons anchored off the coast suffered badly in the storms. Many horses were lost and one unlucky dragoon washed overboard and drowned. The transport *Yazoo* wedged fast on a reef, stranding Colonel William S. Harney and one troop of dragoons. All the men were saved, but fewer than ten of the mounts survived. The relieved dragoons were back on solid ground on March 21, but General Scott noted they were "without effective horses for more than a company, many having been lost at sea, and another large portion rendered unfit for immediate service." Those who were mounted participated in the investment of the city's defenses, others manned trenches with the infantry.[3]

With the rapid fall of Veracruz by March 27, Scott's forces moved inland as quickly as possible to avoid what was called the "vomito," or yellow fever season. Anderson's Company C, along with three others, were in the vanguard of the army's advance over the great highway followed by Hernando Cortes' conquistadors three hundred years before. Anderson's company encamped near Jalapa, forty-six hundred feet above the tropical plain around Veracruz. They continued scouting and carrying dispatches, both hazardous chores due to the numerous guerilla bands on the road between Veracruz and Jalapa. On April 14, for example, a newspaper correspondent noted that "A dragoon, who had been sent down express by Gen. Twiggs, was yesterday found shot by the roadside. His papers had not been touched. It is thought they have killed no less than fifty of our men within the last three days on the road." Two days later the same correspondent encountered Lieutenant Anderson with a small forage party and a company of Tennessee Mounted Volunteers along that road. Anderson's dragoons recorded no encounters with Mexicans, who were mostly irregulars preying on lone riders, but two of the Tennesseans had been wounded earlier after having had "a brief skirmish with a party of rancheros." Such duties meant that Anderson was not engaged two days later at Cerro Gordo.[4]

Well-entrenched Mexican forces were ready to make a stand at Cerro Gordo and Anderson must have been piqued at missing the action. The American infantry assault threw the defenders "into great confusion," and they "fled precipitously." That was the signal to deploy the dragoons, whose pursuit of the fleeing army caused further panic and inflicted a great number of casualties until the exhaustion of their mounts compelled them to halt. A correspondent passing along the road afterward reported seeing "the bodies of Mexican lancers and their horses, cut down by Colonel Harney's dragoons. Almost every man's skull was literally split open with the sabers of our horsemen, and they lay stretched upon the ground in ghastly groups." Scott's nemesis, General Santa Anna, set about organizing another force to contest Scott's advance.[5]

Anderson and three companies of dragoons accompanied Scott to Puebla, the second largest city in Mexico, arriving on May 28. On June 18, Anderson was escorting a wagon train when a strong force of Mexican "guerrilleros" attempted to block the mountain pass of La Hoya. Dismounted dragoons soon drove the Mexicans from the heights around the pass at La Hoya and onto the road, where they encountered other mounted dragoons ready to give chase. The horsemen drove the fleeing Mexicans into a waiting line of American troops who had come out from Perote on hearing the firing. Mexican losses were about thirty killed and wounded, with the American casualties at half a dozen men wounded slightly. It was termed a "skirmish" and the results were decidedly lopsided in favor of the American troops, but it marks the first time one can say with certainty that Lieutenant Anderson was directly engaged in the fighting.[6]

Scott's army continued its advance toward Mexico City from Puebla on August 7, with dragoons leading the way. Mexican cavalry shadowed the army but kept "a respectful distance" until they neared the hacienda of Buena Vista on the 10th. There, Mexican cavalry "of the guerilla breed" appeared in the road about a mile distant. The Mexicans "brandished their lances, and waved their hats, apparently challenging a fight." Anderson's company, led by Captain Hardee, was among three under the command of Major Edwin V. Sumner. All went forward to meet the challenge. The Mexicans continued to taunt the Americans, "yelling, as if to intimidate us," recalled one participant. "But yelling is the last thing they should attempt," he went on, "for our men can make an Indian ashamed of himself any time when they commence hallooing in battle." Sure enough, as the dragoons broke into a canter "the cowardly rascals dispersed in every direction, each man flying for his own safety, leaving the dragoons much disappointed."[7]

Scott's army inched its way across 10,000-foot mountain passes and established headquarters at Ayotla. From there the National Road narrowed to a causeway that ran through marshy lands between Lake Texcoco to the north, and Lakes Chalco and Xochimilco to the south. Mexico City loomed less than twenty miles distant, but the area lying between the lakes was heavily fortified. Scott became convinced that the proper approach to the city was along a road that skirted south of Lakes Chalco and Xochimilco to San Augustin.[8]

Dragoons spent several days probing the extent of the Mexican defenses and alternate routes of approach, but once Scott decided to take the southern route, the harshness of the rocky terrain limited the usefulness of the cavalry. The dragoons advanced at the head of Major General William J. Worth's division to the vicinity of San Augustin, where they quickly drove off a guerilla force after firing a few shots. They entered the town on August 17 after another brief skirmish. On the following day, Scott ordered Worth to probe the road northward that led through the hacienda of San Antonio and thence on to Mexico City. Enemy guns swept the road and a sixteen-pound shell struck Captain Seth Thornton full in the chest, mangling his body "in the most horrid manner." The strength of the Mexican positions prompted Scott to explore other routes. Captain Robert E. Lee found an alternative path through a lava field known as the Pedregal, and engineers and laborers set to work making it suitable for the passage of artillery. A large band of guerillas set upon Anderson and Hardee on August 20 as they guarded the approaches to San Augustin. The skirmish led to the repulse of the guerillas "with the loss of nearly forty horses and a quantity of arms and accoutrements captured by the dragoons."[9]

Anderson was officially distinguished in the engagement at San Augustin. Captain Hardee brought Anderson's behavior to Major Sumner's attention. Sumner, then commanding the regiment, mentioned Anderson by name in his official report. Only five other line officers of the regiment, all captains, warranted comment in the period of August 7 through August 20. One of those was the slain Captain Thornton. Anderson was the only "subaltern" line officer deemed worthy of mention. Though no more vivid account survives, Anderson's behavior was remarkable enough to enable Hardee to lobby for Anderson's promotion to brevet first lieutenant the following spring. The South Carolina legislature recalled his service with gratitude when it presented him with an elegant sword on the eve of Civil War.[10]

Meanwhile, Scott's next move was to use General Worth's 1st Division to attack a cannon foundry housed in a massive stone complex of buildings situated to the west of the park of Chapultepec. The stone-walled foundry of Molino del Rey that gave its name to the battle marked the Mexican left flank that lay "directly under the guns of the castle" of Chapultepec. Another stone building, the Casa Mata, marked the Mexican right flank. With the Artillery positioned in the center, Sumner's dragoons would guard the left flank of the American advance, "hold in check the enemy's cavalry, and give a blow to their horse or not, as opportunity should offer." As the infantry struggled fiercely at the center of the line, Mexican cavalry prepared to fall on the exposed left flank of the attackers. Sumner quickly advanced his men at a brisk trot to meet the challenge. In doing so, he was compelled by unfavorable terrain to pass "within pistol shot" of a large body of Mexican defenders. A pause to find another route would have allowed the Mexican horsemen to reach the infantry, and volleys from the Mexican defenders emptied a number of saddles. Fire wounded five officers and thirty-three soldiers, while seven enlisted soldiers fell dead. Horses fared badly as well, with twenty-seven mounts killed and seventy-seven wounded. Yet Sumner's men—with

Anderson presumably among them—pressed on through that gauntlet, outmaneuvering the enemy at every turn. As a result, the large body of Mexican cavalry became merely "cold spectators of the conflict" according to one of their chroniclers. Sumner particularly commended the actions of Captain Hardee, Anderson's commander, who diligently worked to maintain "order in his squadron during the many evolutions that it was necessary to make with great rapidity." Sumner also noted that his mounted men were unable to pursue the retreating Mexican infantry due to the large force of mounted troops on the left of the line "still maintaining a menacing attitude." Worth's infantry, meanwhile, lost almost a quarter of its strength in the two-hour-long contest.[11]

Scott next determined to attack Mexico City via the fortified hill and castle of Chapultepec, which rose two hundred feet above the surrounding plain and stood as the final significant obstacle to the capture of the Mexican capital. Two days of preparations and artillery bombardment followed, during which time the dragoons were carefully posted near Molino del Rey to guard the left flank of the assault troops. Mexican cavalry periodically threatened an attack, but nothing significant transpired. Finally, on the morning of September 13, 1847, US forces surged forward. Within an hour, Chapultepec had fallen under the determined attack.[12]

Attackers and defenders then crowded the causeways leading to the two main gates of the Mexican capital, but it quickly became apparent that the fight for the causeway would be an infantry and artillery affair. The dragoons were collected and sent back to Tacubaya to guard against any Mexican attacks from that quarter while the rest of the army stormed the city gates. Mexican forces evacuated the city on the night of September 13 and Scott's men immediately took possession of the stricken capital. By 8 AM the next morning, General Scott, accompanied by Major Sumner and his dragoons, now clad in their finest regalia, entered the ancient Aztec city and occupied a central plaza dominated by the National Palace and the great cathedral dedicated to the Assumption of the Virgin Mary. "The band of the Second Dragoons (mounted) played with much spirit the appropriate air of 'Hail Columbia,'" recalled one of the horsemen. As Scott's escort wheeled into line facing north in front of the main façade of the sixteenth-century cathedral, the band broke into "the patriotic strains of 'Yankee Doodle.'" Scott dismounted, removed his hat, and passed along the squadrons of dragoons lining the plaza in front of the cathedral before entering the National Palace on the east side. It was undoubtedly a thrilling moment for the assembled soldiers affected by the enormity of the scene and the "intense enthusiasm" displayed by the troops as Scott entered the city. It marked the first time that an American army occupied a foreign capital. Scott established martial law and warned his troops to refrain from drunkenness and disorderly conduct. Within a short time, however, no thoughts of celebration entered the minds of the occupiers. Hostile shots came from the rooftops and houses fired by stragglers and criminals released from the city's jails by Santa Anna's fleeing army. The ensuing "unlawful war," Scott noted, lasted more than twenty-four hours, during which time the dragoons were engaged in the street fighting. Company K lost one man and five other dragoons were wounded before an uneasy peace settled on the city.[13]

With the quelling of that outbreak of violence, the army settled down to enjoy the fruits of occupation. The reception from the Mexican inhabitants still ranged from violently hostile to collaborative though, with many lower-class citizens continuing to offer sporadic resistance while the upper-class residents were largely more docile. Many of the officers found the company of the city's women much to their liking, and a number of romances blossomed. Henry Heth (he preferred "Harry") told of the adventures of his close friend Ambrose Burnside, whose career as a fickle lover nearly ended at the hands of a jealous, stiletto-wielding senorita. Burnside eventually won back her heart with persistent wooing. Heth seemed particularly delighted to relate tales of the handsome Winfield Scott Hancock, who once professed his love to a Mexican beauty near Cuernavaca. Hancock's tales amused Heth. "I know you have said the same thing to half a dozen girls in the city of Mexico and God knows how many in the States," he declaimed. Hancock merely noted with flawless logic that the US was still at war with Mexico, and "all is fair in love and war." Anderson's social interests are unknown. He never joined the Aztec Club, organized by American officers in Mexico City in October 1847, and headquartered in a stately home on the grand plaza , but among the 160 original members of that social club were many of the future leaders of the Union and Confederate armies, including Ulysses S. Grant and Robert E. Lee.[14]

Meanwhile, other officers found less frivolous ways to spend their time during the occupation. Thomas J. Jackson once wrote home about his intention to remain in Mexico and share his life "with some amiable senorita," but he soon turned to improving his education, learning the Spanish language and exploring Catholicism in his determination to make a study of religion. Others who had sustained painful wounds, like James Longstreet, were first hospitalized before falling under the care of wealthy Mexican families prior to returning home to recuperate further. Despite the largely cordial relations, unsavory incidents also occurred. Bandits all too frequently waylaid and stabbed intoxicated soldiers to death. Soldiers sometimes reciprocated with their own bad behavior. Richard S. Ewell recalled an instance where eight US soldiers broke into a home to rob and kill the owner. One captured man subsequently turned against his fellow conspirators. "It is very much to be hoped that the whole batch will be hung," wrote Ewell.[15]

Until the peace treaty was signed in May 1848, the threat from Mexican forces, guerillas, and bandits remained a concern. Moving supplies and dispatches between Mexico City and Veracruz required escorts provided mostly by the mounted men of the dragoon regiments. Anderson made the trip on a number of occasions, apparently uneventfully. In mid-April 1848, Anderson assumed command of Company F, but he found time to join a number of other officers in exploring the area around Mexico City, specifically the volcanic mountain called Popocatepetl.[16]

Like the Aztec Club, the list of officers interested in exploring that mountain comprised a roster of key leaders during the Civil War, and members of the club showed the most avid interest. Ulysses Grant recollected that the prospective climbers consisted of Anderson, Captain Henry H. Sibley, Captain George Crittenden, Simon B. Buckner, Mansfield Lovell, Andrew Porter, Charles P. Stone, and Zealous B. Tower. Harry Heth was also along, and he noted the presence of a quartermaster and a few assistant surgeons. "And right glad we were, as it turned out, that those 'saw-bones' were with us," he recalled. At the time, the men assessed the summit of Popocatepetl to be between sixteen and seventeen thousand feet, but it is actually a just over a hundred feet shy eighteen thousand feet. At any rate, it was an ambitious undertaking for inexperienced mountaineers, and some probably considered the effort foolhardy. National pride, combined with the climbers' knowledge of well-known ascents elsewhere, overcame any qualms they might have had. They had already proved their mettle as intrepid fighters, and these were not young men inclined to shy from the challenge offered by the brooding, smoking face of Popocatepetl.[17]

Sibley was de facto leader of the band of explorers, and his company of dragoons escorted the expedition. Grant became its quartermaster, and the army furnished the required transportation. Twenty-five officers and seventy dragoons of Company I set off from Mexico City towards the foot of the giant mountain on April 3, 1848. Already at an elevation of 6,000 feet on the plain, Simon Buckner noted that Popocatepetl still rose majestically more than two miles above them, with the snow-capped peak jutting upward "until it seemed but a glittering point in the sky."[18]

The ascent was both difficult and dangerous, and after a few days of misadventures that included a mule pitching off a narrow ledge and an episode of snow blindness among several climbers, Anderson and a handful of other hearty souls finally reached the peak. They took great pride in planting a small flag there and in knowing they were the first Americans ever to reach the summit. Within an hour, they began their descent and were back in the comfortable surrounds of Mexico City within a few days. There, the constituency of the Aztec Club gaily feted Anderson and the others.[19]

By the end of May, with the Treaty of Guadalupe Hidalgo finally ratified, the war was officially at an end and troops began to depart. Anderson and his men made their way slowly towards the new regimental headquarters established at Camp Corrine near Pascagoula, Mississippi, arriving in August. Promoted to the rank of first lieutenant, Anderson was assigned to Company G before being detached for recruiting duty at Carlisle, Pennsylvania.[20]

Chapter 4
From Carlisle to Texas

Secession will be the remedy.

—W. W. Anderson to R. H. Anderson,
September 1850

On October 23, 1848, First Lieutenant Anderson headed east for recruiting duty at the Cavalry School for Practice at Carlisle. At first detailed to the Recruiting Service Headquarters in Philadelphia, he soon fell ill, and by November 23 his commanding officer reported that the lieutenant was "very sick" and "I am sorry to say, there is no possibility of his being fit for duty for some time." He was at Carlisle during the remainder of the fall and winter, but he returned home on sick leave between March and June 1849. His duties from 1850 onward were to keep him in Pennsylvania for an additional three years.[1]

It was the longest period of stability of his entire career, and he made the most of the opportunity. There was the camaraderie of his fellow officers, including two Virginians, Phillip St. George Cooke, whom Anderson had met briefly on the Santa Fe Trail during the Boone expedition; and young Beverly Robertson. Cooke was then writing a series of articles on western life that began running in the *Southern Literary Messenger* in June 1851 under the title "Scenes Beyond the Western Border." Cooke and Anderson must have spoken of their frontier experiences and discussed the brewing sectional strife that would devastate Cooke's family. One of Cooke's sons became a brigadier general in the Confederate army, and a daughter married Rebel cavalryman James Ewell Brown (J. E. B.) Stuart. Cooke and another daughter remained loyal to the Union, a decision that led Stuart to quip: "he will regret it but once, and that will be continuously." The young lieutenant might have sought Cooke's advice when letters from his father expressed strong views on secession and concerns that his son's northern connections could have a serious impact on their own family. There was no question of where Beverly Robertson's loyalties lay, however. He would be dismissed from the army in August 1861 because he had already accepted a commission as captain in the Confederate Army six months earlier.[2]

Carlisle was a more civilized location than any other in which Anderson had found himself during his career, which greatly enhanced the charm of his stay there. The companionship of persons more befitting the interests of a twenty-eight-year-old bachelor soldier held a special delight. The beautiful young daughter of Pennsylvania Supreme Court Chief Justice John Banister Gibson soon attracted his attention, and a romance blossomed. Sarah Gibson had just turned eighteen when Anderson arrived for duty at Carlisle, and her family's station rivaled or exceeded his own. She would make a good match for the stocky South Carolinian. Sarah's father, John B. Gibson, was an eminent jurist and there was a strong tradition of military service in Sarah's family. Judge Gibson's father had served in the Continental Army, and a number of Sarah's brothers and cousins currently served in the Army.[3]

Dick Anderson announced his engagement to Sarah in the winter of 1850. Dr. Anderson assured his son he would "do everything in my power to promote your happiness and make you comfortable . . . and it shall be my delight to promote and cherish the happiness of the lady who is willing to unite her destiny with yours." With the magnanimity of a loving father, he opened his arms and heart to the young woman from Carlisle. "When she becomes your wife," he penned, "she will be my daughter & shall be as one of my own children. She shall not want a home whilst I live," he continued, "and I will do all I can for you to enable you to provide for her if it should be the will of Providence to take you from her." Sentiments alluding to an early death might seem strange in a congratulatory note, but they illustrate the prevalent threat and the uncertain character of life in the mid-nineteenth century, even further compounded by Dick's profession.[4]

The engagement prompted Dr. Anderson to caution his son in financial matters, simultaneously disclosing that his plantation's earnings provided merely a comfortable living for his family. By 1850, cotton cultivation had seriously depleted much of the Upcountry soil. Yearly fluctuations in crop production and prices required economic vigilance. Promising Dick "an equitable portion" of his estate, he nevertheless warned him to adopt thrifty spending habits. "Let me seriously and earnestly impress it upon you as a thing *always* to be remembered & kept in mind, that you will not have enough to allow you to indulge in any sort of extravagance, and allow me my dear son to guard you against the evil of contracting debts. Live on what you have," he counseled, "& 'pay as you go.'" Dr. Anderson's eldest son was undoubtedly well on the way toward developing frugal habits. Despite his meager wages, there is no evidence that he was ever heavily indebted to anyone before his attempts to salvage his father's estate in 1865. Meanwhile, service on the remote western frontier provided few opportunities to spend his money even had he wished to.[5]

Dick Anderson and Sarah Gibson married in early October 1850 as dark clouds began to descend over the country. The nation was reeling in the wake of the controversy over the fate of the territories acquired from Mexico. It was a Constitutional crisis the likes of which had not been seen since the Missouri Compromise, and southerners aggressively sought an expansion of slaveholding lands and maintenance of the status quo in the Congress. All of those pent-up emotions came to a head in the highly charged congressional debates of 1850 that saw some of America's greatest political minds lend their weight to the argument and reach a compromise that once more staved off the threat of secession.[6]

Unfortunately, the compromise left many issues unresolved, and it left many southerners hopping mad. Dr. William Wallace Anderson was one of them. He and Dick had been corresponding throughout the contentious debates, and in one letter it was apparent that the son had well pleased his father. "Your suggestions are very good," Dr. Anderson wrote on September 22, just weeks before the upcoming wedding. "I think Secession will be the remedy. The differences of opinion growing out of the slave question are irreconcilable and must inevitably end in separation of the union and dismemberment of families." He viewed the political situation as volatile, but he did not view all northerners as opponents, instead carefully identifying the South's real foes as abolitionists. Still, since he had not previously asked, nor had his son told him, he now wished to know "How does [*sic*] Judge Gibson & his family stand affected towards the South? I hope they are not abolitionists." He warned his son not to "conceal your sentiments from the family you are about to enter and form the closest connection with." Dick might well have been straddling a fence, trying to appease his father on one side while remaining vaguely non-committal on the other so as not to offend his future in-laws. Dr. Anderson's strong opinions also prompted him to remind Dick of "the unhappy discord which already exists in our family on that subject." In part, this could have been a reference to the death of the doctor's younger brother, Dr. John Wallace Anderson. He had died of fever in Liberia after volunteering for the American Colonization Society, which sought to convince free Blacks to forsake oppressive racial conditions in America for freedom in Africa. For his efforts, John Anderson found only agonizing death and an unmarked grave. His older brother found that a bitter pill to swallow, particularly since they must have disagreed about the propriety of the society's mission to start with. Such was the strength of his conviction, not to mention his uncertainty about his heirs' opinions, that Dr. Anderson later found it prudent to include a restriction in his 1863 will. It stated that "should any of my heirs' scruples of conscience, refuse to be owners of slaves he or she shall forfeit all rights to any portions of them, or to his share, and said share go to the rest of my heirs above named."[7]

The wedding of Dick Anderson of South Carolina and Sarah Gibson of Pennsylvania took place as planned on October 8 at St. John's Episcopal Church in Carlisle. His sister Mary was the only representative of the Anderson family known to have attended the event, though Dick's brother McKenzie had expressed a desire to attend. There is no evidence confirming that he made it. After the wedding, the newlyweds accompanied Mary to Baltimore before going on to South Carolina where Dick introduced his bride to her new family. Sarah, to whom Dick referred always as "Sallie," undoubtedly made a good first impression on her southern kin, enthralling them all with her "superb soprano voice." Sallie was as pleasing to look upon as to listen to, and one admirer reported that she was "one of the loveliest fabrics of creation." Dr. Anderson provided the couple with a sound financial start, having written to his son in September that he "would let you have now five hundred dollars & more at another time."[8] The newlyweds must have enjoyed themselves thoroughly. Anderson extended his original twenty-day leave of absence for ten more days, and he did not return to duty until November 10.[9]

There followed a lengthy period of relative stability in the familiar surroundings at Carlisle, and Anderson formed deep bonds with the Gibson family over the next two years. His attachment to Philip St. George Cooke also continued to grow. The degree to which Cooke's unionist political philosophy may have influenced Anderson's own deliberations during this period are unknown. At Carlisle friends and relatives holding opinions that differed vastly from those of his father surrounded him. Not only had he married into a prominent Pennsylvania family whose members would maintain their fealty to the Union, his own commanding officer with whom he shared close contact was a southerner who believed he owed his allegiance foremost to the nation, not Virginia. Although Cooke's example did little to maintain the integrity of his own family, his opinions of the disturbing events of the early 1850s must have stirred in Anderson some uncertainty about his own views. If looming threats of secession had become a reality then, one wonders whether Anderson would have felt compelled to resign and to ask Sallie to cast aside a lifetime's connection with her kin should a sectional conflict result. Thankfully, the immediate crisis passed, but the possibility of disunion would soon enough return to the forefront of the American political scene. Anderson was surely aware of his father's political involvement as a delegate to the meeting of the Southern Rights Association in Charleston in May 1851, which drafted a resolution calling for southerners to act. It included the statements that while conciliation was preferable, "separate state action is the rightful remedy" to which they pledged support. The delegates also called for an address to other state associations calling for a massed convention at a future date. Despite concerns over unilateral action, the final resolution of the meeting reinforced its embrace of secession as the needed remedy to correct "the wrongs and aggressions" of the North. The body drafted the call to other state associations, eliciting their participation in a future convention designed to bring the southern states together in opposition to perceived northern injustices. Anderson's home state was already leading the way in forging the path to disunion.[10]

Meanwhile, the 1852 birth of a son, also named Richard, further complicated matters and led Anderson to consider leaving the army. He wrote his father in the summer of 1852 about his intentions. Dick's younger brother McKenzie quickly sought to discourage him from abandoning his career. He began his letter with congratulations to "you and sister Sallie on the birth of the young gentleman she has given to our family," then moved on to the matter of his brother's return. Despite McKenzie's empathy for the hardship of army life and his expressed desire that they be together, he concluded that he could "not see at present any prospect by which you would be benefitted [*sic*] by resigning." The financial situation of Dr. Anderson's plantation at that time precluded the possibility. "Pa would no doubt be delighted to have you here & would do anything in his power to promote your wishes," he wrote, "but it does seem to me that it would be a most dangerous experiment, for you to give up the sure income & highly respectable position you occupy, for the very precarious & infinitely more harassing life you would have in the management of the few Negroes that he could afford to you at this time."[11]

McKenzie described the uncertainty of finances at home, as well as his own disenchantment with his work and lifestyle. Their father then held about forty enslaved people to work the main plantation at Riverside, which his son Benjamin was slated to manage upon his graduation from South Carolina College the following year, and the cotton crop generally yielded about 120 bales. In 1851, the crop did not even produce that much. There were other considerations. "A matter more to be considered in planting than the comparatively poor compensation one meets with," he complained, "is the intolerable annoyance a gentleman finds in the detail and management of ignorant & indolent negroes." He concluded with the comment that "nothing could induce me to plant, unless on a scale that would enable me to have an overseer to relieve me from the disagreeable part of the duties, that are inseparable from our system." That disagreeable component of slave labor only worsened over the next decade as the Andersons' slaveholdings increased. However, the growth in the number of enslaved workers on the property is indicative of the family's increasing wealth. By 1860, for example, Dr. Anderson noted for tax purposes that there were 158 enslaved people on the plantation. The records do not indicate whether that growth resulted from an adjustment in the production and profitability of cotton and other crops, or whether Dr. Anderson's overseer eventually excelled as a manager of the plantation and its labor pool. Tripling the size of the workforce in less than a decade, however, was testament to someone's careful management of affairs as well as the decade's boom in cotton prices. The long-range plans for Dr. Anderson's plantation in 1852 likely called for reinvesting profits into purchasing additional enslaved workers, thereby enabling him to plant more acreage and reap even greater profits. The need to divide profits to support Dick and his family would have made such a long-range plan more difficult and the decade's growth in cotton prices was unanticipated at that time. Dick Anderson's father was always supportive of his son, and his letters frequently expressed his love for his family and his devotion to them, but in the summer of 1852, Dr. Anderson had no doubt already convinced his youngest son Benjamin to assume the role of overseer on his plantation upon his graduation. It turned out that Dr. Anderson's faith in his son was rewarded, as Benjamin's diligent oversight contributed to the plantation's expansion. It seems likely that the old man truly would have done anything in his power to advance the wellbeing of his offspring, but the rate of the plantation's growth over the next decade not only was unknown in 1852, its management was destined for Benjamin's hands. In any case, Dick Anderson remained a soldier.[12]

The following year, their brother Benjamin did indeed graduate and assume oversight of daily operations at Riverside, where he lived. McKenzie Anderson by then was engaged in legal practice in Sumter, which must have been lucrative. Despite his professed aversion to planting and to managing an enslaved workforce, he purchased the 1,900-acre plantation known as Hiwassee in February 1859. He acquired a sufficient number of enslaved persons to work the plantation as well, and probably hired an overseer if he continued to divide his time between Hiwassee and his practice in Sumter, though no records from Hiwassee survive to confirm that. Whether his father assisted in the purchase of land or enslaved persons is unknown, but between his August 1852 letter to his brother Dick and the winter of 1859, he had a distinct change of view about the rewards of entering the planter class. Perhaps the growth of his father's holdings and the prospects for profitability contributed to that change. When he marched off to war to join his brother Dick's staff, McKenzie kept his brother's welfare in mind. His will of March 29, 1862 bequeathed the plantation to Dick's son but reserved a life estate to Dick Anderson. When McKenzie died in battle a few months later, the inventory of his enslaved workers indicated he owned at least twenty-seven people valued at over $17,000. One of them, Cicero, was likely in the field with McKenzie when he died, and he must have remained there. Cicero acted as Dick Anderson's servant throughout the remainder of the war.[13]

Meanwhile, with an imminent return to the frontier looming, the difficulties of caring for a family gave Anderson much cause for anxiety, which he must also have expressed to his father. There, the Andersons could be more magnanimous, and McKenzie solicitously entreated his brother to send his family to South Carolina. "As to carrying Sister Sallie & your little boy to the far West," he wrote, "you ought not to think of it for a moment. Bring them on to us. Nothing could be more delightful to us all, and if the summer suns should prove too hot with us, I or Ben could always see them to Carlisle when summer came on, & escort them back in the Fall." There is no evidence that Sallie traveled to Stateburg however, and it is likely she remained in Carlisle with her own family.[14]

Left with little choice, Dick Anderson dutifully parted from his wife and the idyllic home life at Carlisle for a return to the hardships of frontier service. His thoughts of leaving the army remained with him, however, and he struggled with the issue over the next several years. The strain on his family life coupled with the persistent sectional tensions threatening to pit his Southern allegiance against his oath to the Union kept the delicate question alive in his mind. In the meantime, Anderson and Cooke were ordered back to the 2nd Dragoons in late September 1852. Anderson was to report to Fort Graham, Texas, where he arrived for duty with Company F sometime in December 1852. He immediately assumed command of the company until the return of the captain the following June. In early 1853, Anderson was left in charge of the entire post when his former commander, Captain William J. Hardee of Company C, also took leave. In May 1848, Hardee had written letters to two influential South Carolina politicians noting Anderson's "gallantry & intelligence" during his service in Mexico, and recommending him for a brevet promotion. Anderson did receive that brevet promotion, no doubt owing in part to Hardee's endorsement.[15]

Chapter 5

Frontier Service, Texas to Kansas, and Resignation

I have nowhere found a land to prefer to our beloved state.

—R. H. Anderson,
letter, April 28, 1859

Located on the eastern bank of the Brazos River in north Texas, Fort Graham was little more than a grouping of scattered buildings, considered relatively safe since hostile war parties rarely attacked a fortified location. Primarily a base for scouting expeditions and escorts, Fort Graham was strategically located near Native American villages along the upper Brazos River, and the dragoons supported the government's Indian Agents working with the semi-agricultural tribes in that area. With white settlements rapidly expanding westward, Fort Graham soon outlived its usefulness and the Army relocated its troops to keep pace with the increasing rate of settlement. The dragoons began to shift their operations to the San Saba Valley.[1]

The settlers' consumption of resources necessary for the survival of the Native American way of life presented a considerable threat. With the San Saba Valley opened to white settlement, pioneers and prospectors alike poured into the region. One of the routes to the California gold fields took travelers through the San Saba on the road to El Paso. The raiding tradition of the Comanche and Kiowa Tribes compounded the Army's problems. Though their homelands lay in the north, forays against frontier settlements in the south were common. Raids into Mexico and Texas were the primary means by which the tribes amassed huge herds of horses and cattle traded for guns, whiskey, and tobacco. That custom was not easily forsaken, for the route known as the Comanche War Trail was worn deeply into the high desert floor.[2]

In 1851, the Army established a new line of fortifications about 100 miles west of the old line that encompassed Fort Graham. Within that protective inner and outer cordon of forts lay the heart of Texas settlement. On November 9, 1853, Anderson and the two companies of dragoons from Fort Graham set out on a seventeen-day trip of over two hundred miles to occupy one of the new strongholds, Fort McKavett.[3]

Anderson was then the assistant acting quartermaster and assistant acting commissary service responsible for supplying the men with equipment and provisions. Those tasks consumed significant time and effort, as procuring supplies and foodstuffs locally and from the central army depot in San Antonio proved to be challenging. Anderson was soon complaining to Brevet Major James Belger, his counterpart in San Antonio, about damaged or spoiled food shipments arriving from that place, while shortages of some items had already reached a critical stage. Salt—a vital staple for both man and beast—was so lacking that troopers scraped residue from the insides of pork barrels. Anderson requested diversion of a wagon train sent to move another of the dragoon companies. "The distance is not greater and the roads are better," he claimed. "This arrangement would probably furnish an early opportunity to send the supplies that are wanted." Anderson also requested the delivery of another item essential for the health and well-being of the men, though it might also indicate his own developing habit of imbibing spirits. "Send also if you please a barrel of whiskey," he wrote.[4]

Duties at the fort frequently shifted due to the absence of other officers. Anderson temporarily took command of Company G in early March 1854, adding to his frustrations as quartermaster and commissary service officer. The supply difficulties continued for some weeks, perhaps owing to the large-scale movement of troops during that period and the necessity of using the available wagons for that purpose. Anderson soon renewed his plea to Belger, explaining that he had already purchased all the available coffee in Fredericksburg, and anticipated running out of that supply soon. "At about the same time such supplies of sugar, vinegar and salt as are now remaining will have been consumed," he wrote. It was not only the men's diet that concerned him. As for the "public horses and mules," Anderson stated, they "have had no salt for many months and are suffering for the want of it." Desperate by early spring, he informed Belger that he was sending a wagon to San Antonio to obtain coffee, sugar, vinegar, and salt "with as little delay as practicable as I am completely out of the articles stated."[5]

Anderson not only had difficulty obtaining supplies for the men and animals during this period, but he also had his own troubles with the US Treasury regarding the funds expended during his most recent tour of duty on recruiting service. A letter from an auditor in the Treasury Department written in December 1853 implied that Anderson had somehow manipulated accounts to his credit. Admitting to his lack of expertise in financial matters, Anderson nevertheless brooked no imputation of misconduct. "My ignorance of the forms of book keeping and accounting may have led me into gross mistakes and you may entertain as free opinions as you please on this point," he replied, "but I will not allow you to express the slightest insinuation as to my motives or intentions." Anderson dutifully refunded $148.84, but still bristled at the accusation of wrongdoing. "I hope I may be mistaken in supposing that you really mean to insinuate . . . that I sought to obtain credit twice for the same sum. Whilst however your letter even by the most strained constructions may bear such an interpretation I will decline to receive it."[6]

The intemperate exchange only provoked the auditor, who found within a few months a number of other clerical errors in Anderson's quartermaster accounts. He was able to clarify two of the mistakes, but admitted that all "other errors in calculations or addition must be charged against me." He also explained that he received payment for some of the questioned travel expenses prior to receipt of an order changing the reimbursement method. That order did not reach Carlisle until six months after he departed. The tone of the exchange between Anderson and the auditor was decidedly more professional than the earlier encounter, but the auditor was undoubtedly gloating over his discoveries.[7]

The incidents described, while minor, are illustrative of a number of Anderson's personal qualities. First, he was admittedly deficient when it came to mastering the intricacies of the army's bureaucracy—at least on a level that affected him personally. His attention to detail and perseverance in seeing to the needs of his men and the animals under his charge was tellingly different. He performed his duties well when they seemed important to him, yet despite having served for nearly sixteen years as a cadet and soldier, he somehow failed to master the mundane paperwork accompanying his position. Second, Anderson's code of honor made him highly sensitive to personal insult and any allegations that might impugn his integrity, yet, with only one notable exception regarding a dispute with a fellow officer in 1855, he was generally immune from rash or impetuous actions and responses to those insults. Clearly, he was no milquetoast and was perfectly capable of standing up for himself and his integrity. These events depict his willingness to speak out against what he perceived to be unjust accusations, and argue quickly in his own defense. Nonetheless, he was also willing to admit his errors as evidenced by his prompt repayment of twice-credited funds as well as his response to the acting assistant adjutant general for the Department of Texas, who questioned Anderson's failure to acknowledge the receipt of official correspondence properly. He thought the reports he made "from time to time" in the official correspondence "seemed to render more particular replies unnecessary."[8] Nevertheless, he admitted to the oversights and expressed his regret. Anderson's apathy towards his administrative responsibilities was a flaw that continued to vex his superiors. It was one that he probably carried over into his postwar civilian life as well, and which very likely had some impact on his ability to master the intricacies of his plantation's fiscal requirements.

In addition to his administrative duties, Anderson led patrols of dragoons, particularly after General Smith ordered that "All the disposable force" would take the field in detachments comprised of fifteen men each. Eventually, Smith directed that an entire company of dragoons from each of the three northernmost posts "be kept in motion within suitable limits, for the detection and pursuit of marauding parties of Indians." These patrols seldom brought excitement, but the tedium of Anderson's routine was broken in late April 1854, when he left with a detail of sixteen dragoons to arrest Assistant Surgeon Josephus M. Steiner. Prior to the closure of Fort Graham several months before, a personal quarrel between Steiner and Brevet Major Ripley A. Arnold had taken a sudden, bloody turn. In September 1853, Steiner murdered Arnold. His "terrible and untimely 'taking off' caused deep regret among a large circle of friends and comrades," one of them later recalled. Arnold had distinguished himself in Florida as well as at Resaca de la Palma and Palo Alto during the war with Mexico.[9]

On April 16, 1854, Brevet Brigadier General William S. Harney, commanding both the Second Dragoons and the Department of Texas, ordered Anderson to proceed from Austin to Fort Graham to arrest Steiner, a difficult trip of around 140 miles. Harney was careful to add that Anderson should "omit no effort to effect" Steiner's arrest, and then to "adopt such precautionary measures as will render his appearance before the Court perfectly certain." He was to take along a civilian attorney to act as legal advisor, but the lawyer declined to go at the last minute, claiming an illness in his family. "Believing that I understood the case sufficiently well to carry out the instructions without the aid of counsel," Anderson later explained, "I departed without a legal advisor." Subsequent events indicated that a greater degree of patience was in order.[10]

Steiner sought to avoid a military court martial and hoped instead to stand trial in a civilian court, where he stood a better chance of acquittal. The Army thought otherwise and advised Anderson "that if he could place his hand upon him at any time before the sheriff could do so that he was then his prisoner." Moreover, Anderson told his men en route, if anyone tried "to take Doctor Steiner from his custody by force that he was ordered to kill Steiner instantly, and then take care of ourselves." The men now realized there was some danger in their task. On approaching the fort, Anderson dismounted and hoped to surprise Steiner in his home and take custody of him with the least amount of trouble. Anderson took a few men from the detail and approached Steiner's quarters while the rest remained behind.[11]

Anderson found the doctor at home sitting partly dressed. "How are you Dick?" Steiner said. "I suppose you have come after me." Anderson replied affirmatively, adding that he hoped there would be no difficulty. Anderson asked if the doctor could be ready to leave in half an hour. Steiner thought so, though he first had to catch his mare, which had been running loose for several days. In all, about an hour and a half elapsed before the party made its way from Fort Gibson. The delay, probably intentional on Steiner's part, was to be a costly one. The sheriff of Hill County appeared just as Anderson was ordering Steiner to mount his horse. He warned Anderson not to take Steiner, threatened him with the law, and told him that he would regret it. Dr. Steiner, still convinced that justice from the Texas civil authorities would be more satisfactory than a court martial, requested the sheriff to see a judge and obtain a writ of habeas corpus.[12]

With no further interference, Anderson, Steiner, and the dragoons headed out of the fort. Steiner asked to detour through the village of Waco so that he could confer with his attorney before going to Austin. Anderson thought the request was reasonable. Moreover, it had already rained the night before and "the morning gave promise of heavy rain sometime during the day." The route through Waco avoided a number of the streams that might have been subject to sudden flooding. Anderson pushed his tired horses and men about thirty miles or more that day, coming within a few miles of Waco before making camp.[13]

Reaching the banks of the Brazos River at Waco next morning, Anderson found that the fords were already flooded and he was compelled to cross by ferry. The boat was too small to accommodate all the men and horses at once, so Anderson, Steiner, and eight dragoons were ferried across first. As they approached the town, Anderson halted until the others could catch up, but the ferryman did not transport the remaining soldiers immediately. Meanwhile, a resident of the town approached and asked to have a few minutes' conversation with Dr. Steiner in private. Anderson stated he could not let the doctor out of his sight, but that he would accompany them. Leaving a detail to take care of the horses, Anderson, Steiner, and four dragoons went to a house where there were several lawyers waiting, along with another dozen or so citizens.[14]

Once inside, the sheriff "sung out for Doctor Steiner's Guard." The unsuspecting Anderson, now alone in the house with Steiner and his rescuers, immediately called out for his own men to react. More citizens scurried to enter, quickly overpowering and disarming a sergeant rushing to bar the door. "They were armed with rifles full cocked," he recalled, "and there were some hundred and fifty or two hundred of them in the street armed also, and I did not think it my duty to resist." Armed citizens held the other troopers at bay and the sheriff placed them under arrest. Meanwhile, the rest of the dragoons observed the events, forded the dangerous river, and came up at a gallop. They too were compelled to surrender when they saw the size of the armed mob. Anderson and Steiner were both marched to the courthouse. Facing a warrant charging him with "having forcibly removed a prisoner from the civil authorities," Anderson himself now needed the services of an attorney. The lieutenant obtained counsel and was remanded to Hill County. After quickly being tried and acquitted, authorities released the other dragoons next day.[15]

A Hill County magistrate heard the case against Anderson and authorized his release on $1,000 bail with a promise to appear for trial in June. A Grand Jury failed to lodge a bill of indictment against him and the case was subsequently discharged. Anderson returned and took command of Company A on July 2, but the matter was not entirely settled. Anderson had failed in his mission to arrest Steiner as ordered.[16]

Anderson wrote to Colonel Samuel Cooper, the army's adjutant general, fully explaining the circumstances and outlining his rationale for acquiescing to Steiner's request to confer with his attorney in Waco. He noted the road conditions and threatening weather as further support for his decision. He attempted to refute the implication that his delay in Waco had allowed the authorities to catch up with the detail and recover Steiner. "In fact," he explained, "I know now that the news of the arrest of Dr. Steiner reached Waco early in the afternoon of the same day on which it was effected & preparations were made at once to intercept me on any road that I might take." Anderson concluded by stating that he was satisfied of his "integrity and innocence in the matter," and he requested either approval of his actions or a trial before a court martial "as speedily as possible."[17]

Despite his explanation, the Army charged him in mid-September 1854 with several specifications relating to his failure to bring Steiner to Austin. The General Court Martial alleged a combination of misdeeds and charged him with "Conduct to the prejudice of good order and military discipline." The first specification was related to his delay in departing Austin, a second to his failure to return there by the most direct route rather than through Waco, and a third to his having separated himself from the bulk of his command on arrival at Waco. After several days of testimony, the court found him not guilty of the first specification, but found that with some minor changes the facts were as stated regarding the others. Despite that, the court found that there was no criminality attached to Anderson's actions "under the circumstances as shown in the evidence." Though found innocent of the charges, he continued to have difficulties convincing the authorities to pay for his civilian defense attorney. Steiner's difficulties were likewise far from over. Anderson appeared as a witness at Steiner's court martial on November 29. As there was no prisoner, however, there was also no trial. The record is silent as to how the matter finally ended, but a notation in the papers of Secretary of War Jefferson Davis in early 1856 indicates that a civilian court had acquitted Steiner of the charge and he was then inquiring whether the War

Department would accept his resignation. The Army dropped him from its rolls in 1856.[18]

As 1855 began, it must have seemed an opportunity for a fresh start for Dick Anderson. He caught up with Company G in the field in early January in the midst of an expedition in search of marauding Comanche warriors. Anderson took over command from fellow South Carolinian, Captain Patrick Calhoun, son of the former Vice President. Three companies of Texas Rangers joined the dragoons. The expedition gathered at Fort Chadbourne, where Anderson inspected the Rangers, who had supplied their own equipment. A Colt .44 Dragoon Model revolver and a double-barreled shotgun were the weapons of choice. In this case, Anderson found about two-thirds of the men armed with state-issued Mississippi rifles, the rest with shotguns. Anderson also estimated that one-half of the pistols the Rangers carried were "entirely too small for efficient service," indicating that most had not yet obtained the heavier Dragoon or Walker Model guns. Moreover, ammunition was scarce among the Rangers. There were no molds for buckshot, and few ladles for the rifle and pistol molds. This, Anderson reported, meant the men were "obliged to resort to tedious and wasteful expedients." Although there was enough powder, lead, and percussion caps to supply each man with 125 rounds, Anderson found the caps to be "inferior or damaged."[19]

The horses and tack were generally in better shape, but a more serious issue was the lack of adequate clothing. "The men are altogether insufficiently clad," Anderson informed Calhoun, "and should the expedition encounter severe weather much sickness will inevitably ensue." A lengthy expedition would undoubtedly reduce them to tatters. Anderson knew from long experience starting with his expedition with Nathan Boone that the strain on the dragoons was likewise considerable and his familiarity with campaigning probably matched that of cavalryman Edmund Kirby Smith at nearby Fort Mason. "Scouting is extremely arduous," Smith noted. "We move rapidly without equipage, sleep in the open, our own horse blanket for a bed, & saddle for a pillow, pork, flour, & coffee, with game, our only subsistence. We are almost as nomadic as the Bedouin of the plains, feeding our horses on the scattered grass of the prairie & depending principally on our own exertions for subsistence."[20]

The expedition proved largely uneventful, but a pleasant surprise awaited Anderson when he returned to Fort McKavett in late March. Despite legal issues and a court martial, he was promoted to the rank of captain. He immediately applied for a leave of absence for two months, stating, "I have now been nearly thirteen years in the service, and during that period I have had but thirty days of ordinary leave of absence." It was a favorable time to request leave since all of the officers in Company G were then present. His hopes to see Sallie in Carlisle once again were in vain. While he awaited a response, the number of officers in the company rapidly dwindled to one—himself. He remained with Company G until April, when he assumed command of Company A. The spring and early summer of 1855 passed quietly for the men and their dejected commander, but events farther to the north conspired to wreck his long-awaited plans for leave and turn the peaceful interlude into a season of hard campaigning.[21]

Sallie, meanwhile, had to content herself in Carlisle with written correspondence, and in May 1855, she received a solicitous letter from Dick's sister Mary at Stateburg. "I am very anxious to hear from you how you bear this disappointment, in the refusal of furlough to brother," she wrote. "You can't go to him while the Indian fighting is going on, & so you will have to bear it & content yourself with letter communication." She hoped that his promotion to captain would help him "escape some of the annoyances he used to be subject to." Mary had recently received a letter from her brother in which he told her he could not obtain the furlough. "I think they must count those days of drilling soldiers at Carlisle as holiday," she complained, "for surely he is entitled to it now." She went on to inform Sallie about some of the enslaved persons. Henry, for example, was with Dick in Texas, and "from having very little to do is gathering a little money, for his wife, he says, who is, by the way extremely cut down at his not coming." Mary also told her that she had not seen a former house servant Betsy, who appears to have relocated from the Homestead to Riverside. "I hear of her now and then—sometimes she sends for a ticket late in the evening to go back when she has spent the day here, but she never comes to see us, she keeps up her old unsociable ways." Mary's mention to a "ticket" referred to the prohibition against enslaved persons traveling about after dark without permission to do so, and there was considerable risk in encountering a slave patrol at night and being punished if found without a pass. Sallie, meanwhile, was getting along in Pennsylvania without the services of enslaved help, and Mary asked whether she still liked "Dickey's nurse as much as you did? The Irish woman who taught him his prayers."[22]

Mary explained that the family remained in Stateburg that summer rather than having gone as usual to their summer home on the coast. Dr. Anderson had purchased a home on Sullivans Island near Charleston Harbor for $250 in April 1848, and the family frequently went there in the spring and summer. Dr. Anderson went there in the spring of 1855 and had the house shingled after a violent storm struck the area the previous summer, but Mary informed Sallie that the rest of the family "staid [*sic*] at home to economize." Still, she wistfully wrote that the "beach and the waves haunt me like a dream of pleasant things." The letter was full of family news, church matters, and even news of the two family pets. Billy and Fannie were sent to the Smithsonian Institution where they were "getting an education. They were too unruly Mother and Papa thought, & Billy began to butt so I was afraid of him." Her father had corresponded with the museum's curator, Spencer Baird, who assured them that the animals would be taken very good care of. "He had long wanted an antelope," Mary said. Informative and entertaining letters such as Mary's must have helped relieve some of the burden of separation and loneliness the young mother felt, and it would be fall before she was reunited with her husband, then busy campaigning against the Sioux tribe.[23]

The nation had been shocked and outraged by the 1854 Grattan Massacre that saw the death of Lieutenant John L. Grattan and twenty-nine soldiers in Wyoming at the hands of Brulé Sioux warriors. Secretary of War Jefferson Davis recalled Brevet Brigadier General William S. Harney from his leave of absence in Paris and set him to the task of subduing the Sioux. Harney organized a force at Fort Kearny, Nebraska Territory, numbering about 600 men and including companies D, E, H, and K of his own 2nd Dragoons, but it was March of 1855 before the campaign plans were complete.[24]

Anderson's Company A, already in the field, set out from its camp in August 1855 to join five other companies at the northernmost Texas defensive position, Fort Belknap. The six companies of dragoons under command of Major Enoch Steen then marched to Fort Riley in Kansas Territory to take part in the Sioux campaign. Traveling mostly over rolling prairie, Steen thought the route an easy one, but it was a difficult trip for many of the soldiers. Some men became sick briefly from eating badly prepared food or drinking brackish water. The horses, Steen later claimed, were "in only tolerable order" at the start. When the column reached Fort Riley, the animals were in no condition to go on a campaign against hostile Sioux. Many had sore backs caused by new Grimsley saddles that some soldiers were recently issued. Steen's troopers, with Captain Anderson among them, reached Fort Riley after a 495-mile march from Texas. Averaging a respectable fifteen miles per day, the column nevertheless arrived too late and in no shape to take an active part in the campaign.[25]

General Harney had already marched from Fort Kearny, Nebraska Territory in August spoiling for a fight, and he found it within days. After soundly beating the Sioux in one engagement, he pushed into the heart of their country challenging the various bands that had not complied with a previous order to move south of the Platte. No one took up his challenge and the soldiers settled into winter quarters.[26]

Anderson and his company remained relatively inactive at Fort Riley throughout the fall and winter. By the time Dick Anderson arrived there in the fall of 1855, a serious cholera epidemic that had killed the wife of Brevet Major Lewis A. Armistead had passed, but the memory of its ravages could not have escaped his attention. The death of a brother officer's wife under such dreadful conditions must have been an unpleasant reminder of the risks involved in bringing one's family to the West. Despite the danger, Anderson requested a seven-day leave of absence in October 1855. "My object in soliciting this indulgence," he wrote, "is to go for my family and bring them to this post." Presumably the family would have started westward by steamboat, and he would meet them somewhere en route as seven days would hardly have been sufficient to make a round trip to Carlisle. In any event, the family would be together once again, at least when Anderson was not in the field.[27]

One disagreeable incident marred the period spent at Fort Riley, however. While a court martial was in session that added to the number of officers typically present as part of the fort's garrison, Anderson hosted a dinner at his quarters. Seated at his table was Captain Nathaniel Lyon, who was rapidly developing an almost fanatical opposition to slavery. Lyon took the opportunity to launch into a vitriolic harangue of the South and its peculiar institution, despite the presence of Anderson—his host—and a number of southern officers. Stunned by Lyon's diatribe, the northern-born officers were dumbfounded while the southerners appeared indignant. It was not their place to usurp their host's role in confronting this insult at his dinner table, and Anderson simply smiled serenely "and by occasionally addressing a word or two to those nearest to him, [tried] to make the occasion pass as pleasantly as possible under the circumstances." Later that evening, however, as Lyon sat with a group of officers in another colleague's quarters, Anderson found him. He rapidly approached Lyon, rebuking him for his outrageous behavior, "when I from my position was helpless to repel your insults." Anderson then stated that he would not waste his time with a verbal admonishment that "would do very little harm." Instead, he said, "I am going to thrash you." As he began advancing on his antagonist, Lyon remained seated but threatened to kill Anderson. At that, several officers intervened and came between the two men.[28]

Anderson retreated but within an hour, Lyon awakened Surgeon William Hammond with the news that Anderson had issued a formal challenge. Citing the illegality of dueling and professing "conscientious scruples against" it, Lyon stated that he would not accept Anderson's challenge. "Then you will be sent to Coventry without delay," replied an astonished Hammond. "You have grossly insulted Anderson in his own house, and you must give him satisfaction, or you will be run out of the army." After much discussion, Lyon finally agreed to meet Anderson, but he then selected a method of dueling that he anticipated Anderson's second would reject outright. The duel, he asserted, should take place across a table with pistols. At Lyon's insistence, the next day Hammond approached Major Sibley, who was to act as Anderson's second. As anticipated, Sibley rejected the notion out of hand as being "outside the pale of the laws of dueling, and as being barbarous, murderous, unusual, and ungentlemanly."[29]

Hammond and Sibley finally got Anderson and Lyon to agree to submit the matter to a council of officers whose decision would be binding. That council dealt Lyon a blow, concluding that he was guilty of a grave offense and should formally apologize to Anderson in the presence of every officer on the post. Naturally Lyon was at first livid and reluctant to agree, but he eventually calmed and accepted the decision. That night, Dr. Hammond hosted a reception for all the officers and their wives at his quarters. Anderson purposely stationed himself, with Sibley at his side, at the farthest end of the room. Lyon had to stride past each of the officers and their wives to reach him, whereupon he expressed his regret at having spoken so vehemently at Anderson's table. Anderson bowed but said nothing. Lyon bowed in turn before retreating quickly from the room. Neither man offered his hand, nor ever spoke to one another again except when official duties required it.[30]

The incident marks the only known instance where Anderson believed his honor so impugned he had to resort to challenging someone to a duel, but that was not his initial intent. At first, he merely expected to confront Lyon with physical violence, but with fists, not with weapons. When prevented from that course of action, he was compelled to offer a challenge. There was simply no honorable way Anderson could ignore such a gross insult delivered in the presence of his fellow officers and in his own home. That he held his tongue during Lyon's verbal assault illustrates the appropriate level of self-control a gentleman and an army officer possessed, and that illustration was reinforced by the fact that no one else at Anderson's table rose to challenge Lyons then and there. That responsibility lay with the host, but Anderson chose not to escalate it at that moment or to add further to the disagreeable atmosphere created by Lyon's remarks. Moreover, Lyon's words were immaterial to the context of the insult, which stemmed from his abuse of his host's hospitality. Lyon's thoughts and the words he used to convey them mattered less than the manner and the place in which he spoke them. Still, facing an onslaught of hateful venom in a typically congenial setting of fellow officers must have troubled Anderson's mind at a time of strained sectional tensions, and perhaps the incident came to mind a few years later and nudged him more decisively towards resigning his commission.

By the summer of 1856, the force arrayed against the hostile tribes began to disperse, but many of the soldiers remained in place because of brewing trouble in the Kansas Territory. The Kansas-Nebraska Act signed by

President Franklin Pierce in May 1854 set the stage for another round of sectional controversy pitting pro-slavery advocates against antislavery Free Soilers, or Free Staters. By 1856, as the concept of popular sovereignty came into practice, the territory was plunged fully into guerilla warfare, aptly living up to its nickname of Bleeding Kansas. Sectional and family loyalties once more nagged at Captain Anderson, as they did many of the officers. Maintaining a neutral stance on the Kansas controversy was difficult, yet that is precisely what federal troops were required to do. Continual suspicions were raised by both pro and anti-slavery adherents concerning the impartiality of the federal troops, most especially that of the officers. George "Tige" Anderson, a native Georgian, was relieved from his command at Fort Scott because of his demonstrated support for the pro-slavery faction. One newspaper correspondent even tarred all of the officers at Fort Leavenworth with the same brush, despite having no evidence to back his claim. Others accused some officers of favoring the Free Staters, and Colonel Sumner fell under suspicion on that account, as did Captain Lyon of the 2nd Infantry. Dick Anderson's views at that time are unrecorded, but the situation could not have been easy for him. A number of factors tempered Anderson's own stance. He had been away from South Carolina nearly half his lifetime. His wife and her family were Yankees, and the kinship he felt with them could only have added to indecision. Torn by the imminent possibility of raising his sword to quell a civil war between northerners and southerners in Kansas, he could hardly have relished the prospect, yet his sense of duty to his native state and his devotion to his father and family there must have been foremost in mind. Anderson was on sick leave from the end of May until early June 1856, and when ordered to march in late July, he found that he was to be the only officer present with his company. He set aside any misgivings and dutifully led his command from Fort Riley on July 30 en route to Lecompton where it arrived on August 20 along with troops C, F, G, and I. With the prospect of conflict looming, Anderson was gratified that he had recommended weekly target practice, possibly mirroring widespread orders in the Army at that time requiring familiarity with the new rifled muskets that were replacing the old smoothbore models. Anderson thought five rounds "abundantly sufficient" with oversight from officers and non-commissioned officers to guide the dragoons in improving their skill, even suggesting "a small sum of money as a prize," which he believed would provide the strongest "incentive to the acquirement of skill."[31]

In the end, no weapons were fired in action and the sole source of excitement occurred when the dragoons and a company of the 6th Infantry were returning to Fort Riley. Anderson established camp with the men near a small stream where "the grass was extremely tall and dry." After taking precautions against fire, he headed upstream with his fishing rod. Before long, he heard the roar of a prairie fire approaching, and he reached the camp to find that the fire had already passed over and consumed it. It was clear that the blaze did not originate in the camp, and Anderson immediately sent several troopers to apprehend two civilians who had passed by shortly before. The dragoons returned with their prisoners and one confessed that they were indeed responsible for setting the blaze. Despite his intention to turn the culprits over to the civil authorities, one of his subalterns apparently later released them while Anderson was temporarily absent from the camp. Perhaps the dragoons who lost many of their personal possessions took matters into their own hands, for as Anderson later wrote to his commander by way of explanation of the affair, "What punishment they got, by whose direction or by whom inflicted I do not feel it incumbent on me to say." If Anderson's men engaged in any form of vigilante justice, their captain made no effort to hold the responsible parties accountable. Not only had Anderson lost another prisoner, his inattention to administrative details was once again illustrated when he admitted that he "lost or misplaced" the list of public property that was destroyed. He cavalierly told Lt. Col Cooke that it could "easily be recovered by reference to the companies to which the detachments under my command belonged."[32]

Returning to Fort Riley in November, Anderson saw another winter pass without a leave of absence. With his two lieutenants absent, he was stranded. After moving to Fort Leavenworth in late May 1857, he obtained a brief leave of absence from June 21 until July 10. While he was away, his company relocated to Lawrence, headquarters of Free Stater efforts to prohibit slavery in the Kansas Territory and the scene of several bloody encounters between pro-slavery elements and free-state proponents. The governor had requested troops and placed the town under martial law after prominent citizens adopted a town charter not in accordance with the act established by the territorial legislature.[33]

Anderson was uncertain at that point whether he desired any further connection with the unsettling events transpiring in that part of the country. He wrote from Fort Leavenworth on June 10, requesting six months' leave of absence over the coming winter. "I have served above fifteen years without ever having had at any time more than thirty days of ordinary leave of absence," he wrote to Adjutant General Cooper. Since 1849, he noted, he had been "only twice absent from duty, once on a thirty day leave in October of that year and again in the present year I had twenty days leave last June. With the latter exception I have been for nearly five years on continuous frontier service." His statements revealed that he remained troubled by constant separation from his family, torn between his service to the Union and his devotion his state. "In addition to my desire to procure through a leave of absence of some length, relaxation and respite from such service, I have in view the determination of a subject of importance to me—my retirement or continuance in the Army, and I seek the opportunities which a leave of absence for some months would give me to decide this matter without uncertainty or precipitation." He concluded by noting that "the lateness of the season will preclude any active operations before next spring," and that all the officers of his company were present for duty.[34]

Returning to Leavenworth at the expiration of his leave in July, Anderson found no reply to his request for a longer leave of absence. He waited in vain until September 12, when he wrote in frustration to Cooper: "I have the honor to resign the commission which I hold in the 2nd Regiment US Dragoons." That same day he wrote to the regiment's acting adjutant: "I enclose my resignation and have the honor to apply to be relieved from duty so soon as the necessary transfer of Company property can be made." Fortunately, the process of resigning took more than two days, for on September 14 Anderson received notice of the approval of his request for leave of absence. He sheepishly wrote Cooper that he misinterpreted the delayed response to his request for leave and explained that he thought there was telegraphic communication between Washington and Leavenworth City. He had resigned when he learned the 2nd Dragoons were to leave soon for Utah, "the necessity for my going home being imperious." He had "the honor to recall my resignation" and noted that subsequent correspondence could reach him at Carlisle, Pennsylvania. Leaving from Leavenworth meant that he had only to step aboard a steamboat on the Missouri River to begin his journey. He could reverse almost the exact route he first took westward in 1842—down the Missouri to the Mississippi; down the Mississippi to the Ohio; thence overland by rail or canal to Harrisburg and Carlisle.[35]

As it turned out, Anderson was gone for nearly a year, from September 16, 1857 until September 4, 1858. He was on leave for nine months, followed by nearly three more on recruiting duty at Carlisle, thus avoiding further distasteful duty in "Bleeding Kansas." He rejoined his company in September 1858 when it was still in Utah after attempting to coerce recalcitrant Mormons who had rejected the supremacy of federal authorities to abandon their folly. An agreement reached that June avoided outright war with the Mormons, but federal troops remained and garrisoned several forts in the territory.[36]

During the year that he was away from the regiment, Anderson spent most of that period in Carlisle with Sallie's family. He had sufficient time to make some decisions about his continued service with the Army, and several factors influenced his decision to return to duty. Promotion in the

Antebellum Army was notoriously slow, but dragoon officers fared slightly better after the 1855 creation of two new cavalry regiments that drew officers from existing mounted units, thus creating a number of vacancies at higher ranks. Otherwise, promotion opportunities depended solely on a single qualification—seniority. Anderson's elevation to captain in March 1855 probably gave him hope for advancement in the near future. Moreover, Anderson's civilian prospects remained unappealing. Though his father's plantation was growing under Benjamin's supervision, its ability to support another family was for some reason still too uncertain. Why Dick Anderson could not have taken over management of the Riverton plantation after Benjamin's death from illness in the late summer of 1857 is not clear, but perhaps the financial situation was too precarious to cover the cost of supporting Dick, Sallie, and two small children in addition to his father and mother. Striking out alone would be even less secure. Many officers who left the Army found civilian life a struggle, including Ulysses Grant and William T. Sherman, whose failed ventures led both to agree, "West Point and the Regular Army were not good schools for farmers, bankers, merchants, and mechanics."[37] Such uncertainty, coupled with the fact that there was no military retirement system at the time, led many officers to remain in the service as long as possible. Despite the hardships, it was at least an honorable profession and a steady source of income. In addition, the economic downturn following the "Panic of 1857" undoubtedly added to Anderson's concerns about a successful transition. Based on his own financial well-being, it seemed that the balance sheet was adding up in favor of remaining a soldier, no matter how onerous he found the duty.

The fact that violence in Kansas had largely ended after May 1858 also factored into Anderson's deliberations. He must also have considered the increasingly vituperative rhetoric that characterized the controversy in the press and in politics. The rejection of the pro-slavery Lecompton Constitution in August 1858 effectively settled the issue in the territory but left a festering wound on the national consciousness. A temporary plaster disguised the wound, and a surge in long-standing anti-Mormon sentiment eventually supplanted the crisis in Kansas. Many Americans could empathize with at least one of the two legs of the Republican Party platform pertaining to the elimination of polygamy and slavery, and the nation's ire was diverted temporarily. Anderson was spared the prospect of fighting against his fellow citizens. By the latter part of 1858 Army service on the frontier resumed its former characteristics unhindered by the prospects of peacemaking between pro and anti-slavery factions or restraining rebellious Mormons.[38]

During his trip to Utah Territory Captain Anderson and about forty dragoons were bivouacked in present day Wyoming along the banks of the

Big Sandy River. Near sunset, bugle calls from the camp attracted the attention of another party of soldiers about two miles upstream. A surprised Army engineer, Lieutenant Edward Porter Alexander, "had no idea of any white man being within some hundreds of miles," and he rode off to discover the source of the music. He soon encountered Dick Anderson and his dragoons. Alexander was pleased to find Anderson, as he had heard much about him from his classmate Tom Berry who had served with Anderson and wrote of him frequently in letters to his friend. Lieutenant James C. Duane of New York led Alexander's company. It was a brief but pleasant encounter as the three officers chatted easily on the banks of the Big Sandy that fall evening. Dragoons gathered around the campfires, mingling and joking with one another as the sky above the majestic Rocky Mountains turned orange in the setting sun. Pickets paced lazily, listening to the gurgling passage of the Big Sandy as tethered horses munched contentedly nearby. Others went about performing their camp chores, glancing occasionally at the darkening eastern sky where stars slowly began to make their appearance, twinkling with astonishing brightness. Within a few short years, all three officers would long for the peacefulness of a prairie campsite. Darkness in the east and shining stars would portend something very different by then. Alexander became the chief of artillery for James Longstreet's corps in the Army of Northern Virginia and served under Anderson when he commanded the corps in 1864. Duane became chief engineer for the Army of the Potomac. All would become general officers.[39]

Though meeting Lieutenants Alexander and Duane was a delightful experience, Anderson was far less impressed with other aspects of the campaign. He derided the entire affair, opining sardonically, "Brigham Young only raised a fuss with the U. S. to get specie carried to Utah, and that as soon as our army got there and spent their gold he had gained his object, was satisfied, and submitted." His disdain even extended to the ladies he encountered, later remarking that he "never saw women with so repulsive countenances and hard faces as those of Utah."[40]

The arrival of a letter the spring of 1859 informing him of the South Carolina legislature's adoption of a resolution honoring his Mexican War service and awarding him a ceremonial sword adorned with a likeness of John C. Calhoun might have rekindled reflection on his loyalties. The unexpected receipt of the resolution and gift could only have meant one thing that year as politicians struggled with the issue of slavery in the territories and the nation girded itself for a presidential election in 1860 that might decide the fate of the Union. South Carolina wished to gauge where his personal loyalties stood while reminding him that his service as a South Carolinian was recognized. On April 28, 1859, he acknowledged the honor in a carefully worded letter that vaguely hinted at what his response to secession might be. "Twenty-one years ago," he wrote, "I left my home to enter the Military Academy of the United States. Since that time I have revisited my native state only at long intervals, but my affection for it has not been diminished by my absence. I have been led, by my services to our common country, into almost every quarter of this wide and magnificent domain, but I have nowhere found a land to prefer to our beloved state, nor have I ever ceased throughout all my wanderings, to entertain the hope that, at some future day, I may find a home and a resting place upon its soil." Lest the recipients be unclear about his careful parsing of words and his distinctions between their "common country" and "native state," he went on to refer more specifically to his "attachment" to South Carolina, referring to it as "my country," rather than "common country," a phrase he used to describe the Union. Like many southerners, he clearly recognized his native state as his "country" and acknowledged Calhoun's qualities as a worthy model. "The feelings and reflections which your letter excited are all additional incentives to me to prove myself not unworthy of the commendation and reward so generously bestowed, to cherish attachment to the government and institutions of my country, to preserve a high admiration for the noble patriotism of the great statesman whom you name, to be guided by his wisdom, and to emulate the stainless purity of his private life." Anderson's subsequent actions indicate that, despite his misgivings, he understood that his loyalty to his state took precedence. Receipt of the sword prompted him to deliberate intently on his future and to move closer to deciding his course of action should sectional conflict divide the nation.[41]

Anderson and his dragoons slowly made their way back to Fort Kearny over the late spring and summer of 1859, arriving near mid-August. He remained there through 1860 carefully watching the momentous events on the national political scene and as discontented with his situation as he ever was. Fred Childs wrote to Wallace from his post in Texas on December 2, 1860 noting humorously that Mary had "received a very pleasant letter from brother Dick the other day. He says he is not a bit more reconciled to Army life than he used to be & gathers comfort from the fact that Mary is beginning to experience its realities on the frontier, on the principle that misery loves company." There was a bit of good news in the letter as well. Sallie and Dick Anderson were expecting a third child in January. The Anderson family's men maintained close contact as the sectional crisis deepened. In South Carolina by the fall of 1860, "the whole state . . . was in ferment. Many . . . had gone wild on the subject of secession, and were anxious that Lincoln should be elected." Those rash southerners "believed that his election would sweep the South from the Union over the opposition of those who did not favor secession and were regarded almost as traitors."[42]

With Lincoln's victory South Carolina quickly scheduled a secession convention in Charleston to begin on December 17. The convention members took the state out of the Union three days later. Mississippi, Florida, Alabama, Georgia, Louisiana, and Texas soon followed suit. Whatever Dick Anderson's feelings were concerning slavery; despite his torn devotion between two families—one northern and one southern—and despite his qualms, when South Carolina seceded and severed the bonds of union, he was at least prepared to resign his commission in the United States Army, but he did not rush to do so. Notwithstanding his father's preoccupation with the prospect of familial discord over the issue of slavery, no outward friction appeared in Dr. Anderson's immediate family. Still, grave uncertainty marked the period of crisis, and even Dr. Anderson urged caution. In January 1861, Dr. Anderson did not know what to advice to give his son-in-law Fred Childs except to urge him to remain in the army "till things develop." Certainly, he must have advised his sons Dick and Wallace to do the same. His daughter Mary, fierier than the others, was less sanguine that the situation could be defused. "No step backward is her [South Carolina's] motto," she wrote her mother-in-law that month. "She will never be in the Union again—another Union but not this one." Her brother Wallace, then serving as an army surgeon in Texas, eventually resigned his commission, but Mary found his calmness alarming in the meantime. "I don't believe he reads the papers or knows anything about it," wrote an astonished Mary. Wallace hoped to obtain leave at the end of January to return to South Carolina. "He talks of bringing sister Jennie back with him & making her comfortable at Fort Chadbourne as if nothing was the matter. And I believe unless he comes as a Texas volunteer he won't come back at all." In fact, Wallace and his brother McKenzie had considered the situation carefully, and both were equivocal regarding the rush to secession. Wallace responded to McKenzie from Fort Chadbourne regarding his letter of January 2. "I think with you, that our State has pushed matters a little too far and fast, and if the aim of the leading men in the movement is for absolute and unconditional disunion under any and all circumstances, whether the North concedes full redress and security or not, I think they are to be blamed and their counsel opposed as decidedly as that of the Northern fanatical party." In spite of those sentiments, Wallace also declined to impugn the motives of those leading men, instead choosing to believe them motivated by "true patriotism and the unselfish desire to do that which is best, not only for their own State but for the entire South." He, like his sister Mary, was not confident of reaching any resolution other than one that would simply postpone "the evil day. The seeds of aggression have been widely sown at the North and have taken deep root, and the Country is now beginning to reap the fruits in the discord and hate which has now become pretty general between the two sections, at any rate between the South and the Abolition party." He went on to castigate the Abolitionists for their disregard of Biblical teaching and embrace of "lying party newspapers. If they use the Bible it is with the view of making it subservient, by misinterpretation, to the furtherance of their own Devilish Designs. . . . The Grace of God, to which all things are possible, we cannot expect to see poured out upon such men, for they not only do not seek it but absolutely reject and scoff at it." Wallace was apparently as religious as his brother Benjamin had been, and he hoped that religious sentiment would sooth the crisis. "If quiet should now be for a time restored I think that all true Christians should exert themselves to the utmost to spread His Gospel throughout our country and support to the extent of their abilities domestic Missions. By this means I believe that if the fearful struggle cannot be entirely prevented it will yet be deprived of much of its terrible strength and desolating fury." Though no letters from Dick Anderson to his brothers from this period survive, he must have been a party to the discussions and thus aware of their thoughts on the crisis. The fact that he did not rush to resign indicates that he must also have been hoping for some sort of resolution in these days.[43]

Dick Anderson wisely corresponded with his Pennsylvania relatives as well, who likewise urged restraint. Sallie's brother, George Gibson, implored him hold on to his commission "until the last moment in hopes that matters may be arranged." Whether George meant personal matters or national ones is not clear, but in the end, nothing at all was arranged. As for Sallie, her deepest feelings passed unrecorded, but she stood by her husband regardless of any personal misgivings she too might have entertained. Instead, the vivacious Sallie moved easily between camps, devoted to her husband yet never forsaking her family ties to Pennsylvania. "I get homesick sometimes," she wrote during the war, "and then the Penna. Dutch would be as music to my ears."[44]

On February 16, 1861, Anderson wrote to the army's adjutant general, Colonel Samuel Cooper, requesting that his resignation from the Army take effect on March 3. He made a point of specifically asking that his request be acted upon before "the close of Mr. Buchanan's administration," prior to Lincoln taking office. Anderson delayed his departure for a time due to Sallie being ill, perhaps attributable to her pregnancy, but they and eight-year-old Richard along with three-year-old daughter Sallie, soon set off for South Carolina, his "country." Fred Childs, an artillerist serving in Texas also resigned his commission. He and Dick's sister Mary arrived home in South

Carolina in time to meet Mary Chesnut. The inveterate diarist noted that the "very pretty and very interesting" Mary was "in a real South Carolina rebellious spirit" that afternoon. Wallace and Fred's sister Jennie soon followed, though Jennie arrived at her mother's home in Wilmington, NC long before Wallace left Texas. The surgeon apparently delayed his departure for some time in order not to abandon the men prior to the arrival of a replacement and because there was no transportation. He was finally able to resign on April 20, but in the meantime, both Fred and Jennie wrote to the new Confederate government to apprise them of Wallace's situation and his intention to offer his services to the Confederacy. Former officers of the US Army were vying for a place in the new order.[45]

Chapter 6

Charleston to Pensacola Bay

The missiles of death showered upon us.

—Braxton Bragg,
official report, December 4, 1861

Anderson's Confederate service began as a major of cavalry in mid-March 1861, but he was quickly elevated to the rank of colonel and placed in command of the 1st South Carolina Regular Infantry on Sullivans Island near Charleston. His administrative chores there were tedious. One haughty young officer recently graduated from the South Carolina Military Academy was soon vexed by Anderson's casual treatment of a conundrum involving the seniority of the regiment's junior officers who all held identical dates of rank. "Our Colonel seemed entirely oblivious to the importance of a prompt and decisive course of action," recalled First Lieutenant Thomas Huguenin. The arrival from Texas of Lieutenant Colonel Bernard Bee soon resolved the impasse when Bee had the officers draw lots to determine their seniority. Huguenin remained dissatisfied, having to settle for the position of senior first lieutenant. The disappointed Citadel graduate believed himself "much superior in education and in every other respect to others who had been more fortunate in the drawing."[1]

By April 11, when General Pierre G. T. Beauregard issued an ultimatum to Union troops occupying Fort Sumter, portions of Anderson's regiment manned batteries on Sullivans Island while others stood ready to repel anticipated Union attacks. Confederate bombardment of the fort began early on April 12, and several companies from Anderson's regiment served as artillerists. Most men stood by "in readiness to act as reserve or to be thrown on any point where their services were required." Those who took no part in the initial great engagement of the war soon found that the Union Navy's relief force was standing off, leaving Sumter and its beleaguered defenders to their fate. Thirty-four hours after the first shot, Major Robert Anderson, USA, struck his colors and surrendered the fort.[2]

On May 31, Beauregard took command of Confederate forces at Manassas Junction, Virginia, with Anderson appointed commander of the forces around Charleston. He ensured the prompt and efficient execution of Beauregard's instructions regarding the strengthening of the harbor's defenses by overseeing the construction of new fortifications, equipping them with ordinance and ammunition, and assigning troops to handle the guns. The distribution of manpower proved to be a complex task, but it was just one of numerous challenges. The lack of a trained engineers and inadequate funding were both vital issues that led Anderson to write Samuel Cooper to "beg respectfully" for an engineer and the funds necessary for the construction of defensive works. He was likewise sent begging for troops to man the fortifications as most newly arrived men rapidly moved on to Virginia.[3]

In addition to improving the defenses of Charleston Harbor, Anderson was responsible for other defenses along the South Carolina coast as well. By early June, he had obtained estimates for the construction of batteries at Bay Point and Hilton Head and was again begging Cooper for approval and funds. Heavy guns destined for those batteries arrived in the city by rail, while others needed new gun carriages. The shortage of materials to construct the carriages led Anderson to complain that eighteen guns were "consequently lying here useless" and he wondered if any assistance in mounting them was available from the Navy Yard at Norfolk, Virginia.[4]

Anderson detailed an armed schooner to monitor the Union blockading squadron and ensure no enemy boats were able to communicate with the local fishing craft. He also sought to charter a more efficient steamer for the same purpose, noting that it could easily supply transport between the city and the forts. The constant shifting of troops remained the most frustrating issue for Anderson, with some of his original regiments sent to Virginia and others hoping to follow. Few wished to remain idle where the war had already swept past. Anderson could ill afford to see those assigned to him more dissatisfied than garrison duty would naturally render them, and he was sensitive to issues that would foment that dissatisfaction. He understood from first-hand experience on the frontier that garrison troops were subject to low morale if not properly handled. In late June, he was compelled to write to South Carolina's adjutant general, States Rights Gist, regarding a telegraphic dispatch he had received from Major Josiah Gorgas of the Ordnance Department directing him to exchange the rifled muskets then in the hands of troops at Charleston with the inferior smoothbore muskets of Hampton's Legion. Anderson was rightfully miffed firstly that the dispatch did not arrive through proper channels. It had no official signature, and an officer subordinate to Anderson, whom, he noted, was "within the limits of my command," had made the application for the rifles. Moreover, Anderson had not had the opportunity "which is mine by right and courtesy to endorse my remarks" to that officer's request. Anderson declined to comply on that basis, deeming the transfer "inexpedient." Such was the sensitivity of the garrison soldiers that Anderson believed it would "inflict upon the troops a mortification but little less galling than being compelled to lay them down before the enemy." He sought to have the matter adjudicated by the President. Anderson's vigorous defense of his men and their right to retain their arms, notwithstanding his apparent pique over the method making the request, stands as evidence of his effective leadership at Charleston. Everything about his handling of that situation had the hallmarks of a strong leader ensuring the welfare of his troops. The record of the incident does not show whether Wade Hampton was aware of Anderson's role in stopping the transfer of the rifles to the troops of his Legion, but it could have put him on the wrong foot with a powerful political figure from his home state.[5]

By July 1861, South Carolina Governor Francis Pickens recommended Anderson's promotion to brigadier general. Pickens ranked Anderson highest of all the officers in the regular forces of South Carolina because "he was the oldest officer of the late United States Army from the State, and outranked all others." Unhappily for Anderson, he had seen "his juniors in rank promoted over him" since entering Confederate service. One of those was Bernard Bee, appointed brigadier on June 17, 1861. Bee fell at the Battle of Manassas a little over a month later, but not before passing down to posterity a nickname for one of the war's most revered leaders, Thomas J. "Stonewall" Jackson.[6]

Anderson received his promotion on July 19, writing immediately to Adjutant General Cooper to "solicit as a further mark of [President Jefferson Davis'] favor the command of a brigade in active service in the field." He also wrote to the Secretary of War expressing his wish to "be assigned to a command in the field."[7] Elated by his rapid rise from captain in the US Army to brigadier general in the Confederate Army, Anderson cast aside any qualms about his decision to throw in with the Confederacy and embraced his new role with relish. It was a responsibility to take very seriously, and it must have been abundantly clear to all men of even moderate ambition that favorable notoriety in the conflict with the North would bode well for post-war opportunities, particularly since contemporary opinion held that the conflict would be a brief one. It was imperative to make the most of it while the opportunity was present. Moreover, prevailing concepts of duty and honor required men of quality to seek a prominent place at the decisive scenes of action in the war, no matter the danger. Of the latter, Anderson was fully aware. Three days before, the body of General Bee had arrived in Charleston along with those of two prominent colonels from the state. The nearly bloodless engagement at Sumter had been but a gentle introduction to the horrors of war. Casualties resulting from the battle at Manassas on July 21 were light in comparison to those suffered in future contests, but the news of the dead and wounded combined with the solemn arrival of Bee's body indicated that it was now war in earnest.

Personal family tragedy dampened Anderson's spirits at this time, despite his promotion. His daughter Mary McKenzie, born just five months earlier, died on July 1. There is no record of Sallie's whereabouts at that time, but it is most likely that she was with the Anderson family in Stateburg as little Mary was laid to rest there in the Church of the Holy Cross Cemetery just across the King's Highway from the Anderson home. One can only imagine the devastating impact on the parents, but no letters or other comments survive to plumb the depth of that grief. Anderson's responsibilities at Charleston must have at least taken his mind off his sorrow for a time. Sallie and her other children along with a nurse would soon go to join Dick in Florida.

On August 21, 1861, Brigadier General Anderson received orders to report to Brigadier General Braxton Bragg. Bragg commanded the Gulf Coast between Mobile and Pensacola with headquarters at Pensacola's navy yard. Bragg wrote to his wife on September 1 about two generals ordered to report to him at Pensacola, Daniel Ruggles and Anderson. "A. was five years after me, [at USMA] –of course he is a true and valliant [*sic*] Knight. He has arrived."[8] Bragg's opinion of Anderson's knightly qualities would soon change for the worse.

Pensacola Bay was the best on the Gulf Coast, and the navy yard second only to Norfolk, Virginia. Its isolation and transportation limitations detracted from the location's usefulness, while the obstacle posed by forty-mile-long Santa Rosa Island, which stretched across the mouth of the bay and limited entrance to a narrow channel between its western tip and the mainland, proved the most serious restriction. A Union garrison occupied Fort Pickens on Santa Rosa Island, which guarded the entrance to the bay. Lacking the wherewithal to break the Federal stranglehold on the port, Pensacola became the site of only a few minor engagements. One of them took place soon after Anderson arrived.[9]

A small Union naval expedition consisting of about a hundred men aboard a ship's launch and three cutters slipped into the Pensacola Navy Yard before dawn on September 14, hoping to burn the Confederate schooner *Judah* and spike the ten-inch Columbiad gun of a battery located nearby. It was a daring and successful raid with small loss to the attacking force. The *Judah* burned to the waterline, and the incident marked the first bloodshed to occur in Florida during the war. Less than two weeks before the destruction of the *Judah*, another boat's crew of eleven men destroyed a dry dock that they believed the Confederates were planning to use as a channel barricade. A frustrated Bragg, unable to do more, at least determined that his opponent must be "chastised for his annoyances."[10]

With Pickens' massive guns turned inland and trained on the Rebels, the advantage of the badly outgunned Confederates having recovered the navy yard intact was effectively neutralized. Colonel Harvey Brown of the 5th US Artillery commanded the Department of Florida from his headquarters at Fort Pickens. With him was a force of artillerymen and the 3rd US Infantry. Camped outside the fort itself, Colonel William Wilson's 6th New York Volunteer Infantry, known informally as "Billy's" Zouaves, protected the fort and vulnerable batteries outside its eastern walls from an attack. In addition, a roving squadron of Union ships blockaded the bay and added substantial firepower. Unlike Fort Sumter and other former Federal forts in the South that had quickly surrendered to the Confederate forces arrayed against them, Pickens proved a more formidable nut to crack. It fell to Bragg—no doubt to his intense disgust and embarrassment—to command a seaport crippled by the presence of a strong Union force just offshore. Bragg understood that there was no other way to take the fort than "with a regular siege, and we have no means to carry that on."[11]

Bragg instead planned a smaller retaliatory strike against Santa Rosa Island, and he selected Dick Anderson to lead it. On the night before Anderson's expedition, Bragg sent Captain William R. Boggs and another staff officer to the island to determine the feasibility of attacking the guns and defenders positioned outside the fort. Bragg took a hazardous risk in planning a nighttime mission with inexperienced troops under the command of an almost equally inexperienced officer who had led nothing larger than a company or two of mounted troops. Boggs was convinced that Bragg thought his talents were wasted at Pensacola and thought that the assault resulted largely from Bragg's mounting feelings of displeasure at being relegated to a backwater. Bragg decided to press ahead with the attack with the intention of burning Wilson's camp, spiking some of the Union guns, and "avenging the annoyances he had recently caused my command."[12]

The call for volunteers produced an enthusiastic response. For the past several months many men had declined to perform common labor on the area's defenses, noting, said Bragg, "they came to fight." They would soon have an opportunity to show their mettle. Private Richard A. Clayton of the 5th Georgia's Company F recalled that their colonel told the men that he wanted volunteers "for hazardous work tonight." The entire company proved eager to go. His lieutenant then "detailed 17 men from the right," Clayton wrote to his father, "I and Milt were (to our joy) included."[13]

Private W. J. Milner of Company A (Clinch Rifles), 5th Georgia, also recalled his captain calling for volunteers for a "hazardous expedition," telling them that he did "not want any man to go who is not willing to die tonight if necessary." Like Clayton, Milner reported that the request for volunteers to bring their weapons to the shoulder met with a response that, "if he had given the order 'Shoulder Arms' could not have been more promptly and completely complied with." Milner was thrilled to be among those selected. Members of Milner's company busied themselves preparing for imminent battle, using a grindstone to hone the saber bayonets for their Mississippi Rifles "as sharp as butcher knives." None knew yet what their mission would entail, yet all were eager to participate. A disconsolate comrade approached Milner and appealed to him with tears in his eyes and the offer of twenty-five dollars to let him take his place. Milner declined the offer. "Think of conquering an army of such soldiers!" he wrote.[14]

On the night of October 8, 1861, Anderson assembled much of his force at the navy yard and began embarking them onto the steamer *Time* for a short trip across the bay to nearby Pensacola. He divided the soldiers into three battalions. The first, with 350 men of the 9th and 10th Mississippi and 1st Alabama Regiments, was commanded by Colonel James R. Chalmers, a Mississippi lawyer and politician who had Bragg's confidence. The second battalion included three companies of the 7th Alabama, two companies of Louisiana infantry, and two of the 1st Florida, totaling 400 men under the command of Colonel James Patton Anderson. Patton Anderson was a doctor and politician, but he had military experience, having raised and commanded the 1st Battalion, Mississippi Rifles during the war with Mexico. Colonel John K. Jackson commanded the final battalion, numbering 260 men of the 5th Georgia and the Georgia Battalion. Jackson was a Georgia lawyer who had turned his regiment into a finely regarded body of troops. Another fifty-three men from the 5th Georgia Infantry along with a company of artillerymen was lightly armed with pistols and knives. Commanded by Lieutenant James H. Hallonquist, assisted by Lieutenant Llewellyn A. Nelms, their mission was to spike Union guns and to burn and destroy buildings and gun carriages. Five surgeons and twenty men to assist them rounded out Anderson's force.[15]

By 10 PM, Anderson arrived at Pensacola and began dispersing men to the steamer *Ewing* and a variety of barges and flat boats. Darkness led to confusion and a delay that would have serious repercussions for the raid's success. First, the underpowered *Ewing* was unable to tow the tightly packed barges and boats. The steamer *Neaffie* soon arrived to assist and the expedition finally got underway just after midnight. By then, the excitement and anticipation of battle began to settle in. Private Clayton later wrote to his father "Some of us had curious feelings," in the tense and uncertain darkness. "I thought of you—my sisters, brothers and friends—prayed God to bless you and them," he wrote. The crossing went smoothly enough, as did the landing and disembarkation. The tide was in and the ships and barges were able to get fairly close to the beach. Still, many men were soaked from having to wade to shore. Anderson's three battalions formed on the Santa Rosa Island beaches by just after 2 AM, still about four miles from Fort Pickens.[16]

The element of surprise was essential to accomplish the mission and prevent the interception or bombardment of the transports. Anderson explicitly instructed Chalmers and Patton Anderson to maintain secrecy by capturing Union pickets before they gave a warning to their comrades. Chalmers then struck out along the north beach adjacent to the bay, while Patton Anderson set off along the southern beach adjacent to the Gulf. Colonel Jackson followed a few hundred yards behind Chalmers, intending to deploy across the middle of the island once firing began. Lieutenant Hallonquist's detail followed Jackson. The plan was so fully reliant on the element of surprise that early detection and a determined federal response to the attack could have proved fatal.[17]

By the time the columns approached the Zouave camp, situated between the landing site and the fort, the men were exhausted from slogging through the soft sand along the beaches on that "hot and lurid night." Dick Anderson later noted only that the march was "toilsome and fatiguing," but Clayton described more vividly the difficult nature of the movement when he reported that Jackson's command had "marched very fast—way down next to the water. Sometimes the waves would roll high up above our shoes—sometimes almost to our knees." The night's stillness was suddenly broken when Confederates shot down a Zouave picket after he fired wildly at the head of Chalmer's battalion. General Anderson sent Jackson's men rushing through the undergrowth between the beaches. Jackson's men swept aside the Union pickets and burst into the camp, where the company streets were paved with pine boughs and shaded by arbors, but devoid of Zouaves. "The rascals had fled to the fort," thought Private Clayton. Hallonquist's men began firing tents, sheds, and storehouses, the conflagration fueled by dried pine branches above and below. From his vantage on the mainland, Bragg anxiously trained his field glasses on the dark silhouette of the island, relieved to see flames consuming the Union camp. On learning later of the flight of the New Yorkers, Bragg gleefully reported that they "fled in their shirt tails . . . at the first fire."[18]

Bragg's statement belied his fears at the time that the Union defenders could trap the raiders on the island or that the guns of the fort could decimate the transports re-crossing the bay. General Anderson realized immediately that his success in overrunning and destroying the Zouave camp would be the high point of the affair. He ordered his men back to the safety of the ships, but a quick response by other Union forces conspired against his complete success. Wilson's Zouaves did not withdraw entirely from the

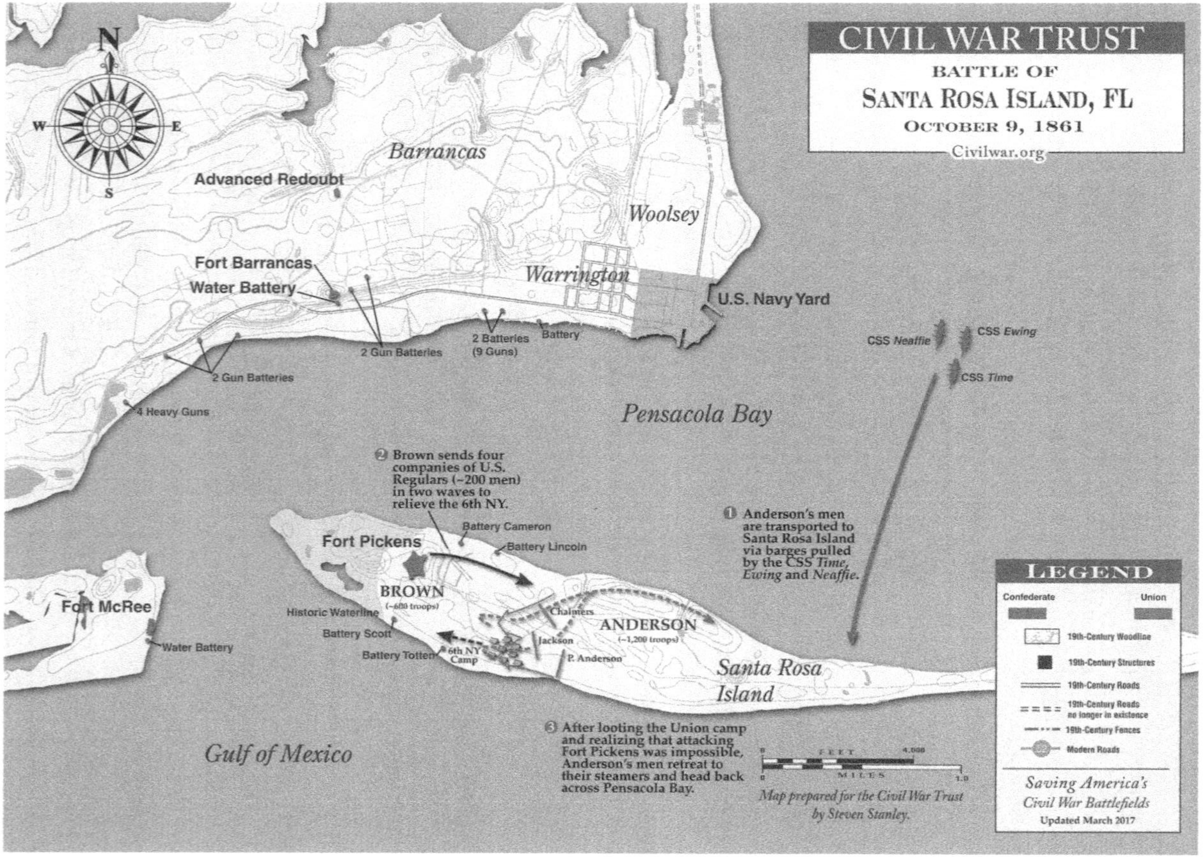

Figure 2. Map of the Battle of Santa Rosa Island, October 9, 1861. Courtesy of the American Battlefield Trust.

engagement, and though confused and overwhelmed, small groups of New Yorkers did offer some resistance.[19]

Wilson's command numbered no more than 250 at that time, and the colonel quickly had them fall out on the drill ground at the first sound of gunfire. The Zouaves returned a volley or two after they received fire from the camp itself, by then engulfed by flames. One New Yorker recalled hearing the Rebels shout, "No quarter to Wilson' men," as they pillaged. The blaze illuminated the area enough for the New Yorkers to see that hundreds of Confederates were milling about and moving to cut them off from retreat. Wilson was unable to restrain his men, and the red-legs "broke for the beach" and headed towards the batteries nearer the fort. Meanwhile, a Zouave sergeant ran into Wilson's flaming tent and managed to save the regimental colors.[20]

Other Union troops in and around the fort rushed to aid the New Yorkers. Major Israel Vogdes led a relief force along the north beach towards the sound of the guns. Colonel Jackson's contingent had begun its retreat, and they soon saw the gleam of Vogdes' bayonets in the firelight, but were unsure whether the troops were friendly or not. A volley from Vogdes' men tore into the Rebel ranks and soon set the matter straight—for a moment at least. Colonel Jackson then rode up and ordered the men to cease firing and form a line, also believing that Vogdes's troops were friendly. Some did not hear the command, however, and the scene remained one of confusion as some Confederates kept up the fire with others shouting "Don't shoot! They are our men." Vogdes, also uncertain which troops he confronted, rode forward and was immediately pulled from his mule and taken prisoner. A Confederate officer then stepped forward requesting the surrender of Vogdes's detachment. Instead, several shots sped in his direction, but superior southern numbers soon brushed the federals aside. Disjointed forces of Yankees and Rebels continued to blunder into one another for a time, until General Anderson finally had the men back on the beaches and ready to load onto the transports.[21]

The dangers of General Anderson's troop dispositions now became apparent. Men scattered along the island would have become easy prey had not the Union pursuers been equally confused and substantially weaker. The expedition was now beginning to feel the impact of its late start. The guns of the fort and ships of the blockading squadron could potentially fire on the fleeing transports as daylight approached and revealed their presence. One of Colonel Brown's first actions was to order the steamer *McClellan* to proceed to the spot where the Confederates had landed, but the *McClellan* attempted to tow the frigate *Potomac* to the scene as well. The ensuing delay prevented either ship reaching the site until too late. Had the *McClellan* set out alone its rifled guns might have driven off or disabled the Confederate steamers and left the force stranded.[22]

There was trouble enough for the retreating southerners. The tide had receded by then and the ships and barges had been compelled to stand off into deeper water. Tired Confederates now had to struggle through the surf to reach the craft. Meanwhile, pursuing Union forces appeared behind the dunes on the beach and began to fire into the mass of Confederates crowded onto the boats. General Anderson himself received a painful wound to the left elbow at that time. Anderson's men were returning fire at a very rapid pace, and bullets whistled over the dunes and through the scrub pines as frantic Confederates sought relief from their precarious spot. From the center of the barge, Private Milner was loading and firing as fast as he could. As the Union fire increased, recalled Milner, so too did the Confederate's "confusion and consternation." The receding tide had left the barge in perilously shallow water, and the added weight of the men soon settled it on the bottom. Soldiers rapidly began to transfer to the crowded steamer in an attempt to free the grounded barge, but even thus lightened it would not budge. One soldier aboard the steamer raised a hatchet to cut the rope anchoring it to the troublesome barge, but a man on the barge raised his rifle and threatened to shoot him if he did so.[23]

A series of calamities kept the hapless Rebel force stationary as the battle raged. Not only was the barge behind the *Time* grounded, a hawser had come loose and become entangled in the propeller of the *Neaffie*. That steamer was dead in the water, its guns useless against the gathering bluecoats. Unable to free the propeller, sailors tied the *Neaffie* and the flat barge she had in tow onto the *Ewing*, but the *Ewing* would not obey her helm with the additional burden. Sailors made some "change in the manner of towing" to relieve that problem, but a third potential disaster occurred when the barges being towed by the *Ewing* came loose from her. Anderson simply noted in his report of the battle that "still further delay was occasioned in recovering them," but the delay seemed an eternity to the men enduring the Union fusillades. Finally, with the wayward barges made fast once again things began to brighten. The *Time* was able to dislodge its barge and begin to move off slowly too, and the little armada steamed away as quickly as possible after men cut away the hawser from the *Neaffie's* prop. They arrived at the docks in Pensacola around 11 that morning, cheerfully greeted by "many ladies with refreshments for the hungry and bandages for the wounded."[24]

Once safely ashore at Pensacola, the wounded attended to, and the rolls taken, the Confederates began to assess the results of their foray. They termed it a great success, having accomplished the rout of "Wilson's pickpockets" and the destruction of their camp and stores. In that regard, they were correct, but not a single Union gun was spiked during the confused fighting. All of the batteries were beyond the Zouave camp, closer to Fort Pickens, and approaching daylight had forced General Anderson to halt the attack and return to his transports. Anderson reported two officers killed, Captain Bradford and Lieutenant Nelms, along with four non-commissioned officers, eleven privates, and one citizen volunteer. Two officers, five non-commissioned officers, and thirty-two privates suffered wounds. Among the captured were five officers, two non-commissioned officers, and twenty-three privates. Prisoners soon corresponded with their friends, and several men reported missing and feared dead were discovered later to be in Yankee hands. One officer received a letter within days from three of his men requesting that he send their blankets, clothing, tobacco, and some money.[25]

The results were notable primarily for their avoidance of a potential disaster. The entire operation was ill conceived. Bragg himself noted in a letter to his wife that it "was a desperate affair, in which success [would be] commended, a failure unpardonable." That he was willing to risk such an "unpardonable" failure undoubtedly reflected a mixture of concern for the morale of his troops, his desire to punish his opponent, and his hopes that success would bring attention to himself. Naturally, Bragg was on tenterhooks throughout the night and only later began to crow that the operation was "entirely successful." He also began to evaluate his troops' performance more critically, citing a propensity for straggling as the cause of many of the casualties. He derided the volunteers' lack of "order and regularity in retiring," noting that they had won the day, but then "could see no impropriety in scattering about and enjoying the walk home." Anderson, whose responsibility as overall commander was to ensure such things did not happen, has to bear the blame for that lapse. The fact that most of his command was comprised of untested recruits undertaking a difficult mission in the dead of night somewhat mitigates the amount of blame Anderson, his subordinate commanders, or the men should bear. Bragg failed to note that most of the losses stemmed from the accidents disabling the transports and the subsequent attempts to rescue them. A more vigorous pursuit by a stronger Union force would have added greatly to the Confederate casualties and been a result of the flawed plan itself, not the actions of the men who implemented it. As for Anderson, Bragg noted in his report that he "conducted the expedition with a zeal and gallantry worthy of high commendation." Commenting on Anderson's wound, Bragg further wrote that "it is trusted we shall not long be deprived of his valuable services."[26] Behind Bragg's outwardly gracious comments, however, a growing resentment against his subordinate was apparently festering.

General Anderson's wound delayed his report of the battle until October 23, with Sallie writing on the fifteenth that he continued "to improve and is sitting up dressed this morning." He might have been mulling the Anderson family penchant for wounds to the left elbow, as a musket shot in nearly the same place disabled his grandfather and namesake at Guilford Courthouse in 1781. Anderson was also concerned for the safety of his family if a retaliatory bombardment ensued. Sallie even spoke of sending the children off to South Carolina should there be any prospect of an "unquiet winter" at Pensacola, and they discussed the possibility of building a shelter in the woods, safely out of range of the Union guns. Financial considerations must have played a part in their deliberations, as housing in the small town of Pensacola was scarce and expensive. When Sallie arrived with their two children in early September, the family of four and two servants had stayed at the Bedell House in Pensacola at a cost of $72.85 for eight days. With pay of $301.00 per month, the family could not have afforded such luxury for long. Despite fears of Union reprisal, Pensacola remained quiet for a time after the raid.[27]

Colonel Brown had proposed a joint artillery assault on Rebel defensive works by all his available batteries supported by ships of the blockading squadron. The bombardment was set for dawn on October 16, but when the Navy ships steamed off in response to an urgent need elsewhere Brown postponed it until November. The lull in activity at Pensacola came to an abrupt end at 9:55 AM on November 22 with the firing of a signal gun from Fort Pickens that heralded the opening of a massive and destructive bombardment.[28]

Captain Boggs noted that the first shells fell into the midst of a panicked crowd of men detailed to unload transports at the navy yard. He later heard that "the appearance of General Richard Anderson walking cooly [*sic*] about" served to check the consternation on the docks. Mrs. Anderson was less calm. An orderly brought her a hastily found horse with no saddle and only an old rope for a bridle. She quickly mounted and little Sallie was boosted onto the saddle of an accompanying soldier. While making her way to safety, she encountered one of the town's prominent citizens. "All at once her womanly instincts returned, and stopping her horse she asked Mr. Moulton to please assist her to adjust her seat and skirts." With shells crashing around them, old Mr. Moulton was in no mood for such niceties. Breathlessly, he informed her "she was doing very well indeed," and rushed onward out of range of the deadly shower of projectiles. Little Sallie's beloved nurse, meanwhile, was not invited to ride along and "was left to shift for herself." Young Sallie could not bear this. She "immediately became unmanageable and demanded to be put down." The nurse gladly accepted a ride behind another of the soldiers accompanying the party and the minor dilemma was resolved to the child's satisfaction.[29]

Meanwhile, Confederate guns responded heartily, absorbing a great deal more punishment than that meted out to the Federals, although one Georgia gunner reported that his battery of two 8-inch Columbiads put thirty-seven holes in the walls of Fort Pickens. Before the fire halted, Bragg's command suffered casualties of six men killed, and nine wounded, two of those succumbing later to their wounds.[30]

When Union shelling resumed the next morning the rate of fire was more restrained but more accurate. The Confederates had suffered on the previous day and were not able to respond as robustly when the duel resumed. Unable to fire any of the brick and slate structures of the navy yard itself, Federal artillerists soon succeeded in burning a part of the town of Warrington adjoining the yard. The sudden change of targets by the Union gunners and the pumping of hot shot into the towns might have reflected their frustration. Despite having disabled a good number of Rebel guns and silencing the fire of many of the batteries, a well-placed Confederate shell knocked one of Fort Pickens' 8-inch Columbiads out of action.[31]

Although evacuated at the start of the shelling, Bragg bemoaned the Union's "barbarous act" of firing into the navy yard's hospital. The surrounding towns suffered most of the damage though. Despite the accurate Union fire on Confederate batteries, there was not a single casualty. Both sides claimed a victory, with Brown writing that the attack on Wilson's Zouaves and Fort Pickens had been avenged, and Bragg calling the shelling a "miserable failure," although he also proclaimed it would "rank with the heaviest bombardment in the world. It was grand and sublime." Bragg closed his report with flowery prose before calling on Psalm 127 for words befitting his impression of the affair as one of great importance. "And in the hour of our trial the missiles of death, showered upon us by an infuriated enemy, respecting neither women, children, nor the sick, have been so directed as to cause us to laugh at their impotent rage. Verily, 'Except the Lord keep the city, the watchman waketh but in vain.'" The bombardment also did little to damage Confederate morale. One soldier of the 1st Alabama wrote that "Old Brown said in October that he could shell us out of this place in two hours, but it seems that he is a false prophet." Conversely, one of Wilson's Zouaves bemoaned the waste of ammunition and the poor Union tactical situation. The discomfited New Yorker criticized Brown's leadership, noting "Under such circumstances wise men do not fight."[32]

Other than Boggs' comment about General Anderson's poise, his role in the engagement is undocumented. His 2nd Brigade was posted largely in the area of the navy yard and its adjacent batteries. He directed those not needed immediately in serving the big guns to form behind the navy yard's north wall. In anticipation of an attempted landing, Bragg held other troops in readiness on the beach throughout the barrage. Bragg noted in his official report that he was indebted to Anderson "for able support and prudent counsel during the whole time," but the precise nature of that support and counsel remains unknown. In the next engagement, Anderson took a more active role that pleased Bragg far less. In a few months' time Anderson would find himself facing serious allegations of misconduct leveled by the prickly Bragg, but even as early as October 13, despite his public statements praising Anderson's role in the attack on Santa Rosa Island, Bragg had begun to express some doubts about Anderson's qualities as a general. Though he declined to criticize his subordinate in his official report of the battle at Santa Rosa Island, he privately expressed his true opinion in a letter to Confederate President Jefferson Davis when he noted that he was sending Ruggles to command the defenses at New Orleans because he was more capable than Anderson was.[33]

Prior to Anderson's fall from grace, one of Bragg's staff officers was also smarting from ill treatment at Bragg's hands. By December 1861, Captain Boggs' relations with Bragg had cooled to such an extent that he had determined to resign his position as Bragg's chief of engineers. He elected to take his leave of Pensacola on New Year's Day 1862, and had gone to visit the Andersons to bid them farewell. The general and his wife were receiving New Year's guests that day, and several officers were already there, all sitting around chatting easily. At around 3 PM a gun from Fort Pickens fired, followed by two more shots. Boggs later claimed that the Confederate guns returned fire immediately and a heavy artillery exchange began within a short time. The officers present all mounted and rode away quickly to their posts. Anderson was then in temporary command while Bragg was visiting Mobile, and he acted decisively. At the navy yard, Anderson dismounted and went rapidly to the top of the parapets to observe the fire. He then called upon the officers of a nearby battery to come up with him so that they could see the effects of their fire and adjust their shots accordingly. The heavy exchange of gunfire continued until dark, with no casualties save the unfortunate burning of a "large and valuable storehouse, with considerable property," in the Navy Yard.[34]

The Union shells that led to the exchange of gunfire had come in response to the appearance of a steamer attempting to make its way to the Navy Yard. Already on his way back from Mobile, Bragg was "privately advised" by telegram of the ongoing engagement.[35] He reached Pensacola at about 4 AM on the morning of January 2 and immediately halted the ineffective fire of the Confederate batteries. Union guns had long since fallen silent.

Apparently, a considerable disagreement ensued among the officers, with one local correspondent reporting, "there was quite a flare up all round—Bragg's man Friday, chief engineers, ordnance officers, and everything else."[36] In fact, the results of the engagement showed clearly that the men had acted rashly, and of course, the blame fell on Anderson, who bore overall responsibility. Anderson's aggression undeniably led the Confederate batteries to continue responding so vigorously to the Union provocation, and it fell to him to disengage from the uneven duel before too much damage had befallen the vulnerable Navy Yard. Instead, he encouraged the exchange of fire, possibly hoping to achieve some notable result in Bragg's absence. Perhaps he felt less compelled to halt the cannonade because of the Federals' previous failure to damage buildings at the navy yard. Still, Rebel guns had caused no visible harm to Fort Pickens or any of the surrounding batteries, and Bragg had lost a warehouse brimming with valuable supplies. The contest had been decidedly uneven, and now someone would have to pay for that setback.

Even Colonel Brown at Fort Pickens expressed surprise at the intensity of the Rebel response. "I am impressed with the belief that General Bragg was not present," Brown astutely reported, "and that a less experienced and more hot-headed officer commanded." Moreover, Brown fired slowly and deliberately, having discovered in November the difficulty of burning Confederate buildings at such distance. Conversely, he reported Rebel fire "not so good as before," though he thought that they expended "considerably more ammunition than on either of the previous days, and with less effect." Since November, Brown had received a supply of rock-fire and carcasses, which he could employ with greater effect than his previous ammunition. Rock-fire was an artillery round filled with incendiaries, while carcasses were hollow oval cases filled with combustibles and thrown from a mortar. Both did their work on that day. Brown ceased his fire at darkness, except for a few of the mortars, which continued to lob their rounds until 2 AM. He noticed the first sign of flames at the navy yard around 9 PM that night, "and in an hour the whole firmament was illuminated." Brown attributed the success of the bombardment to the newly received ammunition and the cool actions of his gunners.[37]

Anderson soon bore the wrath of Bragg's displeasure. Bragg's report began by alleging that a "private steamer had imprudently been allowed to run to the navy yard," thus drawing the federal fire and precipitating the entire affair. He also lamented the useless expenditure of ammunition so needed for defense, and regretted "exceedingly to add that the concurrent testimony of many officers of rank represent Brigadier-General Anderson as so much intoxicated as to be entirely unfit for duty, and that his conduct was very reprehensible." It was a damning condemnation, especially so since

Bragg had made numerous efforts to curb the general drunkenness of the troops around Pensacola. He had already declared martial law in the area, prohibiting the sale of alcohol, arresting offenders, and seizing enough whiskey "to have kept the Army drunk two months." Having held juniors to "rigid accountability," Bragg was most unwilling to "overlook a similar offense in a commanding general under such aggravating circumstances."[38]

Certainly, Anderson must have been drinking that New Year's Day, and he acted imprudently by encouraging the return fire, but he was unaware of Brown's new ammunition that rendered the Confederate facilities susceptible to destruction. Boggs later attempted to excuse Anderson's behavior by suggesting that the general bombardment began of its own volition while Anderson was entertaining guests at home, but evidence disputes that recollection. Colonel Henry D. Clayton of the 1st Alabama reported that his battery at Fort Barrancas received the order to commence firing a little after 3 PM. That is about the time that Colonel Brown at Fort Pickens reported that he fired on the Rebel ship and received a reply from one of Confederate guns. While some response was necessary, not all the batteries opened at that time. Colonel John P. Villepigue was several miles distant from his post—possibly even at the Anderson home—when the firing began, and his batteries at Fort McRee began to reply at around 4 that afternoon. Boggs' admission that the officers at Anderson's quarters immediately mounted and went to their respective posts, coupled with the recollection of Colonel Brown that approximately forty-five minutes elapsed between the initial Rebel shots and the subsequent fusillade, seems to suggest that Anderson must have inflamed the affair. Even if events transpired as Boggs recalled them, it would have been incumbent upon Anderson to take steps to halt the useless fire or slacken its pace. Instead, he rashly embraced the moment as an opportunity to bring about a general engagement. He must have warmed more fully to the occasion in response to the effects of John Barleycorn, and his contrite behavior afterwards indicates some truth to the allegation. An angry Bragg ordered an investigation into the affair. He wrote Secretary of War Judah P. Benjamin that Anderson's "arrest and prosecution would be necessary." Benjamin agreed, writing Bragg on January 8 that he was "equally surprised and indignant to learn of the conduct of General Anderson, and heartily concur in your decision not to overlook it."[39]

Bragg had Anderson placed in arrest that very day, and he was ordered to "take up his quarters" in Pensacola, effectively confining the general to his home. No record exists of events that ensued following Anderson's arrest, but possibly the intervention of influential supporters derailed Bragg's plans for a trial, and he readily assented instead to a transfer to Virginia. Meanwhile, while en route from Pensacola to his home in Georgia, Captain Boggs had learned of Anderson's arrest. He immediately wrote to Bragg expressing his surprise and relating the facts as he knew them. He also wrote to Anderson, informing him that he would happily appear as a witness in his defense should the need arise, but characters far more exalted than Boggs must have lent their weight to Anderson's cause. Certainly, Governor Pickens would not have liked to see one of his state's highest-ranking officers disgraced. It is also possible that the statements of other officers who vouched for Anderson's actions swayed Bragg's resolve in the end. Bragg may have concluded that drink played a smaller role in Anderson's behavior than poor judgment. If so, he probably welcomed Anderson's removal from his command.[40]

On February 12, 1862, Anderson received orders to proceed to Manassas, where he was to report to General Joseph E. Johnston and assume command of the South Carolina Brigade then headed by Brigadier General David R. Jones. Anderson must have departed for Virginia prior to officially receiving orders, for on February 14, Brigadier General J. E. B. Stuart wrote his wife from Centerville, Virginia that "Dick Anderson is here for duty in command of a S.C. Brigade." Two days later, Anderson received further orders from Johnston's headquarters instructing him to report to his old friend and West Point classmate, Major General James Longstreet, who was commanding the second division containing the South Carolina brigade. Longstreet understood his old friend, and thus began an effective and mutually satisfying relationship that later caused a staff officer to remark of Anderson that "Longstreet knew him well and could get a good deal out of him, more than anyone else." After the controversy at Pensacola and his escape from formal charges, Anderson reputedly took a pledge of abstinence as part of the bargain. It certainly was common for officers to grow fond of drink. Entertainment at lonely frontier posts often included much use of alcohol, so if he imbibed regularly, it was part of normal and accepted behavior. At the Anderson home in Pensacola, records indicate that holiday entertaining followed that old Army tradition despite Bragg's prohibitions. On November 28, Anderson paid $10.50 for three gallons of "fine whiskey," and $0.75 for a demijohn. Less than two weeks later, he paid another $16.00 for five more gallons of whiskey. As a senior officer, he undoubtedly entertained frequently and was preparing for the coming holidays, yet clearly, whiskey played some role during the New Year's Day fiasco. Nevertheless, having given his word, Anderson abstained throughout the war. Later, Major Edward N. Thurston of Anderson's staff would tell Anderson's niece that after Pensacola, "the Gen swore off and did not touch another drop during the war."[41]

On his way north to Virginia, Anderson probably escorted his family to his father's home. The old man was as feisty as ever, writing to his son Wallace on March 8 that Dick was then at Centreville. "He is well & I hope at the risk of his life he will serve some of the generals on the Potomac as he did the scamp Billy Wilson at Santa Rosa. I am perfectly confident that we shall in the end be able to conquer the devils and put them to flight." Dick Anderson had many opportunities to try that before long, for soon after arriving in Virginia he was in the thick of hard fighting on the Peninsula from Yorktown through the Seven Days Battles. In early April, his younger brother McKenzie joined him as a volunteer aide de camp on his staff.[42]

Chapter 7

Yorktown and the Seven Days

Go forward men, straight forward, don't halt at all.

—R. H. Anderson,
Edmund Patterson's journal, May 6, 1862

In the spring of 1862, Confederates in Virginia under General Joseph E. Johnston around Manassas Junction were prepared to counter another Yankee invasion. Other southern forces under General Thomas J. "Stonewall" Jackson shielded Johnston's left flank in the Shenandoah Valley. A third force of fewer than 15,000 men led by Major General John B. "Prince John" Magruder manned thinly held lines spanning the lower Peninsula between the York and James Rivers, effectively bottling Union forces neatly at Fort Monroe on the tip of the peninsula and guarding the Confederates' right flank. As Union strategy unfolded that spring, it became apparent that General George B. McClellan was moving his armies by sea to the Virginia Peninsula. The strategy capitalized on Union naval strength and used the navigable waters of Virginia's rivers to best advantage. The Union's *USS Monitor* successfully countered the threat of the Confederate ironclad *CSS Virginia* off Hampton Roads that March, clearing the way for the invasion that forced the evacuation of Norfolk by early May, allowing the Union navy to steam up the James River nearly as far as Drewry's Bluff and provide enfilading fire in support of McClellan's advancing troops. The plan held much promise, and by April 2, 1862, McClellan firmly established the headquarters of the Army of the Potomac near Fort Monroe. The theatrical antics of Prince John, whose skillful manipulation of his small force convinced McClellan that he faced a much larger army, too easily deceived the Union leader. Federal forces crept forward cautiously, and nearly a month passed before McClellan was prepared to lay siege to Confederate works around Yorktown. In the meantime, southern forces in Tennessee had been defeated in a two-day bloodbath near Shiloh Church. Albert Sydney Johnston received a mortal wound, and his army was now retreating towards Corinth, Mississippi with General Beauregard at its head. Days later came news of the fall of Fort Pulaski near Savannah, Georgia, and a week afterwards Union naval forces began shelling Confederate defenses below New Orleans. The fortunes of war had turned decidedly against the South in those early days of spring 1862, and much now depended on the defense of the Confederate capital of Richmond. General Joseph E. Johnston's army thus marched southward from the Manassas line to reinforce—and relieve—Magruder and confront McClellan on the peninsula. Johnston protested the futility of holding a defensive line at Yorktown, instead proposing to withdraw and strengthen positions nearer the capital. He concluded that Yorktown could hold out only briefly before McClellan compelled him to retreat. Lee and Davis, hoping not to abandon Norfolk's vital naval facilities, insisted on a stand. Johnston's men dutifully took up their positions around Yorktown. At Yorktown, Confederate Surgeon J. R. Page saw men anxious to "meet the enemy as soon as possible and to strike him such a blow as to make York Town again the arena upon which the right of self-government was established and would have been entailed to us for ages to come had it not been for Puritanical cupidity and fanaticism." Though anxious to engage the foe, many were unprepared for what lay ahead. Colonel John Bratton of the 6th South Carolina wrote his wife on April 25 from his camp near Yorktown about a recent false alarm that saw his regiment called to arms. "I have never yet had an opportunity to drill the Regt.," he complained. In the meantime, Union artillery had already started to make it very hot on the men manning the breastworks. Troops of the 9th Alabama Regiment quickly began to learn the craft of warfare. They discovered that putting a man on watch for the flash from an enemy gun gave at least some warning of an incoming round and allowed the men to take cover. Private John Mason's captain kept a dog with him, which would run after the spent solid shot as they rolled along the ground, but, like the men, the dog soon enough learned a little something about war. Once a spent round dropped right under the dog and threw him "up in the air about seven feet," he "made for the breastworks" quickly. After that, whenever the lookout would holler out a warning at the flash of a Union shot "the dog would make for the breastworks just as fast as the men would for he had learnt what it meant." Others who endured shelling and skirmishing felt somewhat abused. "I think it is hard we should be kept so hard at work when there are thousands of troops doing nothing," wrote David Maxwell of the 2nd Florida.[1]

Ultimately, Johnston had his way and his well-timed retreat from the Yorktown-Warwick line began on the night of May 3, a few days before McClellan's intended bombardment with siege guns that likely would have annihilated much of the army's artillery or prevented its effective withdrawal. The men saved the field guns before that disaster unfolded, and they would see good service in the coming days. Johnston's men at first took the retreat in stride, showing evidence of their still high morale. One Massachusetts soldier facing Longstreet's division found a humorous ditty scrawled on a canvas tent side in the abandoned rebel camps: "He that fights and runs away, will live to fight another day." The truth of that statement would soon become apparent.[2]

Moving towards Williamsburg on two roads, Johnston divided his retreating army into three wings under Major Generals Daniel Harvey Hill, James Longstreet, and John Magruder, with a reserve force commanded by Gustavus W. Smith. In Longstreet's center wing was R. H. Anderson's brigade of South Carolinians comprised of the 5th and 6th South Carolina Infantry, the 4th South Carolina Battalion, the regiment of Palmetto Sharpshooters, and the Louisianans of St. Paul's Foot Rifles. Virginia artillerymen of Stribling's Fauquier Battery rounded out the command. Because of the first Confederate conscription bill approved by President Davis on April 16, Anderson's South Carolina troops began in late April to reorganize themselves and form new companies and regiments. "The men united at their pleasure to join new companies and these new companies joined as they pleased to form the new regiments," Anderson wrote on April 27. The result created Colonel Micah Jenkins' 1st Regiment of Palmetto Sharpshooters and dissolved the 9th South Carolina Infantry, leaving three South Carolina regiments and the five-company-strong 4th Battalion. Such democratic methods in organizing the troops had varied effects. Perhaps thankful for the support from his men, or wary of their future wrath, Captain James L. Coker of Company E, 6th South Carolina "began a course of discipline and training that was considerate of his men, but at the same time firm and dignified." Flexibility on the part of their officers likely satisfied the men, but in other respects, their condition was not very good.[3]

While marching from Centreville to Yorktown earlier that month, Anderson noted that some soldiers of his command were "in many respects destitute" when it came to clothing. Once again demonstrating a good leader's concern for the welfare of his troops, he requested permission to march into Richmond to purchase the needed supplies. Anderson's brigade included over fifty wagons for the surgeon and the quartermasters, along with "two small two horse wagons" hauling the baggage, tents, and personal items belonging to Anderson and his staff. The record does not indicate whether Anderson was able to divert his troops to the city, but it is more likely that they trudged on in their depleted condition. Fortunately, the weather had been fine and Johnston's army converged on the peninsula over mostly "tolerable roads." Soldiers took time to comment on the physical appearance of the women whom they passed along the line of march, with one noting rather uncharitably "beauty was the exception."[4]

The retrograde movement from Yorktown was quite a different affair, and morale soon began to slip. Soldiers keenly felt the humiliation of leaving their fellow citizens to the mercy of an invading foe. The people of Williamsburg watched sadly as their defenders passed at a funereal pace of about a mile an hour. A bottleneck ensued where two usable routes leading from Yorktown converged into a single well-churned road just outside Williamsburg. The struggle along those muddy paths caused Joe Johnston much concern over fears that a sea-borne Federal force could land upstream and block his passage. He could do little about it except to spur his army onward as rapidly as possible, but Johnston realized he must soon turn and fight to keep the pursuing Union forces at bay. Though the vanguard of Johnston's retreating army marched "leisurely along during the day" on Sunday May 4, those at the rear noted that "the Yankees were pushing us, and all through the 4th they were troublesome; our wagons and artillery moving very slowly on account of the boggy roads." Everyone understood the impending danger however, and the men accepted the developing situation with the cold rationality that soldiers quickly learned to evince. "It was evident something had to be done to check the . . . advance," wrote one, and "I suppose that we will have to fight before we reach Richmond" reasoned another.[5]

Magruder had already prepared defensive works near Williamsburg, where the distance between the York and James Rivers spanned about seven miles, further constricted by two significant creeks on either flank that would funnel Union troops onto an even narrower front. More than a dozen strategically placed redoubts and felled trees along with an earthen bastion named Fort Magruder protected the intersection of the two roads leading from Yorktown. The proximity of the rivers on which the Union Navy was ranging freely would eventually make the line untenable, but it would serve its purpose well on May 5 despite the fact that Magruder, already far past Williamsburg with his columns, had not informed anyone of the exact layout of the defenses. The result was that two of the redoubts on the left of the Confederate line went unnoticed and remained unmanned by the rear guard designated to stem the Union advance.[6]

During the "clear and beautiful" afternoon of May 4, Longstreet received orders to replace the men in the defensive works near Williamsburg with a brigade from his command. Thinking the size of his brigades too small for the task, Longstreet sensibly selected both Anderson's and Brigadier General Roger Atkinson Pryor's brigades. It was nearly dark by the time Anderson's men filed into the lines along with Pryor's Alabama and Louisiana troops. The "air was soft and balmy" recalled one soldier, "and the first half of the night [was] illuminated by the rays of the moon." After the joyless retreat through Williamsburg, the exhilaration of turning to meet the foe led some to march back through the town with a jauntier air, with one Alabamian inspiring his entire regiment into singing the popular song "Shenandoah."

In the absence of a brass band, a lustily sung tune helped settle disquieted hearts that night.[7]

Anderson's men held positions on either side of Fort Magruder, while the 4th South Carolina Battalion advanced as skirmishers. Soon the sky clouded and light rain began to fall. Skirmishers nearly stumbled into the Union lines before forming into groups of three and preparing for a wet and miserable night. It was raining heavily by 2 AM. Near daylight, the enemy's intentions became clear, and Confederate skirmishers could hear Union troops "snapping caps on their guns—to dry the tubes." As the sky lightened, blue-clad soldiers "appeared in large numbers and soon attacked."[8]

Anderson later reported an attack on his skirmish line at around 6 AM on the morning of May 5 that drove his pickets from their advanced position. He sent two companies from the Palmetto Sharpshooters forward with the skirmishers while he and his staff "went to the front to see what was going on and to drive the skirmishers of the enemy back." Anderson personally supervised the advance as they pushed the Federals back into the timber fronting Fort Magruder. As the skirmishers and the leading elements of the Union forces battled in the rain that morning, Union General Joe Hooker brought forward a six-gun battery that was unlimbered on the road and put in a cornfield facing the fort. As more Federals arrived throughout the morning, Hooker deployed them into line but declined to move forward in a general attack. Instead, sometime after noon, Longstreet ordered Anderson to seize the initiative and attack, giving him Brigadier General Cadmus M. Wilcox's brigade as support. Wilcox, an infantryman by trade and an 1846 West Point graduate who favored a straw hat with a wide brim for headgear, would soon show that he had great potential to lead men in battle. He taught tactics at West Point for several years, wrote a manual on the subject, and translated another from German. Despite his nervous and fussy habits that resulted in the nickname "Old Billy fixin'," Wilcox excelled in battle and was destined for promotion. Anderson ordered Wilcox's brigade to occupy some dense pinewoods on the left flank of Hooker's artillery and then attack in an effort to outflank the Union line. Wilcox soon found the enemy and a furious infantry fight ensued. Anderson called for two more brigades, those of Brigadier General A. P. Hill and George Pickett. Along with the units from Roger Pryor's brigade pulled from the redoubts, the Rebel lines expanded even further. With Fort Magruder under heavy fire from Hooker's guns, Anderson went to direct the troops on the right of his line, leaving his own brigade under the command of his capable senior colonel, Micah Jenkins. He soon had Wilcox's brigade on line, with Hill's and Pryor's men to Wilcox's right. Pickett's brigade eventually occupied the far right next to Pryor.[9]

At first, the troops struggled through a slashing of fallen trees in what was previously a heavily forested area. The men struggled laboriously over logs and through tangled undergrowth. A soldier of the 9th Alabama of Wilcox's brigade recalled that just as the firing began, "a mounted officer whom I did not know, but who was, I afterwards learned, Gen'l Anderson of South Carolina, rode up and said, 'Go forward men, straight forward, don't halt at all.'" Anderson apparently then continued down the lines towards the 10th Alabama on the right. Another Alabamian from the 9th recalled that the fallen timber "afforded us a good shelter," but when three companies on the right of the line thought they heard an order to charge. "We went forward into an open space where there was six pieces of artillery firing grape and canister into us hot and heavy to check our speed, but stop wasn't in our language then for we didn't stop till we captured them and planted the Red, White, and Red on them." Wilcox rode up and praised the men heartily for their "little victory," but he also inquired as to the whereabouts of the rest of the regiment. Just then, Colonel Samuel Henry appeared with the missing portion of the regiment and was promptly placed under arrest for cowardice. He later explained that the left companies of the 9th Alabama had inexplicably begun to fall back to the cover of a ravine, and he was compelled to rally his men there and bring them forward to join the other companies. Wilcox must have accepted the colonel's explanation, particularly given the felled timber and the nature of the ground that seriously impaired visibility. Henry remained with the regiment throughout the rest of the fight.[10]

Although Anderson had charge of the entire field on the Confederate right, there was a considerable amount of discretion exercised during the fight which demonstrated the confused nature of battle where commanders maneuvered large bodies of troops while relying only on sight, sound, and the services of staff officers who were sometimes unsuccessful in delivering vital messages. Longstreet had instructed Anderson to "seize the first opportunity to attack the most assailable position of the enemy," and he arrived in time to witness the first assault. "The attacking columns were well arranged and gallantly led by General Anderson and most ably seconded by the gallant brigadiers and other officers." Anderson ordered A. P. Hill forward to Wilcox's support, while Wilcox reportedly sent one of his staff officers directly to Hill with a request for him to move forward immediately. Cavalry commander, Brigadier General J. E. B. Stuart, who later claimed Wilcox had sent *him* word that he needed reinforcement, intercepted Wilcox's message. Stuart relayed that message to the closest command, that of General Pryor, who advanced with a small force. A self-satisfied Stuart remarked later that while "General Anderson commanded in person on the scene of conflict; I frequently found it necessary to take the responsibility of dispatching re-enforcements of artillery, as well as infantry, to points obviously requiring them." Strangely, Wilcox noted specifically in his official report that Hill "had not been instructed to come to my support, and [Hill] referred to General Longstreet." Why Wilcox thought this and chose to mention it specifically in his report despite all other evidence that Anderson did indeed order Hill to Wilcox's support, including Hill's own statement to that effect, is unknown. Wherever Anderson was located on the field when he was personally directing the attack, Wilcox apparently was unable to find him. The capable and ambitious Wilcox often held strong opinions about certain commanders, and he seldom expressed sympathy for their not viewing his own battlefield needs as supreme. Division commanders, however, relied primarily on reports from the brigades in situations where the terrain did not permit them to view the action personally. After the war, Wilcox even denigrated Longstreet's abilities and noted that he only saw that general twice under fire while under his command. "Yet he is spoken of as the hard and stubborn fighter," Wilcox wrote resentfully in 1869. "His troops did fight well, but not from any inspiration drawn from him, and he of course gets the credit for it." Concerning Anderson, however, Stuart's statement implies that Anderson might not have been in his proper place given his advanced responsibilities during the battle. One lesson Anderson learned from this affair was that his place when commanding a division was not directly on the front lines among the fighting men, but instead in a location where his subordinates could easily find him.[11]

The fact that Wilcox failed to acknowledge Anderson's presence is even more puzzling in light of Anderson's assistance with the deployment of Wilcox's brigade, especially the 10th Alabama, which at one point occupied the extreme right flank of the Confederate line. Anderson later wrote that he "was conducting the Tenth Alabama Regiment to the place which I wished it to occupy when just as it was gaining the situation, a tremendous fire was poured upon them, which for a moment produced some confusion and seemed to stagger our men." Two of Anderson's staff members were near him at the time, Captain Edward J. Means and Anderson's brother McKenzie, who had "repeatedly passed and re-passed under the fire, bearing orders and messages with coolness and intelligence which could not have been surpassed." Anderson was then so absorbed with the task of rallying the 10th Alabama and pushing them forward that he was unaware McKenzie had toppled from his mount mortally wounded when a federal bullet crashed through his skull at the right temple and exited over the left ear. It was only later when the Union troops retreated that Captain Means was able to inform the General of the loss of his brother.[12]

By mid-afternoon, despite refilling their cartridge boxes from those of the federal dead and wounded, the attacking rebels were running low on ammunition. Longstreet sent forward his reserve brigade under Brigadier General Raleigh Colston and ordered troops from Major General D. H. Hill's division to come to A. P. Hill's aid. Several participant accounts mention the conspicuous presence of brigadiers such as A. P. Hill, who was ever present, "erect, magnificent, the god of war himself, amid the smoke and the thunder." Yet the colonel of the 10th Alabama declined to mention Anderson's assistance in placing and rallying his command. Anderson could hardly have gone unnoticed under such conditions, yet despite his "signal gallantry and coolness" being mentioned by Longstreet, and the acknowledgement of other brigadiers that he directed them to deploy their forces to specific locations, Anderson's presence went largely unremarked. When Brigadier General Jubal A. Early was directed to support Anderson late that afternoon, he learned that Anderson was not at Fort Magruder, but "somewhere to the right, where his troops were engaged with the enemy," but Early met Longstreet before reaching Fort Magruder and was ordered to the Confederate left flank with his brigade. Longstreet then rode off to the sound of heavy musketry to the right, setting the stage for D. H. Hill and Early to decide on an ill-fated attack from the Rebel left. Why Anderson's actions went unmentioned in most accounts of the battle is puzzling, perhaps illustrating the self-interest of peers hesitant to add recognition to anyone else's contributions. The typical practice of the time was to acknowledge only the behavior of those under one's command, but praise notwithstanding, mention of Anderson in letters and diaries is curiously rare.[13]

The onset of darkness halted the bloodletting on May 5, but not before Early's misadventure on the left marred the day's achievements. On the right of the line, the Confederates had been successful, holding the field confidently by day's end. Anderson noted, "the woods were literally strewn with the dead and wounded of the enemy and with his arms and equipments." On the Confederate left, the two vacant redoubts on the rebel line ultimately caused problems after Federal artillery and infantry under Brigadier General Winfield Scott Hancock occupied them and poured a destructive and dangerous fire into Fort Magruder. Early directed an ill-coordinated attack complicated by a lack of proper reconnaissance, which led to the heaviest losses of the day. He lost at least 600 of his men in this engagement, rendered even more pathetic because he was unaware that the unsupported Union forces were in the act of retiring when he advanced. Early fell victim to a serious shoulder wound himself. The unnecessary casualties cast a pall over what would have been a resounding rebel victory. Two companies from the 6th South Carolina of Anderson's brigade occupying works to the left of Fort

Magruder had joined the ill-starred attack after being cajoled into action by one of Early's staff officers. By the time the South Carolinians moved forward "under the enthusiasm of the moment" the other attackers were already far ahead and enduring a withering fire from the Yankee guns. Fortunately, the federals barely gave notice to the late advance of two small companies on the right of the attacking force. As Early's men faltered and began to seek shelter in the thick woods to their left, the 6th South Carolina withdrew quietly back to the redoubt "from which we had issued, much to our relief, for all of us understood the situation perfectly." Captain James Coker of the 6th considered it good fortune to have escaped unscathed and noted that "the effort to dislodge them [Union troops] was very badly planned. The movement as made was worse than foolish and resulted in the sacrifice of hundreds of brave Confederate soldiers." Only one man was struck in the redoubt over the course of the day despite the constant fire from enemy sharpshooters, to which Coker's men, armed with short-barreled Mississippi rifles, were unable to reply. Corporal John Kelly was fortunate that the shot that struck him in the chest failed to penetrate the Bible that his old Sunday School teacher had given him, "and [it] was spent when it reached the book of Second Kings."[14]

The gruesome aftermath of the day's fighting tempered the euphoria of victory for many of the weary survivors. The task of gathering the wounded and searching for the missing meant a sleepless night for many of the men, driven to strenuous efforts by the realization that the army would soon continue its retreat, leaving those still unfound to the mercy of the advancing Union forces. For Dick Anderson, an agonizing four days passed before he was able to sit and write a letter to his father detailing the circumstances of his brother's death. From his camp on the Chickahominy River on May 9, he began his remorseful missive. "My dear Father," he wrote, "My heart is oppressed with sorrow at the mournful intelligence I have to communicate. A most heavy affliction has fallen upon you and me and all the other members of the family in the death of McKenzie. The suddenness with which this calamity has befallen us renders it appalling." McKenzie's death filled him "with inexpressible grief and wretchedness." Though McKenzie had been at his side for only a month, "his unconcealed satisfaction at being with me, his deep interest in all that was going on, his eager and cheerful performance and his constant anxiety that all should go well with our country's cause increased my attachment—if indeed anything could have done so."[15]

Anderson explained that Captain Means had taken McKenzie into Williamsburg where a Dr. Garrett had prepared the body for burial. A common grave in company with his fellow South Carolinians in Cedar Grove Cemetery was McKenzie's final resting place. Anderson arrived later that night and described seeing the "calmness and sweetness," of his brother's facial expression as being "the most agonizing moment of my life." Dr. Garrett and his wife pressed the general to spend the night at their home, but he could not do so. "I was, therefore, compelled to leave my brother's body to be placed in the grave with none but strangers to attend him," he lamented. He closed his letter with an attempt not only to console his father on his loss, but also with words designed perhaps to restore McKenzie's place in his father's estimations of him. Dick's brother might have spoken initially against the war, perhaps merely being opposed to the idea of secession, but likely not harboring reservations about slavery as an institution as he had become an enslaver himself just a few years earlier with the purchase of Hiwassee. "Whatever may have been his opinions at the beginning of this revolution," Anderson assured his father, "they must have undergone that change which made him a warm and zealous advocate of our cause—for I never heard a word from his lips which did not express the warmest interest in our success and a determination to give his life, if necessary, to secure it." There were many months of bloodletting ahead, but this was to be the most dolorous personal loss for Anderson, perhaps contributing later to his seemingly natural inclination to fall into wistful bouts of melancholy. For now, he could do little else but carry on, sustained and strengthened by his brother's sacrifice and his knowledge that with young McKenzie Anderson's death "our soil is reddened with the blood of no purer patriot."[16]

In just under five years, Dr. Anderson lost two of his adult sons. Benjamin had fallen to illness in 1857, now McKenzie to Yankee lead. How the old man bore up under that burden is unknown, but his other son Wallace apparently had difficulties coming to terms with it. As late as June 21, Wallace's wife Jennie was chastising him for not having written to his father or mentioned McKenzie's death. Jennie was at home in Stateburg at that time, while Wallace was at Meridian, Mississippi. When another letter came that week with no mention of the tragedy, Jennie remonstrated with him. "I may as well say out as I think it, it is not satisfactory," she wrote. She was deeply puzzled by his behavior. "Today I said apologetically to Father I do not think Willie knows what has happened. Oh yes he does said Pa," perhaps being more understanding of the impact of the loss on his son's sensitive nature than was his wife. Dick surely would have written directly to his brother to add some personal touch to the sad news as was the custom of the day, and Jennie had no doubts Wallace was well aware despite her confusion about his silence on the matter. "You really have sensibility—you think and feel aright & have a deep sense besides—then why should you of all people appear wanting at a time like this," she wondered. "Write to your Father feelingly, as is your duty, take pains and make your letter interesting." If Wallace took her advice to heart, the letter has not survived, but tragedy would continue to plague the family. Just two months before, in March, Wallace and Jennie had mourned the loss of their own young son, another William Wallace laid to rest in sight of the Homestead at just over a year old.[17]

Though it could do little to console him as he wrote his somber epistle, Dick Anderson's notable performance led Longstreet on May 9 to seek promotion for his friend along with A. P. Hill. Colonels submitted for elevation to brigadier general included Samuel Garland, Jr. and James L. Kemper, an 1842 graduate of Washington College in Lexington, Virginia who would one day serve as governor. Petersburg, Virginia native and notorious fire-eater Roger Pryor, a distinguished graduate of Hampden-Sydney College, notable lawyer, and former US Congressman also received Longstreet's endorsement.[18]

Longstreet forwarded his recommendations to President Davis, but after General Johnston's wound on May 31 and General Robert E. Lee's assumption of army command, promotions were delayed. By June 7, General Lee was considering ways to reorganize his new command. He responded to a letter from President Davis "in reference to Genl. R. H. Anderson & your conception of his qualifications" and enclosed a note from Longstreet in which he "particularly" recommended Anderson and Colonel Micah Jenkins for promotion. "Gen. Anderson had command of three Brigades at Williamsburg, and two Brigades on the 31st [May, Battle of Seven Pines or Fair Oaks]. He used his forces with much ease and with the greatest effect," Longstreet wrote. As for his own opinion, Lee wrote that he knew "little of Genl A. personally except as Capt of Dragoons. He was a favorite in his Regt. & was considered a good officer." Lee mentioned Bragg's charge of drunkenness at Pensacola, but told Davis that he was "told he is now under a pledge of abstinence, which I hope will protect him from the vice he fell into." Lee accepted Longstreet's estimation of Anderson's qualifications. "Longstreet is a capital soldier," he told the President. "His recommendations hitherto have been good, & I have confidence in him." Unfortunately, Lee had yet to receive information about to the exact number of troops under his command and their present organization, so he was unprepared to commit to promoting Anderson. Someone, perhaps Longstreet, had also recommended that Anderson replace Benjamin Huger, whose ability appeared to be unequal to that required on the field of battle. His performance had been far less than desired, though not entirely owing to his own actions. Longstreet and Johnston both unjustly criticized Huger's failure to bring his troops into position at Seven Pines, when in fact the reason for Huger's delay was that Longstreet's misdirected troops had halted and blocked Huger while they determined which road they were supposed to follow. Longstreet, however, wrote Johnston regarding Huger, "Slow men are a little out of place upon the field." By the end of June, Longstreet's opinion of Huger had been borne out. Moreover, Longstreet's criticism about the delay at Seven Pines deflected blame from himself onto Huger, a fact that must never have come to Lee's attention. Huger's subsequent tardy movements and loss of control over his troops doomed the Confederate attack at Frayser's Farm on June 30 and sealed the general's fate. It was the final straw, for Lee had already noted on June 25 that it would be well to send Huger to Charleston "since Richard H. Anderson can replace him." The recovering General Johnston supported Lee's decision. Johnston's June 24 report of Seven Pines referred to Longstreet's praise of his officers, noting "the manner in which Brigadier Generals [William H. C.] Whiting and R. H. Anderson . . . exercising commands above their grades are mentioned."[19]

Seven Pines had assuredly raised Anderson's stock. Johnston was withdrawing steadily in the face of McClellan's slow advance towards Richmond until discovering that the rain-swollen Chickahominy River divided Union forces into two elements. Johnston was also relieved of the threat of a separate Union force advancing on him from Fredericksburg, Virginia after Stonewall Jackson's exploits drew it to the Shenandoah Valley. Now Johnston's plan called for three columns consisting of approximately two-thirds of his army to advance on roughly parallel routes to Seven Pines, where he hoped to drive a wedge between the left element of McClellan's force and three Union army corps already separated from it by the Chickahominy. Longstreet commanded the right wing of Johnston's force when fighting broke out late in the afternoon of Saturday, May 31, while Dick Anderson led Longstreet's division. Micah Jenkins handled Anderson's brigade. The feisty Jenkins took the Palmetto Sharpshooters along with the 6th South Carolina into action adjacent to the Richmond & York River Railroad line on the left of the Williamsburg road. The South Carolinians, all armed with inferior Mississippi rifles had halted to dress their lines when Jenkins spotted Anderson nearby. Anderson's instructions were "to advance," Jenkins reported, and that is precisely what the men did. Moving forward steadily under fire through thick abatis, Jenkins soon found Union regiments giving way in the face of the determined Confederate advance. After brushing aside those troops, Jenkins turned his men on an oblique to the right and pushed forward to face components of two other brigades. "After a most obstinate resistance and terrible slaughter," Jenkins recalled, those federals also fled grudgingly across Williamsburg Stage Road to Jenkins' right. Placing his men in line in the roadbed facing to the south, Jenkins received notice of a threat to his left flank from advancing Union reinforcements. He quickly determined to eliminate the threat south of Williamsburg Stage Road first before turning to meet the troops advancing toward his position along the road from the east. He dispatched a staff officer to Anderson requesting reinforcement, and no sooner had Jenkins routed the federals south of the road and reformed his men facing east, than word arrived that Anderson had sent the 28th Georgia toward Jenkins' position at the double-quick. Forming a line perpendicular to the road, Jenkins advanced toward the sound of cheering federals in his front. Fierce fighting ensued as the opposing sides closed upon one another in fits and starts. Eventually, the opposing lines were only thirty or forty yards apart as the frenzied rebels spat hot lead into the enemy ranks and took equally galling fire in return. With reinforcements from the 5th South Carolina, the spirited southerners prevailed against far greater numbers, and the opposing blue line began to give ground. As darkness neared, the exhausted men ceased firing, buoyed by the distant sight of small squads of Union troops fleeing across open fields in the fading light of a terrible day of carnage. Anderson ordered Jenkins' men back to the area between Fair Oaks Station and the set of Union earthworks known as Casey's Redoubt that had anchored the Union line at the start of the day. Anderson then sent the 19th Mississippi from Cadmus Wilcox's brigade to further support Jenkins and strengthen his position for the night. Half the men in Jenkins' two color companies had fallen, including ten of the eleven men in the color guard itself. Throughout the course of the fighting, Jenkins noted proudly that the colors had "passed through four hands without touching the ground." At one point Jenkins rode by the spot where one of the fallen color bearers lay. "He raised himself on his elbow and exclaimed: 'For God's sake, Colonel, take care of my flag.'" Anderson thought Jenkins "was of such stuff that soldiers and heroes were made," and one of Longstreet's staff officers, Thomas Goree, later noted "Anderson's S. C. Brigade immortalized itself" that day. He thought Jenkins the "perfect model of a Christian hero." Longstreet too was full of praise for Anderson's men, noting in his report that while "the severest part of the work was done by . . . Hill's division, the attack of the two brigades under General R. H. Anderson was made with such spirit and regularity as to have driven back the most determined foe." Jenkins was particularly daring that day, narrowly escaping death or maiming on several occasions when struck by spent shells. His accoutrements were riddled with holes and his horse received two wounds. His sword was shot nearly in half besides losing its tip and the knob on its hilt. One of Longstreet's staff officers encountered Jenkins as the battle closed. "I met him just as he was coming out of the fight and he was weeping like a child at the destruction of his brave, noble men."[20]

Other men of the 6th South Carolina captured a Pennsylvania captain hiding under a pile of knapsacks in his deserted camp. Confederates pulled him out by his boots and sent him to the rear with a recently wounded South

Carolinian as a guard. The guard soon encountered his wounded colonel, John Bratton, with another man going to the rear. The guard was attempting to assist Bratton when all of them fell into Union hands after wandering into enemy lines. The Union captain "turned the tables on his guard," recalled one of the Confederates, and after hearing later that the Northern papers were very complimentary of the captain, the South Carolinian deemed him "welcome to all the glory he can get out of the battle of Seven Pines." A Richmond paper reported later that Bratton's men "fought gallantly and did their best to sustain the confidence so often reposed in them by their greatly beloved Gen. R. H. Anderson."[21]

Anderson took pride in his South Carolinians and other units that had performed so well under Jenkins' capable handling, but he personally led troops forward on the left of Casey's Redoubt, fighting fiercely after "the Yankees permitted Anderson to get within a few yards of them, when they opened a murderous fire upon him from their cover in the woods. His heroes replied with interest," as D. H. Hill recalled, and the Yankees "were soon in full retreat hotly pursued" by Jenkins and Anderson. Anderson's impression was that his South Carolinians and the single Mississippi regiment from Wilcox's brigade were the only elements of Longstreet's division engaged that day, later writing erroneously that "Pickett's and perhaps Kemper's brigades had some slight skirmishing and brushing next morning, but I do not believe they fired a shot on the day of the engagement." Anderson actually found himself detached from Longstreet's division itself and acting under the orders of Major General D. H. Hill, a puzzling state of affairs that he later recalled lasted "until the evening of the day following the battle." One man from Kemper's Brigade lamented that they "suffered severely from bad management in leading us into the engagement." Many commanders still learning how to manage large numbers of troops in the confusion of battle quickly discovered how difficult the task was. Most were still not yet fully adept at troop handling.[22]

At Seven Pines Anderson also witnessed the almost comic escapades of fellow South Carolinian, Lieutenant Alfred Brevard Jr., son of a Camden physician and cousin of James Chesnut. Taken prisoner in the company of a badly wounded comrade, Brevard and his companion went off with a single Union soldier as guard. When they saw General Anderson and his staff, the two rebels took heart. Brevard seized the Yankee and pinned his arms while his wounded comrade took the man's weapon. The two made their escape, but on returning to General Anderson, he inquired, "With your tremendous strength, why did you not take the Yankee prisoner in his turn?" The "soldierly looking" Brevard, coolly replied that he "was only too glad to be rid of the companionship of the disagreeable creature."[23]

Such episodes give a vague sense of the turmoil on the battlefield, but the fighting on Anderson's portion of the field had been even more confused than just the movements executed by Jenkins' few regiments that day. Largely under Dick Anderson's direction, fellow former dragoon George Burgwyn (G. B.) Anderson's brigade moved generally in concert with Jenkins on the latter's right flank through most of the advance. The 27th Georgia saw especially heavy fighting, even falling back in confusion at one point. G. B. Anderson halted that regiment and reformed it, allowing it to rest before Dick Anderson came back from his advanced position and personally conducted the Georgians to where he desired them placed. As the fighting wound down that evening, the event occurred that caused further confusion in the Confederate ranks and ultimately changed the course of the war. First wounded by a musket ball in his shoulder, General Johnston was soon "unhorsed by a heavy fragment of shell which struck his breast." Command passed to Dick Anderson's West Point classmate, Major General Gustavus W. Smith, who appeared to lack faith in his ability to lead the army. President Davis was unimpressed with Smith's grasp of the battlefield situation and evinced little confidence in him. He believed the army needed a more effective commander, and Smith's tenure was short-lived.[24]

On the afternoon of June 1, President Davis directed Smith to hand over command to Robert E. Lee, who promptly ordered his army back to its original position after the heavy fighting at Seven Pines. It remained there for nearly a month, but determined to seize the initiative, Lee solicited his commanders' input on June 3. Having sent his cavalry on a scout of McClellan's army and dispatched reinforcements to Stonewall Jackson in the Shenandoah Valley, Lee first found it necessary to strengthen his defensive position. Soldiers resented the pick and shovel work their new leader set them to, temporarily earning Lee the sobriquet "King of Spades." Yet untested in the eyes of his men, they remained ignorant of Lee's developing plan to divide his army in order to trap a portion of McClellan's north of the Chickahominy. To do so required a strong presence south of river to hold McClellan in place while Lee thrashed the Union corps to the north. Lee's aggressive nature was soon unveiled, and men thereafter referred to him in more complimentary terms, such as "the first captain of the Confederacy."[25]

If the men initially harbored reservations about Lee, they evinced higher confidence in themselves and in the leaders they had come to know. There were few complaints in the ranks at this time, even after the heavy fighting since May, but on June 17, Anderson had to inquire about the men's pay, which must have been a source of dissatisfaction. Many had "not been paid for nearly eight months and all have been now nearly six months without pay," he told Longstreet. Anderson himself was paid $301.00 per month that spring, and by December 1862, his pay was $337.00 per month, including an added $36.00 in recognition of his twenty years of military service and retention of his seniority from the Old Army. Whether Anderson's inquiries on behalf of his men resolved the issue is not known, but the men thought well of him and he returned the sentiment, building rapport with the troops. On June 14, a Richmond newspaper reported that Anderson presented Coppens' St. Paul's Battalion of Louisianans with a flag, "as a token of his sincere admiration." On May 31, 1862, at Fair Oaks, he had ridden to Coppens' lines and given an order to seize a hill held by two strongly entrenched Pennsylvania regiments. Coppens' Zouaves and the St. Paul's Foot Rifles drove the Yankees off the hill until the enemy realized how small the Confederate force was. They counterattacked, but Coppens' men were able to hold on until reinforcements arrived. One of them proudly told the Richmond correspondent that the flag was "a remembrance that we will always preciously keep . . . it is a sacred relic that the enemy's balls may threaten, but that their profane hands will never tarnish as long as one of us may live to defend it."[26]

Thomas Blackwell of the 6th South Carolina wrote his wife proudly on June 24 that Anderson's brigade "has the praise of being fighting Stock and it looks like if there is a dangerous post to attack we have to do [it] as he does not know but one command and that is 'go on Boys.'" Blackwell thought Anderson "a good man for he is thought a great deal of by the men. The officers presented him with a fine horse Saturday evening in presents [*sic*] of the whole brigade and his Speech was more of a prayer than anything else." Colonel Jenkins called that presentation on June 21 "quite a pleasant ceremony," noting critically, "The Genl is very much loved, although an indifferent officer." The warhorse was presented after a speech by Captain J. D. Wylie of the 5th South Carolina that overflowed with flowery Victorian sentiments typical of the period. Wylie noted that the sons of South Carolina were "all alike—Southern patriots—struggling for independence, fighting for all that makes life desirable or even endurable." Their common cause, however, did not account for the "strong and heartfelt attachment" to Anderson, "which animates the breast of every member of the brigade." Wylie recapped their shared experiences, highlighting some inspiring battlefield scenes when Anderson was "in our midst on the field of Williamsburg, animating the troops with your own cool and dauntless courage! You were with us in the sanguinary conflict of the Seven Pines, and slept with us, after the hard-fought day, on the bloody field and the brief, but ever memorable command, 'Forward, Forward—I have but one command, and that is—Forward,' with which you led us on that bloody day is still ringing in our ears." Wylie then commented on Anderson's personal conduct during his interactions with the brigade, highlighting that he was both "an officer . . . and yet at the same time a gentleman." In the absence of a better gift, said Wyle, the horse, "equipped and ready for the field," was offered as an indication of "the opinion we entertain of our Warrior General as a slight token of the elevated esteem, the unlimited confidence and the deep attachment of the troops of your brigade." Anderson spoke at some length in response to those glowing remarks, and professed that he could "give but very imperfect utterance" to his emotions after such a gift, noting that "the graceful and flattering terms in which it has been presented are both pleasing and embarrassing. My unpracticed tongue cannot express the feelings which fill my heart." He praised the men in turn for their "obedience . . . patient endurance and . . . unflinching fortitude that spirit of indomitable resolution," and he showed both his human side and his sense of history, touched perhaps with a note of melancholy. He told the young men arrayed before him that while they "may not have at present an agreeable appreciation of the scenes and events which are passing, and which each of you is himself a part, you are, nevertheless, laying up for yourselves a treasury of memory, which you will not hereafter exchange for wealth or for honors, or for any considerations whatever." The conclusion did indeed have the hallmarks of an invocation, with wishes "that you may pass safely through these days of trial and trouble to the enjoyment of all the choicest blessings of peace, is my constant prayer." He would have many shining moments over the next few years that would sustain the men's high opinion of him, but Jenkins also captured an impression of Anderson's character as succinctly as was possible in that single comment about his indifference as an officer.[27]

Though not a professional soldier, the twenty-six-year-old Jenkins graduated first in the class of 1854 from the South Carolina Military Academy and was associated with the King's Mountain Military School at Yorkville, South Carolina until joining the Confederate Army in 1861. Anderson, then forty-one years old, had already served twenty years in uniform and was more reserved than the ambitious Jenkins was. Jenkins had quickly gained Longstreet's confidence and favor, so much so that in the fall of 1861 the general had christened him "the best colonel in the army." Though heady praise, it was well deserved. If Longstreet expected much from Jenkins, he gave as expected. Anderson found Jenkins well suited to lead the South Carolina brigade at times when Anderson managed Longstreet's division.[28]

Meanwhile, Stonewall Jackson had set his men in motion on June 17, moving as rapidly as possible from the Valley to join the Lee near Richmond. Jackson arrived first and attended a war counsel with Lee and other commanders that would lead to the series of battles known as the Seven Days. Flushed with confidence after Jackson's highly publicized exploits in the Valley, southerners now expected to gain a great victory on the outskirts of

Richmond as well. To that end, Lee devised a plan of attack using two wings of his newly reorganized Army of Northern Virginia to draw McClellan's army from its entrenchments and force a battle in the open. Huger and Magruder were to hold defensive positions south of the Chickahominy River while Longstreet, D. H. Hill, and A. P. Hill attacked Brigadier General Fitz John Porter's isolated Fifth Corps north of the river. Jackson was to turn the right flank of Porter's line with a surprise attack from the north. Lee drafted General Orders Number 75 outlining the plan of battle that was to open on the 26th. It was somewhat complex in detail, though sound despite its ambitious expectations for an army led by division and brigade commanders still struggling to find their footing. The goal was to push Porter back past Old Cold Harbor and cut McClellan's supply line along the Richmond and York River Railroad. Lee hoped to maneuver Porter out of his positions without much of a fight once the latter realized the threat Jackson presented to his flank.[29]

The lengthy hiatus between the June 1 Battle of Seven Pines and the opening engagement of the Seven Days Battles on June 25 allowed McClellan to create his own scheme. Union forces seized the initiative and opened the week-long contest, surprising Lee by advancing against Huger before Lee's plans were set in motion. The ensuing Battle of Oak Grove led to minimal gains for the Yankees, and the poor outcome caused some to call the action the "Battle of Casualties," since that was the only noticeable result. Huger's men held steady and they would have to do so the next day as well, for Lee determined to stick with his original battle plan and open his attack on the 26th.[30]

Belying his reputation for rapid marches, Jackson proved on this occasion unequal to the task of getting his men into position on June 26. He was about six hours behind schedule. A. P. Hill had been prepared to advance since early morning with troops standing ready to cross the Chickahominy via the Meadow Bridge. They would do so as soon as Brigadier General Lawrence O'B. Branch's brigade crossed the river a few miles above that point and uncovered the crossing for Hill by driving Union forces back towards Mechanicsville. Branch would then join Hill and continue the advance eastwards until they uncovered the Mechanicsville Bridge, where D. H. Hill was waiting to cross, followed by Longstreet. At that point, the Confederates would make a concerted attack on the Union lines in conjunction with Jackson's assault on Porter's right flank. The plan could not proceed until Jackson was in place to execute his part of it. By 3 PM, both Lee and A. P. Hill grew weary of waiting for Jackson. Hill convinced himself that the hard-marching Jackson must surely be near his goal, and he decided to brush aside the few Yankees guarding the bridge in his front. The scanty Union forces retreated, drawing the southerners towards the heavily defended blue line on Beaver Dam Creek, a naturally strong position with a high bank along the eastern side of the creek further strengthened by rifle pits and artillery emplacements. Having seen the rising dust clouds to the north for some time, Union general Porter knew that Jackson was coming, but he put his trust in his strong position and reckoned Jackson would arrive too late to join the battle. He was correct. It was 5 PM before Jackson was in range to hear fighting at Mechanicsville, where Hill's Light Division was being chewed to pieces in the swampy valley of Beaver Dam Creek. Federal troops repulsed futile attacks with heavy losses in A. P. Hill's division and in the lone brigade of D. H. Hill's that made it into the bloody battle that day. Longstreet and Anderson's men were among the last to cross the river and saw no fighting. That would change on the morrow when they moved forward to replace A. P. Hill's battered brigades, but June 26 had been a day of merely marching and waiting. Anderson had his division "roused up by the long roll at 3:30 AM and on the march by five, only to find themselves waiting expectantly for action. "Intense quiet has reigned all along the lines till within a few minutes past when a brisk fire of musketry and artillery has suddenly opened" one man recalled.[31] Another complained of discomfort after having wandered "about in the swamp, waiding [*sic*] mud and water over knee deep. It has rained every night. I have been perfectly wet for several days."[32] Little had gone as Lee had envisioned, and his plan for the Battle of Mechanicsville unraveled in the face of tardiness, miscommunication, and misguided independent action. Despite that failure, Lee still managed to wrest the initiative from McClellan, who determined to withdraw his army to safer ground under protection of the Navy's gunboats. McClellan, as always, believed he was vastly outnumbered. It was a fatal misapprehension embraced by several of his army's leaders, and even Porter later reported that Lee's army on each side of the Chickahominy was equal to the whole of the Union force. The threat of Jackson's columns advancing on his flank sealed the decision though, and McClellan determined to make a retrograde movement that he disdained to acknowledge was a retreat. Desperate fighting over the next few days ensued as Lee pushed the Union troops back towards new positions anchored on the James River.[33]

In order for McClellan to make his dangerous withdrawal successfully, he needed Porter to hold a defensive line north of the Chickahominy and shield his army from attack. Federals again held a commanding defensive position along the line of meandering Boatswain's Creek about a mile east of Gaines's Mill, from which the battle would take its name. Union troops worked feverishly to fell trees in front of their lines. Others put their backs into shoveling up piles of earth to create life-saving rifle pits, but the position was by nature already a strong one. Porter's troops occupied wooded high ground on a plateau that overlooked the terrain around the creek, an area so boggy that locals called it Boatswain's Swamp. Nearly impenetrable undergrowth in the bottomlands adjacent to the creek helped to mask the Federal lines as well. Porter could hardly have occupied a stronger position, as the advancing Confederates would soon discover when they approached the nearly 30,000 defenders and ninety-six guns of Porter's seventeen batteries.[34]

After enduring some heavy shelling before dawn, Confederate troops advanced at first light on the morning of June 27, slowly driving off the remaining Union forces along Beaver Dam Creek. Bridges over the creek were quickly repaired and Lee's army continued its progress with Jackson and D. H. Hill on the left; A. P. Hill in the center; and Longstreet on the right flank paralleling the River Road nearer the Chickahominy.[35]

Lee's plan was similar to the previous one. Jackson, supported by D. H. Hill, would still execute a flank attack against the right of the Federal defensive line—which Lee presumed would be along Powhite Creek—while A. P. Hill and Longstreet would attack from the front and pin the Yankees in place. Both Hills soon discovered Porter's lines were actually farther east behind Boatswain's Creek. It was mid-afternoon before A. P. Hill had his brigades deployed for an attack, with Longstreet's men supporting Hill's right. Hill's troops suffered terribly as they assailed their opponent's position repeatedly over the next two hours, yet none could gain a foothold or crack the strongly entrenched Union line.[36]

Meanwhile, Jackson was delayed once again after traveling for some time along the wrong road. A countermarch consumed valuable time, but Ewell's division entered the fight on the embattled A. P. Hill's left. Ewell's men were also repulsed with heavy losses as they dashed themselves against the Union defenses. Finally, Longstreet received "an urgent message" from Lee to advance and make a demonstration that would divert attention away from Hill and Ewell. Longstreet obligingly sent Wilcox's and Pickett's brigades forward, but it quickly became apparent from the volume of fire received that only a full assault by all of Longstreet's brigades could prevent the disastrous losses that a piecemeal attack would entail. Longstreet later lamented that he was precisely "in the position from which the enemy wished us to attack him." It looked formidable from the Confederate viewpoint—a quarter-mile-wide open plain lay in front of them, with breastworks and sharpshooters stretching up the rising ridge capped by rifle pits on the crest of the plateau. The advancing Rebel line would also be enfiladed by Union artillery firing from south of the Chickahominy. Longstreet later wrote that he sent his brigades forward only to the edge of the woods that provided some cover and ordered them not to cross the open ground. Portions of those brigades attempted to advance "as their blood grew hot," but Longstreet recalled them.[37]

As the sun began to sink on that bloody day, Lee's dispositions were at last complete—Jackson was in position with D. H Hill and Ewell forming the left of Lee's line, A. P. Hill occupied the center, and Longstreet held the right. Around 7 PM, with about ninety minutes of fading daylight remaining on the already smoke clouded field, Lee ordered a coordinated advance all along the line. Longstreet brought Anderson's brigade into line, keeping only Kemper's in reserve. "As my troops reached the crest under which they had rested they came under the full blaze of the battle," Longstreet recalled, "but Pickett and Anderson were comparatively fresh, and dashed through the open and down the slope before the fire had time to thin the ranks."[38] Anderson was with the 6th South Carolina when the battle line was halted to adjust the ranks at the crest of the hill to which Longstreet referred. The men were taking fire from a fresh body of federal troops at the foot of the hill before Anderson, "who had been lying down with us on the crest, until the formation was completed, ordered a charge, before which our adversaries disappeared," recalled one South Carolinian.[39] That rapid advance momentarily placed the men in a position of relative safety at the base of the steep slope on which the main Union line was located. The federal guns on the crest were unable to depress their muzzles sufficiently to fire upon them, and Anderson's brigade soon gained the summit, driving the Federals from their positions. His brigade extended past the right flank of the Union battle lines, so it was nearly a flanking movement, and even Jackson characterized it as such. The lines advanced steadily, overrunning and capturing many of the Union guns and nearly capturing Porter's reserve artillery. A rash and disastrous mounted charge by five companies of the Fifth US Cavalry was made "under a most galling fire until 6 officers out of the 7 had been struck down." The 9th Alabama formed a hollow square as the lancers "came within prod of the bayonet. We had done some pretty good shooting and emptied a great many saddles from the looks of the riderless horses that was going back over the field," recalled one of them, but the forlorn attack caused the onrushing Rebel line to pause long enough for the reserve artillery to be withdrawn.[40]

Darkness put an end to the fighting. It was a costly victory, but Confederate persistence sent Porter reeling back south of the Chickahominy. The battle demonstrated the possibilities of success for simultaneous assaults made along the entirety of a defensive line, although Hill's hours of sacrifice prior to the coordinated push had surely weakened the defenders. On Longstreet's portion of the field, Anderson and Pickett, along with two regiments from John B. Hood's command, captured about 5,000 prisoners and a number of guns. In his battle report, Longstreet acknowledged that Wilcox's, Winfield Scott Featherston's, and Pryor's brigades endured the "severest trials," from skirmishing all day and enduring "a most annoying fire of artillery the great part of the time." As for "individual gallantry," Longstreet first named Anderson as being "conspicuous among those gallant officers and men." Dick Anderson was repaying the confidence the army had placed in him after the misstep at Pensacola. Several more engagements lay ahead before Lee drove McClellan from the Peninsula, and Anderson would continue to perform well. "In his modest way," noted D. S. Freeman of Lee's brigadiers, Anderson was the one "most definitely marked throughout the campaign by soldierly competence."[41]

Whipped decisively at Gaines' Mill, McClellan continued a cumbersome withdrawal towards the James River and its fleet of gunboats. After efficient Federal engineers rebuilt White Oak Bridge in only two hours on the evening of June 28, his troops managed to cross the swamp the next day after a stalemated fight with a hesitant John B. Magruder at Savage's Station on the Richmond and York River Railroad. Jackson's Division, stalled on the north banks of the Chickahominy, once again arrived late to the field. Magruder faced far superior numbers that day and his hesitancy after Jackson failed to make an appearance was understandable.[42]

Lee continued an aggressive pursuit of the rattled Union commander that led to engagements at White Oak Swamp and Frayser's Farm on the 30th. With Jackson falling upon the Union rear guard at White Oak Swamp, Lee hoped to split the retreating Union column into two parts. Once again, poor execution undermined his goals. The timid Huger once more fell short when he dawdled away the day building a new road on which to advance his troops. Jackson's aggressive nature also failed him and he too spent the day unproductively while massed Union guns on the high ground near Malvern Hill bombarded Theophilus Holmes' troops on the right flank into a panicked retreat. Magruder arrived too late to help Holmes, and it was only in the center of Lee's lines where a concerted and potentially effective attack by A. P. Hill and Longstreet took place that could have severed the retreating federal army. Anderson again commanded Longstreet's division, while command of his old brigade fell to Micah Jenkins. By 5 PM, after a lengthy artillery duel that endangered the lives of both Lee and President Davis, and with nearly 50,000 mismanaged Confederate soldiers standing idly by, Longstreet's and Hill's divisions advanced toward a ferocious conflict with the already exhausted, battle-weary troops arrayed before them.[43]

Under the guiding hand of Dick Anderson, the initial line of assault consisting of three brigades arrayed from left to right under Cadmus Wilcox, Micah Jenkins, and James Kemper pushed forward through heavily wooded terrain and across a stream in a somewhat disorderly advance. Wilcox's brigade straddled the Long Bridge Road that led to Glendale as the Confederate line closed with three brigades of Pennsylvania Reserves. E. P. Alexander thought it was a savagely fought contest involving "more actual bayonet, & butt of gun, melee fighting than any other occasion" he knew of during the war. Kemper's previously untested brigade rushed forward impetuously with a yell, outdistancing its support. Sweeping through the woods and into a large field, the Virginians audaciously overran breastworks and a fortified log house, seizing several artillery pieces. The "completely routed" Pennsylvanians took flight in panic down the roads and through the fields where they bolted through the lines of a supporting division.[44]

On the opposite flank, Wilcox was to move left to close with Featherston's Brigade, but Anderson quickly countermanded that instruction and sent Wilcox forward with the other attackers. Meanwhile, other conflicting orders came—Wilcox later griped but never said who issued them—and all the while the brigade was halted under artillery fire. With the confusion finally alleviated, it was clear that the brigade was to do as Anderson had instructed. Wilcox pushed through the dense woods and approached the cleared field on the other side where he found Anderson who ordered him to "press on directly to the front." The Alabamians surged forward through the open fields in the face of withering fire and captured two batteries, setting the supporting infantrymen to flight. The 11th Alabama soon met a counterattack from fresh Union troops. The Alabamians stubbornly resisted giving up the hard-won guns. Desperate fighting ensued in which "the sword and bayonet were freely used." Despite the furious resistance, numbers finally told, and the decimated 11th Alabama was "at length forced to yield and retire to the pine woods." No Union soldiers pursued and the advance of Pryor and Maxcy Gregg's brigades on the left of the field kept the enemy in check.[45]

The center of Anderson's attacking line met with stiffer resistance from the start, and Jenkins' South Carolinians endured a prolonged struggle for possession of a battery of Pennsylvania artillery. After briefly taking the guns, Federal reinforcements drove off the exhausted rebels. Jenkins persisted and once again took the guns with the eventual help of Wilcox's Alabamians on his left. Jenkins left behind at least four companies when they did not realize the others had advanced in the dense woods, but Anderson soon rode up and put that right, ordering those companies forward. Unfortunately, they emerged from the wood to find the Union artillery supported by a large force of infantry. It was then that Wilcox arrived, telling the South Carolinians that Anderson had ordered him to charge the enemy. "At the command to charge, our companies rose up with that well known 'Rebel yell,' and went forward at a run. We soon captured the artillery, killing all the horses. Some of the enemy stood to their guns and fired even in our faces, until shot down by our boys," recalled a man in the 6th South Carolina. It was probably the most hotly contested section of the field, as evident by Jenkins' casualties.

With over 530 men killed, wounded, or missing, his was the greatest loss suffered by any Confederate brigade that day. Nearly seventy percent of Jenkins' regiment of Palmetto Sharpshooters fell around Frayser's Farm. There was still much fighting left to do, however, and Longstreet sent in nearly every one of the remaining brigades at his disposal to support his flanks and relieve the three beleaguered brigades that had carried the brunt of the battle to that point. The subsequent slaughter and all the bravery came to naught however, and at the end of the day, there was little to show for the effort made. Federal reinforcements eventually secured the Union lines, darkness ended the contest, and McClellan's army was able to continue its retreat towards the safety of the James River. Longstreet lost more than one-quarter of his division. A frustrated Lee, angry over the day's failure, snapped uncharacteristically at Jubal Early, who speculated aloud about the increased prospects for McClellan's escape. "Yes," Lee barked in frustration, "he will get away because I cannot have my orders carried out!"[46]

A calmer General Lee later noted in his report of the campaign that the failure on June 30 was attributable in part to Huger's "not coming up," but he provided no excuse or explanation for his tardy subordinate. Of Jackson, he more charitably stated that his failure was the result of "having been unable to force the passage of White Oak Swamp." The distinction is clear. At least Jackson made an effort. Huger's time in command was moving inexorably toward its conclusion, and that end would benefit Dick Anderson.[47]

First, though, another test for the army lay ahead. McClellan had finally consolidated his army at a strong defensive position on an elevated plateau known as Malvern Hill. Lee, confident in his men and suspecting that the retreating federals were demoralized, meant to attack them there. It would be his army's last chance to destroy McClellan's force before it reached the safety of the gunboats on the James. Lee hoped to hold A. P. Hill and Longstreet's divisions in reserve after seeing the hardest fighting the day before. Anderson thus played no role at Malvern Hill on July 1. With Lee feeling somewhat ill that day, he requested that Longstreet ride with him in case he felt too unwell to continue in command. Anderson again commanded Longstreet's division. As for Huger, his troops fought, but not under his command. He had been unaware that morning that the Union forces in his front near Glendale had withdrawn until Longstreet informed him, then Huger further delayed his advance because he "had no one to show us what road to take." General Magruder soon assumed command of Huger's brigades at Malvern Hill. "As I was treated in the same manner at Seven Pines," Huger later whined, "I can only hope this course was accidental and required by the necessities of the service." Lee had already determined to remove Huger, so it can hardly have been accidental. Huger's unsuitability for field command

and the lackadaisical handling of his division made it imperative that Lee place it in capable hands. Nonetheless, the series of uncoordinated southern attacks that were defeated in detail despite the desperate courage shown by the determined attackers indicated the battle was badly managed from top to bottom. Consolidated Union guns that held a far superior position on the hill treated Lee's artillery especially roughly. The valor of the attacking Rebels, ineptly thrown piecemeal into the fray, could not overcome the botched execution of the offensive. Lee's final chance failed at a cost of over 5,000 casualties. Lee stymied McClellan's plan to seize Richmond though, and despite his victory at Malvern Hill, McClellan thought only of retreat and the safety of his army. Several of his generals were incensed, with one railing that the order to withdraw from their commanding position could only have been "prompted by cowardice or treason." Nonetheless, when the morning fog shrouding Malvern Hill dissipated on July 2, the Union army was gone, en route to Harrison's Landing, badly churning the muddy roads and obstructing the route of their flight behind them with felled trees and destroyed bridges. By the time the Army of Northern Virginia caught up, with an optimistic Longstreet in the van, Lee's survey of McClellan's position led him to conclude it was too strong to attack.[48]

Chapter 8

Division Command and 2nd Manassas

Yankee-doodle was most "elegantly beaten."

—Capt. David Lang,
letter, September 7, 1862

McClellan's army remained at Harrison's Landing until mid-August while Lee reorganized his own force. Impressed by Longstreet, Lee marked him for greater responsibilities, greatly increasing the number of brigades under his command while reducing those under Jackson. Meanwhile, Anderson's competence in his role as Longstreet's senior brigade commander set him at the head of the list to replace Huger. Special Orders No. 151 from Lee's headquarters dated July 14, 1862, relieved Huger from command of his division, with Dick Anderson promoted to the rank of major general taking his place. Anderson notified his former brigade members of his appointment, offering a "cordial and affectionate adieu." Always modest, he praised his men and thanked them for their fine performance. "It is with deep emotion that he parts with you and it is with sentiments of profound gratitude that he recognizes & acknowledges how much he owes to your exalted courage & unswerving fidelity," he wrote, acknowledging that it was "to your constancy in the hour of danger & your faithfulness in the discharge of duty he owes his present elevation." He urged them to "continue to maintain the lofty character which you have heretofore borne, to place duty to the states before all other considerations and to persevere steadfastly in the noble cause of independence." It had become clear in that summer of 1862 that achieving independence would be a lengthier endeavor than previously anticipated. Thus, Anderson encouraged them with predictions of "New victories and fresh honors" as well as the rewards of a grateful country and an "admiring posterity [that] will emulate your virtues." With recognition of the bond he had formed with the men of his brigade, he promised to watch their future careers "with unchanged interest" and concluded that his "warmest sympathy and best wishes will always attend you." The following day he affixed his signature to General Orders No. 43 announcing, "the undersigned assumes command of the Division heretofore designated as Huger's Division."[1]

Lee wished to ensure the placement of competent division commanders, but also to ensure those commanders operated effectively under the direction of a corps or wing commander. Unfortunately, the Confederate government had no suitable level of command or rank between major general and general, but in anticipation of a change in the law that would establish the rank of lieutenant general, Lee unofficially divided the army into two wings or corps under Jackson and Longstreet. Anderson's division in Longstreet's wing was to consist of William Mahone's, Lewis Armistead's, and Ambrose (Rans) Wright's infantry brigades. Anderson's old brigade went to the competent Micah Jenkins, precisely as Longstreet had recommended.[2]

Anderson immediately organized a divisional staff. On July 19, he named Captain Thomas Sumter Mills as assistant adjutant general, with Captains Samuel D. Shannon and Robert P. Duncan as aides-de-camp. Mills and Duncan had been with Anderson since May 1861. The division headquarters was near Drewry's Bluff on the James River. There the men constructed defensive works in anticipation of attacks on Drewry's Bluff by naval forces. The men laboring in the summer heat undoubtedly welcomed news of Lee's instructions to suspend all duties with the exception of inspections on Sundays. It was to be a day of rest with opportunities to attend religious services. The men he commanded were far from choirboys, however. Anderson issued a circular on July 27 decrying the "depredations" of some of the soldiers on fatigue detail. He expressed his hope "that he may not again have occasion to admonish them of the sacredness with which the rights of property of our citizens should be guarded, and the great displeasure he feels at the wanton destruction and appropriation of what it should be our pride & pleasure to protect." He instructed his brigade commanders to suppress "so common and unnecessary an offense" and to bring their "officers and men to a rigid accountability for any indulgence or commission of the same." If the experience of Daniel Gilley of the 16th Virginia in Mahone's brigade was common, it was no wonder the men were violating the private property of citizens in the area. "We get meat and flour and some old dry beans to eat and don't get a nuf [*sic*] of that," he lamented to his family. "I am just tired out on it and want some vegables [*sic*] to eat so bad." Even when available for purchase, items were unreasonably high. "Buter [*sic*] is one dollar and twenty five cents a pound, coffee is 2.50, a pound of sugar is 75 cents, and a plate pie is 50 cents a peace. A egg is 1.00 a dozen, molasses is 1.75 a quort [*sic*]." Lewis Miles of the 22nd Georgia in Wright's brigade also commented on the price of goods as well as rumors that their general was attempting to get the brigade home. "Our Brigadier General is R. A. Wright from somewhere about Augusta I think & he says he is going to try to get his Brigade back to Georgia," wrote Miles hopefully before dashing that prospect in the next breath, "but don't let that lift you too high for he may never get them there."[3]

Anderson's posting south of the James River took him out of Longstreet's direct control, and for a time he fell under Gustavus W. Smith's authority, as Smith was "the senior officer with [that] wing of the army." In mid-August, it was apparent that McClellan was evacuating the Peninsula and probably moving to reinforce John Pope's army then concentrating around Culpeper. Lee was on the verge of departing Richmond after receiving a note from Longstreet requesting that Lee join him at Gordonsville, Virginia. He wondered about the need to move Anderson to Gordonsville as well, but decided against that action. Lee ordered Anderson's division to remain part of the Richmond defenses until August 16, when he directed him to move to Louisa Courthouse and await orders there. The loose command structure of the army at that point might have imparted the wrong impression to Anderson. He later told D. H. Hill that "From the time of my promotion to Major General shortly after the battles around Richmond until the formation of the corps for Longstreet and A. P. Hill the division which I commanded constituted a separate body and was subject only to Genl. Lee's orders." Whether such confusion resulted from his misinterpretation of his relationship to Smith's command or from a lapse of memory in the post-war era is unknown, but his characteristic modesty makes it unlikely he was seeking to inflate his role as an independent commander. Longstreet's report of the battle of Second Manassas appears to support Anderson's recollection though. Longstreet related that during preparations for the attack of August 30 he received a message from Lee "offering me Major General Anderson's division." Longstreet would not have interpreted the situation in such terms had Anderson been under his direct command, however, a post-war letter from Lee to former Union General Fitz John Porter contradicts Anderson's interpretation. Lee wrote that by noon on August 29, Longstreet's "whole force except Anderson's Division was up and that arrived before next morning." D. H. Hill commanded the Department of North Carolina and was in a position to know with some precision what Anderson's assignment was. Both Hill and Anderson briefly fell under Gustavus Smith's command when Lee was preparing to join Longstreet at Gordonsville, but Lee also expanded Hill's Department of North Carolina so that it extended from the Cape Fear River to the James River. Anderson, being on the south side of the James, thus also briefly found himself in Hill's Department. The situation undoubtedly generated some confusion. Nonetheless, ambiguity was clarified by the time Lee set the army in motion to meet the threat from Pope.[4]

Lee worked anxiously to consolidate his entire force against Pope. Already Jackson had won an independent victory at Cedar Mountain on

August 9, destroyed the Union supply depot at Manassas Junction on August 27, and attacked Pope's marching columns on the Warrenton Turnpike near the old Bull Run battlefield on August 28. Pope then attacked Jackson's position over the following two days. Meanwhile, Anderson's division left its position on the James, marching first to Richmond on a scorching day, before taking the train to Louisa Courthouse. The marching over the next few days was "very trying" for the men. The weather was exceedingly hot and the supply of rations was spotty and badly managed. One man in the 12th Virginia of Mahone's brigade recalled that "one day we got bread, and not meat; another day got meat and not bread; again we got fresh meat and no salt; and one day we got neither bread, meat nor salt, but were turned into [a] beautiful field of corn, with the injunction to take no more roasting ears than were absolutely necessary."[5]

Anderson's division arrived near Warrenton Springs on the 26th, where he sent a curious note via a flag of truce to Union Brigadier General Rufus King saying that he was returning to Union lines a woman whom his troops had captured that morning dressed in men's clothing. Anderson's arrival there freed Longstreet to march with the bulk of his command to reinforce Jackson, but the note to King gave the Federals their first definite knowledge of the exact whereabouts of Anderson's division. After forcing the passage of Thoroughfare Gap, Longstreet hurried toward the sound of the guns as Pope and Jackson battled one another. His troops arrived on the afternoon of the 29th in time to repulse several assaults. Anderson's division caught up with the rest of the army near Groveton, with elements arriving before daylight on the morning of August 30, "perfectly exhausted." With no one to guide them into position, over 6,000 of Anderson's men marched to a hazardous location on the field, far too close to the Yankee guns that were sure to open at first light. A warning from Hood led them to retrace their steps. The warlike detritus of the previous days' combat was "lying about in the woods," recalled one of Mahone's men, who was glad when he learned the division was to be held in reserve. They were, he stated, "in very poor condition to go into a fight that morning. We had been broken down by continuous marching and fasting." Nonetheless, Mahone's brigade of Anderson's division took position on the right of the line resting on a hill overlooking the fields around Manassas. Lee's headquarters was nearby on the same hill, and the men beheld the rare sight of General Lee and his staff as he directed the battle later that morning. "He was the handsomest and most graceful man I ever saw," recalled an observer. Another later overheard Lee address Anderson. "General," he said to him, "your men are very much in need of rest, but those people must be driven back."[6]

Anderson apparently was not overly fussy about his appearance, but one soldier recalled that he was in the habit of getting "himself up in good style" before a fight. That day he was resplendent in his "best uniform, a fine hat, and white gloves." The men well knew it was to be a day of battle, but it was common for them on other occasions to predict a fight or hear them remark that "Old Dick is dressed up today, and we will catch the Devil." One soldier noted later that, "the men had great confidence in 'Fighting' Dick Anderson, as he was called." As the tide of battle began to turn clearly against the Union attackers, Lee called on his reserve and pressed the initiative. Jackson's force drove the enemy back on the left flank, and Longstreet ordered an advance from the center and right of the Confederate lines. Hood's Texans led the way, with Anderson's division coming up "gallantly" to Hood's support.[7]

Anderson's men at first thought they might escape the fighting altogether that day before the long roll beat them into line, as they had been sent to the rear to cook rations. "We were ordered to throw off our baggage, and 'go in light,'" recalled one of the surprised men. The division moved forward south of the Warrenton Turnpike from the Brawner Farm towards Henry Hill, eventually coming under artillery fire from Union guns on Dogan Ridge. Mahone found it necessary to halt the men of his brigade three times in order to reform the lines after passing through a wooded area. "I have always thought that this was an excellent test of the courage of our brigade—to be halted and dressed (as if on drill) while men were being killed and wounded along the line," said one proud member of the brigade later. The division moved forward steadily until it was suddenly diverted to the right flank to come to Hood's support. His Texas brigade had just fought a spirited duel with the 5th New York Zouaves, whose colorful red pantaloons and fezzes littered the slopes indicating where more than 330 of them had fallen. Anderson's division swept past the cheering Texans as they halted to re-form. In the excitement of that victory, an old man in civilian clothing rode onto the field "throwing his arms about wildly, and he hallooed to us, 'Go on, my boys, and you'll end this war. The Yankees are running like hell.'" The men were puzzled by the excited man's appearance on the field, "for it was an 'unhealthy' latitude for a peaceful civilian," recalled one.[8]

Advancing across two miles of ground covered by enemy artillery was worth the effort that day. When the troops reached Chinn Ridge the fighting there had ended, and Anderson turned his men towards the still raging fight on Henry Hill. Their arrival provided the additional weight needed to turn the day fully in the Confederates' favor, yet the results were not quite so decisive as they might have been. Sending Wright's brigade first to support their fellow Georgians of George "Tige" Anderson's heavily engaged regiments, Dick Anderson then ordered Mahone's brigade to advance along

Chinn Ridge against the extreme left of the Union lines, with Armistead following behind as support.[9]

Mahone quickly discovered his brigade lines extended well past those of his foe, but a stalwart Union battery remained firing shots that nearly enfiladed the Confederate position. Mahone fell wounded and command passed to Colonel David A. Weisiger of the 12th Virginia. The brigade pressed forward across a burning fence and over the Sudley road before pivoting to the left and into woods where they found themselves facing more Union troops as near as fifty yards away. Desperate to hold the vital flank, the blue-clad soldiers poured a vicious fire into the advancing Confederates, some of whom had halted and lain down. One man of the 12th Virginia thought the brigade seemed "to be waiting as if for orders to move forward." Meanwhile, men assisted Colonel Weisiger off the field after he fell with a serious wound. The oft-hoped for flanking movement had presented itself ripe for exploitation, but no order to advance came. Despite a clear edge, none of the officers present on the field appear to have entirely understood how close they were to an even more decisive victory. Anderson's two brigades under Mahone and Armistead, supported by artillery, stood poised to roll up the Union Army's left flank with an advance along the Sudley Road, yet he did not order the men forward aggressively after they reached a certain point. With looming darkness on his mind, plus the lack of further instructions from Lee or Longstreet, and the fear of federal reinforcements attacking his own right flank, he did not act.[10]

There was also the chance of running into other advancing Confederate troops in the confusion of battle and dwindling daylight, but his exact reason for halting remains unknown. He knew his division was Longstreet's last reserves, so if he ran into trouble on his flanks there would be no support forthcoming. The fighting around Henry Hill raged sporadically until well after dark, and Anderson let the opportunity slip away. In hindsight, it seems as though he could have pressed the immediate advantage more vigorously, but the confusion of battle often leads to missed opportunities that seem apparent only later. To be fair, no one else appears to have recognized the full extent of the advantage either except J. E. B. Stuart, who attempted to convince Armistead to undertake a night attack to cut off the Union retreat across Bull Run. Stuart later wrote that he did not "feel authorized to order it, particularly as there was time to communicate with the commanding general." Lee likewise declined to order the attack. As for Anderson's brigadiers, Wilcox's brigade relieved Rans Wright who was first detached to support Tige Anderson's attack; Mahone had received a chest wound that took him out of the fight and would require a few months' recovery time, and Weisiger did not advance the brigade much past the woods near the

Sudley Road before falling wounded. Armistead's troops similarly advanced but also pulled up short of a decisive thrust. Anderson's apparent lack of initiative to follow up on the situation or to call for the support that would have enabled him to do so more securely contributed to a missed opportunity for Lee's army. It was not the only missed chance that day though, and neither Lee nor Longstreet, nor any other person present on the field ever expressed any disappointment with Anderson's performance. His men had fought well under his leadership, but nearly marching them into the Federal lines when they first arrived on the field and failing to pursue aggressively the advantages gained on the day of battle were indications that Anderson's abilities as a division commander were still maturing.[11]

Rain fell heavily overnight, and Jackson's troops began pursuing Pope's fleeing army the following morning in hopes of inflicting more damage before the Federals reached the safety of Washington's defenses. Longstreet's troops remained behind tending to the dead and wounded "till Jackson could have time to stretch out on his new march." Many soldiers replenished their dwindling food supplies from the ample stocks found among the dead and wounded Yankees littering the fields. Alexander Hunter, a Virginian in Kemper's Brigade recalled just how famished the men were then. "Hunger is a fearful thing," he wrote, "and we forgot for a time many a loved comrade who was shot in the battle." The search through Yankee haversacks proved fruitful, with empty southern bellies filling throughout the day with plundered "salt pork, boiled beef and canned vegetables." Other men hoped to find suitable footwear among the fallen. Edgar Warfield of the 17th Virginia was among those almost barefoot at the time, "with the soles of my shoes about ready to leave the uppers." He was far from alone, however, and despite his nearly desperate condition, he was unable to remedy the situation, "as others in a similar state were ahead of me."[12]

By noon that day, Longstreet had advanced Pryor's brigade across Bull Run to occupy the high ground there. Leaving D. H Hill's freshly arriving troops to finish the remaining burial work, Longstreet's whole command set off a few hours later towards Sudley Ford, which they crossed on the morning of September 1. Pushing closer and closer to Washington along the Little River Turnpike, they caught up with Jackson near Chantilly. They arrived too late to help Jackson repulse an attack by two Federal divisions. Both Union division commanders died in the confused fighting that was marked by a severe late-summer thunderstorm adding dramatically to the day's violence. It was a heavy blow to the defeated Union force, but their attack spoiled Jackson's hope of catching Pope. That night Pope retreated to the capital's defenses. The Manassas campaign, a great Confederate success to which Dick Anderson and his division contributed with yeoman's work, was over. Unfortunately, the official records contain no battle reports from Anderson or from any one of the brigade commanders serving under him. Whether they were lost or whether it is further indication of Anderson's lax commitment to the administrative requirements of his position is unknown, but that unfortunate trend continued to plague his record and that of his command as well. The words of one Florida captain, David Lang, at least succinctly captured the essence of the campaign when he wrote in a letter to his cousin Annie: "Suffice it to say that Yankee-doodle was most 'elegantly beaten.'"[13]

Chapter 9

Harpers Ferry to Sharpsburg

The day has gone against us.

—Col. R. H. Chilton to Gen. Lafayette McLaws,
September 14, 1862

In a few short months since taking command, Lee had driven McClellan's army from the gates of Richmond and defeated Pope decisively. Now he had neither the strength for a direct assault on Washington nor the resources necessary to hold his position in Northern Virginia. Instead, he decided to carry the war into Maryland, which was sure to draw the Union Army back into the open where Lee might yet wage a decisive battle. Confederates thus marched toward the Potomac, plagued by the same lack of supplies and matériel that made the march necessary in the first place. Large numbers of men were soon shoeless, and there were scanty food supplies. Those who stuck it out survived for days on little but green corn and whatever fruits they could gather. Many suffered severe diarrhea from the poor diet, but others had simply had enough. "Our men have broke down badly and dropped out," one Georgia officer recalled. Straggling soon grew to epic proportions. Lee issued General Orders No. 103 on September 6, 1862, hoping to inspire the men by announcing Major General Edmund Kirby Smith's "great victory" over Federal forces at Richmond, Kentucky and by exhorting his troops to "press onward! Let each man feel the responsibility now resting on him to pursue vigorously the success vouchsafed to us by Heaven. Let the armies of East and the West vie with each other in discipline, bravery, and activity." In spite of such efforts to encourage the men to even greater exertions, Lee also found it necessary to install a strict disciplinarian as the army's provost marshal in an effort to curb the excessive straggling that was sapping his army's strength. His choice was one of Anderson's brigade leaders, Lew Armistead, who had charge of the provost guard following in the army's wake with orders to "arrest stragglers, and punish summarily all depredators, and keep the men with their commands." Lee ultimately found it necessary to post guards at the Potomac fords near Leesburg. He feared that Union forces might easily scoop up small groups of stragglers. Moreover, Lee was concerned that large numbers of stragglers trailing the main body of the army into Maryland would at best create a bad impression on the residents and at worst increase the chances of depredations against civilian property. The guards were to direct stragglers to Winchester, Virginia, there to be organized into larger bodies subject to military discipline and then sent forth to join Lee.[1]

For several days starting on September 4, Lee's excited troops forded the Potomac, serenaded by the strains of "Maryland, My Maryland." A Virginian in Mahone's Brigade recalled hearing a bugler playing "Maryland, My Maryland" "as loudly as he could," during the crossing, "when all of a sudden the music ceased and the old fellow had stepped into a deep hole, but he got out and struck up again amid the cheers of thousands of men." The army gathered near Frederick, where the tune continued to enjoy popularity. In Anderson's division the 16th Mississippi's band from Featherston's brigade played it as the southerners marched jauntily into town. They "finished up with 'Dixie,' and a loud Rebel Yell was given."[2] Meanwhile, the Army of the Potomac absorbed John Pope's Army of Virginia, with the united force once again under the command of George B. McClellan. By Sunday, September 7, McClellan set his army in motion, probing to determine Lee's whereabouts. Two days later, at Frederick, Lee issued Special Orders No. 191, describing in detail his operational plans for the foray into Maryland. Lee's nemesis would soon have those plans in his own hands; however, setting the stage for one of the Army of Northern Virginia's most critical moments.

Special Orders No. 191 reflected Lee's reaction to the puzzling behavior of the Federal troops garrisoning the strategic town of Harpers Ferry, which lay on a narrow tip of land marking the confluence of the Shenandoah and Potomac Rivers threatening the integrity of Lee's supply route through the Shenandoah Valley. With heights dominating the town from across the rivers and with ridges to the west offering a superior elevation for attacking forces, most sound military minds understood that the place was indefensible without extensive fortification. Lee had anticipated a hasty evacuation once his army had interposed itself between the town and the Union Army at Washington. Instead, despite McClellan's urging to the contrary, General-in-Chief Henry W. Halleck instructed the garrison's commander, Colonel Dixon S. Miles, to maintain his vulnerable position virtually at the bottom of a teacup and prepare to repulse a Confederate assault. In order to rid his vital supply route through the Valley of that impediment, Lee's risky plan called for dividing his army in the face of the enemy. He believed with some degree of confidence that McClellan would move cautiously, allowing him to reunite his army before any real danger arose. Lee dispatched three separate forces to capture Harpers Ferry. Jackson would first capture the Federal force at Martinsburg, Virginia, then march on Harpers Ferry from the west, sealing off the Union garrison's escape route in that direction. Brigadier

General John G. Walker's division would cross back into Virginia and shell the town from Loudon Heights. The two divisions of Lafayette McLaws and Dick Anderson were to make the primary effort to capture the town, with McLaws having overall command due to his seniority. Those divisions would attack from the Maryland side, seizing the inadequately defended Maryland Heights and thereby subjecting the Union force in the town to a devastating, plunging artillery fire from close range that the defenders could not withstand for very long.[3]

Shortly before leaving his camp near Frederick, Anderson said that Lee summoned him to his tent. There, Lee proceeded to outline his "objects, his expectations and his opinions as to the best steps to be taken, etc." Anderson thought it strange that Lee would speak to him "so particularly" about such things, and he must have thought then that Anderson, not McLaws, would be leading the effort. "He repeatedly said 'Harpers Ferry must be taken against Thursday evening,'" Anderson recalled. The conversation must have taken place prior to Lee's actual issuance of written copies of Special Orders No. 191 on Tuesday, September 9, which clearly indicated McLaws and not Anderson was in command, and which specifically mentioned Friday, not Thursday, as the day by which Lee expected his troops to seize the town. Upon reporting to McLaws, Anderson dutifully "went over . . . all that Genl. Lee had said to me." McLaws, however, also received a copy of Lee's written orders, and spoke personally to him because he later wrote that the Lee also called him to his tent and gave verbal instructions. McLaws was apparently somewhat apprehensive, telling Lee that he had never been to Harpers Ferry or its vicinity and therefore was unfamiliar with the terrain. Lee's optimistic response was that it "didn't matter" as he would easily overwhelm the defenders. In the end, Lee's desires did not factor into the outcome. Harpers Ferry would fall on neither Thursday nor Friday. It held out until Monday, September 15 and put Lee's entire campaign in jeopardy.[4]

McLaws and Anderson left their camps near Frederick on Wednesday, September 10, marching first towards Middletown on "horribly dusty" roads, then south towards the small town of Burkittsville at the foot of South Mountain, a northern extension of the Blue Ridge. The men recalled Middletown as "entirely Union, and some of the ladies expressed their opinions quite freely." The Confederates took it in good humor, but none of those passing by Burkittsville later that day suspected that the town's few churches, its schoolhouse, and many other structures would soon transform into a vast hospital complex housing hundreds of soldiers wounded in the ensuing battles. By Thursday, September 11, the column had marched through Brownsville Pass into Pleasant Valley, which ran north and south, bordered on the east by South Mountain and on the west by Elk Ridge. At the southern tip of

Elk Ridge lay Maryland Heights, the key to the capture of Harpers Ferry. From his headquarters in Brownsville McLaws directed Brigadier Generals Joseph B. Kershaw's and William Barksdale's brigades to ascend Elk Ridge along the Solomon's Gap Road on the morning of the 12th, then push south towards Harpers Ferry with Kershaw in overall command. McLaws also ordered Paul Semmes' brigade of his own division along with Mahone's brigade of Anderson's division to remain behind near Brownsville Pass to protect Kershaw's rear as he moved along Elk Ridge while the main force advanced along the valley floor. Wright's brigade of Anderson's division, accompanied by two artillery pieces, marched east to another pass in the Blue Ridge near Weverton in order to protect the expedition from any attack that might originate along the railroad, the canal, or the turnpike running to Frederick. Anderson himself followed Wright later in the day, arriving at Weverton near sundown with Pryor's Brigade, which he "disposed . . . effectually to defend the pass." Two more of Anderson's brigades, Armistead's and Featherston's, joined Brigadier General Howell Cobb's brigade in sealing off the southern end of Pleasant Valley from any federal escape attempt along the turnpike from the village of Sandy Hook, which lay at the foot of Maryland Heights. Later, "several attempts were made by the enemy to pass out by this road," recalled Featherston, "but they were promptly and easily checked and turned back" by his Mississippians.[5]

Kershaw's force, with some difficulty given the steep terrain on Maryland Heights, was able to drive off the last of the outnumbered Union defenders, sending them scrambling down the steep mountainside and across the pontoon bridge into the town by late afternoon of the 13th. Confederate troops remaining below were undoubtedly pleased when fire from a Union battery of heavy guns on the heights ceased, as those guns had been dropping rounds into the valley throughout the day.[6]

Despite having thrown Miles' defenders off Maryland Heights, only infantry had accomplished that task. Artillerymen still had to haul their guns up the steep slopes in order to bombard the town. McLaws in particular appreciated the urgency of accomplishing his mission. Sometime late on the 13th or during the early hours of the 14th, a dispatch arrived from Lee's headquarters urging haste and informing McLaws that it appeared Union troops were moving in his direction in an attempt to relieve the town. By mid-day Cobb's brigade was sent back towards Crampton's Gap, about a mile north of the Brownsville Pass, to reinforce the infantry and Stuart's cavalrymen, but there was little else to be done until Harpers Ferry was reduced. Urgent work had begun early on the morning of the 14th and by 2 PM a rough road was cut and several guns dragged up the mountain. Soon all three separate Confederate contingents were lobbing shells from the surrounding heights.

Miles would undoubtedly be compelled to capitulate, but the untoward events developing rapidly to the north made the situation more than a little uncomfortable for the widely dispersed Confederate force on the Maryland side. McLaws and Anderson were observing the effects of the fire from the top of Maryland Heights, and McLaws was not unduly alarmed upon hearing cannonading from the direction of Crampton's Gap, five miles to the north. He believed the brigades of Semmes and Mahone, the latter commanded by Colonel William A. Parham while Mahone recovered from his wound at Second Manassas, along with J. E. B. Stuart's troopers were sufficient to defend the gap. Moreover, McLaws had received reassurances from Stuart, who had recently arrived from the gap and prematurely claimed that the attacking force constituted no more than a brigade. Nonetheless, realizing the precarious position he would be in should Union forces gain his rear, McLaws dispatched a staff officer to Cobb with encouragement to "hold the gap if he lost his last man in doing it," then set off with Stuart to see the situation himself. Anderson had already gone there, and McLaws made his way to Dick's headquarters. McLaws soon learned the disquieting news that it was not a single brigade advancing up the eastern slopes of South Mountain, but General Henry W. Slocum's entire First Division. One of McLaws' staff officers soon rode up to announce that Slocum had "forced the gap and that re-enforcements were needed." A significant enemy force able to move upon their rear through Pleasant Valley now threatened McLaws and Anderson's scattered divisions. McLaws ordered Anderson to throw his last unoccupied brigade, Wilcox's, into battle.[7]

Anderson and McLaws were fortunate the threat had not come sooner. Lee's assessment of his foe would normally have been correct, but McClellan moved with uncharacteristic rapidity when a lost copy of Special Orders 191 revealed Lee's dangerous plan. Slocum arrived at Burkittsville around noon on the 14th, and formed for an assault by 3 PM. Confederate fire held the attackers 1,000 yards from the base of the heights for over two hours. The Confederate left eventually gave way under enormous pressure, but then a difficult assault across a distance of 80 to 100 yards was needed to dislodge Mahone's Virginians strongly posted behind a stone wall bordering a road running along the mountain's base on the Confederate right flank. Despite several assaults, the defenders held out more than three hours until outflanked and compelled to retreat directly up the steep mountainside. Union troops followed closely in a race up the eastern slopes of South Mountain. Despite the arrival of some reinforcements, Federals eventually began to outflank most of the southern defenders on the heights. Mahone's Virginians and Stuart's dismounted troopers finally began streaming precipitously down the western slopes into Pleasant Valley, carrying the Tenth Georgia from Semmes's brigade that had arrived earlier as reinforcement with them. By then Cobb had been on the scene for some time, but could only watch in horror as Yankees drove his men off South Mountain. "After the lines were broken," he recalled, "all my efforts to rally the troops were unsuccessful." He was able to hold the enemy in check until nightfall ended the Union advance. This "allowed a new arrangement of the troops to be made to meet the changed aspect of affairs," McLaws later noted simply in his report. One member of the 6th Virginia that had stood so valiantly at the stone wall reported that when his company mustered later in Pleasant Valley, only four men answered to their names, and only a total of seventeen in the entire regiment made it back. The sacrifice surely saved McLaws's and Anderson's force from greater disaster and permitted that "new arrangement of the troops."[8]

McLaws returned to his own headquarters around 10 PM where his aide Captain Henry L. King, whom the general judged to be "a very clever young fellow but quite an exquisite," lamented the "very anxious predicament" they now found themselves confronting. Anderson's whereabouts that night are unknown with any certainty, but it is likely he was busy ensuring the effective placement of defensive lines across Pleasant Valley. Possibly he shared the "anxious feeling in all our bones" that King attributed to those on McLaws's staff. Most "sat up late consulting," King recalled, and "all feel that tomorrow will be a bloody day." Knowledge that Union troops had not only forced their way across Crampton's Gap, but were seriously threatening other gaps as well would have compounded their fears if they were aware of that situation. Lee had sent Longstreet from Hagerstown at dawn on the 14th to support D. H. Hill, who was then holding Turner's Gap and Fox's Gap over South Mountain north of Crampton's. When Longstreet arrived, he found Lee already on the scene. Longstreet's troops were hardly fresh after an exhausting march, but they quickly scaled the mountain and took position to stave off the Union attacks until well after dark. Lee ordered his men off the field under cover of darkness, hoping to consolidate into a more defensible position that allowed more options for maneuver and facilitated the reuniting of his dispersed army. Sometime during the night, McLaws received a disturbing note from Colonel Robert H. Chilton, Lee's Assistant Adjutant General. "The day has gone against us," he wrote, "and this army will go by Sharpsburg and cross the river. It is necessary for you to abandon your position tonight." Lee apparently intended to be in a position to re-cross the Potomac near Shepherdstown if necessary, or to threaten McClellan's flanks should his army turn southward to relieve Harpers Ferry, and thus the army began to gather around Keedysville and the nondescript hamlet of Sharpsburg on the banks of the Antietam Creek.[9]

Developing intelligence allowed Lee to refine his thinking throughout the night, and he later wrote McLaws that Longstreet was instead moving to occupy the Boonsborough Valley in order to protect McLaws's flanks from federals advancing from Frederick. Anxious that McLaws was aware of the crisis, Lee followed up on the morning of 15th with more urgent instructions to withdraw immediately from Maryland Heights and join the army at Centreville, also known as Keedysville. "If you can't get off any other way, you must cross the mountain," Lee informed him. "The utmost dispatch is required." It seems unlikely based on McLaws's actions that any of those instructions reached him in a timely manner. McLaws and Anderson continued to strengthen their position and bring more troops into line until word arrived at mid-morning that Harpers Ferry had fallen.[10]

Union troops did not advance against the defenders stretching across Pleasant Valley on the morning of the 15th, but Confederate guns positioned on Maryland Heights opened on the Federals as soon as it was light enough to see. Soon after receiving word from Jackson that Miles had surrendered the town, McLaws set off to confer with Jackson in Harpers Ferry. He left Anderson in command in the valley with instructions to "push the train across the river as fast as possible and follow us with the infantry when the trains were well over." Anderson thus began to withdraw the infantry as the wagons began to cross the Potomac. McLaws later resumed command, but it was not until 2 AM when all the wagons were safely over the river and the weary infantrymen could follow. They marched quickly through the crowded town, and in response to Lee's urging, pushed on another four miles to encamp near Halltown by 8 AM on the morning of the September 16. Anderson and McLaws must have been much relieved to escape the confines of Pleasant Valley. There would have been little prospect of withdrawing the trains and artillery safely over the mountains that hemmed them in, or for any but the infantry to escape until Harpers Ferry fell and the way was clear to cross the Potomac there. The anxiety over that grim situation stayed with Anderson as an unpleasant memory. Never one for hyperbole, he later recalled that they "had the most uncomfortable time of it under Maryland Heights at the foot of Pleasant Valley until Jackson cleared away the road for us."[11]

Lee's anxiety conspired against the men's need for rest, and many had long ago exhausted the meager provisions with which they had set out. Another message arrived from Lee entreating McLaws to rejoin the main body of the army as rapidly as possible. The men were roused and soon on their feet, resuming the march towards the ford at Shepherdstown. When they halted after dark a few miles short of the river, another desperate plea arrived urging the exhausted men onward. They pushed forward with Anderson's division bringing up the rear and arriving near Sharpsburg as the sun was rising on September 17. Armistead's brigade was acting as provost guard and crossed the river last, but Anderson had pushed on too rapidly with Pryor's brigade leading the way. Armistead was thus detached to support McLaws, and some regiments did not reach the field until late morning. According to McLaws, Longstreet instructed Anderson to proceed down the road to the hill beyond Sharpsburg, where he would receive orders."[12]

Longstreet subsequently held Anderson's men in reserve on the Shepherdstown Road west of Lee's headquarters until throwing them into the fray north of the town. From the Piper farm, Longstreet called on Anderson's troops to support D. H. Hill's men holding a sunken road that would soon earn the name "Bloody Lane." Anderson's entire division, about 3,500-men strong, began to advance through Piper's orchard and cornfields as Hill's men in the sunken road fought desperately to hold off the Union assault. Frustrated federal gunners across Antietam Creek were unable to fire effectively into the swarming melee at the sunken road, and instead swept the fields to the rear with shot. Casualties among the infantry and the rebel gunners were heavy, and before he could fully deploy his men behind Hill's line, Anderson himself fell with a wound to the thigh that toppled him from his horse and took him completely out of action that day after he fainted from loss of blood. Command of the division fell to Brigadier General Pryor, the former Virginia politician whose skills proved unequal to the crisis. Pryor wisely appealed to Longstreet for artillery support, but his direction of the troops otherwise proved too weak and ineffective. Pryor inefficiently handled the brigades or badly placed them. The fierce contest at the sunken road raged on before Confederates suddenly and precipitously began to fall back due to some confusion on each end of the line. The momentum of Colonel Carnot Posey's brigade on reaching the sunken road led to him pushing his impetuous Mississippians through the front line and across "Bloody Lane" in an ill-advised counterattack that quickly met with disaster. After falling back to the sunken road, Posey attempted to get his men out of the overcrowded lane, but the rearward movement of the Mississippi regiments only triggered more confusion and a general withdrawal on the entire right of the line. Then there was a similar muddle on the Confederate left in the 6th Alabama from Brigadier General Robert Rodes's brigade, which had been ordered to adjust the line to face an enfilading fire. Having mistaken Rodes's instructions for an order to retreat, the unexpected withdrawal of the Alabamians quickly swept others along with it. Rodes was assisting a wounded staff officer when he was himself struck in the thigh. It was a serious and painful wound, but with the artery undamaged, Rodes concluded it was not dangerous. When he staunched the blood flow and turned back to the field, he found to his horror that his men were "retreating in confusion." The gap that opened in the Confederate line proved fatal, and Union troops poured through, routing the defenders, inflicting heavy losses, and stopping only when massed artillery fire brought them to a halt and allowed the disorganized Rebels time to regroup.[13]

The federal attack stalled at that point when heavy fire from the Confederates concentrated on high ground and along the Hagerstown Pike discouraged any further advance. Meanwhile, only the timely arrival from Harpers Ferry of A. P. Hill's Light Division averted near disaster on the extreme right flank of Lee's line. Despite those nearly calamitous moments, as the sun set over the ravaged landscape that had witnessed the highest casualties of any single day's fighting in of the war, the Army of Northern Virginia held tenaciously onto to its positions. "The dead lay in every direction," recalled one horrified staff officer of McLaws's division, "in numerous places piled on each other, but gladly did I mark that the enemy were 10 to 1 of ours." At "Bloody Lane," the statistics were not so favorable for the Confederates. It had been a disoriented and muddled affair, and Anderson's division was not the only organization thrown into battle ineffectively. Colonel R. T. Bennett of the 14th North Carolina reported observing "masses of Confederate troops in great confusion," as he moved his own men into position during one of the federal assaults. He specifically recognized the 16th Mississippi and 2nd Florida of Anderson's division as having broken "beyond the power of rallying after five minutes' stay" and sweeping two North Carolina regiments of Bennett's brigade away with them. Colonel Richard Floyd of the 8th Florida in Pryor's brigade recalled with frustration the confusion in his search for his regiment that day. The response to his inquiries as to the whereabouts of his command by "officers riding to & from the field was answered by 'I know not—no man can unless by accident find his Brigade in the field[.]'" Floyd was left behind sick when his men marched from Virginia, and he had been struggling vainly that day to locate them. He finally found a few of the men coming off the field with wounds, and discovered the rest were "all killed, wounded, or dispersed." The other Floridians of Pryor's brigade had suffered as grievously. "The next day it was difficult to find any men at all of these Regts, except the wounded who were brought off," Floyd later wrote, but they had repulsed the attacking federal troops and thrown them back before retreating to a new Confederate line that was established several hundred yards to the rear of the sunken road.[14]

Colonel Robert Jones of the 22nd Georgia had led his men to the sunken road at a run before taking command of the brigade after General Wright fell badly wounded. Jones was "shot through the hat and hit in the stomach by a ball penetrating his belt and going through his body," but he survived. His brother, Captain Wesley Jones, received seven wounds that proved mortal.

Given the ferocity of the fighting, Dick Anderson's early thigh wound likely saved him from even greater harm on that bloodiest day of the war, but at the cost of his division's cohesion and effectiveness.[15]

September 18 saw no renewal of the intense fighting, and the exhausted armies lay facing one another in line of battle. Even in the absence of a formal truce, the men gathered in many of their wounded comrades despite the relentless fire from sharpshooters. The trauma inflicted on the army was apparent from the recollections of one 9th Alabama captain who was thankful to have been spared from the carnage along the sunken road, but who spent a fretful day with his comrades all "in dread" of another attack. That night, undoubtedly to the relief of many, Lee ordered his army to re-cross the Potomac. A light fog and drizzle added to the gloomy mood of the troops. The men now hissed and shouted down a band's attempt to play "Maryland, My Maryland." It is useless to speculate on what might have gone differently had Anderson retained command on September 17. What is worth noting is that Pryor's flawed actions, notably in committing troops piecemeal—or not at all—followed by Posey triggering a retreat after his imprudent attempt at a counterattack failed, all contributed to a calamity at an otherwise strongly defended, entrenched position on the field. Likewise, the wounding of Rodes as well as of Colonel John B. Gordon of the 6th Alabama left that regiment in the hands of its lieutenant colonel, who inadvertently brought about the collapse of Rodes's brigade holding the left flank. Anderson left no account of what became of him that day or even afterwards while he recovered. The record is entirely silent until he began to issue written orders once again on November 15. Wilcox had meanwhile returned to duty and superseded Pryor. Wilcox issued his last order as temporary division commander on November 7, placing Anderson's return sometime between then and the 15th.[16]

Wilcox's opportunity to command the division temporarily only sharpened the sting of his failure to gain permanent promotion. Unable to comprehend the delay in his own advancement, he watched as comrades from the class of 1846 surpassed him despite what he saw as his own excellent performance. One of those classmates was Stonewall Jackson. Classmate George McClellan again led the Army of the Potomac, and Wilcox was aware that others like Major General Jesse Reno excelled him in the Union Army as well. Perhaps most galling to him would be the promotion of George Pickett to the rank of major general in October. That Virginian had finished fifty-ninth, the very bottom of the class. Wilcox might have felt even worse had he himself not finished fifty-fourth. Still, he found it hard to swallow. Even A. P. Hill had won promotion in May, and he did not finish the Academy until 1847 after having to repeat a year due to illness. Others soon to advance, like John B. Hood and J. E. B. Stuart, were far younger, having graduated the Academy in the classes of 1853 and 1854 respectively while Wilcox was instructing infantry tactics there. The resentment that was stewing in him would continue to roil and it would spill over later that fall.[17]

Meanwhile, in addition to his concerns over promotion, Wilcox had been seething over the lack of discipline he saw in the army, calling it "little better than an armed mob" whose route of march left desolation in its wake. "They burn fences, pillage orchards, steal the green corn, kill beef, sheep, hogs & poultry," he complained. He did not direct his ire toward the bulk of the army, but rather toward "the marauding stragglers who leave their companies without authority . . . but come back voluntarily after being absent a few days." He must have recognized, however, that some of the straggling was undoubtedly due to the poor condition of the soldiers, who were, he admitted, "sadly in want of clothing especially shoes." The issue of footwear continued to plague the army whose men trudged constantly over the roughest of roads. Wilcox estimated that "5,000 are about useless from the want of shoes."[18]

Despite his army's grim condition, Lee was reluctant to abandon the idea of conducting further operations in Maryland. As he pondered his options, the army continued to suffer and slowly disintegrate, with straggling again reaching enormous proportions. Lee had to reconcile himself to the fact that the army that entered Maryland so cheerfully was no longer the same body of men now by his side. "As far as I am able to judge," he told Davis while considering a possible advance on Hagerstown, "the hazard would be great and a reverse disastrous. I am, therefore, led to pause."[19]

Evidence of the army's disorganization was easy for all to see, but Lee requested an accurate field return to get some official count of the troops available to him. Remarkably, Dick Anderson's division was Lee's strongest, with nearly 6,300 men counted on the rolls of the field return. Exclusive of the cavalry and reserve artillery, the total count for the army was 41,520 men. By October 10, a subsequent field return indicated an increase in the size of Anderson's division to over 10,000 men, while the army overall grew to nearly 71,000 men, again discounting the cavalry division and reserve artillery. Those numbers illustrate how quickly new men arrived to take the place of the fallen, and how stragglers were rapidly returning to the fold. The army had been hemorrhaging men since the battle at Manassas in August, and some remained discouraged. J. J. Wilson of the 16th Mississippi finally wrote home in early October. "I have got my fill of fighting and am willing to let them alone if they will let us alone," he said, lamenting that many dead and wounded comrades were left in the enemy's hands north of the Potomac. Edmund Patterson of the 9th Alabama in Wilcox's brigade sat out the fighting in Maryland while recovering from a wound inflicted at Manassas. He received news of the regiment while at Gordonsville, Virginia by September 22 from another man wounded at Sharpsburg. "The entire regiment numbered only one hundred and thirty men in the battle," he was told, "and ours was a fair sample of the army. Two thirds of the men able for duty were on this side of the Potomac barefooted." The wounded comrade told "of hard times the boys had and I don't doubt it, living for days on green corn and apples don't improve the health of an army." Bailey McClellen of the 10th Alabama sustained an arm wound at Sharpsburg, and at first was doubtful that he would make it to the rear from the regiment's position. He finally found a field hospital before sundown. He and other wounded men started for Shepherdstown the next day, then on to Winchester, before receiving orders to continue south to Staunton on foot. The ninety-mile march "was pretty tough on wounded soldiers and no rations, and through a country which had been overrun by soldiers of both armies," McClellen recalled. After separating from his comrades, he fortunately fell in with the Negro cook from his company who was en route to Richmond. "Dan had money and I had none," remembered the unfortunate soldier, "and it was at a time I felt the great necessity for a friend he used his money as freely for me as he did for himself, and . . . I was saved the necessity of begging ration for the travel. I always had great respect for that old darkey as long as he lived for his kindness to me."[20]

Although the army was reconstituting, some took advantage of the situation in order to wander. John Mason of the 9th Alabama was only recently returned to the regiment after being wounded on the Peninsula that summer. He and two others found their comrades at Martinsburg, and "they were very glad to see us," he recalled, "for they gave us three cheers when we entered the camp." Nonetheless, when the men marched off a few days later, Mason and four others "went to straggling so we could have some fun." Mason threw away his shoes so he would have some excuse for why he was not able to keep up. By the time he caught up with his regiment they had been encamped for three days. Mason left no detailed record of what their "fun" entailed, but young soldiers like him were undoubtedly among those General Wilcox would have liked to see exhibit more discipline.[21]

The *Richmond Enquirer* reported on September 23, that "intelligence" had been received "confirming the account of the recent Confederate victory at Sharpsburg, but adding that our army had not wholly withdrawn to the South-side of the Potomac." The correspondent described the army's condition as "excellent, and the spirit of the troops, flushed with victory, high and warm." Such fabrications also contradicted northern newspaper reports of a Union victory as "sheer and shameless fabrications." The article described the army's withdrawal as "purely a matter of precaution, to provide against possible contingencies." The writer went so far as to say that despite Lee's desire to renew the attack the next day, he found that the federals had withdrawn from his front. An officer writing to the paper from the field named the army's wounded commanders and listed Anderson as having been "severely wounded in hip."[22]

Despite his wound and the devastating loss of leaders in his division, it was Anderson's responsibility to ensure the submission of official reports of the campaign in Maryland and to follow up to see to it that they were received and forwarded to army headquarters. Once again, either Anderson failed to submit his own report or it was lost. The records of his brigades contain the report of only a single temporary brigade commander. Only two after-action reports from the entire division are included in the records, one from the captain of the 16th Mississippi, which suffered the heaviest casualties of any regiment in the division in losing 84 of its 228 men. A second report addressed to Anderson from Colonel William Gibson of the 48th Georgia praised the "daring gallantry and bravery of our commanding General A. R. Wright." Despite receiving a severe wound to his leg, Gibson said that Wright remained on the field and had to be carried forward on a litter so that he could direct the brigade. Of Anderson, Gibson noted that the general "in following our brigade to the field, was also wounded long before reaching our advanced position." Gibson was obviously very proud of the brigade's performance that day in Anderson's absence, and his submission is clear evidence of his desire to make it known to his division commander and the army in general. "Of the gallantry and bravery of Wright's Brigade," he wrote, "let the advanced position they occupied, together with the casualties (in proportion to the number engaged) and the piles of dead Yankees or Irishmen and Dutch in our front, speak."[23]

A report from Wilcox's brigade written by the 8th Alabama's Major Hilary A. Herbert, who assumed command of the brigade when Col. Alfred Cumming was wounded early in the engagement, surfaced in a 1906 history of the regiment. Cumming stated he wrote it in consultation with fellow officers of the regiment in October 1864, and originally submitted it to the adjutant general of Alabama. Though he commanded for a good part of the day after Cumming and another more senior major fell wounded, Herbert reasoned that he never submitted an official report through normal army channels to his division commander "for what appears to me now the clearly insufficient reason that I was not called upon to do so."[24]

Of the divisional artillery, only Captain Marcellus N. Moorman of the Lynchburg Artillery mentioned the battle at all, and that came only in response to Lieutenant Colonel E. P. Alexander's mid-October inquiry about the battery's loss of "two 10-pounder Parrott guns and part of a caisson." Moorman reported only one gun lost at Sharpsburg after it was disabled and "hauled off some 800 yards." Returning later with a new carriage for the gun, Moorman's men found that "someone, supposing the gun abandoned, appropriated it."[25]

The lackadaisical manner in which Anderson treated his administrative responsibilities is both troubling and unfortunate. Division commanders often filled their reports with acclaim for the heroics of their subordinate officers and the men themselves, and such recognition was an obligation that Anderson too often let slip. The men deserved better recognition for their efforts. Moreover, though wounds and deaths often took unit leaders out of action, it was incumbent upon the remaining leaders to reconstruct the events as best they could. As Captain Herbert later claimed, no one had asked him. That is a failure of leadership at several levels, but of course, the ultimate responsibility rests with Anderson as the division commander, though Wilcox certainly must share some blame for not addressing the shortfall during his temporary reign over the division. Modest by nature and apathetic about advancing his own reputation, Anderson's indifference towards the praise anxiously sought by more zealous officers meant that his men also had to be content simply in having done their duty well. Despite those failings, the men in the ranks continued to revere him.

Chapter 10

Fredericksburg

Be resolved therefore to do your whole duty.

—R. H. Anderson, Circular to Anderson's Division, December 15, 1862

Recalling the division commanders in Longstreet's corps, Major Moxley Sorrel of Longstreet's staff echoed Micah Jenkins's evaluation of Dick Anderson as an indifferent officer when Sorrel likewise remarked that Anderson "was rather an interesting character. His courage was of the highest order," he wrote, "but he was indolent. His capacity and intelligence excellent, but it was hard to get him to use them." It is difficult to know whether Sorrel had come to that conclusion on his own, or whether he had overheard or participated in discussions with Longstreet along those lines, but Sorrel wrote those recollections around the turn of the century. His characterization of Anderson in the late fall of 1862 might have differed. Nevertheless, Sorrel's opinions were generally balanced and discerning, and his observations were likely accurate. One thing is clear; Anderson was a very likable man. He was, Sorrel concluded, "withal, of a nature so true and lovable that it goes against me to criticize him." Perhaps then, Sorrel might even have been overly generous in his evaluation. But in the fall of 1862, Anderson still served under Longstreet's able hand, and Sorrel's perceptive observation that Longstreet was able get more out of Dick Anderson than anyone else could was telling. Events over the next several months would illustrate his continued growth as a competent division commander, though there would be some shortcomings as well.[1]

The army's rapid growth after the struggle on the banks of Antietam Creek had badly strained its logistical supply chain, causing suffering from the onset of cold weather and shortages of matériel in the fall of 1862. Edwin Sherwood, an Alabama soldier in Wilcox's Brigade, wrote at the start of October that the army was "getting very short of provisions, we have not drawn anything to eat but beef and bread and it is playing out." More than just food was growing scarce though. Sherwood commented on the lack of pay, and that his regiment had "not had a change of clothes in 5 or 6 weeks. I am as dirty as a negro and almost shoeless," he wrote to his father. Half the regiment was barefooted. One soldier had gone without footwear for three weeks, yet he kept up with the regiment. Anderson found it necessary on November 28th to call the attention of the company commanders throughout his division to a previously issued order directing that the "men use the raw hides of slaughtered cattle in making moccasins for themselves as a substitute for shoes." Men were no longer to "be excused from any duty on account of being barefooted." It was not an ideal solution. The men sewed the green hides onto their feet before gathering closely around the campfires. There the hides would "commence to get dry and draw up and some of them had a nice time getting them off," recalled Corporal Mason of the 9th Alabama, "but when they did get them off they couldn't put them on again so that played the moccasins out very fast. Then they had to get us some shoes, which they did a couple of weeks later."[2]

The Shenandoah Valley provided safety for the army as it regained its strength behind the formidable crests of the Blue Ridge, but by the end of October, McClellan began a slow southward movement towards Warrenton, blocking the passes through the mountains as he went. The advance stirred the dormant Army of Northern Virginia into action, and Lee quickly sent Jackson off to Sperryville and Longstreet to Culpeper Court House. One Alabamian of Anderson's division recalled a forced march of over thirty-two miles in one day, and "when we halted for the night" he later wrote, "the boys were so tired that they lay right down where they halted without further ceremony." After that, the rush seemed unnecessary as others from Longstreet's Corps had already secured the ground near Culpeper. The Alabamians marched only about three more miles the next morning before lying in camp for another few days prior to taking up picket duties along the Rappahannock. Surprisingly, it was already a much-needed interlude. Veterans were unaccustomed to such hard marching after the long interlude since Antietam, while large numbers of new enlistees or those returning from wounds or leave were likewise unconditioned. They would all need time to become more seasoned and into top fighting trim. James J. Kirkpatrick of the 16th Mississippi in Featherston's Brigade noted "not half the army has kept up. Straggling," he opined, "has gone so long unpunished that it has become popular." In the meantime, the Union army's advance slowly ground to a halt around Warrenton under a new leader. Ambrose Burnside had taken command on November 10. He continued to concentrate his army in the hopes that it would lead Lee to believe that Culpeper or Gordonsville were his target, thus keeping the Rebel chieftain focused on the upper Rappahannock while plans for an attack at Fredericksburg took form. While the federals gathered their strength and resupplied, Lee's army remained inactive pending developments.[3]

One unfortunate event in Anderson's division occurred around this time when three members of the 9th Alabama of Wilcox's brigade were sentenced to be shot, most likely for desertion. One member of the firing squad was so distraught that he frantically pleaded with his comrades and offered $100 if someone would take his place. His captain finally had him excused, but nearly all the men played some role in the process of carrying out the sentence. The members of each company loaded the guns of those in the next company, and "when the order came to load the guns I didn't know whether to put a ball in or not," John Mason recalled, "but I came to the conclusion that the more balls the quicker the poor fellows would be put out of their misery. So I jammed her home." The sentenced men were kneeling with hands bound behind their backs, and when the order was given to shoot, Mason could see balls striking the dirt in front of them while others clipped off the branches of trees high over their heads. Some men, perhaps out of mercy, aimed true, and the doomed soldiers collapsed next to their coffins. Mason later wrote, ". . . every man in the regiment looked sorrowful for a few days till it all died away. Then everything got lively again and the order came for us to go on picket at the river." Commanders undoubtedly hoped the event would imprint a more long-lasting impression on the men and positively influence their behavior.[4]

Logistical issues and supply shortages continued to plague the army. Anderson reported in early December that there were still almost four hundred men in his division without arms, with the number increasing daily as his ranks swelled. He sought permission to send an officer to Richmond in an effort to secure needed arms and other supplies. The influx of new recruits also added to the sick rolls as young men previously unexposed to a variety of diseases contracted the many types circulating throughout the army at any given time. Smallpox ran its course through the camps.[5]

Lee had formalized the army's structure in early November. Longstreet and Jackson were elevated to the rank of lieutenant general with command of one of the army's two corps. In Longstreet's First Corps, Virginian George Pickett and Texan John Bell Hood now headed divisions at the rank of major general, joining those of Anderson, McLaws, and Walker, and a number of colonels were elevated to brigadier general to fill positions vacated by promotions or incapacity. Roger Pryor was reassigned from Anderson's division as well, pushed out of the way first by Lee's intended promotion of Carnot Posey to brigade command, and secondly owing to the transfer of three Florida regiments from Pryor's brigade to that of Massachusetts native Edward Aylesworth Perry, former colonel of the 2nd Florida Infantry. Promoted to brigadier general in May 1862, Perry assumed command of his three-regiment-strong brigade of Floridians on November 10. Lee tried to form brigades from regiments drawn from a single state and under a commander who was also a native of that state. This caused one Alabama regiment from Pryor's old brigade to go to Wilcox and one Virginia unit to Kemper's brigade in Pickett's division. Pryor's former brigade ceased to exist and he thus joined Major General Gustavus Smith's command near Richmond.[6]

By November 18, Burnside put his army in motion towards Fredericksburg. Lee responded by assuming defensive positions there as he awaited some definitive indication that Burnside planned a Rappahannock crossing. The inactivity of Burnside's army dragged on once again when he reached the banks of the Rappahannock, allowing Lee to strengthen his lines and entrench where the topography did not naturally support his position. Lee did not intend to oppose Burnside's crossing because the high ground of Stafford Heights on the Federal's side of the river indisputably commanded the floodplain adjacent to the Rappahannock. Instead, Lee left a token force in the city to annoy and delay the Union engineers, bridge-builders, and those who crossed at first in small numbers. He placed his main battle line farther back on higher ground where the men were less vulnerable to the batteries ranged along Stafford Heights. With their exposure reduced, Confederates were strongly entrenched on higher ground with concentrated artillery support, while attacking Union infantry would cross an open plain beyond the river and the city.[7]

On November 19, Anderson's division anchored Lee's left flank at Taylor's Hill, adjacent to the Rappahannock. From Taylor's Hill two lines of hills stretched eastward, the lower range culminated at a point known as Mayre's Heights just behind the town of Fredericksburg, while the upper range of hills provided greater protection against the Union batteries due their greater elevation. On the right, Anderson's lines connected with those of McLaws's division, situated squarely behind the city of Fredericksburg. Robert Ransom's small two-brigade division stood in reserve within easy supporting distance of Marye's Heights. A canal and a millrace that ran parallel to Anderson's front and reduced the likelihood of an enemy crossing there vouchsafed his position. The division stretched from Wilcox's brigade lines at Taylor's Hill, followed by Wright, Mahone, Perry, and Featherston holding the far right on Marye's Heights between the Orange Plank Road and Hazel Run.[8]

Anderson was also concerned with keeping watch on enemy movements near Banks' Ford, the closest natural river crossing which lay a few miles up-river from Fredericksburg. He personally examined the ground around the ford on December 5 to determine whether the enemy's pickets could be overwhelmed and captured there. Longstreet had apparently requested such an exploration, and after making his survey Anderson told his chief that he doubted "the practicability of capturing the picket, but I am prepared to make the attempt and to execute your orders." Longstreet's sensible response to such a lukewarm endorsement was to do nothing. Closer to the Taylor House at the left of the Confederate line was the water works dam, another source of concern for Anderson. He instructed Wilcox to post two of his companies there with another two stationed along the road running down to the river. Anderson advised Wilcox to "keep six men always on guard at the water's edge so as to keep a close watch upon all the doings of the enemy near the Dam." As the army maintained its watch on the river, each commander listened carefully for the pre-arranged signal alarm of "two guns fired in rapid succession" to be given upon the enemy's attempt to cross over. Upon hearing the signal, each unit would form rapidly and remain "under arms awaiting orders."[9]

Activity in the Union camps in the early morning hours of December 11 indicated that an attempt to cross the river was imminent. Before daylight the long-awaited signal guns barked out a warning that drifted across the hills and misty river valley. Anderson's brigades fell into formation at their camps and marched rapidly to take up their positions. Edmund Patterson of the 9th Alabama recalled that "having lain down with my sword and pistol buckled around me, I only had to raise up and shake myself and my toilet was made." Others were equally prepared and "before the echo [from the signal gun] had died in the distance we were up and ready for anything." In the city proper, William Barksdale's brigade of McLaws's division stood poised to dispute the laying of pontoon bridges across the Rappahannock. They were supported by the 8th Florida and the 3rd Georgia of Anderson's division. The Georgians would suffer few losses in disputing the crossing of Union troops that day, but Captain David Lang's 8th Florida had a more trying time. Lang had been associated with Anderson since Pensacola and the Fort Pickens raid in October 1861, when he was a non-commissioned officer with the 1st Florida. The graduate of the Georgia Military Academy was continuing to develop as a sound and effective leader. Lang had the bulk of his regiment posted along the river near an old ferry crossing where Union troops were attempting to construct a pontoon bridge that would become known as the "upper crossing." Barksdale soon saw that federals were also attempting another crossing down-river from a destroyed railroad bridge at the city wharves below the town. This location would take on the name "middle crossing." He instructed Lang to detach three companies to resist the attempt to traverse the river there. Captain William Baya, charged with that task, at first objected heartily upon seeing the spot he was to occupy, claiming that the position was "so exposed and admitting of so little means of escape" that it was foolhardy to attempt to hold it. Lang had to repeat the order before Baya would finally obey. He was to support companies from Barksdale's 17th Mississippi under Captain Andrew R. Govan, but that officer had already posted his own men in the partial cover afforded by nearby buildings and warehouses. Baya's companies occupied a totally exposed location on the riverbank. Perhaps at least wisely if not bravely, Baya acted accordingly given Lee's intent not to seriously contest the crossing. Fearful that fire from Union artillery that enfiladed his lines would decimate his men, Baya repeatedly declined to reveal his position by firing on the Union bridge builders. Eventually the Union artillery did open fire, and despite his expressed desire to retreat by mid-afternoon, Baya had no choice but to hold the spot until surrounded and forced to surrender. Govan, however, later complained that Baya had disobeyed his orders throughout the day out of fear for his safety, and that the capture of his men most likely resulted from "inefficiency and a fear of being killed in the retreat."[10]

The main body of Lang's troops was more heavily engaged repelling the Union engineers and bridge builders upriver at the foot of Hawke Street, but they too came in for some criticism from the officer commanding the 17th Mississippi. Lang dispersed his companies along the riverfront just above the spot where the bridges were slowly taking shape at the upper crossing. The rest of the 17th Mississippi connected to Lang's right flank and held the area directly in front and below the bridge. At first, the Floridians held their own and "acted gallantly," at least until Lang fell with a serious head wound at around 11 AM after a Union shell collapsed a brick chimney on him. After that, the companies "seemed troubled and in want of a commander," reported Lieutenant Colonel John Fiser of the Mississippi regiment. He went so far as to make mention of the odd behavior of a certain Florida lieutenant whose name he later magnanimously claimed he could not recall. That frightened officer "so far forgot himself as to draw his pistol and threaten to kill some of my sharpshooters if they fired again, as it would draw the enemy's fire on his position." Nonetheless, Lang later noted that the fire of the troops holding the riverbank had repeatedly sent the Union attackers scattering for shelter. Furthermore, he contended, "each attempt of the pontoniers to continue their work was met by a well-directed fire from my command." The Floridians held their position despite being "exposed to a galling fire of shot, shell, canister, and musketry" until ordered to withdraw at about 4 PM. Their performance after Lang's wounding remained subject to criticism however, and one Union engineer constructing the bridge even recalled hearing the outraged shouts of the Mississippians calling to the demoralized Florida men—"Why in hell don't you fire!" McLaws complimented Lang in his report of the battle, but stated blandly that after his wounding his regiment "rendered but little assistance." As it was, the 8th Florida sustained the highest losses of any regiment in Anderson's division since few others were actually engaged so directly in the fighting. Seven men were killed, thirty-seven wounded, and forty-four others captured or missing, the latter owing to the surrender of Baya's detached companies.[11]

During much of the battle, most men of Anderson's division remained protected from the sustained Union artillery fire by the hills and undulating ground in front of their position. Walter Moore of the 2nd Florida told his wife that his regiment was held in reserve and "none of us got hurt." During the battle, his regiment received a "beautiful flag" accompanied by a letter from the governor. The reading of the letter frequently halted for a time because "the thunder of the artillery was so incessant." The 9th Alabama likewise suffered no casualties while posted to a relatively safe area in a hollow. Corporal John Mason of the 9th later recalled that, unlike his own regiment, the 11th Alabama of his brigade "was on top of the hill and when the enemy commenced firing the shells would pass over our heads and would bust in amongst them and hit somebody every time." Things were not quite so bad as he thought, however, and the 11th suffered only eight men wounded. Many of the men later remembered the cold weather and exposure during the nights as the primary cause of much of their discomfort. Though the daytime temperatures were unseasonably balmy, Anderson reported afterwards that Featherston's and Perry's brigades had lain "four days and nights in an open field without shelter and without fire." General Kershaw likewise mentioned that the night of December 12 was so brutally cold that one man in his brigade died and another was disabled. Lieutenant Clark of the 9th Alabama recalled that women and children evacuating the city had filed past their lines on the frozen road. Many were in tears and had fled without sufficient clothing to guard against the extreme cold. Clark's men removed their own winter overcoats and distributed them to the freezing women and children.[12]

Meanwhile, as Union forces struggled to complete their bridges, Barksdale continued to resist the crossing. The resolute Mississippian held the town much longer than anyone had a right to expect, allowing additional time for Lee's army to prepare. Time and numbers eventually worked against the defenders and after gaining a foothold on the Confederate side of the river on December 11, Burnside marshaled his forces in preparation for a concerted attack. That would not take place until December 13. Those of Anderson's division in a position to observe the pageantry throughout the day on the 12th had a spectacular view of long lines of Union infantry clad in sky blue overcoats and trousers streaming across the river against the dazzling white background provided by a recent snowfall. The scene increased Lee's confidence that Burnside's entire force was on the field and the crossing there was not just a diversion. He ordered Jackson's corps, until then held in reserve, to move forward to join him. Most of those men filed into line on the army's right flank with sufficient time to prepare to receive the attack coming from Burnside's troops then filing across the pontoon bridges downriver known as the "lower crossing." On Lee's left flank, the men of Anderson's division were fortunate that the brunt of the attack would likely fall elsewhere. As the fog cleared off on the morning of December 13, the booming sounds of artillery fire and rifle volleys emanating from Lee's far right flank began to waft across the valley. Most of Burnside's troops who had crossed near Fredericksburg at the upper and middle crossings appeared to be forming in the town and below it, but not directly in front of Anderson's position. As the Union force gathered in strength, however, both Longstreet and Anderson expressed some concern about the integrity of their own lines. In Anderson's case, this was in part because the terrain on some parts of the field was less favorable than on others, despite the obstacle presented by the canal. The length of Anderson's front and the resulting thinness of the line in several places led him to believe that would be unable to resist a determined attack. Longstreet had already moved Robert Ransom's small division into position along Marye's Heights on the afternoon of the 11th, and after some indecisive shuffling back and forth, Ransom's North Carolinians finally took a permanent place in the battle line supporting Brigadier General Thomas R. R. Cobb's Georgians posted in the sunken road along the Heights. That reinforcement of McLaws's line allowed Anderson to slide Featherston's brigade to the left of the Plank Road and thereby shorten his own division front, yet still he feared he was too weak along other sections of line, and his fear would become even more evident once the Union attack was underway.[13]

Burnside's plan for the assault called for Major General Edwin V. Sumner's Right Grand Division to hold the Confederate left flank in place while other Union divisions assaulted the Confederate right. Sumner's forces assembled in Fredericksburg before moving into the fields that sloped uphill approximately eight hundred yards to Marye's Heights, just to Anderson's right and almost directly above the town. Featherston's brigade was nearest the point of action. Anderson ordered it forward until it was about a hundred yards in rear of Captain Victor Maurin's Donaldsonville (Louisiana) Artillery, whose guns were firing rapidly from behind an épaulement. Featherson recalled that his regiments were "subjected to a very heavy fire from the enemy's artillery immediately in our front, and extending up the river to our left." Despite that, the Mississippians found some protection by lying down as much as possible in a roadbed. He thought the Union artillery fire enfilading his position on its left flank "could not have been more rapid and galling on any part of the line." Anderson instructed Featherston to hold his position and to protect the guns by advancing if Union infantry moved towards the battery. Although brigade after brigade of Sumner's Grand Division soon battered itself to oblivion attacking Brigadier General Cobb's Georgians and Ransom's Tarheels holding a sunken road at Marye's Heights just to Featherston's right, no Union infantry ever ventured directly towards the guns in his front. Featherston endured the Union artillery fire all through the battle, though Maurin's guns in his front received most of the fire. The artillery captain lost one man killed and five wounded in his battery. At one point Captain Osmun Latrobe of Longstreet's staff and Lieutenant R. P. Landry were compelled to assist in manhandling one gun out of its position in the bastion in order to bring it to bear on a group of federals who were concealed from most of the Confederate fire and were making ready to charge Marye's Heights. One gunner was killed almost immediately by a piece of shrapnel from a bursting shell, and the exposed gun was preparing to loose its fourth round when it was disabled by a shot that simultaneously wounded three more of the men. "But the object was accomplished;" Maurin reported, "some fled, some were killed, and the remainder dared not leave their cover." Anderson must not have observed that action as he did not specifically pay tribute to the behavior of his gallant Louisiana artillerymen in his own report, but Maurin came in for accolades in Ransom's report. "His conduct was admirable," he wrote in praise of Maurin, "for during the time he was exposed to a direct fire of six and an enfilade fire of four guns." In addition to Ransom's tribute, and because the Donaldsonville Artillery was attached to Perry's brigade, that officer too complimented the men's behavior noting that they "stood bravely and faithfully at their posts," while "the guns were handled with masterly skill and with great effect."[14]

Anderson did mention General Mahone, recently returned to his brigade after recovering from his wound at Second Manassas. Anderson's reference almost certainly was to Mahone having identified the vital position occupied by Maurin's guns. Mahone's recommendation for placing the guns there was likely due to his having made surveys of the area long ago while with the Valley Plank Road Company. Anderson praised him for pointing it out, as well as for rendering "very efficient service, assisting in the construction of the battery which drove them [the enemy] from their place of shelter." The battery's service was one of the most significant contributions made by Anderson's division in the fight, and through Featherston's brigade's exposure in supporting Maurin, his Mississippians suffered the division's second highest losses in killed and wounded.[15]

Anderson watched with some trepidation as wave after wave of blue-clad infantry charged and fell on the slopes below Marye's Heights to his right. Still, they came on. Cobb's Georgians, facing the brunt of the assaults, eventually reported to McLaws that they were running low on ammunition.

Staff officers hurried ordnance wagons to the front while McLaws shifted reinforcements to the spot. According to McLaws's later recollections, at around the same time—approximately 1 PM—Cobb reported meeting an apprehensive Dick Anderson, who told him, "if the attack was turned on him he would retire his troops to the hills in his rear." Other post-war accounts contend that Cobb received a note to that effect directly from Longstreet. Cobb reacted to the suggestion that Anderson might be compelled to retire and that he should conform to the movements of Anderson's division with the chagrin expected from a commander then hotly engaged with the enemy and in the midst of repulsing repeated assaults. "If they wait for me to fall back," the fiery secessionist supposedly exclaimed, "they will wait a long time." Nonetheless, Anderson feared that Wilcox's more exposed line closer to the river rendered it vulnerable to being thrown back, requiring the division's withdrawal to stronger positions. The impact of such a move threatened to leave Cobb's left flank exposed in the sunken road, thereby compelling his withdrawal. With massed firepower in his front however, Cobb's retreat to higher ground behind the road would have entailed disastrous losses. He sent McLaws word of the troubling communication from Anderson, and McLaws claimed he went immediately to consult with Longstreet to determine if that was the general's understanding as to what Anderson's course of action ought to be if he was pressed hard. Meanwhile, McLaws said he went himself to observe the disposition of Anderson's division, later commenting that the "defenses and preparations to resist an attack were, in my opinion, inconsiderable and incomplete." McLaws asserted in a post-war address long after Anderson's death that he took it upon himself to see that Cobb's flank was secure by having Kershaw's brigade poised to protect it and then sending two of Kershaw's regiments into the fight at the sunken road. That self-congratulatory version of events is suspect, however. Kershaw reported being ordered to send two regiments to support Cobb at around 1 PM that day and "within a few minutes after" being ordered to advance his entire brigade to the sunken road. Upon being informed that Cobb had been wounded, Kershaw rushed forward alone to assume command at the sunken road. The original two regiments dispatched as reinforcements arrived just as Kershaw took command, and it was nearly 3 PM before the remainder of his brigade was able to file into the line. It seems unlikely that the exchanges of notes, the consultation with Longstreet, and McLaws's exploration of Anderson's line could have occurred so quickly, all at around 1 PM when Cobb relayed Anderson's concerns.[16]

Longstreet also dispatched two brigades from Pickett's division to reinforce the most vulnerable points along his front, probably at around 2 PM. One went to support Ransom and another replaced Kershaw's South

Carolinians in the battle line. A note from Longstreet's aide Moxley Sorrel soon arrived telling Anderson that Longstreet had "reinforced the position to your right with all the troops he can well spare at present. If you find them pressed," Longstreet cautioned, "it will be necessary for you to send them assistance." Obviously fearing any surprise reaction or withdrawal on Anderson's part that might uncover the army's left flank, Longstreet further cautioned that he wanted to be "well advised of any movement you make," and that he would endeavor to support his position and that of Ransom's if possible. After Cobb's mortal wounding at the sunken road, Kershaw's entire brigade had rushed down the slope and jumped pell-mell into the sunken road behind the stone wall. With Kershaw then in command of the awful fight raging along Marye's Heights and with the addition of his South Carolinians to the fray, Rebels along the stone wall fronting the sunken road now stood four-deep in many places. Union assaults continued nearly incessantly into the early evening, with a final, impetuous charge setting out at around 5 PM and lasting for over an hour. Some attackers got within thirty yards of the Confederate line, but Kershaw recalled that the ranks of intrepid federals mostly began to shatter by the time they got within 100 paces. Burnside finally called a halt to the senseless slaughter, and with the exception of Featherston's brigade and the two regiments of Floridians who had suffered badly on the 11th, none of Anderson's infantry was directly engaged in any fighting or met with any significant loss, though there were some casualties from the shelling and sharpshooters. In the 16th Mississippi of Featherston's brigade, James Kirkpatrick recalled that a shell burst amongst the regiment, "inflicting some damage," even before the men advanced to their position behind Maurin's battery. Once in position, a corporal of his company was "killed by a Minie ball, shot perhaps from front of Marye's Heights." Featherston himself opined the short casualty list "can only be accounted for under Providence," but also because men were able to remain prone and take "advantage of every hill and crest as a protection."[17]

Anderson's division experienced the battle largely as an artillery fight. The batteries arrayed along the division's front included the guns of Lane's battery of (Alan S.) Cutt's (Georgia) battalion on the far left of the division's line, commanded by Captain John Lane. To their right along the line was Huger's (Virginia) battery directed by Captain Frank Huger, then Lewis's (Virginia) battery under Captain John W. Lewis. Lewis's battery, positioned on the heights overlooking a river ford that ran between Falmouth and Fredericksburg lost one man killed and two wounded, which General Wilcox found to be quite amazing under the circumstances. "It would seem to be almost incredible that the loss should have been so inconsiderable; for, from a point near a mile above Falmouth, on a commanding height, there was a six-gun battery of rifle pieces that enfiladed my line," he reported later, noting also the position of three additional enemy batteries that were located even closer to him. Still others were at least near enough to reach his lines and beyond, so that "there could not have been less than fifty pieces that bore upon us." Lewis himself reported firing about 400 rounds from the time of the initial river crossing through Sunday night after the battle. Next along the front came Lieutenant William T. Peet commanding Captain Charles R. Grandy's Norfolk (Virginia) Light Artillery Blues, followed by Maurin's Donaldsonville Artillery. With the great discrepancy in artillery strength apparent to all, Anderson noted in his report that the while the batteries were subjected to heavy enemy fire, their commanders largely adhered to their orders and declined to engage in an artillery duel despite the provocation. Instead, conscious of their vulnerability and a limited ammunition supply, they focused on the importance of repulsing infantry attacks. Lewis recalled orders not to waste ammunition and claimed he "only fired when certain of doing them damage." Maurin's pieces, closest to the point of the Union attacks, drew exceptionally heavy return fire. He later reported that during the battle on the 13th, as the effect of his guns told on the attacking blue-clad infantry, the enemy maneuvered eight guns into position at the edge of the city to try to neutralize his battery, which had already fired over 200 rounds into the Union infantry formations. The artillery then "opened on me so furiously they succeeded in diverting my fire," Maurin recalled. The battery was fighting for its survival at that point, with enemy shells "so well directed that I could only occasionally give a round to the infantry whenever the opportunity occurred." In the midst of that heavy fire, artillerists heroically dragged the 10-pound Parrott out of its protected cover to break up a concealed mass of Union infantry preparing to assault the Confederate lines as previously noted.[18]

Anderson's fears that the masses of Union troops would be unleashed against his over-stretched lines passed for the time being, but Burnside's huge army stood poised to renew the battle at any point, and even Lee believed Burnside had yet to make his main assault. Once the firing died down that Saturday, the agonizing cries of the many wounded men filled the air, occasionally punctuated by the sounds of entrenching or by shots directed at men desperate or foolish enough to move about or show themselves. As night fell on the grisly scene, some Confederate regiments sought to deter an attack in the darkness by firing random volleys across the field. Anderson's battle line remained unchanged except that Maurin's hard-fought battery withdrew and the Bedford (Virginia) artillery replaced it. No officer whose troops stood in the sunken road agreed to give up that post of honor, and the men of Anderson's division remained on the sidelines as a result.[19]

Little transpired throughout the day on the 14th, and after the morning fog burned off it revealed only "a distant line of cavalry vedettes." Cold and weary men in butternut and gray remained under arms awaiting a renewal of the contest. Burnside had assaulted Lee's right and center, and now it was unlikely but hardly out of the question to think that subsequent assaults could come against the Confederate left. In anticipation of an impending clash, Anderson issued a circular that day with an inspiring message relayed to the troops throughout his division. It began by bringing their attention to "the greatness of the occasion now presented to them. Let every man of us summon all his spirit and all his strength to this encounter," he exhorted them. He noted that a victory now might well end the war, while a defeat would surely lead to many more bloody battles. Anderson sought to put the onus for that victory onto the shoulders of every single soldier under his command, and each was encouraged to feel that on their individual "efforts may hang the success or failure which will be attended with consequences of such magnitude. Be resolved therefore to do your whole duty. Think of this only, and trustingly leave all the rest to the Almighty Disposer of all events." By the 15th, Longstreet must have shared Anderson's trepidation about the outcome of a vigorous assault on the Confederate left despite the water obstacles presented by the canal and millrace along Anderson's front, which would have required Union forces either to span them under fire or to use only the existing small bridges. Nearly all the ground to the north of Fredericksburg between the city and the canal was unsuitable for the passage of large bodies of infantry, however. It was an area known locally as Gordon's Marsh. Burnside could also use the hiatus to try to cross in force above Lee's positions and fall upon Anderson's flank. The situation seemed secure, yet it warranted some caution, and both Longstreet and Anderson remained apprehensive. Longstreet exhorted his friend to keep his men ready and make them "understand that they must hold their ground against anything that comes." He urged Anderson to "Keep them in good spirits, for this will probably be their last battle if they win it." Conversely, he said in echoing Anderson's observations on the previous day, "if they lose it they may have to fight forty more." Longstreet then moved on to what was likely his real purpose in penning such a note. Certainly, he wanted his friend to motivate and inspire the troops, but he also wanted to spur him to greater exertions in leading his men. Anderson's gentle heart must have sunk just a little as he read his old comrade's admonition: "Some of your troops have been unsteady in several battles," Longstreet wrote, "let them know that they now have an opportunity to establish themselves as the steadiest of veterans." The compassionately relayed criticism was implicit nonetheless. As their commander, Anderson bore ultimate responsibility for the conduct of his troops. In light of Longstreet's criticism of the division's performance, the encouragement Anderson hoped to provide to his men as he penned his own missive now boosted his own resolve as well.[20]

Steeling themselves for a continuation of the fight, the men waited anxiously throughout the 15th, yet it too "passed off with little or no firing." Filled with wind and rain, that night was again extremely uncomfortable. Daylight revealed the river valley around Fredericksburg blanketed once again with a heavy fog. As the weather cleared, men could see that Burnside's army had withdrawn back across the river. "Not a vestige of a living Yankee was to be seen," wrote a news correspondent, "and from many hearts went up thanksgiving to God for the victory and for His mercy in sparing our lives." Weary southerners cheered themselves on the triumph and soon trudged back to their camps after having lain in line of battle for five entire days. The mettle of Anderson's division would be tested another time. The battle had been a resounding triumph for Lee's army, and Lafayette McLaws one of its prime architects. In missteps during the Maryland Campaign, he had failed to secure Crampton's Gap, allowed federal cavalry to escape from Harper's Ferry and capture a portion of Longstreet's train, and took too long to reach the battlefield. His performance at Fredericksburg redeemed all. He came in for much praise from both Lee and Longstreet. It was only in conjunction with other commanders whose "gallant divisions" had been "deprived of their opportunity by the unexpected and hasty retreat of the enemy," that Dick Anderson, through no fault of his own, was mentioned.[21]

Chapter 11

Winter Camp on the Rappahannock, 1862–63

Oh Ma, prepare to meet me where there is no separation.

—Miles Lewis to Amy Lewis,
March 23, 1863

Anderson was fortunate to have Sallie nearby in Richmond throughout the fall and winter of 1862–63. She occupied herself in social intercourse with the other female notables of the city, including South Carolina's Mary Boykin Chesnut—one of Anderson's boyhood acquaintances and the wife of former US Senator James Chesnut Jr. Mrs. Anderson proved a popular guest, often called upon to entertain at gatherings, once that winter as part of "matinee musicale" hosted by Mrs. Jefferson Davis where Sallie sang accompanied on harp. Sallie mostly remained safely in Richmond while her husband was in the field, and Anderson devoted his energies to soldiering during much of the fall and early winter when the Union presence immediately across the Rappahannock still offered a threat. The couple probably exchanged visits with some frequency though, particularly after the immediate danger of another Union advance had evaporated in the winter's cold.

Despite the proximity, exchanging visits between the two cities was at that time no simple matter. A trip by rail between the capital and Fredericksburg was just under sixty miles, but with train speeds averaging just fifteen or twenty miles per hour, it could have taken nearly four hours. Sallie came to Fredericksburg for a longer period in the late spring of 1863, but the army did not remain stationary for long after that and she departed when her husband marched off towards Pennsylvania. She was back in Richmond in September 1863 when Major Charles Venable, General Lee's aide-de-camp., and Colonel James Chesnut were at a dinner party "ridiculing the weakness" of some men of importance in revealing news about the army or "secrets of state." The conversation was lighthearted, and Sallie mentioned a recent letter from her husband in which he injudiciously advised her to "remain in Richmond—we may be ordered there at any moment." Mrs. Chesnut, for one, considered Anderson "the most silent and discreet of men," and the party no doubt laughed off his minor indiscretion when one of them exclaimed, "That's nothing! The best of men will tell any lie to keep their wives out of camp. Very few men can bear their wives trailing after them to the army." Anderson was similarly "silent and discreet" in his treatment of newspaper reporters. One *Savannah Morning News* correspondent visited the general near Fredericksburg that winter, finding him unfailingly courteous, but in keeping with his reserved manner, the correspondent went away without a story. "The General disliked publicity," recalled one acquaintance, and "he thought newspaper correspondents did much harm and no good."[1] Personal experience later sustained his opinion.

Although Sallie occasionally visited her husband during that winter, leisure time was an uncommon luxury for most men in the army. Soldiers typically kept busy constructing defensive works, though proper tools were in high demand and short supply. Anderson reported to Longstreet on January 21, 1863, that rifle trenches "on the river above the town are progressing, but are not yet completed. The total insufficiency of the supply of tools keeps back the work," he complained before inquiring if he could "get any more from any quarter?" Besides overseeing such work, Anderson had myriad administrative tasks to perform. That same day he reported to Longstreet that an investigation into "charges against certain officers of the 8th Florida Regiment in the late battle" had not reached "any satisfactory conclusion." This was a reference to the criticism from Lieutenant Colonel John Fiser of the 17th Mississippi, who had officially reported that after Captain Lang's injury on December 11th, the Floridians behaved badly and a lieutenant even threatened to shoot the Mississippi sharpshooters if they continued to fire and expose his position. Anderson identified the lieutenant as Hector Bruce. The investigation also pertained to Captain A. R. Govan's official statements that Captain Baya and his small contingent of Floridians refused to obey commands to fire on the federals who were building the pontoon bridge below the town. Anderson recommended referral of the matter to an official court of inquiry because he found it "impossible to get at the whole truth without having all parties examined." Up to that point, he was able to conclude only that the statements made by the Mississippians were "contradicted by the officers of the [Florida] regiment." By then Captain Lang had returned to duty, "thanks to a thick skull" as he wrote lightheartedly about his concussion.[2]

Anderson's failure to discover the truth of the matter may have been an indication that he was inclined to let the whole thing drop, possibly to avoid making a determination that might reflect badly on his own men. If there was any further investigation, the results must have been equally inconclusive. Lieutenant Bruce, wounded at Fredericksburg, later advanced to the rank of captain. Captain Baya likewise received promotion to major, then to lieutenant colonel in June 1863, so neither suffered any lasting effects from the allegations.[3]

Anderson completed his official report of the battle at Fredericksburg in a timely fashion, as did his brigade commanders. He even found time to catch up on some overdue obligations, such as writing to Adjutant General Cooper recommending Colonel John Bratton of the 6th South Carolina for promotion to brigadier general based on his actions at the battle of Seven Pines. There, Anderson wrote, Bratton led his men against a greatly superior force driving them two miles from the original line. Bratton was captured after he sustained a severe arm wound and accidentally wandered into Union lines during the confused ebb and flow of the battle. By the time Bratton returned to command of his regiment in late October 1862, Anderson was commanding his own division, leaving the 6th South Carolina with Pickett. Anderson failed to acknowledge Bratton's gallantry, but he now sought to rectify that. "His conduct excited my admiration," he told Cooper, "and I am happy to perform this rather tardy act of justice." There was no action taken then however, and Bratton's promotion would not come until 1864. In the meantime, Bratton took it in stride then and later, noting modestly after finding that someone had been promoted over him in early February 1863, "it is a great deal, perhaps, enough for such a man as I am to be spoken of for distinguished position." Even when finally promoted to brigadier general to replace Micah Jenkins in May 1864, the kindly Bratton attributed his elevation to "the merit of my men. They richly deserved it whether I do or not."[4]

The issue of promotions in the army had long plagued the government. President Davis hoped the Congress in Richmond could agree upon some system of ridding the army of incompetent officers, and on October 13, 1862, the Legislature passed a law authorizing the appointment of examining boards to determine an officer's qualifications for command. Once the army was in a position to carry out that task, Anderson embraced the idea at once, issuing orders for boards to "examine into cases of such officers . . . as may be brought to their attention for the purpose of determining their qualifications for the discharge of [their] duties."[5]

The structure of Anderson's division remained unchanged over the winter except that Carnot Posey, formerly of the 16th Mississippi, now led Winfield Scott Featherston's Mississippi brigade. Featherston voluntarily transferred to the Mississippi Department after General Joseph E. Johnston's January request for an additional brigadier general at Vicksburg. Featherston had been absent sick for several months, apparently with some prospect of not rejoining the army. Lee had already submitted Posey's name for promotion to brigadier general in October while Featherston was ill, but he soon returned unexpectedly to his command, thus leaving Posey with no position.

Lee hoped to find another place for Featherston, as he seems to have preferred to have Posey in the job. Posey, a Mississippi lawyer and planter, had attended law school at the University of Virginia and was a veteran of the Mexican War, where he served as a lieutenant in the future President Davis's 1st Mississippi Rifles. He had already demonstrated his capability for command by leading the brigade in Featherston's absence. With Featherson now headed west, Posey was secure in his new role at the head of the Mississippi brigade.[6]

Confederates were constantly on alert that fall and winter, but there was no action after the ignominious end to Burnside's January attempt to make too early a start to the spring campaign. There were sound reasons for armies traditionally settling into winter quarters, largely in consideration of poor road conditions and sheltering the men. Burnside set out on his "Mud March," during what had otherwise been a dry January of 1863. By the end of the first day's march on the 20th, the weather blew decisively in the Confederacy's favor when a slow-moving storm began to drop rain torrentially. Roads and adjacent fields rapidly turned into quagmires. After nearly five days of struggling desperately through knee-deep mud, dejected Union soldiers returned to their camps. The path of the retreat sometimes carried them close to the Rappahannock's banks where they were subjected to further humiliation by the jeers of the elated Rebels, some of whom had tacked up signs reading "Burnside Stuck in the mud" and other insults.[7]

In response to Burnside's march, Anderson's division reinforced the crossing at U.S. Ford on the Rappahannock. The relatively hard surfaces of the Plank Road and the macadamized Orange Turnpike facilitated the Confederates' ability to move more quickly. Nonetheless, once the storm got underway the men suffered greatly because of marching off hurriedly without their supply wagons. Nearly all were compelled to sleep in the open without shelter in inclement weather and severe cold. In the 6th Virginia of Mahone's brigade, which had moved to U.S. Ford on the 15th, many of the men had at least brought a tent fly to provide some modest covering. Others had more warning of the impending movement.

As early as January 16, Anderson had alerted his other brigade commanders to "hold themselves in readiness to move at a moment's notice." Already there had been "indications that the enemy are about to make an advance." Then Wright's brigade had been directed to "move at once" on January 18, as soon as the threat from Burnside began to materialize. The Georgians took up positions about four miles from the ford and Wright established communication with the pickets already on the river. Anderson instructed Wright to try to conceal his movements and his campfires as much as possible. Most of the freezing and soggy soldiers gladly pitched in to construct earthworks in an effort to stay warm, and Anderson further instructed Wright that upon finishing the earthworks around U.S. Ford he should begin to construct rifle pits at Ely's Ford on the Rapidan. As rain continued to fall, Anderson also found it necessary to order that pickets keep their rifles unloaded except when absolutely required. The heavy rains destroyed the loaded ammunition, which he noted was "too difficult to replace to further justify it."[8]

Others in his division suffered less from the bad weather and more from boredom, and at least one Floridian, David Lang, from a touch of ennui. Lang was glad for a few minutes' relief from his companions' "stereotyped remarks" on such topics as the availability of food, Burnside's next move, and "the 'state of the country.'" He instead expounded to his cousin Annie on the "strangely contradictory" idea of "winter in the 'Old Dominion,'" where its "noble sons" had forsaken all the old pleasures of the hunt, "the dinner-party and the merry jingle of the sleighbells." Instead, "the gay sportsman chases now, the larger, yet scarcely more noble game from the 'Faderland' and 'Green Erin,'" he wrote in reference to the Union's immigrant soldiers. Instead of dwelling "in bitterness upon the gay scenes that are gone. Let us rather turn with renewed energy to the stern realities of the present, and the glorious work before us." What his cousin thought of his melancholy musings is unknown, but it seems clear that the dreary and wet days of January 1863 were already affecting more than just men's bodies.[9]

Others were glad to learn that their efforts to prevent a crossing were not in vain, even though they acknowledged that the weather had been the real factor in turning Burnside away. "Apparently our shivering was of some value after all," wrote one. Yet even subsequent sunny weather failed to prevent some writers from descending pensively to the depths of sadness. John Bratton eloquently blamed the bright sunrise on Sunday, January 25, for "utterly deluding the poor little birds who were chirping with all the lividness and gayety of spring. The scene was and is, however, only suggestive to my perverse mind of sad reflections. The bitter disappointment to which the little birds are destined, is indicative of that in store for the high and wise man who will use this glorious and life giving weather in preparation for the deeds of bloodshed and havoc."[10]

Most likely those coming battles were on everyone's mind, and without the distraction of active campaigning many of Anderson's young soldiers waited eagerly for correspondence from home to salve their loneliness and stave off unpleasant thoughts of the future. Some pleaded with friends and relatives to write more frequently. "You must write if you have nothing to say," one chided. Often, they grew tired of waiting and wrote home with barely concealed frustration to "know why you have not written before now. If you do better in the future, I will forgive for the past."[11]

Anderson had written to his brother Wallace on January 9, but his letter contained no melancholy musings of past or pending battles. He told Wallace that he expected no further action until Burnside was replaced, but Burnside's failed campaign less than two weeks later proved that prediction wrong. "They must get up a new hero and make the usual amount of bombastic puffing and prediction as to his great qualities before they can make another move," he wrote. The rest of the letter addressed war events and passing news of camp and home. He expressed disappointment "at the winding up of the Murphriesboro [*sic*] operations" conducted by Braxton Bragg, and he hoped that General Joe Johnston "may still put matters to rights in the West." He also commented on the health of their Mississippi relative Willie McWillie, then serving on Anderson's staff. "I think that dyspepsia is the secret source of all his trouble and is undoubtedly aggravated by the too free use of tobacco," he told Wallace, "but worse than the immoderate use of the weed is his injudicious use of coffee, tea and water at his meals." Anderson observed, "No one could fail of suffering all sorts of disorders to his system who deluges his stomach at meal times with any sort of liquid . . . Willie drinks enough coffee and water at either one of his meals to ruin the strongest digestive apparatus that was ever given to any man." Anderson's concerns were unfounded however. Willie lived until 1922.[12]

He also informed Wallace that Sallie had inquired about their son Dick attending a boarding school in Abbeville, South Carolina. Young Dick was by then about ten years old, and his father found it "deplorable to think of how many of our young men have lost the opportunities of completing their education. It is one of the most serious evils attending the war." He closed by telling Wallace that their father had rented McKenzie's plantation Hiwassee "and will sell enough of the negroes [*sic*] to pay off the debts on the estate. I think he has done wisely," Anderson concluded. Though McKenzie's will left the plantation to his brother Dick, the war prevented him from actively participating in its management. Dick and his father must have concluded that the best course of action was to rent the place, probably with the enslaved workforce remaining in place for the time being.[13]

McKenzie, however, had taken pains in his will to provide instructions regarding a single mulatto enslaved woman by the name of Willoughby and her three children. He specified that he bequeathed them to his brother Dick, stipulating that it was his "will that the said Family of slaves shall be most kindly treated and every privilege allowed them that is consistent with the Laws of the State of South Carolina." McKenzie merely directed the sale of the rest of his enslaved workers with the net proceeds divided equally among his three siblings. He appointed Dick and Wallace executors. Anderson's descendants today still speculate about the reason for McKenzie's concern for Willoughby's future, and it is possible that some relationship existed between them that surpassed that of an enslaver and enslaved. If so, it shows that McKenzie was not unlike many other southern enslavers who engaged in sexual relations with enslaved women, possibly even fathering children by them. Though McKenzie was only recently a planter with an enslaved workforce of his own, he purchased Willoughby from Charles Moody, a close neighbor, and it is possible that a relationship predated his ownership of the woman. As a free woman in 1865, Willoughby made her mark on a labor contract, agreeing to continue to work for the Andersons. Her later whereabouts are less certain.[14]

In addition to Willoughby, another of McKenzie's enslaved workers experienced Dick and Wallace's patronage. With both brothers away from home, it was some time before Wallace was able to return to the Homestead where an appraisal of the enslaved workers took place. One of them, William, was worth very little. He was the father of a former house servant Betsy, and husband to another woman on the Anderson plantation. "You will see by the low price attached to him that he is not regarded of much value," Wallace wrote to Jennie in early 1864. "He is getting old and it will be better to let him remain here with his wife during Papa's lifetime. Rather than have him separated from his wife Brother [Dick] and I would purchase him and leave him where he is."[15]

The incident may illustrate not only the Andersons's paternalism, but also how the relationship between enslavers and house servants—and by extension their families—sometimes created enduring bonds of loyalty. It is also possible of course, that had William been highly valued, financial considerations might have trumped such feelings of allegiance. Another factor illustrated once again is the difference between how enslavers related to their house servants as opposed to field hands, with whom they would have had relations that were more distant and with less frequent contact. One exception to that trend was youngest son Benjamin's reliance on Canada during the time Benjamin managed Riverside Plantation for his father. They clearly developed a close, though sometimes fraught relationship. Canada too made his mark on the labor agreement after the war and elected to remain with the Andersons. The name William also appears on the list of those who remained at the plantation. Curiously, Betsy's name does not.[16]

In the meantime, concerns about the specifics of McKenzie's will doubtlessly garnered little attention from Anderson when military affairs occupied so much of his time. In his division that February of 1863, the men's spirits began to rebound when they found the main body of the Union army completely gone by the 23rd. Wright had dispatched one of his staff officers across the Rappahannock at U.S. Ford to "examine the country opposite." The officer soon returned and reported no enemy troops in the vicinity. Citizens informed him that they had headed for Aquia Landing on the Potomac River. That news ended the maneuvering on the Rappahannock and the constant threat of another Yankee crossing.[17]

With fortifications along the river line completed, Anderson was able to disperse his division more widely. Mahone's and Posey's brigades took up positions on the river to guard U.S. Ford. Wilcox's men saw to Banks' Ford, and Perry's brigade held "the Old Mine road, about 3 miles west of Fredericksburg." Wright's Georgians stood in reserve at Massaponax Church, about eight miles due south of Fredericksburg, not within easy supporting distance in any emergency at the farthest reaches of the division's scattered locations. The circumstances illustrate the difficulties of subsisting a large army concentrated in too small an area for any extended time, but the situation was not an unusual one or reflective of any poor planning on Anderson's part. When Anderson later called up Wright's brigade a few days prior to the fighting at Chancellorsville it arrived in plenty of time.[18]

Soon after the Union forces withdrew, McLaws obtained a leave of absence. One Georgia surgeon observed on February 27, that Dick Anderson was in command of McLaws's division as well his own. He expressed more confidence in Anderson's leadership than in McLaws's. "If we are to have any heavy fighting," the surgeon thought, "it is better so, than that the other should be in command, but I trust that all may be quiet until we get off from the neighborhood of Fredericksburg." Things remained silent for the rest of the winter, but getting off from the neighborhood was not to be.[19]

Furloughs granted selectively during the army's inactivity halted in early spring, and earnest preparation for a new campaign began. Lee ordered surplus baggage sent to Richmond anticipating "a resumption of active operations by the 1st of April." Anderson had already requested permission to order back from Richmond nearly 300 men of his division known to be there on sick leave. Once again, he fretted over an enemy advance across the Rappahannock and he put his troops on alert. He warned Mahone on March 17 to have his men "in the best position for checking any attempt of the enemy to cross at U.S. Ford." He further instructed Mahone—whom he recommended two weeks later for promotion to major general—to strengthen his position if he was able to so, and to examine the river above and below that place to ensure that no other practicable fords existed. Anderson cautioned Mahone particularly to look for one called "The Blind Ford" that was supposedly located just below the confluence of the Rapidan and Rappahannock. He even went so far as to suggest that it might be possible to learn more about U.S. Ford by enticing a Union "picket to come over to exchange papers or to trade." Though federal troops had dispersed for miles around the supply base at Aquia Creek, soldiers from each Union regiment routinely performed picket duties along the river, typically for three-day stints. Whether Mahone attempted to entice any of them to cross over is unknown, but within a few days fickle winter weather had dumped another eight inches of snow on the barren landscape.[20]

A week after that snowstorm, in what was perhaps a true indication that all thoughts were on the coming spring campaign, Lee published orders indicating that President Davis had set March 27 "as a day of fasting and prayer for the nation." As such, Lee suspended all duties and ordered chaplains of regiments to perform "religious services appropriate for the occasion." The prospect of the hard fighting that was to come persisted in preying on the minds of many of the young soldiers, particularly those who had so much to live for. One anxious Georgian in Anderson's division seemed preoccupied around that time with morbid thoughts that he would never see his wife and children again. He pined for his "little bright eyed gal & my blue eyed boy." He hoped to once again behold his "lovely companion's sweet contennace [*sic*] & git under the sound of her cheerful voice." Referring to his wife as "Ma," he professed his love for her and their children, but acknowledged the pain of separation, "I feel never to be reunited again on earth—if not let us meet in heaven." The prayers and reflections of Davis's day of thanksgiving did little to ease his mind, for he wrote again soon afterwards with equal pessimism. "Oh Ma, prepare to meet me where there is no separation," he implored with sorrow at his anticipated demise. "Try to raise our children right." His foreboding was unwarranted though. He survived the slaughter that would soon rage around the tiny crossroads of Chancellorsville.[21]

Meanwhile, Lee learned in mid-February that the Union Ninth Corps had embarked on transports and was steaming down the Potomac River towards Chesapeake Bay. Its destination was unknown, but Lee had to position troops to respond to the danger and "to resist an advance upon Richmond." Lee sent Longstreet with Hood and Pickett's divisions, while Anderson and McLaws remained with the army near Fredericksburg, along with Jackson's Second Corps. Longstreet soon found himself commanding the Department of Virginia and North Carolina that extended from Richmond to Wilmington, North Carolina. The task occupied him for some time, and he missed the opening of the spring campaign. Now on his own, Anderson fell temporarily under Lee's direct command. He remained especially alert on his front as a result.[22]

Chapter 12

Chancellorsville

My brave old general.

—R. E. Lee to R. H. Anderson,
W. McWillie diary

By the end of April, it was clear that the Union Army was again on the move, this time under the command of Major General Joseph Hooker. Men of the 10th Alabama on picket duty along the Rappahannock could distinctly hear their opponents' voices and the movement of wheeled vehicles and artillery. "We were perfectly aware of their purposes to cross the river above," one recalled. Communications between the two army's pickets had continued unabated, and the primary topic that April had been the resumption of campaigning. An officer in Mahone's brigade commanding a battalion of pickets in mid-April found "the Yankees were anxious to converse with our boys." The men attempted to exchange newspapers but the strong current sent their little plank rafts streaming rapidly towards the sea. "We asked when they were coming over," the Virginian recalled, "and they said in a few days and said McClellan was in camp over there." It might have been wishful thinking on the part of the Union soldiers, who almost universally held McClellan in high regard, but they would have to make do with Fighting Joe Hooker for the time being.[1]

Lee fired off a flurry of orders to his First Corps division commanders on Wednesday evening, April 29. Hooker's intentions were unclear, though Lee did know that Union infantry and cavalry had crossed the Rapidan at two fords above the river's confluence with the Rappahannock. Hooker was advancing on two fronts simultaneously, in front of Fredericksburg and upriver at the Rappahannock and Rapidan fords. One of those fronts would be a weaker holding action and diversion, while the other would be the main thrust with the bulk of his army. Lee had to prepare for both until he was certain of Hooker's primary route of advance. Lee instructed McLaws to occupy the same rifle pits above Fredericksburg that the army had occupied during the December battle. If Hooker crossed there, Lee would again offer resistance from the heights beyond the city. Lee next addressed a note to Anderson instructing him to "draw in your brigade at United States Ford, and throw your left back so as to cover the road leading from Chancellorsville down to the river." Recognizing the critical nature of that position, Lee specifically told Anderson that he desired him "to go forward yourself and attend to this matter." Meanwhile, in Richmond, Adjutant General Cooper was busily dispatching reinforcements from around the state, finally reaching out to Longstreet, headquartered at Suffolk, Virginia. "Move without delay with your command to this place," he ordered, "to effect a junction with General Lee," who had already informed President Davis of Hooker's developing attempt to turn the army's left flank. "If I had Longstreet's division, would feel safe," Lee wrote the President.[2]

Meanwhile, reports from prisoners captured by Stuart's cavalry disclosed at least three of Hooker's corps were crossing the river on Lee's left flank with only Anderson's division standing in Hooker's path. With Longstreet still absent, Lee wrote with great specificity to Anderson, then establishing lines near Tabernacle Church, instructing him to "set all your spades to work as vigorously as possible and hold your position firmly." Lee hoped to forward additional support and artillery to assist Anderson, but in the event that Anderson was required to move quickly to support the army elsewhere, Lee also advised him to be prepared to pack his trains so he could move at any moment, and to ensure his men carried two days' cooked rations. In addition, Stuart had sent two of his cavalry regiments to support Anderson. He posted them in front of Anderson's defenses where they could inform him of the enemy's movements and hinder their advance. Lee remained fearful despite the preparations. "I hope you have been able to select a good line and fortify it strongly," he wrote to Anderson. He was also hopeful that Anderson could connect the line to Wilcox's position, which still guarded against an advance from Banks' Ford, closest to Fredericksburg.[3]

As Lee's appreciation of Hooker's intentions developed, he refined his own plans. Special Orders Number 121 issued on Thursday, April 30, directed McLaws to leave one brigade near Fredericksburg to watch Union troops there and then to reinforce Anderson at Tabernacle Church with his remaining brigades as soon as possible. Jackson was to leave one division below Fredericksburg and reinforce Anderson with the rest by daylight on May 1.[4]

Anderson had called Wright's brigade from near Massaponax Church on April 29 to support Major General Early's division near Bernard's Farm at Fredericksburg. Early had been facing Union Major General John Sedgwick's Sixth Corps, which crossed the river south of Fredericksburg with orders to hold Confederate troops in place or pursue them if they attempted to reinforce Lee's left flank. Later that night Wright was directed farther west towards Chancellorsville on the Plank Road to join Anderson and form a line with Perry's brigade to assist in repelling an advance from the Rapidan fords. To convey the urgency, Anderson informed Wright that "the enemy is reported advancing rapidly—Artillery—Infantry & Cavalry."[5]

Arriving at Chancellorsville at midnight, Anderson met with Mahone and Posey and found that Mahone had moved his men to Chancellorsville from U.S. Ford and left only a regiment from his own brigade and five companies of the 19th Mississippi from Posey's brigade to hold the ford as long as possible. After consultation with his two brigade commanders and an examination of the lines, Anderson saw the danger of the position immediately and wisely chose to pull back along the Plank Road to a point where it intersected with the Old Mine Road. The latter road was indefensible by the small force on hand and it led directly to the rear of the present Confederate position near Chancellorsville. A significant Union attack at U.S. Ford might also easily overwhelm the token defensive force there, allowing federal troops easy access to Anderson's rear and cutting him off from Lee's main body. Anderson planned to withdraw beyond that road so that it was no longer in his rear. In the meantime, Wright's brigade arrived on the scene at daylight on Thursday, April 30 after marching since midnight in "drenching rain and impenetrable darkness." Pulling in his small force at U.S. Ford, Anderson began to march eastward using the Plank Road and Orange Turnpike, but not before Mahone's rear guard was set upon by aggressive Union cavalry troopers who reportedly "were so effectually repulsed that we were not further annoyed by them during the movement." The little victory was not so clean as all that, although one participant recalled that they "met and repulsed them without much loss on either side." Nonetheless, the Union horsemen captured several men "because their guns failed to fire, on account of the hard rain that fell the night before." Anderson formed his new lines that day stretching from an unfinished railroad bed south of Tabernacle Church, then northward across the Plank Road and Orange Turnpike, with Old Mine Road now safely in his front. Lee had already dispatched his chief engineer and an assistant to help in selecting the best defensive line, and Anderson found those men waiting for him when he arrived. Once laid out, the entrenching work began immediately amidst some intermittent skirmishing with Union cavalry. One of Stuart's regiments belonging to Brigadier General Fitzhugh Lee's Brigade, the 3rd Virginia Cavalry under Colonel Thomas H. Owen, arrived by afternoon and established a picket line in front and on the flanks of the Confederate lines. On the way to assist Anderson, Owen's men had harassed and delayed Hooker's advance, several times causing multiple regiments to form in line of battle to defend themselves against the mounted Confederates. It was a welcome delay, and Anderson's infantrymen continued to dig vigorously throughout the day and into the following morning.[6]

McLaws arrived with his division just before dawn broke on Friday, May 1 and joined Anderson's men in digging the entrenchments. Within a few hours, General Jackson arrived on the scene with the bulk of his corps closing rapidly behind him. Lee's army was now poised to meet the main thrust of Hooker's advance. The arrival of Jackson's divisions changed the tactical outlook, and after a brief consultation with Anderson, he immediately took control, ordering the men to abandon their spades and ready themselves to move forward to engage the foe. The anxious Confederates had already anticipated it. Seeing Jackson approach resplendent in full uniform, "our boys commenced saying 'Get ready, Jackson is coming, we will soon be on the move.'" By 11 AM, the men began their assault. Meanwhile, Anderson ordered Wilcox and Perry back from the Fredericksburg vicinity to rejoin the division, but their brigades arrived too late to join his advance and they found themselves on the turnpike supporting McLaws instead. Perry and Wilcox eventually formed a line of battle connected to McLaws's and stretching from Banks' Ford nearly to the Old Mine Road. One officer of the 5th Florida in Perry's brigade, Lieutenant Joel Blake, recalled rushing at double-quick time towards the sound of the artillery fire with reports flying down the line "that the Yankees were in thousands a few miles ahead of us, on we went panting like tired sheep," until arriving near the "scene of action." There Blake was stunned to see "what a large force of our troops Gen Lee had concentrated, it looked to me like every Rebel in the land was there or thereabouts." In the usual way the soldier on the battle line typically has no idea what the cause of a certain event is, he commented only that, "our Brigade was for some reason or another temporarily transferred to McClaw's [*sic*] Division."[7]

Blake's company advanced as skirmishers through densely thicketed woods and swampy areas with steeply banked streams that scattered the men. "Some 2 or 3 of our Company were for a time lost but came up after a while, the worst scratched mortals you ever saw, our clothes were torn almost off of us." Some distressing sights illustrated the horrors of war as it affected local civilians, and Blake attributed one atrocity he observed to the retreating Union troops. "We passed a little dwelling they had fired in their retreat and it was distressing to hear the cries of the inmates, the elderly lady of the house had been shot in-to, her head severed from her body. A younger woman, seemingly her daughter, was perfectly frantic and in her fright had run off & lost her two little children." The scene angered Blake and the men of his company. "I tell you the blood boiled in every man along and everyone would then have gladly met the cowardly foe with any odds." Blake's regiment was later withdrawn from the lines after having settled down for the night, but after retracing their steps for about three miles they encountered one of General Anderson's couriers "who stated that there was something wrong about the matter." They soon learned the order to withdraw was an error and the men stumbled through the pitch-black night back to their original positions. Blake estimated the Floridians had marched about twenty miles that day and were all "tired, hungrey [*sic*], sick and sleepy."[8]

Anderson had earlier advanced Mahone's brigade along the turnpike per Jackson's instructions, while Wright and Posey moved forward on the Plank Road. Owens's troopers screened the front and surrounding roads, while several batteries from E. P. Alexander's artillery battalion accompanied the infantry brigades. Mahone temporarily ended up under McLaws's direct supervision while his brigade was sandwiched between the Georgians of Brigadier Generals Paul J. Semmes on the left and William T. Wofford on the right. As skirmishing commenced one officer of Mahone's 12th Virginia recalled hearing "the gallant [Bernard] Hill Carter, Jr.," of the 3rd Virginia Cavalry "halloo out to us, 'Hurry up boys and get a shot at the Yankee Cavalry.'" A mile or so to their front lay the main body of Hooker's army, which reacted quickly to the sight of the oncoming Confederate lines. "They opened on us with artillery, and seemed determined to resist our farther progress," Anderson recalled. Despite having been on the march the previous day for more than twenty hours and covering twenty-seven miles, then digging through the night to create entrenchments, Wright's Georgians, supported by Alexander's artillery, swept aside "a considerable force" of Union troops straddling the Plank Road. Anderson ordered Wright to undertake a flanking movement by continuing to push along the Fredericksburg and Gordonsville Railroad's unfinished track line lying south of the Plank Road, which then positioned Wright squarely astride the Union right flank. Notwithstanding their near exhaustion, the stalwart Georgians marched on to Catherine Furnace, arriving at around six that evening. General Stuart, who had brought his troopers from the west onto the left flank of Lee's force, met them there. Stuart informed Wright of the enemy's position, and Wright aggressively attacked Union troops lying in dense woods north of the Furnace. The Georgians drove the Union troops out of the woods, across an open field, and into the cover of a pine thicket. Wright, uncertain of what he faced in his front, was hesitant to advance rapidly and fearful of falling into a trap. He called on Stuart for artillery to support a continued advance and determine the strength of the force before him. When those guns finally got into position, daylight was nearly gone. Stuart's guns quickly drew an overwhelming response from federal artillery better positioned on elevated ground at Hazel Grove and Fairview. Jackson and Stuart themselves had both come forward to observe the ground in their front just as the cannon fire exploded. One of Stuart's staff officers fell mortally wounded before they could move away from the sudden onslaught of iron. Hopes of continuing the attack and flanking the federal batteries with infantry went unrealized because of descending darkness and the tangled undergrowth, as well as the strength of the federal artillery arrayed against them. Instead, Wright marched his tired men back along the Furnace Road, leaving the field to Jackson's fresher divisions and rejoining Anderson along the Plank Road by around eleven that night. The Georgians had performed yeoman's work that day, their efforts instrumental in helping clear the way for troops forging towards Chancellorsville along the Plank Road and Turnpike.[9]

Meanwhile, Anderson, with Posey's brigade in hand and Mahone's nearby with McLaws, continued a determined advance along those two critical roads converging on Chancellorsville. After dispersing the Union cavalry screen, Mahone's regiments drove back Major General George Sykes's US Regulars. The 12th Virginia was deployed in front of the brigade as skirmishers, and one of them recalled the other regiments coming up "in beautiful style" before the "the whole line went forward with a yell. They stood up well for some time, but we steadily advanced, and when we got to close quarters, they began to give way and retire sullenly." When the Virginians reached a rail fence on an elevated ridge, they were able to pour a "hot fire" into the withdrawing Union soldiers, "which made them break and run." Another Virginian in the 41st Regiment similarly recalled confronting the Yankees until "they faced about and 'done some of the tallest running you ever saw.'"[10]

Posey's brigade likewise swept forward along the Plank Road with Stephen Dodson Ramseur's North Carolina brigade situated on the left between Posey and Wright. Posey had no contact with McLaws, then still advancing with Mahone along the turnpike. Skirmishers of Posey's 12th Mississippi steadily drove back their Union counterparts until coming upon a more substantial line of battle on the road to Catherine Furnace. This too proved no impediment to the oncoming rebel skirmishers, who soon forced their enemy to retire through dense woods. Posey emerged into a marshy area exposed to a concentrated fire of artillery and was compelled to halt his forward momentum. He later wrote proudly to his wife that he made this "grand advance," in Jackson's presence. Jackson "sent his compliments to me and directions to 'push on' the only command he ever gives." Late that night Anderson ordered Posey to move forward as far as he was able. Posey advanced his skirmishers and "with much difficulty" pushed his men through a marshy area, halting again "within a short distance" of the Union lines. His position was a tense one throughout the night, as he believed the Yankee lines on his right were flanking his own position, and possibly even threatening his rear. Relieved early next morning by a brigade from A. P. Hill's division, Posey then moved back beyond the road to Catherine Furnace and rested his men.[11]

As the sun set on the first day's carnage around Chancellorsville, Dick Anderson felt certain that his actions measured up to both Lee's and Jackson's expectations. His troops fought well, but owing to the scattered disposition of the brigades of his division, he had no opportunity to exercise any real independence once Jackson arrived. McLaws effectively controlled the battlefield to the north along the Turnpike, with Mahone's brigade—which was well familiar with the terrain—wisely in the van of his advance. Wilcox and Perry's brigades came up to support McLaws and guarded his flank and rear. Jackson effectively superseded Anderson along the Plank Road to the south. His modest account of his actions so far that morning until Jackson first arrived on the field pleased the general who found no cause for criticism. Anderson had consolidated his force, extracting the brigades from the tangled danger presented by the wilderness surrounding Chancellorsville and withdrawing them to a more advantageous location. His troops were prepared to repel a Yankee attack in the event Jackson did not arrive with timely support. Jackson did arrive, and he chose to accompany the force on the Plank Road. He had already directed the men of his arriving Second Corps to follow in that direction, hence Ramseur's position between Wright and Posey that day. Though he believed Hooker would withdraw in the night, Jackson had immediately understood that open ground farther south of the river would provide more room for maneuver, and in that respect, he had anticipated an opportunity for one of the war's greatest flanking attacks despite having limited familiarity with the ground.[12]

That night Lee and Jackson held a meeting, and Anderson joined them for a time. One man from the 16th Mississippi in Posey's brigade recalled that after halting near the Furnace he and two others from his regiment were detailed to guard the horses and camp where "R. E. Lee, T. J. Jackson and R. H. Anderson [were] holding a council of war." Lee and Jackson sought Anderson's views on the strength of the Union force in his front and the topographical features of the area over which his brigades had ranged since the previous fall. His advice would have helped his chiefs decide the most appropriate course of action. Unable to maneuver on the heavily wooded ground near the river, and with no vulnerability apparent in the center of the Union line, the remaining option was to attack Hooker's right flank. As the men pondered that prospect, Stuart rode up with encouraging news that altered the nature of the discussion. Hooker's right flank, he reported, was unsecured and vulnerable. It was "in the air," as the popular parlance of the day put it. Stuart was dispatched to find a route that could be used by infantry and artillery to strike Hooker's flank, and Lee authorized Jackson to undertake the movement early on the morning of May 2nd.[13]

To make the attack on Hooker's flank, Jackson proposed to use his entire corps with the exception of Jubal Early's division still facing Sedgwick near Fredericksburg. Lee, once again showing that he was willing to take great risks to gain victory, assented to Jackson's proposal. The Second Corps, screened by Stuart's cavalry, would march off with about 33,000 of Lee's men. Lee had only the two divisions of McLaws and Anderson to hold Hooker in place. The decision was not only testimony to Lee's confidence in Jackson's proven ability to execute a turning movement successfully, but also to Lee's confidence in the leadership qualities of the two division commanders left to hold the front. Everyone held the prowess of the fighting men of those divisions in high regard, but there were fewer than 14,000 of them, plus a little more than a regiment of cavalry and the artillerymen of six batteries. In all, there were fewer than 15,000 men confronting Hooker's far superior numbers. Lee was aware that Hooker was constructing defensive works and thus seemed unlikely to take the offensive early on May 2, but he had ample reason not to accept Hooker's entrenching as a decisive indicator of his intentions, for he knew that Hooker was building resources for the fight and being reinforced with every passing hour. Lee's confidence in Jackson and his appreciation for his opponent's weaknesses are often cited as cause for Lee's confidence in dividing his meager force, but no commander could have done so without also having full confidence in the leaders and soldiers tasked to hold the line in the face of such overwhelming power. It does them great disservice to ignore how much that might have influenced Lee's willingness to allow Jackson to march off with more than two-thirds of his entire force.[14]

Undoubtedly apprehensive throughout the day as Jackson's columns moved westward on a mostly hidden route to outflank Hooker's force, Lee knew it was a risk worth taking. In the meantime, he sought to attract Hooker's attention and probe his defenses, yet not bring on a wider engagement. That risk increased when Federals observed Jackson's movement. Union artillery positioned at the elevated clearing known as Hazel Grove opened fire on Jackson's columns as they crossed a clearing near Catherine Furnace to the south. Union Major General Daniel Sickles found the sight irresistible, and he sought permission to slice into the passing line of Confederate troops seen in the distance. Brigadier General David B. Birney's 1st Division of Sickles's Third Corps set out as soon as Hooker gave his assent. Federal commanders ultimately surmised that Lee was retreating, and Hooker thus paid little attention to Sickles's efforts. By the time Sickles got permission to attempt to cut the column, most of Jackson force was already well past the point of danger or had diverted onto alternate routes in response to Union artillery fire. Jackson had ordered a regiment posted at the clearing near the furnace to dispute any aggressive move against his column, and the assignment fell to the 23rd Georgia of Alfred Colquitt's Brigade, D. H. Hill's division. Some passing artillery and infantry at the tail end of the Rebel procession assisted the Georgians and the force was able to hold Union troops in check as Birney's advance took shape. Meanwhile, Anderson had shifted Wright's brigade to fill vacated positions south of the Plank Road formerly held by portions of Jackson's command. Anderson also noted that he moved Posey's brigade slightly "to the rear of the line of battle" at around 7 AM after it was relieved by a brigade from A. P. Hill's division. As the Union assault around the Furnace began to develop sometime around noon, Lee directed Anderson to dispatch assistance to the beleaguered 23rd Georgia. He sent Posey's brigade in that direction. A "warm skirmish" ensued as Posey's Mississippians poured enfilading fire into the flanks of Sickles's men advancing toward the Furnace. Anderson subsequently had to call on Wright to support Posey, who maintained his position "against great odds, and checked the farther advance of the enemy." Posey recalled his line spanning the Furnace Road about 500 yards from Catherine Furnace, where his skirmishers were "hotly engaged during the whole day and part of the night." Each time the Union troops attempted one of its "frequent efforts to advance," the firing of the skirmishers drove them back in confusion. Wright eventually formed on Posey's right flank to the north of the Furnace Road and together the two stalwart brigades held off the threat of an attack by Birney's entire division, also supported by a battalion of Colonel Hiram Berdan's green-jacketed sharpshooters. Timely artillery support and Posey's sudden appearance on Birney's flanks stopped his advance, but it was not in time to save the 23rd Georgia, the bulk of which was captured in the unfinished railroad cut Wright's men had used on the previous day to outflank the Union lines advancing along the Plank Road.[15]

Wright's brigade remained on the left of the Plank Road until around 2 PM, when Anderson sent it rushing to Posey's support. At the same time, he shuffled Mahone's brigade to the left to cover the ground vacated by Wright and support Captain Willis Dance's Powhatan Artillery. In that way Anderson moved at least three of his scattered brigades in closer proximity to himself where he could exert more control over them. The order to help Posey and the resulting precipitous departure of Wright's brigade, however, left the 3rd Georgia in the lurch. That regiment formed a skirmish line in the heavily wooded area in front of the brigade, and just as Wright received the order to go to Posey's aid a large force of Yankees advanced on the skirmishers. Wright sent word to Anderson of the regiment's plight and hurried off to support Posey. After a brief consultation with Posey, Wright formed his brigade line and tried to extend it as far to the right as he could in a desperate attempt to establish contact with the 3rd Georgia. Fearing for the fate of that regiment against apparently overwhelming odds, Wright sent a messenger to its commander, Major John F. Jones, inquiring about conditions he was then facing and urging him to hold at all costs, "as he held the key to our whole line in this quarter." Jones replied that not only was the regiment holding its own, it was "actually advancing upon and driving the enemy before him." A relieved Wright turned his attention back to the ominous threat massing against Posey, but a concerted assault by Birney's men never came. Wright recalled that it was growing dark when he observed large blue-clad masses approaching Posey's lines "with loud cheers." The thin Rebel line was fortunate. By the time Sickles brought up support for Birney's division and adjusted the gap in his lines, word of a calamity on Hooker's right flank began to arrive. Sometime around 5:30 PM, Jackson's line of battle had pitched into that exposed flank, sending most of Major General Oliver O. Howard's unsuspecting and unprepared Eleventh Corps fleeing precipitously towards the Rappahannock fords. Sickles was compelled to fall back on Chancellorsville as Hooker consolidated his lines to resist Jackson's advance. As darkness fell on Wright's front, the 3rd Georgia was withdrawn from its advanced position and formed on the brigade's right. Hooker had not been interested in bringing on a wider engagement there, and the Union advance on the 3rd Georgia's front had been undertaken merely to see if Lee was still there.[16]

Darkness also returned Perry's Floridians to Anderson's control when the brigade withdrew from McLaws's line and bivouacked behind the front. As the Floridians marched behind the battle line held by Wright's Georgians, one of them noticed that Perry's men "were apparently worn out, having been skirmishing all day with nothing to eat, but they were in fine spirits." Some of the passing Florida men recognized their opponents from the previous winter's snowball battle. "You beat us in snow balling," called one, "but we will fight together to-morrow." Mahone's Virginians also commented on meeting their "snowball friends," calling out to them that they knew they could "stand bullets better than you can snowballs, don't let the Yankees whip you as badly as we did." Wright's Georgians had just received three days' rations, and "unmindful of their own wants," crowded around the hungry Floridians sharing the food stashed in their haversacks. Georgians and Mississippians both called out to the passing boys from Florida. "'Here goes the Florida Rebels,' hurrah for Southern Dixie, the cry. 'Go it boys, we are with you, good night, we will see you out tomorrow,' etc." The word was passed quickly down the line as the Florida boys passed, "'Out with your crackers, boys, and feed the hungry.'" Lieutenant Blake received several crackers and "a large slice of delightful ham" from a fellow officer. He "felt grateful enough for it," and made "a fine supper of it."[17]

Meanwhile, Wilcox remained at Banks' Ford where Anderson had dispatched him earlier that morning. The Alabamians observed Federal reinforcements moving along the river's opposite bank en route to support Hooker, and Wilcox kept a strong force of pickets around the ford in case of an attempted crossing there. He would not return to Anderson's direct control until the morning of May 3, when he believed the Union force at Banks' Ford had gone to join Hooker. Only a small detail of pickets remained after that.[18]

Nightfall on May 2 did not bring a long respite in the day's fighting. Darkness merely added confusion on the battlefield. On hearing Jackson's attack, Lee reported later that he directed Anderson and McLaws to probe the Union lines in order to keep Hooker off balance and prevent his moving reinforcements to confront Jackson, but they were not to "attack in force unless a favorable opportunity should present itself." As they advanced, the lines were to incline to their left to reach toward Jackson's in hopes that they could reconnect into one continuous front line as soon as possible. One hazard, however, was that they were also advancing towards Jackson's fire, and some caution was needed to avoid friendly casualties. Posey and Wright did not advance their lines at all after Sickles's withdrawal and the onset of darkness, but skirmishers continued to probe Union positions. One of Mahone's men, however, recalled, "severe fighting through the whole night" by his own and Wright's brigade. Mahone himself recalled "engaging the enemy more or less warmly as the range of his (General Jackson's) enfilading fire would allow." Some of Mahone's skirmishers did take good advantage of Lee's instructions to "feel the enemy," and they were able to do the Federals some damage when Captain W. Carter Williams of the 6th Virginia rushed three companies over some abatis near the Plank Road a little after dark and poured fire into the Union rifle pits. The Virginians captured a number of prisoners and the colors of the 107th Ohio, losing only one officer taken prisoner. "The standard, a most elegantly finished work" was delivered to Lee at his nearby headquarters.[19]

No captured flag, no matter its elegance or the level of success that attended its seizure, could have possibly relieved the pain that Lee was to suffer on the night of May 2, 1863 when he learned that one of his most trusted lieutenants fell with a wound that would later prove fatal. Sometime around 9:30 PM, North Carolinians mistakenly fired at Stonewall Jackson and his staff as they were returning from scouting the enemy lines. A. P. Hill, who was next in line to command the corps, also fell wounded soon afterwards, but he remained on the field to guide division commander Robert E. Rodes, who temporarily took the reins. Meanwhile, with Rodes relatively unknown beyond his own division Lee thought it best that J. E. B. Stuart immediately take command of the corps.[20]

Stuart prepared for an early morning attack while E. P. Alexander placed his artillery to support the infantry. Dawn brought a renewal of the vicious combat as the entire army threw itself against Hooker's defenses. Anderson vigorously pressed forward towards Chancellorsville with the right flank of his line on the Plank Road to the southeast of where it split from the Orange Turnpike, and his left stretching tentatively towards Jackson's corps in the direction of Catherine Furnace. He had placed Perry's Floridians on the left of his lines before first light with instructions "to gain the Catharpin road and move toward the furnace." The Catharpin Road connected the Plank Road with Todd's Tavern to the south, and ran roughly parallel with the Furnace Road. This movement eventually brought Perry into line on the left flank of the division, with Posey to his right, then Wright's Brigade, and finally Mahone, whose right flank rested on the Plank Road. Anderson pressed forward for a time, the troops moving "with spirited impetuosity and with as much rapidity as was permitted by the dense thickets and tangled abatis" driving "the enemy from his intrenchments [*sic*]." Eventually it was necessary to wheel the left-most brigades to the right to face Hooker's lines. Posey reported that his Mississippians made their dispositions "in fine order, under heavy fire of shell and grape as each regiment attained its position."[21]

E. P. Alexander had wisely placed a number of guns on the cleared plateau known as Hazel Grove, a commanding high point that the Yankees unwisely abandoned as they concentrated their lines around Chancellorsville. Perry's brigade passed close to Hazel Grove in its advance northward. As they pushed towards another strategic clearing called Fairview and the Plank Road beyond, to the west of Chancellorsville, James J. Archer's brigade of A. P. Hill's division joined them on their left.[22] Lee's two corps now joined around Chancellorsville in a continuous line. Perry's men continued to claw their way through abatis, which Colonel Lang of the 8th Florida remembered as ranging between "fifty to two hundred yards in width. Over this fallen timber & the breastwork our men quickly went, shouting & yelling," he told his cousin. The men surged towards Fairview and sent Union troops fleeing to the rear "in utmost confusion" until "a shower of grape and canister" opened on the small band of Floridians. Perry ordered the men to lie down and the protection afforded by a slight ridge meant losses were less than anticipated. One lieutenant recalled the men loaded while lying down and then "rising on one knee poured it into them until it got too hot for them, when, as soldiers say they 'got up and got.'" Lieutenant Blake of the 5th Florida was in advance with his company deployed as skirmishers again. They "had as hot work as I ever want to have, balls, shell & grape fell thick and fast around us, and for 15 or 20 minutes I expected every moment to see the company shot to pieces but fortunately the balls passed over, as we hugged the ground very closely. The Company behaved very cooly & bravely," he commented proudly, "many of them firing very deliberately."[23]

To the right of the Florida brigade, Posey's Mississippians likewise drove forward impetuously as the Rebel yell rang out through the dense woods. The men advanced over a broad abatis to the "trenches of the enemy, driving him off with much slaughter and capturing many prisoners." James Kirkpatrick of the 16th Mississippi recalled chasing the Yankees out of the rifle pits, pursuing them as they ran "pell mell" in the direction of the Chancellor House. The Rebels were "loading and firing as fast as possible" before being halted and recalled to the recently vacated rifle pits to reorganize. Those log and earth pits, guarded by abatis about 100 to 150 yards in front appeared to be well made, and, in Kirkpatrick's opinion, ought to have withstood the attack. "It looks like troops of any courage might have held them," he wrote derisively. Anderson was most likely busy issuing instructions to his brigadiers, driving his men forward, or by then directing them as they re-formed their lines. An officer of the First Virginia Artillery, Major Robert A. Hardaway, had been ordered by Lee that morning to "follow General Anderson's movements" with three rifled guns from a Virginia battery. Anderson was already advancing his division from Mine Creek towards the Plank Road/Orange Turnpike and his columns had entered the woods by the time the artilleryman caught up. Hardaway was unable to locate Anderson, however, and he quickly realized that the route was "impracticable for artillery." He did find one of Anderson's staff officers though, and he told him that any attempt to follow the infantry through such terrain would most likely keep the guns "out of the fight altogether." Hardaway instructed the staff officer to inform Anderson that he would place his guns near the other artillery pieces already in position in the clearing around Hazel Grove and thereby bring "the weight of metal . . . to bear against the enemy's flank while he advanced in front." Hardaway's failure to readily locate Anderson illustrates just how densely wooded the area was. It shows not only the difficulties one might have had in locating a particular individual on a division front spread across several miles in such wilderness, but also how it was equally uncommon for the average soldier advancing in battle to have encountered the division commander and preserved an account of it. In other cases, on less tangled fields of battle, it might have been easier to observe the division commander, perhaps conferring with the brigade commander or a regimental leader, but such a sighting might have been so commonplace it was hardly worth mentioning in letters or diaries. Encountering Lee, however, was always an event worth noting.[24]

Anderson paid keen attention to the performance of his troops. He recalled that Wright's brigade was the first to reach Chancellorsville, where it "captured a large number of prisoners." Wright was supposed to connect his flanks to those of Mahone and Posey, but as his front was over a mile in length and having only about 1,600 men, he was unable to do so. Instead, he advanced and attempted to keep equidistant from each of the flanking brigades while guarding his own flanks with strong skirmish lines. Driving Union troops from the wooded area in front of their rifle pits, Wright's Georgians pushed the Yankees back through the abatis and out of their defensive works. The impetuous advance halted there in the face of "the most terrible fire of artillery and musketry I have ever witnessed," Wright lamented. Soon after sending one of his staff officers to find out where Mahone's brigade was and to urge it to advance quickly to his aid, a major commanding Mahone's skirmish line found Wright and conveyed the disturbing news that he also did not know where his brigade was, "except when last heard from it was very far in the rear." Wright reported later that the major left and he saw neither him nor Mahone again that day.[25]

With no support on his right flank, Wright deemed it prudent to shift slightly to the left to close on Posey's flank, and the weight of combined fire soon drove the federals from their entrenchments. Wright was still taking fire from Union troops holding their ground on his right flank. Observing this state of affairs, Anderson quickly ordered Wright to shift the 3rd Georgia to the right to "dislodge the enemy sharpshooters . . . and then push forward for the enemy's battery which was so incessantly playing upon us." Anderson watched the Georgians' advance to Chancellorsville, where federals were "then in some confusion around and in the rear of the brick [Chancellor] house." The disorganized Union troops fled in the face of the spirited charge "leaving us in entire possession of his strong position," whereupon Wright formed his own disorganized brigade along the Orange Plank Road in front of the house. Four companies of the 3rd Georgia were sent forward as skirmishers, and the exuberant Rebels soon overtook the fleeing Yankees, capturing between 600 and 700 officers and men of the 27th Connecticut. Meanwhile, both Lee and Anderson had ridden onto the field at that point, and Wright was ordered to relocate his line "a few rods" down the Plank Road and await further orders."[26]

On the far right of the line, Mahone's men also swept forward, perhaps somewhat belatedly or perhaps too far to the right for Wright to observe them. Wright had shifted closer to Posey after despairing of Mahone's appearance. John Mosely of the 6th Virginia recalled advancing through a "valley with very thick undergrowth on fire between us—it was evident that this was to be a terrible day." Perhaps that delayed or disrupted the progress of Mahone's advance, but advance he did. One officer in the 41st Virginia, for example, remembered that artillery was still massed around Chancellorsville, and he considered it treachery when, after the Union infantrymen raised a white flag at their breastworks, "some guns in the rear of the [Chancellor] house opened on us, killing some of our men. Then they fled." That must have been prior to Wright's men reaching the brick house. In any event, the officer recalled that evidence of the hasty retreat lay all around. "The ground was strewed with knapsacks, blankets, overcoats, hats, oilcloth, Yankee tents, dead men and horses," he told his sister. Such detritus was often a temptation to the more scantily supplied Confederates, causing the men to search out useful items from among the wreckage, but in this case the men were quickly re-formed and poised to face new threats. The forward momentum of Jackson's Second Corps hurtling against Hooker's lines from the west pushed Anderson farther east as the Union defenses contracted. When he brought the men into line once more along the Orange Turnpike they were again east of Chancellorsville.[27]

Hooker was compelled to withdraw into a U-shaped defensive position, anchoring his flanks on the Rappahannock with U.S. Ford in his rear. That afternoon Anderson shifted his division to the northeast along the River Road where it guarded the junction with the Old Mine Road, but not before the horrific scenes around the Chancellor House came to their fiery conclusion. The house "was in full blaze . . . having been fired by Yankee shells, and was the theatre of a most horrible scene." Many of the wounded federals brought to the house before their comrades fell back perished dreadfully in the raging inferno. Lee's aide-de-camp, Major Charles Marshall captured the battle's intensity in a gripping description of a sight that could "never be effaced from the minds of those who witnessed it." Confederate troops pressed forward "with all the ardour and enthusiasm of combat. The white smoke of musketry fringed the front of the line of battle, while the artillery on the hills in the rear . . . shook the earth with its thunder, and filled the air with the wild shrieks of the shells that plunged into the masses of the retreating foe." Floridian Joel Blake likewise recalled that "the cries of the wounded—the groans of the dying on every side filled the air, & the dead, mangled & bruised and torn to pieces in every conceivable way, are scattered over the whole field." The shocked lieutenant and his men began to attend as best they could to the wounded. Confederate soldiers rushed their injured comrades to the rear as quickly as possible, but the victors also tried to succor their stricken foe. "Touched with sympathy for my race, I could feel for our wounded enemies, and . . . administered to them as friends," Blake wrote a few days later.[28]

With Hooker's force now contained in his front, Lee was compelled to look towards Fredericksburg. After much urging from his superiors, Sedgwick began to advance against Early and threaten Lee's flank. Overwhelming numbers began to tell, and Union troops eventually forced the Confederates off Marye's Heights and pushed westward along the Plank Road. Early was occupied with a significant force of federal troops south of the town, and Lee had no choice but to divide his army once again and rush troops to meet the threat. By around mid-day on May 3, Lee ordered Mahone's brigade to join McLaws's division and rush towards Fredericksburg, once more taking the brigade out of Anderson's command. "After three cheers for our brave, brave commander, General Lee, who was then present, we took up our line of march," recalled one of the Virginians. By 4 or 5 PM they "reached the Brick Church" that gave its name to the battle—Salem Church.[29]

Anderson's three remaining brigades held their position along the River Road to block Hooker's access to the Old Mine Road and simultaneously threaten Federals on the opposite bank of the Rappahannock. Anderson had Major Hardaway's thirteen guns at his disposal, and he put those to good use the next morning when they opened just before daylight on "large parks of the enemy's wagons and the camps of some of his troops on the opposite side of the river." He also pushed his skirmishers forward early on the morning of May 4 to "drive back the enemy, and to discover his position and strength." Perry, on the far left of the division, sent the 2nd and 5th Florida Regiments forward about a half mile apart with a line of skirmishers connecting them. Lieutenant Blake recalled that his regiment quickly ran into Union pickets and "after a continued firing for two or three hours, we discovered that the enemy were securely entrenched & trying to decoy us into a trap." Hooker's line was indeed secure and well-fortified on a ridge lying beyond Mine Run. Lee was reassured that Hooker was on the defensive, and that gave him the confidence to send the rest of Anderson's division streaming back towards the threat at Salem Church later that morning as Brigadier General Harry Heth's command filed into line to replace Anderson's men. The transition was not as rapid as Lee would have liked, and he felt the delay even more personally because he was waiting to accompany Anderson and his brigades to see first-hand the state of affairs around Fredericksburg.[30]

As Anderson hurried on his way towards Salem Church, Cadmus Wilcox had just had one of his finest days of the war. Seeing the impending danger to Lee's flank on May 3 and deciding on his own to delay Sedgwick's advance towards Chancellorsville, he deployed his men to block the Plank Road while Early withdrew southward to protect the railroad connecting Richmond and Fredericksburg. Wilcox's brigade repeatedly delayed Sedgwick's advance, forcing him to deploy lines of battle and post artillery to disperse the stubborn Alabamians. McLaws raced to join him as quickly as possible around Salem Church, and by the time the Yankees pushed ahead with their assault on the Rebel lines at the church there were five Confederate brigades spanning both sides of the Plank Road, two of them Anderson's. Wilcox held the center and Mahone was on the far left with Brigadier General Paul J. Semmes's Georgians between. Kershaw stood on Wilcox's right flank and Brigadier General William T. Wofford's command held the southern end. Wilcox's Alabamians would withstand the worst of the Union assault up the Plank Road though.[31]

Wilcox deployed the 14th and 11th Alabama north of the Plank Road with the 10th and the 8th south of the road. The 9th Alabama stood in back of the 10th' with one soldier in the 9th later writing that "we were put in the rear of the 10th Alabama Regiment for they couldn't depend on her." So, it would prove to be. One company of the 9th had been deployed as sharpshooters in a schoolhouse about sixty yards in front of the church. Another company of the 9th occupied the church itself with orders to fire from the windows. In the center of the line between the 11th and 10th Alabama was an interval of approximately eighty yards in which Wilcox placed four artillery pieces. The Union attack on the south side of the road pressed forward with more vigor than on the north side, soon overrunning the company in the schoolhouse. Probably they would have surrendered en masse except that the command from "a sandy whiskered" federal lieutenant to "'Show them no quarter,'" changed their minds. The shocking statement "caused the Confederate inmates to redouble their will and energy and they went to shooting at the squad. The sandy whiskered lieutenant failed to give anymore commands." Wilcox ordered the 9th Alabama forward as the Union attack surged ahead and smashed the 10th Alabama. The 9th quickly repulsed the charge and regained the schoolhouse while Wilcox railed mightily at the broken 10th Alabama. The frenzied advance of the 9th soon carried the rest of the brigade with it. Caught up in the moment, two of Semmes's regiments swept forward along with the re-formed 10th Alabama. Excited Rebels brushed aside yet another hastily formed line until halted by artillery fire and fresh lines of blue-clad soldiers. It had grown dark by then, making it imprudent to advance further. Wilcox and Semmes drew up and casually retraced their steps to their original positions. There was no Union pursuit or counterattack.[32]

Dick Anderson did not observe Wilcox once more demonstrating his considerable leadership abilities. After remaining on the sidelines at Chancellorsville, Wilcox and his Alabama regiments rose to the occasion when called upon. Wilcox's initiative delayed Sedgwick's advance culminating at Salem Church. Although the 10th Alabama briefly faltered, Anderson could take pride in knowing that all his brigades had performed admirably over the past few days. If he had been concerned that his friend Longstreet harbored doubts about the steadiness of some of Anderson's regiments, or lacked full confidence in his ability to inspire them to perform their best,

Chancellorsville and Salem Church showed that he had little cause for concern on both counts.

When Anderson's weary troops reached Salem Church late on May 4, after a daybreak skirmish with Hooker and an exhausting march from Chancellorsville, the Confederate defenses then stretched from Early's lines spanning the Telegraph Road south of Fredericksburg towards McLaws's lines spanning the Plank Road to the west, but with a large gap between them. The two had been unable to complete their junction, and an exasperated Lee ordered Anderson's men to fill that gap. Lee hoped a united Confederate line would be able to push Sedgwick's corps into the river, and though he had urged Early to try to unite with McLaws on May 3, he could not accomplish it before night fell. Now Anderson's men joined Early's left flank with a renewed plan to drive Sedgwick from Fredericksburg while McLaws advanced along the Plank Road. Like his army's commander, Sedgwick had formed his lines with both flanks anchored on the Rappahannock. By the time Lee was content with the disposition of his forces on May 4 it was already around 5:30 or 6 PM when E. P. Alexander's guns furnished the signal for the attack to commence. Anderson and Early moved out, driving the Union troops back towards their escape route over a pontoon bridge situated below Banks' Ford "without much trouble, meeting with but slight resistance." The retreat was so rapid that McLaws could add little but to join in the pursuit of the fleeing bluecoats. In fact, the charging Confederates were only pushing the enemy's skirmish lines back, and while Sedgwick found it necessary to contract his lines in an orderly fashion, they were by no means broken. Darkness ended the assault despite Lee's wishes to the contrary, but the Union general had had enough, and by the next morning, he had disappeared across the river. Leaving Early to guard against Sedgwick's return, Lee ordered McLaws and Anderson to return to the lines at Chancellorsville, where Hooker still waited behind his entrenchments.[33]

Lee was undoubtedly disappointed in the conduct of all three of the most senior commanders on that part of the field. The expected cooperation between Early's advance and McLaws's support never really materialized. Early's attack subsequently came undone and began to lose cohesion. In Anderson's division, only Wright and Posey had advanced towards the Plank Road. Though Anderson later reported that Wright's brigade "advanced with great intrepidity across a wheat field, under a hot fire of grape, and drove one of the enemy's batteries from its position," he neglected to mention that Wright advanced on an oblique that took him directly across Posey's intended route of advance, thus masking that brigade. Meanwhile, Perry had been held in reserve, but John Robarts of the 2nd Florida recalled a bleak moment when Lee himself ordered the Florida brigade to charge across an open field where a battery of a dozen Union guns was deployed. "I thought my time had come," Robarts recalled. "I made up my mind to die." It was a sentiment that gripped much of the brigade. His regiment had been in "good spirits all through the fight till it come time to charge that battery. I tell you she cooled down. Not a word could you hear from a man's mouth in the whole brigade." At that point, the Floridians found that Wright's oblique advance had driven the federal guns from their positions. Perry was the only one who later expressed any optimism about capturing the guns, boasting that his opportunity was ruined by Wright's brigade "swinging across the line of battle, and charging across the field in my front." Wright's advance also covered Posey's front, and Posey noted that Anderson himself accompanied him in leading the Mississippians forward toward the Plank Road. Wright, meanwhile, had been fearful of advancing farther lest he encounter Wofford's brigade that was advancing down the Plank Road. Anderson eventually ordered Wright to halt and hold his position, and that was probably when the Mississippians moved forward. Wright later complained that the order to halt subjected his brigade to a "murderous fire," to which he was unable to respond. In all, it was not Anderson's finest day of battle and even under Lee's critical eye, he was unable to effectively coordinate the movements of the various brigades of his division. Despite his otherwise fine performance over the last few days, it could not have increased Lee's confidence in Anderson, nor provided convincing evidence that he had yet matured into a reliable division commander. Lee most likely concluded that Anderson's record was inconsistent and that he was still learning how to maneuver large bodies of infantry in difficult terrain under adverse conditions. Nonetheless, judging from Lee's after-action reports, he was pleased with Anderson's overall conduct in which truly good moments outweighed less notable ones.[34]

After discovering Sedgwick gone from their front on the morning of the 5th, Anderson's division got on the road back to Chancellorsville at around 4 PM "in the midst of a violent storm," arriving just after dark. The men of the 8th Alabama might have considered it an unlucky omen when a violent crash of lightning coursed through the regiment sending one captain tumbling from his mount and several other soldiers to the hospital. "Every man in the regiment was more or less shocked," recalled one of them. "The hardest kind of a rain" continued to fall through the night as Wilcox and Wright bivouacked on the Catharpin Road, while Mahone, Perry, and Posey set up camp on the Plank Road. The men recovered quickly or blustered robustly. A correspondent for *The Times* of London reported that "the brigades of Anderson's Division came splashing through the mud in wild tumultuous spirits, singing, shouting, jesting, heedless of soaking rags, drenched to the skin, and burning again to mingle in the wild revelry of battle." The 8th

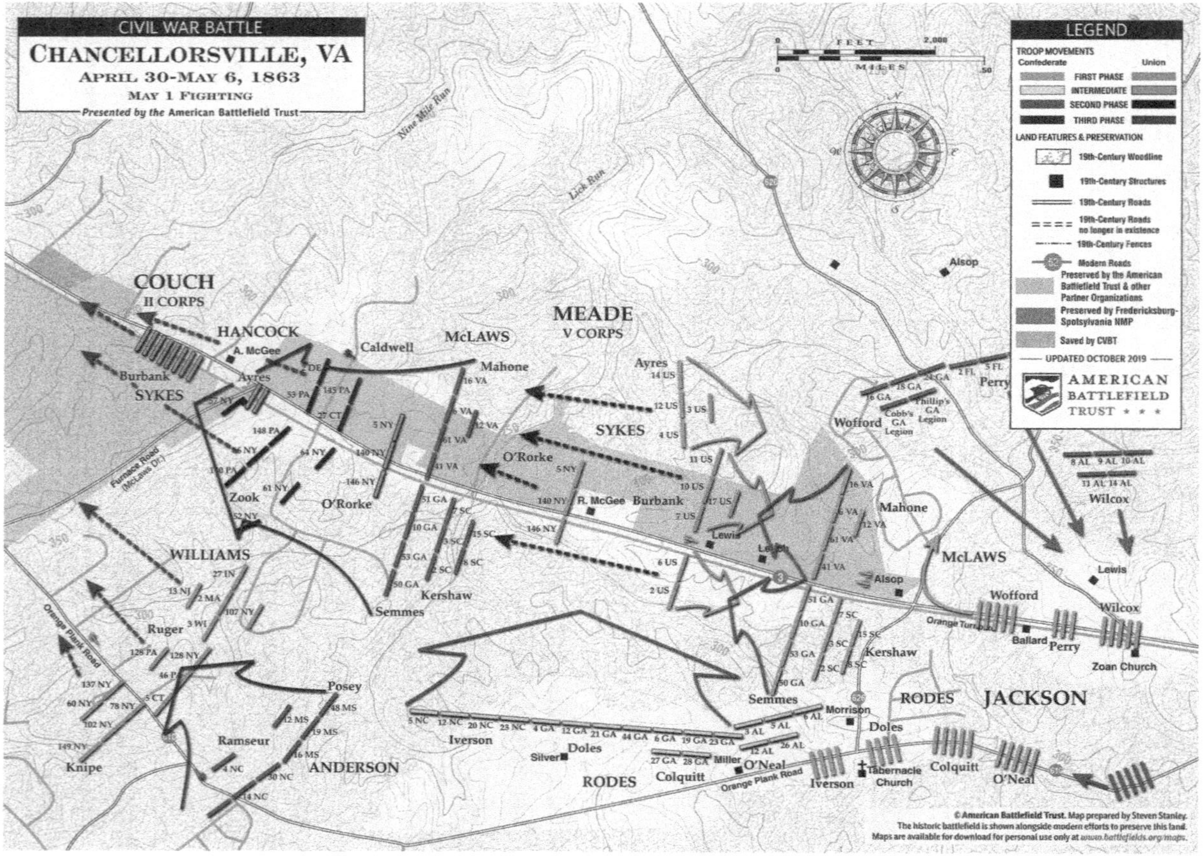

Figure 3. Map of the Battle of Chancellorsville, showing the first day's fighting, May 1, 1863. Courtesy of the American Battlefield Trust.

Alabama advanced towards the Chancellor House as "the half-drowned men filled the air with terrible yells" that passed back and forth along the line. Major Thomas Mills of Anderson's staff demanded to know "'What in the hell are you yelling about?'" A soldier responded that they were trying "to scare Fighting Joe Hooker." By 8 AM on May 6, the division was in place at the junction of Ely's Ford Road and U. S. Ford Road ready to pitch into Hooker's defenses in drenching rain. The advancing skirmishers soon found that their adversaries had made good use of the stormy night by withdrawing across the Rappahannock and posting artillery to command the fords. By late morning, Lee ordered Anderson to return the brigades to the positions they occupied prior to the battle.[35]

Weary soldiers were physically exhausted, and the violence had given most a mental shock. Some considered it the hardest fight of the war so far. "I can't describe the scenes of blood and horror that I have seen it was terrible sickening in the extreme," recalled Virginian John Mosely of Mahone's Brigade. Joel Blake recalled seeing "hundreds of dead Yankees lying about half burnt still unburied, many of their wounded were doubtless burned to death. My God such an [*sic*] horrible sight I hope I may never witness again." A Mississippian wrote his wife with anguish, telling her "the sight I saw I cant [*sic*] pen it down. It is a slaughter pen. It is enough to make the Old Master weep." John Hosford returned from sick leave just after the battle and was in time to see "a column of yankee [*sic*] prisoners near the length of a mile and a half long." Rather than being dispirited, the prisoners "were in good spirits and full of jesting," he recalled, "no doubt glad to get out of the murderous scene they had been witnessing." The relieved Yankees joked that they were headed "down towards Richmond. Hooker had promised to carry them and they had concluded to go without him."[36]

Despite the confused advance of his brigades on May 4, Anderson's performance during most of the multi-day engagement at Chancellorsville and Salem Church must be marked as one of his most significant accomplishments. At one point, he had received Lee's warmest compliments on the field. Lee rode up to Anderson and "raising his hat and bowing low said 'General you have done your country great service. Allow me to thank you in her name.'" Anderson bowed deeply in return, modestly acknowledging the praise. "I am well pleased General if you think so," he replied. Another staff officer recalled seeing Lee ride up to Anderson "and with trembling emotions of admiration and gratitude, salute him as 'My brave old general.'" Lee also acknowledged Anderson's role when he penned his report of the battle after a summer of heavy campaigning that took his army from the banks of the Rappahannock to the bloody fields of Pennsylvania. At Chancellorsville, Anderson was "distinguished for the promptness, courage, and skill with which he and his division executed every order." Lee also gave Anderson special notice for his initiative and aggressiveness in ordering Wright's brigade to use the unfinished railroad cut to turn the Union right flank on May 1, thus prompting Hooker's withdrawal towards Chancellorsville—a move that set the tone for the remainder of the battle and made possible Jackson's flank attack.

As a result of the dispersal of his command to various locations around Fredericksburg and along the Rappahannock, some of Anderson's brigades supported other divisions where needed. Some brigades approached the battlefield on roads that brought them into areas held by McLaws, while others happened to be handy to block the advance of Sedgwick's corps. Nonetheless, until the disjointed assault on May 4, Anderson had maneuvered the troops under his control adeptly and they had fought well as a result. Whether he had his friend Longstreet's words of advice in mind during those trying days, or whether serving under Lee's direct hand had stimulated his efforts, the fact remains that no small part of the laurels for the victory went to Fighting Dick Anderson and his gallant division. If Lee felt Longstreet's absence, Anderson at least did not add to that burden, and in most instances, he rose above the need for any close oversight and direction.[37]

Despite his nervous agitation as Anderson pulled out of the lines at Chancellorsville and rushed to join McLaws at Salem Church, Lee appreciated more realistically in hindsight the time-consuming nature of such a challenge and found no fault, instead acknowledging that Anderson was prompt in executing his orders. Lee would soon have cause to remark that Anderson was *always* quick to advance, and his actions during the recent fighting and marching bore out that observation. There had been few missteps, and no hesitation. He and his brigade commanders had performed skillfully, and Anderson was quick to acknowledge their leadership. He especially praised Posey and his "brave, untiring, persevering Mississippians," whom he also complimented in person on the field. One soldier recalled that the brigade was "commended very highly by General Anderson for charging without any bayonets." Anderson's report noted that their "steadiness" even when outnumbered "saved our army from great peril." He also remarked the "gallant conduct" of Wilcox and his men at Salem Church. Wilcox had indeed showed initiative, and he went to some length to let Anderson know. "I beg to assure the major-general commanding that the conduct of both officers and men of the brigade was in the highest degree creditable," he wrote to Anderson, likely in an effort to deflect attention from the fact that the 10th Alabama briefly gave way at Salem Church. Anderson realized that Wilcox's Alabamians had felt the full weight of Sedgwick's thrust in that engagement and in his own report even Lee singled him out as "entitled to especial praise for the judgment and bravery displayed in impeding the advance of General Sedgwick . . . and for the gallant and successful stand at Salem Church." Mahone's "bold, skillful, and successful management" also merited mention from the division commander, as did "Wright and his high-spirited, fearless Georgians," who "excited the admiration of all who saw them." Comments about Perry rounded out Anderson's coverage of the infantry. Perry and "his heroic little band of Floridians" drew praise for "courage as intrepid as that of any others." He likewise acknowledged the artillery commanders, staff, and other supporting personnel for their distinguished service.[38]

Lee complimented the entire army in a general order on May 7 that conveyed his "heartfelt gratification" for its "heroic conduct." He urged the men to gather on the next Sunday to "unite . . . in ascribing to the Lord of Hosts the glory due unto His name." In the midst of rejoicing, Lee encouraged the troops not to forget those who fell and instead to resolve to "emulate their noble example." He also passed along President Davis's thanks to Lee and the army "for this addition to the unprecedented series of great victories which your army has achieved."[39]

Lee's most grievous loss was Jackson, whose death on May 10 was a blow from which the army never fully recovered. Lee announced the tragedy the next day. He began to construct an inspiring narrative around Jackson's death, telling the men that "his spirit still lives" and would "inspire the whole army with his indomitable courage." A. P. Hill had immediately taken over Jackson's corps before turning over command to Stuart. Hill was able to resume command of the corps by May 6, and Stuart returned to his cavalry command. There remained a question of a permanent replacement for Jackson, but Lee also gave voice to the idea of reorganizing the army even further. On May 20th, Lee wrote to President Davis suggesting that the army's two corps were too large and should be downsized. It was an idea he had been considering for some time, but Jackson's death presented the opportunity to put the idea to Davis. The current corps structure made it too difficult for one commander to "properly handle and keep under his eye in battle" 30,000 or more men. Instead, Lee proposed elevating Ewell to corps command in Jackson's place, then creating a new third corps comprised of one of Longstreet's divisions (Anderson's) and A. P. Hill's Light Division under William D. "Dorsey" Pender, along with three other brigades that would form a third division for Harry Heth. A. P. Hill, whom Lee described as "the best soldier of his grade with me," would command that corps. Lee urged promotion for Hill and for Ewell, whom he touted as "an honest, brave soldier, who has always done his duty well." Lee thought it would be proper to promote those deserving of advancement, as it would be an inducement to all "to believe that their labors are appreciated." As for corps commanders, Lee believed the promotion to lieutenant general would increase their efficiency, "and I do not know where to get better men than those I have proposed," he added. Lee also described Hood and Anderson as "capital officers," adding that they were "improving . . . and will make good corps commanders if necessary."[40]

On that same day, Lee also wrote to Secretary of War James A. Seddon telling him that he still wanted Longstreet back with the army and that D. H Hill should command the department that lay between the James and Cape Fear. Hill's transfer freed another division command position in his army. Now the reorganization of the army and the movement of commanders had given Lee an opportunity to examine his options closely. Despite his general enthusiasm for his subordinate commanders' conduct, Lee occasionally found fault, though seldom grievous in nature. Lee gently chastised McLaws, for example, for his failure to move more rapidly in supporting Early's advance at Salem Church. Such behavior "reinforced his desire to have Longstreet more closely supervise McLaws in future battles." For the time being, Lee could not bring himself to rate McLaws highly enough to be considered for a corps command despite his seniority. He was accumulating a record for disappointing his chief. Instead, he promoted Ewell on May 23. The next day Lee called Powell Hill to his tent and informed him that he was to command a new third corps.[41]

Lee, always cognizant of the effects of his decisions, had weighed his options for corps commanders carefully. Lee did it again in May 1864 when he appointed Dick Anderson in Longstreet's place. Lee's decisions in May 1863 illustrate some of the same considerations he applied in Anderson's elevation. Ewell had been closely associated with Jackson, and some alleged Jackson himself wished Ewell to assume command. Many observers thought him the most obvious choice. Hill seemed just as likely a choice to others. Major William J. "Willie" Pegram thought Hill should get a chance, as once he did "the enemy will fear him as much as they ever feared Jackson." Dorsey Pender noted that "some designing person" seemed bent on injuring Hill's chances for promotion by claiming that Jackson "frequently said he wanted Ewell to have his Corps." Many on Jackson's staff hoped precisely for that outcome however, with one of them complaining that Hill "behaved very coarsely" towards the staff. Henry Kyd Douglas noted, "the personal breach" between Hill and Jackson "never healed." Lingering animosity abided still in some of Jackson's staff. Jedediah Hotchkiss, Jackson's trusted mapmaker, was concerned when Hill assumed temporary command of the corps. Not only was he not a "man of God," Hotchkiss told his wife, there was scant evidence that Hill bore "the sword of the Lord and of Gideon." Most of Jackson's staff anticipated Hill would replace them in favor of his own choices should he be chosen to lead the corps, but Hotchkiss thought, "Lee will not approve of their leaving." He did not, and therefore, in the end, the wishes of the staff may have influenced Lee's conviction that Ewell was the man for the job. Nevertheless, Hill got his own new corps.[42]

The promotion of Hill over the more senior McLaws, however, led to "no little discontent" among a few officers in the army, including Longstreet, whose recent successes in independent command must have added to his dissatisfaction with his role in Lee's army. McLaws was so annoyed that he complained directly to Lee about Hill's promotion over him, while Cadmus Wilcox also smarted after failing to gain a division command. Wilcox had even petitioned for a transfer as early as November 1862 after he learned of Pickett's promotion and grew despondent over his own chances in the Army of Northern Virginia. Lee was conciliatory then, but he could not accommodate his disgruntled subordinate, writing paternally to Wilcox: "you must come and see me and tell me what is the matter. I know you are too good a soldier not to serve where it is necessary for the benefit of the Confederacy." Nonetheless, Lee continued to overlook Wilcox, instead promoting fellow Virginian Robert E. Rodes to division command in place of D. H. Hill. "Everyone is talking of the injustice done me and I am now really sick with disgust,'" wrote the dejected Wilcox in mid-May. To make that choice even more vexing to Wilcox, Rodes was a graduate of the Virginia Military Institute with no regular army service. He was the only non-West Point man serving in Lee's army as a division commander. Non-Virginians, however, felt the latest insult keenly. In Longstreet's view the fact that Ewell and A. P. Hill both "were Virginians made the trouble more grievous." In early June, both McLaws and Longstreet discussed between themselves options for service elsewhere. One idea was for Longstreet to take over command of coastal defenses while Beauregard moved to corps command in the Army of Northern Virginia. Longstreet must have been considering his options for independent command since he received news of Powell Hill's promotion, perhaps believing that the downsizing of his corps had been a vote of no confidence from his chief. Longstreet reached out to Anderson soon afterwards, seemingly to test Dick's willingness to follow him to another command, although the purpose might have been more benign. Anderson received a note from Longstreet on May 30, the day Lee's Special Orders No. 146 officially decreed that Anderson's division was slated to join A. P. Hill's new corps. He wrote back to his comrade immediately, thanking him for his "kindness towards me," but going on somewhat cryptically from there. Longstreet's note does not survive in Anderson's correspondence, but if he inquired about his friend's willingness to join him in departing the Army of Northern Virginia, he must have done so in a rather oblique manner. Anderson's response was somewhat circumspect as well. "Your feelings and my own in the matter proposed," he wisely responded, "are precisely the same in that no private considerations should be suffered to interfere with public duty, and I am therefore ready . . . to render cheerfully and earnestly my best efforts to discharge my duty in any situation in which the Commanding General and yourself may determine that they can be most suitably employed." It is possible such language regarding "the matter proposed" was simply related to Anderson's transfer to Hill's corps. It is also possible that Anderson crafted it to let Longstreet know tactfully that he would certainly be willing to continue to serve under him if Longstreet obtained an independent command, but he was not going to support an abandonment of Lee by non-Virginians over the issue of Hill's promotion. Anderson would go elsewhere only if Lee and Longstreet both agreed it was best. If that was the intent, he attempted to soften his comments even more by closing "with great regard and respect, your obt servt and friend." The matter of there being "'too much Virginia'" in the army was left to simmer and, as Longstreet recalled, "the little quarrel was soon lost sight of,—displaced by affairs of greater moment."[43]

Anderson's transfer to Hill's corps was, however, fraught with the prospect of difficulties, a possibility that Longstreet probably realized immediately, but which the guileless Anderson declined to entertain. Longstreet and Hill had feuded bitterly over newspaper reports giving Hill too much credit for the success of the Battle of Frayser's Farm. Longstreet took umbrage because the article ignored other commanders' contributions, and the "high-strung" Hill lashed out in return. Acrimonious correspondence flew back and forth, Hill was placed in arrest, and Longstreet was challenged to a duel. Lee intervened and resolved the issue, but relations thereafter remained strained. Longstreet saw that his friendship and close relationship with Anderson might be something Hill would hold against Dick, and the situation might provide an opportunity for Hill to strike back at Anderson's expense. Nonetheless, Anderson's kindly nature and sense of duty led him to accept the situation as it was.[44]

By mid-summer in 1863, tattered and hungry Confederates had exhausted the bounty reaped from Yankee knapsacks littering the Chancellorsville battlefields. Worn clothing began to rival complaints about food shortages, which plagued the troops since earlier that spring. Once again, a lack of footwear became a matter of concern. By that time, the army was on the move, heading north to Pennsylvania and the so-called High Tide of the Confederacy.[45]

Chapter 13

Gettysburg

We have reached the shore on which all dreams are wrecked.

—Stefan Zweig,
The World of Yesterday

Anderson's division demonstrated its resiliency in recovering from the grueling experience of Chancellorsville and resuming a more docile routine. As early as May 6, an Alabamian in Wilcox's brigade, already back on picket duty on the Rappahannock, wrote "the boys and the Yankees are abusing each other across the river. All in a friendly way however, as we have a tacit agreement that neither party is to fire at the other when on picket." A Mississippi officer in Posey's brigade wrote his mother from his camp near Fredericksburg on May 15 that after "eight days of constant fatigue and fighting, we have had ample time to become fully rested and are now as able as we ever were to undergo a campaign, being in fine health and good spirits." Another man wrote his wife that despite the daily hard drilling "the boys is [*sic*] well . . . and in hy [*sic*] spirit." Yet another Mississippian, concerned about news from home about "his little squad of darkies" being enticed to run off and follow "the Negro liberators," wrote his sister to inquire if they took anything with them. If they did, he told her of his plan to extract revenge: "I will pay them with interest, that is if we ever go to Maryland or Pennsylvania, which I believe we will do this summer." In that regard, he was correct. Lee indeed was planning to capitalize on his momentum, move north into Pennsylvania and subsist his army on the plentiful bounty there, perhaps even providing some relief for besieged Vicksburg. Moreover, achieving his long-sought goal of winning a decisive engagement, especially on northern soil, might renew the prospect of European recognition and influence the northern political situation and anti-war sentiment as well. Lee's army was riding a tide of successes in the spring of 1863. If the time was not then propitious for a clear success in the North, when could it ever be so? A conclusive triumph there might even render southern reverses elsewhere largely irrelevant.[1]

Lewis W. Miles of Company D, 22nd Georgia in Wright's brigade wrote to his wife on June 2, 1863, "last evening the order was read on dress parade, that Anderson's Division was taken from Longstreet's Corps & put under A. P. Hill with two other divisions which constitute the 3rd army corps in this part of the army. I had much rather stayed under Longstreet." It cannot be said that his fate might have been different had he remained with Longstreet, but Lewis was destined to die in a field hospital south of Gettysburg on July 22 after being wounded in the groin. "Oh Ma," he had written gloomily to his wife in early April as the spring campaign approached, "prepare to meet me where there is no separation, try to raise our children right." Miles survived the carnage at Chancellorsville only to fall in Pennsylvania less than a month later. After the fight at Gettysburg a companion from Miles's company wrote home on July 9, 1863, from his "camp near heggars [*sic*] town Maryland" to tell his sisters: "I can't say how this fite [*sic*] went. Some say we whipped them and some say we got whipped I no [*sic*] we lost lots of men. My company went in the fite [*sic*] with 33 men, an came out with 15 unhurt. There was 7 we don't know what has become of them. Our Captain and colonel were killed on the field." There was to be no decisive victory for Lee on Gettysburg's verdant fields, and while there were many reasons for the diminished outcome, Dick Anderson's first battle under his new corps commander would raise some troubling questions from some of his subordinates. The wheels were about to come off the Army of Northern Virginia at one of the most critical moments of its existence.[2]

Lee withdrew from the Rappahannock starting on June 3. Longstreet and Ewell marched westward towards the Shenandoah Valley while A. P. Hill's corps remained to guard against a threat from Hooker. Hill deployed his divisions to confuse Hooker about Lee's movements, but it was impossible to disguise them completely. Nonetheless, Hooker was unsure if Lee was withdrawing towards Richmond or moving towards the Valley. If Hooker withdrew to protect Washington and Harpers Ferry, Hill was encouraged to pursue him and harass his rear elements. With nothing now standing between his corps and the Confederate capital, however, Hill was undoubtedly concerned a few days later when all signs pointed to Hooker's intention to attack him south of the Rappahannock. Hooker began shelling Hill's positions while elements of Sedgwick's corps crossed on pontoon bridges downriver from Fredericksburg at Franklin's Crossing (Deep Run). Sedgwick established a bridgehead on the river's southern side, capturing "some 40 of Genl. Posey's men . . . in the rifle pits," and carrying on some skirmishing with Rebel pickets. If Lee was moving westward as Hooker suspected was most likely, he thought it best to cross the Rappahannock and "pitch into his rear." Lincoln astutely advised otherwise, telling Hooker in his usual homespun manner that he "would not take the risk of being entangled upon the river, like an ox jumped half over a fence and liable to be torn by dogs front and rear, without a fair chance to gore one way or kick the other." As for Hill, Lee advised that if overwhelmed he was to fall back on Richmond along the railroad and contest Hooker's advance as best he could. In the event, only a rather feeble reconnaissance in force took place. Despite frequent skirmishing and sharpshooting, Lee seemed certain after a time that there was nothing much to it. Anderson's brigades were routinely engaged in the skirmishing, and Jerome Yeats, a belligerent Mississippian in Posey's command wrote his sister that he was "in sight of not less than five thousand Yankees while I write. I would like to have them all in my power," he told her. "I would send them to another world at a double-quick. . . . I think of you every time I shoot at them." A fellow Mississippian was less sanguine about the situation than Yeats was, writing his wife that he was "expecting a fight ever minute. I may never write to you again but as soon as the battle is over I will write if I am spared. I see hard times hear [*sic*]." Ultimately, "there was a good deal of sharpshooting every day but not much damage done on either side," and Hooker's efforts to divine Lee's plans came to naught. After a hard-fought cavalry engagement at Brandy Station on June 9, Lincoln once again advised Hooker that it was Lee's army and not Richmond that was "your sure objective point." By June 13, Hooker accepted with certainty that much of Lee's army had moved towards the Shenandoah Valley. Hooker immediately withdrew towards Manassas and Dumfries. "Old Iron Ewell," as one Virginian in Mahone's brigade called him, was already as far north as Berryville, Virginia by then.[3]

Hill's corps marched rapidly to rejoin Lee. At Hill's headquarters one staff member had eagerly written to a sympathetic friend in the North, whom he thought "would like to hear from the Land of Cotton," that the men were "now in fighting and marching trim," and would be returning once again to northern soil. "Then woe to the Negro thief abbetters [*sic*] and barn burners. Old scores are to be settled," he wrote. "You will no doubt be pleased to hear that we have concluded to beat the lion in his den." Dick Anderson, probably without such vindictive motives in mind, prepared to do his part in that effort. He bid farewell to Sallie, who had just arrived on June 3 and was staying at Idlewild, a stately brick Greek Revival home west of Fredericksburg. It must have been a disappointing visit, for it is doubtful her husband was able to spend much time away from the looming Union threat near Deep Run that developed soon after her arrival. Sallie at least did not disquiet Dick so much as the concern Hill's pregnant wife Dolly had caused her husband when she declined to leave expeditiously. Another of Hill's division commanders, Dorsey Pender, told his wife about Dolly's misguided dawdling, writing "I know you are too good a wife to have given me as much anxiety and trouble as she gave the General." Sallie Anderson was by then as much a veteran of army service as her husband, and she caused no bother.[4]

Anderson's division started towards Culpeper on June 14, reaching Chancellorsville that first day. General Posey was so anxious to move that he neglected to call in a company of pickets from the 19th Mississippi and had to send his adjutant back to find them and hurry them along. The 8th Alabama's pickets were also tasked with giving Yankee pickets the impression the army was preparing to cross at Banks' Ford. Having had friendly relations with the Yanks across the river for some time, the Alabamians considered it a "violation of good faith" to open fire without warning. They therefore chose to withdraw to cover first, calling out over the river "Take care of yourselves, Yanks, we are coming across!" The blue-clad pickets at first laughed it off as a joke, but the Alabamians commenced firing over their heads until they finally sought cover. With both sides safely behind their breastworks, a two-hour exchange of fire ensued with no damage inflicted on either one.[5]

Longstreet had deployed near Culpeper to screen the army's movements and remain near enough to support Hill if needed. Ewell, meanwhile, continued onward and was moving down the Shenandoah Valley. Hill's divisions followed in Ewell's steps. Anderson continued on the Plank Road and crossed his division over the Rapidan at Germanna Ford. Men were undoubtedly pleased to be quit of the gruesome field of Chancellorsville. An officer in Perry's brigade was distraught to see that the site of one mass grave near the Chancellor house was marked by "several streams of blue gas," that were "gushing; plainly visible for some distance," while "here and there an arm or leg [was] protruding where the rains had washed the dirt from shallow graves." A Mississippi soldier wrote his brother that the battlefield was "Very offensive now. Rights of sepulture badly performed." Such sights did little to encourage men who would soon face the brutal test of combat once again.[6]

By June 15, weather conditions were affecting their progress. It was "very hot—many men sunstruck and fainting on the way," recalled one of Mahone's men. Likewise, Charlie Denoon of Mahone's brigade noted, "we suffered much from heat, several men died on the march from fatigue and heat." He was fortunate to have "felt no inconvenience except blistered feet," which he hoped a night's rest would cure. The following day was more temperate as the marching column snaked through the town of Culpeper and halted for the day. Anderson issued instructions for the men to cook three days' rations that night to carry with them, with each regimental wagon hauling three days' more, and four days' worth in the division's supply trains. Edmond Patterson of the 9th Alabama took the opportunity to set off with four of his comrades to do a little foraging. At dinnertime they found themselves "seated in the shade of an old apple tree . . . with about two and a half gallons of butter milk before us, and of course we had a glorious dinner."

Patterson calculated his regiment made about twelve miles when the march resumed on a northwesterly route on June 17, and another reckoned his Virginia regiment made about ten miles that day. Weather was again "terribly hot . . . many fainting and overcome by the heat." Sergeant James Kirkpatrick was pleased to note that his fellow Mississippians "seem generally to keep up and avoid straggling." Adjutant A. L. Peel of the 19th Mississippi recalled General Anderson passing by the marching columns when one man called out "Mr. Anderson your company is mighty tired, let us rest." The general's response went unrecorded, but Peel too noted the impact of the heat. "Our men straggled tolerable badly," he wrote. June 18 saw little respite until it began to rain that evening and the weather cooled. They were now in "hilly and beautiful country," Mosely wrote. Anderson continued to push his brigades closer and closer to the protection of the Blue Ridge Mountains where Chester Gap lay in the distance, but the beauty of the landscape did little to comfort the suffering soldiers that day. Patterson recorded that more than a dozen men of his company had suffered sunstroke. There was not a breath of air under the beating sun and smothering dust that marked the route of many thousands of feet, he complained. Officers permitted no one to fall out of the marching column, but as men began to drop from the heat and exhaustion, their surgeon finally relented and told the weary Alabamians to "stop when they felt it necessary."[7]

June 19 found the men trudging up the eastern face of the Blue Ridge and filing through Chester Gap near Front Royal before crossing the North and South Forks of the Shenandoah River. Their arrival in the Valley was not a welcoming one. A hard rain beat down all night as the soldiers first stumbled along the muddy and rocky roads and then stopped to sleep as best they could. Many found they could rest only by "standing, sitting, or lying in the mud and water." Others "passed a terrible night—never slept a wink." Edmund Patterson had hoped to keep his clothing somewhat dry in crossing the rivers and had removed his boots, socks, and trousers. "By the time I had cut my feet on the sharp rocks, and fallen down a time or two, I regretted it," he recalled. More trouble followed in scaling the steep bank on the opposite side. All the time rain poured in torrents "and the cussing of some the boys was fearfully serious." Patterson finally settled down for the night on several lengths of rail fence placed side-by-side on the ground to keep him out of the mud. "With the darkness and rain for a covering," he glibly commented, he woke next morning "feeling a little stiff."[8]

Sunday, June 21 brought Anderson and his men to Berryville, where they camped in "a beautiful grove of oaks on the edge of the town." Speculation about the army heading back into Maryland seemed more like fact by then. Already the soldiers took note of the perceptible change in the local population's sentiments though. "Union people pretty thick round here," one Virginian mentioned concisely in a letter to his brother. Others knew of staunch supporters in the area. Edmund Patterson, believing his regiment would rest at Berryville for at least another day, set out before breakfast on the morning of the 22nd with two friends "on our day's ramble." While dining with a Mr. Williams at around 4 PM that afternoon their host commented that he thought, "General Anderson's division was the finest looking body of men that he had ever seen." The surprised soldiers asked where he had seen the division and found that Williams had observed it marching through Berryville about 9 that morning. "Here we were four miles in an opposite direction and the regiment had been marching all day," Patterson exclaimed later. "We thought it not worthwhile to grieve," he concluded, and the three friends took their time catching up to the unit near Shepherdstown the next day, well fed and amply supplied with tobacco.[9]

The route to Shepherdstown and the Potomac River fords first took Anderson's division through Charlestown on June 23. There the sentiments of the residents were more sympathetic and the men "met with a most enthusiastic reception." One of Perry's Floridians remarked on the crowds of flag and handkerchief waving ladies that lined the streets as the soldiers tramped by in step to the tune of the "Marseillaise" rendered by "our fine brass band." The 6th Virginia passed by as early as 7 AM and were greeted with "great cheering by the people." Even Edmund Patterson, rushing along to catch up with the 9th Alabama noted that "the people were delighted to see us, and gave us a hearty welcome." It raised the troops' spirits. They would soon be crossing the Potomac into Maryland to find themselves once again in less hospitable surroundings, but Hill had taken advantage of the current good spirits in his corps around that time to issue General Order number 4, in which he told of the forthcoming crossing of the Potomac and the "prospect of a brilliant Campaign." He exhorted the men to give their all and to "resolve to conquer a peace this campaign."[10]

Wilcox's brigade waded the Potomac at a ford below Shepherdstown early on the morning of June 24. The water was three to four feet deep, Patterson recalled, and "it was a little cool but we were all in such fine spirits that we didn't mind it." The hardened Alabamians passed through Sharpsburg once more, "a hard looking dilapidated old town" that still bore many of the scars of the previous September's battle. James Kirkpatrick likewise found Sharpsburg "much dilapidated," as his regiment moved through on the way to Boonsboro, and A. L. Peel observed that the Sharpsburg "women looked sour."[11]

Just before crossing the river that day, James B. Johnson, adjutant of the 5th Florida, met a Baltimore woman whom he described as "an enthusiastic rebel." She encouraged Johnson by telling him that, "Marylanders were just waiting to flock to our army, they will join you by thousands." Johnson later found the facts to be somewhat different. "We had one old man to join us and he had a fit and dropped out the first day," he recalled. "That was all I saw of recruits in passing through Maryland." James Kirkpatrick likewise observed that they found "few signs of sympathy since we crossed the river," while a sergeant in the 2nd Florida wrote in his diary that "everything looks pretty union."[12]

Nevertheless, the men were in high spirits and a good number of veterans filled the ranks. Newer men who had bolstered the army's numbers after Antietam had every right to call themselves veterans after the vicious fighting at Chancellorsville in May, but as the army approached a major battle, Anderson faced a number of minor crises at the brigade command level. He was again compelled to temporarily elevate Colonel David Lang of the 8th Florida to replace Brigadier General Perry, who had fallen ill with typhoid fever soon after the Battle of Chancellorsville. In light of the criticism Lang's troops received while disputing the federal crossing of the Rappahannock on the first day of the Battle of Fredericksburg, the situation might have given Anderson some cause for concern. Meanwhile, in addition to Cadmus Wilcox's previously discussed consternation over his lack of promotion, William Mahone had also raised concerns after tendering his resignation in early June. Mahone argued that his position as president of the Norfolk and Petersburg Railroad Company now required his immediate attention. Those who might act in his place in that capacity, he contended, were "for the most part within the enemy's lines." He received no response to his tendered resignation until well after the battle, when he sent yet another request that Dick Anderson reluctantly approved, with "regret that any such party should compel the resignation of so valuable an officer." Hill disapproved, as did others up to Secretary of War James Seddon, who "concurred fully with Genl Hill's endorsement." Thus, Dick Anderson was about to engage in battle for the first time under A. P. Hill's leadership with one brigade commander absent sick, another brooding over his failure to gain promotion and recognition, and a third who believed his duties lay someplace other than with his brigade. Of the three, only Mahone's behavior would fall puzzlingly short, but forthcoming events would do little to improve the already foul moods of Wilcox or Wright.[13]

As the division moved along the road to Boonsboro, Maryland, General Anderson very nearly saw his leadership problems compounded when Wright and his staff were passing through Keedysville. They were riding well ahead of the Georgia brigade and "were pounced on by a dozen independent cavalry." Rans Wright and his staff quickly wheeled about and spurred their horses back in the direction of their advancing brigade. It was a narrow escape, except that Wright's son William, who had lost his right leg at Second Manassas and was unable to ride as quickly as the others, was "captured and carried off to the mountains." There was no cavalry nearby to pursue, and William spent nearly a year in Yankee prisons before his exchange, but his immediate fate was unclear. Now a fourth brigade commander had reason to be out of sorts.[14]

While not so hostile as the reception received by General Wright and his party, many found the reaction to their presence in Maryland varied. Sergeant George Bernard of the 12th Virginia recalled stopping at a humble, one-story Maryland house with a hallway running from front to back. Bernard solicited a drink of water from a young girl. After bringing the water, the girl said, "Look at Grandma." Bernard was amused to see "the old lady, away back in the hallway, waving an old-fashioned sun bonnet and performing a very dance of jubilee in the privacy of her own dwelling, knowing full well that, did she indulge in public rejoicing, the vengeance of neighbors otherwise affected would be visited upon her after we had passed by." Still, as Bernard admitted, it soon became "painfully apparent . . . that the idea of recruiting our ranks in Maryland was not to be realized." Bernard thought the "quasi-friendliness" of the population an embarrassment to Lee, who was thus unable with good conscience to "draw upon the resources of the country as that of an enemy, nor obtain any substantial support from the inhabitants as allies." Nevertheless, Lee issued orders on June 21 warning against pillaging. Although it prohibited the men in the ranks from damaging or destroying personal property, appropriately designated officers of the Ordnance, Medical, Quartermaster, and Commissary Departments had authorization to purchase goods from willing sellers or to seize them from those unwilling to cooperate.[15]

Captain Charles Waddell of the 12th Virginia found a wild reception in passing through Boonsboro, Maryland, where he "had to submit to having the buttons on the sleeve of my jacket cut off by some four or five ladies—was seized by them in the street & was not allowed to proceed until I gave up the buttons." In Hagerstown, however, Anderson had to order the stores to be opened, "and Confederate money was taken at 50 cts on the dollar." As his regiment moved into Pennsylvania Waddell found that the "people look upon us as Savages, incarnate devils until they are brought in contact & then a most pleasing change comes over them."[16]

By the time Anderson's division reached Pennsylvania, one Alabamian was amused to find that "the people seemed to think that the Rebel army would eat them up without salt or bread." A Virginian similarly found that some of the people "were frightened to death" and "thought we were nothing more than a Grand Gang of Cut throats . . . committing all manner of depredations." He complained that people would not sell anything "either for Silver, Greenbacks, or our money but with few exceptions. . . . Most of the Generals told their men to offer Confed. Money and if they would not take it take what they wanted." Still, some men in the ranks ignored Lee's order prohibiting the seizure of property, with one admitting that his fellow "Alabamians [were] very bad at this, so Mississippians." One of the latter noted, "some of our boys haven't acted right, are in hopes it will stop." Another thought his fellow Mississippians "have acted shamefully . . . it demoralizes the army." One possible reason for their behavior was that Yankee troops had passed through or seized areas of both states. Tales of hardship and depredations filled letters from home. Dr. Robert Peel of the 19th Mississippi expressed the despair many felt. "Amongst the many trials & troubles a rebel soldier has to bear, there is none so bitter & humiliating as the thought that his mother, sister, wife or sweetheart must feel the blow & suffer the horrors of this cruel war." It was little wonder that some distraught and angry soldiers sought to repay northerners in kind. Hill therefore thought it necessary to issue another circular on June 25 reminding his men of the proscription, not to mention the sanctions, "The penalty for such offence is death, and . . . in an enemy Country this penalty can be enforced by Drumhead Court Martial."[17]

Anderson's division passed through Chambersburg, Pennsylvania on June 2, where "our bands gave the citizens an abundance of rebel music," a Mississippian recalled. The head of the long column finally halted at nearby Fayetteville. Anderson's division remained near those towns until July 1, the men still unsure of their destination. "Some think to Washington, others to Baltimore, and others think through Pennsylvania," a Virginian told his parents. Others, perhaps owing to the stimulating effects of being on northern soil and among the foe, were concerned only with living life in the immediate present. William McClellan wrote his sister that on arriving at Chambersburg the women "would turn up their nose and toss their heads to one side as contemptuously as if we were highway Robbers." Young Rebels wasted little time winning their hearts. When the soldiers left many of the women "would ask the Boys to come back and see them the first opportunity." Some had even become engaged to girls, McClellan asserted, and "would have married them in three more days." Fleming Thompson of the 11th Alabama later confessed to his relatives that he "came very near falling in love with one of the Pennsylvania Dutch Gals."[18]

Edmund Patterson of Alabama continued his frequent forays away from camp, and after taking dinner at the hotel in Fayetteville on July 30, he and a few comrades set out into the surrounding country "go get a supper." They were successful as usual, finding a farmhouse where there was a comely young lass who "was Union but called herself a 'copperhead.' I wouldn't mind being bitten by her a few times," Patterson admitted in his journal.[19]

Heth's and Pender's divisions had already marched towards Gettysburg on June 29, leaving Anderson's division to bring up the rear when it set out on the Chambersburg Pike before daylight on July 1. As the column crested South Mountain, several men commented on the nearby ruins of Thaddeus Stevens's iron forge that Ewell's men had fired. One Mississippian noted he "encountered a heavy rain" that slowed the steep march before they were halted on the summit. Others wound down the eastern slope towards Cashtown, and several men later remarked about halting there as well for an indeterminate period ranging from "for some time" to "several hours." Anderson himself recalled "waiting about an hour at Cashtown" until Hill sent orders to continue onward to Gettysburg. Most likely, the halted division stretched from Cashtown back towards South Mountain for a mile or more. From their elevated vantage point, some could see masses of troops moving across the landscape in battle formation. Eventually, all heard the roar of Heth's distant fight, soon joined by the guns of Pender's division and Ewell's corps arriving on the field from the north. As they resumed their march and moved ever closer, rolling volleys of musketry accompanied the booming artillery fire. Most expected going directly into the fight, even though they had marched about twenty miles that day. "The query was in our minds—Why are we not put in? and we answered ourselves by saying, if we were needed 'Marse Bob' would have us there," recalled one Alabama officer.[20]

The battle began somewhat unintentionally despite Lee's injunction against a general engagement until he could concentrate his army. Hill had advanced one of Heth's brigades from Cashtown on June 30 in search of supplies at Gettysburg. Rumor that the town might contain a quantity of shoes was too much to ignore, but the Confederates returned empty-handed with only the additional information that there were federal troops of unknown strength there as well. One salient feature of the town of Gettysburg was the convergence there of several important roads. While Major General George G. Meade, then in command of the Union forces, groped somewhat blindly to find his adversary, Lee too was moving largely in the dark. He did not know the Union Army's precise location because he also did not know the location of his own most reliable source of information—Jeb Stuart's cavalry. Rather than screening Lee's movements, Stuart had once again ridden around his opponent's rear. His exploit did Lee no good whatsoever. Instead of supplying valuable intelligence, Stuart was now searching for his own army. On July 1, he was over thirty miles to the north in Carlisle, Pennsylvania. He would not move to rejoin Lee until the early hours of July 2.[21]

When Heth pressed forward with Hill's blessing on the morning of July 1 he found himself engaged with Brigadier General John Buford's cavalry troopers armed with breech loading Sharps carbines capable of a far more rapid rate of fire than the standard infantry rifle. Buford's dismounted cavalrymen delayed Heth's advance obstinately, and when Heth finally felt confident enough to send two of his brigades forward to capture the town they found not only cavalry to contest their advance, but a rapidly forming line of infantry soon to include the hardened westerners of the Iron Brigade. Buford's delaying tactics allowed Major General John F. Reynolds's First Corps infantrymen to reach the field. The general engagement that Lee had hoped to avoid had begun. From that point onward, each side rushed troops into the fray and the battle assumed a life of its own. Meade converged on Gettysburg, and Lee would have to meet him there. Lee, en route to Cashtown with Longstreet's corps, rushed ahead towards Hill's position as the sounds of battle grew angrier. On the way, he passed the drawn-out column of Anderson's division making its way towards the sound of the guns.[22]

Edmund Patterson of the 9th Alabama observed Lee confer briefly with Anderson as he passed by on the way to the front. The men were soon on their feet and back on the road. Anderson then received a note from Lee around noon saying that the general wanted to see him. He spurred forward and found Lee "intently listening" to the unfolding battle in the distance. Lee lamented Stuart's absence and told Anderson he was "in ignorance as to what we have in front of us here," but his division commander was unable to provide any information to ease his chief's mind. Lee rode on toward the din of battle. Rather than being thrown into the fight as many in Anderson's division anticipated, Lee sent a dispatch instructing the general to take up the positions that Pender's division had occupied before it moved into the fight. Anderson later claimed that Lee's uncertainty about the strength of the Federal force he confronted compelled him to hold the division in reserve, yet he was so puzzled at the time that he again rode ahead to find the General to verify that the courier had delivered the message correctly. Lee confirmed it, telling Anderson then that his division constituted the only fresh troops on hand until Longstreet arrived. By the time Anderson confirmed Lee's order and his brigades were drawing near the battlefield, the day was nearly gone. With it went the opportunity to capitalize on what seemed a rout of the Union troops initially pushed off Seminary Hill, only to rally in greater strength on Cemetery Hill. Later, questions arose about Anderson's sluggish efforts to reach the scene and whether arriving sooner might have ensured Confederate success. Lee and Hill, however, never questioned it or censured Anderson, and it seems Lee did not intend to throw his only available reserve force into the fight that day.[23]

Anderson's division began its march soon after daylight that morning. He and his staff rode well in advance of the division, and he probably encountered Lee near Cashtown before noon. The later meeting held to confirm the placement of his division was likely closer to 2 PM, after Lee arrived on the battlefield six miles past Cashtown. Rearmost elements of the division marched over twenty miles that day. With an aggregate strength of 8,000 men, the column would have stretched about a mile while marching in the standard column of fours, but the length far exceeded that with the attached artillery batteries and divisional supply trains. In addition, the fits and starts caused by mountainous terrain, road conditions, traffic congestion, rain, and heat undoubtedly conspired against a rate of march anywhere near parade-ground figures, likely extending the column length to something closer to two miles. The natural tendency for troops to string out on a difficult march lengthened it still further. If the head of Anderson's division halted at Cashtown at around 2 PM, it seems reasonable to conclude that the tail of the division would have passed that point at least an hour later. Once he heard the firing in the distance, Anderson instructed Lang to quick march Perry's Florida brigade around the division trains and connect with Wilcox, an order the men undoubtedly welcomed after shuffling along behind the wagons in the heavy dust cloud rising from the plodding hooves of horses and mules. General Wright, however, whose brigade was second in the column, claimed that it was within a mile of Cashtown by 10 AM, and halted there behind Mahone's Virginians. Wright left his command that day due to "severe indisposition" and likely remembered the time incorrectly, as all other references to the division reaching Cashtown point to an afternoon arrival. Several accounts put Anderson's arrival near the battlefield itself around 5 PM, but the entire division might not have been up until after six. Other accounts mention that it was nearly dark before they arrived at the point where they deployed into line, and some recalled arriving in time to observe the final phase of the still distant battle. In any event, Lee was fully aware of the precise location of Anderson's troops and had a solid estimate of when they would be available.[24]

Anderson's troops passed lines of wounded men along with Yankee prisoners streaming to the rear. Once on the field, he deployed his brigades along Herr Ridge about a mile south of the Chambersburg Pike and on the far right of the Confederate line. Anderson sent Wilcox with an artillery battery to occupy a position at right angles to the division line near the Black Horse Tavern. With Wilcox's Alabamians holding the right flank, the line ran through Perry's brigade commanded by Lang, then Wright's, Posey's, and Mahone's on the far left. The men slumbered undisturbed on their arms that night, knowing what the dawn held.[25]

Lee determined to press the attack on the Union lines on the morning of July 2, and he directed Anderson to move his division forward about a mile and a half to new positions on Seminary Ridge. The sun was already high when Anderson personally accompanied Wilcox to indicate the position that he wished his brigade to occupy, which was again on the extreme right flank bordering on a wood line called Pitzer's Woods. Unaware that Lee's plan required Longstreet to shift to the far right of the Confederate line beyond Anderson's flank, Dick remained apprehensive about the security of that flank. Longstreet would not be in position for some time.[26]

Some participants later alleged that Lee anticipated Longstreet to get into position overnight. While Lee did not specify an exact time for an attack to proceed, his vague instruction to do so "as early in the morning as practicable" apparently indicated a time much earlier than Longstreet was prepared to meet. According to that view, the plan that developed the previous night called for Ewell to demonstrate on the left while Longstreet made the primary attack on the right. Ewell, naturally, was to capitalize on any advantage gained by Longstreet's advance. Others, including Longstreet, maintained that Lee was still undecided as to how to proceed, and it was not until he returned from a visit to Ewell's positions on the left flank that morning that Lee finally decided that Longstreet's would be the primary assault. Longstreet insisted it was not until 11 AM that Lee issued definitive orders for the movement, and it was not until 2 PM that McLaws's division was finally filing past Wilcox's position and taking its place with the rest of Longstreet's corps on the right flank of the army. The attack was to begin on the far right against a prominence called Little Round Top, towards which Hood's division began to advance around 4 PM Lee's line would attack en echelon, with each brigade moving forward successively in waves as the one on its right advanced ahead of it. It was nearly ninety minutes after Hood's advance before the Mississippians of Brigadier General William Barksdale's brigade of McLaws's division started across the fields towards the Sherfy Farm and the Emmitsburg Road. Wilcox would follow them.[27]

Anderson's line ran generally parallel to the Emmitsburg Road and brigades preserved the same order in which they had bivouacked the previous night. From right to left were the brigades of Wilcox, Perry (Lang), Wright, Posey, and Mahone. Mahone's and Posey's brigades stretched southward from the vicinity of McMillan's Woods; Wright's brigade nearly spanned the gap between there and Spangler's Woods, with Lang's small brigade of Florida troops in those woods and around the Spangler Farm. After an interval of about a hundred yards running through Spangler's Woods, Wilcox's men formed a line from the southern edge of the trees that sloped upwards towards Pitzer's Woods. Other gaps in the line existed where the brigades did not connect, but because they anticipated making an attack and not defending against one, those breaks caused no anxiety. As his men moved into position, Wilcox found two of his regiments engaged in what Anderson would later term a "sharp skirmish" with Union sharpshooters in the woods. The 10th Alabama charged forward and drove the 3rd Maine and the green-clad marksmen of Hiram Berdan's First New York Sharpshooters away. Wilcox later reported the Yankees "fled precipitously" in face of the Alabamians' charge, "leaving 20 or 25 dead and twice that number wounded, and prisoners." The 10th Alabama received orders to lie down when it first received fire, Private Bailey McClellan recalled. The Maine men advanced "shooting at us all they could" until they were less than fifty yards distant. At that point, the 10th rose up and delivered a withering volley that "seemed to produce consternation in their ranks whereupon they made a right about for their rear and with a rebel yell we pursued them some distance. . . ." Berdan noted simply that he withdrew with most of his wounded men after "having accomplished the object of the reconnaissance," but Colonel Moses Lakeman's 3rd Maine suffered the most casualties. The Colonel reported that his men were deployed to fill gaps in the lines of the sharpshooters, who were all hidden behind trees while his own men stood without cover. Still, despite Wilcox's claim about the precipitous flight of his opponents, Lakeman noted that not until ordered to fall back by Colonel Berdan "did a single man leave the ranks." The Maine men delivered a few more volleys as they retreated, keeping Wilcox's pursuit at bay.[28]

With that minor but bitterly fought action concluded, Wilcox completed his occupation of the positions Anderson had laid out for the brigade. To protect his flank Wilcox formed the 10th Alabama at a right angle to the brigade line, which like the rest of Anderson's division was facing southeast towards the Emmitsburg Road and Cemetery Ridge beyond. Anderson could clearly see the Union troops about 1,200 yards distant, positioned on the opposite ridge that was slightly higher than the one occupied by his own men. Between the two opposing forces lay mostly open, undulating farm fields broken by rail or plank fences. Houses and farm buildings dotted the landscape of ripening wheat and young corn, but the men could also see the rail fence that ran along each side of the Emmitsburg Road. Removing the rails and piling them on the banks to form a breastwork, blue-clad soldiers rapidly formed there along with a number of artillery batteries. Anderson finally received word that Longstreet's corps would be coming up on his right for an attack, and that Old Pete's line would be positioned "nearly at right angles" with his own. Anderson's orders to put his brigades into action successively as Longstreet's men came up to connect with his right flank seemed logical, but the awkward, angled positioning of the troops of the two corps would complicate that movement. His brigades faced the Emmitsburg Road, but if executed as described, Longstreet's men would be attacking up that road and across his front. The fact that his division covered an excessively broad front that stretched nearly a full mile in length also contributed to the attack's ultimate failure. Such distance hampered easy communication with his brigades, and had it been possible to hold a strong brigade in reserve there might have been a different outcome.[29]

The precise location of Anderson's headquarters is unknown, but one logical area is the woods slightly behind the ridgeline and the Spangler House along present-day West Confederate Avenue. The spring that fed the house would have watered the horses of the officers, staff, and couriers. That area placed Anderson within approximately 500 yards of the extreme right of his line occupied by Wilcox. It seems logical that he would have expected the greatest burden of fighting to fall to the brigades on the right of his line since they would be the first to be committed to Longstreet's support. It is also possible that he knew from the very start of the engagement based on Hill's orders that he would throw forward only the brigades of Wilcox, Perry, and Wright to bolster Longstreet's attack. That too made his presence nearer those brigades more critical.

Troops "sweated, sweltered, and swore," recalled an 11th Alabama captain who complained, "the sun was fiercely hot and there was no shade or protection for the men." Hours ticked away as the wait for Longstreet's assault dragged on. A Florida soldier commented on the intense heat, made worse by the fact that the men "knew there was desparate [*sic*] fighting ahead of us, and [we] chafed at the delay." Meanwhile, "the enemy kept throwing their shells, grape and canister over us and among us." In the 22nd Georgia Wiley Pope was struck by a stray ball that "went through his nose and lodged in the back of his neck; he bled profusely and went to the rear." Pope walked all the way to Winchester, Virginia and was never again fit for duty. Federal skirmishers deployed within rifle range and some men were unable to resist taking an occasional shot at them even though they had no orders to do so. One Yankee climbed onto a rooftop to take better aim at his targets, but quickly drew attention. "He was such a nice target for the boys' sport" that he soon came down off the roof in a hurry, "fully instilled with the sensible idea that his position was not tenable."[30]

In the suffocating closeness of that July day, Wilcox's men finally saw what they had been waiting for—Longstreet's troops charging forward and pushing the Union lines back. One Confederate soldier on the skirmish line recalled hearing "a cheer such as southern soldiers only can give and a terrible crash of musketry" as Longstreet's assault commenced. Men watched as their comrades advanced twice through the open fields, and on the third charge Wilcox's Alabamians sprang forward with Barksdale's Mississippians to their right. Those in Wilcox's brigade heard amidst the firing a resounding rebel yell on the right of the Confederate line, "and on looking in that direction we could see the Yankees running and our boys after them in full drive and yelling all the time." As the 9th Alabama advanced, John Mason recalled seeing "Longstreet's corps charging in fine style for we could see down his whole line. Our boys stopped charging and pulled off their hats and gave them three cheers." Another observed the retreating Yankees, "and our boys yelling like madmen in hot pursuit." Wilcox first had to shift his brigade to the left as much as 400 or 500 yards to make room for Barksdale, but once clear, Wilcox faced his men by the right flank and struck out for the Union lines. Fearing that Lang was unable to see what was happening far to his right, Anderson sent a dispatch letting him know that Longstreet was driving the federals' left flank in and that Wilcox would soon advance as well. Anderson ordered Lang to send a strong line of skirmishers and move forward with Wilcox. Once the Alabamians advanced, Lang ordered his Floridians to follow, and those who had been engaged in the vice of playing cards "immediately tore them up and threw them away." Wright's Georgians followed Lang's men, all en echelon. The rest of the division stood fast. Anderson withheld most of Posey's Mississippians from the main assault, along with Mahone's brigade. Posey later reported that although he had understood earlier that he was to advance the brigade, he had received an order from Anderson just before the attack began "to advance but two of my regiments and deploy them closely as skirmishers." He sent the 19th and 48th Mississippi forward toward the Bliss Farm, the site of heavy skirmishing throughout the day.[31]

As soon as Wright's Georgians cleared the woods in their front "and came into the open fields the enemy poured a most terrific fire of shells into our ranks," recalled one man. Fortunately, a series of depressions and hollows running parallel to the Emmitsburg Road allowed for some respite from the direct fire, and the Georgians rushed forward successively from the intervening high ground "into each succeeding hollow." By that method, the men worked their way across the open field towards the Union positions, breaking down the fences along the way until reaching the Emmitsburg Road where Yankees stubbornly resisted their advance. Hand-to-hand fighting ensued for a time before the federals gave way. Finally, some of the Union artillery struck for the rear "and the infantry followed at a run."[32]

On the far right, Wilcox's men met with similar success. Edmund Patterson strode forward apprehensively in the ranks of the 9th Alabama praying for the courage to do his duty as Wilcox rode along the lines urging the men forward. "Cheer after cheer filled the air almost drowning the sound of shells that were bursting above and around us," Patterson recalled. As they advanced with their flag waving proudly, the high spirits of the moment led him to speak for all when he later wrote, "we felt that the starry cross must triumph."[33]

In the center of Anderson's three-brigade assault, Lang's Floridians were suffering heavy losses. James Johnson of the 5th Florida recalled Union artillery "making great gaps in our lines." The "air seems filled with musket balls," he wrote, and "our men are falling on all sides." Still, the tiny brigade pressed ahead. One Pennsylvania major later wrote that he had "never before seen such desperation on the part of the rebels, who hurled their columns against us in masses."[34]

By the time the frenzied assault carried the men across the Emmitsburg Road, the obstacles they encountered had disorganized their lines. Many of the Yankee troops fell back in equal disarray, and in some cases were overrun. In other places, Union regiments boldly stood the test or withdrew grudgingly. Thinned rebel ranks pushed on to the foot of Cemetery Hill where the exhausted men halted before a final thrust up the heights. As they stood gasping for breath in the humid evening air amidst the choking smoke of battle, they could see Union artillery and infantry reinforcements surging to stem the tide of the Rebel advance. Wilcox and Wright sent riders to Anderson with appeals for support. It is unclear what troops Wilcox expected his division commander to send to his support, as all the brigades were holding a position in the line of battle and there was no reserve on hand. It was unreasonable to expect that Anderson would simply open a wide gap in his lines in the face of the enemy by withdrawing a brigade and shifting it nearly a mile to the right. Mahone's would have been the only possibility, but it was then supporting artillery batteries and at best, Anderson could have dispatched only a portion of it. The prospect of even a small part of that brigade reaching Wilcox's advanced position in time to support his attempt to scale Cemetery Ridge was highly unlikely. It was a threat to Wilcox's right flank that would ultimately send his brigade streaming dejectedly back to Seminary Ridge, and loss of contact with McLaws's advance rendered it uncertain as to whether Longstreet's assault had achieved its goal. Of Longstreet's troops, only Barksdale's brigade remained huddled behind the rocks and bushes along Plum Run at the base of the heights with Wilcox's Alabamians, and the two brigades were by then "mingled in glorious confusion." Wilcox later asserted that a second supporting line would have provided the impetus for his battered regiments to reach the top of the heights. He did not say where that line of troops might have come from. On Wright's front, Anderson had ordered Posey to advance and he would reiterate the order, but something surely was misunderstood. Posey continued to maintain that he ordered only two regiments forward as skirmishers. That order, he said, came to him from Anderson's aide-de-camp.[35]

Wright, however, expected to see Posey's entire brigade advancing to support his exposed flank. He was caught unawares when Posey advanced only two regiments as skirmishers and began a protracted fight around the Bliss farmyard and buildings, while most of Wright's Georgians claimed that the Mississippians advanced only a short distance and then retired. Wright pressed on nonetheless, achieving the greatest success of the day on reaching the crest of Cemetery Ridge, where they "drove the enemy's infantry into a rocky gorge on the eastern slope of the heights some 80 or 100 yards in rear of the enemy's batteries."[36]

Nevertheless, with Longstreet stalled and federals rushing to stem Anderson's attack, his unsupported and battered brigades had little choice but to withdraw. Wilcox grudgingly ordered his regiments to fall back "to prevent their entire destruction or capture," later complaining he was "without support on either my right or left." Some of his men were also under the impression that Lang's brigade on their left had not advanced, allowing Yankees to get behind the Alabamians' lines. Edmund Patterson was one of the unfortunates who found himself facing a line of federal rifles to his rear. "I saw at a glance that we were 'gone up' and no help for it," he later recalled. He and a large number of men and officers from the 9th Alabama soon found themselves shepherded to the rear behind the Union lines, where they joined another large group from the regiment. "I was glad to see them," Patterson wrote, "for misery loves company."[37]

Lang and his troops, however, were also at the foot of the heights preparing to charge when he received word that Union reinforcements were driving Wilcox's line back. The Floridians thought the withdrawal of the Alabamians allowed federal infantry to advance on Lang's right flank. The two brigades became increasingly disconnected during the course of the advance when the battle began to take on a life of its own, and regiments directed their attention to the threats in front of them rather than to alignment with their neighbors. With the air "filled with sticks, rocks, dust and black smoke, almost suffocating," the extent of the separation was likely difficult to discern or correct. Officers tried their best, but circumstances soon overwhelmed their efforts. Lt. Anderson Peeler of the 2nd Florida was conspicuous in dashing "up and down the line, hurrahing, and encouraging the men on, and keeping the line dressed on Wilcox." Peeler was knocked down and stunned before receiving a serious bullet wound to the head. Such losses undoubtedly contributed to the confusion. On learning of the problem on his right flank, however, Lang went to see the situation himself and found "that the enemy had passed me more than 100 yards, and were attempting to surround me."

He ordered the men back to the Emmitsburg Road, but finding little cover there, he continued to fall back to his original position. David Maxwell of the 2nd Florida grudgingly attributed the success of the Union troops to their "fighting much harder on their own soil & having the best positions."[38]

Wright later claimed that on reaching the heights of Cemetery Ridge, "We were now complete masters of the field, having gained the key, as it were, of the enemy's whole line." He too thought at first that Lang had not advanced across the Emmitsburg Road, but now he found that the Florida brigade "had actually given way and was rapidly falling back to the rear, while on our left we were entirely unprotected, the brigade ordered to our support [Posey's] having failed to advance." Wright fell back as Union troops converged on his flanks. The movement was "effected in tolerable order, but with immense loss" Wright later wrote. One Georgian recalled that while the brigade "had succeeded in taking their Bateries [*sic*]" they had to fall back "without saving the Pecies [*sic*] with grate [*sic*] loss." As quickly as the retreating Georgians cleared the captured artillery pieces, Union gunners rushed to put them back into service with devastating effect. Brutal blasts of grapeshot and canister ripped through their already thinned ranks. Though driven from the high tide of their attacks that day, they faced no concerted counterattack except that a small band of impetuous Yankees chased the 8th Florida, capturing over thirty prisoners and the regiment's flag. Showers of whistling lead and iron were sufficient to speed the retreating Rebels on their way, and the Union defenders were undoubtedly relieved to see them go.[39]

Posey's Mississippians did not advance to an extent that met Wright's expectations, but they had contributed substantially to his success. The 19th Mississippi advanced well past the Bliss Farm and across the Emmitsburg Road, driving away the gunners of a Rhode Island battery that "was playing upon General Wright." To the right of the 19th, the 48th Mississippi was connected to Wright's line, but must have stopped at some point in its advance and engaged in the fighting around the Bliss Farm and across the Emmitsburg Road. Posey afterwards stated that he also sent the 16th Mississippi forward "later in the day," likely at Anderson's urging after hearing Wilcox's and Wright's pleas for support. One Mississippian recorded that his regiment "advanced nearly to the batteries on the hill, and then the enemy, by being re-enforced, would force us back to the orchard," around the Bliss Farm. When Posey received word of his endangered flanks, he personally led forward his last remaining regiment, the 12th Mississippi, and sent word to Mahone requesting support. Posey pushed past the Bliss Farm with the 12th and found his other three regiments well advanced, having "driven the enemy's picket lines into their works and the artillerists from their guns in their front." By then it was nearly dark, and Posey sent to Anderson for instructions. The rest of the division must have already withdrawn by that time, and he ordered Posey to return to his original positions. Despite initial orders to advance only two regiments as skirmishers, Posey's entire brigade had advanced to some extent. Mahone sent no support, however. His brigade was formed that day "in the rear of another division," (Pender's) and his response to Posey's request was that he was unable to aid him as he had been ordered to the right, but whether that meant to support Wilcox or Wright is unknown. Anderson's behavior that day, as well as Mahone's inactivity, would subsequently lead to several recriminations. Mahone's response to Posey seems to indicate that Anderson might well have ordered the Virginians to move to the support of the heavily engaged brigades that were meeting with success, but perhaps he simply wanted Mahone to take a position that was not directly in rear of Pender's Division. That would have placed him in position to support Posey. Yet, he did not move. Despite his love for his men and his desire to be out of the army altogether, it is neither likely nor reasonable to conclude from his wartime record that Mahone would have shirked his duty. Perhaps the order came too late to make a difference, but participants never mentioned it later except that Anderson's aide Lieutenant Samuel D. Shannon alleged that Mahone refused to respond to an order from Anderson relayed by Shannon. Anderson later excused Mahone, stating that he was acting on his direct orders, which were in turn compliant with Hill's wishes.[40]

On the evening of July 2, Anderson's bloodied division once again took up the positions from which it had begun the assault some hours before. Many post-battle accounts written before they had time to analyze the events reflect the men's sheer exhaustion. Most noted only the detached and emotionless comment that they had returned to their positions. James Kirkpatrick of the 16th Mississippi, for example, noted simply that the men were "relieved after dark and returned to our position behind the batteries." Likewise, in the 48th Mississippi, Sergeant Charles Hutchinson wrote simply that they "stayed out until dark and came back to [the] pits. Our adjutant was killed." Later reflections mentioned the suffering and cost. A Georgian noted that his regiment retreated "to where we had started from, what few of us that were left. . . . My company started with forty-five men, and got out with twenty-two, and every man of the twenty-two was hit somewhere with a bullet but one." In a letter to his wife describing the action and the retreat, Wright lamented that, "very few of the brave spirits who so recently had passed over that line buoyant in spirit and confident of success, now answered to the order that calmly sang out upon the air, 'Fall in Wright's Brigade and here we'll stand again.' Of over sixteen hundred that went into the fight, 554 were all that answered to that summons." Once darkness fully descended on the scene of the day's carnage, soldiers roamed the battlefield searching for wounded comrades and carrying them off the field. "I need not tell you," Wright penned, "that sleep was not thought of by me on that night." Moonrise cast a glow over the ghastly panorama of torn and mangled horses and men. Roaming hogs were rooting among the dead in some places, further desecrating mutilated bodies in a final act of indignity. Men holding the advanced picket lines had to maintain their positions, all the while listening to the agonizing cries and pleas for water from wounded and dying men who dotted the fields or lay clustered in clumps where they fell.[41]

Lee's battle plan for July 3 included another assault, aimed nearly at the same point where Wright penetrated the Union line on July 2. This time the attack would be spearheaded by fresh troops from Longstreet's corps with portions of Hill's corps, and supported once again by the men of Anderson's division. Longstreet would use three brigades from Pickett's division; four from Heth's division now under the command of North Carolinian James Johnson Pettigrew after Heth's wounding on July 1; two from Dorsey Pender's division to be commanded by Major General Isaac Trimble; and two of Dick Anderson's brigades—Wilcox's and Perry's (Lang's). The latter were to fall directly under Longstreet's command and the whole of the attacking force would number approximately 15,000 men. Anderson's other brigades were to be held in readiness to exploit any gains made by the main attack. Longstreet argued strenuously against an attack against the strongly defended position, and did not believe success was possible. Longstreet had his say and then turned away to carry out Lee's orders. He later wrote unfairly that he did not understand why Lee did not choose a leader who had more confidence in the plan, particularly since "two thirds of the troops were of other commands, and there was no reason for putting the assaulting forces under my charge." Hill was the only other option, but he was new to corps command and he had been visibly ill on July 1. He spent much of July 2 in close contact with Lee, who might not have been confident in Hill's full recovery. Hill thus had little to do on July 3. Dick Anderson left no account describing his thoughts about the planned assault that day, but he was prepared to do his duty regardless of his thoughts.[42]

The arrangement of the battle lines for the July 3 assault kept Anderson separated from Wilcox and Perry's brigades. Those units were on the far right of the line of attack to ensure the safety of Pickett's right flank. To Pickett's left in the attacking formation were Pettigrew's troops joined by Trimble's. Anderson would directly command only the three remaining brigades of Wright, Posey, and Mahone, which would all advance to support Pettigrew's left flank should the attack be a success. Ewell was to assault Meade's right flank simultaneously. In addition, the charge by Pickett,

Figure 4. Map of the Battle of Gettysburg, July 1–3, 1863. John B. Bachelder (published 1883, compiled 1876). Library of Congress Geography and Map Division.

Pettigrew, and Trimble would follow a heavy artillery bombardment designed to silence the menacing federal guns bristling along their lines. Like many of the plans at Gettysburg, that one too was destined to go awry.[43]

The plan's first setback resulted from Longstreet being unprepared to advance at an early hour. Ewell's men, however, were already engaged on the Confederate left, but were unable to capture the heights. By early afternoon, their power spent, Ewell's troops were no longer in any condition to provide a significant distraction on the Federal right, and yet Longstreet still had not moved. When his divisions finally stepped out into the fields still raked by Union artillery fire despite a furious rebel bombardment, ammunition for the supporting Confederate batteries was nearing exhaustion. The stalwart infantry drove onward through the storm of shot and shell, back across the Emmitsburg Pike with some eventually scaling the heights to engage in vicious hand-to-hand fighting around a copse of trees that marked the aiming point for Pickett's division. On learning from Pickett that his men would soon attain the objective of the attack, Longstreet ordered Wilcox and Lang forward with their brigades to guard Pickett's right flank. Wilcox received the same orders from Pickett, who sent three staff officers through the maelstrom in hopes that at least one would make it to Wilcox. Longstreet likewise sent Anderson forward in support of the left flank when it appeared that two of the brigades on that end of the line were faltering. Unfortunately, the tide of battle turned too quickly. Only a portion of the determined rebel force had fought its way to the top of the heights, but Confederate units on the left flank stalled and began to fall back. It was apparent that Anderson's three brigades could not reach that critical point before it gave way. Longstreet quickly halted Anderson's advance. Wright thought his brigade had advanced only five or six hundred yards by then. Now, with the Confederate left flank exposed, it was also clear that the attackers could not maintain their foothold around the copse of trees, and all along the line, Rebels began streaming back across the fields. Lee had Wright move his brigade farther to the right where he and his officers were ordered to attempt "to rally and collect the scattered troops behind Anderson's division." Anderson returned Mahone and Posey's brigades to their original position in the line and made ready to receive the Union counterattack that typically followed a failed assault.[44]

On the Confederate right, however, no one thought to order Lang and Wilcox to withdraw. Those two brigades continued forward in a costly and futile charge even as the primary assault was failing. Lang was to follow Wilcox's movements, and Wilcox pushed forward when ordered. Some of Lang's men were already bordering on heat exhaustion from having lain all day in the sun with no cover whilst Confederate artillery just to their rear fired over their heads. A depression in the ground supplemented by hastily dug entrenchments gave some "protection from the direct fire of the enemy, and from the sabots and fragments of premature explosions of our own guns which fired from behind us," Lang recalled, but then the men stood and formed for the advance. One soldier from the 5th Florida made it less than a hundred yards before keeling over from the heat. Others already perceived the attack to be a forlorn hope and hesitated to throw themselves again into the same deadly firestorm they had encountered on July 2. "Knowing what we had to incounter [*sic*]," one of them recalled, the attack order "was not obeyed with the same alacrity as was the case yesterday." Lang later reported that Pickett's troops had already retreated beyond his own lines by the time he reached the foot of the heights, where his men once again battled in the rock-strewn valley created by Plum Run, and where Lang was unable to make himself heard above the roar of the cannon and the incessant bark of the rifles. His men were so scattered by that time that the order to withdraw could not be "properly extended," and he feared many of the Floridians were captured as a result of not hearing the command to retreat. Some of the men sheltering behind the boulders in the little valley likely thought it safer to remain there rather than run the lead-filled gauntlet back to their own lines. Others were keener for the fight, such as Lieutenant James Wentworth of the 5th Florida, who was stunned by a close explosion during the advance. Coming to his senses later, he was unaware that his men had already retreated. He began to wave his sword and shout for them "to rally and give them hell." A Yankee private quickly brought the lieutenant back to reality when he approached and told the still reeling Rebel that they would give *him* hell if he did not surrender. Wentworth quickly recovered enough of his wits to demand they produce an officer at least of his own rank so that he could surrender his sword with honor. In the meantime, the 2nd Florida, Lang's left-most regiment, had lost its beautiful silk flag when the 16th Vermont rushed down the slope of Cemetery Ridge into the Plum Run basin and crashed into the Floridians' left flank. That disaster prompted Lang to order his men to move by the right flank through Plum Run valley in order to reach the marginal safety of a ravine that ran perpendicular to the heights and back across the Emmitsburg Road, and which might provide at least some cover from the brutal fire sweeping the field.[45]

Wilcox's regiments had been deployed about 200 yards behind the Confederate artillery line that stretched along the Emmitsburg Road and into the adjacent fields, so when the gunners sprang into action that afternoon the guns were at least not firing uncomfortably over their heads. Still, it was a memorable event. "I thought that I had heard cannonading before" recalled Fleming Thompson from the 11th Alabama; "but not so, or at any rate nothing to compare with [120] pieces firing as fast as they could and at the same time the Shell from the enemy was exploding every where [*sic*] as thick almost as hail." In the 9th Alabama, John Mason had been amused earlier in the day when a nearly spent shell struck the hastily constructed breastwork where his comrades had been sitting with their backs propped against some piled fence rails. The force of the shell "knocked us all about six feet off," he recalled. "It was fun to see the boys getting up and looking at each other to see who was hurt. But as luck happened there was none, only some with a few scratches." Later that day when the Confederate batteries opened, the light-hearted atmosphere quickly grew more serious. "The earth and the air shook for miles with the terrific concussion," Mason later wrote, "which no longer came in volleys, but in a continuous roar."[46]

By the time Wilcox advanced, he must have wondered what his already depleted brigade and the tiny band of Floridians were expected to accomplish since the primary attack had clearly failed. Wilcox's report hardly disguised his frustration, writing, "Not a man of the division that I was ordered to support [Pickett's] could I see; but as my orders were to go to their support, on my men went down the slope. . . ." Like the Florida brigade, Wilcox suffered a severe onslaught of artillery fire while crossing the open fields. He observed the Federal troops moving against the left flank of the assault and quickly spurred his horse to the rear in search of artillery support, only to find that none of the batteries had ammunition. Lang had also dispatched a staff officer on an equally ineffectual mission. Unable to obtain assistance and "seeing none of the troops that I was ordered to support," Wilcox accepted the futility of his advance and ordered a retreat. With Lang's small brigade shattered, the beleaguered Confederates needed little encouragement to fall back. Fleming Thompson described his own frustration with the attack, telling his mother and sister that they had charged "through grape & canister, but to no effect only the loss of men." John Mason recalled that one of A. P. Hill's couriers arrived with orders to withdraw. "His horse was white with froth he was going so fast," he recalled. Mason admitted that many of the Alabamians declined to go back across the open fields to their own lines and "so they lay down behind some rocks at the foot of Cemetery Hill and was [*sic*] taken prisoner." Mason decided to try to escape in the disorderly retreat. "You ought to have seen us going back over that field," he later wrote. "Every time a cannon ball would strike the ground near by you see us drop nearly to the ground and then strick [*sic*] out again, till I was tired out. I fell to the ground to get my breath. I had a load in my gun so I got on my knees I took aim and fired. While doing so a Yank was taking aim at me and came near breaking my leg, the ball went through my pants and pealed the bark off my shin." Mason took off at a run but "was knocked down by some of our men that was going a mile a minute. It was such a stampede that I didn't know where I was going."[47]

Wilcox and Lang's brigades suffered grievously, adding nearly five hundred more casualties to the butcher's bill of the previous day. Despite the lack of explanation for the senseless assault, neither Wilcox nor Lang ever attempted to cast any blame for that day's events, unlike the controversy stemming from Wright and Wilcox's resentment over the previous day's lack of support. Owing to confusion as to who was actually responsible for the brigades that were comingled on July 3, as well as the lack of written orders from Lee that might have clarified the temporary command arrangements, no one apparently took responsibility or blame for the needless sacrifice of Lang's and Wilcox's men. One noted historian probably said it best when he wrote, "Wilcox apparently was under everybody's order and nobody's." Certainly, no one paid a price except those who went—not quite unquestioningly and at least reluctantly—into the maw of battle.[48]

The extensive attention given to the Battle of Gettysburg reflects the sense that the fight had a remarkable impact on the subsequent course of the war and the life of the Confederacy. Historians almost universally agree that something was amiss in Lee's army on those three crucial days in Pennsylvania. Lee's intentions badly miscarried on July 2 and 3, and the reasons for that led to bitter recriminations among participants for the next several decades. In the case of Dick Anderson's performance, the controversy began almost immediately and went public within a few weeks.

A *Richmond Enquirer* article "The Battle of Gettysburg, PA" appeared on July 23, 1863. The correspondent, whose nom de plume was the cryptic initial "A," leveled a number of charges against Dick Anderson starting on the first day. The writer was actually Georgia lawyer, Peter W. Alexander, one of the South's most noteworthy journalists. On July 1, he alleged, Anderson's division had "been unnecessarily halted for more than three hours, . . . at Cashtown." Meanwhile, Heth and Pender were hotly engaging the enemy several miles ahead at Gettysburg and pushing him back. At Cashtown, men clearly heard the sounds of battle, and those halted on the eastern slope of South Mountain could observe the fighting in progress. Nonetheless, Anderson did not advance rapidly to join the fray. Had he done so, "A" contended, Lee's forces would have prevailed by denying Meade the higher ground on Cemetery Ridge. It was, he said, a "fatal blunder," made worse by the fact that all of Anderson's brigadiers were supposedly clamoring for an advance, "but the Major-General would not consent." The correspondent presumed Lee would conduct some inquiry into the matter and asserted that the country deserved an explanation for why several thousand men were prevented from engaging in the fight that day. There was little substance to that particular complaint, however. As previously described, Lee and Anderson met and conversed on at least two occasions after the start of the fighting that day, and Lee had ridden along Anderson's column as he rushed towards the battlefield. He knew precisely where Anderson's men were in relation to the scene of action. The record is entirely silent as to whether Lee desired Anderson to hurry forward to join the attack, but every other existing piece of evidence refutes such a notion.[49]

The writer's complaint of the second day's failure was similar in nature. He praised Wilcox and Wright for the extent of their advance in conjunction with that of McLaws and Hood on their right. According to the correspondent Posey and Mahone both failed to attack, forcing Pender and Heth's divisions to remain stationary as well. Unsupported, Wilcox and Wright were compelled to fall back with heavy losses after overrunning the Federal lines and capturing several guns. Perry's Florida brigade, positioned between Wilcox and Wright, supposedly met with overwhelming force and had fallen back early on, leaving a gap between the other two brigades. Into that gap, maintained the writer, poured a column of Union troops that took the brigades under fire from flank and rear. The failure of Posey and Mahone to advance likewise opened an opportunity for Yankees to fall on Wright's left flank and gain the Emmitsburg Pike in his rear. The lack of support for the attack was disastrous, and for that, the correspondent unabashedly blamed Anderson, stating, "the conviction is general in this army that Maj. Gen. Anderson should be held responsible." As Richmond's largest newspaper, and with a circulation that extended well outside the immediate Richmond vicinity, it was one of the region's most respected journals. The allegations were sure to draw wide attention.[50]

A subsequent *Richmond Enquirer* article on July 28 supported the paper's correspondent, whose comments had unleashed a firestorm of debate. The article in that latest edition, entitled "Anderson and Pettigrew," came from the Savannah *Republican*. Another anonymous author who used the initials "P.W.A." wrote it. The *Enquirer* maintained that the use of the initial "A" in the *Republican's* writer's initials was "wholly accidental" and there was no connection to its own correspondent, but this—like much of the supposedly factual information in the articles—was untrue. The writer in both cases was Peter W. Alexander, the Georgia lawyer turned newspaper reporter who was then "the principle [*sic*] army correspondent." "P.W.A." asserted accurately enough that the advance of A. P. Hill's infantry was "not regular and systematic as it should have been," and Anderson's division "never did get fully into action." He lauded Wilcox's and Wright's advance, noting especially that the Georgians went "boldly forward and excelled all previous performances." Perry's brigade, under Lang, he alleged, advanced only a short distance and "did not become fully engaged." Posey, he claimed, balked at advancing unless Mahone advanced to cover his left flank, while Mahone purportedly refused unless Posey advanced and Pender's division covered his left flank. Pender went forward to examine the ground and fell wounded, producing, the writer alleged, a complete halt as Pender's brigadiers argued the question of who was the most senior, an issue not settled until nearly sunset. The source of that fanciful rendition of the facts was not mentioned. Meanwhile, P.W.A. alleged that Wilcox and Wright struggled on valiantly with no support.[51]

The Savannah *Republican* correspondent also criticized Pettigrew's actions on the next day, alleging that he failed to advance his division to support Pickett's left flank. This led to enfilading fire "being brought to bear upon" Pickett, which caused "him to retire with great loss." The *Enquirer* concluded with the damning statement, "here is probably to be found the real cause of our unfortunate assault."[52]

Mahone and Posey both launched an immediate counter-offensive against the statements pertaining to their brigades and the division, ostensibly in defense of Anderson. The two composed and signed a joint letter to the *Enquirer* that appeared on August 7. First acknowledging their "respect for the good opinion of the public generally," they then professed an unwillingness to be held accountable as soldiers "to any other source than that of our military superiors." They first countered the accusations leveled against Anderson before proclaiming his qualities and his "well-earned reputation as a gallant and accomplished officer, a vigorous and skillful fighter." In response to the supposed halt of three hours at Cashtown, the generals termed it "substantially false," in that Anderson's pause there was no more than forty minutes in duration and was made "in accordance with directions of his superiors." They expressed their opinion that it was also untrue that the brigade commanders were impatient and told Anderson they desired to advance more quickly, and it was absolutely false as it pertained to themselves. Instead, they maintained that the division advanced "as it was called for" and took up Pender's positions after his division had advanced to Heth's support. Pender, they noted, was consistently in advance of Anderson on the march, only engaging with the enemy near the close of the day's action. It is true that the day's battle had been a surprise. No one knew the Union army was near the town in such force, but by around 4 PM Lee and Hill watched from Seminary Ridge as Union troops streamed from the field to take up stronger positions on Cemetery Hill and the high ground to the south. With sufficient daylight remaining to push those federals from the opposite heights, Lee turned to Hill and asked if Heth and Pender's divisions could do it. Hill demurred. His men had suffered enough that day and had given all they were capable of. It was only then that Lee keenly felt the absence of Dick Anderson's division. It was still making its way from Cashtown with little hope it would arrive before dark. Had it been available and if he had been willing to risk using his only reserve, Lee might have sent it into action that evening, but he never expressed any disappointment or dissatisfaction with Anderson not having arrived sooner. It was most certainly a missed opportunity, but Anderson was not to blame for that. Had either Hill or Lee understood the circumstances more rapidly, particularly after learning that the hornet's nest that Heth kicked over that morning contained the battle-hardened westerners of the famed Iron Brigade, they might have urged Anderson to hurry to the scene. Lee had done so numerous times with McLaws on the route to Antietam, but no similar orders came and neither commander expressed any such concerns. As for timing, George Bernard of the 12th Virginia wrote in a postwar memoir that he thought the sounds of an increasingly heavy engagement were clearly heard at around 3 PM, and that Anderson deployed the division into line on a "lofty eminence to the right of the main road" around two hours after that. He estimated they were then about two miles from where Heth and Pender's divisions were engaged. There was, he thought in hindsight, "full time to have thrown our division into action." Had that occurred, he opined, there would have been no battle at Gettysburg subsequent to July 1. Likewise, Lieutenant Colonel Hilary Herbert of the 8th Alabama also recalled halting and forming "on a road from which I could plainly see the smoke of the battle going on & which I took to be about 1 ½ miles from us. . . . I never understood why we were not ordered in." In either case, it was not Anderson's decision, and Lee wisely chose to wait until his dispersed force was gathered.[53]

As for Mahone and Posey failing to move forward on July 2 as part of the alleged "peremptory" order for a simultaneous advance, both generals maintained they received no such order. The brigades of Anderson's division constituted a supporting force for Longstreet's attack on the right, they asserted. In response to the advance of Longstreet's troops, specifically those of McLaws's division, Anderson's brigades were to move successively "by 'echelon'" from right to left. They understood their purpose as supporting Longstreet's attack by holding federal forces in place and preventing an attack on his left flank as he advanced. Posey, moreover, contended that his orders were to send only a portion of his brigade forward to protect Wright's left flank. Mahone asserted that his own brigade formed behind the right end of Pender's battle line as support for the large number of guns positioned there. No action occurred in his front that warranted an advance, and Pender likewise saw no reason to attack. All the other statements in the *Republican* article as to "any hesitancy, discussion or disagreement between Brigadier

Generals Mahone and Posey, or between the former and Major General Pender," or anyone else were "wholly without the shadow of truth."[54]

That same August 7 edition of the *Enquirer* also carried a letter from the Savannah *Republican* correspondent, "P.W.A." seeking to clarify an error in his original story as it pertained to the fighting on July 2. The result was only to shift the responsibility from Anderson to A. P. Hill's shoulders. "P.W.A." explained that he received additional clarification from Anderson in a note dated July 29, which had also appeared in the *Enquirer*. The note informed him that Mahone and Posey were merely following his orders and that Anderson issued those orders "in strict conformity" with the instructions he received from Hill, who supported that interpretation. The correspondent excused his mistake because of having received the information "from so many different sources as to leave no doubt of its correctness." He admitted being wrong in accusing Anderson of negligence in directing his brigades and insinuating that Posey and Mahone had for some reason declined to advance, but his note was hardly an apology. He had not intended to question the Mississippians and Virginians' "disposition to perform their whole duty," nor, he claimed, was it his intention to question the sagacity of Hill's orders. Hill was "known to be one of our best officers," P. W. A. wrote, yet he concluded immediately after that with the observation that "the reader will make his own comments." In reprinting Anderson's note to P. W. A. from the *Enquirer*, the Augusta *Daily Constitutionalist* was equally arcane. It concluded that Anderson's failure to support Wright after having said he would do so was "inexplicable, but we must believe that circumstances caused him to change the order, while Wright and Wilcox were struggling in full view of them against the whole Yankee centre."[55]

The *Richmond Enquirer* claimed to be tiring of the exchanges, yet it was apparently too tempting for circulation purposes not to encourage further debate, this time over the role of Perry's Florida brigade. After prefacing its coverage with the remark that "we hope the matter is finally ended" the paper published a letter from Anderson dated August 6, in which he sought to address an oversight from his previous note. He had neglected to address the accusation that Perry's brigade "advanced a short distance," but was not "fully engaged." Not only did the brigade under Colonel Lang advance "as bravely, as perseveringly, and as far, as any troops could have done in the same situation," they had, he contended, suffered proportionally more casualties than any brigade in the army. A letter to the editors from Lang had already effectively countered the claim from P. W. A. "The loss of more than half of the men carried into this charge," Lang wrote on July 29, "would appear, to unprejudiced eyes, that the brigade did 'become fully engaged.'"[56]

While that closed the public controversy, Anderson, Mahone, and Posey were left to speculate as to who supplied P. W. A. with the information that left the correspondent with "no doubt of its correctness." The official reports of the battle gave some indication of possible sources of that information. Wilcox wrote, for example, that upon nearly reaching the crest of the ridge and being attacked by Yankee reinforcements, he sent Captain Walter E. Winn, his adjutant general, to Anderson to request support, "but no support came." Much later—he did not submit his report until September—Wright likewise complained that he sent his aide-de-camp to Anderson informing him that Posey had not advanced on his now exposed left flank. Anderson was said to have replied, "press on" and he would tell Posey again to advance. Wright went on but soon realized that Posey had not only failed to advance past the Emmitsburg Road, his regiments were falling back. He had written his wife exactly the same thing within days of the fight, telling her he had sent a courier to Anderson to inform him that neither Posey nor Mahone had moved to cover his left flank. He maintained that Anderson's response was that they "had been ordered in and that he would reiterate the order."[57]

The letter Wright penned to his wife dated July 7, appeared anonymously in the pages of the Augusta *Daily Constitutionalist* on July 23. It contained the remarks about Anderson as well as the negative comments about the advance of Lang's Floridians. A group of the 5th Florida regiment's angry officers selected adjutant J. B. Johnson to investigate the identity of the writer. He first went to the army's main news correspondent, P. W. Alexander, who deceptively denied any knowledge of the author, but suggested that he might check with Wright's brigade since the general himself was from Augusta, Georgia, where the news article had first appeared. Johnson reined up in front of Wright's tent and found him seated there in conversation with other general officers. After showing Wright the article and asking if he could help identify the writer, the general asked why he wished to know who wrote it. "Because I replied it is as false as Hell itself," Johnson said. Wright "almost sprang from his seat," Johnson recalled. "He turned red, and I saw he was very angry." Wright told Johnson that the letter "was not intended for publication, it was a private letter to my wife, from information I had." Johnson was not deterred, however. Turning to Wright's adjutant general, Captain Victor Girardey, Johnson asked him what he had observed of Wright and the Floridians' advance on July 2. After first claiming he thought Wright "was sick and at the hospital," Girardey then admitted that he had spoken to Johnson at "the furthest point" Wright's brigade had advanced, and seeing the Union reinforcements pouring into position they had both agreed they would be unable to hold their position. Girardey also agreed that when the time came to pull back, he and Johnson had retired from the field together. "That will do said General Wright, I was misinformed, I will write a correction for publication you can call for it tomorrow."[58]

If true, Johnson's postwar account of the meeting with Wright decisively settles the question of the Floridians' advance, but Girardey's statement that Wright was in hospital and not on the field that day adds a problematic element to Johnson's recollection. Wright had, in fact, been indisposed and left his brigade during the march on July 1, but he was back with the men—as he wrote in his subsequent report of the battle—early on the morning of July 2. Wright also mentioned in his report that soon after he resumed command of the brigade, Anderson himself conducted him to the exact position he wished him to occupy. Given the controversies surrounding that day's actions, Anderson surely would have read the report with some care and noted anything not entirely accurate. Certainly, he would not have countenanced Wright placing himself on the field if he knew he was not there, and he would not have endorsed and forwarded a report containing statements he knew to be false. Johnson's memory might have failed him on that aspect of his conversation with Girardey, but such errors serve to call his version of the affair into question. By virtue of his position with the brigade, Girardey would surely have known that his chief had returned to command and was not still absent, but he was killed in 1864 and could never dispute Johnson's postwar account. Wright died in 1872, and it is unknown whether he ever read Johnson's undated memoir. Johnson's account, however, is bolstered by the memoir of Private William B. Judkins of the 22nd Georgia, who wrote that although Wright had returned and was in command, he "was not in the charge, he was not well, but his Adjutant Genl. Geroda [*sic*] was in command, or led the brigade." Surely, Johnson would have cited Girardey's position as authoritative regarding his knowledge of the circumstances, but it also seems unlikely Wright would have saddled his adjutant with such a responsibility. The usual remedy would have been to name a ranking subordinate to that position, as Wright had done the day before when he absented himself briefly and left Colonel William Gibson of the 48th Georgia in command.[59]

The reliability of Johnson's memoir is questionable, as is Judkins's recollection, but the essential elements are true. One can expect differences in the perspectives of those in the midst of the danger, din, and smoky confusion of a fierce battle fought on undulating ground. Wright published a retraction of his statements in the Augusta *Daily Constitutionalist* on August 6. He admitted he had hastily composed his remarks and based them on second-hand information. In his official report written weeks after the encounter with Johnson, however, Wright again stated that on gaining the enemy's works "it was discovered that the brigade on our right [Perry's Florida Brigade] not only had not advanced across the turnpike, but had actually given way, and was rapidly falling back to the rear." Perhaps he had conducted additional interviews with his officers from the 22nd Georgia, which held the right of his line, and concluded that Johnson's version could not be entirely factual. In any event, the report directly contradicted the assertion that the Floridians advanced as far as Wright's brigade and that they fell back together. More likely, the disorganization that attended the assault produced confusion among the observers. It was clear that the echelon formation of the advance meant the brigades never formed an unbroken line, and that flaw compounded once the fighting was underway in earnest. The rock-strewn woods bordering Plum Run and the broken terrain rising in their front, the disjointed Union defensive efforts, and the organization of the attacking line, meant that units or portions of units naturally would have found it expedient to exploit opportunities to focus on immediate threats. Some undoubtedly targeted artillery batteries or infantry formations that diverted their attention from maintaining the integrity of the attacking formation and a connection with their neighbors. Of those directly involved in the division's attack, only Anderson and his staff could possibly have seen anything approximating a birds-eye view of the events, and even that is doubtful given the distance involved, the undulating nature of the ground, and the smoke that would have filled the air and obscured the field after so much firing.[60]

According to Johnson's recollections, Anderson summoned him to his headquarters soon after meeting Wright and Girardey. The veracity of that tale is not particularly relevant, though interesting, because it indicates what Anderson's reaction to the publication of Wright's letter might have been. Johnson related the story in detail, perhaps attempting to add more credibility to it. Anderson's headquarters tents were set one behind the other, he wrote, so that the outer one could serve as an office and the other as his quarters. Anderson handed Johnson a copy of the newspaper article and told him to take a seat in his office tent at the table filled with maps and papers. He had learned of Johnson's visit to Wright, and asked whether Wright had admitted to writing the letter. When Johnson confirmed that he did, Anderson told him to "impress every word of that conversation upon your memory. I am going to have him court-martialed for it." He was "determined that the officers under me must make their reputations by their swords and not by their pens."[61]

A board to hear the case convened at Orange Courthouse in mid-August. Harry Heth was appointed president, while Brigadier Generals Joseph B. Kershaw, Stephen Dodson Ramseur, Harry T. Hays, and Henry Harrison Walker comprised the board. Wright was placed in arrest sometime around July 14 because of "disobedience of some order regarding transportation in the Brigade." The details of that dispute with Anderson are lost to history, but Wright was charged in Special Orders 196 with "violation of orders, disobedience of orders, disrespect to superior officers, and conduct unbecoming an officer and gentleman." A Georgia newspaper was more direct in referring to the Augusta *Daily Constitutionalist*, where Wright's letter to his wife appeared, adding that the charges related directly to "matters connected with publications." A notice of the trial that appeared in the *Richmond Enquirer* mentioned that "Gen. Wright is managing his own defense," and a subsequent update after the start of the trial indicated that he was doing so "with an ability equal to his well known gallantry on the field." Within days the consensus was that Wright would be exonerated. A Georgian in Wright's brigade expressed his belief on August 24 that Wright would "be released in the course of a few days. He stood the court martial and thus far has been cleared."[62]

With final arguments for prosecution and defense made on August 25, the court was "cleared for consultation." An hour later, the court adjourned, "having reached, as I learn, a decision," one correspondent reported. That decision could not be publicized until a general order was published stating the findings, however, the reporter's "own impression . . . is that a judgment of acquittal has been rendered, and justly so, too, in my opinion. General Wright is a brave man, and reputed a good officer." An Atlanta paper expressed hopes for his acquittal, concluding, "Nobody doubts his gallantry and patriotism, but he is generally considered vain, and ambitious of acquiring popularity."[63]

The court acquitted Wright. No detailed record of the trial exists, so the outcome for specific charges and specifications is unclear. Johnson claimed Anderson was "considerably worried," and had told him that he "would hate to have to escape a court martial by a technicality, but it will have its effect." He acknowledged Wright's bravery and dash though, telling Johnson, "sometimes he has too much dash, a little more coolness would bring better results." Anderson quickly put the incident aside, believing he had made his point in bringing the charges, but strong feelings about it would linger long afterwards in others.[64]

The press coverage and trial ended, but questions surrounding the troubling nature of Anderson's role in the actions and in the failure to act on July 2 remained open. Anderson claimed he was unable to locate Hill after hearing from Wilcox, thus making it impossible for him to send additional support given his previous orders from Hill to hold two brigades in reserve. That statement could equally show an astounding lack of initiative on Anderson's part. Unless he knew the reserve force was intended to repel a counterattack, one may justly ask what its purpose could be if it was not intended to be used to reinforce success. Conversely, if his orders did not clearly give him the ability to advance his other brigades to capitalize on successes achieved by the attack, it would have been a gross violation of orders. The primary attack was Longstreet's to make, with Anderson's troops in a supporting role designed to guard the flank of the First Corps and forestall the movement of Union troops to reinforce their line. In the midst of battle, it is a simpler matter for regimental and brigade commanders to seize opportunities. It is less so an inclination for a division commander much farther removed from the scene of decision. Still, Wilcox and Wright held Anderson culpable for their losses and the failure to capitalize on hard-won success. In their eyes, it was not something that would be very easy to forget or to forgive, particularly in light of what Wilcox learned from his adjutant general. When Wilcox dispatched Captain Winn to seek reinforcement from Anderson, Winn reputedly "found Gen'l A. back in the woods in rear of the Emmitsburg road several hundred yards in a ravine, his horse tied and all his staff lying on the ground (indifferent) as tho' nothing was going on, horses all tied." The picture thus conveyed gives the impression that Anderson and his staff were totally disconnected from events and unconcerned with the welfare of the men. Wilcox went on to state that he doubted Anderson ever saw a foot of the ground over which his brigades had advanced so gallantly. That was a damning statement, though Wilcox knew it was untrue. Anderson personally placed both him and Wright into position that day. Anderson could not have failed to take note of the ground over which the men would advance. Such invective encapsulates the view that Dick Anderson in his first combat under the equally lax A. P. Hill fell short of expectations. The army could ill afford to endure that sort of lethargy. Wilcox tempered his comments somewhat when he subsequently wrote that he might have been wrong in his opinion of Anderson, but he "always believed that he was too indifferent to his duties at Gettysburg." Something undoubtedly miscarried that day, and Anderson's strange lack of aggression in directing his brigades was one of the lowest points of his career. His statement that he was unable to locate Hill at a crucial moment is also puzzling. By some accounts, Hill spent most of the day observing the battle from a distance with Lee. In any case, Anderson and his staff did not find him or receive orders at a time when they most needed guidance. Hill did have Heth's division in reserve, but it was at least two miles away behind Willoughby Run. He could have ordered Mahone to advance, but perhaps by then it was too late to capitalize on the foothold achieved by Wright's men or to add the extra weight to Wilcox's effort to gain the heights. Hill also might have chosen not to commit more men to the fight in which his troops supposedly played a supporting role for Longstreet's attack. The plea for reinforcement from Anderson's brigade commanders reflected in part their excitement at advancing so successfully, as well as the idea that their particular point on the field stood poised to become the decisive one that would lead to victory that day. For them it was the source of much angry frustration over heavy losses that resulted only in a missed opportunity. The conduct of the battle that day fell squarely onto the shoulders of Anderson's brigade commanders with insufficient direction from above. Lee also bears some blame. He too watched rather than direct. In any event, none of the potential actions that might have remedied the setbacks transpired. Everyone, it seems, watched passively on July 2 while brigadier generals and colonels pressed home their attacks unaided by those above them. As for July 3, there was simply no accounting for the pointless slaughter of Anderson's brigades. The men they led truly deserved better on those three crucial days in July 1863.[65]

Chapter 14

On the Rapidan and Rappahannock Line and into the Wilderness

Let me kiss him for his Mother.

—John P. Ordway,
song, ca. 1859

Rain fell heavily on the fields of Gettysburg on July 4 as the adversaries eyed one another warily, anticipating a renewal of the fighting at any moment. Lee spent his offensive power, however, and Meade declined to advance his battered army towards the wounded Rebel force. Lee had already begun to put his wagons and ambulances on the Cashtown road throughout the day with orders to make haste for the Potomac River crossing at Williamsport via the Cashtown Gap. The infantry followed after dark in the direction of the Fairfield Gap, a shorter, southwesterly route to the Potomac. Hill's corps was the infantry vanguard, and Anderson marched his division towards Fairfield throughout the night, struggling through deep mud and water until resting at the eastern foot of the mountains. "The night we left Gettysburg was the darkest in fact as well as feeling I ever experienced," recalled a man in the 12th Virginia. A comrade in his regiment recalled the difficulties of maintaining unit cohesion, noting that it was necessary for the men to "halloo out the names of their companies in order to keep together" as they struggled along the nearly impassable road. Anderson's division defended the mountain pass the next day as Longstreet and Ewell's men trudged towards Hagerstown, Maryland, where they arrived on July 7. Rain fell again that afternoon and continued heavily overnight. The army crept towards the rain-swollen Potomac on the afternoon of July 10, constricting its lines and creating a formidable barrier against a possible Union assault. "[We] expect a fight tomorrow," wrote Sergeant Charles Hutchinson of the 48th Mississippi, "'God defend the right.'"[1]

Meade inched closer, cautiously probing for weakness. Lee's three battered corps stretched from south of Hagerstown, across the vital Boonsboro and Williamsport turnpike, and to the banks of the raging Potomac. Behind them lay the crossings at Williamsport and Falling Waters, key to the army's eventual escape. Anderson's division formed a battle line at a right angle to the turnpike between Boonsboro and Williamsport. With skirmishers placed, weary men set about fortifying their positions amidst some heavy skirmishing. The waters eventually subsided and engineers built a pontoon bridge at Falling Waters. Lee rushed his army across the Potomac to the safety of Virginia's soil. Hill's corps would be the rear guard, and Anderson's division led the difficult march towards Falling Waters after dark on July 13. "It commenced raining soon after we started," James Kirpatrick of the 16th Mississippi noted in his diary, and the latest downpour "put the roads in miserable plight." A Virginian described the night as one of the worst he ever saw as they rushed through the darkness over "roads knee deep in miry mud & rocky."[2]

Lee waited anxiously at the river crossing, fretting over the safety of his rear guard and waiting at any moment to learn that Meade had launched an attack that would prevent Hill from joining the main Confederate body already south of the Potomac. Nearly a third of the army was vulnerable to an enemy assault, its lifeline a rain-swollen ford at Williamsport and a makeshift pontoon bridge at Falling Waters. No other circumstances could have been more stressful for a general with the possible exception of facing a more aggressive commander than Meade under similar conditions. At dawn on July 14, Lieutenant Colonel Moxley Sorrel of Longstreet's staff crossed into Virginia at Falling Waters and informed the army's commander that the way was finally clear for Hill's troops to follow. It was apparent that Lee's "anxiety was intense," and he instructed Sorrel to rush back to Hill and "urge him to the utmost haste in getting his men over." When Sorrel found Hill, the corps was within a mile of the crossing and moving quickly towards it, but Meade's cavalry was nipping at its heels. Anderson's division was still in the vanguard followed by Pender's troops, while Harry Heth, recovered sufficiently from a July 1 head wound and back in command, brought up the rear. Pettigrew had returned to command of his brigade in Heth's division, but the popular North Carolinian suffered a mortal wound that morning when two small squadrons of Brigadier General Judson Kilpatrick's Union cavalry dashed precipitously against his lines and paid for their rashness with heavy casualties. The Rebels had been uncertain at first as to the identity of the cavalry. By the time they opened fire, the mounted men were already thundering rapidly towards them in a wild charge. Heth's men then held off more coordinated attacks by dismounted cavalry, but in the confusion of the retreat the Federals captured around 700 men and several regimental battle flags fell into enemy hands. Lee later contended most of the men captured were stragglers who were simply "worn down with fatigue" and had become separated from their units, while the guns had been lost owing to broken-down horses. There were no prisoners taken in battle during the retreat, he asserted in a letter to Adjutant General Samuel Cooper on July 21, but Lee was misinformed about how close the rear of his army came to being overwhelmed. Meade made no other serious attempts to contest Hill's passage that day, and he had to content himself with that small victory. Meanwhile, Lee closely monitored the progress as Hill's corps made it way towards the river, and when he first learned that morning that Anderson's division was leading the march to safety, he expressed concern with a mild admonishment. "My friend Dick is quick enough pursuing," he said to Sorrel, "but in retreat I fear he will not be as sharp as I should like." Nonetheless, Lee's adept tactical handling of the retreat kept Meade at bay, and Hill's corps made good its escape. Engineers severed the pontoon bridge at Falling Waters from its moorings and the raging waters of the Potomac quickly swept it downstream.[3]

Anderson's division moved south gradually, crossing the Shenandoah River to Front Royal on July 22, but the army could not subsist in the ravaged countryside of the lower Shenandoah Valley. Longstreet and most of Hill's corps made their way out of the Valley through Chester Gap, just south of Manassas Gap, while Ewell's corps lagged behind. Anderson was in motion at daylight on the 23rd, with Wright's Brigade detached to guard Manassas Gap a few miles east of Front Royal. Union cavalry there was probing for routes onto Lee's flank. Wright was then in arrest due to a dispute with Anderson over an unidentified issue related to the brigade's transportation, so command fell to the 3rd Georgia's Colonel Edward J. Walker, the only colonel left in the brigade. The Georgians took up their duties on the very day Meade would attempt to force passage of the Gap to disrupt Lee's withdrawal.[4]

Meade remained on the east side of the Blue Ridge to maintain easy contact with his supply lines while he shadowed Lee's army through the Shenandoah Valley. He hoped to sever Lee's retreating columns by crossing one of the gaps in the mountains, such as Manassas Gap, which carried the railroad line between Manassas Junction and Front Royal that Stonewall Jackson's men had ridden in July 1861 to reach Manassas in the nation's first use of a railroad to move troops into battle. Now Meade hoped to reverse the same route onto Lee's flank. Lee was moving southward by necessity and had to hold the mountain gaps to safeguard the army's flank as he did so.[5]

Colonel Walker deployed his brigade to defend Manassas Gap on its higher western elevation where it emptied into the Shenandoah Valley, and he was alarmed when a large body of Union troops appeared later that morning. By early afternoon, the enemy had deployed for an advance. The Yankee skirmish line alone vastly outnumbered the defending Georgians, and behind that, the thinly stretched Rebels could see three more brigades of infantry, three artillery batteries, and fifteen more regiments in reserve. Walker immediately sent a courier to request assistance from Ewell, whose corps was still marching southward from Front Royal. Ewell dispatched Robert E. Rodes's division, but in the meantime, the Georgians were on their own.[6]

Walker fell wounded soon after the skirmishing began, and the brigade command split between Captain Charles H. Andrews of the Third Georgia and Captain Girardy, Wright's assistant adjutant general. They held the Yankees in check, even forcing them to break off the engagement in order to organize a more effective assault. The Georgians continued to resist "to the utmost of human capacity" but with their ammunition exhausted, Federals pierced the center of the line and the remnants of the brigade retired to a new position about 600 yards to the rear where Rodes's division was located. Rodes must have arrived on the scene well before his infantry reached the field and he had observed much of the fighting, complimenting the "gallant fellows" who repeatedly broke the enemy's advances. He thought the Union officers behaved "generally with great gallantry, but the men behaved in a most cowardly manner," once finding they now faced Rodes's fresh division and not just a single weakened brigade. "The conduct of our men, and of Wright's particularly," he reported, "was the subject of admiration, that of the enemy was decidedly puerile."[7]

Seeing Rodes's division strongly emplaced, the Union attack ground to a halt, allowing the Georgians to withdraw. Ewell ordered Rodes to pull back towards Front Royal that night. Lee's army was by then far south of Manassas Gap and Ewell's corps continued up the Luray Valley to cross the Blue Ridge at Thornton's Gap. For the Georgians that had suffered so grievously on July 2, the fight at Manassas Gap added further to their reduced numbers. The brigade suffered nearly 170 additional casualties at the Gap, with almost half listed as "missing," which likely meant they had fallen into enemy hands in the mismatched fight. Rodes's praise was well deserved though. Even without their commander and most senior officers, the Georgians of Anderson's division acquitted themselves well, holding a vastly superior force at bay for far longer than expected.[8]

Skirmishing continued to occur along the army's route. Anderson detached Mahone's Brigade on July 24 to check enemy cavalry as the wagons and infantry crossed the Thornton and Hazel Rivers, and the division reached the safety of Culpeper Courthouse the next day. The army rested astride the Orange & Alexandria Railroad about midway between the Rappahannock and Rapidan Rivers while the men reflected on their recent travails. Lieutenant Joseph R. Manson of the 12th Virginia was especially disheartened with the reversal north of the Potomac, stating only that he "was sorry when it was begun, and I am glad it is over." He had possessed little confidence in the invasion and had been troubled by the way some of the men had "acted very disgracefully . . . towards the citizens." He accused the officers who did not act against such depredations as being equally guilty. "I was associated with an armed mob," he complained, "not with a disciplined army." Another man in Manson's regiment expressed his thanks "to the merciful God who spared me," but added that he had made up his mind "on the Sojor [*sic*] question and if Providence spares me I will never every [*sic*] play it again." In the 41st Virginia, Charlie Denoon mentioned reversals on other fronts. "The boys were quite lively until they heard of the fall of Vicksburg" he wrote, "Now they are despondant [*sic*]."[9]

Anderson's report of the campaign on August 7 presented a different view of the division's treatment of civilians and their property from that presented by Lieutenant Manson. Much evidence tends to support Manson's claim of the misbehavior. Of that evidence Anderson was either unaware or he deemed it inconsequential compared to his troops' otherwise good behavior. He reported, "peaceable inhabitants suffered no molestation," noting that the men did not seek revenge "for the inhuman wrongs and outrages" then being inflicted upon their southern homes. Rather, he claimed, "in a land of plenty, they often suffered hunger and want. One-fourth of their number marched, ragged and barefooted, through towns in which it was well ascertained that the merchants had concealed supplies of clothing." In addition to defending his soldiers, Anderson praised their "courage and spirit," concluding that no blame for the campaign's failure could be laid at their feet. Perhaps in a sign that he was starting to embrace his faith, or that he was struggling to come to grips with the sacrifice of his men, he expressed the idea that the fault for failure "must be recognized and accepted as the will and decree of the Almighty disposer of human affairs." A more cynical reading of that statement might conclude that he was also absolving himself of any blame. The men were up to the task, but God deemed otherwise and nothing he could do could change that. The post-Gettysburg period once again brought about a great resurgence of religion in the army into the fall of 1863, with many camp meetings held. Harry Lewis of the 16th Mississippi thought the "preaching in the brigade [was] generally indifferent," yet he noted "a growing interest in religion" in the army overall, while John Mason of the 9th Alabama recalled that "a great many of the country boys would get Religion on the brain and would roll around the woods a hollering." Perhaps Anderson had experienced a more dignified reaction, for his statement reflects the wide belief in the army at that time that matters beyond one's control remained in God's hands. There was no other way to rationalize and accept the many inexplicable events and illogical outcomes that the war presented.[10]

News of Vicksburg's fall was most galling for Anderson's Mississippians. John S. Lewis of the 19th Mississippi expressed his angst to his mother when he encouraged her to flee to Alabama with such possessions as she could take. He was fearful that Yankees would soon take "possession of our country," whereupon they would "pillage and plunder, and will take all the negroes [*sic*], besides laying all inhabitants open to insult and oppression." Such concerns for the home front on the part of the soldiers who came from areas occupied by Union troops were difficult to bear, and Lewis bemoaned the Confederacy's failure. It would not have been so "if the whole country had done its duty," he wrote bitterly.[11]

The opposing armies settled into a cautious stalemate around Culpeper. Fraternization and illicit cross-river trade over the Rappahnnock once more relieved the tedium of picket duty until Union Brigadier General John Buford's First Cavalry Division splashed across the river at Kelly's Ford in late July. Buford's men pushed on to Brandy Station on August 1, while outnumbered Confederate cavalrymen fell back and called frantically for assistance. The weight of numbers began to tell as Buford steadily pushed the Rebel troopers back towards Culpeper. Anderson rushed Mahone, Posey, and Lang towards the critical spot. Mahone and Posey's brigades were first on the scene that scorching afternoon, with the lead elements thrown in precipitously and forced to load while advancing at a rapid pace. Anderson's infantry drove the Yankee cavalrymen back relentlessly "without halting but always moving at quick and frequently double quick time." As a result, men dropped from the excessive heat and exhaustion in addition to the enemy's fire. One of Posey's Mississippians later cavalierly dismissed the affair as a trifle. "When we came on the field, they took the back track," he said. "We followed almost to Brandy Station when, darkness coming, it was left to the cavalry to finish putting them across the river." Lang's men had also joined in the attack, and although General Hill likewise dismissed the affair as minor, it was hardly so for the already much reduced Florida brigade. Lang suffered six killed and twenty-three wounded in his tiny force of only 160 men.[12]

Buford's advance towards Culpeper took place while Lee was in the process of withdrawing behind the Rapidan River. He considered the terrain around Culpeper unsuited for battle and began shifting southward towards Orange Courthouse. Hill's three divisions were the last to withdraw, thus positioning Anderson to respond quickly to the Union advance. What Lee did not know, however, was that the cavalry was merely the advance element of Meade's army, which intended to cross at Kelly's Ford and Rappahannock Station once engineers repaired the railroad bridge across the river. Before that work was completed, Lee withdrew Hill's corps south of the Rapidan and concentrated it around Orange while Stuart's troopers screened the movement from Meade's view. Meade had missed his opportunity and Lee's force was now safely entrenched beyond the more defensible Rapidan, where the elevation on the southern side of the river was mostly greater than on the opposite bank.

Casualties at Gettysburg meant the promotion of new division commanders, and Cadmus Wilcox finally got his reward for his hard fighting and steady leadership. He took over Dorsey Pender's division on August 13 with promotion to major general. His former brigade remained in Anderson's division, and Brigadier General Abner Perrin eventually took command in February 1864. A South Carolina lawyer with Mexican War experience, Perrin rose to become colonel of the 14th South Carolina in Maxcy Gregg's brigade of South Carolinians. He later took over command of that brigade from Samuel McGowan when the latter fell wounded at Chancellorsville. The thirty-six-year-old Perrin received his promotion to brigadier general effective September 10 and would lead Wilcox's Alabama brigade once McGowan returned to duty. The relationship that existed between Dick Anderson and his new brigade commander is unknown, except that it was destined to be brief. Some sense of what it might have been comes from a letter Perrin sent to South Carolina governor Milledge L. Bonham on July 29, 1863. Describing the action at Gettysburg, Perrin praised Pender highly and extolled the South Carolina brigade's successes on the first day. Perrin alleged that after driving Union troops through the town Pender told him he had sent back for Anderson's division to come up, "supposing as I suppose[d] of course that Anderson was not far off. But neither Anderson nor his division was anywhere to be found." Meanwhile, they observed federal troops regrouping on Cemetery Ridge. "I suppose you will be curious to know where Anderson was & why he was out of the way at so important a juncture," he wrote. "*His failure to be up was the cause of the failure of the campaign.* I know he had camped some miles in our rear that night preceding the battle, but I know not why. It may have been Gen Hill's fault & it may have been the fault of Anderson himself. I saw nothing of him until the next day." Perrin complained about the behavior of nearly everyone during the battle with the exception of Pender, but such criticism added to speculation that Anderson was derelict in his arrival. One might therefore conclude that Perrin's relationship with Anderson was cool, and Perrin's unbridled ambition likely did not sit well with Anderson's more reserved and statelier demeanor.[13]

In addition to the flap over his performance at Gettysburg, Anderson faced yet another personal crisis. It was likely sometime in July when the general received the terrible news that his sister Mary, married to Frederick Childs, had died. News that reached the family or news that reached the front during the war often traveled slowly or even contained erroneous information that took time to confirm. In this case, Jennie not only lamented her sister-in-law's death in a July 1863 letter to Wallace, but also noted incorrectly, "that brother Richard is wounded. I trust not dangerously." He had come through the recent fighting at Gettysburg unscathed though. Jennie, then in Marion, Mississippi, received the news of Mary's death via a letter from her mother-in-law at Stateburg. "It is a dreadful blow and I am sick and unnerved from the shock," Jennie wrote as she related the latest tragedy to Wallace, whom she affectionately called Willie. Adding to the pathos was the fact that Wallace had intended to return soon to Stateburg. "This is a grief to you I know and to think of your proposed visit being timed just too late to see her again on earth, but you must go and see brother Fred in his sorrow, and say what you can to comfort him." Perhaps recalling Wallace's reluctance to address McKenzie's death promptly in his letters home, Jennie reminded him of his duty. "Poor father's afflictions are crowding upon his old age," she wrote. "Do let him have the assurance of your love." Dick Anderson's reaction to his sister's death passed unrecorded, but it could only have added to the burdens he carried. His sadness over the compounding family losses, the emotional toll of the death and wounding of so many of his soldiers, the criticism of his performance, and his separation from his loved ones must have weighed oppressively on his mind.[14]

By the end of the first week of September 1863, Lee and President Davis concluded to send Longstreet and his First Corps west to Tennessee. News from the Army of Tennessee had been disturbing. Knoxville fell to Union forces on September 2 and Braxton Bragg evacuated Chattanooga six days later. Longstreet's departure left only 54,000 men on the Rapidan, but a display of the army's power might bolster morale. Anderson's division participated in a review of Hill's corps on September 11, a few days after Longstreet's departure. Lee had denied Wilcox's request that his former brigade join his division, but Anderson recognized his outstanding service. "When I left the brigade," Wilcox wrote, "Genl Anderson, the division commander issued an order making it known as Wilcox's Old Brigade." Perrin left no record of how he felt about taking over a brigade linked indelibly with the name of its old commander, but Anderson announced the order well before Perrin's appointment to lead the Alabamians. Perrin was eager to advance and he would work hard to make his own reputation. The Alabamians, however, would never take to him.[15]

Within days of Lee reviewing Hill's corps, Union cavalry occupied Culpeper and pushed Stuart's horsemen towards the Rapidan. By nightfall on September 13, Lee directed Hill to send support to the beleaguered troopers. Hill rushed Anderson's division to their aid, and it reached Rapidan Station just before daylight. When Union cavalry arrived near the Rapidan fords, they found the high ground south of the river occupied by infantry in earthworks. Artillery positions fully commanded the approaches to the river from the north. Attempts to approach the fords were in vain, and Meade declined to push the issue further until he knew more of Lee's strength and intentions. Lee, on the other hand, believed the cavalry was the advance element of Meade's army, and his scouts reported the whole of it under marching orders. Most threatening of all, the enemy was already aware of "the large reduction" in Lee's strength.[16]

Facing uncertainty and conflicting advice from his superiors, Meade crossed his army over the Rappahannock a few days later and came to a halt. Lee did not retreat in the face of this threat, however, and Meade soon realized the strength of Lee's Rapidan line. As he continued to grapple with a lack of direction from Washington, the two armies again settled down to picket the banks of the Rapidan. Meantime, a resounding Confederate victory at Chickamauga in north Georgia had driven the Union army into Chattanooga, Tennessee, immediately besieged by Bragg's forces, including Longstreet. The federal response to that crisis would have a significant impact on events in Virginia. By September 30 Lee informed President Davis that the Meade's Eleventh and Twelfth Corps were headed west under Joe Hooker's command, while Meade was ordered to "fall back on Washington" should the situation in his front require it.[17]

Lee took offensive action within days, and Anderson issued orders for his division to be ready to march "across the Rapidan in the direction of Madison Court House" by 5 AM on October 9. Lee intended to turn Meade's right flank or intercept his retreat, and on October 13, Lee reported that Meade "had been compelled to retire north of the Rappahannock." Meade withdrew along roads leading directly to his destination, while Lee pursued by circuitous routes on his flank, attempting to overtake the retreating columns.[18]

During that rapid march, Lt. Hosford of the 5th Florida was inspired by the presence of some "beautiful girls" lining the road and "giving 'Huzzas' for the 'Rebels'" and encouraging them to throw all the Yankees into the Potomac. One of the excited girls "struck me on the shoulder with her 'kerchief saying 'go it my brave fellow, you are the boys for me,' just then I had a feeling, and felt as though I could fight 'old Meade,' and all his Yankee crew." Hosford got his wish later that day as Anderson's division drew close to Bristoe Station where the Union Third Corps was slowly fording Broad Run. A. P. Hill surveyed the mass of Yankees crowding at the ford and knew that immediate action would catch them in a vulnerable state.[19]

On the afternoon of October 14, Hill's impetuosity set in motion a series of actions that would spell disaster for Harry Heth's division when he sent it rushing headlong into what he thought was a disorganized Union traffic jam at Broad Run. As Anderson's troops marched along the road towards

Bristoe Station, he received an order from Hill to send forward the artillery battalion under Major David McIntosh that had been accompanying his division, and to send two infantry brigades to the right of the road on which they had been marching. Union troops marching along the Orange & Alexandria Railroad tracks leading to Broad Run threatened Heth's advance. Anderson sent Posey and Perry's brigades in an attempt to intercept them. The Yankees disappeared into some pine woods before either of his brigades could catch them, and the Rebels continued to advance toward the railroad. They soon found a strong line of enemy soldiers concealed in the railroad cut and embankment with a battery positioned to enfilade the road and sweep the field across which Anderson's men would have to traverse. Anderson brought them to a halt until he could examine the ground. Brigadier General Armistead Long, Ewell's artillery commander, rode up then and offered to place some of his own guns on a rise that would support Anderson's advance. Having sent McIntosh forward, Anderson was without any artillery of his own. "To this I gladly assented," he reported, "as I deemed it necessary to the farther advance of the troops of my command."[20]

Soon afterwards, Anderson discovered that Ewell's corps was advancing on his right, and orders came to connect his right flank with Ewell's left. He brought up the remainder of the division to join Posey and Perry's brigades. While the battle line was taking shape, Heth "became hotly engaged." Pushing forward at Hill's impatient urging in an attempt to bag the prize presented by the disorganized federal troops, Heth had discovered to his dismay a strong line of Yankee skirmishers posted along the railroad line, perpendicular to his line of advance. That discovery had prompted Hill to call for Anderson's two brigades to guard Heth's right flank. Still, Hill could not resist the opportunity presented by the fleeing Union troops at Broad Run and he boldly ordered Heth forward thinking that Anderson's brigades, then drawing into sight, could easily defend the right flank against whatever small force of federals happened to be there. The excited Hill saw an opportunity to crush the Union Third Corps on the march, but Heth was advancing into a trap.[21]

The Union soldiers concealed behind the railroad embankment that roughly paralleled Heth's line of advance consisted of approximately 3,000 infantrymen of the Second Corps supported by concealed artillery poised to shower deadly volleys of iron through the Confederate flank. Heth's men were compelled to wheel to their right to meet the threat, and they advanced bravely to the railroad line, but with terrible losses. Falling back in disorder, the Rebel infantry rushed past McIntosh, leaving his guns unsupported. Several fell into the hands of pursuing Yankees.[22]

Meanwhile, as Anderson was organizing his battle line, Heth's disaster unfolded rapidly, and Anderson could do little about it. As Heth's brigades gave way, Union troops poured onto the field in hot pursuit. Long could not post his guns in such a tenuous position until Posey and Perry drove the Yankees back. By the time they accomplished that job and when Long got his artillery in position, it was nearly dark. "After a few minutes' cannonading, to which the enemy replied warmly," Anderson later reported, "the firing was discontinued." The day had gone badly for Hill, whose outmatched troops suffered over 1,400 casualties with nothing to show for it.[23]

After Union troops withdrew, Lt. Hosford recalled the gruesome results of Hill's impetuosity. Of interring the Confederate dead, he wrote to his sweetheart with unusual and startling graphic detail. "But of a few of them we could only find some pieces of the body such as a hand or two or three fingers. Sometimes a foot, or part of a foot, sometimes a whole arm, or half of the head, and bodies mangled in every conceivable condition." He lamented their fate and the unattended carelessness with which they went to their graves. "How often I have thought of the song 'I'll kiss him for his Mother,' for it seems to speak a word of sympathy to the grieved."[24]

Anderson's losses were relatively small. He reported eleven killed and just over forty wounded, but the most grievous loss was that of the valiant Mississippian Carnot Posey who fell with a wound to his thigh. The injury itself was not particularly life threatening, but in that era, no one fully understood the role of bacteria. He succumbed to infection after struggling for his life for nearly a month. Posey died in Charlottesville, where he had studied law at the University of Virginia. Colonel Nathaniel Harris of the 19th Mississippi took his place, making two brigades now commanded by colonels. The other was Wilcox's Old Brigade, still under command of Colonel John Sanders until Perrin arrived in February 1864. Harris received promotion to brigadier general in January.[25]

In the meantime, Meade continued his retreat to Centreville. Lee saw little utility in further pursuit or in forcing Meade back into the fortifications surrounding the capital. He returned to the Rappahannock line, destroying the Orange & Alexandria railroad along the way in hopes that "it may prevent the return of the enemy to that river this winter." John Mason of the 9th Alabama in Wilcox's Old Brigade described how railroad ties were piled up and set afire. Rails placed atop the pyre became so hot in the center that the ends of the rails drooped down "forming a graceful bow." Another method of destruction was to heat the rails and twist them around stout tree trunks. The men demolished the telegraph lines and anything else that might prove to be of use to the Yankees. "We thought we'd give them a little trouble fixing them up again," John Mason wrote. Plagued by foul weather, the army arrived safely back beyond the Rappahannock by October 18, with Confederate cavalry remaining to watch for the enemy's maneuvers. Stuart quickly inflicted a severe loss on the Union cavalry, which suffered a humiliating defeat at Buckland Mills. The flight of the enemy was so precipitous that rebel participants afterwards took to calling it "the Bucktown Races."[26]

Lee again halted along the Rappahannock, with Anderson's division positioned upriver from Rappahannock Station, where the Orange & Alexandria Bridge had been destroyed during the most recent Yankee retreat. Major General Jubal Early's division from Ewell's Second Corps held the area around and south of the Station. A pontoon bridge connected both banks and linked Lee's army to a Confederate bridgehead on the northern side comprised of earthen forts and redoubts connected by rifle pits designed to defend against a crossing. Though the Rappahannock line was less easily defensible than the Rapidan, Lee was reluctant to cede more of Virginia's soil to the Yankees than was necessary. Meade moved back towards the river, and by early November, he defeated Early's troops at Rappahannock Station and overwhelmed the Confederate defenses at the critical river crossing downstream at Kelly's Ford. It was a staggering setback that entailed the loss of another 2,000 men from Lee's already outnumbered army. With Meade across the Rappahannock, Lee was compelled to retreat again. It marked a significant turning point for Lee. Never again would his entire army be capable of maneuvering as a whole to pursue offensive action across the upper Rappahannock River. Anderson's division moved towards Culpeper Courthouse on November 8, where James Kirkpatrick of the 16th Mississippi observed federal cavalry far in the distance. They "seemed to like the distance well," he wrote in his diary and the day passed uneventfully. That night, braving cold and wind, with some regiments marching through fields and woods rather than on roads, Anderson's men pressed on to the safety of the Rapidan. Weary and dismayed Confederates crossed the next day and again occupied stronger positions along the southern banks of the river. Hill's corps held the left of the line; Ewell's, temporarily under Early's command, held the right. Rebel cavalrymen roamed on each flank to guard against surprise.[27]

Hoping to settle into winter quarters, Anderson's men prepared for cold weather. Lieutenant Denoon of the 41st Virginia in Mahone's brigade wrote his parents that he was busily constructing a chimney for his tent. Within a week, he reported that they all had "good huts erected" and that he and the other officers were "well fixed at present with chimney and bunks." John Mason of the 9th Alabama likewise recalled having built "nice cabins" before once again commencing picket duty along the river and "a little more trading with our friends on the other side." In the Mississippi brigade, the sad news of General Posey's death began to filter in just after mid-November, marring the welcome prospect of settling in for the winter. The brigade held a meeting "to pass resolutions on the death of our late commander," Kirkpatrick recalled. Posey had been "well liked by his brigade and particularly by our regiment. He was remarkably kind and humane." Another recalled, "many young men of his brigade have had the advantage of his fatherly advice and guardian care." If he had been a father figure to many, the fact that two of Posey's sons were serving on his staff at the time of his death probably rendered the expressions of sympathy even more intense.[28]

In the Florida brigade, Colonel Lang had recently returned from a leave of absence at home. He regretted missing the exciting chase of Meade's army to Manassas, but returned in time to join Lee's withdrawal from the Rappahannock. His opinion was that Meade could do little else "until he drives fifty thousand as good soldiers as ever fired a gun from their own chosen position which they have strongly fortified." Lang, as well as the rest of Lee's army, had much confidence in the strength of their position on the Rapidan.[29]

President Davis visited the army at Orange Courthouse on November 21. Some speculated that the purpose was to discuss sending additional reinforcements to Bragg. Lieutenant Denoon considered the idea plausible and wrote that he did not "feel inclined to swap places at this time, but if it falls to Genl. Anderson's [command] to go [then] I go, willingly, though I would hate to leave Old Uncle Bob." He was hardly alone in his affection for Lee, going on to claim that, "he is believed by the soldiers and citizens of Northern Virginia to be the greatest man now living." Troops demonstrated "a decided preference" in popularity for Lee over Davis, even though the president had been welcomed warmly enough upon his arrival. "Huzza, Huzza was heard from the bystanders though quite feeble," Denoon wrote. When Lee's presence became known, however, "a shouting went up from the crowd that caused the earth almost to tremble beneath our feet."[30]

Despite the speculation, no plan to transfer any other units from Lee's army was afoot. Instead, Lee was certain that offensive operations by his opponent were forthcoming. Lee's immediate concern was the health and subsistence of his army and those issues must have been the subject of lengthy discussions. Food, warm clothing, shoes, and forage for the animals were a great source of anxiety for Lee, and Davis could observe for himself the state of the army as he reviewed the troops. Dick Anderson must have been one of those among "nearly all of the principal officers of the army" who called upon the president during his visit. The day after Davis's return to Richmond, all of those troubles had to take a back seat to the developing threat of a Union attempt to cross the Rapidan.[31]

Confederates watching the fords on the lower Rapidan on November 26 observed the federal advance once the heavy morning fog cleared out of the river valley. Union troops hoping to make a coordinated crossing waited while engineers built a pontoon bridge across the swollen river. Other troops at passable fords were in motion, but the bridge construction took time and the day passed with little accomplished. Meanwhile, the men of Anderson's division, though they heard the cannonading downriver, were largely unaware of the threat. Charlie Denoon complacently wrote his parents about rumors of Meade's impending advance to the Rapidan fords, "all of which may be untrue. The fact is," he told them, "such reports may be heard every day in camp without the slightest foundation." He must have been surprised to receive orders to prepare to march later that evening.[32]

Handicapped by an inability to clearly see the federal movements once the columns had crossed the river, Lee noted, "the country in that vicinity was unfavorable for observation, being almost an unbroken forest." He was thus uncertain whether Meade's target was Richmond or a march up the Rapidan to assault his right flank. It was necessary to maneuver the army in such a way as to prepare for both possibilities. With Ewell still absent sick, Jubal Early got his corps rapidly marching eastwards that night. On his right flank, Hill's corps, including Anderson's division, took the Orange Plank Road while J. E. B. Stuart and Wade Hampton's cavalry rode ahead to screen the advance and scout the enemy's dispositions. "I am concentrating this army upon . . . [Meade's] right flank," Lee telegraphed Davis on the 27th, "with a view to bring him to battle."[33]

Lee soon knew beyond doubt that at least a portion of Meade's army was moving westward towards him, though he was yet uncertain whether that was a diversion. Confederate troops rushed to contest the advance. The 16th Mississippi of Posey's old brigade in Anderson's division had set out at 4 AM from their "comfortable homes" on "roads hard frozen and slippery." The men laughed as comrades slipped and slid along the road, but it was "not so amusing when a loaded gun goes off by contact with ice" recalled James Kirkpatrick. On the right of the advancing Confederate lines, Rebel troopers eventually confronted Meade's cavalry on the Orange Plank Road. Heth's division rushed forward and a "brisk skirmish" brought the engagement to a standstill. North of the Orange Turnpike, Early's men confronted federals at Payne's Farm, but there was no decisive result. Contact with the enemy immediately changed the situation Lee was facing. He now sought to close a gap separating Hill's and Early's corps before federal troops spotted the vulnerability. At Lee's direction, Hill directed Dick Anderson to move his division to the left and establish contact with Early's lines. He soon located Brigadier General Harry T. Hays's Louisiana Brigade and eliminated the threat of a Union advance through the breach that had existed. For some, however, the movement was a challenging one. Kirkpatrick recalled that his regiment "groped about in the dark like blind men in a thicket for a few hours, not finding the right place." Once in place in a pine thicket, the men rested briefly and noiselessly without the benefit of fires before countermarching in the direction they had come from that day. Opting to occupy defensive positions after indecisive clashes on the 27th, Lee withdrew during the night beyond Mine Run where the ground was more favorable for defense. There men constructed breastworks and dug rifle pits in hopes that Meade would dash his troops against well-defended positions. Artillery positions spanned the entire line. Anderson's division rested its left flank on the Orange Turnpike and extended southward to connect to Wilcox's division.[34]

Meade took up the pursuit but his troops faced the same daunting challenges that Kirkpatrick and his Mississippi comrades had confronted, struggling through mud and dense thickets. What faced them a few hundred yards to the west across Mine Run gave them pause. "I never saw a more imposing sight," wrote one Yankee of Lee's ridge top defensive line. Meade spent the remainder of the day surveying the strength of the position, ultimately deciding on a flanking maneuver on Lee's right. Federals were poised to make the assault on the morning of November 30, but the Union Second Corps commander, Major General Gouverneur K. Warren realized his attack would have little chance of success. Anticipating an attack on his flank, Lee had strengthened his lines there. He placed Heth's division, first held in reserve, between Anderson and Wilcox. Artillery fire followed by a charge by their Rebel counterparts drove back advancing Federal skirmishers, and the battle ended nearly before it began. Warren knew he had insufficient strength to carry the Confederate position. "The full light of the sun shows me that I cannot succeed," he wrote to a chagrined Meade that morning after calling off the assault.[35]

Meade's failure shifted the initiative fully to Lee, who waited vainly one more day for the Union general to attack before determining to assault the Yankee lines on December 2. Hill concentrated Anderson and Wilcox on the extreme right of his line, ordering them forward at daybreak. Anderson left no report of the Mine Run Campaign or of the events of December 2, but the experience of Mississippian James Kirkpatrick undoubtedly captures the essence. By daylight, his regiment was on the extreme left flank of Meade's line prepared "to show the enemy that if they are afraid to charge breastworks, we are not." Meade, however, had withdrawn his army during the night. Anderson's division took up the pursuit for several miles, but found Meade already safely across the Rapidan. "One can scarcely imagine his object in coming over and going back without a fight," Kirkpatrick mused. Another

Mississippian told a friend of his disappointment that Meade had retreated "without giving us a trial. I really wanted them to come on," he wrote, "as we had such good ditches and redoubts for our cannons. I believe we could have whipped three to one." As one Richmond newspaper derisively put it, "Meade has marched up the hill and then marched down again."[36]

Anderson's troops returned to their quarters along the Rapidan and settled in for what they hoped would be a quiet winter interrupted only by the occasional discomforts of picket duty. The winter camp of the 16th Mississippi was "erected on a high hill, at the foot of Clark's Mountain, from which position they had a full view of the surrounding country." From the summit "we could overlook the Federal camps, . . . and with the aid of a glass, could discern more than a dozen towns, each of which had been the scene of numerous battles during the last two years." The men could also see all the way eastwards to the plains of Stafford, across from Fredericksburg, while in the opposite direction rose the majestic peaks of the Blue Ridge, "over which we had passed so often." For others, like J. B. Crawford, another winter away from home meant only more loneliness and fretting over family and conditions at home in faraway Mississippi. "I am almost crazy about you and the children," he wrote his wife Martha in December. "I am afeared you will suffer if times dont get no beter [*sic*] and I see no prospect of it going any beter at present. . . . If you cant do no beter . . . do the best you can." As for himself, he complained of not getting enough to eat, but he had "made me a little home. . . . All I lack is a little wife to go with it." Others were concerned about younger brothers at home. Jefferson Wilson advised his to join the cavalry, as it was "a good deal easier than infantry." He also cautioned him not to be too anxious and not to "come out until the conscript age was about to get you. There is not a bit of fun in fighting. I have tried it long enough to know about it." Wilson would be captured the following August and die of acute diarrhea in a Yankee prison camp.[37]

Religious revivalism continued in the army through the winter. "Conversions were frequent, and the songs of religious worship could be heard in the camps of every regiment . . . cheering the drooping spirits of the suffering soldier." Lee did much to encourage the spread of religious sentiment by calling attention to the obligation of "a proper observance of the Sabbath," suspending all duties and labor not considered essential on those days, and instructing commanding officers to schedule Sunday inspections at times that did not "interfere with the attendance of the men on divine service at the customary hour of the morning." Religious services were one alternative to the drudgery of daily routine, but snowfall once again opened opportunities to release the pent-up energies of the young soldiers. Snowball battles sometimes raged for hours that winter, with the officers leading men in mock engagements. Some men were fortunate enough to receive a furlough during the winter months, and Charlie Denoon somehow got two of them. After the first in January, Charlie returned to the regiment two days past the expiration of his furlough. His excuses for his late arrival were reasonable and accepted without question. Perhaps he might have tried harder to return on time if he had witnessed the recent execution of two members of the 16th Virginia in his brigade for being absent without leave. Most men committed to stay the course though, with Jeff Wilson telling his father, "two-thirds of the army has not been home since the war commenced. I would like to get a furlough . . . but there is not any chance for me without I get sick or wounded. I had rather say until the war ends if I have to get a furlough in that way." Always reluctant to grant too many furloughs, Lee eventually increased opportunities in January 1864 once he knew the federals were unlikely to advance again. Rather than two men out of each hundred, the new rate became a dozen.[38]

While most of the men huddled in the confines of their winter huts, clearing and burning as many as 1,000 acres of trees during the cold months of inactivity, higher ranking officers frequently resided in conveniently situated private homes. Dick Anderson probably established his headquarters at some house strategically located in the area occupied by his division. The absence of letters to his wife during this period indicates that Sallie likely ventured forth like many other wives of senior officers to join her husband in the field. A. P. Hill, initially established his headquarters in tents at the base of Clark's Mountain, but knowing how anxious his wife was to join him, a local resident prevailed upon him in mid-December "to bring her to his home." She apparently arrived within a few days and the family eventually took up residence at Mayhurst, a recently built twenty-room Italianate mansion in Orange County. In keeping with normal practice, his staff erected the headquarters tents nearby in the yard. After Ewell returned to command of his corps in early December, his winter quarters with his wife were at Morton Hall, a somewhat more modest Italianate home built in the 1730s. The General doted on the domineering Mrs. Ewell, quite the opposite of Dolly Hill's intense devotion to her husband. His staff found the situation distasteful, though some undoubtedly would never get over the loss of their former great chieftain Jackson, to whom Ewell, with all his eccentricities of manner and appearance would never quite measure up. Similar living conditions surely marked the lives of General and Mrs. Anderson that season, though the identity of their temporary home is unknown. Sallie had taken every opportunity during the war to spend time with her husband, following him first to Florida and then to Richmond and the banks of Rappahannock where she might have spent time knitting socks or mending garments for the troops as many of the other wives did. "I can bear anything rather than separation," she once wrote. General Anderson, moreover, was compelled to remain with the army that winter as he took temporary command of the corps when Hill visited Richmond in January and again during Hill's illness in early February. Though Hill remained at his quarters, his recurring illnesses sometimes incapacitated him for lengthy stretches of time, as was also the case with Ewell, whose horse fell and rolled on him after slipping on icy roads in early January 1864.[39]

The monotony of camp life was broken in February when Federal troops under John Sedgwick surprised southern pickets and crossed the Rapidan at Morton's Ford on Ewell's front. Abner Perrin woke Wilcox's Old Brigade at 2 AM and rushed to contest any further Yankee advance, but Ewell handily bottled up the federal force and drove it back across the river. In the meantime, the Alabamians struggled along roads turned to quagmires by a recent heavy snow and tramping of thousands of feet. Men soon began to straggle badly, so much so that Lee dispatched his chief of staff, Robert H. Chilton, to deal with the stragglers. As Chilton encountered the lagging Alabamians, most claimed that they were part of Perry's tiny Florida brigade, which numbered only around three hundred men and was the butt of jokes about its small size. After several such reports, the exasperated Chilton fumed "My God, Perry counts only three hundred, and I have counted three thousand already." Another Alabamian found cause to joke about size, but this time regarding the excessive length of a cavalryman's nose. The marching troops were approaching a group of rebel horsemen by the roadside, one of whom "had a tremendous long nose," as George Clark recalled. Just then, an Irishman stepped from the ranks of passing troops and addressed the cavalryman with a bow. "My dear sir," he said, "won't you kindly turn your head to one side so the army can pass?" This of course led to fisticuffs and the Irishman "whipped him in three rounds," but it must have been an amusing diversion for the otherwise suffering marchers. They soon learned that Ewell had handled the threat at Morton's Ford, and they returned to their winter quarters around Orange Courthouse.[40]

If the winter passed uneventfully for most of the army, all suffered from food and clothing shortages. Rations were reduced to only a quarter pound of meat daily, and officers who had to purchase their food found it so scarce that they sometimes had to subsist on the charity of their men. With the second highest number of mouths to feed in the entire army, the situation was dire for Anderson's division. Alabamian George Clark recalled that the quarter pound of bacon and pint of meal that as the daily fare was "very hard on me as I had my servant to feed out of this slim amount of rations. We ate only one meal a day," he noted, "which was about eleven o'clock, and in order to protect my servant, before beginning to eat, I would separate the food and turn his over to him for safekeeping." When he returned from furlough in mid-January, Charlie Denoon observed that rations were "as scarce as hen's teeth." Though he brought back provisions, two of his comrades "devoured my sack like hungry wolves." In Mahone's brigade, events earlier that month illustrated the seriousness of the food situation. The theft of some flour led to the issuance of a rifle to "a negro boy named Ben" who slept in the brigade supply tent. The rifle was loaded only with peas, but a soldier who wandered too near the tent in the pre-dawn hours of a dark night received the full load in the head and face, knocking him to the ground, whereupon Ben must have struck him with the rifle and killed him. As news spread throughout the camp, only the intervention of General Mahone and some other officers saved the boy from a mob of incensed soldiers. Civil authorities eventually took him into custody but his ultimate fate went unreported, as were any further thefts of flour.[41]

The food shortages led Lee to complain to Secretary of War Seddon on January 22 that, "Short rations are having a bad effect upon the men, both morally and physically." He noted an increase in the number of desertions, despite taking drastic actions against those apprehended. "Unless there is a change, I fear the army cannot be kept effective, and cannot be kept together." To relieve the strain, Lee was authorizing furloughs at the rate of sixteen per company of one hundred men, and eight per company of fifty men. Lee, whose wife remained in Richmond that winter, also recommended ending the practice carried over from the US Army that permitted officers to purchase food for their families from the Commissary Department. Originally enacted to ease the burden on officers with families serving in remote frontier outposts, Lee maintained it had no basis for continuing in areas where officers could purchase supplies on the local economy. Lee also sought to encourage the soldiers with exhortations drawing on the tradition of the Revolution—"Soldiers! You tread with no unequal step the road by which your fathers marched through suffering, privations, and blood to independence. Continue to emulate . . . their valor in arms, their patient endurance of hardships, their high resolve to be free, which no trial could shake . . . and be assured that the just God who crowned their efforts with success will, in His own good time, send down His blessing upon yours."[42]

The army survived the trial of that difficult winter, and as spring approached, changes both large and small began to appear. Visiting officers' wives began to make their way homeward, soldiers returned from furlough, and the army recovered its strength in preparation for the campaigns that would accompany the arrival of fine weather in Virginia's Piedmont. In the North, Ulysses S. Grant was elevated to the rank of lieutenant general and appointed General-in-Chief. He intended to make his headquarters with Meade's army and direct operations from there. It was change that brought a commander finally willing to act on Lincoln's strategic ideas regarding simultaneous advances on all fronts. Plans for offensives in every theater of the war began to take shape. "Wherever Lee goes, there you will go also," the new commander told Meade. In Lincoln's typical well-turned phrase after hearing of plans for coordinated attacks, he quickly grasped the essence and remarked to Grant "those not skinning can hold a leg." Both concepts—targeting Lee and attacking everywhere—would change the nature of the war in the spring of 1864.[43]

Longstreet's corps returned, reaching Charlottesville by rail on April 20 and making its way on foot to Gordonsville. Lee held "a grand review" in early May, and "the troops greeted the old leader with great enthusiasm," recalled John Bratton of Micah Jenkins's brigade. The event "passed off finely," and the men knew now they were back on familiar ground and in Lee's competent hands. On May 2, Lee gathered his corps and division commanders at the signal station on the summit of Clark's Mountain, with its commanding view of the surrounding countryside that included the bustling Union camps north of the Rapidan. Lee believed that Meade's army would cross the Rapidan on his right flank, but he was not certain. Rather than seizing the initiative, Lee could only order his commanders to have their troops standing by in readiness to march at a moment's notice with three days' rations. Lookouts on Clark's Mountain and an extensive cavalry screen along the Rapidan would serve notice of Meade's movements.[44]

The May 2 meeting was a timely one. The signal station on Clark's Mountain began to observe unusual activity the following evening, which seemed to presage an imminent march. The next morning's scene verified Lee's suspicions. Long lines of Meade's troops with their wagons, artillery, and impedimenta were filing toward Germanna or Ely's Fords on Lee's right flank. By noon, Early's men were headed east on the Orange Turnpike, while Hill's corps set off on the Plank Road. Anderson's division would "watch the movements of the enemy," as he later recalled, "with orders to follow the march of the army when I should be assured that the last of the enemy's forces had moved from Culpepper [*sic*] and that no attempt was to be made by him on our rear." Longstreet marched that afternoon for Brock's Bridge over the North Anna River, a distance of about sixteen miles, from which point he continued moving north before picking up the Catharpin Road that would bring him east. In order to stymie the Union offensive and catch their opponent in the tangled Wilderness, where the unsuitability of the terrain for rapid movement reduced Meade's numerical advantage, it was necessary for the Rebels to march rapidly to meet him. Meade intended to cross at both the fords, move southwards to the Orange Turnpike, then push west on the Turnpike, the Plank Road, or several others that led to Lee's position. He hoped to maneuver Lee out of his defensive works and into open ground where the federal advantage in numbers would be telling. The success of Meade's scheme required the Union force to march quickly as well, but that was not a trait numbered among its proven qualities.[45]

Instead of advancing rapidly through the Wilderness on May 4, Meade halted his men to allow the supply trains to close the gap with the infantry. Lee pressed steadily forward with Ewell and Hill until darkness ended the day's march. Though still without Longstreet close by, and absent Dick Anderson's division, Lee intended to seize the initiative, capitalize on the federal halt, and bring Meade to battle in the tangled growth of the Wilderness the next morning. With luck, Ewell and Hill would pin Meade in place. Longstreet would arrive soon on the Catharpin Road, in all likelihood placing him squarely on Meade's left flank where he could deliver a crushing blow.[46]

The engagement on May 5th around the Turnpike and Plank Roads was brutal with Ewell and Hill battling Meade's army to a standstill, but Anderson's division took no part in it, having moved on May 4 to man the defensive works along the river per Lee's orders. Jerome Yates of the 16th Mississippi was just finishing a letter to a friend that day when drums sounded an orderly call. "Oh, the devil," he wrote, "cook two days rations and get ready to leave is the next order. . . . Well, for Grant and glory. So Goodbye," he concluded. Anderson's men avoided a precipitous departure, however; only evacuating their posts along the Rapidan on May 5 after he concluded there was no threat to Lee's rear. Anderson instructed his brigades to gather near Verdiersville, a crossroads hamlet located where the Plank Road merged with the Orange Turnpike. They began to trickle into Verdiersville by sunset, though the farthest spread units arrived much later in the evening. A courier from Lee's headquarters arrived just after midnight with orders to rush the division onwards. The fighting on May 5 had proven indecisive. Now Lee needed every rifle when the battle resumed in the morning. Groggy men set out on the Orange Plank Road by 2 AM with Mahone leading. Wright, Perrin, Perry, and Harris followed. As they stumbled along the road that morning the nearly sleepless men fought against a tide of ambulances and wounded soldiers pitching forward in the darkness, "some hobbling on guns used as crutches," determined to find aid before succumbing to exhaustion or blood loss. Even though the pace increased as dawn's light began to show, the excruciating march had consumed nearly six hours.[47]

Lee intended to place Anderson's division in a second line along with the rest of Hill's corps, which had been roughly handled in the fighting on May 5. He also anticipated seeing Longstreet's divisions arriving well before daylight, and those units would push ahead of Hill's men to create a fresh line of attack. Despite Lee and Hill's confidence in him, however, Longstreet did not arrive before dawn. Expecting relief imminently, Hill had therefore not reoriented his battle line effectively despite some complaints from Wilcox and Heth on that matter. Wilcox took his concerns directly to Lee, who told him not to worry because Anderson and Longstreet would be up soon to relieve his men. Heth went to Hill, who told him substantially the same thing. Both Wilcox and Heth persisted throughout the night until Hill, again suffering from a malady that did nothing to add to his patience, finally lost his temper. "Damn it Heth," he snapped, "I don't want to hear any more about it; the men shall not be disturbed." On May 6, Ewell's early morning assault on the right of the federal line began. Soon after, Union skirmishers appeared before Hill's disorganized line of battle. With Longstreet still absent, Hill's haphazardly placed divisions now stood to bear the brunt of the Yankee assault developing in his front.[48]

Wilcox's division, slightly in advance of Heth, received the first attack. Elements from two Union corps far outnumbering the Rebels began to force Wilcox's men back, some precipitously and others more stubbornly. Joined by Heth's division, they all retreated several hundred yards where some attempted to form a new defensive line. Others fled heedless of pleas to halt. As the great mass of Union troops continued to advance, threatening to create a wide gap between Hill and Ewell's lines, Lee's army teetered delicately on the brink of disaster. Relying on one of the area's few clearings for the effective use of artillery, Confederate guns had massed in a small clearing around the Widow Tapp's farm, commanding the Plank Road and giving an open view for about three hundred yards along the front. Belching cannon fire spewed hot iron into the advancing bluecoats, finally slowing their advance. At the height of this dilemma, the head of Longstreet's columns at last came into view on the Plank Road, with Texans and Mississippians filling both sides of the dusty road in parallel ranks. Lee watched the soldiers advancing excitedly amidst the confusion, telling John Gregg, the Texan's leader: "when you go in there, I wish you to give those men the cold steel." Other Lone Star State soldiers cheered heartily when Lee remarked, "Texans always move them." The compliment and resultant cheers passed down the Texans' lines until they began to shout "Lee to the rear," swearing they would not advance until their chief had removed to a place of safety.[49]

Hill's two divisions passed to the rear through the advancing First Corps and began forming behind them as had been intended long before. Longstreet and Lee both worked feverishly to throw Longstreet's regiments into line. With the Union advance halted, the Confederates began to drive their adversaries back approximately to the positions they held earlier that morning. One of the most intensive crises of Lee's tenure passed as Longstreet turned the tide of battle. Lee made little of it in correspondence to the Secretary of War, but it was a looming catastrophe of such moment that Lee himself felt compelled to lead the men forward to preserve the lines. In the epitome of understatement, Lee noted merely that as Hill's troops were being relieved that morning "the enemy advanced and created some confusion." Like his description of the near calamity in crossing the Potomac after Gettysburg, Lee minimized some of the army's setbacks, particularly in cases where some censure might have resulted.[50]

Meanwhile, Anderson's division arrived near the battlefield just after sunrise. Their march halted for approximately an hour while the rear elements of Longstreet's corps filed onto the Plank Road at Parker's Store. Anderson fell in behind Longstreet with Mahone still in the lead. Arriving on the field by around 8 AM, Anderson received orders to report to Longstreet. Hill played little part in directing the fight for the rest of that day, perhaps due to illness, and direction of the Confederate right fell entirely to Longstreet. He opted to use Anderson's fresh troops as a strategic reserve, calling on them as needed, mostly to support Major General Charles Fields's division north of the Plank Road. Soon after Anderson arrived, "orders were received to send one brigade [Mahone] to reinforce Longstreet on the right of the Plank Road and another [Wright] to report to A. P. Hill on the left of the same road; to move up two other brigades [Perrin and Perry] in line of battle at a right angle with the road, the right resting on the road, and to attack." Anderson held Harris in reserve. "Everybody was bawling for reinforcements," Anderson later remarked, "and one after another my brigades were sent off until at last I had but one remaining under my immediate command." The brigades were soon "maneuvering as support to different parts of the line," recalled the 16th Mississippi's James Kirpatrick. He termed the musketry "exceedingly heavy," and he could follow the ebb and flow of the fighting when "a well known cheer tells unmistakably who is getting the best of it." Around noon, the Mississippians were resting on the Plank Road when "Minie balls began to play unmusically to our ears," and federals soon appeared in woods on their left. The brigade moved forward and filed into a gap in the lines, quickly throwing up breastworks. Heavy firing resulted, but no determined assault. "Our protection made it an easy matter to hold our line," said Kirkpatrick.[51]

Longstreet had meanwhile decided to conduct a flank attack on the exposed left of the Union line, and he would use Mahone's Virginians for that purpose. Mahone, along with Wofford's Brigade of Kershaw's division, Davis's brigade—commanded by Colonel John M. Stone—of Heth's division, and

George "Tige" Anderson's of Field's division set out on a route that would take them onto the federal flank. Lieutenant Colonel Sorrel, Longstreet's chief of staff, was familiar with the roads and led the troops into place, but Mahone claimed that as the most senior brigadier general he was in command of the force. Nonetheless, both performed marvelously that day. At Chancellorsville almost exactly a year before, Anderson had sent Rans Wright along the same unfinished railroad cut from the opposite direction to get onto Hooker's right flank. Now the attack would come from the west, once again using the cut to achieve surprise. No one in the Federal Army recognized the threat posed by the route even though one of the Union division commanders and one brigadier on that vulnerable flank had been the victim of the assault using the railroad cut the year before. They would soon pay the price for their inattention. The four Rebel brigades reached the railroad cut south of the Plank Road, turned eastward for some distance, formed under its cover, and set off across fields in the direction of the Plank Road hoping to crash squarely into the federal left flank. Mahone remarked proudly that the brigades "in imposing order and with a step that meant to conquer," were soon "descending upon the enemy's left." It took less than an hour for the assault to clear the ground south of the Plank Road and reach that vital thoroughfare.[52]

Dick Anderson's role thus far had been minimal. His other brigades remained dispersed along the Confederate line facing east and straddling the Orange Plank Road. By late morning, Perrin's Alabamians and Perry's Florida brigade were on either side of a First Corps brigade north of the Road, with Harris's Mississippians as support. Wright supported three of Kershaw's brigades south of the Road. The devastating flank attack led by Mahone now made it possible for the main line to press forward along the Plank Road towards the intersecting Brock Road. Longstreet's corps, along with Anderson's division, prepared to strike a telling blow to the reeling Union forces. Before that could occur, however, misfortune struck on the Confederate right.[53]

Longstreet had ridden out the Plank Road to the scene of the flank attack and was sitting on horseback in a group of staff officers consulting with Lee. Back on the Plank Road, Micah Jenkins, commanding a South Carolina brigade rode up just then, joyfully congratulating Longstreet on the Army's success so far that day. Longstreet, Jenkins, Kershaw, and an entourage of staff officers headed down the road, passing in front of their troops. Jenkins turned to his South Carolinians, formed in the road, and hollered to them—"Why do you not cheer, men?" The troops responded heartily, but the sound of their praise had hardly faded on the dense afternoon air when a volley of shots rang out from a nearby wood. Men of the 12th Virginia making their way back to the Plank Road were mistaken for Yankees in the shadows of the dense undergrowth, prompting an exchange of fire before the error was recognized. Jenkins rose in his stirrups. "Steady men!" he shouted. "For God's sake, steady!" It was too late though. The gallant South Carolinian toppled from his mount mortally wounded. Longstreet too "reeled as the blood poured down over his breast." The firing ended as quickly as it began, and the troops soon learned the sad news that the fire came from their own men. Francis Dawson, of Longstreet's staff, rode quickly to the rear in search of a surgeon, and later encountered General Lee as he escorted the ambulance carrying Longstreet. "I shall not soon forget the sadness in his face, and the almost despairing movement of his hands, when told that Longstreet had fallen." One of Anderson's staff officers reported that he heard that when Lee learned of Longstreet's wound he said, "This is an unfortunate field for me, for here I lost my right arm (referring to Jackson) and now I lost my left (referring to Longstreet)." Artilleryman John C. Haskell recalled that Lee rushed to Longstreet's side, and then sent for Anderson. Major General Field, commanding John B. Hood's old division, assumed immediate command of the corps and prepared to press ahead with the attack before Anderson arrived and took charge. The delay caused by Longstreet's fall, however, had allowed the shattered Union line to reform in time to repulse the southerners' attack.[54]

In the midst of the carnage of the Wilderness after Longstreet and Jenkins fell, Anderson received one of the most heartfelt and unsolicited accolades he ever experienced. The men of the South Carolina Brigade in Field's division had scant reason for joy after losing Jenkins so tragically. Nevertheless, as the men sprawled on the ground resting, they found cause to rise up and cheer. They had not seen their former commander for some months, but as soon as they saw Anderson riding up the line, "they rose, with a yell, to welcome him. They had to be silenced because the enemy was nearby. They silently resumed their places, but as Anderson paused they took off their hats and threw them into the air." Stopping near the center of the brigade line, he "turned to the troops, removed his hat, and said simply: 'My friends, your silent expression makes me grateful for your kind remembrance. I thank you sincerely.'"[55]

"Fighting Dick" Anderson took command of Longstreet's corps, while Mahone was elevated to command of Anderson's division. On May 7, Special Orders No. 122 relieved Anderson from duty with Hill's corps and assigned him to temporary command of Longstreet's. He and Mahone took their personal staff with them to the new positions, but the general staff was to remain with "their proper commands." It was a temporary expedient undertaken in crisis, albeit at Longstreet's wish. According to Moxley Sorrel, General Lee had been considering three of his most able generals as possible replacements for the longer term—Early, Edward Johnson, and Dick Anderson—and if Sorrel's recollections are accurate, Lee seemed to be inclined towards Early. Sorrel also thought Early the most capable of the three, but also told Lee that he "feared [Early] would be objectionable to both officers and men" because of his unpopularity in the corps. "His flings and irritable disposition had left their marks," he recalled, and "some ugly feelings had been aroused while operating in concert." In all likelihood he was referring chiefly to the bad effect Early's irascible nature had on Longstreet's staff, not on the rank and file of the corps. Lee astutely realized that a sound working relationship between the commander and his staff was critical for the effective administration of the corps. Sorrel thought Johnson too little known in the corps. When asked his opinion of Anderson, Sorrel told Lee simply, "We *know him* and shall be satisfied with him." It was hardly a ringing endorsement, but an honest one. He had been with the corps as a brigade and division commander until moving to Hill's command. Nonetheless, Sorrel left his dawn meeting with Lee on May 7 with the distinct impression that he would soon be serving General Early, but later that day the order came naming "chivalrous, deliberate 'Dick' Anderson" to the post.[56]

Sorrel's recollection of events rings true. Lee would have been concerned that the experienced and highly capable First Corps staff be able to work smoothly with a new commander. A year earlier, he had interviewed Major Alexander S. "Sandie" Pendleton of Jackson's staff when faced with the task of replacing Stonewall. Lee told Pendleton that the staff ought to remain in place and a new commander should not tamper with it. In that respect, Lee was reflecting the position of President Davis. He had made clear his desire to retain an existing staff as a permanent component of a command and not change it on the whims of a new commander. It made sense to capitalize on the staff's experience, vital to the day-to-day operations of such a large enterprise, but it simultaneously raised the question of whether the new commander would mesh with the inherited staff. In interviewing Sorrel, Lee wished above all to know which of the men under consideration would work well with Longstreet's finely tuned and capable staff. Lee likely bypassed Early because it was also clear that A. P. Hill's health was declining markedly and he might not recover sufficiently to continue in command of his troops. Early would be a suitable choice to replace Hill in that case, and Hill's staff knew Early from his days serving under Jackson. Sorrel's conversation with Lee took place early on the rainy Saturday morning of May 7, when Hill's illness was again worsening. Later that day Hill sat with Lee on the porch of an abandoned farmhouse, undoubtedly hard pressed to conceal his suffering. By the next day, he was unable to sit his horse and Lee appointed Early to temporary command of the Third Corps. Hill soon recovered and resumed his duties, but Early would find new opportunities when Ewell fell ill within a few weeks. Command of Ewell's Second Corps temporarily fell to Early on May 29 in a move that eventually gained permanence. The army would not have received the news of command changes with any great concern, for it had been widely thought since the winter that "a new cut, shuffle and deal in Lieutenant Generals," would not be a bad thing. Ewell's physical deficiencies were suspected to "have impaired his efficiency" in command, while Powell Hill was thought not to have "risen to the requirements of a corps commander." Hill retained command of his corps despite absences during periods of incapacitating illness, but it remained to be seen how the elevation of Early and Anderson would play out.[57]

Lee had made a sound decision in appointing Anderson. He was a good fit with the corps, and it seemed likely that Longstreet would return when healed from his wounds. As Acting Adjutant General and nominal chief of staff-since the latter position did not formally exist in the Army of Northern Virginia—Sorrel welcomed the pipe-smoking, "indolent" Anderson, whom he described at that time as having "a short, thick, stock figure, with good features and agreeable expression." E. P. Alexander, chief of artillery in the Second Corps, also recalled Anderson's appointment with fondness. He "was as pleasant a commander to serve under as could be wished, & was a sturdy and reliable fighter. . . . we were no strangers to him." Others might have held different opinions, such as Rans Wright, who as late as February 1864 had still harbored intense resentment over Anderson's failure to support his attack at Gettysburg on July 2. Wright reassured his daughter when she expressed concerns for her father's safety that she should "feel no uneasiness about" him at that time. Wright was then in command of a division, and in what was likely a veiled reference to his accusation that Anderson was safely behind the lines on July 2, he informed her sarcastically that "therefore by following an *illustrious* example I need not expose myself." Cadmus Wilcox captured the Georgian's sentiments after Gettysburg most succinctly—"Wright never liked him afterwards," he wrote.[58]

One staff member who would later recall his relations with Anderson quite fondly was Francis Dawson. The young Englishman had sailed to the Confederacy as a "landsman" aboard a Confederate steamer in 1862, and he eventually secured a spot as an ordinance officer on Longstreet's staff. He not only enjoyed pleasant relations with Anderson, but he later wrote that "Indeed, we became close friends." Four years after the war, Anderson heartily endorsed the Englishman's application to join the Survivors' Association of Charleston District in South Carolina. "I had constant opportunities to observe the meritorious conduct and gallant bearing" of Dawson's he wrote, which "eminently entitle him to share the privileges and distinctions of a Survivor."[59]

Despite the loss of their commander, the men of Longstreet's corps were in fine fettle on Saturday night, May 7, as was the rest of Lee's army after a sultry day of only light skirmishing. That night a sudden cheer arose from the right flank of the Confederate line "situated in the depths of the wilderness," recalled another of Anderson's staff officers. "It was reechoed with the utmost stretch of human vociferation from right to left throughout the whole line beginning in Longstreet's corps then passing into Hill's and finally into Ewell's." The chilling expression of hard-won victory was a spontaneous outburst of emotion. "The men seemed to proclaim that the day passed without word of the enemy's attack was an acknowledgement of their triumph, an assertion of their power, an unaccepted challenge . . . which Grant and his army dared not take up. . . . I never heard anything so wild, joyous, and thrilling as this outburst from fifty thousand hearts stretching along for miles unseen by each other in that deep forest."[60]

Grant had learned a valuable lesson about the Army of the Potomac, witnessing some weaknesses evidenced by Meade's commanders. He had allowed Meade and his subordinates to handle the tactical details of the fight, and he likely regretted not taking more control over the course of the battle. To truly test the army, however, Grant knew he needed to draw Lee into the open. Rather than withdraw and refit the army to try again another day, Grant again proposed to turn Lee's right flank. Confederates fought him to a draw in the tangled Wilderness, but perhaps marching rapidly towards Spotsylvania Court House would enable him to bring Lee to battle outside his breastworks and under conditions that were more favorable.[61]

Chapter 15

Corps Command at Spotsylvania

In War, the way is to avoid what is strong
and to strike what is weak.

—Sun Tzu,
The Art of War

The relative quiet that reigned on Saturday, May 7 had done little to relieve the horrors of the scene. Many expected a renewal of fighting that morning, and the army spent much time organizing defenses overnight while unnerved pickets fired indiscriminately at the slightest provocation. Incessant pleas or horrendous screams from wounded and dying men punctuated the darkness. Exhausted soldiers saw carnage of a sort rarely before witnessed to this extent, presaging the relentless bloodletting that would unfold over the next weeks. Tangled undergrowth had caught fire in many places, as it had the year before at Chancellorsville, but now fires spread more widely. "The flashes of the exploding cartridge boxes on the dead and wounded could be seen as the long sweep of flame went over them," one man recalled. Red-tinged acrid smoke burned their throats while the stench of burning flesh added to the misery. Wounded men were roasted alive, suffering a fate that must have set even the stoutest men quaking in anger or trepidation. Others had attempted "in the mad energy of despair, to escape" the licking fires by dragging themselves frantically along the ground trailing blood and mangled limbs in their wake. Men assigned to the ambulance corps "rescued many from death, at the peril of their own lives," reported on Mississippian in Anderson's old division. "Every bush seemed hung with shreds of blood-stained clothing," one Union officer recalled. "Hell itself had usurped the place of earth." Rebel survivors assisted many of the injured, sending them westward along the roads crowded with ambulances and walking wounded. Others set about burying the dead and marking the spots with crude headstones.[1]

For Dick Anderson, the responsibility of commanding an entire corps added to the personal discomfort he felt in those hellish surroundings. He now led Field and Kershaw's divisions, the former with five brigades and the latter with four. In addition, he would have three battalions of artillery under E. P. Alexander. Pickett's third division had been detached for service with the Department of North Carolina and would not rejoin Anderson until late

May. Field, a pre-war Dragoon and cavalryman, had received a very serious leg wound at the Battle of Second Manassas in August 1862, and had only recently recovered sufficiently to resume field duties. Kershaw hailed from Camden, South Carolina, near Anderson's birthplace. The two were close in age, but Kershaw had studied law. Although he had no formal military training, he had served during the Mexican–American War as an officer of the Palmetto Regiment. Despite that limited experience, his performance would mark him as one of a handful of non-professional soldiers who rose to division command with Lee's full confidence. Sorrel found him "of most attractive appearance, soldierly and handsome, of medium size, well set up, light hair and moustache, with clean-cut, high-bred features." Anderson knew he had two reliable division leaders.[2]

Frequent Union probes on May 7 indicated that Grant might move towards Spotsylvania Courthouse. Lee directed Stuart's troopers to scout the roads in preparation for shifting the Confederate army in that direction. Sometime late that afternoon Lee told Anderson he had "reason to believe that the enemy is withdrawing his forces from our front and will strike us next at that point." He instructed Anderson to prepare to move towards Spotsylvania. "General Lee . . . directed me to retire the troops quietly and as soon after nightfall as practicable," he recalled. He was to rest the men when he "reached a suitable place in rear of the line they had been occupying," forbidding any fires or noise to be made during that pause in the march. The respite would be a brief one, for he was to have the men again on the march by 3 AM. A guide would show him the route to Spotsylvania Courthouse. Lee emphasized his desire that Anderson ensure the men were moving at the hour he named. "I wish you to be there to meet him, and in order to do so you must be in motion by three o'clock in the morning," he concluded.[3]

Lee instructed his chief of artillery, Brigadier General William Nelson Pendleton, to supply a staff officer to guide Anderson along a new road cut out just that day. The route ran south to the Catharpin Road and across the Po River before encountering the main east-west thoroughfare near Shady Grove Church, where a guide from J. E. B. Stuart's cavalry would conduct Anderson to Stuart's position. The Shady Grove Church Road led back across the Po at Block House Bridge and thence to Spotsylvania. Pendleton accompanied the designated staff officer to meet Anderson and go over the route with him. Anderson either did not mention Lee's instructions to withdraw just after dark and find some place to rest on the way to Spotsylvania before resuming the march by three, or else Pendleton had forgotten later. The artillerist's recollection documented in his report of February 1865 credited Anderson with preparing to start much earlier than the 3 AM time stipulated by Lee. "He was preparing to start at 11 that night," Pendleton wrote, "Those four hours anticipated proved of incalculable value next day." Previous biographers cited that statement as justification that the normally indolent Dick Anderson acted aggressively on May 7 by moving earlier than Lee ordered. He was thus in position to save Lee's army by preventing the Union seizure of the strategic crossroads at Spotsylvania Courthouse the next morning. The impact of the early start was all that Pendleton claimed it to be, but it should not be credited to Anderson's initiative. Anderson himself related the fortuitous circumstances more prosaically.[4]

The diary of the First Army Corps indicates the men starting the march at 11 PM on Saturday, May 7, while Anderson himself reported the movement starting at ten. According to Anderson's recollection, the column marched a mile or two before he began to search for a suitable resting place "at which to allow the men to take some sleep as the General had directed." His own statement contradicts the idea that he decided on his own accord to push aggressively to Spotsylvania in the belief that Grant was already headed that way, and instead indicates he intended to execute Lee's instructions to the letter. He was unable to do so. "I found the woods on fire and burning furiously in every direction," he recalled. "There was no suitable place for a rest." Anderson's next action was a prudent one that reflected the only sensible option at that point. Rather than disperse the divisions along the route of march by allowing them to rest in multiple clearings suitable for smaller groups of soldiers, he wisely pushed on in search of larger spaces that could accommodate more men, thereby preserving the integrity of the corps as a readily available fighting force. There were other considerations as well. "The road by which I was conducted was narrow and frequently obstructed," he continued, "so that at best the progress of the troops was slow, and the guide having informed me that it preserved the same character until near Spotsylvania Courthouse, I decided to continue the march until I should be within easy reach of that place." Finally, just after daylight and within a few miles of Spotsylvania, the column reached open fields a half mile from the Po River crossing where Anderson halted to rest the troops and allow the column to close up.[5]

Within the hour, a frantic courier from Fitzhugh Lee's cavalry reined up and delivered distressing news. A large force of Union horsemen had assailed the smaller Rebel contingent near the Courthouse, and the hard-pressed troopers might soon give way. Kershaw's division was in the van, and Anderson rapidly dispatched it to aid the beleaguered cavalrymen. Field's division had by then "pretty well closed up" and Anderson sent it rushing off in the wake of Kershaw's troops. Before Kershaw had gone far, however, another scout reported to Anderson that a large body of federal infantry was approaching from his left flank on the Todd's Tavern or Brock Road.

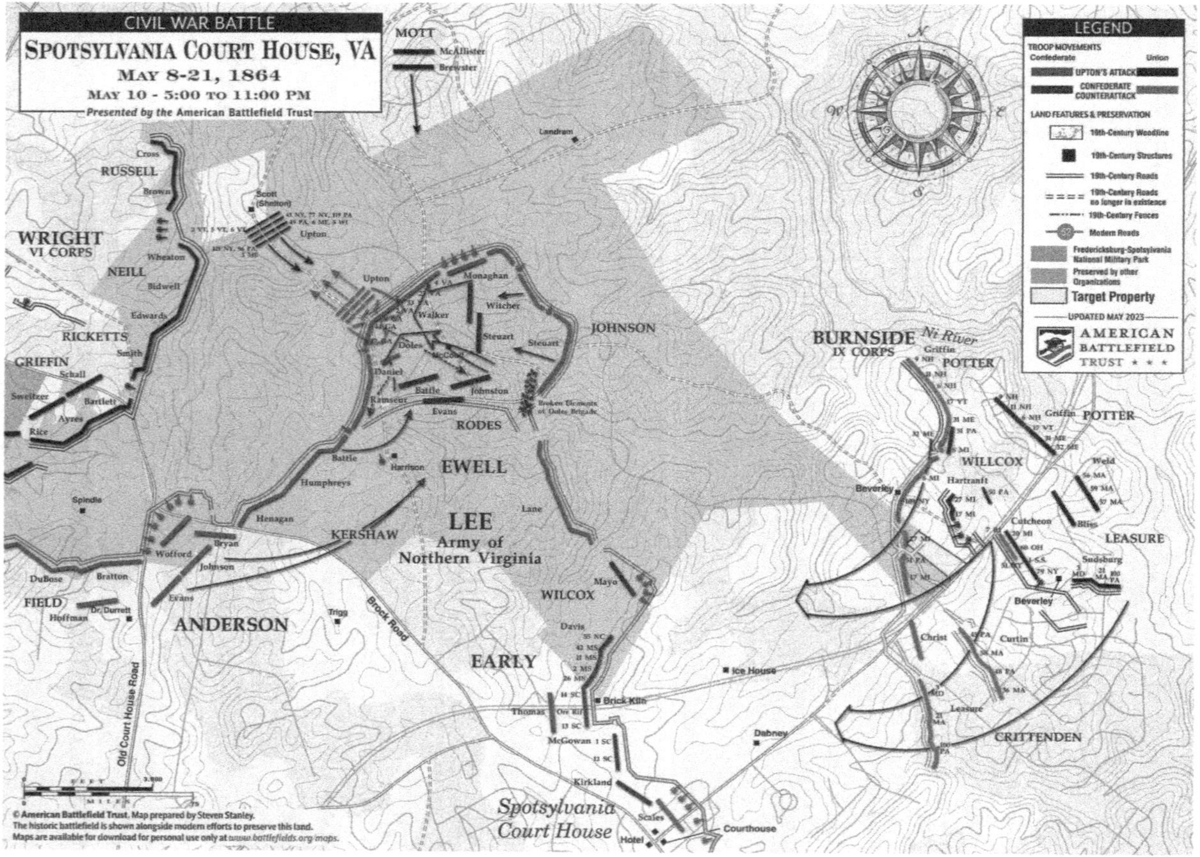

Figure 5. Map of the Battle of Spotsylvania Courthouse, showing Upton's assault on the Mule Shoe Salient, May 10, 1864. Courtesy of the American Battlefield Trust.

Anderson diverted Kershaw's old South Carolina Brigade, now commanded by Colonel John W. Henagan, along with Benjamin Grubb Humphrey's brigade of Mississippians towards the Brock Road to support Fitz Lee at Laurel Hill, while hurrying Kershaw's two remaining brigades of Georgians under brigadier generals Goode Bryan and William T. Wofford ahead to the courthouse itself. As the rest of the corps came up, Anderson rushed it towards the courthouse. At Spotsylvania, Fitz Lee's cavalry had lost possession of the village, but the arrival of Confederate infantry would soon set matters right again. Meanwhile, General Lee had already told Ewell to prepare to move in Anderson's wake. Early on May 8, now more certain of his enemy's movements, Lee ordered Ewell to connect with Anderson, who was already at Spotsylvania, noted Lee, "and may need your support."[6]

Events unfolded quickly that morning around Spotsylvania, and as the Union Fifth Corps took up positions north of the Courthouse it was clear that Ewell's men would indeed be required. All morning long, Fitz Lee's cavalry had contested the Yankee advance southward towards Spotsylvania on the Brock Road, making a fighting retreat along the way until reaching a low ridge constituting Laurel Hill, which lay just to the northwest of the Courthouse. Now the situation turned critical. A Union cavalry division had entered the village of Spotsylvania from the east along the Fredericksburg Road, and after learning of Fitz Lee's position a brigade was preparing to trot up the Brock Road and straight into the Confederate rear at Laurel Hill. The results of Anderson's rapid march to Spotsylvania now paid dividends. If he sought no credit for the corps' timely arrival, he would soon be able to take much credit for his aggressive and adept management once his troops reached the field.[7]

Major John C. Haskell's artillery battalion had been at the head of the corps with the leading brigade when it halted near a squared log structure known as the Block House, where Fitz Lee's courier found it. Haskell immediately sent two of his batteries north on the Old Court House Road leading from the Block House to the Brock Road and Laurel Hill. Stuart was rapidly maneuvering his outnumbered troopers to counter the Union advance, and Haskell soon found that only cavalry skirmishers were supporting his guns, then no one. He arranged the batteries en echelon and spread them apart so that they were somewhat protected by each other's crossfire, but the escalating situation was not a good one for unsupported artillery. When Anderson dispatched Henagan and Humphrey's brigades to that location with orders to report to Stuart, they too followed the same road Haskell took. Anderson eventually raced to the scene himself, probably because the rest of the corps would soon be coming up to support that line after they evicted the federal cavalry from the courthouse. Finding J. E. B. Stuart there and already well familiar with the circumstances, Anderson wisely relinquished command to the more knowledgeable senior commander. Stuart skillfully placed Anderson's two brigades quietly into positions stretching across the Brock Road westward along the ridge line, while Haskell arranged his guns on the left to sweep the field obliquely in their front. Haskell loaded with solid shot, the last of his ammunition. As federal troops advanced, by then only a hundred yards distant from Humphrey's men deploying east of the Brock Road, the unsuspecting Yankees had no idea they were about to square off with Anderson's infantry, not dismounted cavalry.[8]

Meanwhile, with Anderson's brigades arriving at Laurel Hill, Stuart simultaneously sent some cavalry towards the courthouse to stem the Union advance from that direction until Anderson's foot soldiers could arrive there as well. The Federal troopers had brushed aside a small Rebel force holding the village and discovered that a short march north on the Brock Road would land them in Stuart's rear at Laurel Hill. Before that movement got underway, however, word came that Anderson's foot soldiers were advancing from the west. The Yankees prepared to fight but instead were ordered to withdraw. Brigadier General John Bratton, leading the South Carolina brigade of Field's division, reached the courthouse and hurried the Union horsemen on their way, "the enemy retiring before us and abandoning the place without a fight." Bratton quickly changed direction and headed his command up the Brock Road to help in repelling the Union Fifth Corps.[9]

The day had turned exceptionally sultry for early May, and Union troops were not in top form for an assault by the time they arrived in front of the Laurel Hill defenses. With reassurances that they were facing only dismounted troopers, leaders urged exhausted men forward only to be stunned by massed volleys from Confederate rifles and destructive fire from Haskell's guns. The solid shot, recalled Haskell, was "much more efficacious in breaking the charging line than shrapnel or canister which, while disabling twice as many, did not make such a crash." Some attackers fell back in confusion while others went to ground, unable to move in any direction. Still others pushed on with disastrous results. Only on the Confederate left did a handful of determined men of the 83rd Pennsylvania reach the Rebel line, whereas Humphreys recalled, "for the first and last time in my warring, I saw two hostile lines lock bayonets." The wild melee resulted in a number of Confederate soldiers receiving bayonet wounds in their backs as they crouched behind their barricades. Too few in number to prevail, however, the hearty Pennsylvanians finally gave way. Two of them later received Medals of Honor for their actions at the Spotsylvania.[10]

While there are accounts of Stuart riding among the men along Laurel Hill, laughing with them and encouraging them, there is once again no information about Anderson's whereabouts for much of that day. Though less conspicuous than the flamboyant cavalryman, Anderson should be credited for rapidly assisting the hard-pressed horsemen by skillfully dispatching brigades to ensure possession of Spotsylvania Courthouse and bolstering the wavering positions at Laurel Hill. Undoubtedly, he hurried the remainder of the First Corps along and sent additional brigades forward to extend the lines. Men busied themselves scooping out the earth to construct breastworks bolstered by piled logs with firing ports. Meanwhile, Ewell's Second Corps marched rapidly towards Spotsylvania throughout the day as men fell out, drained by the heat. Struggling down the Shady Grove Church Road was Brigadier General Stephen Dodson Ramseur's brigade of North Carolina troops, the lead element of Ewell's corps, which reached Block House Bridge across the Po by around 6 PM. A dispatch rider from Anderson soon reined up with a message informing Ewell of the repulse of heavy Union attacks ahead and exhorting him to greater exertion and speed before federal numbers grew overwhelming. Ramseur read the note first before sending it on to Ewell. He spread the news through his brigade and, knowing the response he would get, asked if the men were able to continue. A resounding "yes" issued from their parched throats and the inspired soldiers rushed on at a grueling pace to aid their comrades. Lee was well aware of the "sharp encounter" with the Union Fifth Corps and that Anderson had thus far "repulsed the enemy with heavy slaughter and took possession of the Court-House." Anderson's two worn divisions had battled all day against the onslaught, and by the time his plea reached Ramseur's hands the prospect of yet another attack was rapidly developing. This time the Confederate defenders would face six enemy divisions, some of which extended far past the right of the Rebel lines.[11]

Darkness was approaching as the next federal attack swarmed forward. On the Confederate left, Anderson's men handily beat it back. The developing assault on the right flank, east of the Brock Road, was more problematic. The line was simply too short and could be outflanked by the superior Union numbers. Indeed, the plan was to fix Anderson in place with a frontal assault while three brigades circled around the exposed Confederate right flank. The presence of a well-placed Virginia battery at the intersection of the Brock Road and Old Court House Road that would have enfiladed the advance of one of the Union divisions led its commander to call off the forward movement of his troops. Farther to the Union left, however, Brigadier General Samuel W. Crawford's Pennsylvanians were picking their way through the darkening woods with two additional brigades from the Sixth Corps, when a wild Rebel yell echoed across the landscape. Once again, Lee's army narrowly avoided disaster, this time saved by the timely arrival of Ewell's Second Corps. Alabamians of Rodes's division led the way, sweeping up elements of

John Bratton's South Carolina brigade that Anderson had sent to support the right flank, and all surged forward crashing headlong into the advancing federals. Rodes continued to feed brigades into the fight that drove the Yankees back, but the exhausted Confederates were unable to sustain their momentum after the enervating rush to reach the field. Disappointed commanders were compelled to give up the assault and their hoped-for rout of the blue-clad force.[12]

Anderson must have agonized over the fate of his corps that day, but he probably had confidence in the timely arrival of Ewell's men. It had been yet another near-run thing, but in the end, Grant was held at bay and Lee held onto Spotsylvania. By nine that evening, Lee was relieved to note that Union assaults had been "again handsomely driven back." Dick Anderson's boldness that day in pushing his brigades forward into critical positions that held up the Federal advance and preserved the critical juncture at Spotsylvania Courthouse was a decisive factor. Always determined in battle, he now demonstrated a skill in handling troops that reinforced Lee's decision in choosing him as Longstreet's replacement. Anderson's lack of hubris and concern for the outcome above all else led him agreeably to welcome Stuart's assistance. There was nothing about Fighting Dick Anderson's performance to criticize. Though it was largely a defensive battle, it nevertheless required adept handling of the troops and sound decision-making. Lee had been unable to start either Ewell or Hill on the way to Spotsylvania until he was certain of his opponent's next move. Sending Anderson there was a critical step, but the First Corps was on its own once Stuart's cavalry withdrew. "Grant would practically have the whole day to picnic with us as he saw fit," recalled E. P. Alexander, "& no one to interrupt him." Anderson won the race to Spotsylvania thanks to the early march that he sustained through the night, along with the stubborn resistance of the Rebel cavalrymen. Once there, Anderson fought calmly and determinedly to retain possession. His infantry fought well, as befitted the reputation of the corps, and E. P. Alexander's judicious placement of his guns meant that the artillery added much to the outcome of the day. Whether his guns could have broken the flank attack that was developing before the timely arrival of Rodes's division is unknown, but for an uncomfortable few hours, Dick Anderson confronted a quandary such as he had never known in battle. As it became clear that Union forces were massing on his right flank, Anderson did not panic. He scribbled a dispatch urging Ewell to hurry, but it was not a panicked act of desperation. Instead, it was a judicious and soldierly exhortation to come to the aid of his corps, and it had the desired effect. As the menace to his flank loomed closer, he began to shift Bratton's regiments there. Rodes's arrival rendered that moot, but Anderson probably had couriers rushing back and forth to keep him informed of Rodes's progress. As early as 11:30 AM that morning Anderson received the "very agreeable information that General Ewell's corps is coming up and is now within supporting distance." He could not have known then that Ewell's progress would not be so quick as he hoped and that he would not see the vanguard of the Second Corps until after six that evening. Nonetheless, his confidence in his men, in his dispositions, and in the progress of Ewell's march all combined to quell any undue alarm. The period between taking command of the corps and nightfall on May 8 was yet another of his finest hours of command.[13]

As the fighting tapered off that night, Ewell's corps extended the defenses north of Spotsylvania east of the Brock Road, but doing so created a bulge necessary to occupy the high ground in front of the Rebel positions. Anderson's corps remained in its original location, with Fields's left flank anchored on the Po. The line then reached eastwards across Laurel Hill to the Old Court House Road, linking there with the Parker's Virginia battery and assorted guns at the intersection of the Old Court House Road and the Brock Road. East of that junction, Kershaw's lines joined Ewell's. Working incessantly through the night, the men strengthened their position in preparation for renewed attacks next morning. Fires again took light and some of the Rebels went out to rescue wounded men. On the 15th Alabama's front enemy pickets opened fire and killed a sergeant. "We got back over the works . . . and then commenced retaliating when they would try to give their wounded relief," a fellow Alabamian wrote. "Such sometimes is war, but it is terrible." On the Confederate right, the salient known as the "Mule Shoe" caused much uneasiness. Ewell gave assurances it could be held, and no changes were made until the Third Corps arrived and extended the right flank southward almost to the courthouse later in the day on May 9.[14]

May 9 passed quietly with only some skirmishers probing Field's lines late that afternoon. Entrenching continued as the generals discussed making an assault, but they deferred when it seemed the enemy might undertake one first. May 10 opened with much "sharp skirmishing along the whole line . . . and heavy shelling." Field's line received several assaults, but all were repulsed until a "most obstinate" attack fell on his position after sunset. That "last and most desperate" charge aimed at two of Dick Anderson's brigades, those of Tige Anderson's Georgians and John Gregg's Texans along with the 3rd Arkansas of Gregg's brigade. Union troops came up to the trenches so rapidly that their assault sent Gregg's Texans reeling down the slope of Laurel Hill where many had already gathered to prepare their supper. Some of the frenzied blue-clad soldiers leaped over the breastworks and jabbed their bayonets at the startled Rebels. The Richmond Howitzers sent double and triple charges of canister down the abandoned trench line, staggering the federals and gaining valuable time. Confederates rallied and swept up the slope, driving the enemy back after vicious fighting with clubbed muskets against Union bayonets. After that action, the Texas and Arkansas regiments requested bayonets, a weapon they had previously disdained to carry. Dick Anderson reported the attack being "repulsed with great slaughter to the enemy and little loss to us," but it had been a day of frantic action. Once again, only darkness ended the bloodletting. Men sheltering behind breastworks learned to accumulate multiple rifles and adopt an expedited loading process that eliminated use of the ramrod. Soldiers fired as quickly as they could before hurling their rifles to the rear where harried officers dropped a cartridge into the barrel and slammed the rifle butt firmly on the ground to seat it. The process took only seconds before they passed a loaded rifle back in exchange for an empty one, vastly increasing the rate of fire. It was a reliable enough method for close range work.[15]

May 11 passed with skirmishing and a heavy rainfall, although Anderson anticipated another attack that day. Instead, by evening, all signs pointed to a Federal withdrawal and Lee prepared to follow. The signs, however, were misinterpreted. The bustle of movement in the Union lines was actually the sound of preparations for an early morning attack on May 12. Just after 4 AM Federal infantrymen surged across the no-man's land between the lines and crashed into Lee's most vulnerable point at the apex of the Mule Shoe, quickly overwhelming the defenders. In the meantime, Lee had withdrawn artillery from critical spots in preparation for following Grant's supposed withdrawal. By the time Ewell realized that Union forces were massing in his front and ordered the guns returned, darkness and confusion resulted in their reaching the lines only in time to be seized by the swarming bluecoats. Major General Edward "Allegheny" Johnson's division bore the brunt of the attack. Federals captured him and Brigadier General George Steuart along with a number of the guns and about two thousand more Confederates. Rodes's division to Johnson's left was also threatened, and Anderson was compelled to extend Kershaw's line to the right so that Rodes could pull troops from the left of his own line to drive the enemy from the salient. A secondary defensive line held by Brigadier General John B. Gordon's division spanned the open end of the Mule Shoe, and Gordon slowly drove the federals back after yet another incident—the second in the past week—where the men insisted that an excited Lee go to the rear and get out of immediate danger before they advanced. On Anderson's portion of the field, "two violent assaults" on Field's entrenchments west of the Brock Road were "repulsed with great loss to the enemy," around mid-morning. Bratton reported later that his men held their fire until the enemy, "advancing beautifully in two lines of battle," was within fifty yards. The ensuing volley proved effective, and "a line of their dead was laid down across the entire front of my brigade." Yankees fled to woods beyond the crest of a hill where they kept up a sustained but useless fire while Bratton's troops waited for another assault. The ineffective Union fire continued for a few hours, Bratton recalled, and "we began to think that by some happy mistake they were fighting themselves. It seemed a heavy battle and we had nothing to do with it." He finally sent a skirmish line forward to the crest, where the South Carolinians discovered the Yankees lying prone and "firing at what did not clearly appear." A Rebel yell and a gallant rush by the skirmish line sent the bluecoats fleeing precipitously across the fields where deadly artillery fire added to their woes and put an end to action on Anderson's front. He had been fortunate that E. P. Alexander had prepared his artillery to move but wisely left the batteries in place in the event of some surprise such as the one that occurred. Earlier Anderson sent Brigadier General William T. Wofford's Georgians to support Rodes at the Mule Shoe, and just before sunset, he dispatched Bratton's South Carolinians and Humphrey's Mississippians to aid Ewell. Both those brigades supported the withdrawal of their comrades that night and strengthened Gordon's position at the base of the Mule Shoe, where a new defensive line formed. Otherwise, the brutal, close quarters combat that raged in rain and mud from before dawn until 4 PM was largely a fight carried on by the Second Corps and portions of the Third. The former "Mule Shoe" had earned a new name—"Bloody Angle."[16]

By the time Lee's forces withdrew from the salient to their new defensive line at around 3 AM on May 13, casualties in the Army of Northern Virginia since May 7 had mounted to 12,000, with the heaviest losses in Ewell's corps. Fighting transformed the trenches of the Mule Shoe into an abattoir, with the dead of both armies lying in places four deep and with the wounded struggling to extricate themselves from beneath the mud and dead weight of fallen men. Anderson's fight from behind stout defensive works meant lighter losses. In his old division still in Hill's Third Corps, however, Abner Perrin fell dead while rushing to Ewell's aid at the Bloody Angle. Not long before Yankee lead riddled his body, the ever-ambitious Perrin had announced boldly that he would emerge from the fight as either a live major general or a dead brigadier. Despite the frightful losses, however, Lee's army was intact, though it would be hard-pressed to carry out any offensive operations. Grant's casualties were even more appalling, with 18,000 soldiers lost. Despite his aggressiveness, Grant could not sustain the campaign without replacements. He remained confident, however, reporting heavy Rebel losses to chief of staff Henry W. Halleck on the evening of May 12, and commenting glibly, "the enemy are obstinate, and seem to have found the last ditch." The next few days passed in relative quiet as Grant prepared for the next phase of his campaign. For Lee, the large number of captured Yankees placed additional burdens on his resources. Some prisoners were undoubtedly glad to have survived the carnage, though they would yet undergo significant trials in captivity. Others, confident of exchange and parole, could not be gotten rid of too soon. Captain McWillie of Anderson's staff remembered one Union major, a martinet "who was quite drunk at the time of his capture [and] wanted the guard to salute him and cursed one of them and told him to present arms. The old soldier looked at him and said 'you are a damn fool. Genl. Lee don't expect that from me himself.'"[17]

Skirmishing on Anderson's front continued until May 14, when pickets finally confirmed a federal withdrawal. He informed Lee that afternoon that the breastworks opposite him were empty, and though still uncertain of "the full extent of the movement," he was "inclined to believe it includes the entire right of the enemy's line." Lee ordered Anderson to shift his corps to the far right of the Confederate line and connect with Early, a move that began at midnight on May 15. By dawn, Field's division took position next to Early with Kershaw in reserve. With no Union forces opposite Field's men, quiet reigned until May 18, when Ewell repulsed an attack mostly with artillery fire. A poorly conducted reconnaissance by Ewell on the 20th resulted in unnecessary loss of 900 men but confirmed the position of Grant's lines. Grant began a complete withdrawal late that night, moving southward once again to sidestep Lee's defenses and confront him in open country.[18]

Chapter 16

South to Richmond and Petersburg

[Anderson] is a regular trump, cool as an ice box, calm and serene.

—Brig. Gen. James Conner,
letter, July 29, 1864

Lee's army began to move on May 19. Ewell headed toward Mud Tavern where the Telegraph Road ran south to Richmond. Anderson followed, marching throughout the night before resting for two hours. Lee issued a number of very explicit directives to his new corps commanders that spring, and Lee provided Anderson with detailed instructions throughout the march. On the evening of May 22, for example, Lee accompanied Ewell to Hanover Junction after instructing Anderson to "keep well closed up with Ewell's corps," while on the move and to "send back and get up all stragglers and see that the proper staff officers attend to the marching of the men and require them to keep with their commands." On the following night, Lee directed Anderson to "have the wagons of your corps packed and everything in readiness by daybreak tomorrow to move in any direction," and on the next evening, Lee responded to a dispatch from Anderson, saying he was glad Dick had "discovered the road intersecting that between Haw's Shop and Atlee's." Lee cautioned him to place a picket there for his own safety and to strike any enemy force moving on that road. "Do everything for the grand object," Lee urged, "the destruction of the enemy." Lee notified Anderson on May 26 that he believed Federals intended to attack on his front. Lee urged him "to be on the alert and be ready to meet it if made" and he directed Anderson to advance his skirmishers to discover what lay in his front. Anderson already knew that Union troops were there in force, and Lee soon followed up with a message withdrawing his orders about the skirmishers. On May 27, Lee notified Anderson of the location of his headquarters and ordered him to have his command ready to move by 3 AM Lee also kept Anderson informed of the movements and locations of the other two corps and shared his plan to seize high ground just east of Atlee's Station to confront Grant on the banks of the Totopotomoy Creek. Later that day Lee also forwarded a suggested route for Anderson's corps to follow.[1]

The existence of such correspondence from Lee has been cited as evidence of his new apprehension and caution in dealing with untested corps

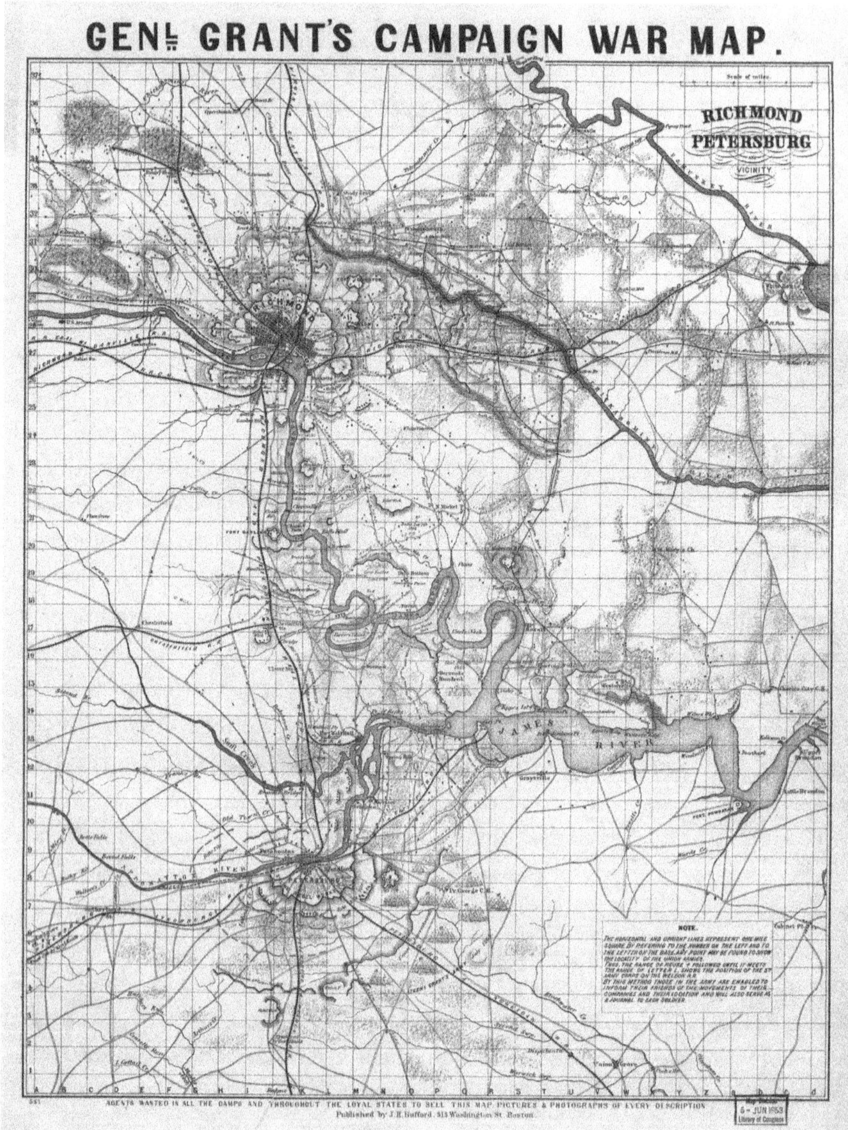

Figure 6. Grant's campaign war map showing Richmond and Petersburg, 1864. Shows fortifications, camps, roads, railroads, street pattern of Richmond and Petersburg, towns, drainage, vegetation, hachures, and houses. J. H. Bufford & Co. (1864). Library of Congress Geography and Maps Division.

commanders as the army confronted a leadership crisis that began with Longstreet's wound and was further complicated by Hill's and Ewell's absences, along with J. E. B. Stuart's death at Yellow Tavern on May 12.[2]

Hill's bad heath detracted from his ability to manage his corps, while Jubal Early finally replaced the ailing Ewell on May 29. Lee's previous style of issuing vague instructions to leaders like Stuart, "Stonewall" Jackson, and "Old Pete" Longstreet were now adapted to compensate for the uncertainty arising from the uneven performances of their successors. This increased oversight caused Lee and his staff additional burden, but in reality, things were now as they should have been all along. Moreover, considering the dangerous circumstances the army faced, exercising more control was judicious. Lee had been fortunate to have Stuart's, Jackson's, and Longstreet's initiative to rely on, but still missteps had occurred, if not from lack of clear direction, then at least from a prevailing sense that the discretion implied by Lee's vague orders also encompassed occasionally not doing precisely what he intended. Lee surely must have taken some lessons from that experience, and in several instances, he should have been more direct and specific even with those three trusted chieftains. Now he would find it prudent to be so, but such caution was a valid response to having new leaders inexperienced at that level of command, and was not necessarily a reaction to any particular shortcomings. Lee had to provide them an opportunity to grow into their roles, and it was his responsibility to ensure they did so without constituting a danger to his army.

Added to the drawback of novice corps leaders, but often ignored, was the fact that Grant's constant attempts to slip around Lee's flank constituted an entirely different kind of campaigning to which neither army had thus far been accustomed. Lee's outnumbered army was in mortal danger and potentially fighting for its survival each day of the campaign. He could hardly afford to be anything less than specific in his instructions regarding troop movements during that period, and it seems quite likely that no matter who led his three corps, the guidance might have been similar. There simply was no longer any margin for error when even slight mismanagement could invite a calamity from which the army might never recover. Rather than view Lee's detailed guidance as evidence of his concern about Anderson's ability, particularly after having so amply demonstrated it since taking command, one might make the point more effectively regarding Ewell. During much of this period, Lee chose to remain near Ewell, whose behavior from the start of the spring campaign had been uneven at best and alarming at worst. Not only did Lee fear Ewell's health would suddenly render him incapable of command, but indecision had marred his performance at the Wilderness on May 6. At Spotsylvania, the disposition of his corps in a manner that created the vulnerable "Mule Shoe" salient was a mistake, but more telling was Ewell's loss of composure when his lines were broken on May 12. The excited Ewell was assailing his fleeing men with angry epithets and whacking crazily at their backs with the flat of his sword when Lee intervened. Cautioning him to restrain himself, Lee then asked how he could expect to control his troops if he could not control himself. "If you cannot repress your excitement," Lee said, "you had better retire." Lee issued only a handful of such stern rebukes during the war. Lee undoubtedly recalled the episode years later when he told his secretary that Ewell had been "too much overwhelmed to be efficient," that day. Lee must have seen his duty afterwards as remaining close to his old warrior, but if he was in any way concerned about Dick Anderson's abilities, those concerns were certainly supplanted by his anxiety first over Ewell and secondly over the fate of his army and the prospects of defending the capital.[3]

Lee's army prevailed once again in a footrace to the North Anna River, where the general chose to pause on May 22. Uncertain about Grant's next move, Lee marched rapidly on the Telegraph Road where Ewell and Anderson's strung-out corps had been vulnerable to attack. Hill's corps used roads farther west, and only Hampton's thin cavalry screen stood between the Federals and the lines of weary Rebels trudging southwards. With the rain and the earlier spring heat wave over, the weather was mostly fine with mild temperatures. Anderson's corps bivouacked on the south side of the North Anna River with Ewell to his right and Hill on his left. Pickett's division finally arrived that day too, but hardly in the mood for fighting. "The men are calling loudly for bread," Pickett lamented, "we must get something or the Div'n will be more than useless." Ordered to report to A. P. Hill on May 23, Pickett stood in reserve on the far left of the Confederate line where the Federals had crossed unopposed at Jericho Ford and were pushing Hill. When firing began that morning, Anderson was immediately concerned for a few South Carolina regiments stationed on the north side of the river, one manning earthworks at Fox's Bridge on the Telegraph Road. E. P. Alexander quickly dispatched some guns to support those stranded regiments, but there was little Alexander's fire could do for them. Terrain features kept the attackers out of sight of the guns and several men from the Palmetto Regiment fell into enemy hands as a result.

Around dusk, Generals Lee, Anderson, Early, and others met under a large oak tree in a clearing to discuss how best to arrange their lines to meet the assault that was expected early next morning. Troops moved into position throughout the night and scraped out trenches in anticipation of Grant's attack. The next few days were critical for the army defending the railroads and the route to Richmond, but Hill, who had just resumed command of his corps on May 21, was still not in top physical form. His indecisive response to the crossing at Jericho Ford on May 23 apparently disappointed Lee. Moreover, Lee himself was by then feeling the strain of the last weeks, and his own ill health was becoming a factor in his ability to manage affairs. Lee later downplayed his illness when he wrote to his wife on May 29. "I have not been very sick," he said, though he admitted that he had been unable to mount his horse for several days. "I am better now and hope to be well tomorrow." His adjutant general, Walter Taylor, also thought Lee was improving, noting early on the morning of May 30th that Lee had until then "been somewhat indisposed, and could attend to nothing except what was absolutely necessary for him to know and act upon." Ewell had to relinquish command to Early on May 27, so Lee, A. P. Hill, and Ewell were all unwell at that time. Dick Anderson was the only senior commander whose health was unimpaired from May 23–26, but his spirit might not have been as robust as his body.[4]

In the middle of May he received news of more family misfortune. This time it was correspondence from Wallace reporting that their father had died on May 10. Dick probably knew his father was failing, but Wallace lost no time in trying to ease his brother's mind. Wallace had the good fortune to be at home then and could provide comforting details of their father's death. It had been a warm day and old Dr. Anderson lay on a sofa to catch the breeze from an open door. He asked to have the news read to him, which included one of Lee's dispatches describing his son Dick as being in command and driving the enemy from Spotsylvania Courthouse with small loss. The report cheered the old man. "He died with the news of victory on his ears" Wallace wrote, "and with the gratifying knowledge that you led our advancing columns in their victorious onset and passed through the conflict in safety."[5]

Probably due to Lee's indisposition, he allowed an opportunity to attack and destroy one element of Grant's divided army south of the river to pass. Believing Grant was going to move east in another attempt to get around his flank, Lee had not prepared stout defenses on the North Anna. When Grant remained in his front and seemed inclined to attack, Lee formed his lines in an inverted "V" shape, with the point anchored on high ground marked by steep bluffs around Ox Ford on the North Anna, which transformed a vulnerable weak spot into a nearly impregnable one. The legs of the "V" extended southeast and southwest from that apex. Hill anchored his corps on the Little River, while tidewater marshes around Hanover Junction protected Ewell's line. At Ox Ford, Anderson's line began with Kershaw on the left flank, extending southeasterly to connect with Field's division, which ran due east towards the Richmond, Fredericksburg and Potomac Railroad and linked with Ewell's corps. It was a formidable position that had the advantage of interior lines, while Grant's forces would be compelled to split into two separate wings in order to assail it. The formation of that battle line required Lee to pull back slightly from the river, a move he hoped would entice Grant to send his army across if he thought the Rebels were retreating. Lee could then destroy at least one of the separate elements of the Union force. Grant took the bait, pushing Hancock's corps across the North Anna along the front held by Anderson and Ewell. If Hill could hold his own in his defensive positions on the Confederate left flank, Anderson and Ewell could take the offensive against Hancock's troops isolated south of the river.[6]

Lee's army did not turn to the offensive, however. The general's intestinal illness took a turn for the worse and virtually prostrated him as the opportunity to crush Hancock passed without action. Had Longstreet or Jackson been present, some historians have maintained, Lee might have handed over the reins of the army to carry out such an attack. He was desperate to strike a blow, yet he chose to remain idle, perhaps not trusting the fragile Ewell or the relatively inexperienced Anderson to beat Hancock decisively. Ewell, as senior corps commander, would have been the most natural choice to deliver a crushing defeat, but Lee must have feared that an attack absent his own guiding hand could miscarry. Lee also might have been thinking of the recently passed engagements. Gettysburg was the last time Lee stood by as an observer, allowing his corps commanders the freedom to carry out his orders. There, all had failed him. At the Wilderness and Spotsylvania, Lee found it necessary to insert himself at points of imminent danger to inspire the men to advance or to hold on. The refrain "Lee to the rear" sounded on two recent occasions as the general made clear his intention to lead from the front. Now, lying on his cot, powerless to act, Lee could not risk placing the army in another's hands. In his memoir of his service on Lee's staff, Walter Taylor neglected to mention anything about Lee's illness and incapacity at that time, instead asserting only the disparity of numbers prevented Lee from assailing one of the Union army's vulnerable wings south of the North Anna. A private remark in a June 1 letter to his future bride more accurately reflected the uncertain feelings around Lee's headquarters during that period. Taylor told her that since his illness Lee had remained "quiet" and was directing the army's movements from a distance. "This is as it should be," he went on, "& if we had capable lieutenants 'tis the course he might always pursue." Taylor did not specify whether he was referring to all three of the corps commanders, but in light of recent events involving Ewell and Hill such a comment is not surprising. Thus far, Dick Anderson's only flaw was the novelty of his new role, but he had given Lee no cause for concern otherwise. Nonetheless, Lee declined to take advantage of the circumstances presented by Grant's exposure. Grant withdrew to the north bank of the swollen river overnight on May 26, after a rain-lashed encounter with Ewell's men demonstrated the strength of the Rebel positions. Once again, Grant began sidling around Lee's right flank. Instead of frustration, however, Grant and his army were encouraged by Lee's failure to strike an offensive blow on the North Anna. Grant interpreted that as a sign that Lee's army was substantially defeated already, while others saw it as a sign of lost confidence. Events would soon show that this was far from the case.[7]

With confirmation that Grant was gone from his front on May 27, Lee set his army in motion once more. Anderson started his trains across the South Anna immediately, with his corps trudging southwards towards Ashland following the Richmond, Fredericksburg and Potomac rail line. Pickett's division marched with Hill but rejoined Anderson that night. Lee informed him that evening that he was making his headquarters at the Jenkins' House near Hughes's Shop. He advised Anderson to make his men "as comfortable as possible for the night," but by 3 AM he should again be on the march to Atlee's Station, the nearest telegraph office north of Richmond and a stop on the Virginia Central Railroad about five miles northwest of Mechanicsville. Unfortunately, road congestion prevented the First Corps from adhering to Lee's orders. The corps' diary for May 28 noted, "Move early for Atlee's Station, or rather ordered to move early, but we are greatly impeded by the Second [Corps], which is on the same road and is ordered to move at the same hour." Lee was feeling better by then, but staff work and coordination apparently were suffering even in such routine situations as deconflicting the daily order of march and its timing. Both corps had arrived near Hughes Crossroads after marching on two different routes, but now they would need to use the same roads to reach the area around Atlee's Station. Under those conditions, it would not be difficult to keep closed up on the rear of the Second Corps, now in Early's hands due to Ewell's ongoing illness and resultant incapacity. Grant, meanwhile, had crossed the Pamunkey River and fought a cavalry battle at Haw's Shop. Lee intended to establish a line at Totopotomoy Creek. Anderson's corps finally reached its destination and went into bivouac along Shady Grove Road near Shady Grove Church and Hundley's Corner. Hill's corps faced north and lay to the north and east of Atlee's Station with Breckenridge to his right, while Early's line faced east around Pole Green Church. Anderson occupied a position ready to support either element of the army.[8]

After the cavalry engagement at Haw's Shop on the 28th, Lee was certain that Grant had crossed his infantry over the Pamunkey. As Grant maneuvered to discover Lee's positions, he pushed troops across Totopotomoy Creek and again found his opponent strongly entrenched. Lee could do little but wait to see what Grant's next move might be, but already he was growing uneasy about potential weak spots in his line. By mid-afternoon on May 29, Lee was cautioning Anderson to "be prepared to move in any direction." Soon after that, Rodes asked Anderson to post vedettes to watch the ground between his position on Early's left flank and Breckinridge's right where there was a gap in the lines fronted by swampy ground. Lee then advised Anderson to prepare to move up and cover Early's left, but an hour later, he was instructed to send staff officers to Hill and Early so that he could be aware of the conditions on each front and then exercise his judgment "in moving to the support of the point where you may be required." As an afterthought, and out of concern for the gap between Early and Breckinridge, Lee advised Anderson to send another staff officer to familiarize himself with the situation. "The country is regarded as impractical;" that note read, "the creek is difficult of passage, yet you had better be prepared to ford it." Anderson deployed his divisions to support three separate sections of the defenses. Kershaw stood by in support of Breckinridge's north-facing line near the Atlee Station Road, while Pickett buttressed Early's east-facing line where it stretched north of Pole Green Church. Field covered the swampy gap between Breckinridge and Early, despite the unlikelihood of an attack there.[9]

As Lee's comprehension of Grant's troop dispositions began to solidify, he determined that it would be best to attack the Union forces that were extending their lines southward towards the Chickahominy River in front of Early's Second Corps. By doing so, he might be able to get astride Grant's left flank and stop any further progress. At 11 AM on May 30, Lee notified Anderson that he had authorized Early to make an attack if he thought he could do so advantageously. Anderson was to render whatever support needed, and Lee instructed him to communicate with Early immediately to determine his role. Early informed Lee by noon that he proposed to move forward with the attack, and that he and Anderson agreed that Field's division would shift right into Early's line as the Second Corps shuffled to the right. Early would send Rodes's division forward to probe the enemy lines near Bethesda Church. If Early decided to attack with his entire corps, Anderson's other divisions would join Fields and replace Early's men in the defensive line. Should he meet with success and begin to drive the bluecoats back, and if Lee thought it "proper," Early opined Lee could send Anderson down Old Church Road in his wake. Lee approved of Early's plan, notifying Anderson of that fact at 2 PM, as well as leaving room for his corps commander to use his discretion by stating his desire that Anderson should take the actions agreed upon, "if circumstances permit."[10]

Rodes did meet with success—at first. His attack along the Old Church Road smashed one Union brigade, but then began to falter as it encountered two others. Rather than turn north and roll up the federal left flank, however, Rodes was compelled to consolidate his lines and await reinforcement. Early thought it a wise decision and he likewise brought the momentum to a halt as they waited for another of the Second Corps divisions to arrive. Meanwhile, Early sent word to Anderson requesting him to move forward and attack the Union lines in his front while his own divisions crashed into their flank. When Brigadier General Stephen D. Ramseur finally arrived on the field, the overzealous new division commander pressed Early to attack immediately. By then, however, enemy defenses had stabilized along the Shady Grove Church Road as Union brigades shifted to face the looming threat. Unaware of the increasing number of federal troops by then south of the Totopotomoy, Early sent forward a single brigade of Ramseur's division—John Pegram's commanded by Colonel Edward Willis. The surprised Confederates were repulsed after senseless slaughter that accomplished nothing. Anderson, meanwhile, had started Pickett's division forward on Shady Grove Church Road, but Pickett abandoned the effort after realizing the strength of the Union defenses. Little support for Early came from that movement, and while Early griped about it, most of his own troops laid the blame on Ramseur for pressing forward too hastily after convincing Early to approve the attack. Early deserved censure for permitting it, and for failing to ensure adequate reconnaissance of the enemy's strengthened position, yet he could not resist displacing liability for the ill-advised attack. He complained to Lee that night that he had requested "Anderson to advance a division along the road to Old Church and take the enemy in flank, and when I supposed he was advancing I sent forward two brigades." In fact, Early sent only Pegram's brigade forward, and no others. Finding his opponent in heavy numbers and well entrenched, "and hearing nothing from Anderson," Early carped, he called off any further advance by his corps. He added to the complaint more specifically the following day in another note to Lee, stating, "if Anderson had moved down the road from Hundley's Corner, I think we could have struck the enemy a severe blow. As it is," he continued, "all we have to regret is the loss of valuable officers and men in Pegram's brigade, which is one I much deplore." The entire incident illustrates the difficulties of coordinating the complex movement of units separated by distance and hampered by erratic communications. Early's attack never effectively employed his three divisions, and for Pickett to make a significant impact the timing would have had to be much more precise. Either Anderson or Early might easily have exhausted their offensive punch before the other was fully prepared to engage in the attack. By the time Early did attack, moreover, he faced precisely the same difficulty that confronted Anderson; the assault ran up against well- entrenched enemy forces. Early had missed the opportunity to turn the

Union left flank, and, in his frustration, he lashed out at Anderson for his failure to participate.[11]

Anderson, as noted, did send Pickett eastward along Shady Grove Road, but he also sent Field's division forward as well, though the exact location of that advance is unclear. The precise location of Anderson's lines is vague in part because of some confusion most likely due to unfamiliarity with road names or laxity in referring to them. Old Church Road was a continuation of the Mechanicsville Pike that led to Old Church, but the Shady Grove Church Road, lying approximately two miles north of Old Church Road, also led to Old Church because it intersected Old Church Road. Early advanced on Old Church Road, which he later interchangeably termed "the Mechanicsville road," and though he stated he wanted Anderson to "move down the road to Old Church," he could not have meant on Old Church Road itself but only in that direction. He intended that Anderson should advance a division along Shady Grove Church Road, from Hundley's Corner, which is what he did. To do otherwise would have led him into Early's rear rather than onto the federal flank or front. Field's advance unfortunately encountered strong resistance, and with darkness rapidly approaching, Anderson suspended any further advance. By 8 PM, he notified Lee that he was withdrawing all his troops to their original position. He shifted the line back to the left to reconnect with Breckinridge's right flank, where a large gap opened while he supported Early. Early likewise began to withdraw and form a new line connected to Anderson's right flank.[12]

On May 31, Anderson's corps shifted to the right, past Early's corps, and extended the lines farther south towards Cold Harbor, with Kershaw on the right followed by Pickett in the center and Field on the left. Lee's headquarters was by then located on the road from Shady Grove leading to Mechanicsville. There he fretted about the strength of the force on hand to confront Grant's growing might and constant attempts to stretch his lines towards the Chickahominy beyond Lee's right flank. Anderson received a circular that day in which Lee urged his commanders "to get every available man in the ranks by tomorrow." Lee expected them to gather up stragglers and return them to their units, and he wanted the field hospitals scoured "for every man capable of performing the duties of a soldier. . . . Let every man fit for duty be present." The arrival of nearly 7,000 men in four brigades of Major General Robert F. Hoke's division, which had come to Lee's support from Bermuda Hundred, was undoubtedly a significant relief to him. The weather had turned very hot that day and Hoke's troops had marched from Richmond along the sun-scorched Mechanicsville Turnpike. Water was scarce, and the men were exhausted by the time they arrived near Cold

Harbor. That evening Anderson sought clarity as to whether Hoke's division was to be under his command or was "a separate and co-operating force," and Lee responded that Hoke would, "whilst occupying his present relative position to you, be under your control." He informed Lee that Hoke's troops had extended the extreme right of his line, with their left near Beulah Church and their right extended slightly beyond Cold Harbor. Anderson intended to push forward in the morning with two strong columns on the road leading to Beulah Church and along the Old Cold Harbor Road. Early had informed Anderson he was convinced no Union infantry was yet south of Matadequin Creek, and Anderson himself thought that "nothing but cavalry" lay in Hoke's front, but he intended to "find out positively" what was before him. Prisoners taken that day reported that the Union Fifth Corps was entrenching along those roads, so the matter was unsettled. Anderson did push forward in the morning, but with decidedly unsatisfactory results that led to a deadly repulse. After that failed morning advance on June 1, Anderson sent a dispatch to Lee at around 1 PM on discovering that a column of Yankees numbering around 15,000 along with artillery had been observed to his right on the Old Cold Harbor and Black Creek Church Road. "I will march at once to attack them," Anderson concluded. Despite that aggressive response that must have reassured Lee, Anderson's performance that day proved unequal to the occasion.[13]

Anderson first failed to coordinate the advance of Hoke's division with his corps during that morning's maneuvers. Hoke later claimed that his orders were not to begin his attack until Anderson's advance was well under way, but no record of that order survives and there is only anecdotal evidence from one of Hoke's brigadiers that Anderson did not have a simultaneous advance in mind. Anderson had sent Kershaw's division southward as the van of his corps, and Kershaw selected his old brigade to lead the assault toward Beulah Church on the road north of Old Cold Harbor. Col. Lawrence M. Keitt then commanded the brigade. He was the most senior but also the most inexperienced colonel available after Kershaw's elevation to division command. Keitt came to the brigade as commander of 20th South Carolina, which had joined Kershaw's brigade on the North Anna in late May after longstanding garrison duties on the South Carolina coast. With over a thousand men on its rolls, the 20th was jokingly called "The Twentieth Army Corps" by the old soldiers of Kershaw's other depleted regiments. It was larger than the entire brigade it had joined. As the regiment passed the watching veterans of the 1st South Carolina of Jenkins's Brigade on the road to Cold Harbor, Frank Mixon of the much-reduced 1st recalled the great size of the 20th and the resulting banter. On asking what regiment they were passing and learning it was the 1st, one of the 20th's men quipped that "this must be only one company of it. But," as Mixon later wrote, "they soon learned how fast members could diminish."[14]

With the 20th leading, the eager but inexperienced Keitt advanced towards the waiting Union defenders. They were Brigadier General Wesley Merritt's brigade of entrenched cavalry troopers from Brigadier General Alfred Torbert's division. Four of Merritt's regiments had Sharps breech loading rifles, and one regiment wielded seven-shot Spencer carbines. Each produced a much more rapid rate of fire than any muzzle-loading gun. The result was predictable. Within minutes, raked by a sheet of flame from the Union line, the 20th was shattered, losing over sixty men. Colonel Keitt, mounted on a prancing iron-gray charger at the head of the regiment, received a fatal wound while attempting to rally the faltering South Carolinians shaken by the Union volleys. A second assault failed as badly as the first, and the band of the 1st New York Dragoons soon added to the cacophony of the battle. The Yankee musicians "gave them 'Dixie'" as the Rebels fell back after the first attack, then when they advanced again the band "gave them 'Hail Columbia' on the horns, while the boys put in the variations with their carbines." Hoke, who was to attack toward Old Cold Harbor, did not join the fight at all, and a disappointed Anderson, stunned by the Union firepower, cancelled the attack and reformed his lines. When Hoke finally did move forward, he discovered more strongly entrenched Union soldiers. These too were "nothing but cavalry," but Hoke wisely conducted a "careful reconnaissance" and found the position too strong to attack.[15]

Yankee cavalry commander, Major General Phil Sheridan, had been less sanguine about the chances of Torbert's division holding Old Cold Harbor. Sheridan knew from prisoners taken that Torbert faced at least three infantry brigades of Hoke's division, but after driving off Kershaw's morning advance, Sheridan wrote to army headquarters around 9 AM that he had "been very apprehensive, but [Major] General [Horatio] Wright is now coming up." In response to the arriving federal infantry of Wright's Sixth Corps, Hoke withdrew with the rest of the Confederate First Corps and began to fortify his lines. If Hoke understood his orders correctly, he deserves no criticism for not attacking after Keitt's assault was well under way, for it was substantially finished before it began in earnest. Brigadier General Johnson Hagood of Hoke's division recalled hearing gunfire from Kershaw's direction, but a courier soon informed Hoke "that the attack was foregone." Anderson might indeed have sent couriers speeding to Hoke when he realized Kershaw was unable to advance further, and thereby prevented Hoke's assault continuing on its own. However, if Anderson's objective had been only to discover what was in his front rather than to drive away the federals and seize Cold

Harbor, the later observation of Lieutenant Colonel William Wallace of the 2nd South Carolina was a valid one. "A few skirmishers thrown out would have accomplished the object of a reconnaissance, and would have saved the loss of many brave men," he complained.[16]

Anderson may have learned two valuable lessons, and one he would not be anxious to repeat. The first was that too hasty an advance into the unknown was decidedly unwise; the second was that an infantry attack on well-armed and entrenched cavalry was equally inadvisable. Earlier in the war, infantry might have brushed aside mere dismounted cavalry with derision, but with increased firepower and the now routine propensity to erect some kind of fortified defensive works, the tenacity of the troopers could not be so cavalierly dismissed. With the benefit of hindsight, E. P. Alexander provided a better plan for Anderson's advance. He suggested that an attack by Hoke on Sheridan's left flank might have been more successful. In the event, Hoke securely held Lee's critical right flank next to Kershaw, while Fitz Lee's cavalry on Hoke's right screened the infantry. Pickett remained on the left of Kershaw's division, followed by Field to Pickett's left. The aggressive advance of Federal reinforcements rendered Anderson's intention to attack the large force he saw moving across his front that afternoon impossible, and he was soon defending against strong infantry assaults on his lines instead.[17]

Lee had declined to interfere with Anderson's operations that morning, writing at 11:15 AM to tell him that one of his staff officers, Major Henry B. McClellan, had just returned from the right flank where he found that Hoke was not advancing. Lee merely suggested that Anderson might send some additional force to the right to assist Hoke in the event the strength of the enemy's position in his front prevented him from advancing "as you designed. . . . Of course you will not alter your plans if they are practicable in the way you intend," Lee graciously admitted. "It may be that Hoke has moved since Maj. McClellan left, but I deemed it proper to give you the information he brought that you might not be misled." Lee must have been unaware at that point that Kershaw's advance failed and that of Hoke cancelled. Possibly Hoke was still awaiting word from Kershaw that he should move forward, as Hagood alleged was to occur before Hoke joined the assault. Lee's comment to Anderson regarding Hoke not advancing "as you designed," seems to confirm that Anderson intended a concurrent attack by both Hoke and Kershaw. That it did not occur must be attributable to the corps commander's flawed management of the troops under his command that day.[18]

The Yankee troops that Anderson observed moving into position were indeed Wright's Sixth Corps followed soon after by William F. "Baldy" Smith's Eighteenth Corps. It was now abundantly clear that the Confederate army would have to remain entrenched behind its defensive works, and

Lee moved his headquarters from Shady Grove Church Road to a clearing just west of New Cold Harbor so that he could be closer to the most critical point of impending action. Two years of determined fighting had brought the army back near the very spot where Lee had first taken command and prevailed at Gaines's Mill. Many veterans must have pondered the turn of events and the growing preponderance of Union power now facing them. Grant, it was abundantly clear by now, was cut from a different cloth than George McClellan. He was anxious to throw the Sixth and Eighteenth Corps against Lee's lines around Cold Harbor, which meant that Anderson's corps and Hoke's division would endure the worst of the assault. Unfortunately for the southern defenses, no one took heed of a gap between the right of Kershaw's line where Wofford's Georgians stood, and the left of Hoke's division where Brigadier General Thomas L. Clingman's Tarheels were entrenched. Once again, it fell on Dick Anderson's shoulders to ensure the proper placement of his divisions and that no vulnerable gaps existed. The area between the brigades consisted of a steep and heavily thicketed ravine through which one of the area's many small streams meandered, and most observers thought it to be impassible. Clingman thought otherwise, and he appealed to the Georgians to shift to the right to connect with his brigade and close the gap. Failing to gain cooperation, Clingman was preparing to shift his own lines to the left to cover the interval when Hoke informed him that he was sending Hagood's South Carolina brigade to hold that position. According to Clingman, Hoke later ordered Hagood to another point on the line and the gap remained unguarded. That shift was a result of the extension of Grant's lines farther to the south well beyond Old Cold Harbor. Lee found it necessary to extend his own lines to the right, stretching them nearly to the breaking point, and Hagood's brigade rushed off in that direction. Clingman, whose 8th North Carolina held the left-most position on his brigade line, was apparently not aware that Hagood had been moved and later claimed he would have sent companies of his command into the gap had he known. How Hagood's relocation was unnoticed is unclear.[19]

Soon after Hagood extended the Confederate lines to the south and left the gap between Hoke and Kershaw unattended, Generals Wright and Smith sent their troops forward in a determined assault primarily targeting Hoke and Kershaw. It was around 6 PM when Smith's Eighteenth Corps advanced its three divisions in column of brigades, six men deep; Wright advanced each of his brigades in column of regiments, eight men deep. The thin line of Rebels, two men deep, stood poised behind breastworks, ready to receive the onslaught. Once southern skirmishers withdrew to the main battle line, volleys of lead and iron poured into the serried ranks of Yankees. Everywhere the assault failed with heavy losses with the exception of the supposedly impassible gap between Kershaw and Hoke. There, while the maelstrom raged around them, elements of two Union brigades moved inexorably through the eye of the hurricane into the vortex created by the undefended ravine. Hidden by its steep sides and the wooded terrain, the federals poured through the gap and into the rear of Wofford and Clingman's brigades.[20]

Clingman at first thought the troops he saw advancing through the trees on his left flank were Hagood's men falling back, and he held his fire. By the time he realized "their true character," the bluecoats were only one hundred yards distant, but his men drove them back. During that time, others had struggled through the ravine unobserved by either Clingman's men or Wofford's Georgians on the opposite side of the gap. Clingman's brigade gave way as determined federals poured into its flank and rear. The Tarheels engaged in a seesaw fight to recover the lines, while the few men Hoke could spare rushed to help. Meanwhile, to the north of the ravine, more Union soldiers streamed onto the flank and into the rear of Wofford's brigade. The result was that the entire brigade ran precipitously from the line to save itself, forming again farther north on the 10th Georgia of Brigadier General Goode Bryan's brigade, where they refused the line along another of the ravines intersecting the Confederate works. This opened a gap about a half-mile long between the 10th Georgia and the Clingman's North Carolinians. Learning of the breach in his lines, Anderson quickly dispatched other troops to contain the breakthrough. Field was able to spare Gregg's brigade to help Wofford regain his position, while Eppa Hunton's Virginians from Pickett's division rushed to assist Hoke. Despite the reinforcements, Confederates were unable to push the Yankees completely off the stubbornly held ground. Instead, a salient formed as southerners dug in on either side of the ravine forming a new line angled back from the main one. During the night, Alexander moved some guns into position to cover vulnerable portions of the salient, and the line began to stabilize. Nonetheless, Anderson was not fully aware of the circumstances on Hoke's end of the line, writing Lee at 10 PM that he had dispatched Sorrel to find out what the conditions were on Hoke's side, but he had not yet returned to provide a report. At that point, Anderson knew only that Kershaw had lost contact with Hoke's line when Wofford was driven back. Anderson's last word from Hoke was that the enemy was "pressing him with heavy forces." That was when Hunton's Virginians arrived to drive federals from Clingman's lines. Vicious night fighting ensued in which the enemy's muzzle blasts provided the only targets at which to fire. In the confusion, however, Anderson still feared that Federals had driven Hoke too from his defenses, and now with the line broken and Yankees likely in possession of Hoke's defenses, he knew "they must either be expelled or the present line abandoned." He could still hear some firing in that direction, and he felt sure that Grant would press the advantage he had gained and that the enemy would renew the attack at daylight. In places, the lines were for a time within fifty yards of one another.[21]

Anderson must have been reassured when Sorrel finally returned. The reinforcements Anderson sent had been sufficient to reestablish much of the line, though as one artilleryman recalled, "they were left in very bad shape." To remedy that, Anderson brought in more reinforcements from Field's division so that a total of three of Field's brigades and one of Pickett's supplemented Hoke and Kershaw in working throughout the night to establish a stronger, concave shaped line that constituted a pocket encompassing two vulnerable ravines that intersected the line. Massed Rebel firepower from front and sides would now greet attackers. The breach in the lines that day could have been disastrous had Union forces been able to follow up their initial success immediately. Fortunately, for Dick Anderson and his reputation, federal reinforcements were not forthcoming and his officers steadied the lines. While blame for such a calamity would have necessarily fallen on him as the corps commander, the oversight in leaving the gap unguarded was one for which several others closer to the scene bore more immediate responsibility. No one at the division, brigade, or regimental level had taken corrective measures, and in that situation Anderson's staff officers should have inspected the lines as well, although they might have thought Hoke had taken steps to close the gap. Perhaps most egregious then was Hoke's withdrawal of Hagood's brigade, apparently without informing Clingman that the ravine was again unguarded. Hoke was not operating independently however. Although not assigned to Anderson's corps, Hoke was temporarily under his command. Had catastrophe befallen the Army of Northern Virginia on June 1, the blame would have rested on Anderson. Lee was largely silent on the near disaster, reporting on June 2 only that the enemy had penetrated the lines between Anderson and Hoke, but that Hoke had recovered his lines and Anderson had established a new one a "short distance in rear of that it first occupied." There the matter rested, but the events surely did not hearten Lee.[22]

Overnight on June 1 and into the dawn hours of June 2 Union troops once again began to shift towards the Chickahominy. The leading division of Hancock's Second Corps reached the Cold Harbor area by around 6 AM with the remaining divisions straggling after. The difficult overnight march left Hancock's men exhausted and in no condition to undertake an intended dawn attack. Other logistical problems plagued the Union army that morning, and Meade was compelled to delay the assault until dawn on June 3. Lee shifted Breckinridge's division south to extend his own lines, but despite the critical threat Hancock presented, Breckinridge failed to move with a sufficient sense of urgency. The division's march, while exhausting, was indirect and marked by frequent halts to rest. Lee expected to receive an early morning attack, but Breckinridge was still some miles from the army's right flank at dawn. All the while, that flank stood vulnerable to a Union attack that would have spelled disaster. With Breckinridge overdue, an anguished Lee sought other ways to strengthen his right. At 10 AM that morning, he sent a dispatch to Anderson stating that it had come to his attention that two of Field's brigades were not in the line of battle. Lee inquired whether Anderson could thus "take more ground to the right so as to liberate some of Gen'l Hoke's troops. . . . the line on that flank requires strengthening." Lee eventually got Breckinridge in place along with the divisions of Wilcox and Mahone from Hill's corps. Meade's decision to delay the attack allowed the newly arrived Confederates time to lodge securely on Lee's right flank. Anderson's corps remained strongly entrenched in the center, while Early and then the remnants of Hill's corps held the Confederate left after Early assaulted the Union lines and drove them back on June 2. With the lines now configured like a reverse fishhook, Early's corps held the hook and curved portion, while Anderson and those on his right held the shank of the hook. The defenses thrown up were formidable. On Anderson's segment of the line, a sergeant of the 4th Alabama in Law's brigade paused to admire his lieutenant vigorously attacking the ground with a shovel. "My goodness, Lieutenant, you can certainly beat any of us at it," the sergeant exclaimed. "Yes," the officer shot back, "and if you realized what is going to happen in the morning you would be at it yourself." Apparently, the Alabamians, like the rest of Anderson's men, took heed. By morning, there was a parapet five feet high with a slightly shallower ditch in front. The trench behind the parapet had a banquette built into it so that the men could stand on that and fire over the edge. It would prove to be of great value with the coming dawn. Entrenching was becoming the norm, and there was no possibility of withstanding persistent attacks by such large numbers of enemy troops otherwise. The men did not like it, but they knew it could save their lives.[23]

It was barely daylight on the foggy and rain-misted morning of June 3 when pickets in front of the 4th Alabama of Field's division let loose a few shots and scurried back behind the main battle line. "Look out," men shouted, "they are coming." All along Anderson's front and southward towards the Confederate right flank wave after wave of Union soldiers staggered forward in the face of withering fire. It was only just nearing 8 AM that morning when Kershaw noted that he had already "repulsed 14 assaults. We are sustaining little loss. Damaging the enemy seriously." He reported his lines strong and secure, with enemy artillery fire "very heavy but not very effective. . . . If they keep up the game long we will have them," he optimistically predicted. The slaughter in Kershaw's front was particularly appalling. Anderson realized that enemy troops were massing in front of the salient in Kershaw's line and he reinforced that position. Union troops drawn into the concavity of the Confederate lines at that point were assailed from front and sides by a crushing onslaught of iron and lead. On the left of the 15th Alabama, Colonel William C. Oates benefitted from a well-placed artillery piece whose rounds of double canister sent a "blaze of fire from it at each shot [that] went right into the ranks of our assailants and made frightful gaps through the dense mass of men." Behind the 4th Alabama, Bryan's Georgia Brigade lay prone on the ground loading for the Alabama boys in the trenches whose fire rapidly decimated another charge. To the south, a brief breakthrough on Breckenridge's front was stabilized by reinforcements from Finnegan's Florida Brigade of Mahone's division and the 2nd Maryland of Breckinridge's. Once again, the tiny Florida Brigade of Anderson's old division had thrust itself unhesitatingly into a maelstrom and helped recover the lines.[24]

Lee undoubtedly welcomed reports like Kershaw's, announcing as it did such an auspicious start to the day. Hoke followed with a similar note reporting not only the great slaughter of the enemy but the more important fact that "up to that time he had not had a singled man killed." The lopsided nature of the fighting prevailed all along the lines with the exception of the temporary breakthrough of Breckinridge's defenses. Union attacks were uncoordinated, and they sputtered quickly with relatively minor losses in some places, but the main thrust along Anderson's front was a hellish scene that rivaled Dante's version. Dead and wounded attackers littered the field, while many still unhurt lay prone and sought what little cover they could find in an effort to avoid the terrible hail of Rebel fire. The recollection of Brigadier General Evander Law of Field's division succinctly captured the results of the federal assault. Law had witnessed the hecatomb at Fredericksburg when waves of doomed Union soldiers surged to their deaths in front of the sunken road on Marye's Heights. He recalled the carnage at Second Manassas when Jackson's men laid waste to John Pope's ambitions as an army commander. All of that paled in comparison, thought Law. "I had seen nothing to exceed this," he wrote of Cold Harbor. "It was not war; it was murder."[25]

At the time, Anderson's men were jubilant at the destruction of their detested foe. Some officers observed that men were much at ease, laughing and talking as they went about their deadly work from the relative safety of their trenches. Yankees later accused dastardly Rebels of shooting at wounded men, or even peppering the bodies of the slain with additional lead simply for the sport of it. Certainly, the reaction to the slaughter must have varied among individuals, ranging from joy to pity, but Dick Anderson left no thoughts on his own feelings. One can only imagine, however, that a man with his gentle nature was on one hand gratified by the military success but at the same time mortified by the senseless sacrifice of life. Others were entirely practical in their view. One untutored North Carolina infantryman in Hoke's brigade wrote simply, "tha made severl triles to run our men out of our brest works but tha could not do it. . . . I can tel you we kil aheap more of the yankeys than tha of us. . . . It is a site to see the battle field after a fight." Despite their courage, the Union soldiers balked later in the day when Grant ordered a renewal of the assaults, expressing by their action a final verdict, "silent, yet emphatic, against further slaughter." There was, however, no outright refusal to advance, only a tacit acceptance of the impossibility of it. Towards the end of his life, even Grant agreed. "I have always regretted that the last assault at Cold Harbor was ever made," he wrote sadly in his memoir. Nonetheless, Anderson's First Corps diary reported that "another furious assault" was made on Hoke's right as darkness fell, while Hunton's brigade was also "severely engaged." That wording gives a false impression however. Martin's brigade of Hoke's division aggressively charged forward around 8 PM in an ill-advised attack. Yankees undoubtedly took delight this time in turning the tables and easily repulsing Martin's three advancing regiments from the relative security of their breastworks. The fact that no one at Anderson's headquarters apparently understood the circumstances indicates his complete lack of awareness of the planned assault. Hoke's authorization for the doomed advance can only be presumed, but in any case, the failure to coordinate any such movement with the corps commander to whom Lee had instructed Hoke to report was both a military faux pas as well as a personal affront to Anderson. The kindest interpretation is that Hoke might have acted under the assumption that he was to confer with A. P. Hill since he now held the right of the Confederate line with two of his three divisions, and Mahone's brigade of Hill's corps was supporting Hoke's lines. Moreover, the Florida brigade of Mahone's division had earlier that evening attempted a similar assault on Union troops in front of the line that been broken and restored that morning. It resulted in similar slaughter for another hundred or so of the Floridians, but that at least had been Hill's responsibility, not Anderson's. Hunton's actions that evening are unknown, though his brigade occupied a portion of the line in the midst of Anderson's corps and he could not have advanced without his knowledge. Most likely, a serious renewal of the firing in Hunton's front, but probably not an actual assault, led to him being "severely engaged."[26]

Modern estimates propose Union losses on June 3 alone at around 6,000 killed, wounded or captured. On the Confederate side, losses probably ranged from 1,000 to 1,500 men. While there were bloodier days for both armies, June 3, 1864 numbers among the more lopsided engagements at a critical time when Lee could ill afford to have sustained such losses himself.[27]

After some wrangling between the army's commanders, a long-awaited truce went into effect between 6 and 8 PM on June 7, permitting men to recover the wounded and bury the putrefying dead. Brigadier General Hagood recalled that the dead in front of his lines at Cold Harbor were already so decayed that it was difficult for the burial details to handle them. Instead, they contented themselves with shoveling small mounds of dirt over each corpse. It was grim work, but the men must have welcomed the opportunity, for by then the stench had permeated everything. "We breathed it in every breath, tasted it in the food we ate and water we drank," recalled one suffering soldier. The truce also provided a respite from the relentless shower of projectiles. One Mississippian complained that in places the opposing armies were "so close together that almost any sound causes heavy fire," and that "rifle fire—buzzing like bees—sounds constantly."[28]

In Baltimore, Maryland on that Tuesday, June 7, 1864, Republican delegates to the National Union Convention gathered to nominate Abraham Lincoln for a second term, reaffirming the Republican platform and Lincoln's prosecution of the war. That the Party would sustain Lincoln in the midst of one of the bloodiest campaigns ever fought in America is testament to a grim determination to see the war through. It was an ominous sign for a struggling Confederacy that could not easily replace its losses. Lincoln's reelection would drive yet another nail in the Confederacy's coffin, despite the optimism felt among many southerners that summer of 1864 that Grant's heavy losses had demoralized the army, led to discontent among northerners, and that "their patience would soon come to an end." Indeed, many of the men in blue standing to arms around Cold Harbor would never get a chance to cast a vote. Vicious fighting would take the lives of thousands over the course of the next few months, and June 7 was for them just another day of warfare. Grant had already begun shifting to the left, possibly towards a crossing of the Chickahominy River, and on June 6, Lee directed Anderson to cooperate with Gen Early "to endeavor to find out where the enemy is and which way he is going."[29]

Early's Second Corps was especially active as their leader continued to test his mettle aggressively in his new role, possibly concerned that Lee might feel obliged to return the recovered Ewell to his former position. Early drove his men hard on June 6, pushing forward relentlessly to discover the enemy's whereabouts in accordance with Lee's instructions. One man of the 13th Virginia complained after a day spent chasing an elusive enemy that "Old Jube will not be satisfied until he finds out where he has gone, so he keeps us on the run until he finds him. He doesn't know that I have no shoes and but little breeches, torn from pockets to bottom." That graphic picture of the tired Virginian's condition was undoubtedly applicable to the bulk of Lee's army by then, not just the men laboring under Early's pugnacious proclivities. Based on Early's estimate of the location of the Yankee picket lines on the 6th, Lee asked Anderson to see whether it would be possible to "ascertain the direction of this line and let Alexander place artillery to explode it?" Lee instructed Anderson to consult Early to discuss whether they could arrange a "systematic advance from which good results might be obtained." Anderson must have thought not, but Early pressed on alone in his quest for the Union line, clearly hoping for some decisive result. Ramseur's division found that line when it ran squarely into works manned by Burnside's Ninth Corps. A sharp engagement ensued, with Burnside's men finally repulsing the attack. Unsatisfied with knowing the location of the enemy troops, Early assertively pushed his men forward again on the 7th after having discussed the situation with Anderson the previous day. Early "drove the enemy back, and established batteries, from which I opened on him" he claimed. Finding no support, however, he complained that he was compelled to withdraw. He was frustrated with the day's results, again blaming Dick Anderson for failing to come to his aid. "I could not find either General Pickett or yourself on the line," he carped. "Your skirmishers did not move forward to connect with mine, and after continuing the fight until nightfall, I withdrew, as I could do no good without cooperation."[30]

Early had apparently been ruffling feathers continuously since taking command of the Second Corps, seemingly justifying Sorrel's fears about Early's potential assignment to the First Corps some weeks earlier. Two of the best men on Early's staff had already asked to be relieved. "He is kicking up a row in everything he comes near," wrote Ewell's stepson, Major Campbell Brown, a disgruntled staff officer who found even his new commander's mere gaze disconcerting. Early, he complained, looked at him "like a sheep-stealing dog." Anderson, however, was in no mood to suffer chastisement by the fiery Early, and shot back a caustic response voicing his disagreement with the way Early had been managing his troops. "I am sorry to see that a consciousness of the folly, which you repeated on yesterday, of sacrificing some eighty or a hundred of your men to obtain a little information, which added nothing to what was already known, has put you in a bad humor," Anderson wrote. "If you mean by cooperation, committing equal folly with yourself, I grant that I did not cooperate." Anderson also bristled at the notion that Early had a tactical grasp of the situation that was somehow superior to his own. "Your opinion as to the best point for attacking . . . is very obligingly given. I have not, however, a high appreciation of your judgment, and I decline to be guided by it." Anderson concluded brusquely with a "recommendation" that

Early communicate any future opinions as to the movement of his command "to the Commanding General, instead of to me." The harsh tone of the letter from the normally even-tempered Dick Anderson must have given Early pause to reconsider his complaints, and the two were soon outwardly reconciled when a more temperate note arrived from Early that evening. "I respect and admire the tone and sentiments of your note of this evening," Anderson responded, admitting to having "felt offended at what seemed to me to be the ill-tempered and unjust reflections of your first note." Once again, Anderson's indignation showed when he thought he had been unfairly maligned. In his usual courteous manner, he rapidly restored his equilibrium and reassured his colleague that his "private feelings will not be permitted ever to interfere with my public duty." Moxley Sorrel sustained Anderson's position, commenting later that Early was "much given to forced reconnaissances" which were "unnecessary and wasted men by death and wounds." Both Sorrel and Anderson were very likely correct in maintaining that accurate information about enemy strength and morale could have been "gathered by scouts and picked men without sacrificing the ranks but General Early thought differently." As early as May 1862 Early was criticized for rashly assaulting fortified redoubts on the Confederate left near Williamsburg with disastrous results. Absent proper knowledge of the ground and without waiting for the rest of his brigade, Early impetuously led a single regiment across an open field in a fiasco that could have only one result. Early fell wounded and left the field before the worst of the carnage, but far too many men fell in the senseless charge and the precipitous retreat that followed. Perhaps that set the tone for his peers' estimation of his abilities. Anderson was fighting on the right flank at Williamsburg, but a complete disaster on his left caused by Early could have seriously compromised the integrity of his entire battle line. More recently, Early had complained to Lee about the fighting around Bethesda Church on May 30, bewailing the lack of support from Anderson that day and the resultant failure to "have struck the enemy a severe blow." Their failure to cooperate easily must have concerned Lee and added to his strain.[31]

After more than a month in command of the corps, Anderson's men had taken his measure and had become acquainted with his style. Having been a brigadier among them, many knew him well enough already. Action had been nearly continuous, and Anderson had shown "commendable prudence and an intelligent comprehension of the work in hand." His modesty would never permit him to push himself forward as the hero of Spotsylvania whose aggressiveness and foresight led to an all-night, forced march that outraced Grant to that strategic crossroad. He freely admitted that his only reason for not following Lee's orders to the letter had been that he could find no suitable place to rest the men. Had he been able to do so, it is likely that Grant would have stolen a march on Marse Robert that night. Moxley Sorrel probably had it right once again when he recalled of Anderson that "he was a very brave man, but of a rather inert, indolent manner for commanding troops in the field, and by no means pushing or aggressive." As noted, such indolence often extended to his lifelong disdain of mundane paperwork, which meant that in times of inaction he left the day-to-day minutia of running the corps to his staff. Sorrel characterized him as having a "meditative disposition . . . constantly soothed by whiffs from a noble, cherished meerschaum pipe in process of rich coloring." His soldierly appearance was impressive. A soldier of the 16th Mississippi, told his mother that "Anderson is a fine looking, dignified man; hair slightly touched with grey and with a very fine eye."[32]

That he was cool under fire and possessed of marked physical courage there can be no doubt. Nor is there any question that the men he led grew to love him, as evidenced by the heartfelt greeting his fellow South Carolinians bestowed on him at the Wilderness. Soldiers who undergo the severe trials of battle, asked to put their lives in great peril at the behest of a man appointed over them, cannot display affection towards a commander in whom they have no faith or confidence. Clearly, that was not the case with Dick Anderson. Those close to him had many opportunities to view his behavior under fire and found his composure inspiring. At the North Anna River on May 23, for example, Anderson's headquarters was at a stately house known as "Ellington." A grove of trees stood adjacent to the large home flanked by two tall brick chimneys stretching above the roof peak on each side of the house. Frequent shelling from Union guns marred the natural beauty of the grove, however. Bursting shells sent "small fragments flying everywhere" and caused such annoyance, "that most of us got under the lee of a gable," recalled Sorrel. Anderson, however, remained "coolly walking about the grove, sucking his big pipe." He eyed the men lolling on the grass near the house and warned his staff that if a round struck the brick chimney, they might regret having taken shelter too near it. Events soon proved him correct. A shell eventually found the mark and sent bricks crashing down on the two dozen or so officers and orderlies sitting on the ground. None of his staff was injured, but two couriers lay amid the fallen rubble, one with broken bones, the other dead. Artilleryman E. P. Alexander survived with only bruised feet and ankles. He had been quick enough to jump up onto a basement windowsill and flatten himself against the house so that the falling rubble missed his head and the pile covered only his feet.[33]

Another incident earlier in the war also supports the picture of Anderson's calm under fire. Colonel Benjamin H. Rutledge related a story after the war when "Old Dick," as he called Anderson, hitched his horse to a tree limb and took a seat at the foot of a pine tree while "bullets were raining around them and the shells tearing up trees overhead." His nervous staff expected to be killed at any moment by shells bursting in the treetops, but as wood splinters fell on him, Anderson merely brushed them off with his gloves and remained serene. Rutledge finally brought their concerns to his attention, but Anderson "gave me a pleasant smile, saying 'Keep cool, we will cut our way out in proper time.'" After a time, Anderson "rose to his feet, shook his old Mexican spurs, mounted his horse, said, 'Send me a courier or two, Jackson has opened.' And we did cut our way out and we soon realized that the noble old soldier was obeying orders to hold what he had until he heard Jackson's guns; then to advance, which he did." One listener of Rutledge's tale chimed in with: "It was just such incidents . . . as you mention which made Anderson's division idealize him to a man. . . . They had perfect confidence in the coolness, bravery and judgment of 'Fighting Dick.'"[34]

Despite his perseverance in battle and his nom de guerre of "Fighting" Dick Anderson, the general's nature would not permit him to feel animosity towards his enemy. Once when someone expressed the thought that the only objection to General Lee was that he did not hate Yankees enough, Anderson responded, "No one has an individual hatred of them. We all treat them well when we get them in our power." E. P. Alexander was quick to agree, but attributed that behavior only to self-respect. Otherwise, it was clear that Alexander himself had no love for his enemy. "It is my greatest comfort to know I have killed some of them with my own hands," he said. "If they were to kill me today and I had but time for one thought before I died it would be that my account with them was more than even."[35]

Anderson kept his men on alert for the next several days of June in preparation for another sudden movement to intercept Grant, but news soon reached Richmond that Union forces were advancing through the Shenandoah Valley. Lee and Davis recognized the importance of expelling the Federals from that vital area and despite the risk on Lee's front, he had already dispatched Breckinridge's men, followed on June 13 by Early's corps. By then, Grant was moving towards the James River. Lee ordered Anderson to march towards the Chickahominy as soon as his front was clear of Union troops. From that point, Anderson continued southward until Lee could determine whether Grant meant to move on Richmond after crossing the Chickahominy or continue across the James and attack Petersburg. On June 13, Anderson crossed the Chickahominy at McClellan's Bridge and marched down the Charles City Road, halting near the 1862 battlefield of Frazier's Farm.[36]

Lee was sensitive to the sufferings of the civilians in the countryside, cognizant that any destruction might affect the area's contribution to supporting his army. When he instructed Anderson to use certain roads in order to avoid shelling by Union gunboats at Deep Bottom, Lee specifically advised him to personally ensure that his men avoided trampling fields or tearing down fences, and that they camped in woods and gardens rather than in houses or cultivated fields.[37]

During the night of June 16, General Beauregard, who commanded the department south of the James River, informed Lee that he was abandoning his line on Bermuda Neck to withdraw to Petersburg because he had insufficient force to hold both places. An alarmed Lee, fearing for the lines of communication between Richmond and Petersburg, ordered Anderson to rush Pickett's division across the James to occupy Beauregard's positions. He instructed Beauregard to hold his pickets and skirmishers in place until Pickett arrived. Lee himself hastened to Drewry's Bluff on the James along with Pickett's men, arriving there by mid-morning on June 17. Meanwhile, Lee had ordered Anderson to take another of his divisions to the James and take command of affairs there. Sensing the urgency, Anderson rushed ahead to the scene with Pickett and one of the Virginian's leading brigades, arriving about an hour before Lee and the rest of the division. By that time, with Field's division closing just behind them, they found that Beauregard had pulled out of line and Union forces already occupied the abandoned works. Anderson's troops quickly drove them out and reoccupied Beauregard's partially completed second lines of defense. Nightfall prevented any further advance.[38]

Lee planned an assault designed to recover the whole of Beauregard's former lines for late the next afternoon, but "in consequence of differences of opinion as to the relative merit of the two lines," Lee ordered Anderson to take some engineers and make a more careful study of the existing positions. Anderson's cautious nature and unwillingness to risk his men led him to conclude that the attack was unnecessary and that the present line was sufficient. The order cancelling the scheduled attack, however, did not reach Pickett in time to prevent him from advancing. Field had been with Anderson when the decision was taken, but when he saw Pickett's advance there was little else to do but move forward to support him. Fortunately, Anderson's concern for the welfare of his troops that day was largely unwarranted, for they easily pushed the Yankees back and recovered the original lines. Lee complimented Anderson "upon the conduct of the men of your corps. I believe that they will carry anything they are put against." Lee also hoped "his loss has been small." Anderson proudly responded that he was "happy to know that the conduct of the troops has pleased you and that they have your confidence. It will be a pleasure to me to make your commendation known to them." In his typically courteous fashion, Anderson also found reason to pay a compliment his chief. The result of the attack, he said, had "altogether verified the correctness of your judgement [*sic*]," and the loss had been "very small."[39]

Grant assailed the Confederate lines around Petersburg for four consecutive days from June 15 through June 18, losing over 8,000 men before deciding that he could not overcome the city's defenses by direct assault. The two opposing forces settled into siege lines after failed assaults on Sunday, June 19. Grant's strength was over 110,000 men, while Lee's defenders stood at less than half that number strong. Lee, A. P. Hill, Anderson, Pendleton, and others found time that Sunday to attend "a delightful service at St. Paul's Church, where they have chimes like St. Michaels [*sic*], sweet music, & a minister . . . who reads beautifully & preached an admirable sermon." After weeks of hard campaigning, the leaders of the great army massed around Petersburg and Richmond were relieved that day to have repulsed all of Grant's attacks and to be in the hospitable embrace of a beautiful Episcopal church. Its austere elegance with ornate capitals and soaring steeple inspired hope and awe in all who viewed them.[40]

Kershaw's division crossed the James on the evening of June 18 and rejoined the corps on the south side, but by 3 AM, it was pushing on to Petersburg, followed by Field's division. Anderson left Pickett to secure the line between the James and Appomattox Rivers now that it was clear that Grant was south of the James and focused on Petersburg. Over the next several weeks, however, Anderson shifted the men constantly to meet various threats or to support attacks. At times, miscommunication plagued the army's operations, perhaps in part owing to the uncomfortable fact that Beauregard, who had formerly commanded a department and an army, now assumed a subordinate role under Lee's command. On the morning of June 24, for example, Lee directed Beauregard to carry out an assault on the Union left flank with Hoke's division, supported by two of Anderson's divisions. The attack stalled when Field's division failed to advance to Hoke's support. Field asserted he had not advanced further once it became apparent that Hoke's attack had broken down, while Hoke conversely claimed the attack could not have succeeded unless Field carried out his part. Lee called both men to account at his headquarters afterwards. Despite Beauregard's detailed battle plan, it was clear only that the implementation did not mirror his aspirations. Lee gently concluded there had "been some misunderstanding as to the part each division was expected to have performed." Though Lee seemed disinclined to cast blame, the results of the action must have moderated the impact of Anderson's reassurances to his chief on the night of June 22, when he wrote that he was sure he could promise on behalf of his corps the "zealous and determined execution of whatever they may be called on to perform." Beauregard's instructions called for Anderson to "place as soon as possible a brigade in the abandoned lines of the enemy, on which shall rest the left flank of Hoke." Anderson's view was that Hoke never drove any federals from their lines. Hoke's attack was repulsed, and rather than abandoning his lines, the enemy heavily reinforced them instead. Lee concluded something similar, writing, "As far as I am aware, the enemy was never driven from his lines." If Lee was growing frustrated with such failures, he did not display his feelings, most likely because successes like those of Pickett's on June 18 demonstrated to Lee the residual prowess of his army that tended to offset the blunders.[41]

Anderson took the repulse in stride, and like Lee, he restrained his emotions other than a mild frustration with the course of events. As he rode back to headquarters, he remarked to his staff that "he would go back to camp and sleep off his chagrin [and] that he never had any great grief that he could not sleep off." He then said, "he thought Quinn the Irish actor was right when his servant came in and woke him and told him it was raining and the breakfast was spoiled. He said, pulling the blankets over his head 'Well John, wake me about this time tomorrow.'" Such coping mechanisms seemed to reflect the sort of reaction one might expect from a man prone to some degree of melancholy, and that trait became increasingly evident in Anderson's behavior as the war with all its horrors dragged on and the likelihood of southern victory waned. Contributing to Anderson's glum mood was the fact that one of his old friends and original staff officers, South Carolinian Major Thomas Mills, became a prisoner on June 22. Mills was sent towards the right flank with an order from Anderson but somehow "missed the right of the line and must have ridden straight into the Yankee lines." With the lingering chivalry that marked the relationship between professional soldiers, Union Brigadier General Seth Williams wrote to Walter Taylor, his counterpart on Lee's staff, personally confirming Mills was a prisoner and not wounded. Taylor referred the letter to Anderson for transmission to Mrs. Mills, "as it may be more satisfactory to have positive evidence of the Major's being unhurt, though a prisoner." Mills later received a lighthearted letter at Fort Delaware from Anderson's wife, expressing her sorrow that he had "got into the hands of the Philistines." Dick Anderson had written Sallie that he hoped to obtain Mills's exchange, and Sallie told Mills that when she returned to Richmond for a visit she intended to "attack everyone on the subject and endeavor to obtain your release. I think of offering myself as a suitable exchange." Nonetheless, over eight months passed before Mills returned.[42]

Sallie had entertained notions of traveling to Pennsylvania that summer, but she gave up the idea and contented herself with writing to Mary Lieper regarding Mills's status. The July letter traveled from Stateburg via Nassau, Bahamas to Lieper's Pennsylvania home, informing her of her brother-in-law's capture around Petersburg. By that point in the war, with all its heartache and loss, Sallie was moved to put an optimistic face on a situation that would earlier have been hard to bear. "I am too sorry they have our dear

Thomas in durance vile," she wrote, "but I hope he will be well treated, and as I told your sister, how much better it is to be taken prisoner with a certainty of being exchanged than to be killed or badly wounded." In her view, the time for heroic valor was fading.[43]

Mills's brother-in-law, Templar Fayssoux, lost his brother Clement at Petersburg on July 5, but in a letter to his mother, he took time to reassure his sister that there were ongoing efforts to ensure Mills's well-being. He noted that, "Gen'l Anderson has shown a great deal of kindness, in making inquiry after Tom [Mills], and has sent me all the information he could get." Fayssoux was also pleased to relate that Mills was "spoken most highly of" by his fellow officers, "giving him the credit of the success of the Gen'l, which certainly was very gratifying to me, as they did not know me." The reaction to Mills's capture indicates that both Dick and Sallie Anderson felt the loss keenly. Not since McKenzie's death two years earlier had Dick Anderson lost a close member of his staff.[44]

Anderson continued to shift his troops over the next weeks, countering Grant's efforts to pierce the southern defenses while Lee tried to divine his enemy's intentions and his strength. On the evening of July 8, Lee ordered his artillery to fire all along his lines and the men to cheer as though they were about to charge. It caused much consternation in the Yankee lines, and a furious response from their cannon belched forth. Otherwise, the ruse had little result other than to give Lee a sense of Grant's strength.[45]

Confederates devised additional ways to generate further consternation and annoy their besiegers. Anderson instructed his men increase their fire at night whenever they suspected the enemy was relieving his skirmish line, "it being possible that some damage may . . . be inflicted upon the enemy's relieving parties and his skirmishers as they come out of their pits." Some Rebels had already decided the game was up by then and deserted to the enemy. Anderson cancelled an attack by Field's division scheduled for July 18 when it became apparent that the Union troops were well prepared for the assault. "It was supposed that two deserters from [Evander] Law's Brigade had gone over to the enemy and had given information," he reported later. Otherwise, the days dragged on marked by "occasional shelling and the usual incessant sharpshooting."[46]

That some beleaguered Confederates should give up the fight is easily understandable. Life in the trenches was difficult for many of them, as it was nearly impossible to move about safely during the day outside the protection of the earthworks. "Indeed" recalled one man, "few have escaped who attempted" it. In most cases, there was little shade along the lines and men huddled beneath the broiling sun in the airless pits. Some busied themselves creating "little contrivances for comfort" that served as a distraction from the misery. The dry, trampled soil made dust a constant problem where a cooling breeze was "more a nuisance than a comfort as it stirs the sand and dust. We eat, drink and breathe dust, and our provisions are covered with sand and dirt." On being temporarily relieved from the trenches and provided an opportunity to wash and cool off, one suffering officer mused to his wife about how "a clean man feels badly at first from the dirt and sand, which blown by the wind and knocked off the parapet by the balls of the enemy, he feels grinding between his neck and shirt collar, but when he is once thoroughly soiled, he does not mind small annoyances like dirt on his collar, regains his cheerfulness and only grumbles when a clod of dirt or handful of sand is knocked into his dinner, which frequently occurs." A routine soon developed in Anderson's corps, with men rotating into the trenches for six days, followed by two days' rest behind the lines. On some portions of the lines there were tacit agreements not to fire at one another indiscriminately, much as the adversaries had previously agreed when facing off across the Rappahannock or the Rapidan.[47]

Farther south along the Petersburg front, Pennsylvania coal miners had quietly dug a tunnel that terminated under the Confederate trenches. It was nearing completion in late July. Grant planned a diversion north of the James designed to weaken the Confederate lines around Petersburg in anticipation of an assault coinciding with the detonation of the explosive-packed mine. After securing a bridgehead across the James from Bermuda Hundred at Deep Bottom, Grant intended to send Hancock's Second Corps and two of Sheridan's mounted divisions towards Richmond. Lee was compelled to meet the threat by first ordering Anderson early on July 23 to send Kershaw's division with orders to "examine the enemy's position at Deep Bottom, & see what could be done." Lee hoped that Kershaw would act quickly to drive back the Union lodgment, but Kershaw deployed in a defensive position and rested his men after the difficult march. Lee again pressed Kershaw to attack and he directed Ewell, now commanding the Department of Richmond, to oversee the attempt to dislodge the federals. "We cannot afford to sit down in front of the enemy and allow him to intrench [*sic*] himself wherever he pleases," Lee wrote somewhat testily to Ewell on July 24. Kershaw's subsequent assaults drove back some of the Union troops, but counterattacks brought them to a halt. The stalemate would not last long. Hancock's Second Corps began crossing the James during the evening of July 26. Kershaw's division held high ground at Tilghman's Gate along the New Market Road, a position that commanded the approaches from the Union bridgeheads at Deep Bottom, but Hancock wasted little time before attacking on the morning of July 27 while gunboats on the James lobbed huge shells into the Confederate lines. Initial successes ground to a halt, owing in part to a courageous

Confederate cavalry assault that slowed Hancock's momentum, but the meager Rebel force evidently needed assistance. Ewell was not inclined to send that help, however, even suggesting that Lee order local defense troops to hold Chaffin's Bluff instead. By the afternoon of July 27, Lee detached Harry Heth's division from the Third Corps to reinforce Kershaw and instructed Dick Anderson to move north of the James and take over command there. He arrived just after dark and consulted with Ewell at Chaffin's Farm, where the river anchored the right flank of Confederate defenses.[48]

Anderson learned that Hancock had advanced up the New Market Road, and he determined to attack early the following morning. Despite Lee's instructions to "examine the enemy's position" and "endeavor to ascertain his strength," Anderson seemingly relied only on second-hand information in formulating his plans. Leaving Heth with a force sufficient to hold the breastworks from Chaffin's Bluff to New Market Heights, he sent four brigades—two from Wilcox's division, all now under Kershaw's immediate command but led by Brigadier General James Conner of Wilcox's division—to turn the federal right flank along the Long Bridge Road. By the time the men stepped off at around 10 AM, the attacking force shrank to only three brigades, though no record exists as to the cause of that reduction. Either it was not up in time to join the attack, or Anderson deemed it more important to hold other positions. The trimming of the attacking force was the first misstep of the day, followed quickly by the results of Anderson's failure once again to conduct adequate reconnaissance and instead rushing headlong to the attack. The terrain over which the Confederates advanced and their prescribed route of march led to much disorganization of the troops. The resulting encounter with Union troops was a desperate one, but the lack of coordination soon took its toll. One North Carolinian later admitted, "we had our asses whip off us if the truth was knone [*sic*]." Anderson had ridden to the field and joined the men at a new defensive line where he worked to calm and rally the troops in anticipation of a Union counterattack. It may have been around that time that Brigadier General Conner of South Carolina had his first opportunity to observe Dick Anderson in battle. The recently promoted Conner would go on to serve under Anderson at the head of Kershaw's brigade, and from what he observed that day, he must have been delighted with that assignment. "It is the first time I ever was under Anderson," he wrote his mother the next day, "and he is a regular trump, cool as an ice box, calm and serene when the enemy were all around us, and the fight going on seemingly all around the circle. I never saw anyone less excitable; I was charmed with him."[49]

Anderson concluded it best to hold his position and await reinforcement, including the much-needed artillery that he had strangely failed to call for in yet another misstep that day. Lee obliged by forwarding a cavalry division along with Field's division, while also instructing artillery chief, W. N. Pendleton, to ensure Anderson had sufficient support from his guns. By the time Anderson had reconnoitered effectively, deployed the reinforcements that slowly arrived, and made a plan to assault, Hancock had pulled back across the James. Field's skirmishers advancing on the morning of July 30 found the Union troops gone from their front, but Grant had accomplished his goal. It is unlikely that at around 5 AM anyone north of the James River heard the massive but muffled underground explosion of the mine that created both a crater and a salient in the Confederate lines on the Petersburg front. Startled Confederates quickly recovered the salient and the attackers were bloodily repulsed. The attack at "The Crater" failed dismally. With the threat at Deep Bottom seemingly neutralized that morning, Anderson informed Lee at 9 AM that he supposed "they have only their picket at Deep Bottom," and as a result he was moving Heth and Conner closer to Drewry's Bluff. Heth was soon returned to Petersburg and Kershaw was afterwards moved south of the James near Bermuda Hundred. Field's division remained to man a section of the defenses north of the river, and once more the armies settled back into the drudgery and danger of trench warfare.[50]

Chapter 17

Valley Sojourn and the Siege

The pale horse of the Apocalypse.

—Stefan Zweig,
The World of Yesterday

Events in the Shenandoah Valley that spring presented Lee with a difficult choice. There, Union Major General David Hunter faced only a small force under Major General John C. Breckenridge, whose efforts to stop Hunter soon faltered. On June 13, therefore, Lee started Jubal Early's Second Corps towards the Valley to contest Hunter's advance. Eight thousand veteran troops crossed the Blue Ridge Mountains while Lee faced Grant's overwhelming numbers. Lee had the uncertain impression that Grant would remain inactive for some time. On the very morning that Early's troops began their march, however, Lee discovered that Grant had slipped away overnight and moved towards Richmond and Petersburg.[1]

By early August, Federal strength in the Shenandoah Valley was growing. Grant appointed Sheridan to lead field operations there, and Lee ordered Anderson to take Kershaw's division to Early's support. After dark on August 7, Anderson and portions of Kershaw's division left by rail for Mitchell's Station, between the towns of Orange and Culpeper. Kershaw's remaining brigades joined them over the next four days along with a battalion of artillery and Fitz Lee's cavalry division. Forage was scarce that late in the summer and Anderson informed Lee that the grass was "abundant but very much parched." He had his quartermaster scouring the neighborhood and was successful in finding some oats around Orange Courthouse. Soon after reaching Culpeper, Anderson received a letter from Early requesting reinforcement of his position at Strasburg. Union cavalry, greatly superior in numbers, was threatening his right flank around Front Royal and in the Luray Valley. Lee, responding to that same news from Early, urged Anderson to, "move up to Sperryville and be governed by circumstances."[2]

When Anderson reached Front Royal with Kershaw's division on the afternoon of August 14, he found Union troops on the road between that point and Early's position at Fisher's Hill, just southeast of Strasburg. He was anxious to make an assault, but only in conjunction with an advance by Early. Hearing nothing from Early on August 15, he sent Fitz Lee to seek out Early's headquarters at dawn on the 16th. Unable to use the most direct road, Fitz Lee had to cross the precipitous ridges and valleys of Massanutten Mountain by mule. Nonetheless, he was back at Anderson's headquarters by daylight of the 17th with plans for a coordinated attack.[3]

In the meantime, a growing Union presence across the North Fork of the Shenandoah River led Anderson to fear that additional enemy reinforcements might hinder his using the fords there. He sent some of his troops across the river to establish a lodgment on August 16, leading to a fight at Guard Hill, initially successful until Confederate cavalry pushed ahead "with too much boldness into the open ground north of Crooked Run." Anderson's primary goal had been to establish a strong position on Guard Hill, but advancing beyond Crooked Run was unnecessary. In the ensuing melee, the Rebels "were rather roughly handled and driven back to Guard Hill." Anderson was content with retaining possession of Guard Hill, and Federal reinforcements from George Custer's cavalry brigade were unable to lodge a foothold on the south side of Crooked Run. The loss of men and at least two flags was an inauspicious start to Anderson's expedition though, and he should have exercised closer oversight or issued instructions that were more specific. Moreover, not only the cavalry was manhandled. Confederate infantry crossed the river near the forks of the north and south branches of the Shenandoah and were likewise repulsed with loss. Anderson neglected to mention any of that in his report of the affair, instead complimenting the cavalry's cross-river dash and seizure of the heights, which he termed "handsomely accomplished." That things deteriorated from that point passed with less emphasis.[4]

Plans for a coordinated attack changed by the morning of August 17, when Confederates found that Union troops had withdrawn, burning barns, grass, and grain along their route. Anderson immediately started towards Winchester while Early also took up pursuit of the fleeing vandals. He kept only one squadron of cavalry with him. The rest of the horsemen sped ahead in advance to try to stop the wanton destruction of vital property. Only a lone squadron from the 15th Virginia Cavalry escorted Anderson and his staff, acting as an advance guard since the general was riding far in front of the infantry. Suddenly, a few shots rang out and the Rebels came clattering rapidly to the rear. An irate Anderson could hardly contain himself. "What manner of men do you call yourselves," he cried out to them. "Oh, if I had my sabre!" Seeing only a small contingent of Union cavalry on the road in their front, Anderson turned to his staff members and nearby couriers with terse orders to "Charge those people in front." Moxley Sorrel, Osmun Latrobe, Peyton Manning, and Thomas Walton of his staff rushed forward to establish order among the cavalry, and with the remnants of the 15th Virginia and several of Anderson's couriers, they set the Yankees to flight. Englishman Francis Dawson recalled that "a glorious race down the Turnpike to the suburbs of Winchester" resulted in the capture of a few of the Yankee contingent, while one of Early's outposts along the road near Winchester scooped up the rest. Dawson seized a "very good McClellan saddle," as his share of the plunder. Anderson magnanimously attributed the cavalry's initial flight to a heavy dust cloud raised by the Union force that concealed the small size of the enemy patrol.[5]

Once united with Early at Winchester, the two generals advanced on Charlestown hoping to bring on a general engagement. Sheridan instead withdrew to Harpers Ferry, skirmishing heavily along the way. Failing to entice Sheridan from his strongpoint after another week of maneuvering, Early took up positions near Bunker Hill and Anderson returned to Winchester by August 30. Frustrated by an inability to grapple with Sheridan's main force, he proposed crossing the Blue Ridge into Loudon County with Kershaw. By then Lee was already anxious to have Anderson and Kershaw's troops back, writing Early on August 26 that he did not think Early could operate successfully north of the Potomac against Sheridan's superior numbers. If Anderson's troops were not needed, Lee thought they should move into "Loudoun or Fauquier County and return to Culpeper." At that point, Lee acknowledged his awareness that Anderson was senior in rank to Early, who must have voiced some concern about the command structure. Lee, however, by then had taken Anderson's measure as a man and as a leader. "I apprehend no difficulty on that score," he reassured the prickly Early. Anderson had already written to Lee on August 23 he was "Consulting solely the best means of success and believing it not to have been your intention that I should supersede Early I have not assumed command but will continue to act in concert with him." It was an awkward situation. Later Anderson told one of his staff members that the mutual understanding between the two generals was that Early would not ask for advice, "because in giving advice he [Anderson] would take over the command." Lee continued to urge Anderson's return with Kershaw's troops, telling Early, "if they can be spared from the Valley, or cannot operate to advantage there, I will order them back to Richmond."[6]

Lee was pleased that his troops drove Sheridan back to Harpers Ferry, but on learning of the circumstances of Anderson's attack at Front Royal, in which his subordinate acknowledged the loss of some three hundred men, mostly prisoners, Lee offered guidance for future engagements. Lee chided that he feared the "enemy at Front Royal was too strong for the force you sent against him," and cautioned, "in all cases it is best to employ all our available force without reference to the weakness of the enemy. If we have the advantage of numbers, it renders success more certain and the loss less. . . . I hope you will endeavor to bring your whole force to bear upon the enemy when practicable," Lee advised, "as in that way alone can superiority of numbers be made valuable." This was the second recent occasion where Lee had observed Anderson's failure to bring all his available force to bear. On July 28, the defeat of Anderson's troops at the Darby Farm during the Battle of First Deep Bottom was in part due to his failure to make a concentrated attack with more of his troops. Anderson might have recalled Lee's gentle chastisement later when he met the enemy again at Berryville, but there he would have little choice but to commit every man available.[7]

Although Lee was anxious about the return of Kershaw's division, Anderson remained in the Valley until September 3, when he set off towards Berryville intending to enter Loudon County. The morning before his advance, he had received a note from Early telling him that Lee had again expressed a dire need for Kershaw's division. "Of course I cannot decide this question," Early told his colleague, "but I think I would respectfully suggest that you had better hold it in readiness to move at a moment's notice if required." Early went on to suggest that Anderson cross the mountains at Ashby's Gap, "so as to give the appearance of moving on Washington." Anderson must not have agreed with Early's suggestion, and he most likely intended to cross at Snicker's Gap and maneuver in central Loudon County rather than on the southern edges of it, where Ashby's Gap would have led him. Either route presented a threat to Washington. Early, meanwhile, proposed to take his own troops back to Charlestown and "attack the enemy wherever I find him." The movement of Anderson and Early's separate forces presented a dilemma for Sheridan.[8]

As Anderson marched towards Berryville, Sheridan had coincidentally started to march towards the same place. Fitz Lee thought it merely another cavalry raid, as Union troopers were discovered threatening Front Royal and Newtown on the Valley Pike. Anderson's move towards Berryville would conveniently threaten the raiders' line of communication, but at the time, he was completely unaware of the Yankee incursion. Anderson also had no expectation of encountering the infantry pickets his men clashed with a few miles outside Berryville. He immediately advanced a line of battle. Kershaw's advancing troops drove the enemy picket line steadily back towards the town, where Anderson could see that a strong force was massing to meet them. It was a portion of Colonel Joseph Thoburn's division facing west astride the Berryville Pike, preparing to face the brunt of the rebel assault. It was nearly evening by then, and Kershaw immediately sent a brigade to attack Thoburn's left flank while his two remaining brigades advanced along the Pike. "With great spirit and gallantry" the infantry assault combined with artillery fire easily swept the Federals aside and crushed Thoburn's flank, but blue-clad reinforcements were already filing into place. The Union front soon stabilized. A counterattack pushed Kershaw back to the high ground overlooking the town as darkness fell and the contest settled into a desultory stalemate.[9]

By morning, Federals were strongly entrenched with Sheridan's entire force deployed along the roads from Berryville towards Summit Point and Charlestown. Early arrived around 9 AM and proposed to attack the Union right flank while Anderson renewed the assault on the left. Early soon found that Sheridan was too strongly posted and he deemed it "inadvisable" to carry out the plan. Instead of sacrificing his outnumbered force in a frontal assault, he wisely chose to withdraw. Anderson returned with his trains to Winchester on September 5, abandoning the idea of moving east of the Blue Ridge or rejoining Lee's army.[10]

After the battle on the evening of September 3, South Carolinian William DuBois of Kershaw's brigade wrote to this wife, "the little affair of Saturday evening was considered, I hear, by Early & Anderson quite a handsome thing as we were much inferior to the enemy in force." DuBois was relieved that the men had performed well, as Early "had begun to laugh at us for letting the Yankee cavalry pick us up at Front Royal and Charlestown." On August 28 Early had written Anderson about a Yankee prisoner who commanded a cavalry unit that two days earlier had captured over seventy of Kershaw's skirmishers from the 15th South Carolina, including a number of officers. The prisoner said he did not intend to attack them until he observed that they "were sitting down roasting corn, and no person paying any attention, many of them having their backs to the line." Indeed, several mishaps marred the campaign thus far. The opening fight at Front Royal in which Jed Hotchkiss thought Anderson "got the worst of it," has already been described, but his inadvertent encounter with the bulk of Sheridan's army at Berryville had very nearly added to the tally. Staff officer Francis Dawson believed later that it was only Anderson's audacity in "presenting as bold a front as if the whole of the Army of Northern Virginia were with us," and attacking aggressively on September 3 that prevented Sheridan's superior numbers from overwhelming his force. The lateness of the hour and the disorganization among the scattered Union forces, however, made such an outcome unlikely. Still, it was another opportunity for Early to make light of the events. Dawson recalled that upon arriving on the morning of September 4, Early's "first salutation was: 'General Anderson, those Yankees came mighty near getting you yesterday.' General Anderson's only reply was: 'Yes General, and it is not your fault that they did not.' It was a strange business anyway." With Fitz Lee off chasing the Federal cavalry, Anderson must have been blind to what was in his front until it was too late and too hazardous to halt his advance. Boldness and an appeal to Early for support were the only options, but even some ordinary soldiers were aware that all was not well at the upper levels of command. George Peyton of the 13th Virginia in Early's corps noted in his diary on September 4 that he supposed, "we made this move to help Anderson whip Sheridan, but he and Old Jube fell out and nothing was done." The previous day's diary entry seemed to blame Anderson. He "did not press the attack at all," Peyton wrote, "but held back as soon as Old Jube started to join him." The comment illustrates how men in the ranks did not entirely grasp the scope of the situation the generals faced, but the recognition that there was dissension between the army's commanders is telling. Peyton also noted that there had "been considerable friction between Old Jube and Kershaw."[11]

In response to Lee's continual entreaties for his return, Anderson issued orders to return to Culpeper. The Valley foray was bookended by misfortune however; the first at Front Royal and now near Berryville. On September 13, while preparing to depart, Federal "cavalry dashed upon the picket on the Berryville Road and captured it without any resistance." The picket of about 150 men was from the 8th South Carolina under Colonel John Henagan. While Union troopers deployed in his front and to his left, a third column galloped up the Pike and into his rear. Henagan fell back into some woods and attempted to reach his brigade, but found the enemy now blocking his way while others pressed forward behind him. Union cavalrymen dismounted and set out through the timber while mounted comrades rode along the edges of the woods shouting for the Confederates to surrender. The colonel must have thought the situation hopeless and he soon complied with the enemy's calls to give up. Fourteen officers and ninety men laid down their arms. A few escaped notice by climbing up into the trees. Strangely, Henagan lost not a single soldier in the exchange, although the bodies of several dead Yankees were discovered at the scene later. His brigade commander, James Conner, withheld "all expression of censure" based on Henagan's previous gallant behavior, but Anderson was less kind. He found the conduct inexcusable. "The post was one which any lieutenant might have defended for some time against any odds," he wrote. Noting Henagan's unquestioned courage and the regiment's bravery, he could only express his dismay. "Why they should have surrendered so tamely can only be known when they return from captivity [and] show the causes." Henagan would never make a report of the circumstances however. He died in captivity at Johnson's Island, Ohio in April 1865, weeks after Lee's capitulation. By then the incident had passed into distant memory.[12]

Anderson finally left the Valley on September 15, reaching Gordonsville before a telegram from Lee on the afternoon of September 23 instructed him to hurry Kershaw's division and a battalion of artillery back to Early's aid. Old Jube had met with disaster in twin defeats at Winchester and Fisher's Hill. Kershaw set out at daylight on the 24th. Sheridan's inaction had led to the decision to return Kershaw to Lee's front. Now, Early was to have Kershaw's troops, but not Anderson. The failure of Anderson and Early to "harmonize," as Brigadier General Conner later put it, led to the decision to withdraw Kershaw's division and opened the door to Early's defeats. Conner misread the situation now, however, writing home of how "comforting" it was "to think that 'Robert' does not need us, for he wrote General Anderson to leave our division up there, and to return himself to Petersburg." Yet another statement indicating Dick Anderson's growing melancholy serves to sum up the Valley campaign of August and September. While marching to Culpeper through the Luray Valley the fine weather had put Anderson's staff in excellent spirits, but he was somewhat despondent. "Looking up at the blue peaks which were frowning down upon us," Anderson could only comment wistfully, "it would be the height of happiness . . . to lie on the top of one of those mountains all day long and roll rocks down its rugged side." Many a weary soldier would have welcomed a day of mindless dawdling, but a commander who shared such sentiments with his staff was clearly in the midst of some crisis. After all, he was shuttling between two components of a vastly outnumbered army, neither of which seemed to have much real hope of prevailing against the enemy. Anderson had also been somewhat preoccupied with forlorn hopes that the impending presidential election in the North would prove favorable for the southern cause. Writing from Winchester on September 6, he noted that he "had begun to entertain some vague sort of hopes for peace" as a result of McClellan's candidacy. "McClellan was never a fanatical war man," he wrote. "In fact he and Lincoln split upon the question of the proper conduct of the war." If Anderson saw little prospect of military success on the horizon, he at least drew some hope from the prospect of a political solution. He might have been further encouraged had he been aware of Lincoln's August 23 memorandum acknowledging the probability that he would lose the election. It would then be his duty, Lincoln had informed his Cabinet, to cooperate with McClellan to save the Union prior to the inauguration, "as he will have secured his election on such ground that he can not possibly save it afterwards." James Conner thought likewise, when he wrote his mother on August 13 of the "peace feelings" in the North. He speculated hopefully, "Old Abe [had] lost ground amazingly of late, and it may be he too will come out the strongest peace man of all." Meanwhile, many of the men wondered at the futility of the marching and countermarching in the Shenandoah that led to naught. Dawson recalled that Early and Anderson "swung corners and chasséed in every direction to no good purpose, that any of us could see." Still, they had not been sitting in sun-baked trenches outside Petersburg, and Dawson considered it "a delightful sort of military pic-nic, and in that sense everybody enjoyed it." The men lost or captured assuredly would not have agreed. The wounding of Brigadier General Benjamin Humphreys on September 3 was an especially hard blow as his services were lost for the rest of the war. Colonel Henagan was en route to a Yankee prison, while Brigadier General Wofford suffered a nasty fall from his horse when the animal was shot from under him during the fighting for Guard Hill. The division had only two brigadier generals at the head of its brigades as it rushed back to help Early that September, and by the time it returned to Anderson's First Corps in mid-November there were none.[13]

Dick Anderson arrived at Chaffin's Bluff at around 11 AM on the morning of September 29. He reached Richmond on September 26 but did not receive orders until two days later. A note from Lee's adjutant, Walter Taylor, instructed him to take command of the troops north of the James River and that the line of works there be "pushed forward as vigorously as possible and everything done to make the entire defensive line secure against any attack of the enemy." The cause for the delay in Anderson's orders is unknown, but the delay was a luxury Lee could ill afford. His need for a leader north of the James was acute, for the present situation entailed a confusing split between Department Commander Dick Ewell and the commander of supporting troops from Lee's Army of Northern Virginia. Anderson sped to the scene on September 29 after meeting a courier from Ewell who told him that fighting was then raging around Chaffin's Farm. Ewell greeted him there with the unwelcome news that two Federal corps had advanced from Deep Bottom, driven troops from the New Market Line, and seized Fort Harrison on the outer defensive line. The divided command situation had created yet another serious problem for Lee. Although five lines of defense stretched around Richmond, there were insufficient troops to man a continuous exterior line. Instead, a rapidly responding force of mobile reserves strengthened threatened points. Rapidity and divided command authority, however, are seldom compatible concepts. Still, Confederate defenders had stubbornly resisted the advance except at the lightly manned Fort Harrison, and they subsequently brought forward sufficient force to stabilize the lines and counterattack.[14]

An alarmed Lee rushed reinforcements to Anderson, and those troops, along with naval gunboat fire, helped repulse a Union assault on Fort Gilmer, on the intermediate line northwest of Fort Harrison. Augmented by additional troops, Anderson sent one small brigade that evening to retake the exterior lines from the James River to near Fort Harrison, and restore that section. Lee himself reached the scene on the 29th, and Hoke arrived with four more brigades overnight. The increase in their force gave Lee and Anderson confidence in a counterattack designed to recapture Fort Harrison, and the morning of September 30 found Lee, Anderson, and Ewell riding along the front to determine the best place to attack the Federal positions. Ewell sustained a serious injury when his horse stumbled and he fell. He returned to the front several hours later with his head entirely swathed in bandages except for two eyeholes and "two small breathing spaces." Whatever happened that day would be in Dick Anderson's hands. They decided to assault on the Union center at Fort Harrison, but it met with failure, which Anderson dismissed as having been due to the "premature advance of [G. T. "Tige"] Anderson's Brigade" of Field's division. Tige Anderson's brigade was to have moved forward from some woods in front of Fort Johnson to the cover of a swale that bisected the line of advance, and there wait for John Bratton's brigade to form behind it prior to advancing. Tige Anderson seems to have lost control of his brigade once it was in motion, however. It did not halt in the depression, and the momentum of its advance pushed it forward directly into the charge. This compelled Bratton to move out at double-quick time to catch up and support the attack. Bratton's last regiment to deploy had to run the entire way and never did get into line with the rest of the brigade. Meanwhile, Hoke, who had so far since his elevation to division command demonstrated a distinct failure to cooperate well with his colleagues during attacks, had deployed his men obliquely to Field's right and about 500 yards northwest of Fort Harrison, and adhered strictly to its orders to advance at 2 PM. By then it was abundantly clear that Tige Anderson and Bratton had been repulsed. Anderson's Georgians met a withering fire as they emerged from the swale in which they were to have halted, and their attack was shattered. The men fell back pell-mell and further disorganized Bratton's struggling brigade. Hoke's attack at 2 PM was hopelessly under-strength and disjointed, and one may wonder why, after seeing the destruction wrought on Tige Anderson's and Bratton's men, he would have advanced only a portion of his division—or at all. While the complicated plan was of Lee's own making, the lack of decisive action on the part of Dick Anderson that day is again a mysterious point. Lee's and Anderson's precise locations during the entire assault remain unknown; although it is likely they positioned themselves either in the area of Fort Gilmer or possibly even closer, at Fort Johnson. If so, they would have had a clear view across the 1,000 yards of open ground lying between Fields's starting point and the walls of Fort Harrison. The confused attack and Tige Anderson's "premature" advance must have been immediately visible to them. Apparently, no one sent a staff officer to Hoke telling him either to advance immediately with Field's attacking units or not to advance at all, but it is possible that the corps commander and the army commander were both too distant to have done so in a timely manner. Hoke advanced feebly and did not throw all his available weight behind the attack, but by then it was merely a useless sacrifice of valuable soldiers. With Lee on the scene helping to rally the remnants of the bloodied units, it is difficult to excuse his lack of direction or allow him escape criticism for the plan or its execution since he had been present from the start to witness the lopsided battle. Lee's adjutant, Walter Taylor, gently passed off the failed assault as being "not an energetic nor systematic one." Another officer thought Lee wore "a face as long as a gun barrel" after that defeat. Anderson succinctly disposed of the affair in his official report, but the sight afterwards of several captured rebel battle flags waving contemptuously from the fort surely caused great mortification. Fort Harrison was destined to remain in Union hands, but a correspondent for the Richmond *Examiner* dismissed its loss as meaningless. "Instead of Richmond," he wrote, "the enemy got Battery Harrison." Despite the correspondent's glib observation, Lee's long face was well warranted. He had wanted the line strengthened to avoid just such a catastrophe. Now he had to form a new one.[15]

Lee abandoned further attempts to retake Fort Harrison, and Anderson's men took up a new defensive line the next day. By afternoon, fearing an assault, Anderson learned of an enemy advance along the Darbytown and Williamsburg Roads. Lee sent him off with reinforcements to counter that Union thrust. Marching in heavy rain, he arrived near dusk at the intersection of those two roads, lying within the main line of defenses, and found that the enemy had merely reconnoitered the positions and withdrawn without attacking. He returned with his troops next day to Chaffin's Bluff.[16]

Several days passed with the men at work with pick and spade strengthening their new lines of defense. Blue-clad soldiers were likewise busy extending their lines from Fort Harrison and entrenching. As that line reached northward, Lee directed Anderson to move Field's and Hoke's divisions to new positions lying between the Darbytown and Charles City Roads. Law's brigade was already on the way to reinforce Brigadier General Martin Gary's cavalry brigade on the Charles City Road. In an effort to prevent any further extension of the Union lines, Lee personally conducted an attack to turn the enemy's right flank on October 7. Gary's and Law's brigades set off at sunrise along the Charles City Road, while Field and Hoke simultaneously struck out on the Darbytown Road. Both quickly drove off the cavalry they encountered on those roads. Confederates captured nine pieces of artillery and ten caissons as the Union cavalrymen broke and fled, not halting until they reached the shelter of their works on the New Market Road. Anderson quickly re-formed his troops in a battle line facing the New Market Road, which stood perpendicular to the enemy's line of works stretching north and south across that road. With Field positioned on the east side of the Union works and Hoke on the west side, Anderson sent them forward toward the Yankee right flank now refused on the New Market Road. The advance was a difficult one, and the men struggled through "thick abatis and an almost impenetrable swamp" before Field finally reached the Union position. In the ensuing melee, Brigadier General John Gregg fell dead at the head of his Texas Brigade with a bullet through the neck, while John Bratton also sustained a serious shoulder wound but was still able to sit his horse and direct the action.[17]

Once again, Hoke's division did not join in the attack, and though Field nearly gained the enemy's works, he was compelled to fall back when Yankees enfiladed his right flank, just where Hoke ought to have been. Whether his absence at that point was due to his own failure to advance, or to Lee not ordering him to do so is unknown. Johnson Hagood alleged in a postwar memoir that Hoke's division was acting as a "reserve," and that Lee had been present with that element of his force "most of the day, and just before and during the last assault." Some in Field's division still blamed Hoke for the failure to support them, but Lee's presence might absolve Hoke in this instance. Still, the failure rankled Field's men. Field's aide was not present that day and only learned the details later, but the version he heard was sufficiently damning to lead him to write his mother in November that the attack would have succeeded "had Hoke supported us, but as usual he was slow or showed the white feather." Dick Anderson's role that day is not clear, but he might have been attempting to deflect blame by noting in his report of operations that Lee "had in person conducted the attack." That statement of course contradicts Hagood's claim.[18]

Anderson's men were next set to work building fortifications extending from Fort Gilmer to the Charles City Road, where the exterior line of the Richmond defenses intersected it. An enemy advance up the Charles City Road early on October 13 drove in Gary's cavalry pickets and threatened Field's left flank. Confederates quickly adjusted their lines after some morning skirmishing, and turned back an afternoon assault on Field and Gary with little loss. Near the Charles City Road, Field refused his line to guard the left flank. Defenses there consisted of substantial rifle pits and abatis. The advance of Union Brigadier General Adelbert Ames's three brigades against a point where he thought no defensive line even existed partly exposed his left flank and the movement "met with considerable loss." That successful defense marked the end of Dick Anderson's tenure as the First Corps commander. Longstreet returned to active duty and command of his old corps on October 19. Although Dick Anderson turned over to his old chief a securely defended line, the abject failures to retake Fort Harrison on September 29 and the October 7 setback on the Charles City Road marred the record of events since his return from the Valley. Both of those defeats, however, took place under Lee's direct eye, and in the latter case, possibly under his immediate direction. In both instances, it must be said that the failure was a joint one.[19]

Chapter 18

Petersburg to Appomattox

> They dair not rase their heads. If they do
> some of us will try their skelps.
>
> —Rice Lucas,
> letter, December 5, 1864

Longstreet's return presented Lee with the question of what to do with Anderson. With no corps available for a lieutenant general, it became necessary to create one. Anderson's Fourth Corps would not be an insignificant command, at least on paper. In December 1864, it counted nearly 13,000 men present for duty. It was only slightly smaller than the First and Third Corps, each having around 15,000 men, but it was considerably larger than Early's Second Corps, then numbering fewer than 9,000. Lee was not satisfied with the situation, however, most likely because Anderson's troops belonged to Beauregard's force. He thus continued to seek a more stable command for Anderson that did not rely on borrowed troops. Even as late as January 10, 1865, Lee indicated to Davis that he was still searching for a position that would be appropriate for Anderson. He inquired about Lieutenant General William J. Hardee, then battling Sherman in Georgia and the Carolinas. "Gen Hardee informs me that he has no command for Gen R. H. Anderson, though he would like to have his assistance," Lee told Davis. Dick Anderson was destined to remain with Lee, however, and there is no indication Lee had lost confidence in Anderson's abilities, only that sufficient forces were unavailable to constitute a corps that was worthy of the name.[1]

Anderson's new corps consisted of only two divisions, one commanded by Major General Bushrod Rust Johnson and the other Hoke's, both detached from Beauregard to meet the emergency around Petersburg and Richmond. The Ohio-born Johnson had graduated the US Military Academy two years prior to Anderson, resigning from the army after fighting in Mexico as an infantry lieutenant. Captured at Fort Donelson in early 1862; then wounded by at Shiloh in April that year, he came east for service in Lee's army after the Knoxville Campaign. Johnson's division had been in the trenches around Petersburg from the start of the siege and had helped drive back Union troops at the Battle of the Crater. There, Johnson's reputation suffered grievously as a result of his strange lethargy after the Union mine exploded a huge gap in his line, burying guns and men alike. The more energetic Billy Mahone redeemed the day for the Confederates, with Johnson contributing only belatedly to an afternoon assault. Having recently arrived from the West, Johnson's failure to show more aggression in the wake of the near disaster did little to endear him to his men or to the commanders of his brigades. His lackluster performance, moreover, took place directly under Lee's gaze. Mahone received promotion to major general; Johnson was ignored. The pairing of Johnson and Anderson, whose personalities together may have lacked the confident and aggressive nature needed to serve the Confederate Army well in the waning days of its existence, was to have telling consequences.[2]

To make matters worse for Anderson, Lee found it necessary on December 20, 1864 to transfer Hoke to Wilmington, North Carolina where nearby Fort Fisher was under threat. With twin threats from Sherman's advance on Savannah and pressure on Fort Fisher, Beauregard had frantically requested the return of Hoke and Johnson, but Lee argued that he would be compelled to abandon Richmond if he lost both divisions. Until then Hoke had remained in place manning the lines in front of Richmond, and had never physically joined Anderson's new Fourth Corps at all, now consisting only of about 5,000 men of Johnson's four brigades—William H. Wallace's South Carolinians, Archibald Gracie's Alabamians, Matthew W. Ransom's North Carolinians, and former governor Henry A. Wise's Virginians. The Virginia brigade was frequently under the command of Colonel John T. Goode in Wise's absence. Supplementing them were four battalions of artillery led by Colonel Hilary P. Jones along with "a small body of reserves under Colonel [Fletcher Harris] Archer" that numbered just 250 men. Lieutenant Colonel Archer's unit was eventually designated the 3rd Battalion Virginia Reserves, whose members were drawn from the under- and over-age male population of Petersburg and surrounding counties. Archer's successful defense of the Petersburg lines on June 9, 1864, in the so-called Battle of Old Men and Young Boys cemented his reputation. His tiny band had held off Union cavalry for nearly two hours until reinforcements arrived and ended the federals' bumbled opportunity to capture the nearly defenseless city. Archer's force began to dwindle after joining Anderson until reassigned to Seth Barton's brigade in the Department of Richmond in January 1865.[3]

The makeshift organization of Anderson's new command also entailed some necessary shakeup among his staff officers since he could bring none of the First Corps staff with him, although some of his old division staff members transferred with him. At least one of the First Corps staff members was disappointed. The young Englishman Francis Dawson found Longstreet too reserved and "the principle members of his staff, with two exceptions, . . .

positively disagreeable." Colonel Osmun Latrobe was courteous, he thought, and Colonel Peyton Manning was Dawson's only real friend, but the rest of "the staff had 'no use' for me . . . and I was on no better terms with them in 1864 than I had been in 1862." Dawson would have welcomed the chance to remain in Anderson's circle, but despite early promise, his desires came to naught. The circumstances as explained by Dawson illustrate Anderson's acknowledgement of military protocol.[4]

> General Anderson had been promoted to the rank of Lieutenant-General, and was to take command of a corps at Petersburg when General Longstreet should return to duty, and he was kind enough to tell me that if Colonel Baldwin, the Chief of Ordnance of the army, would consent to the transfer, he would take me with him to Petersburg, and make me Chief Ordnance Officer of his corps. This would have given me the rank of Major or Lieutenant-Colonel. I rode over to Petersburg to see Colonel Baldwin, and he told me that he would be delighted to see me promoted, and would order the assignment to be made. Unfortunately, though properly, General Anderson, upon reflection, came to the conclusion that it would not be just to Captain E. N. Thurston, who had been his Ordnance Officer while he was in command of a division, to promote me over his head, and that he ought to make Captain Thurston his Chief Ordnance Officer. I assented, of course, but was determined to seize any opportunity that offered to leave Longstreet's Corps.[5]

Dawson ultimately found a place on General Fitz Lee's staff, departing Longstreet in November 1864. Never one to display emotions, Longstreet apparently valued Dawson more than he knew, as Longstreet was not pleased to lose him. "I must say," Dawson later wrote peevishly, "that he did not show any particular interest in retaining me as long as no one else wanted me."[6]

Johnson's division eventually occupied trenches from Hatcher's Run to the Appomattox River on the southwestern portion of the Petersburg defenses, but when Anderson took command, it was still positioned on the southeastern portion of the line in the vicinity of the Crater. The division stretched very thinly to cover not only its own front, but also the entrenchments once occupied by Hoke's division and two of Mahone's brigades. Lee's need to shift his forces constantly to meet immediate threats naturally weakened portions of his defenses, but by the end of October, Anderson's thin line was bolstered by the return of Mahone's two brigades. Johnson's division, along with Archer's battalion and Mahone's two brigades, stretched approximately six miles from the Appomattox River to Battery No. 45 on the

Boydton Plank Road, with Johnson and Archer's lines alone running from the Appomattox to the vicinity of Lieutenant Run. On October 27 and 28, Heth and Mahone's divisions repelled attacking elements of three Union corps seeking to cut the Boydton Plank Road and the Southside Railroad near Burgess Mill to the southwest. In the rain and darkness of October 27, some Union troops also got into a portion of Anderson's works after deceiving the Confederate sentinels by telling them that they were comrades returning to the lines after being relieved from picket duty. The Yankees were "driven out as soon as their true character was discovered," General Anderson later reported. A lieutenant and fourteen men were captured, and "the whole party would have been destroyed or captured," had the Officer of the Day not brought a halt to the fire. Anderson subsequently could find no fault with the officer or the men, as "they were all in their places. I cannot discover that there was any lack of vigilance." The opposing entrenchments within a few hundred yards left of the Crater were at that point in very close proximity to one another, and Anderson determined to expel the enemy from his rifle pits and occupy them with his own troops. His own nighttime attack was a success, but the Rebels were compelled to abandon their gains and return to their own defenses after daylight when it became clear they were unable to hold the position. Anderson blamed the lack of entrenching tools that would have permitted the troops to fortify the trenches to oppose attackers from the Union side of the line.[7]

Such shortages continued to plague the army. At the end of October, the strength of Johnson's division was reported as 6,399 officers and men present; the largest infantry division in the army, but hardly a corps. Adverse conditions soon whittled away at those numbers. As fall gave way to colder weather starting in November, General Anderson strengthened the defenses and constructed bombproof shelters. Confederates scaled back and eventually abandoned the effort altogether because of the scarcity of timber and the difficulties of transportation. By the time the cold weather struck in force, Anderson described the various means of transport by wagon and rail as "rarely sufficing . . . to keep up a scanty supply of fuel and forage.[8]

November 8 was the long-awaited day of the presidential election that might confirm that northerners had "become certainly convinced of the impossibility of subjugating us," as an officer in the 43rd Alabama hoped. Many of the men, he said, believed Lincoln would be "reelected by fair means or by foul," but that regardless of the outcome there would be peace in 1865. That prediction was to be borne out by events, but not in the manner the Alabamians anticipated that November. In the meantime, formal truces relieved some of the suffering that resulted from skirmishing. On Election Day General Anderson agreed a one-hour truce proposed by his old friend

Hancock, who faced him across the shell-swept no-man's land. The ceasefire was limited to the immediate vicinity of a skirmish that had occurred on the night of November 5 in which Moody's brigade had captured the enemy picket line and thirty-one prisoners with no loss. Wallace's South Carolinians had also met with initial success but then suffered high casualties when Federals brought an enfilading fire to bear on the lines they captured. The frequent informal truces that had been a prominent feature of the war had become less common, gradually giving way to the frustrations of trench warfare. Pickets could only be relieved under cover of darkness and by crawling along ditches to and from their posts, and officers encouraged the pickets to keep up a consistent fire to prevent friendly interaction with the enemy. Though the pickets did not always comply with that directive, the danger of picket duty was often worse when the Union troops were black. One Virginian of Pickett's division wrote in December 1864 that the pickets "had a lively time while we were firing at the yankey Negroes. They keep their Negroes on picket nearly all the time but they dair not rase their heads. If they do some of us will try their skelps." Quiet now reigned along the lines, he continued, "for there is white men on."[9]

Sustained attentiveness was required of the men on the line. To soothe Lee's mind about the possibility of a surprise attack, Anderson reported in late November that one of his staff officers had inspected the entire picket line. He also forwarded to Lee copies of instructions describing the duties of the officers of the day. To ensure efficient oversight, General Anderson divided his line into two wings and designated a division officer of the day for each wing. Beneath them were brigade and regimental officers of the day. "Every possible precaution is taken to secure vigilance," he wrote reassuringly.[10]

December saw the much-lamented loss of General Gracie. On the day he died, Gracie had been granted a leave of absence to visit his wife and day-old daughter in Richmond. While overseeing some work on his lines before departing, he was peering through a telescope, exposing the top of his head above the parapet. Shrapnel from an exploding Yankee shell fractured his neck and caused three wounds to his shoulder. Anderson termed Gracie's death a "heavy loss" to the country and his division, calling him an "indefatigable and brave officer." Command of his brigade fell to Colonel Young M. Moody. Just a few weeks earlier in an attempt to find a solid replacement for Henry Wise, Anderson had also tried to obtain the services of Lieutenant Colonel William J. "Willie" Pegram, whom he mistakenly thought had been elevated to the rank of brigadier general. The bespectacled young leader would have been a suitable choice in place of Colonel Goode, who was then commanding Wise's brigade, but Pegram had not yet received his promotion.[11]

Anderson keenly felt the effects of the "incessant fire from the enemy" that led to daily casualties of "seldom less than five, and frequently amounting to ten or fifteen." The constant danger added to the men's misery in what was quickly turning into an "unusually severe and protracted winter." The lack of firewood, inadequate clothing and food, and Yankee enticements to forsake the cause led to increased desertions throughout Lee's army. The constant rain of mortar shells on the trenches, the threat of sharpshooters, and the lack of shelter from blistering sun and drenching rains had all added to the men's misery. On December 26, Johnson's morning report to Anderson noted the desertion of seven men from Ransom's Brigade, four from Wise's, and two from Gracie's. The latter included a lieutenant from the 43rd Alabama. Johnson also reported two men wounded. Anderson forwarded the report to Lee, who sent it on to the Secretary at War "that he may judge of the condition of this army. Scant fare, light clothing, constant duty, no recruits, have discouraged it." Clearly, Lee shared the agony of his troops, but with little means to relieve their suffering the plague of desertions continued, sometimes in even more alarming numbers. In mid-February, Ransom reported that he thought twenty men of one regiment deserted to the rear in an effort to get to their homes, raising the question of how well the division provost guard was doing its work. On a single night the following week Johnson's division lost fifty-seven men to desertion to the enemy and three to the rear. Relying on the services of "good men" as informers, Johnson also reported that same night the discovery of a plot involving a mass desertion of around fifty-to-sixty men from Wallace's brigade. After almost nine months without relief in the trenches of Petersburg, however, Johnson's division was finally withdrawn for a respite that Anderson hoped would restore its vigor. Moreover, newly arrived conscripts or men returning to the army from lengthy detachment to commissary or quartermaster department duties required drilling and re-acquaintance with the routines of infantry life. The removal to a less active part of the lines would provide that opportunity. In early March Anderson relocated his corps to the extreme right of Lee's defenses near Burgess's Mill and took command of that section of the Petersburg defenses. There his small corps would at least experience one of the highest concentrations of troop density of any point along Richmond and Petersburg defenses, with approximately 1,600 men per mile.[12]

Anderson hoped that the change would stem the tide of desertions, but it did not. This he attributed in large part to "the depressed and destitute condition of the soldiers' families," citing "the chief and prevailing reason as conviction among them that our cause was hopeless and further sacrifices were useless." If Anderson too was by then on the verge of despair, he at least persisted in his duties and hid his feelings from the troops. Still, he recognized that "it was within the capabilities of the meanest soldier and most unreflecting to calculate the chances of a further prosecution of the war and to perceive how immensely the odds were against us." The growing strength of the Union Army as well as the relative weakness of Lee's force was clearly visible. Enemy "numbers, his equipage, his transportation, and his ammunition were ostentatiously exhibited to our half-starving, poorly equipped, depleted ranks," Anderson reported, so that his own force "disheartened and discouraged . . . entered upon the campaign of 1865 with but little of the former spirit of former days." It is noteworthy, however, to observe that Johnson's daily reports frequently mentioned a small number of Union deserters coming into the lines throughout the fall months, but by December those notations faded away to be supplanted by an increasing number of his own men abandoning their duty.[13]

On Friday, March 10, Lee wrote to President Davis encouraging him to speedily implement the newly passed law authorizing the use of black troops in the southern armies. Lee hoped to see a considerable number of volunteers, though likely not in time to "be of service during the present campaign." It was thus a sign of both optimism and desperation. Lee had already polled the men on the use of black troops, and Anderson reported to Lee on February 20, that "the troops . . . acquiesce in the proposed measure of enlisting such slaves as may volunteer to bear arms in consideration of receiving their freedom at the close of the war. They are prepared for this or any other step which Congress and the President may deem necessary or expedient." Meanwhile, the lack of reinforcement left recourse only to prayer. Lee had thus designated March 10 as a day of "observance" marked by church services throughout the army. General Ransom, for example, permitted one third of the officers and men of his brigade to attend a service at the brigade wood yard. He, Anderson, and Johnson also joined Lee in Richmond at the stately Greek Revival St. Paul's Episcopal Church across from Capitol Square.[14]

Under the dire siege conditions, Dick Anderson must have prayed fervently for relief for himself and his family. Wallace's wife Jennie was then in Fayetteville, North Carolina, and Dick probably held thoughts similar to his brother, who wrote to Jennie on March 20. "I do not know but that you may be still subjected to the dangers and humiliation of being surrounded by our vile enemies. I hope however they have all left Fayetteville by this time and that you are breathing the air of freedom once again." Clearly agonized by the thought of her plight, Wallace expressed "a firm trust in the protecting power of that Merciful and good Providence which has so often shielded us from harm, and which orders all things for the ultimate good of those who believe in Him with full faith." Wallace's situation at that time was not so critical, though his experience illustrates how precipitously the Confederacy clung to life. He had recently spent three nights making the relatively short trip from Charlotte to Raleigh, North Carolina. Those three nights passed "on a box car with my overcoat for my only covering and trunks and boxes for a bed," he told Jennie. Still, his position provided him with the luxury of going on to Stateburg the next day, where he hoped to employ an overseer and "see the plantation under weigh [*sic*] for a crop." After that he intended to return to Raleigh and hold himself "in readiness to make a start for Fayetteville as soon as it may be practicable."[15]

Despite their pessimism, many stout Confederates adhered to their duty and did their best. When Lee authorized an attack on Fort Stedman at Hare's Hill on March 23, Anderson sat out the affair but contributed Ransom's and Wallace's brigades to the effort led by Major General John B. Gordon. Gordon sent his force across 150 yards of no-man's land before daylight, totally surprising the federals and easily taking Fort Stedman. From that point, the plan miscarried, and stout Yankee resistance compelled Lee to order a withdrawal by 8 AM. By that time, daylight had turned the prospect of retreat into a veritable death trap, as a vicious storm of shot and shell swept the terrain between Stedman and the Confederate lines. Despite the pleading of their officers, many chose to lay down their arms rather than risk retreating across that dangerous ground. The heavy fire struck down many others who tried to brave the storm, while some miraculously reached their lines safely. Anderson reckoned the loss in his two brigades at around 1,200 men. The army's entire loss from the assault and retreat probably totaled 3,500 men, of which nearly 2,000 were prisoners.[16]

Fortunately, for the reeling Confederates the counterattack that typically followed a failed assault did not come immediately on the heels of the repulse. Nevertheless, when it came, it was strong enough to gain possession of a portion of the line held by Moody's brigade. "The line was soon recovered," Anderson recalled, "but not without considerable loss." Elsewhere along the line, more Confederates fell into the hands of the foe. The final estimate of total casualties among Lee's army that day is between 4,400 and 5,000 men, with somewhere around 2,800 captured.[17]

Union forces continued to probe Anderson's defenses for the next several days. He thought they must have had the impression the Confederates were preparing to abandon the works. Lee had hoped that the attack on Stedman would secure his lines and negate the arrival of Sheridan's army from the Valley, but now Sheridan was moving to turn the Confederate right flank and sever the remaining supply lines into Petersburg. Gouverneur Warren's

Fifth Corps and Andrew Humphreys's Second Corps supported Sheridan. That operation began on March 29, when a strong enemy force crossed Hatcher's Run, drove in Anderson's pickets, and seized the Quaker Road and Boydton Plank Road. General Anderson sent Johnson forward to dislodge the Yankees, but they were unable to drive them back despite some initial success. General Anderson was on the field with Wise's brigade as it forced Union troops back that afternoon, but as a counterattack drove back a portion of Wise's Virginians along the Quaker Road, Anderson directed Johnson to bring Wallace's brigade to its support. Union troops eventually rallied and repulsed Wise and Wallace. By late afternoon, he ordered the men withdrawn to a position across the Boydton Plank Road. There they remained until dusk, when Anderson recalled them to their breastworks. The series of back-and-forth actions centered around the Lewis Farm led to nearly equal casualties on both sides, but it left Union troops in possession of the important junction of the Quaker Road and Boydton Plank Road. The position not only cut yet another supply road into the city, it also left the federals poised to assault Anderson's positions on the White Oak Road.[18]

Anderson's lines ran westward along White Oak Road from Burgess's Mill until reaching Claiborne Road and turning northward to Hatcher's Run, almost directly south of Sutherland Station on the South Side Railroad. Lee, realizing that the size and power of the force that accompanied Sheridan's movement portended not a raid on the railroad but rather a full-scale attempt to turn his right flank, began to funnel his reserves towards the scene that was unfolding a few miles to Anderson's right. Soldiers on both sides suffered as a teeming rain fell unabated through the night of March 29 and throughout the following day. Lee's few reinforcements struggled to make their way to their new positions, while their enemies likewise struggled along roads that turned to mud or worse. By morning, Pickett's division from the First Corps had taken up position on Anderson's right flank. Lee arrived and convened a war council with Anderson, Pickett, and Harry Heth, whose troops held positions on Anderson's left flank. Lee instructed Pickett to head west on the White Oak Road to support the cavalry holding the vital junction at Five Forks and attack the Union force at Dinwiddie Courthouse. Lee added Ransom and Wallace's brigades from Anderson's corps to the expedition. Union cavalry probes along the way necessitated halting the column and forming lines of battle that delayed Pickett's march. Pickett accomplished little on March 30 as a result, but delays occasioned by the poor road conditions equally bedeviled the Yankees.[19]

Rain continued periodically on the morning of March 31, and Grant decided that no operations would take place that day. Lee decided differently. He had discovered a gaping hole in the Union lines between the infantry in

Anderson's front and Sheridan's cavalry positioned farther west. Johnson's reduced division, reinforced by Samuel McGowan's brigade of South Carolinians from Cadmus Wilcox's Third Corps division and Eppa Hunton's Virginia brigade from Pickett's division, achieved a stunning success as they swept forward and drove back two Union divisions that morning in the Battle of White Oak Road, which would stand as Lee's final counteroffensive in the defense of Petersburg. Some retreating federals were sent "running to the rear in a most demoralized and disorganized condition," as one Union officers later reported. Ultimately, the success could not be sustained and the attack stalled when the battle-weary Rebels encountered a fresh line of Union defenders. Without reinforcement, Confederate troops were compelled to fall back. Anderson later wrote only that the attempt to force the enemy back that day "failed to accomplish the aim," but the degree of his involvement in the affair is poorly documented. Direct tactical command of the attacking force fell to Johnson, while Anderson appears to have had a minimal hand in the affair other than to direct Johnson to withdraw the exhausted troops to the rifle pits vacated by enemy skirmishers south of the White Oak Road. Lieutenant James Caldwell of McGowen's staff documented Anderson's presence and his humanity. During the withdrawal, McGowan sent Caldwell to Anderson to request artillery support for the South Carolinians' exposed flank. Caldwell rode across the field by the most direct route through a hailstorm of federal fire, finding Anderson and some of his staff officers sitting their horses in front of the Confederate works where they had observed Caldwell's daring ride. Caldwell, despite the urgency of his mission, asked Captain Langdon Haskell of Anderson's staff for an introduction to the general. Anderson excitedly interrupted the attempt at an introduction, exclaiming that he did not think anyone could possibly make it through such a firestorm unharmed. "I said to Haskell," he continued, "That man will certainly be killed." After Caldwell relayed McGowan's request, Anderson insisted that he remain with him out of harm's way, telling the young officer that his brigade would, "be back here in a few minutes; and then you can join them." Caldwell continued to argue that it was his duty to return to McGowan with a report and that it was not so dangerous because "the enemy fired very high," but the general insisted he remain. "I will not consent to your exposure to that fire again," he told him. "Stay with me till your brigade reaches the works and then show them into their places on the right of us." Anderson finally took pity on the young officer's distress and told him that he could return to McGowan if he promised to take a circuitous route through the woods. "But," Anderson continued with a smile, "there is no need for you to go out at all. Your people will be in very soon, and then I trust the enemy will come up and let us have a chance at them." Caldwell set off as instructed nonetheless, but his thoughts were more on Anderson's kindness to an unknown subaltern than on the battle raging around him. No artillery support was forthcoming either, and Caldwell later remarked that it was "the chief peculiarity of the whole battle," in that no Confederate artillery at all fired a shot. The enemy did not give Anderson his "chance" though. The Union assault eventually drove the rebels out of the rifle pits and back to their main line of breastworks, eliminating all of the morning's gains and adding to Lee's woes when federals established themselves securely across the road and threatened direct communication with Pickett at Five Forks. Johnson estimated his casualties at around 800 men, a loss he could hardly afford in exchange for such an ineffectual result.[20]

A few miles to the west, Pickett's attack on Sheridan at Dinwiddie Courthouse initially met with success, but stout resistance brought him to a halt. He retired through the night to a precarious position at Five Forks. The morning of April 1 found the federals gone from Anderson's front, but by late afternoon heavy firing from the vicinity of Five Forks indicated that those troops had moved west to join the assault on Pickett.[21]

The events of April 1, 1865 illustrate the general debilitation of Confederate leadership and foreshadow the rapidly approaching collapse of the army. Thomas Taylor Munford, a talented cavalry commander and Virginia Military Institute graduate who commanded Fitzhugh Lee's division wrote many years later to a comrade, "Fitz Lee and Pickett went back to wagon train where Rosser had a bake of shad from Nottoway River and the usual condiments." The "condiments" referred to alcoholic beverages because Munford continued to say, "they all got on a bender and remained there until well after six o'clock when you saw Genl Pickett straining his horse under fire to get back to the already routed infantry. I had sent every staff officer and courier I had with me and notified them of the approach of the 5th Corps" concluded the still frustrated Munford. His adjutant, Major Samuel Griffin finally found Pickett and Fitz Lee, "two miles in rear enjoying a shad lunch." The infamous shad bake hosted by Tom Rosser took place north of Hatcher's Run, over a mile behind Pickett's line. Not only did Pickett ignore multiple notices of a Union advance, several of his officers had no idea where he was or how to locate him.[22]

Despite some desperate fighting, ceaseless federal assaults overwhelmed Confederate forces at Five Forks. Wallace's brigade broke on two occasions, the first when cavalry gave way and allowed Union troops to pour onto his left flank until Munford sent William Terry's brigade from Pickett's division onto that flank, forcing Wallace's men back into position. Eventually ammunition ran low and the left flank again collapsed under sheer weight of numbers. Still, many stubborn Rebels gave ground grudgingly, but Ransom's brigade fell back without orders, causing Ransom to assert command over the 14th Virginia of Pickett's division and to use that regiment to halt the flight and establish a line on which his men and some of Wallace's could re-form. Such determination came to naught. Repeated attacks drove the beleaguered Rebels back towards the South Side Railroad, Lee's last source of supply. The day ended in a crushing Confederate defeat that saw 600 of Pickett's men wounded or killed, and approximately 4,500 more captured by the surging tide of Union troops. Six priceless artillery pieces fell into federal hands. Ransom and Wallace lost nearly their entire brigades. Munford later placed much blame for the debacle on the absence of Pickett and Fitz Lee. Had they been on the field, he asserted, they might have informed Lee of the situation and caused him to throw the remainder of Anderson's corps onto the flanks of the attacking federals. Instead, Anderson and the troops remaining with him stood by within earshot but without orders while the catastrophe unfolded. He still held a vulnerable section of the Confederate line and he would have been derelict in abandoning it without direct orders from Lee to rush to Five Forks.[23]

In the post-war era that saw former Confederate comrades-in-arms trading accusations and engaging in contentious bickering regarding wartime events, Dick Anderson came under criticism for his role at Five Forks despite the fact he was not even present, or perhaps because critics—Fitz Lee most prominently—thought he *should* have been. The source of the controversy was Fitz Lee's April 22, 1865, report to Lee on the actions of the Cavalry Corps, in which he asserts most damningly that Anderson failed to come to his aid. The claim is entirely without merit and smacks of a disreputable effort to deflect blame that rightly falls on Fitz Lee's shoulders. "Genl [Fitz] Lee's own chosen men [who] blasted his strategy," Munford wrote in a 1916 letter to Anderson's niece, in which he asserted that her uncle became the scapegoat. Munford was well aware that Pickett and Fitz Lee "never came to their commands until the battle had been lost & with between 4,000 & 5,000 men captured." He referred her to his adjutant for verification, concluding that he disliked "to say unkind things but the truth if told will vindicate Genl R H Anderson." Munford admitted to only slight acquaintance with Anderson, "but his reputation was of the first order."[24]

In the wake of the disaster, Lee sent Anderson that evening with Johnson's two remaining brigades and Eppa Hunton's brigade to Church Crossing near Ford's Depot on the South Side Railroad. The troops marched through the night, all the while listening to a constant roar of artillery fire from the direction of the Petersburg, perhaps realizing even then that the roar marked the knell of the Confederacy. Arriving at Fitz Lee's headquarters near Church Crossing just before daylight on April 2, Anderson was unable to find out anything regarding Pickett and his men. His own troops required rest after the long march through the night. Fitz Lee's horsemen were equally worn, and little occurred until near noon when they once again took to the roads en route to the Appomattox River crossing at Bevil's Bridge. Fitz Lee's troopers acted as a rear guard and skirmished constantly with Union pursuers nipping at their heels. Anderson had learned by late morning that the crashing artillery fire heard throughout the previous night had indeed portended disaster. Lee's lines to the east of Petersburg had been broken. All that remained to do then was to withdraw to a more secure position. To that end, Lee ordered all the now isolated troops west of Hatcher's Run to fall back across the Appomattox towards Amelia Courthouse on the Richmond and Danville Railroad line. The entire army evacuated the defenses of Richmond and Petersburg overnight on April 2 into the morning of the third, retreating steadily to converge at Amelia Courthouse.[25]

Anderson rode ahead to ascertain the best route to take in the confusing withdrawal as constant skirmishing on April 2 turned to a more serious threat that evening when southern cavalrymen detected a much larger force of Union horsemen closing on the retreating columns. Fitz Lee requested Johnson's brigades deploy to face the developing menace, "and hasty barricades of rails were thrown up on the high ground about one mile and a half south of Namozine Creek" around Scott's Crossroads. From their makeshift protection the Confederates repulsed three separate charges without significant loss. The fighting died down after 8 PM and the bulk of Union cavalry withdrew. Leaving Hunton's brigade to hold the bridge, Johnson took his troops across Namozine Creek that night, eventually followed by Hunton and the cavalry who covered the crossing and made "several attempts to feel" the enemy's lines.[26]

One more obstacle remained at Deep Creek before the separated force could reunite with the rest of the army, and Johnson started his march toward one of the remaining bridges at 6 AM on April 3. He took the right-hand road where it split near Namozine Church and had advanced at least two miles or more by the time word from Anderson reached him that the creek was impassable. The general instructed Johnson to turn back and take the Namozine road that split to the left at the Church and to head towards Brown's Bridge instead. Fortunately, he found an intersecting road leading west to Namozine Road, and Johnson was able to get back on track without returning all the way to the crossroads nearer the Church. Just south of that point, hard-pressed cavalry and a small infantry force were still entrenched on the banks of Namozine Creek attempting to hold Union horsemen at bay long enough for the infantry to make good its escape. There is no record of Anderson's exact whereabouts at this time, but it is likely that he did not rejoin Johnson immediately and was still exploring the most appropriate escape route for Johnson and Fitz Lee to take. It would soon become clear to Lee, however, that Anderson's force was in an ideal position to screen the army's westward movement from the probing federals, who could clearly see the long lines of rebel troops filing towards the bridges across the Appomattox where the river made an abrupt turn northwards. Lee surely anticipated that Grant's aim was not to chase the battered rebel force, but either to get ahead of it and intercept it, or break the column on the march.[27]

Johnson's rear guard skirmished with pursuing federals throughout the day while Fitz Lee's troopers rushed ahead towards Brown's Bridge, which they found already in possession of the enemy. Johnson sent forward a strong skirmish line that cleared the Union troops from the area. The brigades came up behind the skirmishers, filed off the Namozine road to the right, and crossed Deep Creek unmolested. With determined Rebel cavalry once again holding the rear-guard position and the bridge in flames, the infantry pushed north and east to the vicinity of Bevill's Bridge over the Appomattox. Most likely, that is where they found Anderson, along with some remnants of Pickett's shattered division and the surviving elements of Ransom's and Wallace's brigades.[28]

Though some portion of the army was disintegrating, having been either cut off, captured, or given up, most of Lee's beleaguered force pressed westward on the north side of the Appomattox in a rapid attempt to escape the closing grip of Grant's juggernaut. The greatest threat to their escape lay with the Union forces shadowing Lee's southern flank, which could surge northward to intercept Lee's bedraggled columns as they struggled over muddy roads and rain-swollen watercourses. Aware of that great danger to his army, Lee revised his instructions to Anderson. Rather than cross the Appomattox at Bevil's Bridge and rejoin the other fleeing columns, he was now ordered to remain south of the river and act as a blocking force against any federal advances from that direction. He was to continue towards Amelia Courthouse, shielding Lee's retreat and the wagon trains carrying much needed equipment and ammunition. Thus, on April 3, 1865, Dick Anderson embarked on one of the most critical assignments of his long career. Failure meant exposing Lee's flanks to assaults that could sever the retreating procession or lead to the loss of the wagon trains, and ultimately to the destruction of the army. To check the probing Union forces and prevent that catastrophe, the former commander of the proud and robust First Corps now had at his disposal the broken remnants of Pickett's and Johnson's divisions, Hunton's intact brigade, and elements of Fitz Lee's cavalry, in all probably no more than 3,500 men. Over the next few critical hours as Lee's army north of the Appomattox struggled along roads churned to viscous mud and mire attempting to escape Grant's clutches, Dick Anderson and his small band of reliable fighters would fend off all Union attempts to reach Lee's columns before they consolidated at Amelia Courthouse. His success was of short duration, but was still among his finest hours as a soldier.[29]

In his subsequent report of the activities of his corps during those days of retreat, Anderson noted dryly on April 4 that his troops marched towards Amelia Courthouse and skirmished all day, but such scant adornment downplays his contribution to the army's preservation. Anderson had Pickett's brigades up by 4 AM and on the road soon after with nothing to eat but parched corn. Johnson's men followed by 8 AM, and all slogged westward on Bevil's Bridge Road away from the Appomattox crossing. When the column reached the intersection of Tabernacle Church Road, Union troops were discovered advancing northward along that thoroughfare threatening to sever Anderson's column, gain access to the road leading directly to Amelia Courthouse, or even expose Lee's retreating columns farther north on Goode's Bridge Road to disaster. Anderson quickly formed a line of battle facing south and spanning the intersection that was so crucial to preserving Lee's line of retreat. Throughout the day, his supply wagons filed slowly through the intersection on Bevil's Bridge Road to the sound of artillery fire while Pickett, Hunton, and Johnson's weary troops joined by some elements of Harry Heth's division skirmished with probing federal horsemen of Brigadier General Thomas C. Devin's First Cavalry Division. Devin's entire division with several regiments of dismounted troopers was unable to drive Anderson away from that vital juncture. The concerted attacks diminished to skirmishing lasting late into the evening. By 10 PM, Devin had withdrawn and headed westward to join George Custer's Third Cavalry Division at Jetersville. Anderson rested the men until 3 AM on April 5 before continuing towards Amelia Courthouse through another wet dawn.[30]

Arriving at Amelia Courthouse on April 4, Lee was unable to move on. He had hoped to resupply with food and ammunition there before moving south towards Danville and uniting with Joe Johnston's force in North Carolina. Lee's army remained badly strung out and separated with much of it still scattered on the roads between the Appomattox River and the Courthouse. Even if Lee had wanted to move south along the railroad that night to sweep aside the Union cavalry forming a barrier at Jetersville, he could not have done so. Not only was his army still widely dispersed, the anticipated commissary supplies he hoped to find at Amelia Courthouse were nowhere to be found. Meanwhile, Anderson's command was naturally among those troops delayed in arriving, in his case by the need to deploy in line of battle and skirmish with Union cavalry on the Tabernacle Church Road. His column was still four miles from the courthouse when it resumed marching again early on April 5. Anderson finally arrived at the army's rally point later that afternoon after resting near Tunstall's Station and allowing Mahone's division to pass by. Anderson's depleted corps, with Pickett now attached, passed between Hill's corps and Ewell's commands before pressing on towards Jetersville. Desperate for provisions, Lee now hoped to encounter them along the rail line from Danville. He pushed his army southward paralleling the Richmond and Danville railroad tracks in the direction of Burksville, anxiously anticipating a chugging trainload of supplies on its way to his relief. Instead, he found Sheridan's cavalry in his path with infantry coming up rapidly to block the route south. Lee judged the force too strong to assault. Pivoting westward at Amelia Springs, Lee headed towards Farmville where he hoped to find provisions sent from Lynchburg on the Southside Railroad.[31]

Anderson's wagons had preceded his infantry columns, arriving at Amelia in time to join other wagons headed on a safer northern route. Anderson was dismayed to note that, "the trains were put upon another road, but had not gone ten miles from the Court-House before they were captured and the Reserve Ordnance and Medical wagons all destroyed." Grant's army, spearheaded by constant probes from Sheridan's horsemen, was gradually tightening the noose around the fleeing Confederates. Nothing seemed to be going Lee's way, yet he and the army were not without hope.[32]

Anderson's corps, with Pickett in the lead and trailed by Johnson, plodded through the night behind Mahone's division, which was trudging along at the rear of Longstreet's First Corps. Longstreet interposed his wagon train between Mahone and Pickett for protection. Ewell came up behind Anderson followed by the army's remaining wagons while the Second Corps now under John Gordon and accompanied by Rooney Lee's cavalry provided the army's rear guard. The bottlenecks caused by the wagons' slow progress added to the men's exasperation. Tired, hungry, and soaking, the disgruntled Rebels endured the agonizing stops and starts that marked the snail's pace of progress on the route to Rice Station on the Southside Railroad. Another wet dawn on April 6 would be the harbinger of more misfortune on that most dreadful day for Lee's army.[33]

As the slow-moving columns entered the valleys created by two tributaries of the Appomattox River, the usual vulnerabilities of a retreating army on the march grew more pronounced. The rolling terrain bisected by Big and Little Sailor's Creeks lent itself readily to disorganization of the marching lines of men, guns, and wagons. Frequent probes on the left flank as Sheridan's troopers, riding on a road south of the Confederates, sought every opportunity to strike Lee's strung-out columns and the vulnerable wagon trains compounded the difficulties of geography and water crossings.[34]

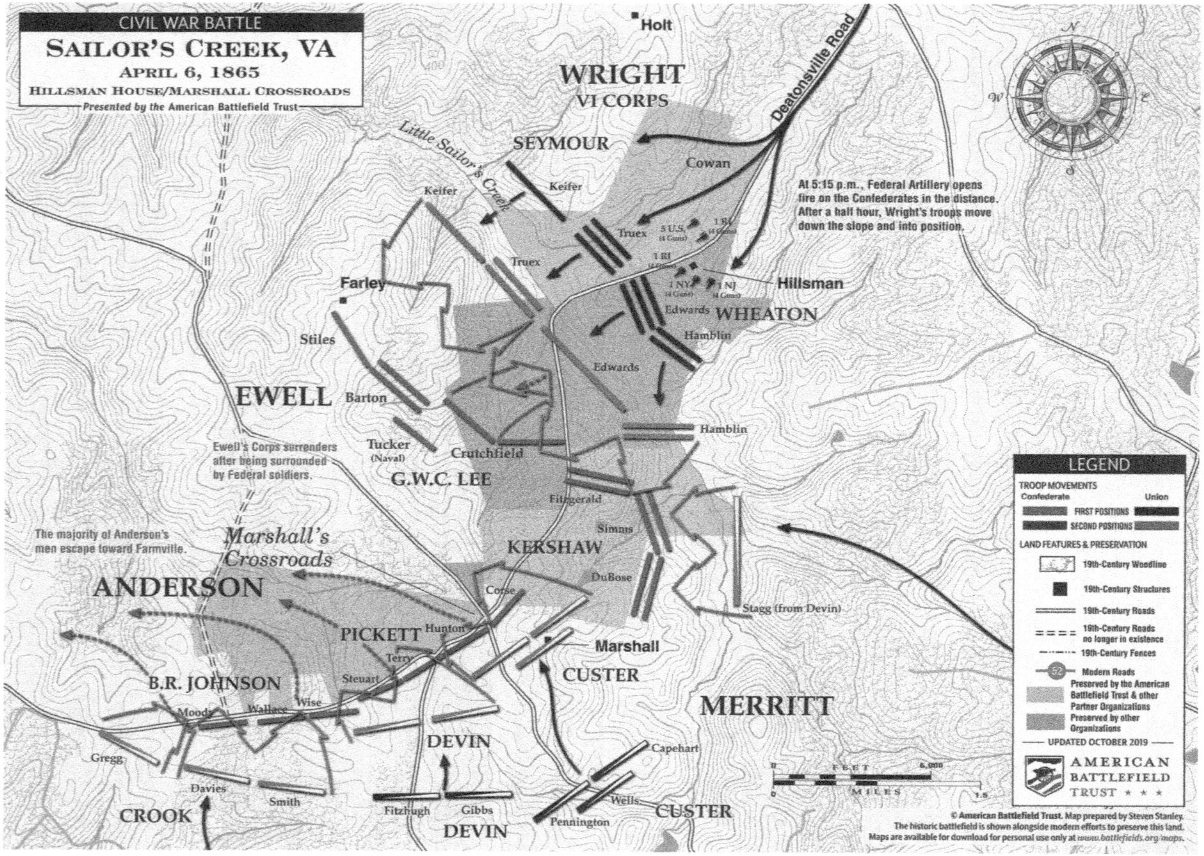

Figure 7. Map of the Battle of Sailor's Creek, showing Anderson's corps, April 6, 1865. Courtesy of the American Battlefield Trust.

Those hit and run assaults eventually led to the disaster that was to befall Lee's army that day. At an intersection known as Holt's Corner late on the morning of April 6, four regiments of Brigadier General Charles H. Smith's Union cavalry brigade threatened the left flank of the retreating columns where Johnson's rear connected with Major General Custis Lee's division of Ewell's troops. This caused Anderson to halt and deploy Johnson's men into a line of battle behind hastily assembled breastworks while Pickett reversed direction to aid him. The affair ultimately amounted to little more than a skirmish, but the disruption had a devastating impact on the integrity of Lee's columns. Anderson noted that the march that day had been "greatly impeded by wagon trains which still blocked up the road," and thus some gap must already have existed between the wagon train at Mahone's rear and Anderson's vanguard. Through either oversight or mischance, that situation worsened when no one notified Mahone that Anderson had been compelled to halt. It took little time for Mahone's troops to widen a gap between their column and Anderson's stationary position; a distance soon catastrophically extended to about two miles.[35]

Hunton's brigade, now in line on the right of Pickett's division, was positioned to observe Mahone's men and the wagons fading into the distance. Hunton informed Pickett, who then notified Anderson, "asking permission to move on after Mahone. But Gen. Anderson had been directed to hold on in connection with Ewell's command. Thus we delayed." Anderson had few options. He could not continue the march with the Yankees pressing his flank. Possibly as many as two or three hours elapsed by the time he thought it safe to continue on towards Marshall's Crossroads, but that delay permitted the arrival of Major General Horatio Wright's Sixth Corps, which was now approaching the rear of the Confederate column. Anderson rushed Pickett ahead across Little Sailor's Creek where Union horsemen had already fired on some of Longstreet's vulnerable wagons and fallen upon the fleeing artillery. Huger's First Corps artillery battalion bore the brunt, losing all its guns until Pickett drove off the Yankees and saved two of the valuable weapons. Meanwhile, Gordon sent word that the rear of the column was being "heavily pressed," and urged that they move forward more rapidly. In an effort to relieve the deadlock on the roads caused by the slow-moving wagon trains, Ewell most likely ordered the train that was following him to cut off at Holt's Corner on a less exposed northwesterly route nearer the Appomattox River. In yet another puzzling instance of miscommunication, no one informed Gordon that the intention was that only the wagons should take that route. In his ignorance, Gordon naturally followed the rolling column completely unaware that Ewell's infantry had continued straight ahead. Ewell's rear now lay exposed to the rapidly advancing infantry of the Sixth

Corps while Gordon continued to spar with pursuing troops from the Union Second Corps.[36]

Finding his progress blocked by a strong force of Union cavalry posted in a commanding position atop a ridge, Anderson was forced to fight an uphill battle to dislodge an estimated two divisions of horsemen. First, however, he conferred with Ewell and suggested two options—they could join forces and attempt to break through the Union force, or they could set off through the woods to their right and search out a road that would lead them to Farmville. Ewell preferred the latter course of action, but claiming ignorance of the geography, he deferred the decision to Anderson. Just at that point, Union infantry was discovered closing on Ewell's rear and preparing to attack. Anderson chose to attempt the breakthrough in front if Ewell would hold back the Yankees massing to their rear. Ewell obligingly faced east to form a line of battle that stretched across the road and ran parallel to Little Sailor's Creek, which lay about 300 yards to his front. There, without a single piece of artillery for support, he prepared to meet the attack of the Union Sixth Corps. With his men placed in a position of relative safety beyond the brow of a slight rise and protected to some degree from the Union artillery massed on the Hillsman Farm, which had opened fire sometime after 5 PM, Ewell rode off to see how Anderson was faring.[37]

Ewell had no sooner ridden away near 6 PM, when the federals poured down the slopes from the Hillsman Farm, struggled across swollen Little Sailor's Creek, and received a well-directed volley from the Rebel line that staggered them temporarily. Anderson had dispatched his aide, Captain Shannon, with a note encouraging Ewell's men to hold out a little longer as he had begun his own advance. Shannon found Kershaw instead of Ewell, who sent back an encouraging reply and continued to repulse the Union assaults.[38]

In the meantime, Johnson's division fell into line with Pickett's men and began skirmishing heavily with the bluecoats in their front. Wise, apparently without notifying Johnson, advanced two regiments that drove the Yankees from their commanding position on the crest of the hill. Johnson, who was then engaged on another part of the front, was unaware of Wise's success and did not order an advance of his entire line. From Anderson's perspective, however, it appeared that his troops were driving the enemy back. He quickly sent word to Johnson to advance. There came a delay while Johnson, still unaware of Wise's progress, argued that his troops were merely holding their own positions. Finally learning the facts, Johnson began to form his men for an assault on the federals south of the road leading to Rice's Depot, while Pickett formed on his left flank. Anderson, knowing the critical situation with Ewell's troops, urged Johnson to press the attack. Johnson moved forward with three of his brigades before halting to allow his fourth brigade to catch up. Pickett soon implored him to remain halted while he brought his men up onto Johnson's left. Unfortunately, Johnson had outdistanced Pickett's men and Yankees lost no time interposing themselves in the gap. With fire tearing into them from flank and rear, not only from Union carbines but also from the artillery on the Hillsman Farm, Johnson's rattled brigades broke and fled in an effort to escape the trap. Anderson, watching with Ewell but unable to observe the full extent of the rout, was soon informed that his troops had broken. He spurred his horse rapidly towards the battle while Ewell rushed back towards his own lines.[39]

Anderson ordered Pickett to withdraw "and try to cut his way out in any manner he could." Each time Pickett attempted to move, Union cavalry made another mounted charge and the men had to turn and fight. Wise received orders to pull back and "form at right angles to his [Pickett's] line." During that movement, Wise later claimed, "Pickett's whole command stampeded." On Wise's left flank, Wallace's brigade fled into the woods north of the road. Farther to the left, a small squadron of federal cavalrymen had gotten behind Pickett's line and was bearing down towards the general and his staff. A few men nearby checked the horsemen with a volley while Pickett and his staff "ducked their heads down by their horses' necks and galloped ingloriously to the rear." Other Confederates turned to face the Union troopers "and killed the last man of them."[40]

Regiments were retreating at the double-quick amidst the incessant musketry, cannonading, and yelling, recalled surgeon William Taylor from the 19th Virginia, one of Hunton's regiments. He thought the rapid retreat at first "remarkably orderly," as he "trotted along on foot . . . in reasonably good spirits. But presently a little unsteadiness manifested itself, which quickly became a decided wobble, and then, in a moment, as though it had exploded, the whole organization flew to pieces. It was a wonderful and startling sight. Those heroes of a hundred glorious fields had instantaneously lost their manliness and become reduced to the grade of a flock of terror stricken children." Taylor's account aptly captures the scene as men fled the onrushing Yankee cohorts. "And so we plunged along, puffing and blowing, enveloped in all the hideous noise of battle, helter-skelter, higgledly-piggledy, each for himself, God for nobody, and the devil take the hindmost—by the nine gods of war, I swear it was a mess."[41]

The scene unfolding before Anderson as these once proud elements of the army melted away under the staggering onslaught of Yankee arms must have brought home fully the realization that the game was finally up. It was apparent from the streaming lines of enemy troops on all fronts that Ewell had given way as well. With little to do in the face of such inordinate disarray, and with small chance of organizing a defense in the midst of an overwhelming disaster, Dick Anderson decided that surviving to fight another day was the most appropriate choice. Thus, he too put spurs to horse and fled the field along with Johnson and Pickett. It was a sad and ignominious end to a distinguished career for the stunned South Carolinian. Undoubtedly the indignity of it all would later embarrass him, and along with his reserved nature compel his hesitancy to ask much of his fellow veterans. His life henceforth would instead seem less a celebration of his contributions to the cause than atonement for his role in its final days.

Ewell, along with nearly all of his command, as Anderson had quickly surmised, had been taken prisoner, but Wise's men and portions of Wallace's Brigade made good their escape. On either end of the shattered Confederate line the men were more rapidly flanked and overwhelmed, compelling a more rapid and wholesale surrender. Nonetheless, scattered remains of Pickett's division along with remnants of Ransom's and Moody's Brigade got away. The corps' artillery batteries under Colonel Hillary P. Jones suffered just as badly, losing all fifteen of their remaining guns. Federals captured three brigadier generals, but five others escaped with their troops. Adding to Anderson's mortification was the fact that while over 1,500 of his men were abandoned to their fate and taken prisoner, nearly 3,300 fighting men remained to lay down their arms two days later at Appomattox Courthouse. Now, however, many of those men were scattered, disorganized, and weaponless, constituting little more than a rabble.[42]

The confusion that accompanied the retreat from the Richmond and Petersburg lines left many commanders of decimated elements of the army without a force to lead, while other units were detached from their normal organizational structure. Pickett's division, for example, had been isolated south of the Appomattox after Five Forks and thus fell under Dick Anderson's command. Similarly, Kershaw's division separated from the First Corps and fell under Ewell's command during the withdrawal. When A. P. Hill was killed on April 2, Longstreet assumed informal command of the Third Corps. Lee entrusted Hill's old corps to his most dependable subordinate rather than to the corps' most senior general officer, Harry Heth. With Pickett and Kershaw no longer with Longstreet, the added numbers from Hill's divisions would barely bring the vaunted First Corps to some semblance of full capacity. Perhaps Lee would have reorganized his remaining troops more efficiently had the army survived longer, but the most sensible thing for him to do amid the turmoil of those days was to utilize to best effect the men he most trusted. For Anderson, the near total collapse and disintegration of both Pickett's and Johnson's divisions at Sailor's Creek left him with so few troops to command that the battered remnants were more easily absorbed into viable units that remained intact. Pickett's few survivors fell in with Longstreet's corps, while Johnson's old division joined Gordon's Second Corps.[43]

According to General Mahone's memoir, Mahone rode to General Anderson after the disaster, and coming upon him "discovered at once that he had lost his heart in the cause. He was the picture, the sad picture of a man who was whipped." Mahone related the news that General Lee wished to see him, and when they reached him, Lee turned his head toward Anderson and "with severe emphasis" instructed him "'take command of these stragglers and go to the rear'—signaling his emphasis by a violent sling of his left hand." Recognizing his chief's anger and frustration as well founded, a dejected Anderson rode off to carry out Lee's order.[44] General Longstreet inserted a lengthy section of Mahone's memoir in his own book, *Mannasas to Appomattox*, which included Mahone's recollection of a much repeated quote from Lee as he observed the effects of the loss at Sailor's Creek: "My God! Has the army dissolved?" In a less than modest tone, Mahone boldly responded that his own troops were "ready to do their duty." Lee was then said to have replied: "Yes, General, there are some true men left. Will you please keep these people back." Longstreet, who admitted to knowing nothing of the events at Sailor's Creek until the next day, took Mahone's recollection at face value, but he pointedly declined to include Mahone's description of Lee's adverse reaction to Anderson's appearance. Instead, he noted that the "stand and fight" made by Ewell and Anderson "on that trying march were among the most soldier-like of the many noble deeds of the war."[45]

Anderson spent the next two days with other officers attempting to "get together the fragments of the command," but he succeeded only in finding between 150 and 200 of his men. He must have been aware that those of his troops who had remained together under General Wise were marching towards the safety of the Appomattox River at High Bridge. He did not consider them technically as stragglers to be gathered, and, given Lee's instruction, he did not join them and take command of the only element of his smashed corps still able to muster any resistance. On the morning of April 7, Lee instead ordered Wise to take command of all the stragglers from Bushrod Johnson's division, while a shame-faced Johnson sat his horse nearby within earshot of Lee's command. Wise, angry at Johnson's abandonment of the field at Sailor's Creek, gloated over his former chief's humiliation, which had been compounded by Lee's summary dismissal of Johnson with another curt wave of his hand immediately after the previous day's debacle. In the meantime, Mahone reached High Bridge and sought out Anderson, who had posted pickets there to halt stragglers. He found Anderson and Gordon nearby discussing the fate of the army. Both were of the opinion that the "army had gone so fully to pieces, that the time had come for surrender." Mahone agreed and the three decided that Anderson ought to go to Longstreet with their conclusions and suggest that he see Lee about the possibility of obtaining suitable terms of surrender. Anderson must have demurred under the circumstances, as he did not deliver that news to Longstreet, and William Nelson Pendleton later claimed he was the one chosen to approach Longstreet. The latter asserted in his memoirs that he did not agree when a delegation representing a number of senior officers represented by Pendleton took the proposal to General Lee, who proposed instead to fight on a while longer. That night a note arrived from General Grant initiating the correspondence that led to Lee's capitulation. Before that, however, Lee finally found time on the afternoon of April 8 to issue orders formally discharging Anderson, Pickett, and Johnson. Despite Lee's apparent ire, nothing in the written orders implied any censure of the men being relieved. Anderson wrote in his report fourteen months later that he had been "relieved from duty and directed to repair to my home or any other place I might select, and report there to the Secretary of War. Part of these orders providence has permitted me to execute and part has been suspended indefinitely." Anderson and Lee never again set eyes on one another, but if Lee's uncharacteristically harsh treatment of Anderson, Johnson, and Pickett at Sailor's Creek is any indication, he must have harbored some angry feelings towards them all. Those would dissipate over time, at least in Anderson's case. Their subsequent correspondence was marked by nothing but mutually friendly and cordial tones, and Anderson never spoke of Lee publicly in anything less than glowing terms. Pickett, who claimed not to have received Lee's dismissal order, remained with his troops, and upon seeing him, Lee is supposed to have remarked unkindly "I thought that man was no longer with the army."[46]

Thoroughly beaten in body and spirit, Dick Anderson voiced no complaint about his fate. He quietly accepted Lee's order to return to his home and set off immediately to comply with the final directions from the chieftain he had followed so faithfully for the past three years. Lee's army existed for only another day, laying down its arms on April 9, 1865. The wording of Lee's orders dismissing Anderson included the leeway for him to try to reach Johnston's force in North Carolina, where he might have been of some service, but there is no evidence that he undertook that course of action. In the event, Johnston's surrender came on April 26 and the war was truly at an end. Though he did not surrender at Appomattox with Lee's remaining band of stalwarts, Dick Anderson could at least console himself with the thought that his service entitled him to include himself in Lee's encomium to his vanquished soldiers when he told them that—"You will take with you the satisfaction that proceeds from the consciousness of duty faithfully performed."

Anderson, no matter his flaws, had faithfully performed his duties under Lee's command. His career as a soldier was now at an end. His war was over. A new one was poised to begin.[47]

An 1894 letter Longstreet wrote to his former staff officer Thomas Goree provides evidence of such a war, this one conducted with words. Longstreet, who despised John Gordon, added condemnation to that officer's conduct at Sailor's Creek and attributed the day's failure in part to Gordon's actions. Longstreet listed a litany of complaints before unfairly criticizing Gordon's "run of fourteen miles as rear guard on the day of Sailor's Creek, and quitting his duty as such, taking with him the artillery on that route, and leaving Ewell and Anderson without a gun, to take his duties as rear guard." Those comments illustrate the danger of many postwar evaluations, when tensions between former comrades sometimes ran higher than those between old adversaries. In the pages of their memoirs, and especially in the papers of the Southern Historical Society, former Rebels created more than just the tale of the Lost Cause. The lack of focus on a cause and the consequent absence of its former unifying tendencies led many former comrades to the cast off the kid gloves and give vent to long simmering resentments. There was, to be sure, conflict among the senior officers during the war itself, but that frequently took a back seat to the war effort. With that unifying element eliminated, veterans wielded words like a rapier. Men who struggled side-by-side frequently re-fought the war in writing, attempting to cast blame on others, display the superiority of their views and military acumen, and generally re-shape the history of the war to suit their agenda. Anderson's refusal to be drawn into the postwar debates illustrates his gentlemanly qualities, but such a complete withdrawal from the public arena also adds credence to possibility that as the war wound down, he simply wished to be done with it. Added to that is his humiliating loss at Sailor's Creek, which, if nothing else, illustrated the perils of a fighting withdrawal. One might also suspect that a man as modest as Anderson would view his actions, no matter how devoted and skillful at times, as the mere performance of his duties. It is likely his humility led him to conclude there was simply nothing to crow about, and his unpretentious report of the march to Spotsylvania is an example. Another man might have tried to make much more of those circumstances, billing themselves as the savior of Lee's army. Anderson, as always, was content with the knowledge that he had done his duty, which really *had* done much fortuitously to save Lee's army.[48]

Failures and struggle marked the ensuing years for Anderson, as it did for many in the war-ravaged South. His future mirrored the fate of his state, and his suffering rivaled that of its people as they all sought to find their way in a new world turned upside down. Outwardly, he would try his best to support his wife and children and to retrieve his family's fortunes, but one is tempted to ponder whether inwardly he felt keenly some personal need to atone for his role in bringing his homeland and the South to ruin and desolation. He had been a key military leader in the conflict undertaken to achieve independence. Instead, his efforts and those of his peers led to subjugation and misery. The humiliation of the war's final days could only have added to his desire for atonement, and all of that might have reinforced his natural reticence. Over time, accolades would again pour forth from his fellow South Carolinians, but for far too long a piercing silence would hold sway over his wounded spirit.

Chapter 19

Ruin and Reconstruction

For the history of the world will not tolerate intruders; it chooses its own heroes and implacably dismisses those not summoned to that rank, however hard they may try; someone who has fallen off the carriage of fate as it goes along will never catch up with it again.

—Stefan Zweig,
Twilight

In Camden, South Carolina, Mary Chesnut's "Sunday evening reception" of May 7, 1865 included Camden-born Samuel D. Shannon, who until recently had served on Dick Anderson's staff. The sometimes-petty Mrs. Chesnut held Shannon in low regard, once noting disdainfully that unlike the way her own husband removed his hat "grandly, like a prince of the blood," Shannon doffed "his hat like a footman." That night, however, she listened achingly and noted in her diary that Shannon had "seemed sulky—grey & dressed to death" as he "gave a painful account of Pickett's division & Bushrod Johnson—under Dick Anderson" at Sailor's Creek.[1]

Within days of that reception, word spread of former Confederate President Jefferson Davis's capture in Georgia. Mary Chesnut, Anderson's boyhood acquaintance, seemed unprepared to relinquish her embrace of the Confederate cause and had little empathy for those too quick to forsake it, writing, "We heard of Jeff Davis's capture. Fighting Dick Anderson, and [Brigadier General] Stephen Elliott of Fort Sumter memory are quite ready to pray for Andy Johnson and submit to the powers that be. But not so our belligerent clergy. 'Pray for people when I wish they were dead?' cries Mr. [Richard S.] Trapier. 'No! Never! But I will pray for President Davis till I die.'" Mary's sentiments leaned towards those of the Reverend Trapier, and she was clearly not "in such a hurry to be Yankee*ecised*."[2]

In the aftermath of war, Anderson eschewed public life and turned his attention to the salvation of his family's plantation. Out of necessity, he focused primarily on providing for his family, and as he had no other opportunities, he could do so only by farming. It was, however, a time of much uncertainty for southern landowners. Before committing to planting and incurring expenses in that effort, it was necessary to seek resolution on a number of pressing issues regarding land ownership and labor conditions. Such was the level of uncertainty that John B. Irving, a Charleston District planter, wrote to Brigadier General John P. Hatch, commanding the Northern District, Department of the South, in June 1865 to inquire as to whether his land still belonged to him. That issue that would not be resolved until President Andrew Johnson's September 1865 mandate that former Confederates who satisfied the requirements for pardon were to have their lands returned to them. Many of the issues raised by Irving were those that to some degree plagued other former enslavers. While many formerly enslaved persons were cautious and calculated that remaining in familiar circumstances was in their best interest, emancipation set many freedmen in motion in search of family members, better working conditions, or a separation from the familiar surroundings they now equated disdainfully with their former status. Did persons unknown to the plantation owner have a right to come onto the plantation and settle there, Irving inquired? What power did the owner have to compel unwanted persons to leave? Some freedmen declined to work, Irving complained, but he was uncertain what recourse he had to force them to do so, or to leave his property altogether. Planters were required under threat of penalty to sign contracts with formerly enslaved workers, but Irving thought the freedmen were under no such threat if they refused to sign. If they did work, expectations for the number of hours per day the freedmen could labor were unclear. Those details had to be satisfactorily resolved before the successful implementation of a workable labor system. For former high-ranking Confederate officers like Richard Anderson, however, it was first imperative to resolve the issue of a pardon and to relieve those individuals of their personal anxieties over their ability to function as full citizens.[3]

One of the state's other prominent general officers, Wade Hampton, faced similar concerns, and he too would soon face bankruptcy with debt exceeding a million dollars. Hampton, however, inserted himself back into public life almost immediately, devoting his energies to politics and embracing a leadership role in the state's and the South's post-bellum affairs. Realizing that salvaging any of their former rights would require every citizen's "statesmanship" and "patriotism," Hampton publicly called on his fellow ex-Confederates to take the oath of allegiance to the United States. "I invoke my fellow citizens—especially those who have shared with me the perils and the glories of the last four years—to stand by our State manfully and truly." Anderson's views on the matter remained private, but he needed no urging to come to the same conclusion for himself. On July 17, 1865, ten days before Hampton's public plea, and less than three months after the surrender of Joe Johnston's army in North Carolina effectively ended hostilities in the East, Anderson wrote to President Johnson, to whom it was necessary to appeal directly for pardon because of having been a general officer in the

Confederate Army. He provided the rationale supporting his application, asserting above all that his resignation from the US Army was not treasonous. In his mind, his resignation and its acceptance released him from his oath of loyalty to the Constitution—"First, although I was an officer of the U.S. Army, my resignation was duly tendered to Mr. Buchanan & accepted by him. Secondly, I acknowledge the defeat of the South and yield without animosity or vindictiveness to the final decision of the sword. Thirdly, I accept the consequences of the defeat & yield the question which led to the strife. Fourth, I am ready to enter upon the new order of affairs in good faith and with earnest, hopeful spirit." A letter to President Johnson from a friend in Carlisle, Pennsylvania followed in early August and supported Anderson's application for pardon. That writer was "convinced Mr. Anderson went into the Rebellion with reluctance, urged by the circumstances which surrounded him, and however little justice there was in his conclusions, his parental regard dictated the result."[4]

That astonishing, though admittedly self-serving, statement supports the notion that in the years leading to the outbreak of the conflict Anderson struggled with his conscience, influenced by familial devotion on one hand and loyalty to his oath and his Pennsylvania relations on the other. The writer, however, was actually "more anxious" for Anderson's pardon "on account of his lovely wife, who is the daughter of my old and esteemed friend Chief Justice Gibson . . . and whose anxiety renders her unhappy. I have seen Mrs. Anderson here lately," the writer continued, "and that with a letter from Mr. Anderson, satisfies me that he will heartily cooperate with the Administration in the restoration of his State." Anderson subsequently swore allegiance and took an oath at Sumter on August 24, 1865. He was described then as being of "dark complexion, dark hair, grey eyes; . . . five feet seven inches high, aged 44 years; by profession a Planter." That, at least, was his intended profession, and he would make a game attempt at it before forsaking the difficult work. To begin anew, Anderson also sought to make matters right with his state after taking the oath of allegiance to the United States.[5]

Writing to provisional Governor Benjamin F. Perry on September 5, 1865, he acknowledged "the defeat of the South, and being resolved to abide by the consequences of the defeat and to give earnestly and hopefully my adherence and cooperation to the new order of affairs I am desirous of returning to my allegiance to the Government of the United States." Perry originally held anti-secession views that he laid aside once South Carolina took its fatal step in December 1860, and President Johnson appointed him governor on the strength of his former unionist sentiments and despite his adamantly racist beliefs. Anderson had learned well from his classes in ethics at West Point, which schooled him in Blair's *Rhetoric* and Paley's *Moral*

Philosophy. The former strove to teach him the invaluable use of rhetoric as a means to social advancement. He therefore had learned to wield the pen eloquently and persuasively, and he had done so throughout his career. To the Enlightenment theories of utilitarianism espoused by William Paley, Anderson owed his grounding in morality and a sense of political obligation. For those reasons, it seems unlikely that his letters seeking pardon and voicing a desire to be reconciled with his country were anything less than heartfelt and genuine. He must have looked to the future with an "earnest, hopeful spirit" as he settled down to await the government's final determination about his status.[6]

Anderson's October 1865 letter to Major Thomas Mills, formerly of his staff, provides further evidence of his sincerity. "Have you made your application for pardon?" he asked Mills. "I made mine long ago but have heard nothing from it yet. I will go to planting—upon the wreck of my father's estate and upon a plantation which my brother McKenzie left me. But I can do nothing until I get a pardon. I am not despondent-and with God's blessing hope to live to see the day when I can say that all has happened for the best. At any rate since we are beaten I accept the results and am resolved to give the new order of affairs an unprejudiced and earnest trial. Then if I find the change intolerable I will quit the country." Later, his economic situation would become so dire that he would at least entertain a chimerical flirtation with the idea of relocating to California. For the present, he was determined to press ahead with his plans to revive the plantation.[7]

Anderson's course of action at the outset of the sectional strife could have been no different than it was, however. Raised a proud South Carolinian and steeped in the masculine southern ideals of chivalry and honor, he could not have turned his back on his family or his native state, and least of all on his father, from whom he stood to inherit around 2,000 acres of property that included a stately home and nearly 150 enslaved persons. By 1865, the family's capital investment in enslaved persons was gone, as were all investments in Confederate bonds. Confederate money itself was valueless, but in 1860, practical considerations as well as ideals guided his personal behavior and shaped his character.

Tempering the youthful influence of the era's immensely popular Walter Scott novels with a careful reading of Cervantes's *Don Quixote*, however, would have served him better. In *Don Quixote* one finds a protagonist whose chivalric flights of fancy stemmed from having lost his grip on reality after reading too avidly about knights-errant, consequently leading to his many misadventures. Anderson, as well as countless other young southerners, could have drawn valuable lessons from the fate of the binge-reading knight of the woeful countenance. Instead, conceptions of chivalry and honor reinforced by Scott's characters bred in many southerners a prickliness that arose whenever their homes and their peculiar institution fell under criticism. Anderson rejected ostentatious displays of southern masculinity, however. There is no evidence that he ever engaged in duels or in any physical violence over points of honor with the single exception of his being provoked to challenge Nathaniel Lyon, though he was quick to wield his pen in defense of his integrity. While Anderson certainly adopted the best characteristics of gentlemanly and chivalric behavior in his personal life, he also adopted to some degree—consciously or unconsciously—the southerner's usual sensitivity to criticisms of Dixie and its ways, perhaps, enhanced by the atmosphere in his boyhood home and his sense of filial devotion. Such sentiment naturally reinforced the devotion he felt to his native state, to his family, and to the way of life he knew best. If his heart was not entirely committed to the Confederacy, and if he agonized over the decision to resign his commission from the US Army, all his misgivings fell away for a time as he threw in his lot with the war of the rebellion. He saw it as his duty to do so, but he reflected on his interpretation of duty with thoughtful sincerity. Doubts resurfaced from time to time, affecting his moods and adding to his melancholy tendencies, and even influencing the effort and energy he devoted to his duties. In any matter of faith, however, whether in God or in a cause, the most vital attribute is the ability to overcome doubts and persist in one's beliefs. His record as a Confederate officer illustrates that Anderson most assuredly strove to do so. In 1865, he embraced a new belief—that he could be a successful planter.

Anderson's younger brother, Wallace, ended his military service in Columbia, South Carolina, as "Medical Inspector with Superintendence of Vaccination of the Armies, Hospitals and Camps of Instruction of the Confederate States." He likewise returned to his stepmother's home in Stateburg along with his wife, Mary Virginia (Jennie). She would later play a major role in salvaging the family home, but in 1865, Dick and Wallace set about attempting to transform themselves from military men to plantation owners. In Wallace's case, his career as a planter would have been only a part-time endeavor as he had his medical skills to rely on as well. At some point after his return, he rented Acton, a nearby plantation home. Dick was the primary manager of the original Anderson plantations at Riverton and Hiwassee as a result.[8]

After coordination with the military authorities of the Freedmen's Bureau in September 1865, Dick and Wallace duly entered into "Articles of Agreement" with "the Freedmen and Women of their plantation." The

Freedmen's Bureau, established in March 1865 under the War Department was woefully short-staffed and underfunded for the first eighteen months of its existence. It at first provided immediate assistance to many in the form of necessities like food and clothing, but it also oversaw all other matters related to formerly enslaved persons. The Bureau's policies and oversight addressed at least some of the questions raised that summer by planters such as John Irving, but the relationship between former enslavers and freedmen remained fluid and chaotic. The records from the Anderson plantation indicate that the Union officer who represented the Bureau received a small fee to negotiate the articles of agreement for Anderson's laborers. The articles stipulated that freedmen would continue, "to reside upon and devote their labor to the cultivation of the Plantation . . . and conform to such reasonable and necessary plantation rules and regulations as they may prescribe." Some of the restrictions included not keeping a gun or pistol, not leaving the plantation without permission, avoiding drunkenness, and conducting themselves in an orderly, quiet manner. In addition, they could not leave the plantation without the permission of their employer. A Provost Court or a Military Commission would adjudicate any deviations from the contract, and workers dismissed from the plantation forfeited their claims to a percentage of the crop. As recently as 1863, over 160 enslaved persons labored for their father. While some may have viewed the proximity of Union troops as an opportunity to escape slavery, most remained on or near the Anderson plantation. Though Union troops passed very near during the final months of the war, none disturbed the Anderson home as General William T. Sherman's army marched through the state.[9]

Later, however, on April 9, 1865, the day of Lee's surrender, Union troops commanded by Brigadier General Edward Potter faced off against a small local militia force at Dingle's Mill, about three miles south of Sumter. Potter's larger force drove the militia back and continued on to Camden, returning along the King's Highway past Stateburg and skirmishing with Confederate troops along the way. Fighting at Beech Creek just a short distance north of the Anderson home in Stateburg marked the end of hostilities on April 19. Possibly as many as ten thousand Upcountry enslaved persons trailed Sherman's army in hopes of freedom, and it was claimed that as many as five thousand followed in Potter's wake, but most realized the war was nearly over and did not abandon homes where, "although they sowed as slaves [that spring], they stood to reap on other terms." Eighty-five of the now free persons on the Anderson plantations affixed their mark to the contract that fall. The arrangement at face value appeared suitable to all, and many of those who signed the agreement had lived on the plantation for generations and established deep ties to the place. Some undoubtedly hoped the federal government eventually would give them some of the land they had worked.[10]

The Andersons appear to have continued their father's practice and gone a step further than required in attempting to appease the freedmen who agreed to work on their plantation. Sometime during the construction of the plantation outbuildings and his doctor's office, their father built a pisé structure adjacent to the Homestead that served as a schoolhouse. Later, probably early in 1855, Dr Anderson built additional pisé structures, including quarters, at Riverside Plantation where the majority of enslaved people lived. In March 1855, Dick's sister Mary wrote to Wallace with the news that she and her parents had ridden "up to the plantation . . . to see the pisé cottages and they are very good & the negroes very comfortable." Although antebellum state laws proscribed education for the enslaved, the staunchly religious senior Dr. Anderson encouraged church attendance and Bible study among his workers. It is likely that training for the enslaved was limited to reading instruction, which was permissible under the laws. The brothers retained a teacher to instruct the plantation children as the records from Riverside Plantation indicate they paid seventy-five cents per month for each pupil enrolled. The cost in June 1866 amounted to $29.35 including a one-dollar book and a four-dollar miscellaneous "purchase." Mr. K. E. Knott, likely the teacher, appended a note to that record stating that he would send a monthly list "of the freed people as also the amt for which they have drawn on you, and which you have accepted." It is not clear how Knott was paid, but the amount drawn on the plantation account by the freedmen would be deducted from their share of the crop. They were not supplying an education at no cost, and it further complicated plantation administration, but it held benefits for Anderson and the freedmen alike.[11]

The contract permitted the Andersons to deduct expenses prior to distributing a portion of the crop to the workers. For each work animal used exclusively in cultivating crops, they deducted seventy-five bushels of corn. They also subtracted the amount of cotton equal to the cost of bagging and rope for baling. Cotton seed was to remain the property of the plantation. After making those deductions, the Andersons were to allocate one-half of the remaining cotton, corn, rice, peas, potatoes, wheat, and any other crops to the freedmen. In addition to furnishing "necessary medical care" for the freedmen, women, and children, a general stipulation open to broad interpretation called for them to be "treated in a manner consistent with their freedom." With the labor agreement already proscribing a number of rights normally held by free persons, it is unclear precisely what that statement might have meant, but one possibility is that former enslavers were no longer free to apply corporal punishment. There is no direct evidence of that happening on the Anderson plantations, but it was a common complaint made to the Freedmen's Bureau.[12]

The experience on John Frierson's plantation on nearby Pudding Swamp provides an illustration of the process of enlisting the freedmen for labor. Frierson called for the freedmen on his plantation to gather in front of his house. Standing on his piazza with the labor contract in his hand, he addressed them in a brief speech explaining the purpose and contents of the contract and expressing his hope that, though they were now free to leave if they wished, they would remain and continue "to work and behave yourselves." If they did so, he told them, they would share in a percentage of the harvest on January 1, 1866. Most of the contracts signed between freedmen and former enslavers stipulated that the workers receive a percentage of the crop as settlement, though house servants and skilled laborers typically negotiated cash payments. Though such arrangements were not ideal, they began to instill some order and stability to both the agricultural system and the method of hiring servants for the home. With the assistance of the Freedmen's Bureau, male plantation owners hiring field hands had a distinct advantage over the women in their households. Enslavers and their overseers had kept records of plantation matters that left them better prepared to maneuver in the new free labor economic conditions, and Dick and Wallace Anderson undoubtedly referred to those records as a first step to understanding the operation of their father's plantation and establishing reasonable expectations for their hired laborers. Their stepmother and their wives, however, very likely found themselves at first performing many of the household tasks formerly carried out by enslaved women. Wallace's wife Jennie had grown up with both free and enslaved servants in her home, and since her marriage had continued to rely either on enslaved workers or both. Dick Anderson's wife Sallie had also grown up with free servants in her Pennsylvania home, and in the years since her marriage, she too had grown accustomed to enslaved helpers. Nonetheless, they were all unprepared to negotiate the requirements of their new roles as employers of freedwomen in the positions of cooks, cleaners, washers, and nursemaids. Some freedwomen chose to embrace the tangible evidence of their freedom by abandoning their former enslavers. Mary Chesnut noted succinctly in her diary that June, "The black ball is in motion. Mrs. DeSaussure's cook shook the dust off her feet and departed from her kitchen today, free, she said. The washerwoman packing to go." But whether the formerly enslaved remained or departed, conditions changed. Employers of freedwomen now had to consider market conditions such as how much a servant might charge, expectations about the exact tasks to be done, and their availability and working hours. Former mistresses generally had no records or paper trail to guide them in negotiating those things, while freedwomen who had been performing those tasks knew precisely how much time it took to do them and could set the value of their labor accordingly.[13]

While over half of the original workforce on the Anderson plantations signed the labor agreement in 1865, the whereabouts of the remainder is unknown. Perhaps many had shaken the dust from their feet like Mrs. DeSaussure's cook, while others might have remained idling in the area until they saw how events unfolded. Officers representing the Freedmen's Bureau in Orangeburg District, which adjoined Sumter District south of the Santee River, noted in June 1865 that, "it is found very difficult to disabuse the negroes of the false and exaggerated ideas of freedom they have received. . . . They have been led to expect that all the property of their former masters was to be divided out to them; and the most reasonable fancy which prevails, is that besides receiving their food, clothes, the free rent of houses and gardens, and the privilege of keeping their hogs and poultry, they are to take for themselves all day Saturday and Sunday and to receive half the crops." With inadequate numbers of mounted troops, Bureau officials were unable to cover the long distances in the departments, and the Bureau's judicial boards could therefore investigate only a small number of complaints brought by freedmen and former enslavers. This, thought a captain serving as Chairman of the Orangeburg Commission on Contracts, also led to "an alarming increase of vagrancy throughout the country, and the idleness, halfway work, and turbulence of a large portion of the negro population." Some planters resorted to a return to previous norms and the captain further noted that, "in districts remote from our posts of occupation the plantation discipline still prevails, and cases of flogging and shooting are continually brought to the notice of the Commission. . . ."[14]

Conditions thus remained volatile, but the Bureau's officers attempted condescendingly to convey to the freedmen the meaning of their new independence. In one standard speech, they were told that the only difference they could discern "between slavery and freedom, is that neither you nor your children can be bought or sold." Officers encouraged no rosy picture of a future life of ease. "You may have a harder time this year than you have ever had before; it will be the price you pay for your freedom." Officials warned them not to think of leaving the plantation "where you belong." They would find no work in Charleston, for example, and nothing to eat.[15]

Sumter District experienced similar difficulties. There, in the late summer of 1865, the officer commanding the district noted that around two-thirds of the freedmen there anticipated receiving land as compensation, and many assumed it would be the land they had worked in slavery. He seemed unable to change their minds on that point. "'I have been about the district' he explained, 'and done all that is in my power to do away with the expectation, but I no sooner get back than there is another story started.'" Those freedmen declining to labor for the Andersons might have been ill disposed towards the labor contract's terms of employment as a fulfillment of emancipation's promises—real or imagined.[16]

With Freedmen's Bureau agents haranguing them to work and behave, strictures on their supposed freedom, and the prospect of laboring in the same fields with little improvement in their overall condition, it is no wonder that discontent was rampant. One can imagine that in the summer of 1865, formerly enslaved workers expected at least to reap the rewards of their supplemental labor attached to their own gardens that they planted in spring, the livestock they raised, and other commodities they created. Even under the pre-emancipation gang labor system, expectations were for around ten hours' work daily. Evenings, Sundays, and holidays were frequently devoted to supplemental activities, which often resulted in production of a marketable surplus. Many enslavers encouraged subsistence production by allowing designated time for the cultivation of a local food crop that added substantially to the variety of workers' diets and relieved the enslaver of the obligation to supply such foodstuffs. Longstanding habits and customs in that regard often instilled some sense of entitlement that mitigated the enslaver's total dominance of their lives and provided the enslaved with a vague impression of independent ownership and control over that small aspect of their lives. After emancipation, most former enslavers carried on with those traditions, but it raised uncertainty about actual ownership of land and livestock that added to the confusion of the post-bellum situation.[17]

Dick and Wallace Anderson had to borrow money to make a start at planting, but turbulent events soon overwhelmed the inexperienced farmers. To start with, the family was already in debt, and in December 1865, Wallace had to post a $5,275 bond to satisfy a single debt owed by his father's estate to the estate of his father-in-law, Judge Thomas Waties. Poor weather, drought, and strained labor conditions hindered good results and pushed the plantation further into debt. Results of the first post-bellum harvest were disappointing throughout the state, further discouraging disappointed freedmen who reaped little from their labor and grew increasingly reluctant to enter into new labor agreements. In the meantime, the state legislature had enacted a series of laws termed the "Black Code," which sought to restrict Freedmen's rights and reassert a white supremacist tone to social and labor relations. This not only led to further discontent among freedmen, it provoked northerners who were already opposed to President Johnson. Within two years, Dick Anderson was beginning to show signs of despair as debt mounted and successful harvests eluded them. In the summer of 1867, the brothers' trust in their labor source was betrayed, first through the workers' absence from the fields at a critical time, and then for more odious reasons. "At last, when corn and cotton began to ripen," Anderson complained to his friend D. H. Hill, "a system of bare faced, indiscriminate plundering of the field commenced and much of the little which we were going to make had been stolen already. We are about finished I suspect." Contributing to the unreliability of some workers was the perceived diminished value of the freedmen's labor, as well as the indelible memories tying cotton to slavery. Freedmen often received less in wages than former masters had paid owners for rental of their slaves. In addition, cotton passed out of the freedmen's hands into the larger economy rather than into their mouths like the food crops so badly needed for their support. Moreover, many enslaved workers felt shortchanged because of the poor harvests in the previous two seasons, believing they had not received compensation commensurate with the amount of work necessary to grow the crops. In this case, Anderson did not specify whether the "plundering" was done by his own workers or by other freedmen who were not employed at his plantation. If the former, it could have been the case that previous years' crop failures frightened the laborers into seizing usable or marketable crops sooner than Anderson planned in an effort to at least get something out of the work they performed and recoup past shortages. If the latter, it was unfortunate that those who labored diligently were cheated out of fair compensation. In any case, the severe drought that summer followed by excessive rainfall created tension that led some white landowners to drive freedmen from their lands without pay, or sent forth freedmen of their own volition off in search of other work. The agricultural conditions in the state were as unstable as they had been in the spring of 1865, and the impact on the Andersons was marked as they fell increasingly into debt.[18]

As November turned the fields to brown in 1867, Dick Anderson's gloomy pensiveness was evident. Writing to Hill, he woefully expressed his desire to see his "dear, good friend," but "unless you can come here, I see not any prospect of our meeting." Anderson thought even his trusted old warhorse was similarly dispirited. "I am unable to move any further from home than my old black horse can carry me and he grows so dejected and hangs his lower lip to so melancholy a length when I make him go more than three or four miles from his stable that I fear if I undertook to travel much further upon him he would insist on my doing so on my own legs and not upon his." Anderson's dire condition was evident in the example provided by his horse, which derived "small comfort and very short rations" at the stable to which he seemed so attached. Anderson felt trapped in his current predicament. He plaintively described his circumstances as similar to that of watching a beetle, snug inside a dry log suddenly cast onto a campfire. Though the insect emerges and sees the danger that surrounds it, it runs back into its familiar home only to perish in the smoke and flames. "And you have wondered that the poor infatuated, stupid beast did not run off by the end of the log and fly from certain destruction into the broad forest where there were plenty of old logs and good homes." Anderson too would have moved, but he told his friend despairingly, "I cannot get away! . . . Ruin and destruction stare me in the face and yet I cannot fly."[19]

Anderson's despair was not complete, however, and he did plan a move, but only from his stepmother's home to his own plantation at Hiwassee a few miles distant. There, he would be giving "up almost every comfort . . . for there is but a poor and incommodious house on the place." He believed the move to be essential and intended to persist in planting for another year. "It will be my last effort," he told Hill. "If I fail next year then I must truly cease to be like an infatuated bug, and must act like a rational creature—fly from the burning home and seek a new one in the 'wide wide world.'" Anderson's sentiments illustrate his close relationship with Hill, so critical to him at that time when failure loomed. He found it "cheering and comforting in times like these to receive assurances of undiminished love and regard. Be assured that it is no small comfort to me to know that I have your love," he told Hill.[20]

Other than his correspondence with Lee and D. H. Hill, Anderson kept mostly to himself for the first few years of his new civilian life. Within three months of the surrender at Appomattox, however, Lee sent a cordial letter to Anderson indicating that he wished to ensure "the bravery and devotion of the army of N. Va. be correctly transmitted to posterity." To that end, Lee planned to compile a complete history and sought missing reports of battles. Many reports had been lost or destroyed shortly before the army reached Appomattox. Lee asked him to forward copies of any reports he had, or those he was able to reconstruct from memory, along with duplicates of Lee's orders or other correspondence. He was particularly interested in Anderson's operations covering April 1–9, 1865. Anderson obligingly reconstructed the report, pointedly ending it on April 8, the day he was relieved of command with Lee's army. His response to Lee followed the trend of his lackadaisical administrative efforts in the army, however, and he did not send his completed report until June 1866, although he solicited information from his former staff officer Major Thomas Mills as early as October 1865. "My Dear General," he began his cover letter, "I am at last able to give you some account of the operations of the troops which I commanded," though he had to admit immediately that he had no papers to refer to and "relied upon my memory for the strength of my command at different times & its losses." He promised continued efforts to obtain more information and concluded by relaying Mrs. Anderson's sincere thanks "for your kind remembrance of her and your friendly message and unites cordially with me in wishing you and your family good health prosperity and every blessing." If there was lingering resentment over his dismissal, the courteous Dick Anderson had clearly put them aside, signing, "I am with true regard and respect Your Obt. Servt & friend."[21]

Though he maintained cordial relations with Lee, he never asked his former chief for anything. Jubal Early, however, whom Lee removed from command near the end of the war, requested recommendations attesting to his conduct while under Lee's command. Anderson, despite his genuinely friendly feelings of admiration and respect for his former chief, never sought to capitalize on that friendship and instead struggled unaided in the immediate postwar years. Even Sallie eventually grew bitterly frustrated with her husband's humility, which she viewed as a flaw in his character. As their fortunes declined, she complained to her son late in 1870 that despite his father's "uncommon talents and excellent head and heart and good education, [he] still is no more able to make his way in life than an infant six months old, and all from excessive modesty, delicacy and want of self assertion."[22]

Around March 1868, Anderson received a letter from Hill inquiring as to how affairs stood then and whether he might be interested in relocating to California. Hill mentioned he was departing soon on a trip that would span several months, so Anderson did not respond for some time. He did not see how he could go to California then, "as circumstances seemed to tie me down to this place." A subsequent letter to Hill in January 1869 restated that conclusion. He added that he had been living on his own plantation and "entertained some hope that my presence might do something towards restraining the stealing and plundering and securing more diligent attention on the part of the Negroes. My expectations in these respects have been totally disappointed and I have to record a third year's complete and disastrous failure in my crops. This winds up the business for me," he sadly informed his friend. He could see no other prospects for success "under the present system, or anything like it." It was time, he said, "to seek for some other mode of making my bread." He was then wrapping up his affairs at home, and as soon as he concluded that, he intended to "set out in search of something to do and better luck." Still, the thought of moving west seemed appealing, if only a dream. "California runs in my head in various enticing views" he told Hill, "and if I can scrape the means of migrating so far I think it not unlikely I may be found somewhere on the Western slopes of the Rocky Mountains before the end of the year."[23]

It was not to be, however, and Anderson remained in South Carolina, appearing on the 1870 Federal Census records enumerated on June 16 in Sumter Township with an occupational title of "Ex Rebel General." His real estate holdings were valued at $7,000 but his personal estate was valued at only $500. Living with him at that time was his wife Sallie, listed as "Keeping House," and his son and daughter. Richard was by then eighteen and listed as a "Civil Engineer." Young Sallie, at twelve, was "Attending School." Anderson and his family relocated to the town of Sumter sometime in early March 1870, and he was elected soon afterwards as a warden and one of two delegates to the Diocesan Convention for the Episcopal Church of the Holy Comforter on North Main Street. A Charleston newspaper reported that he traveled to Clarendon Courthouse in May, "owing to an interest connected with the South Carolina Central Railroad." The notice was otherwise vague about precisely what the "interest" was, and the reporter apparently thought readers would be more interested in knowing that the General was "looking well and appears to be in excellent health."[24]

Anderson began to reappear at public functions, dutifully attending public events and taking on a role commensurate with his stature in Sumter except that he persisted in avoiding political affairs. On a hot July day in 1870, for example, he stood next to the Bishop of Charleston and read the program during the "Distribution Exercises" of St Joseph's Academy, a girls' boarding school run by the Catholic Sisters of Mercy. Earlier that spring he was elected warden at Sumter's Episcopal Church of the Holy Comforter as well as delegate to the diocesan convention. Now distanced from the idea of planting, Anderson began to seek opportunities to build a new career, which exposure through public engagements might assist. His reputation as the state's most senior former military officer would begin to play a role in his search. By September, he was back in Charleston staying at the stately Classic Revival-style Charleston Hotel. Near the end of that month, he visited Cincinnati to attend the city's Grand Industrial Exposition as a representative of the South Carolina Railroad, indicating that he must have secured some official position with the rail line by that time. With him were a number of other prominent Charleston residents representing the Chamber of Commerce, Board of Trade, Agricultural Society, and the South Carolina Institute.[25]

Anderson also began to associate with war veterans and others befitting his social status in Charleston. "The State Survivors' Association" in Charleston elected him first vice-president in November 1869. Wade Hampton was president. The Association meeting ended with a dinner and series of toasts, one of which was to "The Army of Northern Virginia." A rousing "rebel hurrah," followed, and Dick Anderson's brother Wallace "made an eloquent response to the toast." A year later, Anderson was seated on the platform along with former members of Lee's staff, as well as General James Conner, Colonel C. Irvine Walker—who would become Anderson's first biographer—and Major Edward N. Thurston of Dick's staff, when a meeting was held at the city's Hibernian Hall to honor Lee's memory. Lee had died peacefully in Lexington, Virginia five days earlier. Anderson was called upon to make remarks, and his esteem for Lee was evident. "Since the day of the Father of our Country," he said, "no man has arisen whose fame and whose deeds have shed so splendid a luster upon the land of his nativity." He extolled Lee's exceptional physical appearance, deeming it to be "as nearly as possible to the perfect man." Moreover, he advocated as "a lamp and a guide to ourselves, and to our posterity throughout all generations," the memory of Lee's "Christian virtues [and] the emulation of his blameless example," Anderson's remembrance of his personal embarrassment at Sailor's Creek and Lee's frustrated, peremptory dismissal of him there had faded quickly from his mind.[26]

Anderson's efforts to begin anew in Charleston were haunted by the recent past however. A judgment issued in a common pleas court case brought against both Dick and Wallace Anderson by several creditors marred the Christmas season of 1870. On the first Monday in January 1871, the court ordered the sale of Dick Anderson's 1,900-acre Hiwassee Plantation at a public auction held at the courthouse in Sumter. His attorneys filed bankruptcy paperwork with the district court within weeks. The inventory of personal property by then sadly consisted of clothing for himself and his family valued at only $100, and the sword presented by the state of South Carolina, also valued at $100. His accumulated debts were simply insurmountable. In 1867, he had borrowed $7,000 from a private individual, William Roberts, a civil engineer from New York. Anderson secured the loan through a lien on real estate, most likely Hiwassee, to which he held life rights, after which it was to pass on to young Richard in conformance with Mackenzie's will. Though he would have faced the same outcome had he borrowed from a bank, the loan illustrates the difficult financial conditions in the post-war South. Few banks existed there, and private investor funds were the source of most loans. Anderson's unsecured debts accrued in 1868 and 1869 totaled over $6,800 and were all payable to local planters, merchants, and cotton factors in Baltimore and Charleston. The dearth of local banks and consequent shortage of capital led to a common system of loans whereby a lien on the yearly crop provided security for repayment. The crop failures in those years made it impossible for Anderson to fulfill his obligations in that regard.[27]

With outstanding debts totaling nearly $14,000, or approximately $318,500 in 2022 value, Anderson was fortunate to own real estate valued at approximately $15,000. His 1,900-acre Hiwassee plantation in which he held a life estate interest was only valued at around $4,000, in part because a portion of that acreage was unusable swampland. That was likewise the case with his interest in the original Anderson plantation at Riverton, or Riverside as it was sometimes termed. It comprised 2,500 acres valued at $10,000 along with another 150-acre tract in the village of Stateburg containing the Homestead. That tract was valued at $1,000. The bankruptcy process discharged his debt, and he emerged with his personal belongings and his cherished sword. In an odd twist of fate, the bounty land warrant issued to his grandfather Richard Anderson in 1790 that provided the means to obtain the original plantation land was attributable to Richard's heroic service in the Continental Army during the Revolution. Now, his grandson and namesake stood poised to lose the benefits of that land warrant in part because of his own service in a revolutionary endeavor with a less successful outcome.[28]

The proximity of the Episcopal Church that stood within sight of his home meant that the Anderson family's gravesites were located there, not on the troubled home property as was so often the case in more rural areas. Dick's younger brother Mackenzie was destined to rest forever in a common grave in the South Carolina row of Cedar Grove Cemetery in Williamsburg, Virginia, now part of the Confederate section marked by an obelisk with no individual names listed. Mackenzie's presence there is traceable only by the notation in the caretaker's book. His family could not recover his remains and bring them home, and in a war where that was common in families with means, it seems a particularly pathetic indication of the Andersons's diminished stature that the brother of a prominent general officer should be consigned to rest for eternity in a common grave. Dick Anderson himself would later rest beneath only a rude wooden headboard in a South Carolina churchyard, a condition that persisted for several years after his death in the economically depressed conditions that plagued the rural South.[29]

Wallace subsequently made several efforts to save the family home, but it was not until seven years after its loss in bankruptcy proceedings that Wallace's wife, Jennie, was able to secure the Homestead and about fifty acres of surrounding land. Jennie had inherited a home in Alexandria, Virginia from her father. The proceeds from the sale of that house allowed her to return the Homestead to the family's ownership in May 1877. Troubles lay ahead, however, and as late as 1888 Jennie sought a loan for $4,500 to satisfy claims against the plantation. By 1916, however, the family's holdings had increased to over 1,500 acres. The property remains in the family's hands and was added to the National Register of Historic Places in 1972.[30]

Previous biographers indicated that Anderson at first was compelled to work at a menial job laboring in the rail yards of the South Carolina Railroad when he went to Charleston in 1870. If true, it must have been for a very short time before his status with the railroad came to the attention of its president, William J. McGrath. It seems unlikely that anyone would have selected Anderson to represent the railroad at the Cincinnati Exhibition in late September if he was then working at such a humble level and without McGrath's knowledge. His elevation in status at the hands of McGrath must have come quickly since Anderson was not even resident in Charleston until earlier that same month. McGrath reputedly brought Anderson to work in his own office before appointing him as the Railroad's agent in Camden in early December 1872. His life in Charleston could hardly have long been that of laborer in a menial job. By May 1871, eight months after his arrival in the city, his friends and admirers circulated a petition of nearly 1,000 names proposing his nomination for mayor. The notice appeared in the *Charleston Daily News*, along with Anderson's response. He first thanked his Democratic supporters sincerely before going on to urge them to desist in the matter. "In ordinary times," he told them, "I would not hesitate to accept the nomination, but in the present condition of affairs, I . . . request that the gentlemen who have so kindly named me do not press my nomination, if any arrangement can be made by which a heated political contest can be avoided, and all good citizens be brought into earnest and harmonious co-operation for the re-establishment and preservation amongst [us] of good order and prosperity." The contest that August did indeed turn out to be heated, with Democratic candidate and former general of Confederate militia troops, John A. Wagener prevailing by 800 votes over the Reconstruction Era Republican incumbent Gilbert Pillsbury, a staunch abolitionist who served as a Freedmen's Bureau agent before becoming governor. Pillsbury's election in 1868 had led to months of acrimonious legal challenges before he was able to take office in May 1869. Similar controversy over distribution of political spoils followed Wagener's victory. Anderson had advocated for "'a division of the city offices,'" and offered that his name be used "'in any way that may seem favorable to such a consummation.'" Anderson wisely avoided direct involvement in the ugly political fray. Wagener's opponents subsequently sullied his name with corruption charges throughout his tenure and he served only one term because of that damage.[31]

Escaping the effects of a widespread yellow fever epidemic in the city that summer, followed closely by a severe hurricane, Anderson remained in Charleston until relocating to Camden in December 1872. The *Camden Journal* published a notice of his appointment, expressing certainty that it would "gratify the General's numerous friends, and his well-known courtesy and competency will render it a sources of satisfaction to all . . ." Anderson embraced his new circumstances in Camden, though often it was a struggle. His devoted wife, Sallie, had returned from a northern vacation with her family and contracted typhoid fever, dying in Charleston on August 11, 1872. A Roman Catholic convert, Sallie was laid to rest in the city the following day after a morning service at St. Mary's Catholic Church. Her death was especially painful because it was widely held that the sudden decline of her family's fortunes exacerbated her natural inclination to nervousness and led to "an unnatural state of mind." Little about that condition could have contributed directly to her death, but the stamina needed to survive a bout of typhoid might have long deserted her delicate mental constitution.

Adding to Anderson's melancholy was his now complete loneliness as a widower who was soon separated from his children as well. Accepting the job in Camden in early December took him from Charleston and his children, and his isolation was a source of despair. In a letter to his daughter, then living with the Sisters of Charity in Charleston, he lamented his behavior before departing the city for Camden. On the day of his departure, he was supposed to return to bid her a final farewell prior to leaving. He apologized for not doing so, writing pathetically that it was, "partly because when the day was over, I felt exceedingly weary, and partly because I then began to realize the bitterness of the situation, and I knew that I would not be able to behave myself quite so bravely as I did in the morning, and would distress you instead of encouraging you." He told his daughter that she should write to him frequently "if you only have ten words to say they will be received with as much pleasure as ten hundred from anyone else." He urged her to use their correspondence to fill the gap in their distant separation and urged her to write, "just as you would say it to me if I were near you."[32]

During the summer of 1873, Anderson was suffering from recurrences of the diarrhea and dysentery he experienced while serving in the Deep South, which he believed was a mild form of cholera. In addition, financial stability remained elusive. That June, before visiting his son and daughter in Charleston, he was awaiting disbursement of a portion of his inheritance from Sallie's estate. If it arrived too late, he intended to send the children money to visit him in Camden instead. Absenting himself from his position for a time that summer apparently presented no obstacle to his going to Charleston, but without the money from the inheritance, he could not afford to travel. Nevertheless, summer was a far less demanding time on the railroad. The volume of freight transfers during the summer typically fell until cotton shipments increased after the fall harvest. He told his son that, "the business of the Road has fallen off to little or nothing. We have nothing to do except fan ourselves and fight the flies, varied occasionally with the highly intellectual employment of twirling our thumbs. You may imagine how eagerly I look for you and your sister." When the dutiful father did send his son $18 to purchase tickets to come to Camden with Sallie, he informed him of "a very good eating house at Branchville," but cautioned him to "be sure you get into the right train after dinner, or you may find yourselves back in the city instead of at Camden."[33]

Anderson's duties as the agent at Camden involved ensuring the prompt shipment of goods, particularly cotton; however, he sometimes had to address complaints about slow or missing shipments. In September 1873, for example, a Baltimore merchant complained of not receiving three barrels of whiskey his company had purchased from a Camden supplier in July. Anderson explained in a letter to the railroad's president, McGrath, that a Deputy Collector of Internal Revenue had issued an injunction prohibiting the transfer of the whiskey. The whiskey was still at the Camden depot, Anderson reported, and "subject (as far as I understand the case) to the orders of the Deputy Collector." Meanwhile, the Baltimore firm claimed to have written twice to the agent at Camden and not received a reply. Anderson noted only that, "their letters have not been received." Things were more serious the following year when Dick again had to write McGrath after the president had expressed his annoyance over reports "concerning irregularities, and short comings, in the conduct of business" in Camden. Anderson did not deny problems existed, but thought that on learning the facts McGrath would "admit that there have been palliating circumstances." Over the slow summer months, the railroad's superintendent had ordered the discharge of Anderson's clerk and a laborer. Anderson had requested their restoration for the usual busy season between October and April, but the superintendent denied him, citing "the falling off of the business and income of the Road." Anderson explained that there had been no decline in the railroad's business at Camden, citing figures to show that the combined tonnage of freight received and shipped from that station exceeded the previous year's figures for October by over a million tons. How that amount of freight could be properly "handled and accounted for with no clerk and one laborer less than had been formerly allowed," was a mystery to him. "It was simply impossible for me to manage the business of the station with the force I had," Anderson complained. Another visit from the superintendent clarified the issue. He authorized Anderson to hire more labor and sent an experienced clerk from Charleston to assist with setting matters right. Anderson was apparently displeased that the superintendent's action had brought the matter to the attention of the president of the railroad. For all his courteous manners, Anderson retained his combativeness when insulted. He was certainly not one to brook accusations of misdeeds, and the former general pressed the attack. His parting shot in response to McGrath laid the blame clearly at the superintendent's feet. "I doubt however that his mode of relief will prove as economical in the end as his having allowed my very reasonable request would have been."[34]

Young Sallie remained a faithful correspondent with her father, enduring his good-natured chiding with poise equal to that of her father's gentle nature. He wrote consolingly to her in January 1874 after Sallie had fallen on ice and was resting in the infirmary. She had sent him a recent photograph, and he inquired in return as to "what old Sea Captain lent you his overcoat . . . to sit in. I am sure you must have borrowed the one represented in the picture from some old salt or perhaps a policeman. Did ever mortal man see such buttons on a young girl's garment?" After his droll chiding, he quickly turned his pen upon himself. "Some day when I get an approving response from my looking glass I will go and sit for my likeness and send it to you," he told her. "We have no very good artists in Camden, but such as we have, can certainly do better than the bungler who gave me that intensely silly smirk in the likeness which I am glad to hear has been 'misplaced' or 'lost.'"[35]

Anderson's good humor was likely attributable to the fact that he had finally compelled the attorney who was settling his wife's estate to "transfer to my own hands my share of it." He reckoned about $1,500 was forthcoming. In addition to that windfall, he was pursuing a new relationship by then, for he was to wed once more before year's end. He and Martha Ellen Mellette, nicknamed Mattie, were married on Christmas Eve 1874. Christmas season weddings were common in that era, when family members often traveled some distance to gather at home. Martha, daughter of Dr. Robert S. Millette and Sarah Ann Millette of Stateburg, was then only between seventeen and nineteen years old. The records disagree but point more decisively to the former age. General Anderson was five years older than Mattie's father was, but such age discrepancies were also common then. They were destined to be together less than five years. Mattie would survive him by nearly fifty years, living until 1928 and marrying twice more.[36]

Writing to Sallie in mid-August 1878 while she was enjoying a "visit to the hills" with her "Uncle Wallace" at the Homestead and her cousin Willie at Millbrook, Anderson informed her that everything was "going on here . . . in the usual routine." That routine apparently was quite boring in the dog days of summer, when heat and lethargy still plagued daily life. "There has not been even a Church ice cream or a benevolent lunch to arouse our energies and tax our powers of enjoyment," he complained. Despite the improvement in his personal affairs, employment problems again plagued the former general. In the fall of 1878, as his earliest biographer put it— "the faithlessness and dishonesty of a trusted employee, involved [Anderson] and he had to bear the responsibility and thus lost this employment" as "Agent of the Railroad at Camden." The date of his sudden unemployment in not known, but a notice appeared in the October 17, 1878, edition of the *Camden Journal* noting that Anderson had been replaced as agent.[37]

That sudden change in circumstances sent the Andersons back to Charleston in late October, where they stayed at the Waverly House, a sprawling four-story King Street hotel. Anderson was happy to find many old friends and acquaintances among the guests. "It seemed to me that I had only been away for a few months instead of some years," he told Sallie. Despite the friendly and familiar surroundings, Anderson was once again not sanguine about his employment prospects in the conditions brought on by the Panic of 1873, which caused a lengthy depression that dragged on until early 1879. He had notified some of his friends that he "was again adrift and in search of employment," but the response was similar to that received on his first trip to Charleston in 1870. Friends promised to try to help, but "the city was more thronged than ever it was with seekers after employment and times are harder and prospects worse" than during his first visit. The couple spent a few days sightseeing leisurely in the city before Anderson set out to determine whether there were any realistic chances for a job. He thought that it would take only a few days to make inquiries, and if the results were not promising, he intended to head to Baltimore, Maryland, to "stir up my friends and relations in that city."[38]

Sometime soon afterwards, Dick and Mattie did travel to Baltimore, where they received a distressing letter from Sallie in early December. A longstanding beau with whom she had seriously discussed marriage had peremptorily jilted her. She welcomed her father's gentle response. "It cheers and comforts me," she wrote, "that I have your love and sympathy in my troubles." After four years of courtship, the couple had reached the understanding that "as soon as he was in a position to marry and able to support a wife we would go to you," for permission. Suddenly the cad broke the news that he was engaged to another. Her reaction after the initial shock showed her truly to be her father's daughter. With great magnanimity, she declined to "attach any reproach to him" and claimed she had not "a shadow of resentment," in her broken heart. To make matters worse, in just over two weeks she was to act as bridesmaid in a Christmas Eve ceremony, an obligation which she now chose to fulfill only "with great reluctance," owing to her recent disappointment. She promised to leave Camden on the 26th and would reach Mattie and her father in Baltimore two days later. Instead, a heartbroken Sallie appended an update to her letter the following morning, explaining that she would indeed forsake her obligation as a bridesmaid and depart for Baltimore within a few days' time.[39]

The political situation in South Carolina vacillated wildly after the war. From the initial period of Black Codes during the lenient period of Johnson's administration, Congress quickly pushed for more control over affairs in the defeated southern states, repudiating presidential reconstruction and embarking on passage of a series of Reconstruction Acts that included suffrage for the freedmen. Congressional Reconstruction thus began in 1867, changing the dynamics of southern politics for the next decade. Many white southerners resisted what they perceived as Republican efforts to establish black rule, and that resistance often included intimidation and violence. In addition to Ku Klux Klan activities, South Carolinians armed themselves under the guise of hunting and recreational rifle clubs in an effort to prevent freedmen from engaging in political affairs. Democrats eventually seized back control in South Carolina with the 1876 gubernatorial election pitting former Confederate general Wade Hampton against the Republican incumbent, Daniel H. Chamberlain. Hampton outwardly espoused a moderate view and appealed to Black voters, but his supporters were far more aggressive. Confederate General James Conner organized the state's rifle clubs, thought to number around 240 with a membership of 20,000 to 30,000, into a statewide entity. Other supporters began wearing red shirts, perhaps copied from the uniform adopted by Italian patriot Giuseppe Garibaldi's followers and worn by the Confederate Garibaldi Legion during the war. Mounted men wearing those red shirts soon became the most visible symbol of Hampton's campaign, leading the push for revanchism among white South Carolinians. The 1876 campaign energized those voters to reassert long-held Confederate sentiments, using racial and gender tropes to stir white anxieties. Widely characterized as a choice between "Hampton" and "Hell," the campaign took on tones of a religious revival, a redemption from the grip of black Republican rule, and salvation through the restoration of white Democratic governance.[40]

Hampton's whirlwind campaign involving highly orchestrated speaking engagements across the state galvanized the Democratic Party and propelled him to a somewhat questionable and probably fraudulent victory. Nonetheless, the Republican incumbent chose to resign in April 1877, when Republican president Rutherford B. Hayes declined to throw his support behind Chamberlain in the disputed election. With Democrats once more firmly in control of the state's political apparatus, Reconstruction there effectively ended. No evidence of Anderson's position, or whether he actively supported the campaign survives in personal or public records, but given his past behavior it is likely he again avoided active involvement in political affairs.[41]

With Reconstruction in South Carolina ended, and financial conditions related to the depression driving voters away from the Republicans, southerners began to consolidate their former power both nationally and at the state level and thus stood poised to assist veterans like Dick Anderson. As the holidays approached, Anderson was aware that the possibility of an appointment in South Carolina loomed. Before he left for Baltimore, Sallie had written that her father should "write or telegraph that I should know your movements" in case those working on his behalf were successful and he was "called back to Carolina." Indeed, political machinations were at work on the part of his supporters, who sought some government office for him. Friends and admirers rallied to his cause, circulating petitions and making speeches on his behalf. A December article from the Columbia *Register*, widely disseminated in other papers even sought to play on the people's emotions, asking "Are we an ungrateful people and have we forgotten all that was glorious in the past?" The writer was leading up to a description of how Anderson, "an educated and high-toned gentleman . . . whose worth is only equaled by his modesty," had until recently been employed in a humble position, but had lately been "driven . . . from our borders to seek employment in another State." The writer then urged Anderson's appointment as Superintendent of the State Penitentiary in place of the "present incumbent carpet-bagger." He called on the state's old soldiers to rise up and force the issue. "Can a carpet-bagger hold a fat office and Dick Anderson wander a poor exile? Think of it." Former Brigadier General Arthur M. Manigault nominated Anderson for the position, seconded by South Carolina congressional representative and former Colonel William A. Walker, but on December 21, 1878, his nomination was defeated in the legislature on the second ballot.[42]

After being elected to a second term as the state's governor in November 1878, Wade Hampton quickly found himself named Senator-elect by the state legislature in December 1878. Hampton was then at home recovering from a badly broken leg incurred in a hunting accident, one so severe that it required amputation, but on hearing that Anderson's nomination had been defeated, he urged Lieutenant Governor William D. Simpson, acting in his stead, to appoint Dick to the position of railroad commissioner. Simpson, however, had promised that position to former general and congressional representative Milledge L. Bonham, on whose staff Simpson had served in 1861. Instead, a newly created, lesser position as Inspector of Phosphates went to Anderson.[43]

While the appointment was a welcome relief, it was not all that Anderson had hoped for, at least on the surface. The Penitentiary position would have netted $2,400 per year, and the railroad commissioner's salary was $2,100 per year. His new post paid only $1,200 per year, and he would have to relocate to the coastal town of Beaufort. His friends thought the position unequal to Anderson's stature, and some suspected he might reject it. Fearful that a more lucrative opportunity might not arise, however, the ever-modest Dick Anderson sprang at the opportunity for steady employment earning a salary about three times greater than his previous job with the railroad. More importantly, a careful reading of the new act that created the position indicated an even greater potential windfall. The Phosphate Inspector was to receive one percent of the royalties collected by the state at the rate of $1.00 per ton shipped. With about a dozen phosphate companies mining just in Beaufort County waters alone, Anderson's income stood to be significantly higher than his base salary. The state received revenues of $199,365 in 1879, and he could have seen his percentage add nearly $2,000 to his salary.[44]

The post of state phosphate agent, as Simpson would recall later, was the best position available at the time to alleviate Anderson's financial distress. A legislative act created the position on December 24, 1878, and Anderson's appointment as "Special Agent" was effective as of January 1, 1879, but Simpson did not sign his formal commission until January 24. Anderson had meanwhile signed the oath of office that acknowledged the supremacy of the US Constitution over that of the state's, and pledged his loyalty to the federal document and to the South Carolina Constitution of 1878. His duties included "supervising and inspecting the navigable rivers and streams of the State containing Phosphatic rocks and deposits, and the work of all persons and bodies corporate mining or gathering therein such rocks or deposits." His primary purpose was to protect the state's interests from unlicensed mining and monitor the quantity of phosphate extracted to ensure the payment of royalties to the state. The latter was especially vital to the state's phosphate agent, as the royalties also funded his base salary in addition to the one percent bonus. Phosphate mining was a significant source of South Carolina's revenue, providing about ten percent of state funds, with about one-third of the mined material consumed domestically and two-thirds exported, primarily to England. Beaufort was the center of the state's phosphate industry and generated the bulk of the profit until the Great Sea Island Hurricane of 1893 left thousands of workers dead and much of the equipment destroyed. The power invested in the state's agent was considerable, but some asserted testily after Anderson's death that the office was nothing more than a "useless and expensive sinecure." Hampton had finally been able to act decisively on Anderson's behalf. That he did not do so sooner is likely due to Anderson not appealing to him, as so many other job seekers had done, during his first term in the governor's office, when Anderson had worked for the railroad in Camden. As it developed, losing that position was hardly a misfortune. It brought Anderson's plight to the attention of those in a position to assist him, and though there is no record of him having

June 30, 1877.] FRANK LESLIE'S ILLUSTRATED NEWSPAPER. 285

A WASHING-HOUSE FOR CLEANSING THE PHOSPHATE ROCK.

LABORERS WASHING THE PHOSPHATE ROCK.

SOUTH CAROLINA.—THE CHARLESTON PHOSPHATE INDUSTRY.—SCENES AND INCIDENTS OF THE PREPARATION OF THE MATERIAL FOR MARKET.

Figure 8. "The Charleston Phosphate Industry, Scenes and Incidents of the Preparation of the Material for Market." *Frank Leslie's Illustrated Newspaper,* June 30, 1877. Courtesy of the South Caroliniana Library, University of South Carolina.

direct contact with Hampton, it is clear that there were supporters who put Anderson's case before him. His unemployment lasted a little more than two months, but now he stood in the most stable and prosperous position of his post-bellum career.[45]

Dick and Mattie Anderson reached Beaufort sometime near the end of January 1879, lodging at the city's hotel for two weeks until they found accommodations in an elegant boarding house located at 800 Prince Street. Local planter William Wigg Barnwell had the house built circa 1816. Named in honor of its original owner, the three-story clapboard home with a deep two-story front porch stood facing south toward the river, about six blocks from the water, though in the twentieth century it was relocated to 501 King Street where it stands today distinctively restored as one of Beaufort's reminders of its prosperous past. A large garden fronted the house on Prince Street, and it was considered one of the best homes in Beaufort. One wartime admirer evoked stereotypical images of the Old South, describing its "deciduous and persistent shade trees that continually wave obedience to the soft air fragrant with the orange and lemon and vine." In 1862, the home served as Union Hospital #4. Barnwell's descendants moved away in 1871, but they retained possession of the property, which served as a boarding house for the next decade. Anderson wrote his daughter Sallie in mid-February that a widow named Mrs. Givens managed the home, and the board cost him twenty dollars a month each "with the understanding that you were to be provided for at the same rate whenever you rejoin us." He hoped that she would indeed join them in Beaufort, but he explained that unless she had money to make her own way sooner, she would have to wait until the start of March when he expected to receive his pay. Though the Barnwell House was not his own, it was nonetheless a home of some stature and refinement. The Andersons certainly could not have been embarrassed to reside in a boarding house of such dignity, although he told Sallie that he had heard of a number of homes for rent "at very reasonable rates and we debate the question of whether to continue boarding or try housekeeping." He thought they would put off a decision until warmer weather was upon them.[46]

The Andersons had received "an exceedingly hospitable and kind welcome." He professed to "like the place and its inhabitants." It was not Charleston with all the charms of that larger city, but as he explained, there were "considerations, especially to people with short purses which weigh heavily in a comparison of the two places." The new position saved Anderson from further financial degradation and positioned him for an opportunity to recover both his fiscal security and his pride. The process, however, got off to a difficult start. He did not receive his pay for March until April 20, first owing to what he termed "negligence in the office of the Comptroller

General" but also, he admitted, to his own carelessness. The Comptroller did not send his pay in a timely manner, but then sent the money to Charleston instead. Moreover, Anderson's negligence in not revoking an old request at the post office there directing that his mail be forwarded to Baltimore caused further delay. Meanwhile, "some pin money that Mattie had put away," tided the couple over. He was finally able to send Sallie money in April to finance her trip to Beaufort, but she did not come after all. Sallie was then living with her maternal grandmother and her aunt and uncle in Chester, South Carolina, and she wrote her father on May 3 begging his advice. Sallie's grandmother had died on April 29 and her desire to be with her father and Mattie conflicted with her obligation to her aunt and uncle. Her aunt was "utterly crushed by her terrible affliction," she told him. "She has been more kind and more tender to me than anyone but my own dear Mother could have been and I know that it will be dreadfully hard for her to be left alone with this grief." Unable to make up her mind, she asked her father to do it for her. "It has not been often my dear Father than I have come to you to decide for me, not as often as it should have been, but I do ask you now to write and tell me what you think it best for me to do." Sallie was unwilling to disappoint either her aunt or her father, but she seems to have been leaning towards the latter, and she wrote in such a fashion as to ensure his agreement with her underlying emotions. "I feel maybe that I am selfish in wanting to go away when they have all been so good to me," she wrote plaintively. "I want you to understand that it is my desire to be with you but if you think that an opportunity has been given me to repay in some measure the kindly consideration which has been shown me I will set aside my own wishes and stay until you think it right to leave." Sallie made it clear that she was not merely seeking counsel, but instead promised to "abide faithfully by what you advise." While Anderson was undoubtedly anxious to see her, he understood her obligation under those circumstances and Sallie remained in Chester. Undoubtedly, she would not have done so had she suspected that her father had so little time remaining to him.[47]

Anderson soon befriended the young editor of the *Beaufort Crescent*, Samuel Henry Rodgers, a veteran of the 23rd South Carolina Infantry whose editorial offices became his habitual stopping point as he walked from his workplace to his home. On June 26, 1879, he dropped into Rodgers's offices to chat and scan the latest news. He complained about the intense heat that day, and said he was on his way home to prepare lemonade in an effort to keep cool. He went off with a bag of lemons. Whether he ever made the drink is unknown, for within an hour or two the startling news arrived that he had died at 5 PM that afternoon of "a sudden attack of apoplexy." His new friends and neighbors rushed to the home to assist Mattie and console her in her grief. Her departed husband was just fifty-seven years old. His life was marked by twenty-seven years of arduous service to his nation and to the Confederacy, followed by fourteen years of bitter disappointment and failures. Now, when he had finally secured a position with some promise of security for his future, that small satisfaction was denied to him. Leaving his family entirely without means of support upon his death far outweighed any sense of contentment from the fulfillment of his long-expressed desire to be a burden to no one.[48]

Local newspapers quickly spread the sad tidings, with the Beaufort *News and Courier* noting that the "community has just been painfully shocked. . . . There is universal sorrow an[d] gloom over the sad event, for the General was a favorite with all." The following day saw nearly the entire population of the city turn out for "Fighting Dick" Anderson's funeral at St. Helena Anglican Church. First, about forty members of the Beaufort Volunteer Artillery marched to Anderson's residence, leaving their cannons at the nearby armory to fire a salute during the interment of his remains. The town's distinguished citizens bore the body from the house to the hearse, and the funeral cortege set off towards the church. A drum corps beating a slow march on its muffled instruments led the procession, followed by the Beaufort Artillery with one member bearing Anderson's ceremonial sword, the long-ago gift from the state. The hearse followed behind, with pallbearers and then citizens in carriages and afoot completing the long line of mourners. On reaching the church, the artillerymen formed on either side of the pathway to the doors, rendering a final salute as the coffin passed. Pallbearers passed though the double doors and under the choir loft and pipe organ, placing the General's coffin reverently in front of the chancel while the soldiers formed in the center aisle and stood throughout the services. Afterwards his earthly remains were borne to the adjacent cemetery and lowered into the newly prepared grave. Three of the Beaufort Artillery guns fired from the armory, while the bells of the church tolled the gallant soldier's final honor. His family's straitened circumstances prevented the immediate placement of a suitable stone marker, and a wooden headstone had to suffice. Supporters instead directed subsequent fundraising efforts toward Mattie and Sallie's relief, and the modest wooden marker would stand for several years as a result.[49]

Mattie soon moved back to Stateburg to live with her parents, and the state legislature voted in early December to pay her $700.00, the balance of Anderson's yearly salary. As early as August 1879, veterans were already coming to her aid. Members of the 12th South Carolina met that month and formed a committee designed to receive contributions to assist Mattie and Sallie "who, we are informed are without means of support." A memorial eulogy was read, "referring to his brilliant military record . . . and the modest, unassuming life he had led." The speaker noted especially that Anderson's salary in his former position as agent for the railroad had been only $400 per year. A memorial "signed by many distinguished officers of the Confederate army," solicited aid for Anderson's family, which it said was struggling "in indigent circumstances." Many of the state's survivor associations received the solicitation, and Anderson's old comrades rallied to the call. General James Conner and General Johnson Hagood, among others, had circulated the request to aid Anderson's family, which was then "left in very needy circumstances. Every Confederate should remember the brilliant services of Gen. Anderson, and aid in this time of their necessity his wife and children." His postwar involvement in state and local Confederate survivors' associations assured a robust response to the call for aid. Just a year earlier Anderson had received a special invitation, along with General Charles Field, to attend the August 1878 reunion of the 6th South Carolina Infantry in Chester. Despite his avoidance of publicity and the troubling financial woes that undermined his status and dignity, the old soldiers remembered their former leader fondly. Those who had shared with him the deadly trials of combat could not forget him.[50]

At the 1879 reunion of the 6th South Carolina Regiment soon after Anderson's death, the veterans applauded General John Bratton when, in his speech to the old soldiers, he noted that "South Carolina had no more devoted son, or valiant and distinguished warrior than that modest and unassuming gentleman, 'Fighting Dick Anderson.'" At that same reunion, a committee formed to draft resolutions related to Anderson's death, noting that in him the men "beheld a leader whose courage and skill obtained the confidence of those he commanded, while his unassuming manners and high qualities of heart won our esteem and affection."[51]

By 1888, as the southern economy had recovered more fully from its postwar financial crisis, an effort began in the state to raise funds for a statue to Anderson. At the urging of the Beaufort Volunteer Artillery, the Survivors' Association of the Charleston District adopted a resolution in November 1889, appointing a committee of five members to head a fundraising campaign to erect "a suitable monument to the memory of Lieut Gen. Richard H. Anderson." The committee members noted that Anderson's grave in Beaufort was "marked by a plain head board," with no other memorial to such a distinguished soldier "who deservedly held an exalted position in the regard and confidence of the troops he commanded. . . ." They envisioned marking his resting place with "a monumental shaft which, in its strength and simplicity, shall fitly symbolize the character of the dead soldier, and, at the same time, shall bear witness to the loving remembrance of his comrades in arms." The committee's circular was distributed for publication in newspapers "which approve of the object for which the committee was appointed." The circular expressed the hope of placing the monument as quickly as possible and requested that supporters forward funds to Anderson's former staff officer, Francis Dawson, who was acting as treasurer. The effort was a success, with the Society of the Cincinnati in Charleston also contributing generously. Anderson had been a proud member of that organization, whose membership was limited to descendants of officers who served in the American Revolution. Previous fundraising efforts had faltered. An attempt made in early 1888 to raise funds for a monument to Anderson apparently met with less success, though the *Sumter Watchman* urged local citizens to "send in their mites," noting that the claim upon the citizens of Sumter was stronger "from the fact that he was one of us." The Survivors' Association likely absorbed into its own efforts any funds initially raised.[52]

Finally, at 5 PM on October 7, 1891, the seventieth anniversary of his birth, the granite memorial over his grave was officially unveiled in a well-attended ceremony. An iron fence donated by Danish immigrant and former Union officer Captain Neils Christensen, then a notable Beaufort businessperson, surrounded the monument. One of those chosen to address the gathering was former Major Thomas A. Huguenin, who reinforced Anderson's widely known propensity to avoid self-promotion and characterized his modesty as "almost morbid." Only those who observed Anderson's actions were fully aware of their importance, he asserted. "Simplicity and modesty were so entwined with his courage and patriotism as to make his life and public services unknown to all but eye witnesses of the actual events." He cited one example where a fellow senior officer's postwar reminiscences failed to give Anderson the credit that was due him. A former staff officer urged him to respond in print and correct the slight. The old general declined, replying gravely, "It will ill become me to join in the general scramble for honor and notoriety; it fully suffices me to know that in every battle . . . I did my duty as a soldier, and that I enjoyed the confidence of the men I commanded."[53]

Unfortunately, tragic circumstances continued to plague Dick's family. His only son, Richard G. Anderson, suffered a mental collapse and died from self-inflicted injuries in Deadwood, South Dakota on December 2, 1898, at age forty-six. Young Dick Anderson had gone west, first to Iowa and finally to Deadwood in 1877, where he worked variously in mining and engineering. Dick wrote Sallie at that time of his concerns for his son and his search for some "regular and remunerative employment." The General probably recalled his own younger days on the frontier with some fondness as he told her that Dick's "roaming sort of life has some novelty which makes it attractive I suppose, but there is no profit it. It is better however to wander about in the far West until he finds an opening than to drag along in the older States on a salary barely sufficient for his maintenance." Only twelve years old when the war ended, young Dick had received an inferior education as a young man and undoubtedly suffered further setbacks with the decline of his father's fortunes that made his advancement in life more difficult. He had to fend largely for himself though eventually he received enough education and training to claim the title of engineer.

His sister, Sallie, by then Mrs. William D. Blanding survived him. Sallie had married at the old Anderson residence in Stateburg, then the home of her Uncle Wallace in December 1881. Sallie's only son, Richard Anderson Blanding, died at the age of nine. Her daughter Sarah Gibson lived until 1985. She was a noted educator and president of Vassar College from 1946–1964. General Anderson's brother Wallace died at age eighty-six in July 1911, leaving his wife, two sons, and three daughters. Mackenzie was honored in 1888 when his name was listed among 336 others on the face of a monument honoring Sumter's Confederate dead.[54]

On June 28, 1916, the *Abbeville Press and Banner* lamented the fading reputation of Dick Anderson. An article advertised that the United Confederate Veterans (U.C.V.) and the United Daughters of the Confederacy (U.D.C.), spearheaded by the "Dick" Anderson U.C.V. Camp and the U.D.C. chapter in Sumter, were proposing "a most worthy movement to redeem this ingratitude of our people, by the publication of his life." The state's U.D.C. president expressed hopes that every member would "aid in this most splendid work to rescue from oblivion the name of one of South Carolina's greatest heroes." Former Lieutenant Colonel C. Irvine Walker subsequently published a biography of Anderson in Charleston in 1917. A fellow South Carolinian, Irvine was a Citadel graduate who served with the Army of Tennessee. He had a distinguished post-war career in business as well as with the state's militia, reaching the rank of brigadier general after Wade Hampton became governor. Upon Hampton's death, Walker rose to command of the U.C.V.'s Army of Northern Virginia Department, later becoming commander in chief of the organization. He wrote prolifically, and before his death in 1927, he published several more works, most dealing with the war or the 10th South Carolina Regiment. His biography of Anderson received fulsome praise, in large part because it would "keep bright the recollections of one who was 'brave as a Paladin of old, gentle and modest as a woman.'"[55]

Then on December 18, 1925, *The Camden Chronicle* ran an article describing ambitious plans to honor each of the southern states on a memorial at Stone Mountain, Georgia, where an artist would carve the likenesses of five military leaders from each state. Naturally, as South Carolina's most senior soldier at the start of the Civil War, the state proposed that Dick Anderson occupy one of those spots. The article provided a very brief biography of the five nominees, noting that Anderson had achieved greatness in part by his actions at Spotsylvania. Undoubtedly, Anderson would have been mortified to know that his biography was reinforcing the inflated version of his rapid movement to Spotsylvania Courthouse in popular memory despite his own claims to the contrary. The article writer further contended that after the defeat at Sailor's Creek just prior to Appomattox, Anderson was making his way towards Johnston's army in North Carolina and thus did not surrender with Lee's army, though there is no other evidence of this.[56]

Though Anderson was an obvious choice for inclusion on the monument, an article several weeks earlier in the *Camden Chronicle* noted that supporters of Wade Hampton were working to elevate his status. Hampton, his supporters urged, should be included in the "central group on the mountain—the group which includes Jefferson Davis, Robert E. Lee and 'Stonewall' Jackson . . . men who belong to the entire Confederacy rather than to any one particular state." The article did not elaborate on how or why the monument committee in South Carolina thought Hampton fit that description. Nevertheless, representatives from the "Dick" Anderson Camp of the United Confederate Veterans assured Dick's nomination for a place on the monument.[57]

Although Anderson might have disagreed with well-meaning supporters touting his actions at Spotsylvania as the ultimate testimonial to his long career, the subsequent series of events that saw controversy and discord mark the monument's progress were even more troubling. First was the involvement of the Ku Klux Klan in promoting the monument and its placement on grounds that were a traditional gathering place associated with the resurgence of the Klan since 1915. The effort suffered further by the dismissal of the original sculptor and a reduction in the large number of figures planned. Moreover, fundraising and progress remained slow, and the monument became a cause célèbre for segregationists reflecting many southerners' forceful resistance to integration and the civil rights movement. The committee finally appointed the artist who substantially completed the project in 1963. A dedication ceremony followed on May 9, 1970. Dick Anderson and the other Confederate heroes were not part of the final plan, which included only Lee, Jackson, and Jefferson Davis. The monument itself remains a matter of controversy.[58]

Modern readers might also be tempted to conclude that Dick Anderson's support for the Confederacy as one of its most senior military figures is sufficient justification to mark him as a figure worthy of censure, but such a reaction is an oversimplification, not only of a long and complex life, but also of history itself. We can hope to understand individuals only in the context of the times in which they lived. In that regard, Anderson's upbringing as the son of a wealthy member of the slave-owning planter elite set the stage for the course of his life and his beliefs, even if at times he might have questioned the rectitude of those beliefs. It is true that he too owned slaves and held racial views common among most nineteenth century Americans. Despite that, there is no commentary from Dick Anderson to support disdain for either enslaved persons or freedman, and no expressions of resentment after the Southern Confederacy was defeated militarily. Instead, he expressed his eagerness to work within the bounds of the new order and bring some normalization to his life. He was justifiably proud of the service he rendered and as a former professional soldier—his life's work—he eventually involved himself in and supported veterans' organizations in his state.

There is no evidence to suggest that he worked against progress in any respect or that he had any connection to groups such as the Klan or even the Democratic clubs, rifle clubs, or militia organizations that sought to advance Democratic political efforts and deny freed people their rightful place in society. His sense of honor and his enthusiastic statements that acknowledged his returned loyalty to the United States argue persuasively against any opposition to its goals. His immediate embrace of the terms of his oath of loyalty constitutes, if anything, a display of contriteness and personal ambivalence about his role in the war. In addition to his natural modesty, personal conflict and a desire for repentance reinforced his hesitancy to capitalize on his former military status during the immediate postbellum years of hardship and led him to withdraw from public view. His rejection of the proposed nomination for Charleston's mayor at a time when the struggle to regain control of the political machine was raging indicates he did not count himself among the unreconstructed Confederates of his time.

Instead, Anderson did as he had done throughout his life, he conducted himself in accordance with his devotion to duty and to service. It is true that he fought in an insurrection meant to split the American nation in two, one whose central aim was the perpetuation of human bondage. In that war he fought hard, sometimes courageously, and he bore witness to the greatest battles and bloodshed that have ever taken place in North America. But when the battles were over, Anderson put down the sword and returned home to face the new realities wrought by war. Unlike so many other former Confederates, he did not continue to pursue the war by other means. He did not take up arms as a member of the Ku Klux or the paramilitary rifle clubs as did Nathan Bedford Forrest or fellow South Carolinian Martin Witherspoon Gary. While it is true that he also did not lead forces to put down such efforts, as did his fellow corps commander James Longstreet, very few white southerners ever did. Instead, Anderson attempted to navigate the postwar world, one forever altered by the realities of emancipation and the attendant decline in personal and financial status that resulted, as best he could for himself and his family.

Just as Anderson never took up the sword after the Confederate surrender, he also never took up the pen to write turgid volumes in support of the Confederate cause as did Jefferson Davis, Jubal Early, and so many others who had participated the failed rebellion. He did not engage in the Lost Cause mythologizing meant to absolve himself and others for the actions that had contributed to the loss of very nearly a million American lives. In return, Anderson has slowly faded from memory, and has never been held in the same regard as the other luminaries of the Confederacy such as Lee, Jackson, Longstreet, or even Wade Hampton.

Anderson's posthumous memorialization, and lack thereof, speaks to his place within postwar memory. While the granite marker at his gave was erected at the dawn of the great period of monument building in service of the Lost Cause, its placement in a modest cemetery was more fitting with the earlier era of monuments dedicated to mourning the soldiers killed at war. Like the man himself, the low-slung monument demands little attention, instead fading into the background of the surrounding cemetery. It differs greatly from the imposing equestrian statue of Wade Hampton III, erected just a few years later in 1906, that dominates the public square at the South Carolina State House. And while there was a brief effort to include Anderson among the pantheon of Lost Cause heroes immortalized at Stone Mountain that effort ultimately came to naught. Perhaps if Anderson had taken up the pen in service of the creation of Lost Cause mythology as many of his fellow officers in the Army of Northern Virginia had done, he would have been remembered more widely and more favorably. But such self-promotion was not within the nature of the man. And so, Anderson has largely slipped out of memory. But perhaps Dick Anderson would have preferred nothing more than to slowly fade away and be forgotten. This book, however, has been an effort to return Anderson to our collective consciousness. To remember his place within the momentous events that rocked the nation in the years 1861–1865 and to take the final measure of a man whose sense of duty shaped the course of his life as a soldier of the South.

Acknowledgments

How do I begin to thank all the wonderful people who have assisted me over the past few decades of researching and writing this work? It would truly be a daunting task to name everyone, but I would be remiss in not mentioning two people who were instrumental in getting my research efforts off the ground. The first is John Coski, formerly of the Museum of the Confederacy, now the Museum of the American Civil War in Richmond, Virginia. John was kind enough—and I'm sorry to say foolish enough—to allow me to walk away from the museum with the microfilmed copy of General Anderson's letter book, which I took so long to read through and return that he probably thought it had disappeared forever from the museum collection. Despite my abuse of his kindness, John has remained a valuable source of information about General Anderson and other relevant figures whose papers are in the museum's manuscript collection.

The second person I feel compelled to thank personally is no longer with us; that is, Mrs. Mary Greenleaf White Anderson, who died in 2016 at the age of 94. In 1948, Mary married a naval officer, Richard Kerfoot Anderson. Anderson was a descendent of Dr. William Wallace Anderson, brother of General Richard H. Anderson, and the couple inherited "The Borough House," as the original Anderson plantation home became known. When I first met Miss Mary in August of 1999, I was welcomed graciously and with open arms into that elegant and historic pisé de terre home built largely by General Anderson's father. What a thrill to sleep in that wonderful old home so steeped in history, that saw the heavy tramping of British soldiers and Patriot troops in the Revolution or heard the soft tread of enslaved house servants as they laid the table for the morning meal. The voices of Joel Poinsett and General Thomas Sumter echoed in the high-ceilinged rooms, and in the old schoolroom adjacent to the house, which now housed the family's remarkable collection of diaries, letters, and plantation records, one could imagine the chattering voices of the young children anxious to be free to roam the plantation grounds. As for me, I could think of no place finer to be on a hot summer afternoon than sequestered in that pisé schoolhouse among the tangible remains of the lives of those who had once inhabited that home. It was the first of several very enjoyable visits, and eventually I met other distant and very kind relatives, including Joseph Cantey Elliott, author of *Lee's Noble Soldier*.

Just over two years later, the horrific events of 9/11 temporarily derailed my research and writing. For several years afterward, I served on active duty with the US Air Force, and more often than not I found myself deployed from home for extended periods. Nevertheless, as soon as opportunities were afforded, I continued my research on General Anderson, even though in fits and starts. Over many years, that research has taken me from Pensacola, Florida, to Carlisle, Pennsylvania, with innumerable stops in between at museums, battlefields, manuscript repositories, and even General Anderson's final home in Beaufort, South Carolina. My research efforts invariably met with able and congenial assistance wherever I went, and to all those who aided my work I extend my deepest gratitude.

I also thank American Public University System for a generous research grant that allowed me to travel to several of those important locations. In addition, many others happily assisted by telephone or correspondence, answering my inquiries about people, locations, or battle movements that added a level of professional knowledge I would have otherwise not risen to on my own. Thereby I learned more about such things as the Texas frontier forts of the 1850s, the location of the Great Salt Plain of Anderson's first military expedition with Nathan Boone, or the importance of phosphate mining in South Carolina. To all those whom I never met personally but who gave freely of their time and expertise I likewise extend my deepest thanks.

Last, I dedicate this book to the memory of my esteemed mentor, Russell F. Weigley, and to my great friend Michael A. Cavanaugh, both of whom continue to inspire my efforts. I hope this work would have met with their approval.

In a final acknowledgment of Miss Mary's great assistance and friendship, I will end here with the words she often used to close her correspondence: "Onward and Upward!"

Edward J. Hagerty
Rockbridge County, Virginia
Spring 2025

Abbreviations

BHA	Borough House Archives, Sumter, SC
CCHS	Cumberland County Historical Society, Carlisle, PA.
CMLSC	Confederate Memorial Literary Society Collection, Richmond, VA
DU	Duke University, NC
FHQ	Florida Historical Quarterly
FSNMP	Fredericksburg & Spotsylvania National Military Park, VA
GLI	Gilder Lehrman Institute of American History, NY
GNMP	Gettysburg National Military Park, PA
HU	Harvard University, Cambridge, MA
LOC	Library of Congress, Washington, DC
MHSM	Military Historical Society of Massachusetts
NARA	National Archives and Records Administration, Washington, DC
NCSA	North Carolina State Archives, Raleigh, NC
RNBP	Richmond National Battlefield Park, VA
SCHS	Sumter County Historical Society, Sumter, SC
SCL	South Caroliniana Library, University of South Carolina, Columbia
SHC	Southern Historical Collection, University of North Carolina, Chapel Hill
SHSP	Southern Historical Society Papers
USAMHI	US Army Military History Institute, Carlisle, PA
USMA	US Military Academy Library, West Point, NY
VHS	Virginia Historical Society, Richmond, VA
WLU	Washington & Lee University, Lexington, VA
W&M	William & Mary

Notes

Introduction

1. "Notice of Sale by Assignee in Bankruptcy," *Watchman* (Sumter, SC), November 29, 1871.
2. "South Carolina. Convention (1860–1862), Declaration of the Immediate Causes Which Induce and Justify the Secession of South Carolina from the Federal Union; and the Ordinance of Secession," Evans & Cogswell, printers to the Convention, 1860.
3. Stateborough, Stateboro, and Stateburg represent three variations of the place names used during various periods, with Stateburg being the most current, modern iteration. Stateburg is used throughout the text for the purpose of standardization, but it refers to the same location depending on the period under discussion.
4. Map showing the distribution of the slave population of the southern states of the United States. Compiled from the census of 1860, Library of Congress Geography and Map Division Washington, DC, http://hdl.loc.gov/loc.gmd/g3861e.cw0013200.
5. US Census Bureau, 1860 Census; DesChamps, "Free Agricultural Population," 82.
6. Woodward, ed., *Mary Chesnut's Civil War*, 830. Throughout her diary, Anderson's childhood friend and neighbor Mary Boykin Chesnut used the term "sandhill tackey" along with the term "country cracker" to describe lower class or poor white people.
7. Known as the Homestead during Dick Anderson's time, the plantation has been styled as The Borough House since the early twentieth century. Likewise, Riverton was the name most commonly used for much of the nineteenth century, but the name Riverview also appears in reference to the same property.
8. Morgan, "Task System," 555–56.
9. Loan Document, W. W. Anderson and William Ellison from Francis Sumter, undated, ca. 1846, BHA.
10. Walker, *Anderson*, 156.
11. Between 1854 and 1859, the Kansas Territory was plagued by a continual series of violent clashes between pro-slavery and anti-slavery proponents seeking to influence the territory's fate as a slave or free state.
12. Stokes, ed., *An Everlasting Circle*, 371.
13. One thousand dollars in 1871 equates approximately to $25,601 in 2024 inflation-adjusted dollars.
14. The sword is currently in the possession of his descendants at the family's ancestral home, the Borough House in Stateburg.
15. Eliott, *Lee's Noble Soldier*, 137–39, 142–43.
16. Saclarides, "Morbidity and Mortality," 762.
17. Freeman, *Lee's Lieutenants*, 1:xix.

Chapter 1: The High Hills of Santee

1. Grants and Indentures, The Borough House Archives, Stateburg, SC (cited hereafter as BHA); US Department of the Interior, National Park Service, National Register of Historic Places Inventory—"Nomination Form, 1–2," n.d., Sumter County Historical Society, Sumter, SC.
2. Higginbotham, *War of American Independence*, 361.
3. White, "The Borough House," BHA.
4. White, "The Borough House," BHA; Parler, "Afterglow," 74–75; Elliott, *Lee's Noble Soldier*, 13.
5. "Colonel Richard Anderson of the Maryland Line, Continental Army," typescript, n.d., BHA; Higginbotham, *War of American Independence*, 359–60, 366–67.
6. Anderson Family Genealogy, n.d., BHA; "Biographical Sketch of William Wallace Anderson," Ann Catherine Anderson Saunders, ca. December 1914, BHA.
7. US Census Bureau, 1820 Census, Richland District, SC; Anderson Family Genealogy, n.d., BHA; Elliott, *Lee's Noble Soldier*, 14; "Biographical Sketch of William Wallace Anderson," Ann Catherine Anderson Saunders, ca. December 1914, BHA; William Wallace Anderson to Richard H. Anderson, April 25, 1852, BHA.
8. NPS, Nomination Form, 1–2, 1–6; Anderson, "The Borough House, Stateburg, South Carolina," typescript, ca. 1983, BHA.
9. Slave Purchase Receipts, BHA; Berry, *Pound of Flesh*, 11.
10. Elliott, *Lee's Noble Soldier*, 16.
11. US Census Bureau, 1830 Population Schedule, Sumter District, SC.
12. Sobel, "Personal Ethics," in *Black and White*, ed. Ted Ownby. 59; Berry, *Pound of Flesh*, 36–37.
13. See Berry, *Pound of Flesh*, and Sobel, "Personal Ethics" for discussions of relationships between enslaved and white plantation children; Conway, *Testimonies*, 5–6.
14. Drago, *Broke by the War*, 13. Sumter is used throughout the text; however, the town was called Sumterville until 1855.
15. For a discussion of physicians' certificates, racism and slave trading in Sumter County see Tadman, *Speculators and Slaves*, and Drago, *Broke by the War*.
16. Kolchin, *American Slavery*, 94; Williams, ed., *Diary from Dixie*, 293; Stern, *Mary Chesnut's Civil War*, 175–76.
17. Woodward, ed., *Mary Chesnut's Civil War*, 198–99.
18. John Benjamin Anderson Diary, September 17, 1855, November 30, 1855, December 1–2, 1855, May 1, 1856, May 20, 1856, December 15, 1856, BHA.
19. W. W. Anderson to Mary V. Childs, May 12, 1855, BHA; Mary V. Anderson to Ann Childs, December 15, 1857, BHA; Mary A. Childs to Ann Childs, January 13, 1861, BHA.
20. US Census, 1850 Population Schedule, Baltimore, MD; 1850 Slave Schedule, Familysearch.org, accessed June 24, 2024, https://www.familysearch.org/ark:/61903/1:1:HRW8-HGW2?lang=en; Frederick Childs to Ann Childs, June 13, 1858, BHA.
21. For discussion of slave revolts see Aptheker, *American Negro Slave Revolts*.
22. For more on slave labor conditions, see McDonnell's "Work, Culture, and Society" and Joyner's *Down by the Riverside*. See also *South Carolina Encyclopedia*, "Slave Labor," accessed May 16, 2024, https://www.scencyclopedia.org/sce/entries/slave-labor/.

23. Glymph, *House of Bondage*, 3–4, 19, 49–52; Phillips, *American Negro Slavery*, 323, quoted in Glymph, *House of Bondage*, 19.
24. Glymph, *House of Bondage*, 21,
25. Edgehill Academy Receipts, December 1834 and October 1835, BHA; Bakewell, Philosophical Conversations, 4–5; Sixtieth Anniversary Meeting of the Dick Anderson Division, United Daughters of the Confederacy, November 5, 1957, SHS; Elliot, *Lee's Noble Soldier*, 17.
26. William McWillie Diary, 1864, MDAH.
27. Williams, ed., *Diary from Dixie*, 267.
28. William W. Anderson, *Medical Diary*, n.p. BHA.
29. Anderson, *Medical Diary*, n.p.; Anderson, "Case of steo-sarcoma," 315–18; Gibson, *Institutes*, 436.
30. Saunders, "Biography of William Wallace Anderson," *Edgefield Chronicle*, September 20, 1915, BHA; Hume, "Ornithologists," 1318; Marcy, *Prairie Traveler*, 254.
31. Records Relating to USMA, 1812–1867, Record Group (cited hereafter as RG) 94, National Archives and Records Administration, Washington, DC (cited hereafter as NARA); Morrison, *The Best School in the World: West Point, the Pre-Civil War Years, 1833–1866*, 62–63.

Chapter 2: From West Point to Mexico

1. Anderson reported in late May or early June for preparatory instruction before the start of the plebe year.
2. Pappas, *To the Point*, 236–40.
3. Morrison, *Best School*, 40–41; Wert, *Longstreet*, 29; Sorrel, *Recollections*, 242.
4. Pappas, *To the Point*, 240–42.
5. Morrison, *Best School*, 77–82; Pfanz, *Richard S. Ewell*, 18.
6. Official Register, USMA, 1841 and 1842, USMA Library; Morrison, *Best School*, 90–99; 160–63.
7. Morrison, *Best School*, 8–11, 15–16.
8. Cullum, *Register*, 2:143; Official Register, USMA Library; Monthly Regimental Returns, 1st Dragoons, July 1, 1842–July 15, 1844, RG 94, NARA; Warner, *Generals in Blue*, 111.
9. Cullum, *Register*, 2: 140; Warner, *Generals in Blue*, 492–93; Morrison, *Best School*, 183.
10. Rodenbough, *Everglade to Cañon*, 245–46.
11. Rodenbough, *Everglade to Cañon*, 246.
12. Monthly Regimental Returns, 1st Dragoons, RG 94, NARA; Flynn, "Reminiscences," USAMHI, 2; Cullum, *Register*, 1:612, 2:49.
13. Monthly Regimental Returns, 1st Dragoons, RG 94, NARA.
14. Frazer, *Forts of the West*, 120; Agnew, *Fort Gibson*, 29–30, 104–5; Prucha, *Sword of the Republic*, 240–45.
15. Flynn, "Reminiscences," 2–3.
16. Flynn, "Reminiscences," 4–5; Rodenbough, *Everglade to Cañon*, 439.
17. Pelzer, *Marches*, 189; Flynn, "Reminiscences,"10; Regimental Records, 1st Dragoons, NARA.
18. Pelzer, *Marches*, 191–92.
19. Pelzer, *Marches*, 193–95.
20. Pelzer, *Marches*, 197–99.

21. Pelzer, *Marches*, 199.
22. Pelzer, *Marches*, 183–85, 201–5.
23. Pelzer, *Marches*, 207; Flynn, "Reminiscences," 8.
24. Pelzer, *Marches*, 208–10.
25. Pelzer, *Marches*, 211; Flynn, "Reminiscences," 11.
26. Pelzer, *Marches*, 213–23.
27. Pelzer, *Marches*, 235–37.
28. Sorrel, *Recollections*, 243.
29. Frazer, *Forts*, 125–26.
30. Pierce M. Butler to W. W. Anderson, May 22, 1844, BHA.
31. Monthly Regimental Returns, 2nd Dragoons, RG 94, NARA; Rodenbough, *Everglade to Cañon*, 93–94.
32. Anderson to R. Jones, March 31, 1846 and April 30. 1846, Letters Received, Adjutant General's Office (AGO), NARA; Sales Receipt for Wilkes House, ca. April 1848, BHA.

Chapter 3: The Mexican–American War

1. Anderson to R. Jones, June 2, 1846; R. B. Mason to R. Jones, July 14 and August 12, 1846, Letters Received, AGO; Monthly Regimental Returns, 2nd Dragoons, RG 94, NARA.
2. Monthly Regimental Returns, 2nd Dragoons, RG 94, NARA; Henry, *Mexican War*, 139–40.
3. Rodenbough, *Everglade to Cañon*, 134; Henry, *Mexican War*, 262–66.
4. Kendall, *Dispatches*, 207–8; Cullum, *Register*, 143; Anderson to George W. Cullum, March 25, 1860, USMA; Official List of Officers Engaged in the Battles of Mexico, Elizabeth Boykin Collection.
5. Kendall, *Dispatches*, 210–20; Rodenbough, *Everglade to Cañon*, 138–40; Henry, *Mexican War*, 282–87.
6. Rodenbough, *Everglade to Cañon*, 146–47; Henry, *Mexican War*, 303.
7. Rodenbough, *Everglade to Cañon*, 150.
8. Henry, *Mexican War*, 322; Scott, *Forgotten Valor*, 104.
9. Rodenbough, *Everglade to Cañon*, 151–52; 522; W. Hardee to H. Woodward, May 26, 1848, BHA; Anderson to "Sir," April 28, 1859, Anderson Letterbook, CMLSC, VHS.
10. W. Hardee to H. Woodward, May 26, 1848, BHA; Anderson to "Sir," April 28, 1859, Anderson Letterbook, CMLSC, VHS.
11. Henry, *Mexican War*, 348–55; Ex. Doc. 1 Sen., 30th Cong., 1st Sess. 361–66, 373–74 (1847); Rodenbough, *Everglade to Cañon*, 156.
12. Henry, *Mexican War*, 357–62; Rodenbough, *Everglade to Cañon*, 157.
13. Henry, *Mexican War*, 362–67; Rodenbough, *Everglade to Cañon*, 158–59.
14. Scott, *Forgotten Valor*, 106; Morrison, *Memoirs*, 57–60, 68–69; Aztec Club, "Index of Biographies," accessed April 4, 2023, http://www.aztecclub.com/bios/bio-index.htm.
15. Robertson, *Stonewall Jackson*, 71–73; Wert, *Longstreet*, 45; Pfanz, *Richard S. Ewell*, 57.
16. Rodenbough, *Everglade to Cañon*, 159, 437–53; Monthly Regimental Returns, 2nd Dragoons, RG94, NARA.
17. Grant, *Memoirs*, 1:180–81; Morrison, *Memoirs of Henry Heth*, 62–63; Thompson, "Winfield Scott's Army," 563, 566.

18. Buckner, "Visit to Popocatepetl," 410.
19. Thompson, "Pioneer Alpinists," 571–72; Buckner, "Visit," 415–16.
20. Monthly Regimental Returns, 2nd Dragoons, RG 94, NARA.

Chapter 4: From Carlisle to Texas

1. Monthly Regimental Returns, 2nd Dragoons; Phillip St. Geo. Cooke to Assistant Adjutant General, November 11, 1848, Letters Received, AGO; Charles A. May to AAG, November 23, 1848, Letters Received, AGO.
2. J. E. B. Stuart to John R. Cooke, January 18, 1862, Cooke Family Papers, VHS, quoted in Thomas, *Bold Dragoon*, 95; Warner, *Generals in Gray*, 259.
3. Middleton, "John Banister Gibson," 8–9, 25, CCHS; Kohn, *Eagle and Sword*, 115–16.
4. W. W. Anderson to R. H. Anderson, January 19. 1850, BHA.
5. W. W. Anderson to R. H. Anderson, January 19, 1850, BHA.
6. See Freehling, *Road to Disunion*, 487–510; Craven, *Growth of Southern Nationalism*, 70–103.
7. W. W. Anderson to R. H. Anderson, September 22, 1850, BHA; Anderson Family Genealogy, BHA; Elliott, *Lee's Noble Soldier*, 27–28; Will of W. W. Anderson, 1863, BHA; R. H. Anderson, Bankruptcy Petition, District Court of the US District of South Carolina, January 13, 1871, BHA.
8. Equivalent to over $20,000 of purchasing power in 2025 dollars.
9. *American Volunteer* (Carlisle), October 17, 1850 and *Herald* (Carlisle), October 16, 1850; "W. M. Roberts to daughter, October 7, 1872," cited in Elliot, *Lee's Noble Soldier*, 23; W. W. Anderson to R. H. Anderson, September 22, 1850, BHA.
10. Proceedings of The Meeting of Delegates 5, 10–13, 26.
11. Edward Anderson to "My Dear Brother," ca. August 1852, Boykin Collection.
12. Edward Anderson to "My Dear Brother," ca. August 1852, Boykin Collection; Anderson Plantation Slave Book, BHA; Koger, *Black Slaveowners*, 144–45.
13. Miscellaneous File, BHA; Hiwassee (typescript record of ownership), BHA; E. M. Anderson Inventory and Appraisement of Personal Property, September 15, 1862, (typescript) BHA.
14. Edward Anderson to "My Dear Brother," ca. August 1852, Boykin Collection.
15. Monthly Regimental Returns, 2nd Dragoons, RG 94; Hardee to H. Woodward, May 26, 1848, BHA.

Chapter 5: Frontier Service, Texas to Kansas, and Resignation

1. Myres, "Fort Graham," 33–35; A. J. B., "The Indian Reserves of Texas," The Texas Almanac for 1859, 130–31.
2. Sullivan, *Fort McKavett*, 5–6; Utley, *Indian Frontier*, 56; Utley, *Frontiersmen*, 63–64.
3. Utley, *Frontiersmen*, 72–74; Sullivan, *Fort McKavett*, 9–10; Monthly Regimental Returns, 2nd Dragoons, NARA.
4. Anderson to James Belger, January 29, 1854, Anderson Letterbook, VHS.
5. Anderson to Belger, March 7 and 21, 1854, Anderson Letterbook, VHS.
6. Anderson to P. Claytin, February 13, 1854, Anderson Letterbook, VHS.
7. Anderson to Claytin, n.d., ca. April–May 1854, Anderson Letterbook, VHS.
8. Anderson to Alfred Gibbs, March 21, 1854, Anderson Letterbook, VHS.
9. Sullivan, *Fort McKavett*, 18–19; Rodenbough, *From Everglade to Cañon*, 169, 453.

10. General Court Martial (cited hereafter as GCM), San Antonio, Texas, September 19, 1854, NARA ; Anderson to D. C. Buell, May 17, 1854, Anderson Letterbook, VHS; Anderson to Samuel Cooper, August 10, 1854, Anderson Letterbook, VHS.
11. GCM, NARA.
12. GCM, NARA.
13. GCM, NARA; Anderson to Buel, May 17, 1854, Anderson Letterbook, VHS; Anderson to Cooper, August 10, 1854, Anderson Letterbook, VHS.
14. GCM, NARA.
15. GCM, NARA; Anderson to F. J. Wood, April 23, 1854, GCM File; Anderson to Buell, May 17, 1854, Anderson Letterbook, VHS; Anderson to Cooper, August 10, 1854, Anderson Letterbook, VHS.
16. Anderson to Buell, May 17, 1854, Anderson Letterbook, VHS; Anderson to Cooper, August 10, 1854, Anderson Letterbook, VHS.
17. Anderson to Cooper, August 10, 1854, Anderson Letterbook, VHS; GCM.
18. J. H. Powell to Miss Morrison, May 10, 1933, GCM, NARA; Davis, Papers of Jefferson Davis, Vol. 6, 1856–1860, 29; Regimental Record Book, 2nd Dragoons, NARA.
19. Anderson to Calhoun, January 17, 1855, Anderson Letterbook, VHS; Robinson, *Men Who Wear the Star,* 110–11.
20. Anderson to Calhoun, January 17, 1855, Anderson Letterbook, VHS; Edmund K. Smith to Francis M. Webster, September 1, 1856, Smith Kirby Webster Black Family Papers, USAMHI.
21. Monthly Regimental Returns, 2nd Dragoons, NARA; Anderson to Don Carlos Buell, April 1, 1855, Anderson Letterbook, VHS.
22. Mary Anderson to Sallie Anderson, May 29, 1855, typescript, BHA.
23. Mary Anderson to Sallie Anderson, May 29, 1855, typescript, BHA.
24. Utley, *Frontiersmen,* 113–15; Beck, *First Sioux War,* 55–56.
25. Monthly Regimental Returns, RG 94, NARA; Rodenbough, *Everglade to Cañon,* 170–71.
26. Monthly Regimental Returns, RG 94, NARA; Utley, *Frontiersmen,* 116–17.
27. Lowe, *Five Years a Dragoon,* 153–54, 157–58; Anderson to T. J. Wright, October 3, 1855, Anderson Letterbook, VHS.
28. Hammond, "Nathaniel Lyon and R. H. Anderson," *The Watchman and Southron,* June 2, 1885, 1; Phillips, *Damned Yankee,* 85.
29. Hammond, "Nathaniel Lyon and R. H. Anderson," *The Watchman and Southron,* June 2, 1885, 1; Phillips, *Damned Yankee,* 85.
30. Hammond, "Nathaniel Lyon and R. H. Anderson," *The Watchman and Southron,* June 2, 1885, 1; Phillips, *Damned Yankee,* 85.
31. Mullis, *Peacekeeping,* 23–24; Monthly Regimental Returns, 2nd Dragoons, NARA; W. W. Anderson to "My Dear Son," September 22, 1850, BHA; Anderson to T. J. Wright, April 15, 1856, Anderson Letterbook, VHS.
32. Anderson to Cooke, December 18, 1856, Anderson Letterbook, VHS.
33. Monthly Regimental Returns, 2nd Dragoons, RG 94, NARA; Cordley, *History of Lawrence Kansas,* n.p.
34. Anderson to Cooper, June 10, 1857, Anderson Letterbook, VHS.
35. Anderson to Cooper, September 12 and 14, 1857, Anderson to Buford, September 12, 1857, Anderson Letterbook, VHS.
36. Newell, *Regular Army,* 36.

37. Newell, *Regular Army*, 49–50.
38. Freehling, *Road to Disunion*, 140–44.
39. Gallagher, ed., *Fighting for the Confederacy*, 9, 365.
40. McWillie Diary, MDAH.
41. Anderson to "Sir," April 28, 1859, Anderson Letterbook, VHS.
42. Frederick Childs to W. W. Anderson, December 2, 1860, BHA; Govan and Livingood, eds., *The Haskell Memoirs*, vi.
43. Mary Anderson Childs to Ann Childs, January 13, 1861, BHA: W. Wallace Anderson to McKenzie Anderson, January 26, 1861, BHA.
44. Woodward and Muhlenfeld, eds., *Private Life of Mary Chesnut*, 29; Elliott, *Lee's Noble Soldier*, 30; Sallie Anderson to Thomas S. Mills, ca. July 1864, BHA.
45. Anderson to Samuel S. Cooper, February 16, 1861, Anderson Letterbook, VHS.

Chapter 6: Charleston to Pensacola Bay

1. Huguenin Memoirs, copy in possession of descendant, Ellen Gray Hogan, South Boston, VA, provided to author by Robert K. Krick, Fredericksburg & Spotsylvania National Military Park.
2. *Official Records* (cited hereafter as *O.R.*), 1, 1:36, 39–43. Citations are for Series One unless otherwise noted.
3. "General Orders No. 42, Head Quarters Provisional Forces, Charleston S.C. May 27th, 1861," Miscellaneous Files, BHA; *O.R.*, 2:896; Anderson to Cooper, May 29, 1861; Anderson to S. R. Gist, June 7, 1861, Anderson Letterbook, VHS.
4. Anderson to Cooper, June 10, 1861; Anderson to Gist, June 18, 1861; Anderson to "Chief of Ordnance," June 20, 1861, Anderson Letterbook, VHS.
5. Anderson to "Capt Bonneau," June 10, 1861; Anderson to Cooper, June 11, 1861; Anderson to Gist, June 24, 1861, Anderson Letterbook, VHS.
6. Pickens to Walker, July 11, 1861, NARA, M409, "Letters Received by Secretary of War."
7. Anderson to Cooper, July 29, 1861; Anderson to Walker, July 29, 1861, Anderson Letterbook, VHS.
8. Special Orders No. 130, Richard H. Anderson, Compiled Military Service Record, RG 109, NARA; Braxton Bragg to wife, September 1, 1861, LOC.
9. McWhiney, *Braxton Bragg*, 177.
10. US Navy Department, Naval War Records Office, *Official Records of the Union and Confederate Navies in the War of the Rebellion*, Series 1, Volume 16: 670–73, (cited hereafter as *O.R.N.*). Citations are for Series 1 unless otherwise noted; *O.R.*, 6:437–38, 458.
11. *O.R.*, 6:438; McWhiney, *Braxton Bragg*, 165.
12. Boggs, *Military Reminiscences*, 14; McWhiney, *Braxton Bragg*, 188; *O.R.*, 6:458.
13. Bragg to wife, April 24, 1861, Bragg Papers, LOC; Smedlund, *Camp Fires*, 255.
14. Milner, "Reminiscences."
15. *O.R.*, 6:460–61; McWhiney, *Braxton Bragg*, 181–82; Warner, *Generals in Gray*, 7.
16. *O.R.*, 6:461; Smedlund, *Camp Fires*, 255.
17. *O.R.*, 6:461.
18. *O.R.*, 6:461; Morris, *History*, 57; Smedlund, *Camp Fires*, 255; Braxton Bragg to Samuel Cooper and Elise Bragg, quoted in McWhiney, *Braxton Bragg*, 194.
19. McWhiney, *Braxton Bragg*, 193; Hewitt, *Supplement to the Official Records of the Union and Confederate Armies* (cited hereafter as *O.R.S.*), Part I, Vol. 1:449, 453. Citations are for Part 1 unless noted otherwise.

20. *O.R.*, 6:447–48; *O.R.S.*, 1:453; Morris, *History*, 57. M. W. Shanahan to James Ham, October 13, 1862, M. W. Shanahan Letters, Abraham Lincoln Presidential Library.
21. *O.R.*, 6:448–49; *O.R.S.*, 1:454–55; Milner, *Reminiscences*, UNC.
22. *O.R.*, 6: 450; Morris, *History*, 63.
23. *O.R.*, 6:451; Milner, *Reminiscences*. UNC
24. *O.R.*, 6:462; Milner, *Reminiscences*, UNC.
25. *O.R.*, 6:445, 462; Dr. J. H. Randolph to "My Dear Sir," October 17, 1861, PHS; *O.R.S.*, 1:453, 459.
26. McWhiney, *Braxton Bragg*, 193–95; *O.R.*, 6:458–59.
27. Sallie Anderson to Mary Anderson Childs, October 15, 1861, quoted in Elliott, *Lee's Noble Soldier*, 34; Bills and Accounts, September 7, 1861, BHA.
28. *O.R.N.*, 16:703; *O.R.*, 6:469; Pearce, *Pensacola*, 120–22.
29. Boggs, *Reminiscences*, 18–19; "General Richard Heron Anderson," Blanding Papers, HU.
30. *O.R.S.*, 1:464–66, 471; Pearce, *Penscacola*, 124.
31. *O.R.S.*, 1:467, 485; *O.R.N.*, 16:776, 781; *O.R.*, 6:485.
32. *O.R.N.*, 16:783–84; *O.R.*, 6:485, 491, 493; *O.R.S.*, I:469; Morris, *History*, 67.
33. *O.R.*, 6:494–95; *O.R.N.*, 16:783; Crist and Dix, eds., *Jefferson Davis*, 357.
34. Boggs, *Reminiscences*, 20, 105–6.
35. *O.R.*, 1, 6:497.
36. Boggs, *Reminiscences*, 107.
37. *O.R.*, 6:496; Morris, *History*, 72; Pearce, *Pensacola*, 136–37.
38. *O.R.*, 6:497–98.
39. Boggs, *Reminiscences*, 106; *O.R.*, 6:496–98, 802; *O.R.S.*, 1:481–83.
40. Special Orders No. 8, HQ Army of Pensacola, January 8, 1862, CMSR, RG 109, NARA; Special Orders No. 8, HQ Department of Northern Virginia, February 15, 1862, BHA; Crist and Dix, eds., *Jefferson Davis*, 357.
41. Sorrel, *Recollections*, 128; Freeman, ed., *Lee's Dispatches*, 10; J. E. B. Stuart to Flora Stuart, February 14, 1862, Stuart Papers, VHS; Bills and Accounts, BHA; W. A. Saunders to C. Irvine Walker, January 28, 1926, BHA.
42. William Wallace Anderson to "My dear son," March 8, 1862, BHA; Richard H. Anderson to "My dear Father," May 9, 1862, BHA.

Chapter 7: Yorktown and the Seven Days

1. Freeman, *Lee's Lieutenants*, 1:148–55; *O.R.* 11, 1:405–11; James T. Petty, April 24, 1862, Petty Diary, VHS; J. R. Page to "Dear Georgia and Tuck," April 25, 1862, Grinnan Family Papers, UVA; Bratton to "Dear Bettie," April 25, 1862, Bratton Letters, SHC; Mason, "Three Years in the Army", GNMP, 7–8; Maxwell to "Dear Father," April 25, 1862, Maxwell Papers, VHS.
2. Sears, *Gates*, 62.
3. Sears, *Gates*, 68; R. H. Anderson to Thomas G. Rhett, April 15, 21, and 27, 1862, Anderson Letterbook, VHS; Coker, *6th S.C. Regiment*, 51.
4. R. H. Anderson to Thomas G. Rhett, April 27, 1862, Anderson Letterbook, VHS; Petty Diary, April 12, 1862, VHS.
5. Sears, *Gates*, 69; Petty Diary, May 4, 1862, VHS; Coker, *6th S.C. Regiment*, 52; Barrett, *Yankee Rebel*, 18.
6. Sears, *Gates*, 70, 73, 78.

7. Petty Diary, May 4 and 5, 1862, VHS; Mason, "Three Years in the Army," 8, GNMP.
8. Anderson to Moxley Sorrel, May 11, 1862, Anderson Letterbook, VHS; *O.R.*, 11, 1:580–82; Reid, *Fourth Regiment*, 80.
9. R. H. A. to W. W. Anderson, May 9, 1862, BHA; Anderson to Sorrel, Report, May 10, 1862, Anderson Letterbook, VHS; *O.R.* 11, 1:565, 580–81, 582, 584–85, 590–93; Dubbs, *Defend*, 95–97; Freeman, *Lee's Lieutenants*, 1:179; Pfanz, *Gettysburg*, 362; Patterson, *Blue to Gray*, 25–27.
10. Barrett, *Yankee Rebel*, 20; Mason, "Three Years in the Army," 8.
11. *O.R.*, 11, 1:564–65, 571, 576–77, 591; Cadmus Wilcox to Edward P. Alexander, February 6, 1869, Wilcox File, Participant Accounts, GNMP.
12. R. H. Anderson to W. W. Anderson, May 9, 1862, BHA.
13. Robertson, *A. P. Hill*, 55; *O.R.*, 11, 1:567, 576, 584–85, 597, 606.
14. Freeman, *Lee's Lieutenants*, 1:188; Anderson to Sorrel, Report, May 10, 1862, Anderson Letterbook, VHS; Osborne, *Jubal*, 80–81; Coker, *6th S.C. Regiment*, 54–56.
15. Richard Anderson to William Wallace Anderson, May 9, 1862, BHA.
16. Richard Anderson to William Wallace Anderson, May 9, 1862, BHA.
17. Mary V. Anderson to W. W. Anderson, June 21, 1862, BHA; Thomas Atkinson to Mary V. Anderson, March 13, 1862, BHA.
18. Crist, *Jefferson Davis*, 8: 170–71.
19. Lee to Davis, June 7, 1862; Lee to Davis, June 25, 1862, Virginia Military Institute, original in Lee–Davis Correspondence, Virginia State Library (cited hereafter as VSL); Longstreet to Lee, June 6, 1862, General Officer Files, CMSR; James Longstreet to Joseph E. Johnston, June 7, 1862, Longstreet Papers, Huntington Library, quoted in Wert, *Longstreet*, 125; Freeman, *Lee's Lieutenants*, 1:611–12; *O.R.*, 11, 1:935.
20. Sears, *Gates*, 119–20; *O.R.*, 11, 1:940. 944, 947–50; R. H. Anderson to E. P. Alexander, October 4, 1867, Alexander Collection, SHC; Coker, *6th S.C. Regiment*, 63–64, 69; McWillie Diary, 1864, MDAH; Langston James Goree, V., *Thomas Goree Letters*, 1: 151–52, 155, 162.
21. Coker, *6th S.C. Regiment*, 68–69; "The Sixth South Carolina Regiment," *Richmond Daily Dispatch*, June 5, 1862.
22. Anderson to D. H. Hill, November 14, 1867, D. H. Hill Collection, NCSA; Petty Diary, June 1, 1862, VHS.
23. Woodward, ed., *Mary Chestnut's Civil War*, 400; Woodward and Muhlenfeld, eds., *Private Mary Chestnut*, 211.
24. *O.R.*, 11, 1:951; Johnson, *Memoir*, 89; Smith, J. O., *Confederate War Papers*, 181–85; Smith, G. W., *Seven Pines*, 103–4.
25. Reardon, "From 'King of Spades,'" 312–13; *O.R.*, 11, 2:796.
26. Pay Vouchers, April and December 1862, CMSR, NARA; Hawkins and Nairsain, "Coppens' Zouaves," *Richmond Dispatch*, June 14, 1862.
27. Anderson to Sorrel, June 17, 1862, Anderson Letterbook, VHS; Thomas J. Blackwell to "My Dear Wife," June 24, 1862, RNBP; Micah Jenkins to Wife, June 22, 1862, Micah Jenkins Papers, SCL.
28. "Committee," *Lancaster Ledger* (SC), July 16, 1862; Warner, *Generals in Gray*, 155; Wert, *Longstreet*, 119.
29. *O. R.*, 11, 2:498–99, 552,; Burton, *Extraordinary Circumstances*, 36–37; Sears, *Gates*, 194–95.
30. Sears, *Gates*, 183–89; Burton, *Extraordinary Circumstances*, 44–51.

31. *O. R.*, 11, 1:623; Burton, *Extraordinary Circumstances*, 61–75; Sears, *Gates*, 195–207; Wheeler, *Sword Over Richmond*, 296–300; Petty Diary, June 26, 1862, VHS.
32. Bohannon, "Six Sons," 8.
33. *O.R.*, 11, 2:222.
34. *O.R.*, 11, 2:224, 492; Freeman, *Lee's Lieutenants*, 1:518–19; Sears, *Gates*, 213–15.
35. *O.R.*, 11, 1:756.
36. Sears, *Gates*, 221–26; *O.R.*, 11, 1:837.
37. *O.R.*, 11, 1:757; Freeman, *Lee's Lieutenants*, 1:526; Longstreet, *Manassas to Appomattox*, 127.
38. Longstreet, *Manassas to Appomattox*, 127–28.
39. Coker, *6th S.C. Regiment*, 74.
40. Longstreet, *Manassas to Appomattox*, 128; *O.R.*, 11, 2:46, 555; Mason, "Three Years in the Army," 10.
41. Petty Diary, June 28, 1862, VHS; *O.R.*, 11, 2:758; Longstreet to Lee, June 6, 1862, CMSR, NARA; Freeman, *Lee's Lieutenants*, 1:652.
42. Sears, *Gates*, 249, 256, 269–70, 274; Eicher, *Longest Night*, 291.
43. Sears, *Gates*, 283–93; Wert, *Longstreet*, 140–43; Eicher, *Longest Night*, 290–92.
44. Gallagher, ed., *Fighting for the Confederacy*, 107; *O.R.*, 11, 2:111.
45. *O.R.*, 11, 1:776–78.
46. Sears, *Gates*, 295–99, 307: Coker, *6th S. C. Regiment*, 81–83; Warfield, *Memoirs*, 78–81; Robertson, *Lee*, 55; Freeman, *Lee*, 215.
47. *O.R.*, 11, 1:495.
48. *O.R.*, 11, 1:790; Sears, *Gates*, 313, 318–21, 338–41; Wert, *Longstreet*, 148; Freeman, *Lee's Lieutenants*, 1:599–603.

Chapter 8: Division Command and 2nd Manassas

1. Freeman, *Lee*, 223; *O.R.*, 11, 1:642; R. H. Anderson, Farewell Address to Brigade, Anderson Letterbook, July 15, 1862, VHS.
2. Freeman, *Lee's Lieutenants*, 1:670–74.
3. Wright's Brigade Order Book, June 18, 1862–December 31, 1862, USAMHI; Daniel Gilley to "Dear Father and mother and sisters," July 13, 1862, Gilley Papers, VHS; Lewis Miles to "Dear Companion," August 5, 1862, USAMHI.
4. Dowdey and Manarin, *Wartime Papers*, 244, 254–55; Anderson to D. H. Hill, November 14, 1867, NCSA; R. E. Lee to Fitz John Porter, October 31, 1867, WLU; Anderson to D. H. Hill, August 5, 1862, Blanding-Anderson Papers, SCL; *O.R.*, 12, 2:566.
5. Todd, "Reminiscences," 30–32, SHC.
6. *O.R.*, 12, 2:349; Todd, "Reminiscences," 30–32, SHC; Hennessy, *Return to Bull Run*, 309.
7. Todd, "Reminiscences," 39, SHC.
8. Todd, "Reminiscences," 40–41, SHC.
9. Dowdey and Manarin, *Wartime Papers*, 282; Hennessy, *Return to Bull Run*, 415.
10. Hennessy, *Return to Bull Run*, 415–17; Todd, "Reminiscences" 40–41, SHC.
11. Hennessy, *Return to Bull Run*, 417–21; Todd, "Reminiscences," 42–43, SHC; *O.R.*, 12, 2:737; Hennessy, "Historical Report," NPS, 490–91, 495, 515.
12. Freeman, *Lee's Lieutenants*, 1:128–29; Longstreet, *Manassas to Appomattox*, 192; Hunter, "High Private's Account," SHSP, 505; Warfield, *Memoirs*, 91.
13. *O.R.*, 12, 2:566; Longstreet, *Manassas to Appomattox*, 192; Groene, "Letters of Colonel David Lang," FHQ, 343.

Chapter 9: Harpers Ferry to Sharpsburg

1. *O.R.*, 19, 2:592, 596; Bohannon, "Six Sons," 8; Hopkins, *Bull Run to Appomattox*, 55.
2. Evans, *Sixteenth Mississippi*, 114; John Sale to "Dear Aunt," January 31, 1863, Grinnan Family Papers, UVA.
3. *O.R.*, 19, 2:603–4; *O,R.*, 19, 1:44–45, 757, 852.
4. Anderson to D. H. Hill, November 14, 1867, NCSA; Oeffinger, *McLaws*, 29.
5. Henry King Diary, September 10, 1862, FSNMP; *O.R.*, 19, 1:852–53; Evans, *Sixteenth Mississippi*, 114; Featherston, "Memoir," USAMHI.
6. *O.R.*, 19, 1:854.
7. *O.R.*, 19, 1:854–55.
8. Sears, *Landscape*, 120; *O.R.*, 19, 1:380, 394, 870, 877; Henry King Diary, September 14, 1862, FSNMP.
9. Oeffinger, *McLaws*, 115; Henry King Diary, September 14, 1862, FSNMP; *O.R.*, 19, 1:839, 1021: Dowdy and Manarin, *Wartime Papers*, 307–8.
10. *O.R.*, 19, 2:608–10; *O.R.*, 19, 1:855; Harsh, *Taken*, 248–52.
11. *O.R.*, 19,1:855–57; Henry King Diary, September 13, 1862, FSNMP; Anderson to D. H. Hill, November 14, 1867, NCSA; Freeman, *Lee's Dispatches*, 93.
12. *O.R.*, 19, 1:857–58; Armistead's Brigade, Antietam Studies Collection, NARA.
13. Harsh, *Taken*, 397–98; Wert, *Longstreet*, 197–98; Sears, *Landscape*, 241–42, 244–45; *O.R.*, 19, 1:1023–24; Walker, *Anderson*, 110; *Richmond Dispatch*, "From our Army on the Rappahanock," September 2, 1862.; Evans, *Sixteenth* Mississippi, 115; Collins, *Rodes*, 169–70.
14. Waters and Edmonds, *Small but Spartan Band*, 37–38; Pryor's Brigade, "Eighth Florida," Map with 1895 Participant Notations, LOC; *O.R.*, 19, 1:1048; John B. Hughes to R. D. Parker, February 25, 1900, CPL.
15. Bohannon, "Six Sons," 8.
16. Glatthaar, *General Lee's Army*, 172–73; Sears, *Landscape*, 304; Wright's Brigade Order Book June 18–December 31, 1862, USAMHI.
17. Patterson, *Blue to Gray*, 50–51; Robertson, *A. P. Hill*, 12; Warner, *Generals in Gray*, 142, 296.
18. Patterson, *Blue to Gray*, 50.
19. Harsh, *Taken*, 443–67; Dowdey and Manarin, *Wartime Papers*, 322; *O.R.*, 19, 2:627.
20. *O.R.*, 19, 2:621, 660; Evans, *Sixteenth Mississippi*, 119; Barrett, *Yankee Rebel*, 64–65; McClellen, Bailey G. "History of Company D," 1901, copy from the *Anniston* (AL) *Evening Star*, GNMP.
21. Mason, "Three Years in the Army," 12.
22. *Richmond Enquirer*, "Movements of our Army in Maryland," September 23, 1862.
23. *O.R.*, 19, 1:812, 884–85; *O.R.S.*, 3:568–70.
24. Fortin, "Herbert's 'History of the 8th Alabama Regiment,'" 77–81.
25. *O.R.*, 19, 1:847.

Chapter 10: Fredericksburg

1. Sorrel, *Recollections*, 128.
2. Edwin Sherwood to "Dear Father," October 1, 1862, Edwin Sherwood Papers, VHS; Wright's Brigade Order Book, November 28, 1862, USAMHI; Mason, "Three Years in the Army," 14.

3. Harsh, *Taken,* 477–79; Warner, *Generals in Blue,* 57; Mason, "Three Years in the Army," 13; Evans, *Sixteenth Mississippi,* 124; O'Reilly, *Fredericksburg Campaign,* 11–12, 21.
4. Mason, "Three Years in the Army," 13–14.
5. R. H. Anderson to "Captain," December 4, 1862, Anderson Letterbook, VHS; Mellon, "A Florida Soldier," 247, 248; Evans, *Sixteenth Mississippi,* 124.
6. Special Orders 234, Wright's Brigade Order Book, November 6, 1862, USAMHI; *O.R.,* 19, 1: 697–98; *O.R.,* 21, 1:1017, 1036; Freeman, *Lee's Lieutenants,* 1:264–66; Warner, *Generals in Gray,* 236; Holzman, *Adapt or Perish,* 59–60.
7. O'Reilly, *Fredericksburg,* 33–35; *O.R.,* 21, 1:552.
8. *O.R.,* 21, 1:608; *Yorkville Enquirer,* "Fredericksburg," December 14, 1887.
9. Anderson to Longstreet, December 5, 1862; Anderson to Wilcox, December 2, 1862, Anderson Letterbook, CMLSC, VHS; Wright's Brigade Order Book, December 2, 1862, USAMHI.
10. *O.R.,* 21, 1:603, 619; Waters and Edmunds, *Small but Spartan Band,* 43–44; Barrett, *Yankee Rebel,* 86–87; O'Reilly, *Fredericksburg,* 64, 81, 85–86.
11. O'Reilly, *Fredericksburg,* 78, 81–82; *O.R.,* 21, 1:579, 603, 610.
12. Walter Moore to wife, December 26, 1862, USAMHI; Featherston "Memoirs," USAMHI; *O.R.,* 21, 1:588, 609; Clark, *Glance Backward,* 27.
13. O'Reilly, *Fredericksburg,* 250; Wert, *Longstreet,* 216; *O.R.,* 21, 1:569–70, 615.
14. Featherston, "Memoir," Civil War Times Illustrated Collection (cited hereafter as CWTI), USAMHI; *O.R.,* 21, 1:618, 620–21, 628.
15. *O.R.,* 21, 1:609–10.
16. O'Reilly, *Fredericksburg,* 250; McLaws, "Battle of Fredericksburg," UCV, 83; *O.R.,* 21, 1: 580, 588–89; Freeman, *Lee's Lieutenants,* 1:359 n 3. Freeman characterizes McLaws' recollection as "confused," and notes that no official reports support his memory while some "at least inferentially" contradict him.
17. *O.R.,* 21, 1:570, 589–90; , Orders, "Headquarters 1st Corps," December 13, 1862, Alexander Collection, SHC; Evans, *Sixteenth Mississippi,* 128–29; Featherston, "Memoir," USAMHI.
18. *O.R.,* 21, 1:611–14, 620.
19. O'Reilly, *Fredericksburg,* 430–33.
20. Longstreet to Anderson, December 15, 1862, Alexander Collection, SHC; Circular, Anderson's Division Headquarters, December 15, 1862, Wright's Brigade Order Book, USAMHI; *Richmond Dispatch,* "Head'rs Anderson's Div'n, December 15, 1862," December 22, 1862.
21. *O.R.,* 21, 1:613, 571; *Richmond Dispatch,* "Interesting Account of the Battle of Fredericksburg," December 22, 1862.

Chapter 11: Winter Camp on the Rappahannock

1. Woodward, ed., *Mary Chestnut's Civil War,* 433, 445; Black, *Railroads of the Confederacy,* 81; United Daughters of the Confederacy, "Souvenir Program, State Convention, U.D.C.," SCHS.
2. Anderson to Longstreet, January 21, 1863, Anderson Letterbook, VHS; Groene, *Civil War Letters,* 345.
3. Civil War Florida Infantry Rosters, Eighth Florida Infantry, Florida Genealogy Trails, n.p.

4. Anderson to Cooper, January 21, 1863, Anderson Letterbook, VHS; Warner, *Generals in Gray*, 33–34; Bratton to "Dear Beattie," February 4, 1863 and to "Dear Wife," July 2, 1864, SHC.
5. Wilfred B. Yearns, *The Confederate Congress*, 104–5; Special Orders No. 91, April 1, 1863, Wright's Brigade Order Book.
6. Freeman, *Lee's Lieutenants*, 1:263–64; Featherston, "Memoir," CWMC, USAMHI; *O.R.*, 19, 2:697.
7. Winters, "The Battle That Was Never Fought," 33–35; Hagerty, *Collis' Zouaves*, 168.
8. Wright's Brigade, Order Book, January 18 and 22, 1863, USAMHI.
9. "Letters of Colonel David Lang," 346–47.
10. Bratton to "Dear Bettie," January 25, 1863, SHC.
11. Denoon, *Charlie's Letters*, 43, 46.
12. Anderson to "My Dear Wallace," January 9, 1863, BHA. Anderson's reference to Murfreesboro, Tennessee referred to Bragg's reverse there at the Battle of Stones River fought December 31, 1862 to January 2, 1863.
13. Anderson to "My Dear Wallace," January 9, 1863, BHA.
14. E. M. Anderson, Will, typescript copy from Sumter County Estate Papers, Bundle 144, SC Archives, BHA; Articles of Agreement, September 20, 1865, BHA.
15. W. W. Anderson to Jennie, February 2, 1864, BHA.
16. Articles of Agreement, September 20, 1865, BHA.
17. *O.R.*, 25, 2:641.
18. *O.R.*, 25, 1:849.
19. James Gaston letter, unknown, February 27, 1863, SHC.
20. Army of Northern Virginia Headquarters (cited hereafter as HQ, ANV), General Orders No. 24, March 21, 1863, Wright's Brigade Order Book, USAMHI; Anderson to Chilton, March 11, 1863, Anderson Letterbook, VHS; Anderson to Mahone, March 17, 1863, Anderson Letterbook, VHS; Lewis Miles to Amy Lewis, March 21, 1863, USAMHI.
21. HQ, ANV, General Orders No. 46, March 23, 1863, Wright's Brigade Order Book, USAMHI; Miles to Amy Lewis, March 23 and April 6, 1863, USAMHI.
22. Dowdey and Manarin, *Wartime Papers*, 405–6.

Chapter 12: Chancellorsville

1. McClellen, "10th Alabama," n.p., GNMP; Denoon, *Charlie's Letters*, 47–48.
2. *O.R.*, 25, 2:759–61.
3. *O.R.*, 25, 2:761.
4. *O.R.*, 25, 2:762.
5. *O.R.*, 25, 1:849–50, Wright's Brigade Order Book, April 29, 1863, USAMHI.
6. *O.R.*, 25, 1:850, 865, 1046–47; Furgurson, *Chancellorsville*, 101–3; Denoon, *Charlie's Letters*, 52.
7. *O.R.*, 25, 1:850, 855; Freeman, *Lee's Lieutenants*, 2:528; Evans, *Sixteenth Mississippi*, 147; Reaver, "Letters" 17–18.
8. Reaver, "Letters," 18–19.
9. *O.R.*, 25, 1:850, 866; Todd, "Reminiscences," 93, SHC; Furgurson, *Chancellorsville*, 133–34.
10. Furgurson, *Chancellorsville*, 125–26; Todd, "Reminiscences," 93–94, SHC; Denoon, *Charlie's Letters*, 52.

11. Furgurson, *Chancellorsville*, 127; Glatthaar, *General Lee's Army*, 245; *O.R.*, 25, 1:871.
12. Freeman, *Lee's Lieutenants*, 2:528–31.
13. Evans, *Sixteenth Mississippi*, 147–48; Freeman, *Lee's Lieutenants*, 2:538–42.
14. Freeman, *Lee's Lieutenants*, 2:546–47; Furgurson, *Chancellorsville*, 239.
15. *O.R.*, 25, 1:798, 851, 867, 871; Furgurson, *Chancellorsville*, 150–54; Sears, *Chancellorsville*, 255–56.
16. *O.R.*, 25, 1:387, 851, 867: Denoon, *Charlie's Letters*, 55.
17. *O.R.*, 25, 1:851; Waters and Edmunds, *Small but Spartan Band*, 53.
18. *O.R.*, 25, 1:851, 855, 874–75.
19. *O.R.*, 25, 1:799, 862–64; Denoon, *Charlie's Letters*, 52.
20. Freeman, *Lee's Lieutenants*, 2:567–71, 582–83
21. *O.R.*, 25, 1:799–800, 851, 872.
22. At Chancellorsville the Orange Plank Road split in two directions. The Orange Turnpike continued eastward towards Fredericksburg. The Plank Road ran southeast for a time before again paralleling the Orange Turnpike and intersecting it again west of Salem Church. West of Chancellorsville to the area of Wilderness Church and Dowdall's Tavern, the Orange Turnpike and Orange Plank Road ran together and was called Plank Road. The Plank Road then ran southwesterly towards Orange Courthouse and the Turnpike continued towards Culpeper.
23. Furgurson, *Chancellorsville*, 245; *O.R.*, 25, 1:875; Groene, "Letters of Colonel David Lang," 353; Waters and Edmunds, *Small but Spartan Band*, 54; Reaver, "Letters," 21.
24. *O.R.*, 25, 1:872, 878–79; Evans, *Sixteenth Mississippi*, 150–51.
25. *O.R.*, 25, 1:851, 867–68.
26. *O.R.*, 25, 1:868–69; Snead, *Third Georgia*, 9
27. *O.R.*, 25, 1:867; Mosely, "Confederate Diary," May 3, 1863, GNMP; Denoon, *Charlie's Letters*, 55–56.
28. Reaver, "Letters," 22; Maurice, *Aide-de-camp*, 172–73.
29. Furgurson, *Chancellorsville*, 265–8; *O.R.*, 25, 1:800–801, 851; Denoon, *Charlie's Letters*, 56.
30. Furgurson, *Chancellorsville*, 269; *O.R.*, 25, 1:852, 875; Dowdy and Manarin, *Wartime Papers*, 455.
31. Furgurson, *Chancellorsville*, 266–67, 273–74; Sears, *Chancellorsville*, 374.
32. *O.R.*, 25, 1:801, 858–59; McClellen, "10th Alabama," 2; Sears, *Chancellorsville*, 383.
33. *O.R.*, 25, 1:802, 852, 869; Sears, *Chancellorsville*, 402, 411, 417; Freeman, *Lee's Lieutenants*, 2:631–4; Dowdy and Manarin, *Wartime Papers*, 455.
34. *O.R.*, 25, 1:852, 876, 872, 869; Waters and Edmunds, *Small but Spartan Band*, 55–56.
35. Reaver, "Letters," 23; Fortin, "Herbert's 'History of the Eighth Alabama,'" 108; Lawley, "Great Battles on the Rappahannock," *Liverpool Mercury*, June 17, 1863; *O.R.*, 25, 1:802, 852; Freeman, *Lee's Dispatches*, 90.
36. Mosely, "Confederate Diary," May 6, 1862, GNMP; Reaver, "Letters," 23; Evans, *Sixteenth Mississippi*, 154; Mellon, "A Florida Soldier," 249.
37. McWillie Diary, 1864, MDAH; Duncan, "Wants His Comrades' Help," *Atlanta Constitution*, July 20, 1890; *O.R.*, 25, 1:797, 803.
38. *O.R.*, 25, 1:553, 803, 852–3, 858–59; Evans, *Sixteenth Mississippi*, 158.
39. *O.R.*, 25, 1:805.

40. Dowdey and Manarin, *Wartime Papers,* 485; Warner, *Generals in Grey,* 315; Freeman, *Lee's Dispatches,* 93; *O.R.,* 25, 2:782, 810–11.
41. Oeffinger, *McLaws,* 37; Freeman, *Lee's Lieutenants,* 2:696.
42. Robertson, *A. P. Hill,* 192; Douglas, *Rode with Stonewall,* 148; Hotchkiss, *Map,* xxv, 145.
43. Piston, *Lee's Tarnished Lieutenant,* 38–40; Longstreet, *Manassas to Appomattox,* 332–33; Patterson, *Blue to Gray,* 51–52, 58; Freeman, *Lee's Dispatches,* 92; *O.R.,* 25, 2:840; Anderson to Longstreet, May 30, 1863, Anderson Letterbook, VHS.
44. Robertson, *A. P. Hill,* 96–97.
45. Glatthaar, *Lee's Army,* 215–16.

Chapter 13: Gettysburg

1. Barrett, *Yankee Rebel,* 103; Evans, *Sixteenth Mississippi,* 161, 164, 165; Coddington, *Gettysburg Campaign,* 6–7.
2. Lewis W. Miles to Amy M. Lewis, "Dear Companion," June 2, 1863, USAMHI; Thomas E. Waldrip, July 9, 1863, Waldrip Family Papers, USAMHI.
3. Thomas, *Lee,* 290; Robertson, *A. P. Hill,* 198–9, 201; Coddington, *Gettysburg Campaign,* 52; *O.R.,* 27, 1:30–31, 38; Denoon, *Charlie's Letters,* 68; Evans, *Sixteenth Mississippi,* 170; Dowdey and Manarin, *Wartime Papers,* 501–2; Long, *The Civil War Day by Day,* 365; Sale, "Letters, June 10, 1863," Grinnan Family Papers, UVA.
4. J. G. C. to Geo. Peter, Esq., May 23, 1863, USAMHI; Robertson, *A. P. Hill,* 199.
5. A. L. Peel, Diary, June 14, 1863, Ancestry.com; Fortin, "Herbert's 'History of the Eighth Alabama,'" 110–11.
6. Peel, Diary, June 14, 1863, Ancestry.com; *O.R.,* 27, 1:613; Robertson, *A. P. Hill,* 200; Waters and Edmunds, *Small but Spartan Band,* 60; Evans, *Sixteenth Mississippi,* 169.
7. Mosely, "Confederate Diary," June 15–18, 1863, GNMP; Wright's Brigade Order Book, June 16, 1863, USAMHI; Barrett, *Yankee Rebel,* 105–6; Waters and Edmunds, *Small but Spartan Band,* 60; Peel, Diary, June 17, 1863, Ancestry.com.
8. *O.R.,* 27, 1:613; Evans, *Sixteenth Mississippi,* xxv, 171; Mosely, "Confederate Diary," June 19, 1863; Peel, Diary, June 20, 1863, Ancestry.com; Barrett. *Yankee Rebel,* 107.
9. Evans, *Sixteenth Mississippi,* 171; Denoon, *Charlie's Letters,* 69; Barrett, *Yankee Rebel,* 108–9.
10. Waters and Edmunds, *Small but Spartan Band,* 61; Mosely, "Confederate Diary," June 23, 1863, GNMP; A. P. Hill, General Orders No. 4, June 22, 1863, "Wright's Brigade Order Book," USAMHI.
11. Barrett, *Yankee Rebel,* 109; Evans, *Sixteenth Mississippi,* 172–3; Peel, Diary, June 24, 1863, Ancestry.com.
12. Johnson, "A Limited Review," GNMP; Waters and Edmunds, *Small but Spartan Band,* 61.
13. Warner, *Generals in Grey,* 236; Waters and Edmunds, *Small but Spartan Band,* 65; William Mahone to Samuel Cooper, July 18, 1863, HU.
14. Sale to "Hard," July 27, 1863, Grinnan Papers, GNMP; Judkins Memoir, USAMHI; Loyless, *Georgia's Public Men,* 16.
15. George Bernard, "Memoir," SHC; Robert E. Lee, General Orders No. 72., June 21, 1863, Broadside, Dickenson College.
16. Charles E. Waddell Diary, June 25, 26, and 30, 1863, CMLSC, VHS.
17. William McClellan to "Dear Sister," July 9, 1863, GNMP; Sale to "Hard," July 27, 1863, Grinnan Papers, GNMP; Giambrone, "'God Defend the Right',"

62; A. P. Hill Circular, June 25, 1863, Wright's Brigade Order Book, USAMHI; Peel, Diary, June 27, 1863, Ancestry.com; Robert Peel to "Dear Sister," December 24, 1862, Ancestry.com.

18. Evans, *Sixteenth Mississippi*, 173; Denoon, *Charlie's Letters*, 70; Moseley, "Confederate Diary," June 26, 1863, GNMP; William McClellan to "Dear Sister," July 9, 1863, GNMP;
19. Barrett, *Yankee Rebel*, 112
20. *Mosely, "Confederate Diary," July 1, 1863, GNMP; Charles E. Waddell Diary, July 1, 1863, VHS; Sale to "Hard," July 27, 1863, Grinnan Papers, VHS; Barrett, Yankee Rebel,* 112; Waters and Edmonds, *Small but Spartan Band*, 65; Evans, *Sixteenth Mississippi*, 175; Fortin, "'Eighth Alabama,'" 114.
21. Pfanz, *Gettysburg*, 20–21; Coddington, *Gettysburg*, 265: Thomas, *Bold Dragoon*, 245–56.
22. Coddington, *Gettysburg*, 267–69; Freeman, *Lee's Lieutenants*, 3:78–81; Longstreet, *Manassas to Appomattox*, 351–52.
23. Barrett, *Yankee Rebel*, 112–13; *O.R.*, 27, 2:613; Campbell, "'Sacrificed,'" 107–8; Longstreet, *Manassass to Appomattox*, 357; Coddington, *Gettysburg*, 316–17.
24. Lackey, "Notes on Civil War Logistics," n.p.; O.R., 27, 2:613, 622; Evans, *Sixteenth Mississippi*, 175; Waters and Edmunds, *Small but Spartan Band*, 66; Dobbins, *Grandfather's Journal*, 148.
25. Ott, "Diary of James J. Kirkpatrick," 117; *O.R.*, 27, 2:613–14, 616: Pfanz, *Gettysburg*, 98.
26. Pfanz, *Gettysburg*, 98–99; *O.R.*, 27, 2:613, 617.
27. Harwell, *Lee*, 327–32; Coddington, *Gettysburg*, 370–71; Pfanz, *Gettysburg*, 98–99; *O.R.*, 27, 2:613, 617.
28. *O.R.*, 27, 1:507, 515: *O.R.*, 27 2:613–14, 617; Pfanz, *Gettysburg*, 98–99, 114; David Lang to John Bachelder, October 16, 1903, GNMP; McClellen, "10th Alabama," 2.
29. *O.R.*, 27, 2:614, 617; Campbell, "'Sacrificed,'" 109; Andrews, "Another Account," *Atlanta Journal*, March 9, 1901.
30. Clark, *Glance Backward*, 36; Johnson, "A Limited Review," 1, GNMP; Judkins Memoir, GNMP, 57; McClellen, "10th Alabama," 2.
31. *O.R.*, 27, 2:631; McClellen, "10th Alabama," 2; Fleming Thompson to "My Dear Sister & Mother," July 17, 1863, USAMHI; Mason, "Three Years in the Army," 17; Coddington, *Gettysburg*, 430; *O.R.*, 27, 2:618, 633; Barrett, *Yankee Rebel*, 115.
32. Army Correspondence, *Daily Constitutionalist* (Augusta), July 23, 1863, GNMP; Andrews, "Another Account," 4.
33. Barrett, *Yankee Rebel*, 116.
34. Johnson, "Limited Review," 1, GNMP; Waters and Edmunds, *Small but Spartan Band*, 69.
35. Pfanz, *Gettysburg*, 373–80; Barrett, *Yankee Rebel*, 117; *O.R.*, 27, 2:618.
36. *O.R.*, 27, 2:618, 623; "Wright's Brigade," *Daily Constitutionalist* (Augusta) July 23, 1863, 4.
37. *O.R.*, 27, 2:618; Barrett, *Yankee Rebel*, 117.
38. *O.R.*, 27, 2:618, 632; Maxwell letter, July 8, 1863, Maxwell Papers, VHS; Waters and Edmunds, *Small but Spartan Band*, 70; Lindstrom, "Perry's Brigade," n.p.
39. *O.R.*, 27, 2:623–24; Garrett Diary, July 2, 1863, GNMP; Heiser, "Emmitsburg Road," *The Morningside Notes*, 6.
40. *O.R.*, 27, 2:633–34; Winschel, "Part 2: Posey's Brigade," 98; Campbell, "'Sacrificed,'" 119; Gottfried, "Mahone's Brigade," 72.

41. Evans, *Sixteenth Mississippi*, 176; Giambrone, "'God Defend the Right.'" 63; Judkins Memoir, 59, USAMHI; Wright to "My dear Wife," July 7, 1863, GNMP; Johnson, "A Limited Review," 2, GNMP; Pfanz, *Gettysburg*, 427, 433.
42. Coddington, *Gettysburg*, 460–62; Wert, *Gettysburg*, 102–4; *O.R.*, 27, 2:620; Freeman, 3:144–46.
43. *O.R.*, 27, 2:320; Coddington, *Gettysburg*, 454; 462–63.
44. Freeman, *Lee's Lieutenants*, 3:158–61; Wert, *Gettysburg*, 238; *O.R.*, 27, 2:360, 615, 625.
45. *O.R.*, 27, 2:632–33; James Wentworth, "Dairy of Civil War Days," *Perry News-Herald* (FL), GNMP; Coles and Waters, "Forgotten Sacrifice," 44; Groene, "Letters of Colonel David Lang," 355; Elmore, "Florida Brigade," 54; Lang to John B. Bachelder, October 16, 1893, GNMP.
46. Fleming Thompson to "My Dear Sister & Mother," July 17, 1863, USAMHI; Mason, "Three Years in the Army," 17.
47. *O.R.*, 27, 2:620; Mason, "Three Years in the Army," 17.
48. Wert, *Gettysburg*, 240; *O.R.*, 27, 2:620; Freeman, *Lee's Lieutenants*, 3:185.
49. Risley, "Peter W. Alexander," 35–36; Styple, ed., *Writing and Fighting*, 5; A, "The Battle of Gettysburg, PA," *Richmond Enquirer*, July 24, 1863.
50. A, "The Battle of Gettysburg, PA," *Richmond Enquirer*, July 24, 1863.
51. Johnson, "Limited Review," 5, GNMP; P. W. A., "Anderson and Pettigrew," *Richmond Enquirer*, July 28, 1863; Risley, "Georgia's Civil War Newspapers," 68–69.
52. Johnson, "Limited Review," 5, GNMP; P.W.A., "Anderson and Pettigrew," *Richmond Enquirer*, July 28, 1863, 4.
53. William Mahone and Carnot Posey, "To the Editors," *Richmond Enquirer*, August 7, 1863, 2; Robertson, *A. P. Hill*, 213; Hilary Herbert to E. P. Alexander, August 18, 1903, Alexander Collection, SHC.
54. William Mahone and Carnot Posey, "To the Editors," *Richmond Enquirer*, August 7, 1863, 2; Robertson, *A. P. Hill*, 213; Hilary Herbert to E. P. Alexander, August 18, 1903, Alexander Collection, SHC.
55. P. W. A. "To the Editors of the *Enquirer*," August 2, 1863, *Richmond Enquirer*, August 7, 1863; "General Anderson," Augusta *Constitutionalist*, August 4, 1863.
56. R. H. Anderson Letter, "To the Editors," *Richmond Enquirer*, August 6, 1863, USAMHI.
57. P. W. A. "Letter," *Richmond Enquirer*, August 7, 1863, 4; *O.R.*, 27, 2:618, 623; Freeman, *Lee's Lieutenants*, 3:125–26.
58. Johnson, "A Limited Review," 5–6, GNMP.
59. *O.R.*, 27, 2:622; Judkins Memoir, 68, USAMHI; Atkinson, "Masters of the Field," 212.
60. Waters and Edmunds, *Small but Spartan Band*, 91; *O.R.*, 27, 2:623–24.
61. Johnson, "A Limited Review," 6, GNMP.
62. "Court Martial," *Richmond Enquirer*; Andrews, *3rd Georgia*, n.p.; Special Orders No. 196, NARA; "Court Martial of General Wright," *The Countryman* (Putnam County, GA), August 18, 1863; "J.A., Letter to the Editor," *Augusta Daily Chronicle & Sentinel*, August 30, 1863.
63. X, Our Own Correspondent, "From General Lee's Army," *Richmond Enquirer*, August 25, 1863; *Southern Confederacy* (Atlanta), August 18, 1863.
64. Johnson, "A Limited Review," 6, GNMP.
65. Patterson, *Blue to Grey*, 59–67; Robertson, *A. P. Hill*, 219.

Chapter 14: On the Rapidan and Rappahannock Line and into the Wilderness

1. Coddington, *Gettysburg*, 537–38; Dowdey and Manarin, *Wartime Papers*, 539–40; *O.R.*, 27, 2:615; Bernard, "Memoir," GNMP, 19; Todd, "Reminiscences," 135, SHC; Giambrone "'God Defend the Right,'" 64.
2. *O.R.*, 27, 2:615; Coddington, *Gettysburg*, 537–38; Evans, *Sixteenth Mississippi*, 178–79, 181; Mosely "Confederate Diary," July 13, 1863, GNMP.
3. Sorrel, *Recollections*, 165–66; Wittenberg, Petruzzi and Nugent, *One Continuous Fight*, 285, 293–95; *O.R.*, 27, 2:638; Dowdey and Manarin, *Wartime Papers*, 557–58; Coddington, *Gettysburg*, 571.
4. *O.R.*, 27, 2:615; Andrews, *3rd Georgia*, n.p.
5. Dowdey and Manarin, *Wartime Letters*, 558.
6. *O.R.*, 27, 2:560, 626.
7. *O.R.*, 27, 1:490; *O.R.*, 27, 2:560, 626.
8. *O.R.*, 27, 2:561; Collins, *Rodes*, 299–300.
9. Mosely, "Confederate Diary" July 23, 1863, GNMP; Joseph R. Manson to "My Dear Mother," July 30, 1863, USAMHI; Sale to "Hard," July 27, 1863, Grinnan Papers, GNMP; Denoon, *Charlie's Letters*, 72.
10. *O.R.*, 27, 2:616; Evans, *Sixteenth Mississippi*, 198; Mason, "Three Years in the Army," 19.
11. John S. Lewis to "My very dear Mother, July 211863," "Battle of Gettysburg," *Woodville Republican*, July 19, 1924.
12. Denoon, *Charlie's Letters*, 75–76; Evans, *Sixteenth Mississippi*, 187; Waters and Edmunds, *Small but Spartan Band*, 86.
13. Freeman, *Lee's Lieutenants*, 3:202; Bonham, "Little More Light," 523.
14. Jennie Anderson to W. W. Anderson, July 11, 1863, BHA.
15. Wilcox, "Report," Participant Files, GNMP; Patterson, *Blue to Gray*, 70.
16. *O.R.*, 29, 2:720; Hunt, *Meade and Lee*, 140–41.
17. *O.R.*, 29, 2:757–59.
18. *O.R.*, 29, 1:406–7, 410; Wright's Brigade Order Book, October 8, 1863, USAMHI.
19. Mellon, "A Florida Soldier," 258.
20. *O.R.*, 29, 1:429.
21. *O.R.*, 29, 1:429; Freeman, *Lee's Lieutenants*, 3:242–45; Robertson, *A. P. Hill*, 234–35.
22. Freeman, *Lee's Lieutenants*, 3:245; Robertson, *A. P. Hill*, 238–39.
23. *O.R.*, 29, 1:428–29.
24. Mellon, "A Florida Soldier," 255. The song title was most likely a reference to the popular 1860 ballad "Let me kiss him for his Mother," by John P. Ordway.
25. Fortin, "Eighth Alabama," 131.
26. *O.R.*, 29, 1:407; Freeman, *Lee's Lieutenants*, 3:261–62; Mason, "Three Years in the Army," 20.
27. Graham and Skoch, *Mine Run*, 5–6, 28–29, 36; Freeman, *Lee's Lieutenants*, 3:264–65, 267–69.
28. Denoon, *Charlie's Letters*, 84–85; Mason , "Three Years in the Army," 20; Evans, *Sixteenth Mississippi*, 219; Conerly, *Quitman Guards*, 57.
29. Groene, "Letters of Colonel David Lang," 360.
30. Denoon, *Charlie's Letters*, 86.
31. Graham and Skoch, *Mine Run*, 37, 43; Freeman, *Lee's Lieutenants*, 3:269; *Richmond Dispatch*, "From General Lee's Army," November 27, 1863.

32. Graham and Skoch, *Mine Run*, 44–47; *O.R.*, 29, 1:825; Denoon, *Charlie's Letters*, 87.
33. *O.R.*, 29, 1:827; Dowdey and Manarin, *Wartime Papers*, 626.
34. *O.R.*, 29, 1:827–29, 896; Graham and Skoch, *Mine Run*, 59; Evans, *Sixteenth Mississippi*, 221–22.
35. Graham and Skoch, *Mine Run*, 69, 78–79; *O.R.*, 29, 1:896; *O.R.*, 29, 2:517; Conerly, *Quitman Guards*, 59–60.
36. *O.R.*, 29, 1:896; Evans, *Sixteenth Mississippi*, 222–23, 226; *Richmond Dispatch*, "From Gen. Lee's Army," December 8, 1863.
37. Conerly, *Quitman Guards*, 60–61; Evans, *Sixteenth Mississippi*, 225, 227, 311.
38. Conerly, *Quitman Guards*, 61; Dowdey and Manarin, *Wartime Papers*, 668–69; Denoon, *Charlie's Letters*, 92; Evans, *Sixteenth Mississippi*, 230.
39. Glatthaar, *General Lee's Army*, 225; Pfanz, *Richard S. Ewell*, 345, 351; Gordon, *Reminiscence*, 230; *Richmond Dispatch*, "From General Lee's Army," January 14, 1864; Letter, "Camp 15th Va Cavalry, 1st February, 1864," *Richmond Dispatch*, March 9, 1864; Robertson, *A. P. Hill*, 246, 250; Sallie Anderson to Mary Childs, October 15, 1861, quoted in Elliott, *Lee's Noble Soldier*, 24.
40. Clark, *Glance Backward*, 46.
41. Pfanz, *Richard S. Ewell*, 357; *O.R.*, 33:1076–77; Clark, *Glance Backward*, 44; Denoon, *Charlie's Letters*, 92; *Richmond Dispatch*, "Soldier Killed," January 5, 1864.
42. *O.R.*, 33:113–17; Dowdey and Manarin, *Wartime Papers*, 658–59.
43. Williams, *Lincoln and His Generals*, 306–8.
44. *O.R.*, 36, 1:1070; Rhea, *Wilderness*, 20; Pfanz, *Richard S. Ewell*, 361; Bratton to "Dear Bettie," May 3, 1864, Bratton Letters, SHC.
45. *O.R.*, 36, 1:1054, 1070; Anderson to Leigh Robinson, February 26, 1875, William & Mary College (cited hereafter as W & M); Rhea, *Wilderness*, 54.
46. Rhea, *Wilderness*, 55, 120.
47. Waters and Edmunds, *Small but Spartan Band*, 99–100; Evans, *Sixteenth Mississippi*, 246, 248. It was widely known at the time that Grant had come east and was in the field with the Army of the Potomac, and thus many refer to Grant's army at the start of the campaign, rather than to Meade's. In an awkward arrangement, Meade retained tactical command of the Army of the Potomac while Grant exercised strategic oversight. Unsatisfactory results on May 5 led Grant to assert even greater control over Meade's force. In the press and the public's eye, Meade was relegated to the background despite his official capacity as the army's commander.
48. Rhea, *Wilderness*, 277–82; Freeman, *Lee's Lieutenants*, 3:353–54, Robertson, *A. P. Hill*, 261–63.
49. Freeman, *Lee's Lieutenants*, 3:356–57; Rhea, *Wilderness*, 294; Poague, *Gunner*, 88–91.
50. Freeman, *Lee's Lieutenants*, 3:359–60; "The Great Struggle for Richmond," *Richmond Dispatch*, May 9, 1864.
51. Freeman, *Lee's Lieutenants*, 3:359–60; Sorrel, *Recollections*, 236; Longstreet, *Manassas to Appomattox*, 561; R. H. Anderson to Capt. Edward B. Robins, May 14, 1879, MHSM; Anderson to Leigh Robinson, February 26, 1875, W & M; Evans, *Sixteenth Mississippi*, 248–49; Rhea, *Wilderness*, 313.
52. *O.R.*, 36, 1:1055; *O.R.*, 40, 3:775; William Mahone to T. S. Mills, Report, 1864, Alexander Collection, SHC; Mahone to Edwin B. Robins, May 9, 1878, John

Codman Ropes Papers, GNMP; Rhea, *Wilderness*, 362; Sorrel, *Recollections*, 241; Krick, *Lee's Colonels*, 360.

53. Rhea, *Wilderness*, 352–53.
54. Dawson, *Reminiscences*, 115–16; Wert, *Longstreet*, 386–87; McWillie Diary, 1864, MDAH; Haskell, "Memoir," (typescript), 44, DU.
55. Blanding, "General Richard H. Anderson, 1821–1879," Address to the Daughters of the Confederacy, n.d. HU.
56. *O.R.*, 36, 2:967; *O.R.*, 36, 3:873; Special Orders, Headquarters Army of Northern Virginia, June 4, 1864, R. E. Lee HQ Papers, Series 7, Folder 2, VHS; Sorrel, *Recollections*, 238–39.
57. DiNardo, "Command Crisis," 83, 85–87; Robertson, *A. P. Hill*, 268; Pfanz, *Richard S. Ewell*, 352, 396; *O.R.*, 36, 3:846.
58. Sorrel, *Recollections*, 243; Gallagher, *Fighting for the Confederacy*, 365; Ambrose Wright to "My Dear Daughter," February 7, 1864, Ambrose Wright Letters, VHS; Cadmus Wilcox, Draft Report, July 1863, GNMP.
59. Dawson, *Reminiscences*, 116, 179.
60. Dowdey and Manarin, *Wartime Papers*, 723; McWillie Diary, 1864, MDAC.
61. Porter, *Campaigning*, 66, 69–70.

Chapter 15: Corps Command at Spotsylvania

1. Evans, *Sixteenth Mississippi*, 249; Porter, *Campaigning*, 72–73.
2. Matter, *If It Takes All Summer*, 361; Longacre, *Pickett*, 150; Warner, *Generals in Gray*, 87–88, 171; Freeman, *Lee's Lieutenants*, 3:xx; Sorrel, *Recollections*, 233.
3. Dowdey and Manarin, *Wartime Papers*, 723; R. H. Anderson to Longstreet, "Extract from Genl. R. H. Anderson's account of operations of 1st Corps," ca. May 1864, Anderson Papers, DU; Anderson to Robins, May 14, 1879, MHSM.
4. *O.R.*, 36, 1:1041; *O.R.*, 51, 1:248.
5. Anderson to Robins, May 14, 1879, MHSM; Anderson, "Extract from account of operations," May 1864, DU; Freeman, *Lee's Lieutenants*, 3:381 n 28.
6. *O.R.*, 36, 1:1056; Anderson to Robins, May 14, 1879, MHSM; Anderson, "Extract from account of operations," May 1864, DU; Rhea, *Spotsylvania*, 51–52; Dowdey and Manarin, *Wartime Letters*, 724–25.
7. Freeman, *Lee's Lieutenants*, 3:381–82; Rhea, *Spotsylvania*, 49–52.
8. *O.R.*, 36, 1:1056; Freeman, *Lee's Lieutenants*, 3:382; Rhea, *Spotsylvania*, 52–54; Matter, *If It Takes All Summer*, 57–61; Alexander to "Dear Father," May 29, 1864, Alexander Collection, SHC; Haskell, "Memoir," 45, DU.
9. Freeman, *Lee's Lieutenants*, 3:384; Matter, *If It Takes All Summer*, 69; *O.R.*, 36, 1:1065.
10. Rhea, *Spotsylvania*, 54–56; William P. DuBose, "Reminiscences," SHC; Haskell, "Memoir," 45, DU.
11. Rhea, *Spotsylvania*, 64, 81, 83; Matter, *If It Takes All Summer*, 86; *O.R.*, 36, 2:974.
12. Rhea, *Spotsylvania*, 83–85.
13. Gallagher, *Fighting for the Confederacy*, 66; *O.R.*, 36, 2:974; *O.R.*, 51, 1:248.
14. Rhea, *Spotsylvania*, 89–91; Jordan, *Some Events*, 78; Matter, *If It Takes All Summer*, 106; Freeman, *Lee's Lieutenants*, 3:392.
15. Dowdey and Manarin, *Wartime Papers*, 726–27; *O.R.*, 36, 1:1056–57, 1089; Anderson to Lee, May 10, 1864, Venable Papers, SHC; Matter, *If It Takes All Summer*, 154; Stocker, ed., *Huntsville to Appomattox*, 169.

16. *O.R.*, 36, 1:1057, 1066, 1072; Rhea, *Spotsylvania*, 250; Gallagher, *Fighting for the Confederacy*, 374, 379.
17. Rhea, *Spotsylvania*, 324; Porter, *Campaigning*, 111–12; Warner, *Generals in Gray*, 235; McWillie Diary, 1864, MDAH.
18. *O.R.*, 36, 1:1057.

Chapter 16: South to Richmond and Petersburg

1. *O.R.*, 36, 3:824, 826, 828, 834, 838; Dowdey and Manarin, *Wartime Papers*, 746.
2. C. Irvine Walker, Anderson's earliest biographer asserted in 1917 that Lee initially offered command of the cavalry to Anderson, who respectfully declined and recommended Hampton. Though Joseph Elliot's 1985 biography repeated the claim in more detail, it seems an apocryphal tale that simply does not ring true given the unstable situation among the infantry corps commanders at that time as well as the availability of a perfectly acceptable option already serving with the cavalry. Wade Hampton was elevated to command on August 11, after a period during which the cavalry division leaders reported directly to Lee's headquarters and Hampton, as senior cavalry leader, served only as nominal commander of the entire force.
3. *O.R.*, 36, 3:844, 846; Pfanz, *Richard S. Ewell*, 389.
4. Rhea, *North Anna*, 231; Hotchkiss, *Map*, 206–7; *O.R.*, 36, 1:1058; Pickett to Sorrell ca. May 23, 1864, Alexander Collection, SHC; Gallagher, *Fighting for the Confederacy*, 388–90, 599 n. 5; Robertson, *A. P. Hill*, 273–76; Freeman, *Lee's Lieutenants*, 3:496–97; Dowdey and Manarin, *Wartime Papers*, 756; Taylor, *Four Years*, 134.
5. W. W. Anderson to R. H. Anderson, May 10, 1864, BHA.
6. Rhea, *North Anna*, 285, 323–24, 344; Freeman, *Lee's Lieutenants*, 3:497–98: Freeman, *Lee*, 396.
7. Freeman, *Lee*, 397; Taylor, *Four Years*, 133; Tower, *Lee's Adjutant*, 165; Trudeau, *Bloody Roads South*, 245.
8. *O.R.*, 36, 1:1058; Rhea, *Cold Harbor*, 97.
9. *O.R.*, 36, 1:1058; *O.R.*, 36, 3:846–47; Rhea, *Cold Harbor*, 108.
10. *O.R.*, 36, 1:1058; *O.R.*, 36, 3:851, 854.
11. Trudeau, *Bloody Roads South*, 255–58; Osborne, *Jubal*, 241–42; Collins, *Rodes*, 370; *O.R.* 36, 1:1058; *O.R.*, 51, 1:245.
12. *O.R.*, 36, 1:1058; *O.R.*, 36, 3:854.
13. *O.R.*, 51, 2:974; Circular, Headquarters, Army of Northern Virginia, May 31, 1864, Alexander Collection, SHC; Anderson to Lee, May 31, 1864, Venable Papers, SHC; Rhea, *Cold Harbor*, 162–63.
14. Dickert, *Kershaw's Brigade*, 365, 370; Mixon, *Reminiscences*, 86.
15. Furgurson, *Not War But Murder*, 90–92; Rhea, *Cold Harbor*, 199–200.
16. *O.R.*, 36, 3:411, 470; Hagood, *Memoirs*, 256–57.
17. Rhea, *Cold Harbor*, 201–4; *O.R.*, 36, 1:1058–59; Furgurson, *Not War But Murder*, 92–93; Gallagher, *Fighting for the Confederacy*, 399; Hagood, Memoirs, 256–58.
18. Lee to Anderson, June 1, 1864, Alexander Collection, SHC; Hagood, *Memoirs*, 255–56.
19. Rhea, *Cold Harbor*, 202; Furgurson, *Not War*, 103–4; Trudeau, *Bloody Roads South*, 269; Clingman, "Second Cold Harbor," 5: 198; Hagood, *Memoirs*, 257.
20. Gallagher, *Fighting for the Confederacy*, 400; Rhea, *Cold Harbor*, 243–44.

21. Clingman, "Second Cold Harbor," 5: 202–4; Rhea, *Cold Harbor*, 245–47, 250; *O.R.*, 36, 1: 1049, 1059; *O.R.*, 51, 2:976; Gallagher, *Fighting for the Confederacy*, 400–401.
22. Stiles, *Four Years*, 275; Rhea, *Cold Harbor*, 254–65; *O.R.*, 36, 3:858, 867.
23. Rhea, *Cold Harbor*, 279–80, 291–92, 307; Lee to Anderson, June 2, 1864, Alexander Collection, SHC; Stocker, *Huntsville to Appomattox*, 173–74; *O.R.*, 36, 3:870.
24. Stocker, *Huntsville to Appomattox*, 174; Kershaw to Walter H. Taylor, June 3, 1864, Alexander Collection, SHC; Rhea, *Cold Harbor*, 326, 348; Oates, *The War*, 366–67; *O.R.*, 36, 1:1059.
25. *O.R.*, 36, 1:869; Taylor, *Four Years*, 135; Law, "'Half-dozen,'" 488.
26. Rhea, *Cold Harbor*, 354, 383–84; Law, "'Half-dozen,'" 488; Jesse Hill to Emoline Hill, June 8, 1864, Jesse Hill Papers, VHS; Swinton, *Campaigns*, 487; Grant, *Memoirs*, 2:276.
27. Rhea, *Cold Harbor*, 382.
28. Trudeau, *Bloody Roads South*, 304, 308; Hagood, *Memoirs*, 262; Dobbins, *Grandfather's Journal*, 198–99.
29. Lee to Anderson, June 6, 1864, Alexander Collection, SHC; Law, "'Half-dozen'," 489.
30. Peyton and Swank, *Stonewall Jackson's Foot Cavalry*, 61; Lee to Anderson, June 6, 1864, Alexander Collection, SHC; Jubal Early Letter, "Spicy Correspondence Between Generals Early and Anderson," *Cincinnati Daily Commercial*, March 31, 1865.
31. R. H. Anderson Letter, "Spicy Correspondence Between Generals Early and Anderson," *Cincinnati Daily Commercial*, March 31, 1865; Osborne, *Jubal*, 243–44; Sorrel, *Recollections*, 252; *O.R.*, 11, 1:565–67, 603–5, 608; *O.R.*, 51, 2:975; Longstreet, *Manassas to Appomattox*, 78.
32. Sorrel, *Recollections*, 242; Evans, *Sixteenth Mississippi*, 196.
33. Sorrel, *Recollections*, 247–48; Alexander to "Dear Father," May 29, 1864, Alexander Collection, SHC; Gallagher, *Fighting for the Confederacy*, 389; *O.R.*, 36, 1:1058.
34. Thomas S. Sumter, "Idolized by His Men," n.d., BHA.
35. McWillie Diary, 1864, MDAH.
36. Lee to Anderson, June 13, 1864, Alexander Collection, SHC; *O.R.*, 40, 2:647; *O.R.S.*, 7:249.
37. Lee to Anderson, June 14, 1864, Alexander Collection, SHC; *O.R.*, 36, 1:1060.
38. Dowdey and Manarin, *Wartime Papers*, 785–86; *O.R.S.*, 7:250.
39. *O.R.S.*, 7:250; Lee to Anderson, June 17, 1864, Alexander Collection, SHC; Anderson to Lee, June 17, 1864, Venable Papers, SHC.
40. Long, *The Civil War Day by Day*, 521–24; Emerson and Stokes, eds., *Faith, Valor, and Devotion*, 286.
41. *O.R.S.*, 7:250; *O.R.*, 40, 1:797–99, 804–5; Trudeau, *Last Citadel*, 87; Anderson to Lee, June 22, 1864, Venable Papers, SCH; Barefoot, *Hoke*, 210–13.
42. McWillie Diary, 1864, MDAH; Krick, *Staff Officers*, 222done; R. P. Duncan to "Mrs. Mills," June 25, 1864, BHA; S. Williams to "Col. Taylor," July 7, 1864, BHA; Sallie Anderson to Mills, ca. July 1864, BHA.
43. Sallie Anderson to Mary Lieper, July 11, 1864, Anderson Family Papers, BHA.
44. Templar Fayssoux to Rebecca Fayssoux, July 26, 1864, typescript copy from A. Waldo Jones Family Papers, BHA.
45. Bratton to "Dear Bettie," July 9, 1864, Bratton Letters, SHC.
46. *O.R.*, 40, 2:675; *O.R.S.*, 7:251–52.

47. Bratton to "Dear Wife," July 2, 7, and 13, 1864, Bratton Letters, SHC.
48. Cavanaugh and Marvel, *Battle of the Crater*, 28; *O.R.*, 40, 3:795–96, 809; *O.R.S.*, 7:252; Dowdey and Manarin, *Wartime Papers*, 825, 826; Price, *First Deep Bottom*, 81, 88, 95–96, 104–5.
49. *O.R.S.*, 7:252; Dowdey and Manarin, *Wartime Papers*, 826; Price, *First Deep Bottom*, 124–25, 142, 152; Moffett, *Letters of General James Conner*, 144.
50. *O.R.S.*, 7:252–53; *O.R.*, 40, 3:813–16, 818–19; Cavanaugh and Marvel, *Battle of the Crater*, 40: Anderson to Lee, Telegraph, July 30, 1864, Venable Papers, SHC. *O.R.*, 51, 2:929; Matter, *If It Takes All Summer*, 348.

Chapter 17: Valley Sojourn and the Siege

1. Duncan, *Lee's Endangered Left*, 255–57; Trudeau, *Bloody Roads South*, 310, 316; Freeman, *Lee's Lieutenants*, 3:518–24.
2. Pond, *Shenandoah Valley*, 120; *O.R.S.*, 7:253; *O.R.*, 43, 1:997; Anderson to Lee, August 11, 1864, BHA.
3. *O.R.S.*, 7:567, 597; *O.R.*, 43, 1:999.
4. *O.R.S.*, 7:567–68; *O.R.*, 43, 1:472–73.
5. *O.R.S.*, 7:567; Latrobe Diary, August 17, 1864, VHS; Dawson, *Reminiscences*, 121–22.
6. *O.R.*, 43, 1:569, 1006; Anderson to Lee, August 23, 1864, BHA; Hinrichs Diary, February 25, 1865; private collection, copy in possession of Robert K. Krick.
7. Anderson to Lee, August 23, 1864, BHA; Lee to Anderson, August 29, 1864, GLI; Price, *First Deep Bottom*, 128.
8. *O.R.S.*, 7:568–69; *O.R.*, 43, 2:862.
9. *O.R.*, 43, 1:367, 590; *O.R.S.*, 7:569.
10. O.R., 43, 1:572; *O.R.S.*, 7:569–70.
11. Emerson and Stokes, *Faith, Valor, and Devotion*, 304; *O.R.*, 43, 1:1007; Latrobe Diary, August 26, 1864, VHS: Hotchkiss, *Map*, 222; Dawson, *Reminiscences*, 123; Peyton and Swank, *Stonewall Jackson's Foot Cavalry*, 103–4.
12. *O.R.S.*, 7:570; *O.R.*, 43, 1:592–93; Krick, *Lee's Colonels*, 189.
13. Elliott, *Lee's Noble Soldier*, 116; *O.R.S.*, 7:599, 604; *O.R.*, 42, 1:875; *O.R.*, 43, 1:571; *O.R.*, 43, 2:878; Moffett, *Letters of General James Conner*, 147, 154, 158; Dawson, *Reminiscences*, 123; Anderson to Mrs. Mills, September 6, 1864, Borough House Archives; Donald, *Lincoln*, 529.
14. *O.R.S.*, 7:258; *O.R.*, 42, 2:1298; Walter Taylor to Anderson, September 28, 1864, Alexander Collection, SHC; Sommers, *Richmond Redeemed*, 14–15, 17–18.
15. *O.R.S.*, 7:258–59; *O.R.*, 42, 1:880, 938; Tower, ed., *Lee's Adjutant*, 195; Sommers, *Richmond Redeemed*, 116–17, 133, 136–41, 148; Trudeau, *Last Citadel*, 117.
16. *O.R.S.*, 7:259; Latrobe Diary, October 1, 1864, VHS.
17. *O.R.S.*, 7:259–60; *O.R.*, 42, 1:876; Latrobe Diary, October 7, 1864, VHS; Stribling, *Gettysburg Campaign*, 273–74.
18. Hagood, *Memoirs*, 308–9; *O.R.S.*, 7:260; Corbin, *Letters*, 77.
19. *O.R.S.*, 7:260; Latrobe Diary, October 13, 1864, VHS; *O.R.*, 42, 1:682.

Chapter 18: Petersburg to Appomattox

1. *O.R.*, 42, 3:1362; Freeman, *Lee's Dispatches*, 315.
2. Warner, *Generals in Gray*, 157–58; Welsh, *Medical Histories*, 117; Cummings, *Yankee Quaker*, 288–300.

3. Hagood, *Memoirs*, 315; Latrobe Diary, December 20, 1864, VHS; *O.R.*, 44, 1:966; *O.R.*, 46, 2:1262; *O.R.S.*, 7:817–18; Trudeau, *Last Citadel*, 11.
4. Dawson, *Reminiscences*,128.
5. Dawson, *Reminiscences*, 128–29.
6. Dawson, *Reminiscences*, 132.
7. *O.R.S.*, 7:818–19; Anderson, "Narrative of Services October 1864 to April 1865," Lee Headquarters Collection, VHS; *O.R.*, 42, 1:906; *O.R.*, 42, 3:1140, 1180; Anderson to Walter Taylor, November 10, 1864, BHA.
8. *O.R.*, 42, 3:1186; *O.R.S.*, 7:818.
9. *O.R.*, 42, 1:909–10; *O.R.*, 42, 2:1195; *O.R.*, 42, 3:559; Quintas Adams to F. A. Royal, November 8, 1864, CWTI Collection, USAMHI; Burgwyn, "Thirty-Fifth Regiment," in Clark, ed., *Histories*, 2:625; Lucas, Letter, December 5, 1864, HCWRT Collection, USAMHI.
10. Anderson to Walter Taylor, November 27, 1864, BHA
11. *O.R.S.*, 7:818–19; Welsh, *Medical Histories*, 86; Anderson to Samuel Cooper, November 10, 1864, BHA.
12. Burgwyn "Thirty-Fifth Regiment," in Clark, ed., *Histories*, 2: 624–25; *O.R.*, 42, 3:1311; *O.R.*, 46, 2:1239, 1261; *O.R.S.*, 7:818–19; Adams to "My Dear Mother," January 25, 1865, CWTI Collection, USAMHI; Hess, *In the Trenches*, 440.
13. *O.R.S.*, 7:819–20; *O.R.*, 42, 1:896–925.
14. Dowdey and Manarin, *Wartime Papers*, 914; Anderson to Walter Taylor, February 20, 1865, BHA; Pearce, ed., *Chambers*, 249.
15. W. W. Anderson to "My Darling Wife," March 20, 1865, W. W. Anderson II File, BHA.
16. Freeman, *Lee's Lieutenants*, 3:647–51; *O.R.S.*, 7:820.
17. Freeman, *Lee's Lieutenants*, 3:651; *O.R.S.*, 7:820.
18. *O.R.S.*, 7:820; *O.R.*, 46, 1:1263, 1286–87; Greene, *Campaign of Giants*, 212–15; Calkins, *Appomattox*, 21.
19. *O.R.S.*, 7:820; Greene, *Breaking the Backbone*, 219–20.
20. Greene, *Breaking the Backbone*, 226–29; Bearrs, *Petersburg*, 435; Walker, *Anderson*, 207; Caldwell, *History*, 212; Caldwell, "The Fight at Gravelly Run," *Yorkville Enquirer*, March 15, 1883; *O.R.*, 46, 1:892, 1288; *O.R.S.*, 7:820.
21. *O.R.*, 46, 1:1288.
22. Munford to Irving, July 26, 1895, Munford Papers, VSL; Gordon, *Pickett*, 149.
23. Welsh, *Medical Histories*, 182; Burgwyn, "Thirty-Fifth Regiment," in Clark, *Histories*, 2: 626; Munford, "Battle of Five Forks," n.d., Munford-Ellis Family Papers, DU; Hess, *In the Trenches*, 456; *O.R.S.*, 7:821.
24. Thomas Munford to Kate Saunders, June 15, 1916, BHA. For full discussion of Fitz Lee's assertions see C. Irvine Walker's rebuttal in his biography of Anderson.
25. *O.R.*, 46, 1:1288; *O.R.S.*, 7:820–21; Dowdey and Manarin, *Wartime Papers*, 928.
26. *O.R.*, 46, 1:1125, 1288–89; *O.R.S.*, 7:821.
27. *O.R.*, 46, 1:1289; *O.R.S.*, 7:821; Grant, *Memoirs*, 456.
28. *O.R.*, 46, 1:1289; *O.R.S.*, 7:821; Marvel, *Lee's Last Retreat*, 30.
29. Marvel, *Lee's Last Retreat*, 31, 44–45; Cummings, *Yankee Quaker*, 336, n. 63; *O.R.S.*, 7:821; *O.R.*, 46, 1:1289.
30. *O.R.S.*, 7:821; Marvel, *Lee's Last Retreat*, 45, 53; *O.R.*, 46, 1:1125, 1289.
31. *O.R.S.*, 7:821; *O.R.*, 46, 1:1289; Marvel, *Lee's Last Retreat*, 59; Freeman, *Lee's Lieutenants*, 3:692–93.

32. *O.R.S.*, 7:821.
33. Marvel, *Lee's Last Retreat*, 65.
34. Calkins, *Appomattox*, 99; Freeman, *Lee's Lieutenants*, 3:698–700; Marvel, *Lee's Last Retreat*, 67–70.
35. Calkins, *Appomattox*, 105; Freeman, *Lee's Lieutenants*, 3:701.
36. Harrison, *Pickett's Men*, 155; *O.R.S.*, 7:821; *O.R.*, 46, 1:1294; Freeman, *Lee's Lieutenants*, 3:700–701; Calkins, *Appomattox*, 105; Cummings, *Yankee Quaker*, 322–23.
37. *O.R.*, 46, 1:1295.
38. *O.R.*, 46, 1:1284.
39. *O.R.*, 46, 1:1290, 1295; Freeman, *Lee's Lieutenants*, 3:704–5; Cummings, *Yankee Quaker*, 324–25.
40. Harrison, *Pickett's Men*, 157; Cummings, *Yankee Quaker*, 325; Wise, "The Career of Wise's Brigade, 1861–1865," 18; Hunton, *Autobiography*, 122.
41. Taylor, "Some Experiences," 112–13.
42. *O.R.*, 46, 1:1275; Freeman, *Lee's Lieutenants*, 3:706–7; Calkins, *Appomattox*, 111–12; Cummings, *Yankee Quaker*, 326.
43. Marvel, *Lee's Last Retreat*, 61; Freeman, *Lee's Lieutenants*, 3:721.
44. Mahone, "Memoirs," CWTI Coll., USAMHI, 9.
45. Longstreet, *Manassas to Appomattox*, 614–15.
46. Mahone, "Memoirs," CWTI Coll., USAMHI, 11–12. Longstreet, *Manassas to Appomattox*, 618–19; Gallagher, *Fighting for the Confederacy*, 528; Freeman, *R. E. Lee*, 96–97, 112; Cummings, *Yankee Quaker*, 327–28; *O.R.S.*, 7:821–22; *Watchman*, "Lecture on Lee," February 1, 1871.
47. Freeman, *Lee's Lieutenants*, 3:752.
48. Cutrer, *Longstreet's Aide*, 177.

Chapter 19: Ruin and Reconstruction

1. Woodward and Muhlenfeld, eds., *Private Mary Chestnut*, 238.
2. Williams, *Diary from Dixie*, 536; Woodward and Muhlenfeld, eds., *Private Mary Chestnut*, 251.
3. Hahn, *Freedom*, ser. 3, vol. I: *Land and Labor, 1865*, 97–98; Abbott, *Freedmen's Bureau*, 12.
4. Cisco, Wade Hampton, 167, 198–99; NARA, Amnesty Papers, RG94, M1003, Roll 44.
5. NARA, Amnesty Papers, RG 94, M1003, Roll 44.
6. NARA, Amnesty Papers, RG94, M1003, Roll 44; Official Register, USMA Library, "Synopsis of Course of Studies."
7. R. H. Anderson to Thomas Mills, October 5, 1865, BHA.
8. Special Orders 246, Adjutant and IG Office, Richmond, October 16, 1863, BHA; Edward M. Anderson Will, Miscellaneous File, BHA.
9. Abbott, *Freedmen's Bureau*, 20, 52; Articles of Agreement, September 30, 1865, BHA; Slave Book, April 15, 1863, BHA; Plantation Account Book, BHA.
10. Paul Anderson, "Potter's Raid," June 20, 2016, in *South Carolina Encyclopedia*, accessed April 15, 2021, https://www.scencyclopedia.org/sce/entries/potter%c2%92s-raid/; Saville, *Work of Reconstruction*, 15.
11. Mary Anderson to W. W. Anderson, March 4, 1855, BHA; Riverside Plantation Records, Miscellaneous Files, BHA.
12. Articles of Agreement, September 30, 1865, BHA.

13. Gregorie, *Sumter County*, 274; Glymph, *House of Bondage*, 139–41, 150; Woodward, ed., *Mary Chesnut's Civil War*, 823.
14. Hahn, Freedom, ser. 3, vol. 1, "Land and Labor," 215–22; After Slavery, "A Northern Military Officer," Lowcountry Digital History Initiative, accessed July 16, 2024, https://ldhi.library.cofc.edu/exhibits/show/after_slavery_educator/unit_one_documents/document_four.
15. Saville, Work of Reconstruction, 27; After Slavery, "A Northern Military Officer," Lowcountry Digital History Initiative, accessed July 16, 2024, https://ldhi.library.cofc.edu/exhibits/show/after_slavery_educator/unit_one_documents/document_four.
16. Saville, *Work of Reconstruction*, 20.
17. Saville, *Work of Reconstruction*, 8.
18. Anderson Plantation Records, BHA; Abbott, *Freedmen's Bureau*, 69, 71, 76; Gregorie, *Sumter County*, 276; R. H. Anderson to D. H. Hill, October 26, 1867, Hill Papers, VHS; Foner, *Reconstruction*, 107–8.
19. R. H. Anderson to D. H. Hill, November 14, 1867, D. H. Hill Papers, NCSA.
20. R. H. Anderson to D. H. Hill, November 14, 1867, D. H. Hill Papers, NCSA.
21. Robert E. Lee to R. H. Anderson, July 31, 1865, W&L; Anderson to Mills, October 5, 1865, BHA; Anderson to Lee, June 15, 1866, R. E. Lee HQ Papers, VHS.
22. Robert E. Lee to Jubal Early, March 30, 1865 and November 22, 1865, Jubal Early Papers, LOC; Elliot, *Lee's Noble Soldier*, 154.
23. R. H. Anderson to D. H. Hill, January 11, 1869, D. H. Hill Papers, NCSA.
24. Richard H. Anderson, Population Schedules of the Ninth Census of the United States, 1870, Sumter County, South Carolina, NARA Series M593, Roll 1509; *Watchman*, "Church of the Holy Comforter," April 27, 1870; *Charleston Daily News*, "Personal," April 30, 1870, May 9, 1870.
25. *Watchman*, "St Joseph's Academy," July 6, 1870, "Church of the Holy Comforter," April 27, 1870; Spiess, "Exhibitions and Expositions," 173.
26. *Winnsboro-Fairfield Herald*, December 1, 1869; *Charleston Daily News*, "Memory of Lee, Remarks of General Anderson," October 17, 1870.
27. *Watchman*, "Common Pleas," December 13, 20, 27, 1870; R. H. Anderson Bankruptcy Schedules, BHA; Foner, *Reconstruction*, 394.
28. R. H. Anderson Bankruptcy Schedules, BHA; *Watchman*, "Notice of Sale," November 8, 1871, 2.
29. Earl Hastings to Mrs. Anderson, December 11, 1999, in author's collection. The Swem Library at William & Mary College contains the daily journal of local undertaker Richard M. Bucktrout, which contains information pertaining to McKenzie's burial.
30. Miscellaneous Documents and Tax Receipts, 1877, 1888, 1916, BHA; National Register of Historic Places, "Single Property Listings, South Carolina, Reference No. 72001224." National Park Service, 2018.
31. *Charleston Daily News*, "The Mayoralty," May 27, 1871; *Watchman*, "Gen. R. H. Anderson," May 31, 1871, 2.
32. Fraser, *Charleston!*, 293; *Camden Journal*, "Our Railroad Agent," December 19, 1872; Walker, *Anderson*, 242; Elliott, *Lee's Noble Soldier*, 142, n. 29; Anderson to "My dear daughter," December 10, 1872, Anderson Papers, SCL.
33. R. H. Anderson to Richard Anderson, Jr., June 24, 1873, Anderson Papers, SCL.
34. R. H. Anderson to William J. McGrath, September 25, 1873 and November 18, 1874, McGrath Papers, SCL.

35. Anderson to "My dear daughter," January 20, 1874, Anderson Papers, SCL.
36. Anderson to "My dear daughter," January 20, 1874; Walker, *Anderson*, 243; Martha E. Mellette, Population Schedules of the Ninth Census, 1870, FamilySearch.org, accessed October 3, 2021, https://www.familysearch.org/; Martha Ellen Mellett Allen, "Find a Grave," accessed October 3, 2021, https://www.findagrave.com/memorial/30835194/martha_ellen-allen (Mellett is spelled variously as Mellette in some records).
37. Walker, *Anderson*, 243; *Camden Journal*, October 17, 1878; R. H. Anderson to "My dear daughter," August 15, 1878, Anderson-Blanding Papers, SCL.
38. R. H. Anderson to "My dear daughter," October 27, 1878, Anderson-Blanding Papers, SCL.
39. Sallie Anderson to R. H. Anderson, December 7 and 8, 1878, Anderson-Blanding Papers, SCL.
40. Cisco, *Wade Hampton*, 226; Poole, *Never Surrender*, 118–19.
41. Foner, *Reconstruction*, 581–83; Rubin, "Reconstruction," June 20, 2016, in *South Carolina Encyclopedia*, accessed October 10, 2021, https://www.scencyclopedia.org/sce/entries/reconstruction/.
42. Sallie Anderson to R. H. Anderson, December 7–8, 1878, Anderson-Blanding Papers, SCL; *News and Herald*, "Fighting Dick Anderson," December 17, 1878.
43. Thomas Smith to R. H. Anderson, n.d., ca. 1878, Anderson Papers, SLC.
44. Thomas Smith to R. H. Anderson, n.d., ca. 1878, Anderson Papers, SLC; Davis, "Coosaw Rock Alchemy," 280, 282; Shuler and Bailey, "History of Phosphate Mining," 28.
45. R. H. Anderson, Appointment to Position of State Phosphate Agent and Oath of Office, January 24 and January 16, 1879, Anderson Papers, SLC; "Phosphates of the World," May 8, 1879; *Intelligencer* "The Phosphate Agent," July 31, 1879; Davis, "Coosaw Rock Alchemy," 269, 271.
46. *Intelligencer* (Anderson, SC), "South Carolina News," January 23 1879; Parker, *Barnwell House*, 3, 7–8; "Barnwell House," National Register of Historic Places Inventory, March 24, 1971; R. H. Anderson to "My dear daughter," February 18, 1879, Anderson Papers, SCL.
47. Sallie Anderson to R. H. Anderson, May 3, 1879, Anderson-Blanding Papers, SCL.
48. *Intelligencer*, "'Fighting Dick' Anderson," July 3, 1879.
49. *Intelligencer*, "'Fighting Dick' Anderson," July 3, 1879.
50. *News and Herald*, "Legislative Proceedings," December 9, 1879; *Yorkville Enquirer*, "Survivors' Reunion," August 7, 1879; *Yorkville Enquirer*, "South Carolina News," July 24, 1879.
51. *News and Herald*, "Address of the Late Dr. Grier At the Reunion of the Sixth Regiment at Winnsboro in 1879, With General Bratton's Introduction," May 25, 1910 Memorial Edition,; *News and Herald*, "The Old Sixth," August 9, 1879.
52. Watchman and Southron, "Fighting Dick Anderson," February 15, 1888; Walker, Anderson, 256–57.
53. Walker, *Anderson*, 258–61.
54. *Watchman and Southron*, "Death," December 7, 1898, "Death," July 1, 1911; R. H. Anderson to "My dear daughter," August 15, 1878, Blanding-Anderson Papers, SCL.
55. *Abbeville Press and Banner*, "U.D.C. Honor the Great Gen. R. H. Anderson," June 28, 1916; *Watchman and Southron*, "Fighting Dick Anderson," December 15, 1917.

56. *Camden Chronicle,* "Gives Life Sketches of five South Carolina Generals," December 18, 1925.
57. *Camden Chronicle,* "General Kershaw Selected with Four Others for Place on Stone Mountain Memorial Carving," November 27, 1925.
58. Freeman, *Carved in Stone,* 62, 78–80, 167, 175–76.

Bibliography

Newspapers

Abbeville (SC) *Press and Banner*
Anniston (AL) *Evening Star*
Camden (SC) *Chronicle*
Camden (SC) *Journal*
Charleston (SC) *Daily News*
Charleston (SC) *Mercury*
Constitutionalist (GA)
The Countryman (GA)
Daily Constitutionalist (GA)
Daily Phoenix (SC)
Intelligencer (SC)
Lancaster (SC) *Ledger*
Liverpool Mercury (England)
News and Herald (SC)
Richmond (VA) *Enquirer*
Sumter (SC) *Banner*
Sumter (SC) *Watchman and Southron*
Wallace (SC) *Constitutional*
Winnsboro Fairfield (SC) *Herald*
Woodville (MS) *Republican*
Yorkville (SC) *Enquirer*

Manuscript Collections

Abraham Lincoln Presidential Library & Museum, Springfield, IL
Shanahan, M. W. Letter, October 13, 1861, 9th Mississippi Infantry
Brake Collection
2nd Georgia Infantry
Judkins, W. B. Memoir
Chicago Public Library, IL
Parker, R. D. Letters, American Civil War Documents, Series 15
Confederate Memorial Literary Society Collection (Formerly at Museum of the Confederacy)
Anderson, R. H. Letterbook
Gilley, Daniel. Papers
Hill, Jesse. Papers
Miles, Lewis. Letters
Petty, James T. Diary
Smith, John O. Papers

Cumberland County Historical Society, Carlisle, PA
  Middleton, William S. "John Bannister Gibson, Chief Justice of Pennsylvania"
Dolph Briscoe Center for American History, The University of Texas at Austin
  Thompson, Fleming W. Letters, 1861–1865
Duke University, Perkins Library, Durham, NC
  Anderson, R. H. Papers
  Haskell, John C. Memoir
  Munford-Ellis Family Papers
Fredericksburg Spotsylvania National Military Park, Fredericksburg, VA
  Long, Henry L. Diary, Copy from the Southern Historical Collection, University of North Carolina, Chapel Hill
Gettysburg National Military Park Library, Gettysburg, PA
  Garrett, William. Diary and Related Papers
  Johnson, James B. "A Limited Review of What One Man Saw of the Battle of Gettysburg."
  Mason, John. Memoir, "Three Years in the Army or the Life and Adventures of a Rebel Soldier," typescript donated by James Mason
  McClellan, Bailey George. Civil War Memoir "10th Alabama" (copy from Columbus State University Archives, GA)
  McClellan, William. Letters
  Mosely, John W. "Confederate Diary" typescript
  Ropes, John C. Papers
  Wilcox, Cadmus M. File, Participant Accounts.
Harrisburg Civil War Roundtable Collection
  J. G. C. Letter (May 23, 1863)
  Lucas, Rice D. M. Letters
  Jordan, William C. Letters
Harvard University, Schlesinger Library, Cambridge, MA
  Blanding, Sarah Gibson. Papers, Correspondence Related to Gen. R. H. Anderson
Harvard University, Houghton Library, Cambridge, MA
  Dearborn, Frederick M. Collection, William Mahone Resignation
  Lucas, Rice D. M. Letters
  Mahone, William. Memoirs
  Wright's Brigade Order Book
Library of Congress
  Map Collection
  Pryor's Brigade, "Eighth Florida," with 1895 Participant Notations
Military Historical Society of Massachusetts
  Robbins, Edward B. Papers
Mississippi Department of Archives and History, Jackson, MS
  McWillie, William. Diary, McWillie Family Papers
National Archives and Records Administration, Washington, DC
  Antietam Studies Collection, NA-A5
  Population Schedules, Census Records, M593
  Record Group 94, Records of the Adjutant General's Office
    Compiled Military Service Records
    General Officer Files
    Monthly Regimental Returns

Records Relating to USMA, 1812–1867
Regimental Record Book, 2nd Dragoons
Record Group 109, Confederate Records
Compiled Military Service Records
Record Group 153, Records of the Judge Advocate General
General Court Martial
Record Group 393, Records of the U.S. Army Continental Commands, 1821–1920
Headquarters Records, Fort Gibson, Indian Territory, 1830–1857
New York Historical Society
Gilder Lehrman Collection, The Gilder Lehrman Institute of American History
North Carolina State Archives, Raleigh, NC
Hill, D. H. Papers
Sumter Historical Society, Sumter, SC
US Department of the Interior, National Park Service, National Register of Historic Places Inventory—"Nomination Form, 1–2," n.d.
South Carolina Historical Society, Columbia, SC
United Daughters of the Confederacy, "Souvenir Program, State Convention, U.D.C."
Stubbs, Thomas McAlpine Collection
United States Military Academy, West Point, NY
Record Group 104, Records of the United States Military Academy
Official Register of the U.S. Military Academy, 1841 and 1842
United States Army Military History Institute, Carlisle, PA
Flynn, John. "Reminiscences of Some Incidents in the Career of an United States Dragoon Between the Years 1839 and 1844"
Civil War Miscellaneous Collection
Miles, Lewis W. Letters
Moore, Walter R. Letters
Waldrip, Thomas E., Waldrip Family Papers
Civil War Times Illustrated Collection
Adams Family Papers
Featherston, Winfield Scott Memoir
University of North Carolina, Southern Historical Collection, Chapel Hill, NC
Alexander, Edward P. Collection
Bernard, George. Papers
Bratton, John. Letters, 1861–1865
DuBose, William P. Reminiscences
Gaston, James McFadden. Papers
Herbert, Hilary A. Papers Milner Family Papers
Milner, Willis J. Reminiscences
Todd, Westwood A. Reminiscences
Venable, Charles. Papers
University of South Carolina, South Caroliniana Library, Columbia, SC
Anderson, Richard H. Papers
Blanding-Anderson Papers
McGrath, William Joy. Papers
University of Virginia Library, Charlottesville, VA
Grinnan Family Papers, Box 1, Correspondence 1860–1869

University of West Florida, John C. Pace Library, Pensacola, FL
Murphy Family Papers
Virginia Historical Society, Richmond, VA
Anderson, R. H. File
Latrobe, Osmun. Diary
Lee, Robert E. Headquarters Papers
Maxwell, David E. Papers
Stuart, James Ewell Brown. Papers
Wright, Ambrose. Letters
Virginia Military Institute
Baker, Isaac N. Memoirs
Virginia State Library, Richmond, VA
Munford, Thomas T. Papers
Washington and Lee University, Leyburn Library, Lexington, VA
Lee, Robert E. Collection
William & Mary University, Williamsburg, VA
Bucktrout-Smith Papers
Anderson, R. H. Letter

Private Collections

Borough House Archives, Anderson Family Papers, Stateburg, SC
Anderson, Mary W. "The Borough House, Stateburg, SC"
Jones, A. Waldo Family Papers
Anderson, William Wallace II File
White, Mary V. S. "The Borough House, Stateburgh, High Hills of Santee"
Boykin, Elizabeth. Private Collection, copies in possession of author
Hinrichs Diary, copy in possession of Robert K. Krick
Huguenin Memoirs, copy in possession of Robert K. Krick

Primary Documents

Proceedings of The Meeting of Delegates From The Southern Rights Association of South Carolina Held At Charleston, May, 1851. Johnston & Cavis, 1851.

South Carolina. Convention (1860–1862). Declaration of the Immediate Causes Which Induce and Justify the Secession of South Carolina from the Federal Union; and the Ordinance of Secession. Charleston, SC: Evans & Cogswell, printers to the Convention, 1860.

US Congress. Executive Document No. 1. *The War With Mexico.* 30th Cong., 1st sess., 1847, S. Rep. 361–421.

US Navy Department. *Official Records of the Union and Confederate Navies in the War of the Rebellion.* 30 vols. Washington, DC: Government Printing Office, 1894–1927.

US War Department. *The War of the Rebellion: A Compilation of the Official Records of the Union and Confederate Armies.* Four series, 70 vols. in 128 vols. Washington, DC: Government Printing Office, 1880–1901.

Electronic Documents

After Slavery: Educator Resources. "A Northern Military Officer Advises Former Slaves on Freedom." Lowcountry Digital History Initiative. Accessed July 16,

2024. https://ldhi.library.cofc.edu/exhibits/show/after_slavery_educator/unit_one_documents/document_four.
The Aztec Club of 1847. "Index of Biographies." Accessed July 31, 2011. http://www.aztecclub.com/LeadPg.htm ().
Anderson, Richard H. 1870 United States Federal Census [database on-line], FamilySearch, Accessed October 10, 2021. https://www.familysearch.org/ark:/61903/1:1:M8RB-F93?lang=en.
Cordley, Richard. *A History of Lawrence, Kansas From the Earliest Settlement to the Close of the Rebellion.* Lawrence, KN: E. F. Caldwell, 1895. Accessed December 5, 2010. https://archive.org/details/historyoflawrencoocordrich/page/n1/mode/2up
Fort Sumter National Monument Manuscript Collection, "A Sketch of the Life of Thomas Abram Huguenin."
Hawkins, Gerald, and Serge Noirsain. "Coppens' Zouaves: 1st Bataillon of Louisiana Zouaves," Confederate Historical Association of Belgium, January 19, 2015. Accessed January 12, 2021. http://www.chab-belgium.com/pdf/english/Coppens%20Zouaves.pdf.
Hennessy, John. "Historical Report on the Troop Movements for the Second Battle of Manassas, August 28 Through August 30, 1862." Denver: National Park Service, 1985. Accessed October 23, 2019. http://www.npshistory.com/publications/mana/hennessy-1985.pdf.
Lackey, Rodney C. "Notes on Civil War Logistics: Facts and Stories," (Table 2 "Approximate Column Length & Pass Time"), unpublished paper, n.d., n.p., US Army Transportation Corps.
Myres, Sandra L. "Fort Graham: Listening Post on the Texas Frontier" *West Texas Historical Association Yearbook* 59 (1983): 33–51. Accessed May 18, 2016. http://www.forttours.com/pages/fortgraham.asp.
New York Historical Society, Gilder-Lehrman Collection, ID#GLC2702.
Peel, Albert L. "Civil War Diary," Ancestry.com. Accessed December 4, 2020, http://freepages.rootsweb.com/~peel/family/peeljune.html.
Peel, Robert Hunter. "Letters During the Civil War Era." Ancestry.com. Accessed December 4, 2020. https://freepages.rootsweb.com/~peel/family/peeljune.html
Rhea, Gordon. "June 1, Morning: Anderson Stumbles at Old Cold Harbor." History E-Library, US National Park Service. Accessed May 25, 2025. https://www.npshistory.com/publications/civil_war_series/11/sec10.htm
Shuler, Kristina A., and Ralph Bailey, Jr. "A History of the Phosphate Mining Industry in the South Carolina Low Country," Brockington and Associates, Inc., Survey Report for the National Register, South Carolina State Library, 2004, 1–47.

Books

Abbott, Martin. *The Freedmen's Bureau in South Carolina, 1865–1872.* University of North Carolina Press, 1967,
Adams, George Rollie. *General William S. Harney: Prince of Dragoons.* University of Nebraska Press, 2001.
Agnew, Brad. *Fort Gibson: Terminal on the Trail of Tears.* University of Oklahoma Press, 1980.
Aptheker, Herbert. *American Negro Slave Revolts.* 1943. Reprint, International Publishers, 1974.

Bakewell, Frederick C. *Philosophical Conversations: In Which Are Familiarly Explained the Causes of Many Daily Occurring Natural Phenomena.* Boston: Carter, Hendee & Co., 1834.

Barefoot, Daniel W. *General Robert F. Hoke: Lee's Modest Warrior.* John F. Blair, 1996.

Barrett, John G., ed. *Yankee Rebel: The Civil War Journal of Edmund DeWitt Patterson.* University of North Carolina Press, 1966.

Bearrs, Edwin C. *The Petersburg Campaign.* Vol. 2, *The Western Front Battles, September 1864–April 1865.* Savas Beatie LLC, 2014.

Beck, Paul N. *The First Sioux War: The Grattan Fight and Blue Water Creek, 1854–1856.* University Press of America, 2004.

Berry, Diana Ramey. *The Price for Their Pound of Flesh: The Value of the Enslaved, from Womb to Grave, in the Building of a Nation.* Beacon Press, 2017.

Black, Robert C., III. *The Railroads of the Confederacy.* University of North Carolina Press, 1952.

Blake, Nelson Morehouse. *William Mahone of Virginia: Soldier and Political Insurgent.* Garrett & Massie, 1935.

Boggs, William R. *Military Reminiscences of Gen. Wm. R. Boggs, C.S.A.* The Seeman Printery, 1913.

Brown, Peter A. *Mosby's Fighting Parson: The Life and Times of Sam Chapman.* Willow Bend Books, 2001.

Brown, Thomas J. *Civil War Canon: Sites of Confederate Memory in South Carolina.* University of North Carolina Press, 2015.

Burton, Brian K. *Extraordinary Circumstances: The Seven Days Battles.* Indiana University Press, 2001.

Burgwyn, William H. S. "Thirty-Fifth Regiment." In *Histories of the Several Regiments and Battalions from North Carolina in the Great War, 1861-'65.* Vol. 2. Edited by Walter Clark. Nash Brothers, 1901.

Caldwell, James F. *The History of a Brigade of South Carolinians.* King & Baird, 1866.

Calkins, Chris M. *The Appomattox Campaign, March 29-April 9, 1865.* Schroeder Publications, 2008.

Cannan, John. *The Antietam Campaign, August-September 1862.* Combined Books, 1994.

Cavanaugh, Michael A., and William Marvel. *The Petersburg Campaign: The Battle of the Crater, "The Horrid Pit," June 25-August 6, 1864.* H. E. Howard, 1989.

Chesnut, Mary Boykin. *A Diary from Dixie.* Edited by Ben Ames Williams. Houghton Mifflin Company, 1949.

Cisco, Walter B. *Wade Hampton: Confederate Warrior, Conservative Statesman.* Brassey's, 2004.

Clark, George A. *A Glance Backward: or Some Events in the Past History of My Life.* Rein & Sons, 1914.

Clingman, Thomas L. "Second Cold Harbor." In *Histories of the Several Regiments and Battalions from North Carolina in the Great War, 1861–'65.* Vol. 5. Edited by Walter Clark. Nash Brothers, 1901.

Coddington, Edwin B. *The Gettysburg Campaign: A Study in Command.* Charles Scribner's Sons, 1968.

Coker, James L. *History of Company G. 9th S.C. Regiment, Infantry, S.C. Army, and of Company E, Sixth S.C. Regiment, Infantry, S. C. Army.* Walker, Evans & Cogswell, 1899.

Collins, Darrell L. *Major General Robert E. Rodes of the Army of Northern Virginia: A Biography*. Savas Beatie LLC, 2008.
Conerly, L. W. *A Historical Sketch of the Quitman Guards, Company E, Sixteenth Mississippi Regiment, Harris' Brigade*. Isaac T. Hinton, Printer, 1866.
Conway, Moncure D. *Testimonies Concerning Slavery*. Chapman and Hall, 1864.
Corbin, Richard W. *Letters of a Confederate to His Family in Europe during the Last Year of the War of Secession*. Neal's English Library, n.d., ca. 1902.
Craven, Avery O. *The Growth of Southern Nationalism, 1848–1861*. A History of the South, Volume Six. Louisiana State University Press, 1953.
Cullum, George W. *Biographical Register of the Officers and Graduates of the U. S. Military Academy at West Point, N.Y. From its Establishment, in 1802, to 1890*. Vols. 1 and 2. Houghton Mifflin Company, 1891.
Cummings, Charles M. *Yankee Quaker, Confederate General: The Curious Career of Bushrod Rust Johnson*. Farleigh Dickinson University Press, 1971.
Cutrer, Thomas W., ed. *Longstreet's Aide: The Civil War Letters of Major Thomas J. Goree*. University Press of Virginia, 1995.
Davis, Jefferson,. *The Papers of Jefferson Davis*. Edited by Lynda L. Crist, Mary S. Dix, Kenneth H. Williams, and Suzanne S. Gibbs. 12 vols. Louisiana State University Press, 1971.
Dawson, Francis W. *Reminiscences of Confederate Service, 1861–1865*. Louisiana State University Press, 1980.
De la Cova, Antonio R. *Cuban Confederate Colonel: The Life of Ambrosio José Gonzales*. University of South Carolina Press, 2003.
Denoon, Charles E. *Charlie's Letters: The Civil War Correspondence of Charles E. Denoon, 41st Virginia Infantry, Mahone's Brigade, Army of Northern Virginia*. Edited by Richard T. Coutier. C.W. Historical, 1989.
Detzer, David. *Allegiance: Fort Sumter, Charleston, and the Beginning of the Civil War*. Houghton Mifflin Harcourt, 2001.
Dickert, D. Augustus. *History of Kershaw's Brigade with Complete Roll of Companies, Biographical Sketches, Incidents, Anecdotes, Etc.* Elbert H. Aull Company, 1899.
Dobbins, Austin C. ed. *Grandfather's Journal: Company B, Sixteenth Mississippi Infantry Volunteers, Harris' Brigade, Mahone's Division, Hill's Corps, A.N.V., May 27, 1861-July 15, 1865*. Morningside House, 1988.
Donald, David H. *Lincoln*. Jonathan Cape Random House, 1995.
Douglas, Henry Kyd. *I Rode with Stonewall*. University of North Carolina Press, 1940; Reprint, Mockingbird Books, 1976.
Dowdey, Clifford, and Louis H. Manarin, eds. *The Wartime Papers of R. E. Lee*. Little, Brown and Company, 1961.
Drago, Edmund L. ed. *Broke by the War: Letters of a Slave Trader*. University of South Carolina Press, 1991.
Dubbs, Carol Ketenburg. *Defend This Old Town: Williamsburg During the Civil War*. Louisiana State University Press, 2002.
Duncan, Richard R. *Lee's Endangered Left: The Civil War in Western Virginia, Spring of 1864*. Louisiana State University Press, 1998.
Eaton, Clement. *A History of the Southern Confederacy*. The Free Press, A division of Macmillan Publishing, 1954.
Eaton, Clement. *The Mind of the Old South*. rev. ed. Louisiana State University Press, 1967.

Eicher, David J. *The Longest Night: A Military History of the Civil War*. Simon & Schuster, 2001.

Elliott, Joseph Cantey. *Lieutenant General Richard Heron Anderson: Lee's Noble Soldier*. Morningside House, 1985.

Ellis, Billy. *Tithes of Blood: A Confederate Soldier's Story*. Southern Heritage Press, 1997.

Emerson, Eric W. and Karen Stokes. *Faith, Valor, and Devotion: The Civil War Letters of William Porcher DuBose*. University of South Carolina Press, 2010.

Evans, Robert G., ed. *The Sixteenth Mississippi Infantry: Civil War Letters and Reminiscences*. University Press of Mississippi, 2002.

Faust, Drew Gilpin. *The Creation of Confederate Nationalism: Ideology and Identity in the Civil War South*. Louisiana State University Press, 1988.

Foner, Eric. *Reconstruction: America's Unfinished Revolution, 1863–1877*. 1988. Reprint, HarperCollins Publishers, 2014.

Fraser, Walter J. *Charleston! Charleston! The History of a Southern City*. University of South Carolina Press, 1989.

Frazer, Robert W. *Forts of the West: Military Forts and Presidios, and Posts Commonly Called Forts, West of the Mississippi River to 1898*. University of Oklahoma Press, 1965.

Freehling, William W. *The Road to Disunion*. Vol 1, *Secessionists at Bay, 1776–1854*. Oxford University Press, 1990.

Freehling, William W. *The Road to Disunion*. Vol. 2, *Secessionists Triumphant, 1854–1861*. Oxford University Press, 2007.

Freeman, David. *Carved in Stone: The History of Stone Mountain*. Mercer University Press, 1997.

Freeman, Douglas S. *Lee*. 4 vols. New York: Charles Scribner's Sons, 1934. Abr. ed. by Richard Harwell, Touchstone, 1997.

Freeman, Douglas S. ed. *Lee's Dispatches: Unpublished Letters of General Robert E. Lee, C.S.A. to Jefferson Davis and the War Department of The Confederate States of America, 1862–65*. G. P. Putnam's Sons, 1915.

Freeman, Douglas S. *Lee's Lieutenants: A Study in Command*. 3 vols. Charles Scribner's Sons, 1942–1944.

Freeman, Douglas S. *R. E. Lee: A Biography*. Vol. 4. Charles Scribner's Sons, 1934.

Furgurson, Ernest B. *Chancellorsville, 1863: The Souls of the Brave*. Alfred A. Knopf, 1992.

Furgurson, Ernest B. *Not War But Murder: Cold Harbor, 1864*. New York: House, 2000

Gallagher, Gary W., ed. *The Antietam Campaign*. University of North Carolina Press, 1999.

Gallagher, Gary W., ed. *Fighting for the Confederacy: The Personal Recollections of General Edward Porter Alexander*. University of North Carolina Press, 1989.

Gallagher, Gary W., ed. *Lee, The Soldier*. University of Nebraska Press, 1996.

Gibson, William. *The Institutes and Practice of Surgery: Being the Outlines of a Course of Lectures*. Vol. 1. James Key, Jr. and Brother, 1845.

Glatthaar, Joseph T. *General Lee's Army: From Victory to Collapse*. Free Press, a division of Simon & Schuster, 2008.

Glymph, Thavolia. *Out of the House of Bondage: The Transformation of the Plantation Household*. Cambridge University Press, 2008.

Gordon, John B. *Reminiscences of the Civil War*. Charles Scribner's Sons, 1903.

Gordon, Lesley J. *General George E. Pickett in Life and Legend*. The University of North Carolina Press, 2000.

Goree, Langston James, V., ed. *Thomas Jewett Goree Letters*, Vol. 1, *The Civil War Correspondence*. Family History Foundation, 1981.

Govan, Gilbert E., and James W. Livingood, eds. *The Haskell Memoirs: John Cheves Haskell*. G. P. Putnam's Sons, 1960.

Graham, Martin F., and George F. Skoch. *Mine Run: A Campaign of Lost Opportunities, October 21, 1863-May 1, 1864*. H. E. Howard, 1987.

Grant, Ulysses S. *Personal Memoirs of U. S. Grant*. 2 vols. Charles L. Webster & Co., 1885.

Greene, A. Wilson. *Breaking the Backbone of the Rebellion: The Final Battles of The Petersburg Campaign*. Savas Beatie LLC, 2000.

Greene, A. Wilson. *A Campaign of Giants–The Battle for Petersburg*. Vol. 1: *From the Crossing of the James to the Crater*. University of North Carolina Press, 2018.

Gregorie, Anne K. *History of Sumter County South Carolina*. Library Board of Sumter County, 1954.

Hagerty, Edward J. *Collis' Zouaves: The 114th Pennsylvania Volunteers in the Civil War*. Louisiana State University Press, 1997.

Hagood, Johnson. *Memoirs of the War of Secession*. Columbia, SC: The State Company, 1910.

Hahn, Steven, Steven F. Miller, Susan E. O'Donovan, John C. Rodrigue, Leslie S. Rowland. *Freedom: A Documentary History of Emancipation, 1861–1867, ser. 3, vol. 1, Land and Labor, 1865*. University of North Carolina Press, 2013.

Harrison, Walter. *Pickett's Men: A Fragment of War History*. D. Van Nostrand, 1870.

Harsh, Joseph L. *Taken at the Flood: Robert E. Lee and Confederate Strategy in the Maryland Campaign of 1862*. Kent State University Press, 1999.

Hartwig, David S. *To Antietam Creek: The Maryland Campaign of September 1862*. Johns Hopkins University Press, 2012.

Harwell, Richard. *Lee: An abridgement in one volume by Richard Harwell of the four-volume R. E. Lee by Douglas Southall Freeman*. 1961. Reprint, Touchstone, 1997.

Hennessy, John J. *Return to Bull Run: The Campaign and Battle of Second Manassas*. Simon & Schuster, 1993.

Henry, Robert Selph. *The Story of the Mexican War*. 1950. Reprint, Da Capo Press, 1989.

Hess, Earl J. *In the Trenches at Petersburg*. University of North Carolina Press, 2009.

Hewitt, Janet B. *Supplement to the Official Records of the Union and Confederate Armies*. 100 vols. Broadfoot Publishing, 1994–2001.

Higginbotham, Don. *The War of American Independence: Military Attitudes, Policies, and Practice, 1763–1789*. *The Macmillan Wars of the United States*. Edited by Louis Morton. Macmillan Company, 1971.

Holzman, Robert S. *Adapt or Perish: The Life of General Roger A. Pryor, C.S.A.* Archon Books, 1976.

Hopkins, Luther W. *From Bull Run to Appomattox*. Fleet-McGinley, 1908.

Hoptak, John D. *The Battle of South Mountain*. The History Press, 2011.

Hotchkiss, Jedediah. *Make me a Map of the Valley: The Civil War Journal of Stonewall Jackson's Topographer*. Edited by Archie P. McDonald. Southern Methodist University Press, 1973.

Hunt, Jeffrey W. *Meade and Lee at Bristoe Station: The Problems of Command and Strategy After Gettysburg, from Brandy Station to the Buckland Races, August 1 to October 31, 1863*. Savas Beatie LLC, 2019.

Hunton, Eppa. *Autobiography of Eppa Hunton*. William Byrd Press, 1933.

Johnson, Bradley T. *A Memoir of the Life and Public Service of Joseph E. Johnston*. R. Woodward & Co., 1891.

Johnson, Michael P., and James L. Roark. *Black Masters: A Free Family of Color in the Old South*. W. W. Norton & Company, 1984.

Jordan, William C. *Some Events and Incidents During the War*. The Paragon Press, 1909.

Joyner, Charles. *Down by the Riverside: A South Carolina Slave Community*. University of Illinois Press, 1984.

Kendall, George Wilkins. *Dispatches From the Mexican War*. Edited by Lawrence Delbert Cress. University of Oklahoma Press, 1999.

Killian, Ron V. *General Abner M. Perrin, C.S.A.: A Biography*. McFarland & Co., 2012.

Knight, Oliver. *Life and Manners in the Frontier Army*. University of Oklahoma Press, 1978.

Koger, Larry. *Black Slaveowners: Free Black Slave Masters in South Carolina, 1790–1860*. McFarland & Company, 2011.

Kohn, Richard H. *Eagle and Sword: The Beginnings of the Military Establishment in America*. The Free Press, 1975.

Kroger, Larry. *Black Slaveowners: Free Black Slave Masters in South Carolina, 1790–1860*. McFarland, 1985.

Krick, Robert E. L. *Staff Officers in Gray: A Biographical Register of the Staff Officers in the Army of Northern Virginia*. University of North Carolina Press, 2003.

Krick, Robert K. *Lee's Colonels: A Biographical Register of the Field Officers of the Army of Northern Virginia*. 4th ed. Press of Morningside Bookshop, 1992.

Kolchin, Peter. *American Slavery, 1619–1877*. Hill and Wang, 1993.

LeClercq, Anne S. W. *An Antebellum Plantation Household: Including the South Carolina Low Country Receipts and Remedies of Emily Wharton Sinkler*. University of South Carolina Press, 1996.

Light, Rebecca Campbell, ed. *War at Our Doors: The Civil War Diaries and Letters of the Bernard Sisters of Virginia*. American History Company, 1998.

Long, E. B. *The Civil War Day by Day: An Almanac, 1861–1865*. Doubleday & Company, Inc., 1971.

Longacre, Edward G. *Pickett: Leader of the Charge: A Biography of General George E. Pickett, C.S.A.* White Mane Publishing Company, 1995.

Longstreet, James. *From Manassas to Appomattox: Memoirs of the Civil War in America*. 1896. Reprint. Blue and Gray Press, n.d.

Lowe, Percival G. *Five Years a Dragoon: ('49 to '54) And Other Adventures on the Great Plains*. University of Oklahoma Press, 1965.

Loyless, Thomas W. *Georgia's Public Men, 1902–1904*. Byrd Printing, 1902.

Luvaas, Jay, and Harold W. Nelson., eds. *The U.S. Army War College Guide to the Battle of Antietam: The Maryland Campaign of 1862*. South Mountain Press, 1987.

Mackowski, Chris. *Strike Them a Blow: Battle Along the North Anna River, May 21–26, 1864*. Savas Beatie LLC, 2015.

Marcy, Randolph B. *The Prairie Traveler: A Handbook for Overland Expeditions*. Harper & Brothers, 1859.

Martin, Samuel J. *The Road to Glory: Confederate General Richard S. Ewell.* Guild Press of Indiana, 1991.
Marvel, William. *Lee's Last Retreat: The Flight to Appomattox.* University of North Carolina Press, 2002.
Matter, William D. *If It Takes All Summer: The Battle of Spotsylvania.* University of North Carolina Press, 1988.
Maurice, Frederick, ed. *An aide-de-camp of Lee, being the papers of Colonel Charles Marshall, sometime aid-de-camp, military secretary, and assistant adjutant general on the staff of Robert E. Lee, 1862–1865.* Little, Brown, 1927.
McDonnell, Lawrence. "Work, Culture, and Society in the Slave South, 1790–1865." In *Black and White Cultural Interaction in the Antebellum South*, edited by Ted Ownby, 125–47. University Press of Mississippi, 1993.
McWhiney, Grady. *Braxton Bragg and Confederate Defeat.* University of Alabama Press, 1991.
Mixon, Frank M. *Reminiscences if a Private.* 1910. Reprint. J.J. Fox, 1990.
Moffett, Mary Conner, ed. *Letters of General James Conner, C. S. A.* R. L. Bryan, 1950.
Morris, Gouvenor. *History of a Volunteer Regiment: Being a Succinct Account of the Organization, Services and Adventures of the Sixth Regiment New York Volunteers Infantry Known as Wilson Zouaves.* Veteran Volunteer Publishing Co., 1891.
Morrison, James L., Jr. *The Best School in the World: West Point, the Pre-Civil War Years, 1833–1866.* The Kent State University Press, 1986.
Morrison, James L., Jr., ed. *The Memoirs of Henry Heth.* Greenwood Press, 1974.
Mullis, Tony R. *Peacekeeping on the Plains: Army Operations in Bleeding Kansas.* University of Missouri Press, 2004.
Murfin, James V. *The Gleam of Bayonets: The Battle of Antietam and Robert E. Lee's Maryland Campaign, September 1862.* Louisiana State University Press, 1965.
Newell, Clayton R. *The Regular Army Before the Civil War, 1845–1860.* Center of Military History, 2014.
Newsome, Hampton. *Richmond Must Fall.* The Kent State University Press, 2013.
Newsome, Hampton, John Horn, and John G. Selby, eds. *Civil War Talks: Further Reminiscences of George S. Bernard & His Fellow Veterans.* University of Virginia Press, 2012.
Niven, John. *The Coming of the Civil War, 1837–1861.* The American History Series. Harlan Davidson, 1990.
Oates, William C. *The War Between the Union and the Confederacy.* Neale Publishing, 1905.
Oeffinger, John C. ed. *A Soldier's General: The Civil War Letters of Major General Lafayette McLaws.* University of North Carolina Press, 2002.
Olivia, Leo E. *Soldiers on the Santa Fe Trail.* University of Oklahoma Press, 1967.
O'Reilly, Francis A. *The Fredericksburg Campaign: Winter War on the Rappahannock.* Louisiana State University Press, 2003.
Osborne, Charles C. *Jubal: The Life and Times of General Jubal A. Early, CSA, Defender of the Lost Cause.* Louisiana State University Press, 1992.
Pappas, George S. *To the Point: The Unitec States Military Academy, 1802–1902.* Praeger Publishers. 1983.
Parker, Penelope H. *The William Wigg Barnwell House.* Historic Beaufort Foundation, 2010.
Paskoff, Paul F., and Daniel J. Wilson. eds. *The Cause of the South: Selections from De Bow's Review, 1846–1867.* Louisiana State University Press, 1982.

Patterson, Gerard A. *From Blue to Gray: The Life of Confederate General Cadmus M. Wilcox*. Stackpole Books, 2001.

Pearce, George F. *Pensacola During the Civil War: A Thorn in the Side of the Confederacy*. University Press of Florida, 2000.

Pearce, T. H., ed. *Diary of Captain Henry A. Chambers*. Broadfoot's Bookmark, 1983

Pelzer, Louis. *Marches of the Dragoons in the Mississippi Valley: An Account of Marches and Activities of the First Regiment United States Dragoons in the Mississippi Valley Between the Years 1833 and 1850*. State Historical Society of Iowa, 1917.

Peyton, George Quintus, and Walbrook D. Swank. *Stonewall Jackson's Foot Cavalry: Company A, 13th Virginia Infantry*. Burd Street Press, 2001.

Pfanz, Donald C. *Richard S. Ewell: A Soldier's Life*. University of North Carolina Press, 1998.

Pfanz, Harry W. *Gettysburg: The Second Day*. University of North Carolina Press, 1987.

Phillips, Christopher. *Damned Yankee: The Life of General Nathaniel Lyon*. University of Missouri Press, 1990.

Phillips, Ulrich B. *American Negro Slavery: A Summary of the Supply, Employment and Control of Negro Labor as Determined by the Plantation Regime*. 1918. Reprint, Louisiana State University Press, 1966.

Piston, William Garrett. *Lee's Tarnished Lieutenant: James Longstreet and His Place in Southern History*. University Press of Georgia, 1987.

Poage, William T. *Gunner with Stonewall: Reminiscences of William T. Poague*. University of Nebraska Press, 1957.

Pond, George E. *The Shenandoah Valley in 1864*. Charles Scribner's Sons, 1883. Reprint. Broadfoot Publishing, 1989.

Poole, Scott W. *Never Surrender: Confederate Memory and Conservatism in the South Carolina Upcountry*. University of Georgia Press, 2004.

Porter, Horace. *Campaigning with Grant*. Century Company, 1897.

Price, James S. *The Battle of First Deep Bottom*. History Press, 2014.

Priest, John M. *Before Antietam: The Battle for South Mountain*. White Mane Publishing, 1992.

Prucha, Francis P. *The Sword of the Republic: The United States Army on the Frontier, 1783–1846*. University of Nebraska Press, 1969.

Reid, Jessie W. *History of the Fourth Regiment of S.C. Volunteers from the Commencement of the War until Lee's Surrender*. 1891. Reprint, Morningside Press, 1975.

Rhea, Gordon C. *The Battle of the Wilderness, May 5–6, 1864*. Louisiana State University Press, 1994.

Rhea, Gordon C. *The Battles for Spotsylvania Court House and the Road to Yellow Tavern, May 7–12*. Louisiana State University Press, 1997.

Rhea, Gordon C. *Cold Harbor: Grant and Lee, May 26–June 3, 1864*. Louisiana State University Press, 2002.

Rhea, Gordon C. *To the North Anna River: Grant and Lee, May 13–25, 1864*. Louisiana State University Press, 2000.

Robertson, James I., Jr. *General A. P. Hill: The Story of a Confederate Warrior*. Penguin Random House, 1987.

Robertson, James I., Jr. *Robert E. Lee: A Reference Guide to His Life and Works*. Rowman & Littlefield, 2019.

Robertson, James I., Jr. *Stonewall Jackson: The Man, The Soldier, The Legend*. Macmillan Publishing, 1997.

Robinson, Charles. *The Men Who Wear the Star: The Story of the Texas Rangers.* Penguin Random House, 2000.
Rodenbough, Theophilus F. *From Everglade to* Cañon *with the Second United States Cavalry.* 1875. Reprint, University of Oklahoma Press, 2000.
Rosen, Hannah. *Terror in the Heart of Freedom: Citizenship, Sexual Violence, and the Meaning of Race in the Postemancipation South.* University of North Carolina Press, 2009.
Royall, William L. *Some Reminiscences.* Neale Publishing, 1909.
Ruff, Martin. *Between Slavery and Capitalism: The Legacy of Emancipation in the American South.* Princeton University Press, 2014.
Saville, Julie. *The Work of Reconstruction: From Slave to Wage Laborer in South Carolina, 1860–1870.* Cambridge University Press, 1994.
Scott, Robert Garth, ed. *Forgotten Valor: The Memoirs, Journals, & Civil War Letters of Orlando B. Willcox.* Kent State University Press, 1999.
Sears, Stephen W. *Chancellorsville.* Houghton Mifflin Company, 1996.
Sears, Stephen W. *To the Gates of Richmond: The Peninsula Campaign.* Ticknor & Fields, 1992.
Sears, Stephen W. *Landscape Turned Red: The Battle of Antietam.* Ticknor & Fields, 1983.
Simkin, Francis B., and Robert H. Woody. *South Carolina During Reconstruction.* University of North Carolina Press, 1932.
Smedlund, William S. *Camp Fires of Georgia's Troops, 1861–1865.* R. J. Taylor, Jr. Foundation, 1995.
Smith, Gustavus W. *The Battle of Seven Pines.* C. G. Crawford, 1891.
Smith, Gustavus W. *Confederate War Papers.* Atlantic Publishing & Engraving, 1884.
Snead Claiborne. *Address at the Reunion of the Third Georgia Regiment at Union Point on the 31st of July, 1874.* Chronicle and Sentinel Job Printing Establishment, 1874.
Sobel, Mechal. "Whatever You Do, Treat People Right: Personal Ethics in Slave Society," in *Black and White Cultural Interaction in the Antebellum South,* edited by Ted Ownby, 55–88. University Press of Mississippi, 1993.
Sommers, Richard J. *Richmond Redeemed: The Siege at Petersburg.* Doubleday, 1981.
Sorrel, G. Moxley. *Recollections of a Confederate Staff Officer,* Edited by Bell Irvin Wiley. McCowat-Mercer Press, 1958.
Southern Rights Association. *Proceedings of The Meeting of Delegates From The Southern Rights Association.* Johnston & Cavis, 1851.
Spruill, Matt, III, and Matt Spruill IV. *Decisions at Second Manassas: The Fourteen Critical Decisions that Defined the Battle.* University of Tennessee Press, 2018.
Stampp, Kenneth M. *America in 1857: A Nation on the Brink.* Oxford University Press, 1990.
Stern, Julia A. *Mary Chesnut's Civil War Epic.* University of Chicago Press, 2010.
Stickles, Arndt M. *Simon Bolivar Buckner: Borderland Knight.* University of North Carolina Press, 1940.
Stiles, Robert. *Four Years Under Marse Robert.* 3rd ed. Neale, 1904.
Stocker, Jeffrey D., ed. *From Huntsville to Appomattox: R. T. Coles's History of the 4th Regiment, Alabama Volunteer Infantry, C.S.S., Army of Northern Virginia.* University of Tennessee Press, 1996.
Stokes, Karen, and James Everett, eds. *Everlasting Circle: Letters of the Haskell Family of Abbeville, South Carolina, 1861–1865.* Mercer University Press, 2019.

Stribling, Robert M. *Gettysburg Campaign and Campaigns of 1864–1865 in Virginia.* The Franklin Press, 1905.

Styple, William B. *Writing & Fighting the Confederate War: The Letters of Peter Wellington Alexander, Confederate War Correspondent.* Belle Grove, 2002.

Sullivan, Jerry M. *Fort McKavett: A Texas Frontier Post.* Texas Parks and Wildlife Department, 1993.

Sumter, Thomas S. *Stateburg and Its People.* 2nd ed. Sumter Printing, 1949.

Swinton, William. *Campaigns of the Army of the Potomac: A Critical History of Operations in Virginia Maryland and Pennsylvania from the Commencement to the Close of the War, 1861–1865.* Charles Scribner's Sons, 1882.

Tadman, Michael. *Speculators and Slaves: Masters, Traders, and Slaves in the Old South.* University of Wisconsin Press, 1989.

Taylor, Walter H. *Four Years with General Lee.* Edited by James I. Robertson, Jr. Bonanza Books, 1962.

Teetor, Paul R. *A Matter of Hours: Treason at Harper's Ferry.* Fairleigh Dickinson University Press, 1982.

Thomas Emory M. *Bold Dragoon: The Life of J.E.B. Stuart.* Harper & Row, 1986.

Thomas Emory M. *Robert E. Lee: A Biography.* W. W. Norton, 1995.

Tower, R. Lockwood, ed. *Lee's Adjutant: The Wartime Letters of Colonel Walter Herron Taylor, 1862–1865.* University of South Carolina Press, 1995.

Trudeau, Noah A. *Bloody Roads South: Wilderness to Cold Harbor, May–June 1864.* Little, Brown and Company, 1989.

Trudeau, Noah A. *The Last Citadel: Petersburg, Virginia, June 1864–April 1865.* Little, Brown and Company, 1991.

Tucker, Spencer. *Brigadier General John D. Imboden: Confederate Commander in the Shanandoah.* University Press of Kentucky, 2003.

Utley, Robert M. *The Indian Frontier of the American West, 1846–1890.* University of New Mexico Press, 1984.

Utley, Robert M. *Frontiersmen in Blue: The United States Army and the Indian, 1848–1865.* Bison Books, 1981.

Walker, C. Irvine. *The Life of Lieutenant General Richard Heron Anderson of the Confederate States Army.* Art Publishing, 1917.

Warfield, Edgar. *Manassas to Appomattox: The Civil War Memoirs of Pvt. Edgar Warfield, 17th Virginia Infantry.* EPM Publications, 1996.

Warner, Ezra J. *Generals in Blue: Lives of the Union Commanders.* Louisiana State University Press, 1964.

Warner, Ezra J. *Generals in Gray: Lives of the Confederate Commanders.* Louisiana State University Press, 1959.

Waters, Zack C., and James C. Edmunds. *A Small but Spartan Band: The Florida Brigade in Lee's Army of Northern Virginia.* University of Alabama Press, 2013.

Weigley, Russell F. *A Great Civil War: A Military and Political History, 1861–1865.* Indiana State University Press, 2000.

Welsh, Jack D. *Medical Histories of Confederate Generals.* Kent State University Press, 1995.

Wert, Jeffry D. *Gettysburg: Day Three.* Simon & Schuster, 2001.

Wert, Jeffry D. *From Winchester to Cedar Creek: The Shenandoah Campaign of 1864.* Simon & Schuster, A Touchstone Book, 1987.

Wert, Jeffry D. *General James Longstreet: The Confederacy's Most Controversial Soldier—A Biography.* Simon & Schuster, 1993.

Wheeler, Richard. *Sword over Richmond: An Eyewitness History of McClellan's Peninsula Campaign*. Harper & Row, 1986.

Williams, Ben Ames, ed. *A Diary from Dixie*. Houghton Mifflin Company, 1949.

Williams, T. Harry. *Lincoln and His Generals*. Alfred A. Knopf, 1952.

Williams, T. Harry. *P. G. T. Beauregard: Napoleon in Gray*. Louisiana State University Press, 1955.

Wittenberg, Eric J., J. Davis Petruzzi, and Michael F. Nugent. *One Continuous Fight: The Retreat from Gettysburg and the Pursuit of Lee's Army of Northern Virginia, July 4–14, 1863*. Savas Beatie LLC, 2011.

Woodward, C. Vann, ed. *Mary Chestnut's Civil War*. Yale University Press, 1981.

Woodward, C. Vann, and Elisabeth Muhlenfeld, eds. *The Private Mary Chestnut: The Unpublished Civil War Diaries*. Oxford University Press, 1984.

Woodward, Harold R., Jr. *Defender of the Valley: Brigadier General John Daniel Imboden C.S.A.* Rockbridge Publishing, 1996.

Yearns, Wilfred B. *The Confederate Congress*. University of Georgia Press, 1960.

Zuczek, Richard. *State of Rebellion: Reconstruction in South Carolina*. University of South Carolina Press, 1996.

Articles and Essays

A. J. B., "The Indian Reserves of Texas." *The Texas Almanac for 1859*. Texas State Historical Association, n.d., 130–31.

Anderson, William W. "Case of Steo-sarcoma of the Lower Jaw, Successfully Treated by Amputation of that Bone." *American Journal of the Medical Sciences* 10 (1832): 315–18.

Atkinson, Matt, "'We Were Now Complete Masters of the Field:' Ambrose Wright's Attack on July 2." *The Second Day at Gettysburg: Papers of the 2006 Gettysburg National Military Park Seminar*, Gettysburg, PA, 2006.

Buckner, Simon B. "A Visit to Popocatepetl." *Putnam's Monthly: A Magazine of Literature, Science, and Art* 1, no. 1 (January 1853): 408–16.

Bohannon, Keith. "Six Sons for the Confederacy: The story of the Jones brothers, 22nd Georgia Infantry, as Seen Through the Letters of Robert H. Jones." *Military Images* 7, no. 4 (January–February 1986), 6–8.

Bolté, Philip L. "Lonely Command." *Civil War: Magazine of the Civil War Society*, no. 61 (April 1997), 42–47.

Bonham, Milledge Louis. "A Little More Light on Gettysburg." *Mississippi Valley Historical Review* 24, no. 4 (March 1938), 519–25.

Campbell, Eric A. "'Sacrificed to the bad management . . . of others.': Richard H. Anderson's Division at the Battle of Gettysburg." In *High Water Mark: The Army of Northern Virginia in the Gettysburg Campaign*, Programs of the Seventh Annual Gettysburg, Seminar. Gettysburg National Military Park, National Park Service, 1999, 103–37.

Civil War Florida Infantry Rosters, Eighth Florida Infantry, Florida Genealogy Trails (from Fred L. Robertson, Soldiers of Florida in the Seminole Indian—Civil and Spanish American Wars, Board of State Institutions, 1903, n.p.

Davis, John Martin, Jr. "Coosaw Rock Alchemy: A Short History of River-Phosphate Mining in Beaufort County." *South Carolina Historical Magazine* 109, no. 4 (2008): 269–94.

DesChamps, Margaret Burr. "The Free Agricultural Population in Sumter District, South Carolina, 1850–1860." *North Carolina Historical Review* 32, no. 1 (1955): 81–91.

DiNardo, Richard L. "Robert E. Lee and the Command Crisis of 1863–1864." *North & South*, February 1998: 82–89.

Elmore, Thomas L. "The Florida Brigade at Gettysburg." *Gettysburg Magazine*, no. 15 (1996): 45–59.

Fortin, Maurice S. ed. "Colonel Hilary A. Herbert's 'History of the Eighth Alabama Volunteer Regiment, C.S.A.'" *Alabama Historical Quarterly* 39, nos. 1–4 (1977): 5–321.

Giambrone, Jeff T. "'God Defend the Right': The Civil War Diary & Letters of Sgt. Charles E. Hutchinson, 48th Mississippi Infantry." *North-South Trader Magazine* 30, no. 3 (2004): 60–65.

Gottfried, Bradley M. "Mahone's Brigade: Insubordination or Miscommunication?" *Gettysburg Magazine*, no. 18, (1998): 67–76.

Gottfried, Bradley M. "Wright's Charge on July 2, 1863: Piercing the Union Line or Inflated Glory?" *Gettysburg Magazine*, no. 17 (1997): 70–82.

Groene, Bertram H. "Civil War Letters of Colonel David Lang." *Florida Historical Quarterly* 54, no. 3 (1976): 340–66.

Heiser, John. "Action on the Emmitsburg Road: Gettysburg, Pennsylvania July 2, 1863." *The Morningside Notes* (An Occasional Publication of Morningside Bookshop), (1983): 1–8.

Hunter, Alexander. "A High Private's Account of the Battle of Sharpsburg." *Southern Historical Society Papers* 10, no. 11 (1882): 503–12.

Hume, Edgar E. "Ornithologists of the United States Army Medical Corps (Part 1)." *Bulletin of the History of Medicine* 8, no. 9 (November 1940): 1301–88.

Law, Evander McIvor. "'A half-dozen take the place of every one we kill:' from the Wilderness to Cold Harbor," in *Battles and Leaders of the Civil* War, one volume edition. Edited by Ned Bradford. Appleton-Century, 1956.

Lee, Robert E. General Orders No. 72., HQ Army of Northern Virginia, June 21, 1863, Broadside. Dickenson College Archives and Special Collections.

McLaws, Lafayette. "The Battle of Fredericksburg." *Addresses Delivered Before the Confederate Veterans Association of Savannah, Ga., 1898–1902*. United Confederate Veterans, Georgia Division, Confederate Survivor's Association Camp No. 756, Savannah.

Mellon, Knox, Jr. "A Florida Soldier in the Army of Northern Virginia: The Hosford Letters." *Florida Historical Quarterly* 46, no. 3 (1968): 243–71.

Morgan, Phillip. "The Task System and the World of Lowcountry Blacks, 1700 to 1880." *William and Mary Quarterly* (October 1982): 563–99.

Nowak, Timothy R. "From Fort Pierre to Fort Randall: The Army's First Use of Portable Cottages." *South Dakota History* 32, no. 2 (Summer 2002): 95–116.

Parler, Josie Platt. "Afterglow: A Record of Two Centuries of Living at Borough Plantation." *South Atlantic Quarterly* 37, no. 1 (1938): 73–85.

Reardon, Carol. "From 'King of Spades' to 'First Captain of the Confederacy': R. E. Lee's First Six Weeks with the Army of Northern Virginia," in *Lee the Soldier*. Edited by Gary Gallagher. University of Nebraska Press, 1996.

Reaver, J. Russell, Jr., ed. "Letters of Joel C. Blake." *Apalachee: The Publication of the Tallahassee Historical Society* 5 (1957–1962): 5–25.

Risley, Ford. "Peter W. Alexander: Confederate Chronicler & Conscience." *American Journalism* 15, no.1 (1998): 35–50.

Saclarides, Theodore J. "Morbidity and Mortality of the Confederate Generals During the American Civil War." *American Surgeon* 73, no. 8 (August 2007): 760–64.

Spiess, Philip D., II. "Exhibitions and Expositions in 19th Century Cincinnati." *Cincinnati Historical Society Bulletin* 28 (Fall 1970): 170–92.

Taylor, William H. "Some Experiences of a Confederate Assistant Surgeon." *Transactions of the College of Physicians of Philadelphia*, ser. 3, vol. 28, (1906): 91–121.

Thompson, Jerry. "Winfield Scott's Army of Occupation as Pioneer Alpinists: Epic Ascents of Popocateptl and Citlapetl." *Southwestern Historical Quarterly* 105, no. 4 (2002): 549–80.

Wallace, Edward S. "The United States Army in Mexico City." *Military Affairs*, (Fall 1949): 158–66.

Waters, Zack. "'Tell Them I Died Like a Confederate Soldier': Finegan's Florida Brigade at Cold Harbor." *Florida Historical Quarterly* 69, no. 2 (1990): 156–77.

Wilcox, Cadmus, "Letter from General C. M. Wilcox" March 26, 1877. *Southern Historical Society Papers* 4 (July–December 1877): 111–17.

Winschel, Terrence J. "Part I: Posey's Brigade at Gettysburg." *Gettysburg Magazine*, no. 4 (January 1991): 7–15.

Winschel, Terrence J. "Part 2: Posey's Brigade at Gettysburg." *Gettysburg Magazine*, no. 5 (July 1991): 89–101.

Winters, Harold A. "The Battle That Was Never Fought: Weather and the Union Mud March of January 1863." *Southeastern Geographer* 31, no. 1 (May 1991): 31–38.

Wise, Henry A. "The Career of Wise's Brigade, 1861–1865." *Southern Historical Society Papers*, -25 (January–December 1897): 1–22.

Dissertations, Theses, and Unpublished Academic Papers

Gabler, Henry. "The Rebel Press: Six Selected Confederate Newspapers Report Civil War Battles." MA thesis. College of William & Mary, 1971.

Grant, Arthur Vernon, Jr. "Unity of Command: The Command Relationship Between Generals Grant and Meade in the Campaigns of 1864–1865." MA thesis. Rice University, 1974.

Lindstrom, Andrew F. "Perry's Brigade in the Army of Northern Virginia." MA thesis, University of Florida, 1966.

Moore, John A. "The McLaws/Kershaw Division in 1864 and 1865: A Case Study into the Causes of the Military Demise of the Army of Northern Virginia." Independent Study Project, American Military University, 2002.

Ott, Eugene M., Jr. "The Civil War Diary of James J. Kirkpatrick, 16th Mississippi Infantry, C.S.A." MA thesis, Texas A&M University, 1984.

Risley, J. Ford. "Georgia's Civil War Newspapers: Partisan, Sanguine, Enterprising." PhD diss., University of Florida, 1996.

Index

Page numbers in italic refer to figures.

Walker, C. Irvine, 348, 365, 393n2